SHAPERS OF URBAN FORM

People have designed cities long before there were urban designers. In *Shapers of Urban Form*, Peter J. Larkham and Michael P. Conzen have commissioned new scholarship on the forces, people, and institutions that have shaped cities from the Middle Ages to the present day.

Larkham and Conzen collect new essays in "urban morphology," the people-centered predecessor to contemporary theories of top-down urban design. *Shapers of Urban Form* focuses on the social processes that create patterns of urban forms in four discrete periods: pre-modern, early modern, industrial-era and postmodern development. Featuring studies of English, American, Western and Eastern European, and New Zealand urban history and urban form, this collection is invaluable to scholars of urban design and town planning and to urban and economic historians.

Peter J. Larkham has authored more than sixty papers for refereed journals, edited three books for Routledge, and authored *Conservation and the City* (1996) and edited theme issues of *Town Planning Review* and *Built Environment.* He is associate editor of *Urban Morphology* and has recently served as associate editor of *Planning Perspectives.* He is professor of planning at Birmingham City University, UK.

Michael P. Conzen is professor of geography at the University of Chicago, U.S.A. where he has taught urban and historical geography since 1976. He is the author and editor of more than a dozen books, including *World Patterns of Modern Urban Change* (1986); *A Scholar's Guide to Geographical Writing on the American and Canadian Past* (1993); *Thinking about Urban Form* (2004); and *The Making of the American Landscape* (2nd ed.), 2010.

SHAPERS OF URBAN FORM

Explorations in Morphological Agency

Edited by Peter J. Larkham and Michael P. Conzen

Routledge
Taylor & Francis Group
NEW YORK AND LONDON

First published 2014
by Routledge
711 Third Avenue, New York, NY 10017

and by Routledge
2 Park Square, Milton Park, Abingdon, Oxon OX14 4RN

Routledge is an imprint of the Taylor & Francis Group, an informa business

Cover images: Bibliothèque nationale de France, Baron Georges-Eugène Haussmann (1808–1891) / Album of the Scheibler-Grohmann Company, 1921, in the Łódź Muzeum Historii Włókiennictwa / Photo by Anngret Simms / Eugen Huhn, Universal-Lexikon vom Grossherzogthum Baden. Bearbeitet und herausgegeben von einer Gesellschaft von Gelehrten und Vaterlandsfreunden. Mit 14 Stahlstichen, 8 Planen und 6 Tabellen / Adolphe Yvon, Portrait of Napoleon III / World Telegram & Sun photo by Phil Stanziola / Photo by Sailko.

Library of Congress Cataloging in Publication Data
Shapers of urban form : explorations in agency / [edited by] Peter Larkham and Michael P. Conzen.
pages cm
1. Cities and towns – History. 2. Urbanization– History.
I. Larkham, P. J. (Peter J.), 1960– editor of compilation.
II. Conzen, Michael P., editor of compilation. III. Lilley, Keith D., author. Royal authority and urban formation.
HT111.S325 2014
307.7609–dc23 2014005594

ISBN: 978-0-415-73889-7 (hbk)
ISBN: 978-0-415-73890-3 (pbk)
ISBN: 978-1-315-81706-4 (ebk)

Typeset in Bembo
by HWA Text and Data Management, London

Printed and bound in Great Britain by
TJ International Ltd, Padstow, Cornwall

For Jeremy William Richard Whitehand

Imaginative contributor to, patient teacher in, and tireless advocate for the international study of urban morphology and its relevance in shaping urban futures over more than half a century.

CONTENTS

List of Figures x
List of Tables xiii
List of Contributors xiv
Acknowledgments xix
Foreword by Ivor Samuels xxi

PART I
Introduction **1**

1 Agents, Agency, and Urban Form: "The Making of the Urban Landscape" 3
Peter J. Larkham and Michael P. Conzen

PART II
Agency in Pre-Modern Settings **25**

2 Royal Authority and Urban Formation: King Edward I and the Making of His "New Towns" 27
Keith D. Lilley

3 Ecclesiastical Authorities and the Form of Medieval Towns 46
Terry R. Slater

4 Urban Corporate Governance and the Shaping of Medieval Towns 63
Anngret Simms

PART III
Agency in Early Modern Settings **81**

5 Absolute Decisions: Towns Fit for a King 83
Katharine Arntz Thomas

6 Haussmann: Reconsidering His Role in the Transformation of Paris 97
Michaël Darin

7 Colonial Regime Change and Urban Form: How Russian Novo-Arkhangel'sk Became American Sitka 114
Michael P. Conzen

PART IV
Agency in Industrial-Era Settings **135**

8 Squeezing Railroads into Cities: Creating Variable Solutions in Britain and the United States, 1820–1900 137
Arthur J. Krim

9 Shaping the Housing of Industrialists and Workers: The Textile Settlements of Księży Młyn (Łódź) and Żyrardów in Poland 152
Marek Koter and Mariusz Kulesza

10 Residential Differentiation in Nineteenth-Century Glasgow: A Morphogenetic Study of Pollokshields Garden Suburb 173
Michael Pacione

11 The Imprint of the Owner-Builder on American Suburbs 193
Richard Harris

PART V
Agency in Late Modern and Postmodern Settings **217**

12 Modernism against History: Understanding Building Typology and Urban Morphology among Italian Architects in the Twentieth Century 219
Nicola Marzot

13 A New Vision: The Role of Municipal Authorities and Planners in Replanning Britain after the Second World War 230
Peter J. Larkham

14 In search of New Syntheses: Urban Form, Late Flowering Modernism, and the Making of Megastructural Cumbernauld 251
John R. Gold

15 Morphological Processes, Planning, and Market Realities: Reshaping the Urban Waterfront in Auckland and Wellington 267
Kai Gu

16 "Birmingham Needs You. You Need Birmingham": Cities As Actors and Actors in Cities 285
Tim Hall and Phil Hubbard

PART VI
Envoi **301**

17 Agents and Agency, Learning, and Emergence in the Built Environment: A Theoretical Excursion 303
Karl Kropf

Index 323

FIGURES

2.1	The location and distribution of Edward's new towns in England and Wales	28
2.2	Diagram of the suggested relationships between key agents of change and the decision-making processes involved in founding a medieval 'new town'	31
2.3	New Winchelsea, Sussex, England, reconstructed plan of town c.1300	32
2.4	Conwy's historic townscape	33
2.5	The new towns of Flint and Rhuddlan (founded 1277)	38
2.6	The new towns of Conwy (1283–4) and Beaumaris (1295–6)	41
2.7	The plans of Conwy and Beaumaris compared	42
3.1	Reconstruction of the archiepiscopal city of Gniezno, Poland, *c.*1000	48
3.2	Model of the ecclesiastical enclosure of St. Peter's Abbey, Münster, Germany	49
3.3	Ecclesiastical precincts in Winchester, England, *c.*1000	50
3.4	Plan of the new town of Battle, Sussex, England	51
3.5	The planning of tenth- and eleventh-century Worcester, England	53
3.6	Siena, Italy	56
3.7	The parish church of St. Thomas of Canterbury, Winchelsea, England	58
3.8	The plan of thirteenth-century New Salisbury, England	60
4.1	Reconstruction of Viking houses and house-plots in Fishamble Street, Dublin	65
4.2	The foundation of Bern, Switzerland, in 1191	65
4.3	Houses in Rostock, Germany, with stepped gables built in brick Gothic style	71
4.4	Medieval parish church of St Mary's in Rostock	72
4.5	Medieval town-hall on the new Market Square in Rostock	72
4.6	Medieval weighing-station in Rostock	73
4.7	Medieval Hospital of the Holy Spirit in Rostock	74
4.8	Medieval university building in Rostock in former town-hall	74
4.9	Medieval town-house in Rostock of the Cistercian monastery at Doberan	75
4.10	Changes in medieval plot-patterns around the market square in Wrocław	76
4.11	Location of different occupational groups in medieval Göttingen, Germany	77
5.1	The town extensions of Potsdam, Germany	85

5.2 Gutenbergerstraße 26–29, Potsdam 86
5.3 Breite Straße 26–27, Potsdam 87
5.4 Charlottenstraße 107–108, Potsdam 90
5.5 Brandenburger Straße 21–24 93
5.6 Town plan of Karlsruhe, as it had developed to 1843 93
6.1 Baron Haussmann and Emperor Napoléon III 99
6.2 *Les grandes percées*, Paris, France, 1848–1870 106
7.1 Plan of Sitka in 1845, produced by the Russian–American Company 117
7.2 Sitka's Russian townscape: the view from the harbor, looking east 117
7.3 Sitka's Russian townscape: the view from Castle Hill, looking east 118
7.4 Plan of Russian Sitka at transfer, 1867 125
7.5 Plan of Sitka in 1914 126
7.6 Plan of Sitka in 1927 127
7.7 Plan of Sitka in 1999 128
7.8 Lincoln Street east of the cathedral, c.1885 and 2006 129
7.9 Streetscape along the old admiralty, 1868 and 2006 130
7.10 District northeast of the cathedral, 1868 and 2006 131
8.1 Railroad lines and stations in central Liverpool, 1825–1900 141
8.2 Railroad lines and stations in central Manchester and Salford, 1825–1900 141
8.3 Railroad lines and stations in central Baltimore, 1828–1900 146
8.4 Railroad lines and stations in central Philadelphia, 1832–1900 146
8.5 Terminal stations in relation to the metropolitan railroad patterns of the four cities in 1900 148
9.1 'Scheibler's Empire': panoramic view of the industrial complex of Księży Młyn, Łódź, in the 1880s 155
9.2 The early growth stages of Łódź 156
9.3 The first cotton spinning mill at Księży Młyn, Łódź (1870–3) 157
9.4 The second cotton spinning mill at Księży Młyn, Łódź (1877) 157
9.5 Workers' housing at Księży Młyn, Łódź (1870–3) 158
9.6 The Herbst villa (1876) 160
9.7 Panoramic view of the industrial complex of Żyrardów in 1899 162
9.8 Linen spinning mill at Żyrardów (1833) 163
9.9 Plan and spatial structure of the historic core of Żyrardów 164
9.10 Workers' housing at Żyrardów (1867–71) 165
9.11 'Karl Dittrich's palace' (1885–90) at Żyrardów 167
9.12 'New School' for workers' children (1892–6) at Żyrardów 168
9.13 Market square and Catholic parish church (1900–3) at Żyrardów 169
10.1 Glasgow, Scotland 178
10.2 The City of Glasgow in 1782 179
10.3 Design plan for Kinninghouse, 1834 181
10.4 Feuing plan for Pollokshields, 1849 182
10.5 Pollokshields in 1865 183
10.6 Pollokshields in 1883 184
10.7 Plan of Pollokshields, 1894 185
10.8 Villa development in West Pollokshields 186

10.9 Tenements in East Pollokshields 186
10.10 Mapping of six-cluster grouping of socio-morphological characteristics of Pollokshields, 2001 188
11.1 Peoria, Illinois, in 1950 195
11.2 Anarchic development, Carola Avenue, Creve Coeur, Illinois, 1956 197
11.3 Controlled development, Knoll Crest, Peoria, Illinois, 1947 199
11.4 Sketch of the Barnevolt house, Peoria, Illinois, 1996 201
11.5 Advertisement for owner-builder housing service offered by a leading Peoria lumber dealer 203
11.6 Privately-assisted self-help housing in the Reinhard Addition, Pekin, Illinois, 1995 205
11.7 The basement of the Andrews' house, Peoria Heights, Illinois, 1947 206
11.8 Constrained owner-building in Hamilton Park, Peoria, Illinois,1995 209
11.9 State-assisted self-help housing in Wil-Mar Knoll, Bartonville, Illinois, 1995 210
11.10 Privately-assisted self-help housing: the King's house, El Vista, Illinois, 1940 211
12.1 EMPAS headquarters, Via dei Mille 9, Bologna, Italy 224
12.2 Monte Amiata housing complex, Gallaratese district, Milan, Italy 226
12.3 Casa-Parcheggio, via Domenico Mazza 30–48, Pesaro, Itlay 227
13.1 J. Nelson Meredith, Thomas Sharp, Herbert Manzoni, Patrick Abercrombie 232
14.1 Photograph of Cumbernauld Central Area, Stage 1, *c.*1980 252
14.2 Model of Cumbernauld's first phase 259
14.3 Artist's impression of the different deck levels 259
14.4 Demolitions on north side, Cumbernauld 262
15.1 The inner fringe belts of Auckland and Wellington, New Zealand 269
15.2 The waterfront areas adjacent to the CBDs in Auckland and Wellington 271
15.3 The formative processes of the waterfront areas in Auckland and Wellington 272
15.4 Principal plan units in Auckland and Wellington's waterfront areas 273
15.5 Areas of fringe-belt alienation and adaptation in Auckland and Wellington 276
16.1 The Bull Ring Shopping Centre in Birmingham, England 294
16.2 Press hyperbole? Mediating the new Birmingham 294
17.1 Leighton Buzzard, Bedfordshire, England 305
17.2 The simple circuit of learning 306
17.3 The loop of calibration 307
17.4 'Design by committee': mutually modifying circuits of learning 311
17.5 The sub-circuit of 'generate and test' as part of a larger circuit of learning 313
17.6 Form in use by a group: mutually modifying circuits can lead to common forms of behavior 314
17.7 The hierarchy of scale emerges from alternating acts of aggregation and codification of types fed by reproduction 315
17.8 The typological process 318

TABLES

4.1 Morphological agents and components in thirteenth-century Kilkenny, Kalkar and Sopron 68
13.1 Plan numbers and types of author 232
13.2 Numbers of known plans by named consultant authors 234
13.3 Comparison of fees charged by a range of consultants 236
13.4 Fees charged by Thomas Sharp for reconstruction plans 236
13.5 Regional Controllers of the Ministry of Town and Country Planning, 1947 246
15.1 Characteristics of streets, plots, and buildings of the plan units in Auckland's waterfront area 274
15.2 Characteristics of streets, plots and buildings of the plan units in Wellington's waterfront area 275
15.3 Key urban planning and design documents prepared for Wellington's waterfront redevelopment 279
15.4 Key urban planning and design documents prepared for Auckland's waterfront redevelopment 279

CONTRIBUTORS

Michael P. Conzen is professor of geography at the University of Chicago, where he is chairman of the Committee on Geographical Studies. Trained at the universities of Giessen, Cambridge, and Wisconsin, he has held visiting professorships in Germany, Austria, Switzerland, and the United States. His research interests include historical and urban geography, comparative urban morphology, landscape history, and the history of cartography. Among his major publications are *The Encyclopedia of Chicago* (2004, cartographic editor); *Thinking about Urban Form: Papers on Urban Morphology, 1932–1998* by M. R. G. Conzen (2004, ed.); *Mapping Manifest Destiny* (2007, with Diane Dillon); and *The Making of the American Landscape* (rev. ed., 2010, winner of the 2012 Noble Book Prize). He is a corresponding member of the Austrian Academy of Sciences and past president of the International Seminar on Urban Form.

Michaël Darin, a licensed architect, is professor of architectural history and urbanism at the École nationale supérieure d'architecture de Strasbourg, France, and has long been associated with the Laboratoire de recherche histoire architecturale et urbaine - sociétés (LADRHAUS) of the Ecole d'Architecture de Versailles. His academic work reflects his interest in the relationship between society and urban space. Among his many works are *De la rue d'habitation a la voie secondaire* (1998, with Odile Meillerais and Francois Bodet); *La place: espaces et societies: morphologies et sociogénèses des sepaces urbains publics a l'âge modern et conemorain* (2005, with Corradino Corradi); *La Cómedie Urbaine: voir la ville autrement* (2009); and *Patchworks parisiens: petites leçons d'urbanisme ordinaire* (2012, with Gilles Targat).

John R. Gold is professor of urban historical geography and a member of the Institute for Historical and Cultural Research at Oxford Brookes University, United Kingdom. A frequent radio and television broadcaster, he is the author or editor of fourteen books on architectural and cultural subjects. His major books include *Place Promotion: The Use of Publicity and Marketing to Sell Towns and regions* (1994, with Stephen V. Ward); *Representing the Environment* (2004, with George Revill); *Cities of Culture: Staging International Festivals and The Urban Agenda, 1851–2000* (2005, with Margaret Gold); *The Practice of Modernism: Modern Architects and Urban Transformation, 1954–1972* (2007); *Olympic*

Cities: City Agendas, Planning, and the World's Games, 1896 –2012 (2007, with Margaret Gold); and *The Making of Olympic Cities* (2012, with Margaret Gold).

Kai Gu is a senior lecturer in the School of Architecture and Planning at the University of Auckland, New Zealand, and Secretary-General of the International Seminar on Urban Form. He has studied at Zhenzhou University (BEng), South China University of Technology (MA), and the University of Waterloo (PhD). He is interested in urban morphology and urban design, methods of characterizing and managing the urban landscape, and urban planning and design with particular reference to Chinese cities. He has written and co-written many journal articles, including "Comparing traditional urban form in China and Europe: A Fringe-Belt Approach"; *Urban Geography* (2012) with Jeremy W. R. Whitehand and Michael Conzen; and is co-editor of *Urban Morphology and Urban Transformation: Continuity and Change in the Pattern of Urban Growth and Form* (2014).

Tim Hall is professor and head of the School of Applied Social Studies at the University of Winchester, United Kingdom. His research interests include urban geography, globalization, and the significance of criminal organizations in the contemporary global economy. He has also been involved in applied research for clients such as the Countryside Agency, the European Union, Gloucestershire Environmental Trust, and the Gloucestershire National Health Service Trust. His books include *Urban Geography* (4th ed., 2012, with H. Barrett); *The Entrepreneurial City: Geographies of Politics, Regime and Representation* (1998, with Phil Hubbard); *The City Cultures Reader* (2000, with M. Miles and I. Borden); *Urban Futures: Critical Commentaries on Urban Futures* (2003, with M. Miles); and *The Sage Companion to the City* (2008, with Phil Hubbard and John R. Short).

Richard Harris, professor and associate director of the School of Geography and Geology at McMaster University, Canada, studies how the built world is reflected and shaped by the lives of its inhabitants, with a particular focus on American and Canadian housing and suburban development. He is also interested in urban development in the British colonies, 1920s–1960s, with particular reference to Trinidad, British Guiana, the Gold Coast/Ghana, Kenya, and Singapore. His publications include *Changing Suburbs: Foundation, Form and Function* (1999, with Peter Larkham); *Unplanned Suburbs: Toronto's American Tragedy 1900–1950* (1996); *Creeping Conformity: How Canada Became Suburban 1900–1960* (2004); and *Building a Market. The Rise of the Home Improvement industry, 1914–1960* (2012).

Phil Hubbard is professor of urban studies in the School of Social Policy, Sociology and Social Research at the University of Kent, United Kingdom. He is interested in the city as a site of social conflict and urban "disorder." He draws on theories of the city developed in urban sociology and urban geography for his research in addition to engaging with debates in criminology and socio-legal studies. This approach is illustrated in his monograph *City* (2006) and his recent publication, *Cities and Sexualities* (2011). Some of his other publications include *Geographies of Politics, Regime, and Representation* (1998, with Tim Hall); *Thinking Geographically: Space, Theory, and Contemporary Human Geography* (2002); and *The Sage Companion to the City* (2008, with Tim Hall and John R. Short).

Marek Koter is a professor emeritus and former director (1981–2007) of the Department of Political Geography and Regional Studies at the University of Łódź, Poland. He was a member of Geographical Sciences National Accreditation Commission of the Polish Academy of Sciences. He specializes in historical, urban, and political geography. His work has focused both on urban morphology in Poland and on borderlands and regional differences. In addition to many studies on Łódź and its region (in Polish), his published works include *Region and Regionalism: Social and Political Aspects* (1995); *Historical, Ethnic and Geographical Problems of Borderlands* (2005, with Marek Sobczyński); and *The Role of Borderlands in United Europe: The Borderlands and Integration Processes* (2005, also with Marek Sobczyński).

Arthur J. Krim, an architectural historian in Boston, Massachusetts, United States, is a survey consultant and preservation planner for the Massachusetts Historical Commission. He has degrees from the University of Chicago (MA) and Clark University (PhD). He has held academic positions at Clark University, Boston University, Salve Regina University, and Boston Architectural College. His interest in roads and railways is evident from his published monographs, which include *The Innovation and Diffusion of the Street Railway in North America* (1967); *Northwest Cambridge: Survey of Architectural History in Cambridge, vol. 5* (1977); *Carriage House to Auto House: a Guide to Brookline's Transportation Buildings to 1940* (2002, with Roger Reed and Greer Hardwicke); and *Route 66: Iconography of the American Highway* (2005, with Denis Wood).

Karl Kropf is the director and owner of the consulting firm Built Form Resource. He received his education at the University of California, Berkeley, California, United States, Oxford Polytechnic, and the University of Birmingham, United Kingdom, where he is a member of the Urban Morphology Research Group. He also teaches a module at Oxford Brookes University on using the built environment as a design resource. His varied activities focus on the interplay between theory and practice and using one to inform the other. His work through his firm involves masterplanning, urban design, cultural landscapes, heritage and sustainability. He co-edited the book *Theories and Manifestoes of Contemporary Architecture* (1997) and is currently working on a *Handbook of Urban Morphology*.

Mariusz Kulesza is head of the historical geography and heritage section of the Department of Political Geography and Regional Studies at the University of Łódź, Poland. His interests center across the whole range of rural and urban settlement history, with special reference to Poland. He has contributed to many academic monographs in both English and Polish, including *Morfogeneza miast na obszarze Polski srodkowej w okresie przedrozbiorowym: dawne województwa leczyckie i sieradzkie* (2001); *Wybrane problemy geografii historycznej* (2008); *Geografia historyczna jako determinanta rozwoju nauk humanistycznych* (2009); *Rola wspólnot wyznaniowych w historii miasta Lodzi* (2010); and *Zagadnienia morfogenezy i rozplanowania miast sredniowiecznych w Polsce* (2011).

Peter J. Larkham is professor of planning in the Birmingham School of the Built Environment at Birmingham City University, United Kingdom. His interests span the fields of urban morphology, planning history, and heritage conservation, to all of which he has made copious research contributions. He is a member of the Urban Morphology Research Group in Birmingham, associate editor of *Urban Morphology*, and a former editor of *Planning History*. His publications include *Urban Landscapes: International Perspectives* (1992, edited with J. W. R. Whitehand); *Conservation and the City* (1996), *Changing Suburbs: Foundation, Form, and Function* (1999, edited with R. Harris); and *The Blitz and Its Legacy* (2013, edited with M. Clapson).

Keith D. Lilley is a reader in historical geography at Queen's University Belfast, Northern Ireland, United Kingdom and specializes in the study of historic landscapes through the use of maps and mapping techniques. His innovative approach combines spatial technologies such as GIS and GPS to explore the character and content of historic landscapes. He received a PhD from the University of Birmingham. He is a member of the Board of Historic Towns Trust and is a contributor to a pan-European heritage project, People, Localities, Archives and Cultures in Europe (PLACE). He is the author of, among others, *Topographical Frameworks and the Concept of the Morphological Frame* (1992); *Urban Life in the Middle Ages 1000–1450* (2002); and *City and Cosmos: The Medieval World in Urban Form* (2009).

Nicola Marzot has been an associate professor of architecture at Delft University of Technology since 2006. He has held previous positions at the Faculty of Architecture of Ferrara, Hosei University and Lund University. He received his PhD from the Faculty of Engineering of Bologna. His research is primarily focused on the theory and method of architecture and urban design strategies in close relation to urban morphology and building typology. He also runs his own architectural firm, PERFORMA A+U and has been recognized in several international design competitions. He has published *Bologna: architettura, cittá, paesaggio* (2006, with Pierluigi Giordani and Giuliano Gresleri); *Il consumo della città* (2009); and *Architettura per un territorio sostenibile: città e paesaggio tra innovazione tecnologica e tradizione* (2010, with Marcello Balzani).

Michael Pacione is chair of geography at the University of Strathclyde, Scotland. He was educated at the University of St. Andrews (MA) and the University of Dundee (PhD). In 2009, he was awarded the Research Medal of the Royal Scottish Geographical Society for his contributions to geographical knowledge. He has also taught at Queen's University, Belfast, the University of Guelph, Ontario, and the University of Vienna. He has published twenty-five books and more than 130 professional research papers. His recent work has focused on the processes of urban restructuring in cities of the contemporary world, sustainable urban development, and land use conflict and public participation in local planning. His most recent books include *Glasgow: The Socio-Spatial Development of the City* (1995); *Applied Geography: Principles and Practice* (1999); and *Urban Geography: A Global Perspective* (2009).

Ivor Samuels is an architect and town planner trained at the Architectural Association and Edinburgh University, with experience in the public and private sectors in the United Kingdom and abroad. He is a former director of the Joint Centre for Urban Design at Oxford Brookes University, where he is Visiting Fellow. He has been a visiting professor at universities in Denmark, France, Italy, Spain, and Switzerland; Latin America; the United States; and Australia and was a consultant to the Civic Trust Regeneration Unit on Town Centre Masterplans. His publications include *New Use for Old Stones: The Practice of Using Old Environments for New Cultural Activities* (1982); *Towards an Architectural Analysis of Urban Form: Conservation Studies in Britain and Italy* (1983); *Urban Morphology in Design* (1985); and *Urban Forms: Death and Life of the Urban Block* (2004).

Anngret Simms is professor of historical geography emerita at University College, Dublin, Ireland. Her professional work has been dedicated to the social and spatial expressions of medieval European urbanism, with special emphasis on urban morphology. For many years, she has chaired the European Historic Towns Atlas Project of the International Commission on the History of Towns, overseeing the multinational publication of hundreds of historic town atlases. Her recent publications include *Irish Towns: A Guide to Sources* (1998, with William Nolan); a contribution to *A History of Settlement* *in Ireland* (2000); *Dublin: Through Space And Time c. 900–1900* (2001, with Joseph Brady); and *Dublin in the Medieval World: Studies in Honour of Howard B. Clarke* (2009). Her academic career also served as inspiration for the volume *Surveying Ireland's Past: Multidisciplinary Essays in Honor of Anngret Simms* (2004).

Terry R. Slater is an honorary senior research fellow at the School of Geography, Earth and Environmental Sciences at the University of Birmingham, United Kingdom. He is also director and trustee of Moseley Community Development Trust. His research interests include English medieval town planning, town-plan analysis, North American colonial urban development, urban conservation, pilgrimage and religious faith. His recent publications include *Towns in Decline, AD 100–1600* (2000); *Edgbaston: A History* (2002); *Celebrating a Century of Christ: The Diocese of Birmingham 1905–2005* (2005); and *A County of Small Towns: The Development of Herfordshire's Urban Landscape to c. 1800* (2008, with Nigel Goose). He is currently preparing *An Historical Atlas of Warwickshire* for publication.

Katharine Arntz Thomas is a freelance editor and translator living in Kempen, Germany. She received her PhD from the University of Birmingham, United Kingdom, in 2002 with a thesis entitled "Evolving residential landscapes: Changing forms, images and representations of house and home in Berlin, Germany, 1890–1945." She was a member of the Urban Morphology Research Group there, and assistant editor of *Urban Morphology,* in which her article "Authoritarian townscapes and *laissez-faire* change: Understanding central Potsdam's built form" appeared in 1998. She published *Building Regulation and the Shaping of Urban Form in Germany* (2002).

ACKNOWLEDGMENTS

Photo credits

Fig. 2.4 Keith D. Lilley.

Fig. 3.2 Münster Stadtmuseum, photograph by Tomasz Samek.

Figs. 3.6, 3.7 Terry R. Slater.

Figs. 5.2, 5.3, 5.4, 5.5 Katharine Arntz Thomas.

Fig. 6.1 Bibliothèque Nationale, France; Walters Art Museum, Baltimore, U.S.A..

Fig. 7.2 Elmer E. Rasmuson Library, University of Alaska Fairbanks.

Fig. 7.3 Oliver Family Photograph Collections, Bancroft Library, University of California Berkeley.

Fig. 7.8 (upper) Historical Collections, Alaska State Library.

Fig. 7.9 (upper), 7.10 (upper) Lone Mountain College Collection of Stereographs by Eadweard Muybridge, Bancroft Library, University of California Berkeley.

Figs. 7.8 (lower), 7.9 (lower), 7.10 (lower) Michael Conzen.

Figs. 9.3, 9.4, 9.5, 9.6, 9.8, 9.10, 9.11, 9.12, 9.13 Mark Koter and Mariusz Kulesza.

Figs 10.8, 10.9 Michael Pacione.

Fig. 11.3 Mel Schmidt.

Figs. 11.6, 11.8, 11.9 Richard Harris.

Fig. 11.7 Mary Andrews.

Fig. 11.10 Wahlfeld Manufacturing Company.

Fig. 12.1 Giancarlo Cataldi.

Fig. 12.2 Gabriele Basilico. Courtesy: Collezione Francesco Moschini e Gabriel Vaduva AAM Architettura Arte Moderna.

Fig. 13.1 *Bristol Evening Post*, Sharp Collection, Newcastle University Library Special Collections, Mirrorpix and the RIBA Library Photographs Collection.

Figs 14.1, 14.4 Royal Commission on the Ancient and Historical Monuments of Scotland.

Figs 14.2 North Ayrshire Council.

Fig. 15.2 (upper) Ports of Auckland, Ltd.

Fig. 15.2 (lower) Kai Gu.

Fig. 16.1 West Midlands Police.

Sources for other illustrations

Fig. 3.1 after Zurowskiego in J. Widawski (1973) *Miejskie Mury Obronne w Panstwie Polskim do Poczatku XV Wieku*, Warsaw Wydawnictwo Ministerstwa Obrony Narodowej, for the Instytut Sztuki Polskiej Akademii Nauk Fig. 70.

Fig. 3.3 after M. Biddle (ed.) (1976) *Winchester in the Early Middle* Ages, Oxford Oxford University Press.

Fig. 4.1 P. F. Wallace (1992) *The Viking Age Buildings of Dublin*, 2 parts, Medieval Dublin Excavations 1962–81, Ser. A 1. Dublin Royal Irish Academy for the National Museum of Ireland.

Fig. 4.2 Buergerbibliothek Bern.

Figs. 4.3, 4.4, 4.5, 4.6 4.7, 4.8, 4.9 Vicke Schorler (1578–1586) Handwritten Chronicle of Rostock, Municipal Archives of Rostock.

Fig. 4.10 R. Czaja (2010) 'Die Gestaltung des Stadtraumes und das Sozialgefüge mittelalterlicher Städte am Beispiel Polens', in F. Opll and C. Sonnlechner (eds) *Europäische Städte im Mittelalter*, Forschungen und Beiträge zur Wiener Stadtgeschichte 52 203–216. Innsbruck Studien Verlag.

Fig. 4.11 after D. Denecke (1987) 'Sozialtopographie der mittelalterlichen Stadt Göttingen', in D. Denecke and H.M. Kühn (eds) *Göttingen. Geschichte einer Universitätsstadt* 1 199–210. Göttingen Vandenhoeck & Ruprecht.

Fig. 5.6 from H. Straub's *Plan von Carlsruhe 1843* (1843) Karlsruhe Verlag von C. Macklot.

Fig. 6.2 after P. Pinon (ed.) (2002) *Atlas du Paris Haussmannien la ville en héritage du Second Empire à nos jours*, Paris Parigramme.

Fig. 7.1 Arndt, K. L. and Pierce, R. A. (2003) *Sitka National Historical Park historical context study a construction history of Sitka, Alaska, as documented in the records of the Russian-American Company*, 2nd ed., Sitka, Alaska Sitka National Historical Park, National Park Service, p.129.

Fig. 9.1 *Album of the Scheibler-Grohmann Company,* 1921, in the Łódź Muzeum Historii Włókiennictwa.

Fig. 9.7 Eckert Pflug, Kunstverlag Leipzig–München, Muzeum Mazowsza Zachodniego.

Figs. 10.3, 10.4 Strathclyde Regional Archives.

Figs. 10.5, 10.6, 10.7 Mitchell Library.

Fig. 11.2 Sanborn Map Company (1956) *Sanborn Fire Atlas, Peoria, Illinois*, New York the Company, plate 94.

Fig. 11.4 Walter Barnevolt.

Fig. 11.5 *Peoria Journal Transcript*, 3 March 1940, section 1-10.

Fig. 12.3 Carlo Aymonino. Courtesy: Collezione Francesco Moschini e Gabriel Vaduva AAM Architettura Arte Moderna.

Fig. 14.3 Royal Commission on the Ancient and Historical Monuments of Scotland, drawing by Michael Evans.

The following figures are the work of the authors of the respective chapters Figs 2.1, 2.2, 2.3, 2.5, 2.6, 2.7, 3.4, 3.5, 3.6, 3.7, 3.8, 5.1, 7.4, 7.5, 7.6, 7.7, 8.1, 8.2, 8.3, 8.4, 8.5, 9.2, 9.9, 10.1, 10.2, 10.8, 10.9, 10.10, 11.1, 15.1, 15.3, 15.4, 15.5, 16.2, 17.1, 17.2 17.3, 17.4, 17.5, 17.6, 17.7, 17.8.

FOREWORD

Ivor Samuels

On being asked to write a foreword to this volume I had two immediate responses. The first was to question the appropriateness of an architect writing the first words in a collection that is penned predominantly by eminent geographers and historians. In the interest of fostering interdisciplinary dialog, though, it seemed reasonable to accept. The second was that this book recalls an earlier one edited nearly twenty-five years ago by one of the contributors to this volume (Slater 1990), prompting the thought that today it is possible in the field to focus a group of original essays such as this around a more tightly-structured theme. It may be helpful to situate this present collection within a broad context of writing on urban form to trace its roots in earlier developments and in particular to an individual to whom it is in very large part a tribute.

The connection between my two reactions can be found in the way the field of urban morphology – as a distinct and methodologically innovative approach to the study of urban form – has evolved over the last twenty-five years. Its scope has widened both geographically, to include in its discussions representatives from five continents, and professionally, with contributions from a variety of disciplines interested in urban form, including architects. Architects from early on had figured prominently in the discourse of urban morphology in some countries, for example Italy, but until recently not in others, like Britain.

From an international standpoint, this evolution was marked by two significant initiatives. The first was the establishment in 1996 of the International Seminar on Urban Form (ISUF), following two years of informal meetings in Lausanne with participants from eight countries (the first president of ISUF, Anne Vernez Moudon has described its foundation, Moudon 1997). The second was the inauguration of *Urban Morphology*, the journal of ISUF, in 1997. In both of these initiatives Jeremy Whitehand has been and continues to be a towering – literally in the case of meetings – presence. As Editor of *Urban Morphology* he has been a member of the Council of ISUF since the group's modest beginning, helping steer it to its present position as a creative international force in helping define how urban forms worldwide should be understood and managed. As such, ISUF sponsors annual conferences which alternate between European venues and cities in Asia, Australia, the United States and Latin America and attract more than 300 delegates. Whitehand has also been instrumental in establishing ISUF's valuable website (www.urbanform.org).

Under Whitehand's editorship *Urban Morphology* has grown into a recognised major refereed academic journal. He has been indefatigable in maintaining its high standard, and while the journal is published in English he has labored hard to include the research of writers whose native languages are not English, making it *truly* of international scope. The published volumes of the journal now constitute in themselves an invaluable reference source for urban morphology in different regional contexts, while being catholic in its coverage of conceptual formulations in an academic world where some methods approach the exclusivity of cults. In particular those fourteen papers (and counting) that examine the study of urban morphology in different countries represent a unique collection of knowledge. However, he has also maintained the journal as a lively publication with a wide attraction: it is much more than a rather dull vehicle for esoteric papers submitted by academic authors trying to raise their research scores, which has been the fate of some sister journals. Furthermore, his inclusion of personal viewpoints renders the journal topical, which is unusual in a biannual publication.

After having taught in the Universities of Newcastle upon Tyne and Glasgow, Whitehand joined the Department of Geography of the University of Birmingham in 1971 where he was appointed Professor of Urban Geography in 1991 and has been Emeritus Professor since 2005. In addition to his undergraduate teaching, in 1974 Whitehand established the Urban Morphology Research Group (UMRG) as a forum for postgraduate and professional studies. It became an international focus for doctoral students, academics and professionals both at the University of Birmingham and from other institutions both academic and professional in Britain and abroad. The significance of this initiative, based in Britain but wholly outward-looking, as well as its quiet but crucial role in the international development of urban morphology, can hardly be overstated.

It was through this group that I first learned of the work of British urban geographers and historians in the field of urban morphology. We live in a digital age in which cross-disciplinary contacts have become common, and it is perhaps now difficult to understand how impervious were the boundaries between professions and also intellectual contexts before the establishment of the UMRG and, two decades later, ISUF. I was trained as an architect in the 1960s and my perspective on urban form was determined by the work of Cullen and the townscape school and Lynch, and I became aware of the Italian typomorphologists during a period of practice in Italy. I was only made aware of the work of Conzen and Whitehand in 1981 by a geographer colleague after joining the Centre for Urban Design at the then Oxford Polytechnic. The two schools, Italian and British, were brought together at a remarkably fruitful seminar held by the UMRG in 1982. As a result many urban design graduates from Oxford have continued their doctoral studies with Jeremy Whitehand through the UMRG, and as a consequence have gone on to apply urban morphology concepts in planning practice.

The international character of the UMRG has been continuously maintained by the presence of students from France, Germany, the Netherlands and Iceland. More recently there have been a number of Chinese postgraduates at Birmingham as a result of Jeremy Whitehand's considerable involvement in matters of urban form and conservation in the context of the rapid urbanization of China.

Behind all the organizational engagement with and encouragement of urban morphological work on the part of others lies a major body of personal scholarship by Whitehand himself. In several monographs and numerous articles, he has presented original research on many of the key questions raised by theoretical advances in the field. Drawing on ideas formulated by M. R. G. Conzen, he pursued urban fringe-belt studies in the 1960s and 1970s, refining the concept and ultimately connecting it to the empirical evidence of business and development cycles (Whitehand 1987a). In the 1980s, he examined the nature of morphological change as city centers underwent modernization, and moved on to study residential growth under planning constraints (Whitehand 1984, 1989). By the

1990s he explored the morphological character of 20th-century British suburbs (Whitehand and Carr 2001a). During this period of three decades Whitehand also collected, summarised, and interpreted the results of studies by himself and others in a series of often edited works that lent coherence to the field (Whitehand and Patten 1977; Whitehand and Larkham 1992; Whitehand 1987a, 1992). And in many articles and two synthesizing books, he outlined the developing intellectual character of urban morphology in the second half of the twentieth century, and particularly the debt the British school owed to M. R. G. Conzen (Whitehand 1981, 1987b, 1992, 2001). With the new millennium Whitehand took a keen interest in the relationship between the Italian typomorphological and the British geographical schools of morphological theorizing, and pressed more vigorously for international comparative study (Whitehand 2003a, 2003b).

Over the last decade, Whitehand has led by example, making a serious foray into Chinese urban morphology, and with the help of Kai Gu introducing and testing many western theoretical concepts of urban morphogenesis, particularly Conzenian ones, against the Chinese historical record, and by direct comparison with the European one (Whitehand and Gu 2006; Whitehand, Gu and Whitehand 2011; Conzen M.P., Gu and Whitehand 2012). He has worked on several Chinese historic cities, and among other appointments he has been Urban Planning Consultant to Pingyao County, Shanxi Province since 2006.

Through much of this work there runs a constant theme: the role of agency, individual and institutional, in morphological change. 'Agency' has been implicit in a great deal of work in the field over the decades, but Whitehand succeeded in making it more explicit, aligning it more comfortably with the scholarly traditions of urban history and planning history (Whitehand 1983, 1984; Whitehand & Carr 2001). Morphological studies since have shown some tendency to pay more attention to individual and group decision-making in the production of the spatial patterns on the ground and in the third dimension that are the stock-in-trade of morphological analysis. It is this awareness, and this commitment to understanding agency in the built environment that situate this collection squarely in the conceptual movement that Whitehand has promoted.

In his most recent Urban Morphology editorials Whitehand has dealt with two fundamental themes in the urban morphology discourse. The first is that "as major embodiments of culture, the physiognomies of cities should therefore be a high priority for debate and research". He then notes that although this may be so obvious as to need no emphasis, especially across cultures, nevertheless, he continues, "there is insufficient recognition of this priority in research and practice" (2012, p. 99). The second theme relates to the interconnection of research and practice: "It may seem self-evident that the production of new urban forms and, even more obviously, the modification and conservation of existing ones should be grounded on an understanding of present urban forms and their past development. But in reality this elementary requirement frequently remains unfulfilled" (Whitehand 2013, p. 3). He goes on to note that, while "understanding the way in which urban form has been developed should be fundamental to urban design . . . copying and pasting an existing form is a risky design strategy unless it stems from an understanding of how such form has arisen" (Whitehand 2013, p. 4). This volume, which discusses the agents that have influenced great changes across a wide range of urban contexts and through different time periods, attempts to redress some of the shortcomings Whitehand has identified and represents, therefore, a major contribution to both these themes.

Ivor Samuels
Oxford Brookes University
Urban Morphology Research Group

References

Conzen, M. P., Gu, K., and Whitehand, J. W. R. (2012) Comparing traditional urban form in China and Europe: a fringe-belt approach. *Urban Geography*, 33: 22–45.

Moudon, A. V. (1997) Urban morphology as an emerging interdisciplinary field. *Urban Morphology*, 1: 3–10.

Slater, T. R. (ed.) (1990) *The Built Form of Western Cities.* Leicester: Leicester University Press.

Whitehand, J. W. R. (1981) Conzenian ideas: extension and development. *Institute of British Geographers, Special Publication,* 13: 127–52.

Whitehand, J. W. R. (1983) Land-use structure, built-form and agents of change. *Institute of British Geographers Special Publication,* 14: 41–59.

Whitehand, J. W. R. (1984) *Rebuilding Town Centres: Developers, Architects and Styles.* University of Birmingham Department of Geography, Occasional Publication no. 19.

Whitehand, J. W. R. (1987a) *The Changing Face of Cities: A Study of Development Cycles and Urban Form.* Institute of British Geographers, Special Publication 21. Oxford: Basil Blackwell.

Whitehand, J. W. R. (1987b) M. R. G. Conzen and the intellectual parentage of urban morphology. *Planning History Bulletin,* 9: 35–41.

Whitehand, J. W. R. (1989) *Residential Development under Restraint: A Case Study in London's Rural-Urban Fringe.* University of Birmingham School of Geography Occasional Publication no. 28.

Whitehand, J. W. R. (1992) *The Making of the Urban Landscape.* Institute of British Geographers Special Publication 26. Oxford: Basil Blackwell.

Whitehand, J. W. R. (2001a) British urban morphology: the Conzenian tradition. *Urban Morphology,* 5: 103–9

Whitehand, J. W. R. (2001b) The creators of England's inter-war suburbs. *Urban History,* 28: 218–34.

Whitehand, J. W. R. (2003a) From Como to Alnwick: in pursuit of Caniggia and Conzen. *Urban Morphology* 7: 69–72

Whitehand, J. W. R. (2003b) Gianfranco Caniggia and M. R. G. Conzen: remarkable parallels, in C. D'Amato Guerrieri and G. Strappa (eds.), *Gianfranco Caniggia: dalla lettura di Como all'interpretazione tipologica della città,* 109–14. Bari: Mario Adda.

Whitehand, J. W. R. (2012) Editorial comment: thinking cross-culturally. *Urban Morphology,* 16: 99-100.

Whitehand, J. W. R. (2013) Editorial comment: urban morphological research and practice. *Urban Morphology,* 17: 3–4 .

Whitehand, J. W. R., and Carr, C. M. H. (2001) *Twentieth-Century Suburbs: A Morphological Approach*. London: Routledge.

Whitehand, J. W. R. and Gu, K. (2006) Research on Chinese urban form: retrospect and prospect. *Progress in Human Geography,* 30: 337–55.

Whitehand, J. W. R., Gu, K., and Whitehand, S. M. (2011) Fringe belts and socioeconomic change in China. *Environment and Planning B: Planning and Design* 38: 41–60.

Whitehand, J. W. R., and Larkham, P. J. (eds.) (1992) *Urban Landscapes: International Perspectives*. London: Routledge.

Whitehand, J. W. R., and Patten, J. (eds.) (1977) Change in the town. *Transactions of the Institute of British Geographers,* NS 2 (3).

PART I

Introduction

1

AGENTS, AGENCY, AND URBAN FORM

"The Making of the Urban Landscape"

Peter J. Larkham and Michael P. Conzen

Like all human phenomena, the "look" of cities—their spatial composition and the content of their built environments—has intrigued commentators and philosophers since virtually the beginning of urban life. A vast array of descriptive knowledge of urban forms has accumulated over the centuries, encompassing every region with an urban tradition, but only in comparatively recent times has the drive to understand the complexity of urban forms and their varied paths of intertwined development taken root as a systematic quest. The literature that has emerged, while inherently interdisciplinary by nature, owes much to the disciplinary perspectives of its contributors. This is not a bad thing, but a fuller understanding can come only from continued international and inter-disciplinary cross-fertilization of ideas and modes of inquiry.

Specialized branches of knowledge relating to urban morphology have sprung up in the professional disciplines of history, geography, anthropology, sociology, art history, architecture, landscape architecture, and engineering, to name only the most prominent, but the task of interpreting urban form itself, in all its varied physical manifestations, does not lie at the existential core of any of these fields. At the end of the day, historians focus on human decisions and actions; geographers on spatial logics and their resulting place-to-place differences; anthropologists on the shaping influence of cultures; sociologists on the interactions between people, and between individuals and society; art historians on the visualizations of artists and their audiences; architects on the challenge of designing workable and expressive buildings; landscape architects on the functional and decorative aspects of open spaces; and engineers on conforming their infrastructural systems with the laws of physics and chemistry. However, when researchers in any of these fields choose to study the genesis and functioning of the built environment of cities, past or present, they are, in fact, making contributions to the field of urban morphology.

A growing perspective in the study of urban morphology over the last couple of decades has been the increasing concern with the role of the "agent" in creating urban forms. This interest may hardly seem new, in the sense that all urban forms clearly emanate from decisions and actions taken by individuals and groups. Yet that proposition is easy to assert but less easy to demonstrate in the detail called for by the nature of the forms being studied. It is not always simple to ascribe "authorship" to the myriad buildings and environments that have accumulated incrementally over time in any given place and for which the record of multiple "authors" may well be hidden, lost, or at best difficult to reveal and reconstruct. Even where a "plan" is known, it is usually, and often over-simplistically, attached to the name of a "great planner." So the growing interest in "agency" in urban morphology represents a valuable movement to better account for the ways in which specific urban forms and particular configurations of urban space have come about. It moves beyond the descriptive accounts of evolution and "sedimentation" in space, which too often carry something of an aura of inevitability about them, as if change and (especially) progress were somehow automatic and to be expected. And it moves beyond the sort of structural explanations that suggest agency only indirectly through the composite character and changes that can be measured in the built forms themselves but without the personalized data behind them.

For most people, the built environment is merely a background to their lives. They live, work, relax, and sleep amid a complexity of buildings, infrastructure, and spaces. For many, though, the urban structure is more than a mere container. We are more than mere consumers; and consumption is not merely a passive action. We are curious about, and sometimes actively involved in, our ever-changing built surroundings. For all urban areas do change, in some cases with extreme rapidity. Lack of change often signals a failure to react to changing social and economic trends, demands, and opportunities: it suggests, in a word, stagnation. Even towns whose economy and fame rests to a significant degree on their heritage of iconic built forms—Paris, Rome, Bath—change and adapt all the time.

People become involved in many ways, large and small. They may design, construct, or indeed demolish buildings and whole areas. They may promote or control development through mechanisms such as planning regulations and local, regional, and national municipal and political organizations. They may, as individuals or groups, seek to restrict the scale or speed of change. Some, and often this may be a majority, may remain uninvolved. They may never seek to extend their houses, protest at development proposals, or actively welcome innovations. Yet they are, nevertheless, affected by urban change. They will shop in new superstores, although they may regret the passing of the corner shop. They will drive along the new bypass, welcoming its speedier movement, although they may regret its intrusion into the landscape. But questions often arise in the minds of many people, whether they are directly or indirectly, actively or passively, involved. "How did this get built? Why did they demolish that? Who designed that? Why isn't something done about this?" Answers can be found to all of these types of question, although finding the information can be a lengthy process. In many cases, complete information is unobtainable, and appropriate inferences have to be drawn. When such research is done, it often fascinates locals, informs professionals, and can be revealing at scales from the most local to the national and indeed international.

This book seeks some of these answers by exploring one specific intellectual approach to the study of urban change: that of tracing the stories of development, identifying the agents and agencies involved, and how they influence the outcomes in the urban landscape. In short, this is the process of "making the urban landscape." In using this phrase, we deliberately paraphrase both Hoskins's early discursive approach to the broader landscape and Whitehand's detailed analytical approach to urban landscape development (Hoskins 1955; Whitehand 1992a). A crucial element is awareness of the significance of change over time: for "the landscape we see is not a static arrangement of objects. It has become what it is, and it is usually in the process of becoming something different" (Darby 1953: 7).

Origins of Early Research Approaches

The broad field of research covered by this book is now commonly referred to as "urban morphology." Literally this means "the study of urban form," but the academic concerns and approaches of the new millennium have developed far from the roots of this field in late-nineteenth century German-speaking Europe. It is helpful, therefore, to summarize this intellectual development, as it sets the scene for our detailed research agenda and approach and also serves to refute some misconceptions about the whole field of study.

Some of the earliest work on the urban landscape[1] was undertaken in the German academic and intellectual tradition in Europe toward the end of the nineteenth century and was principally an extension of wider concerns of landscape evolution within the developing discipline of geography and cognate fields. One of its earliest results was an essay on German town layouts by Johann Fritz (1894), who used visual inspection of town plans as his main source to draw a distinction between eastern and western German medieval towns.

This comparative overview appealed to Otto Schlüter. In his mid-twenties, Schlüter bravely reacted against the emphasis in Volume 1 of Friedrich Ratzel's *Anthropogeographie*, which appeared to align human geography with the investigation of human dependency on nature (Ratzel 1882–99). Schlüter proposed the morphology of the cultural landscape (*Kulturlandschaft*) as the central goal of cultural geography (*Kulturgeographie*), just as geomorphology was central to physical geography. He was interested in understanding the forms created by human activities, but also, and important for our argument, he considered their origins and their development through the course of time. This was not mere description but an integration of form, function, and historical development. Schlüter applied this framework to studies of settlement geography (1899a), a study of the ground-plans of towns (1899b), and a detailed monograph on the settlements of north-eastern Thuringia (1903). Empirical field-based research underpinned his approach. He felt that the urban landscape (*Stadtlandschaft*), that is, the physical form of a town, was the main object of research in its own right (Schlüter 1899a).

Schlüter's influence spread beyond his own publications, especially through the dissertations he supervised at the University of Halle. Prominent among these were studies by Walter Geisler and Rudolph Martiny, who both worked extensively on comparative studies of urban form and the classification of town plans (Geisler 1924; Martiny 1928). The 1920s was a period of intensive work in German-speaking urban morphology (Dörries 1930) but, as Jeremy Whitehand has pointed out, they "allowed themselves to be pushed by the enormous scope of their projects into merely morphographic classification, producing profuse nomenclature with little meaning. Thus, they aggravated a tendency towards mere morphography already apparent in the poorer types of settlement monographs" of the period (Whitehand 1981: 4).

The limitations of this simplistic morphographical approach were noted earlier by Erich Keyser (Keyser 1958). In particular, the small-scale town maps commonly used at the time had insufficient detail to allow recognition of details of street and plot alignments crucial to revealing distinct stages of growth. The use of contemporary plans also tended to obscure developmental stages that might be revealed through comparison of a series of historical maps. Further, the theories and evidence of other disciplines, including urban constitutional, social and economic history, and archaeology, were to add much to the morphographical approach.

German-speaking historians had also become interested in issues of urban form, topography, and development at much the same time as geographers. However, their exploration of documentary sources led, in some cases, to different conclusions. Siegfried Rietschel (1897), for example, showed the ubiquity of deliberate town founding and the characteristic duality of planned market settlement and pre-urban nucleus. Motivating historians such as Rietschel was the fact that many town records were incomplete, and it led to an early recognition that the existing urban landscape could be used as a form of historical data source and the basis for a new research method: urban constitutional topography (*städtische Verfassungstopographie*; Frölich 1938).

Similarly, German-speaking architects developed a significant research base in historical urban form during the early-twentieth century. Eduard Siedler (1914), for example, reviewed the plan of every medieval town in the Elbe-Oder region, identifying numerous examples of multi-period composite plans, but he did not *map* plan types. As Whitehand has recognized, "The fact that their professional training produced early awareness and technical understanding of the significance of artifacts on the ground partly explains why architects were interested in the socio-economic context of medieval urban origins and development that urban historians were discovering" (Whitehand 1981: 6).

Despite these complementary research traditions, however, the references in their published work suggest that even the German geographical morphologists paid little heed to this work until near the end of the inter-war period. The classifications of Geisler, Martiny, and others were criticized for being both ends in themselves and being of little value in advancing the discipline. These works were referred to as *erschöpfend*, a word having the dual meaning of exhaustive and exhausting (Schöller 1953). Hans Bobek was particularly critical, and argued that the study of form *per se* should not neglect the dynamic forces creating those forms (Bobek 1927). However, in light of these criticisms and notwithstanding the relative disregard for extra-disciplinary contributions, the Geographical Institute at the University of Berlin contained teachers (including Bobek and the geomorphologist Herbert Louis) who spurred an interest in settlement geography and urban morphology on the part of M. R. G. Conzen, who would later advance the field in one particularly important respect. His was an education that placed urban morphology in the rounded context of geology, geomorphology, and urban history (Whitehand 1981: 8–9). Significantly, Conzen left Germany in the very year that Walter Christaller's ground-breaking study introducing central place theory was published (Christaller 1933), which would spark a strong disciplinary reaction against morphological topics for decades, both in Germany and in English-speaking countries, and which still influences research today (c.f. Parr 2002; Meijers 2007).

In the English-speaking academic world, approaches were very different, and there was little contact with the German literature. There is a long tradition of study of British medieval towns, which has long included descriptions of regular street patterns; some of this work included detailed archaeological and historical data on origins (e.g. Hope 1909, on Ludlow); others were more general and comparative (Tout 1917; Hughes and Lamborn 1923: chapter 2; Fleure 1931; Dickinson 1934). Probably the first use of the term "urban morphology" in English is the study of some Swedish towns by an American, John Leighly (1928). Ironically, Leighly was a product of an intellectual tradition, the Berkeley school of cultural geography, established by Carl Sauer, that harked back directly to German geographical roots. However, the lasting impact of this school lay in rural landscape study rather than on towns, with Leighly's study a conspicuous exception (M. P. Conzen 1993: 30–31).

The most direct British link with German ideas on town formation came through the publications of R. E. Dickinson in the 1940s (Dickinson 1945, 1951), although his emulation of the earlier German literature brought no advance in theory or method and therefore garnered little influence. It is perhaps a telling factor that M. R. G. Conzen, after his arrival in England, found little familiar or challenging work in English with which to engage.

Postwar Developments

Progress in urban morphology in the postwar period was slow in any discipline or language area.[2] During these years both publications, whether merely descriptive or more analytical, and serious scholars, in any discipline or profession, with a focus on urban morphology were rare. Geographical urban morphologists in the United Kingdom were less interested in conceptualizations of process than in ideographic description and classification, exemplified by Arthur Smailes's general review of contemporary townscapes based on rapid reconnaissance surveys (Smailes 1955) and Maurice Stedman's (1958) characterization of Birmingham's urban landscape. Urban landscapes were seen almost solely in terms of the land uses they contained (e.g. House and Fullerton 1955). American land-use models pioneered by Ernest Burgess, Homer Hoyt, and others of the Chicago School had come to dominate much research and teaching in the name of urban morphology in the English language,[3] despite the fact that this work has little explicit concern for physical form. This led to contemporary criticism of this approach as neglecting the inherent dynamism of the city, producing "merely a synoptic study of a town at a particular time with little or no reference to the forces at work within and without the town which may cause its condition to change" (King 1962: 280).

The preoccupation with land use, more as a functional attribute of cities than a morphological one, continued well into the 1960s and beyond (e.g. Davies 1968). Concepts based on urban economics and the study of land-use patterns were developed in the United States and widely diffused (Sargent 1972). They remain popular (for example, Arnas et al. 1998), but the perspective of the urban geographers who adopted these concepts was "morphological only in its concern with land-use patterns: town plan and building form were generally treated only as land-use containers, if considered at all" (Whitehand 1987: 255). This was a time when quantitative methods were developed (e.g. Grimshaw et al. 1970) and widely applied. Studies employing them were largely morphographic, describing physical forms rather than analyzing their origins and development, and stirred little replication. Meanwhile, some relevant work was being done in other disciplines, including urban history and archaeology (Aston and Bond 1976; Barley 1976; Reps 1965).

It was in 1960, however, with the publication of M. R. G. Conzen's town-plan analysis of Alnwick, Northumberland, that a whole new conceptual avenue of research was opened up (Conzen 1960). This monograph was "widely, and favourably, reviewed and sold well by the standards of the time" (Steel 1984: 59). It presented a remarkably complex, integrated, and new theoretical conception of the morphological evolution, structure, and interrelationships between the townscape's basic elements than had ever appeared before. It introduced dozens of new conceptual terms, such as the morphological frame, fixation lines, the burgage cycle (including burgage series, accretion, repletion, plot heads, and tails), market concretion, morphotopes, urban fringe belts (including fringe belt development, aureoles, alienation, and translation), hierarchically nested plan units, and morphogenetic regions within towns, to name just a few. This comprehensive model of a town's morphogenetic history and spatial composition, though applied to a small market town in Northern England, was conceived as systematic and general enough to be applied potentially to urban forms anywhere. The monograph was followed two years later by an article that applied the conceptual scheme to central Newcastle upon Tyne, by contrast to Alnwick a large multifunctional city (M. R. G. Conzen 1962). Both had a transformative influence on subsequent work in urban morphology, though the diffusion of Conzen's ideas was at first slow owing to the general neglect of the field in many quarters. Whitehand championed Conzen's groundbreaking work, finding in it inspiration for his own considerable agenda and research results in the field and spurring many others to come to grips with Conzen's analytical scheme. He edited a collection of four of Conzen's papers, with detailed introductory and evaluative essays (Whitehand 1981). Much of the further development in Conzen's morphological ideas is summarized in a posthumous collection of his widely dispersed articles, *Thinking About Urban Form* (M. R. G. Conzen 2004).

The Turn toward Agency

Parallel with Conzen's work, a significant broadening of "morphological" research orientations, methods, and sources has occurred, most particularly during the last quarter of the twentieth century. To paraphrase Guelke, urban morphology might "be defined as the study of changes in thought expressed in human activity on the surface of the earth. This definition has the potential of providing a foundation for a stronger and more coherent field" (Guelke 1982: 3, originally referring to historical geography).[4] The study of urban landscapes has been linked more explicitly to the types of agents and the specific organizations and individuals responsible for their creation. "Each pursues particular goals, the nature of which can result in conflict over the form of the built environment. It is important therefore to understand the motives underlying the behaviour of these key agents" (Pacione 1991: 162). This focus on process is a significant advance in morphology and forms the central focus of this volume.

An early contribution to this strand was Harold Carter's work on Llandudno (1970). He distinguished between "primary" decision making, such as the creation of new planned units, and "secondary" decision making, largely concerned with issues of detail. He was concerned more with process than urban product but was driven by the desire to provide a sound theoretical basis for urban morphology, to develop it beyond the "barren elaboration of extremely complex systems" of morphographic classification (Carter 1970: 66, commenting on Jean Tricart 1954). Accordingly, Carter drew upon recent study of those who make decisions and the process of decision making in "the behavioural environment" (a phrase of William Kirk, [1963]). Most influential was Stuart Chapin's conceptual system, quoted by Carter (with his own comments added in square brackets) thus:

> in its most basic form, and viewing the components in reverse order, this framework seeks explanation for any man-induced phenomenon being studied [in this instance town plan] in terms of human behaviour [patterns of activity], with behaviour patterns being a function in turn of people's values [or the attitudes held concerning those activities]. A fourth element of the framework has to do with control processes [strategies or plans] that influence the interplay among the first three components.
>
> (Chapin 1964: 56, as amended by Carter 1970: 67)

This bold attempt at theory building went largely unheeded at the time, as did Carter's demand that "both urban historians and urban geographers" (that is, urban morphologists, in our terms) should develop "a more acute awareness of social processes rather than an obsession with the events of history or the "phenomenal" facts of geography" (Carter 1970: 77). Whitehand (1977) suggested that the value of a decision-making approach was problematic because of the illusive nature of the process of decision making. This caution can, arguably, be minimized given the detailed data sources previously mentioned. The closing chapter in this book, furthermore, demonstrates what can now be done in this regard.

Notwithstanding the early concerns, some seed must have taken root, for the nature of morphological work changed significantly from the late 1970s, especially in English-speaking academe. The "passive view of human agency" (Ley 1988) became *passé*. Gordon (1984) constructed a conceptual framework in which decision makers were seen as "actors" on the stage of changing urban form. A significant amount of relevant work in this respect has been undertaken by urban historians and archaeologists (for example, Palliser 2008; Palliser et al. 2000; Bowler 2004); hence the historical perspective has remained strong. Yet these are, perhaps, unusual historians: they have demonstrated a clear concern for the development and change in urban physical structure: the *product*, rather than simply the people and activities behind it.

The developing research on medieval towns has built on documentary research (for example, Beresford's classic documentary study of the creation of medieval new towns [1967]) to explore the impacts on urban form of landowners including the church (Slater 1987; Slater and Rosser 1998; Baker and Holt 2003), aristocratic families (Lilley 2001), and town corporations (Boogaart 2004). The "agency" concerns have, however, not obscured more refined work on physical form itself. The metrological analysis of plot dimensions, for example, has revealed particular patterns allowing more detailed consideration of *processes* of plan formation and town layout in the medieval period, to supplement the patchy availability of documentary sources (Slater 1996; Lilley 1999). Earlier towns are more difficult to examine in this manner; nevertheless there have been efforts to discuss process, product, form, and meaning in even the earliest cities (Smith 2007).

Some work on the development of towns during the industrial period has shown the impacts of landownership, especially on the conversion of agricultural land to urban use (Springett 1982; Hooper 1985; Graham and Proudfoot 1992), the detail of particularly suburban development, and its usually small-scale nature—for example, proceeding on a field-by-field basis—leading to considerable variation in form and character over space (for example, Dyos 1968; Beresford 1988; Moudon 1986; Sandweiss 2001). New perspectives on historic urban form were developed, for example with Johnston's (1966) exploration of race, caste, and class and the urban form of nineteenth-century Philadelphia, and Paul Groth's study of the multi-class residential hotel in America and its various forms (Groth 1994).

More researchers have paid attention to the period since the mid-nineteenth century, when sources permitting detailed building-by-building analyses became available, for example, in the United Kingdom in the form of building plans submitted to local authorities (Roger 1981). This has, for example, allowed consideration of speculation and design in Headingly, Leeds, and the emergence of a local architectural profession (Trowell 1985). For the post-1947 period, similar data have been recovered from the records of local authority planning departments (Larkham 1988a). Significant work has been carried out using such data in exploring decision-making processes.

Attention turned to what Paul Knox (1987), after Lefebvre, termed "the social production of the built environment" and of building form (King 1984):

> the built environment is not only an expression of the economic and political power exerted at different times by various individuals, social groups and governments: it is also a means by which the prevailing system of power and socio-economic relationships are maintained.
>
> (Knox 1984: 107; although see Unwin 2000 for a critique; Knox 2011; Shaw 2004)

For example, in the United Kingdom, the range of agents active for commercial development (Freeman 1990; Whitehand 1992b; Whitehand and Whitehand 1984), for suburban development (Whitehand and Carr 2001), and for conservation planning (Larkham 1988b) has been explored, leading to examination of the effects of their characteristics on the urban landscape. This significant body of research has produced some interesting findings, although it has only scratched the surface of the information available in a small number of locations in only one country; although

Whitehand's recent work has begun to explore morphology and conservation in China (Whitehand et al. 2010), and the social production approach, especially looking at the contribution of élite groups, has attracted interest, for example, with Domosh's work on contrasting land allocation in retail districts in nineteenth-century New York, with a "splintered élite," and Boston, with a "ruling élite" (Domosh 1998).

In other cultural contexts, agency is often implicit in studies of changing urban form, for example, the cultural and economic control of Chinese communism (Lu 2006). In the same context Gaubatz (1996) explores the cultural, social and economic structures of urban form on the Chinese frontiers; the impact of multiculturalism is significant, for example where Chinese, Tibetan, and Muslim cultures intersect and create or transform urban landscapes containing elements particular to each cultural tradition. In Dubai, the astonishing new built forms emerging in that city's explosive urbanism have been explored in the light of the oil economy, globalization, and policy development (Elsheshtawy 2010). Although such work sheds new light on changing urban forms, processes, and agency, its drawback is that there has been little theoretical development based on international comparative analysis. The complex politics of the postwar period also sometimes seems to limit what can explicitly be said, for example, in relating agency to the mapping of striking urban changes in Lhasa following the Chinese occupation (Larsen and Sinding-Larsen 2001).

Key questions can be explored once agents are identified: for example, whether they are based local to, or distant from, a development or whether speculators are building for their own occupation. Such studies have introduced the concepts of innovation diffusion and distance decay into urban morphology, hitherto found particularly in architectural history, and have also suggested that there is often a geographical link between agents, places, and the nature of physical changes planned and implemented. This can be summarised in Whitehand's comment that

> it seems inescapable ... that boardroom decisions taken in the metropolis against a background of national scale operations would have produced different results from those taken by local individuals with a field of vision ending abruptly at the edge of their town's sphere of influence. (Whitehand 1984: 4).

This strand of research has led to deep and detailed involvement with legal/administrative systems of town planning and urban landscape management, largely a result of the production of major data sources by bureaucratic processes, and their contemporary dominance in the processes of urban change. Other studies have reviewed the place of specific types of agent in the development process, including estate agents and elected councillors (McNamara 1984; Witt and Fleming 1984). This identification and examination of agents of change in relation to the development process led to the classification of agents as "direct" (e.g. owners, architects, developers) and "indirect" (local planning authorities, interested third parties; Larkham 1988b: 150) and hence a better understanding of the power relationships and complex processes of contemporary urban change.

Other perspectives on agents and agency have emerged in recent years. In particular there is a tendency for agency to be assigned to "things" or even "processes" rather than people or institutions. The use of actor-network theory, for example, has offered a new agency-based perspective on urban change, where the actors in the complex sets of associations that shape places can be non-human as well as human: Essex and Brayshay (2007) have seen the 1943 reconstruction plan for Plymouth in this light. Agency has also been assigned to skyscrapers themselves, in a study of architectural forms and the production of architectural and urban form. They should "be understood 'relationally'" in terms of their role as connecting agents in colonial and post-colonial economies (McNeill 2009: 6). In a similar vein, perhaps cultures and values can be seen as playing important roles in shaping places: for example, in how migrant communities reshape the urban surroundings in which they find themselves (Preston and Lo 2000; Nasser 2003; Edwards 2004). Likewise, the economy, and especially issues such as globalization, shapes the actions of individuals and organizations and the landscapes that they produce (Gad and Holdsworth 1987; Stewart 1999).

It is worth noting that, although the "agents of change" approach has tended to be focused at smaller spatial scales, even at the level of changes to individual houses (Whitehand and Arntz 1999; Whitehand 2001), it is also capable of application at the largest scales at which urban morphology can operate. This can include the decision-making processes underlying entire settlement patterns, such as the transfer of urban ideas from the borders of the Duchy of Austria to the kingdom of Bohemia in the thirteenth century (Nitz 2001) or colonial and corporate town plantation (Rego and Meneguetti 2008).

A further outgrowth of the "agents of change" approach may be seen in the abstract modeling of urban environments by the use of computer algorithms. Complex mathematical models have been developed to account for highly organized theoretical urban spatial patterns generated by relatively simple sets of rules and assumed processes (e.g. Batty 2005). Most applicable in contemporary urban planning contexts, such "agent-based modeling" is generally not concerned with historical and cultural settings, and time is conceived, for the most part, as a mechanical, iterative dimension.

The perspective on agents and agency, on decisions and decision making, offers a far more complex and detailed set of responses to the problems raised in understanding the form and development of the urban landscape, even if some of those answers remain partial and derived from inference. It is a more conceptually rich perspective than—and a far cry from—that offered by a range of writers (often from the architectural profession) in the late nineteenth and early twentieth centuries discussed by (and quotations translated by) Catherine Maumi (2003). Léonce Reynaud (1863), for example, suggested that "The layout of a town is the work of time rather than that of architects"; for him, the creation of a town was so complex that it was beyond unaided human achievement. "It was therefore risky to trust one man, one office, one state" (Maumi 2003: 870). Gustavo Giovannoni (1931) agreed, recognizing the influence of a myriad of actors: "No human mind can foresee and manage such a complex phenomenon as the birth or the growth of a town in a rigorous way; no individual force can replace the reunion of wills and interests of thousands of individuals, institutions or firms." Maybe not; but that does not preclude our seeking to understand the complex "reunion of wills and interests" that exists at all times and in all places.

Exploring Agency: The Structure of This Volume

This book, therefore, presents an approach to understanding agency in the built environment that focuses directly on players and the shaping circumstances of the decisions they make, and have made, and links those interactions to the resulting forms. The book also explores this theme in a wide variety of times and places, both to demonstrate its richness and to caution the reader not to apply too simple a model of agency to any one place or historical period, particularly across borders of time and space. So vast a topic mandates selectivity to fit within a single volume. Therefore, the cases collected here represent an exploration, not a compendium. Yet they form a coherent body of ideas and there is a strong rationale underlying its composition.

For exploratory purposes, therefore, the chapters that follow examine the character and range of urban morphological agency within the context of broad European cultural development and some of its global extensions. Even here, limitations of space have imposed further selectivity. Nevertheless, the topics covered offer, we hope, an instructive panorama of many agents, operating in numerous conditions, and always intertwined in their complex effects upon the form of cities.

The primary ordering principle follows the sweep of time. Centuries of development have radically changed the cast of characters involved in the physical shaping of cities, so the role of specific types of agents belongs to a particular time and place. The sequence in the book is chronological and grouped in historical periods fundamental and enduring enough to capture the underlying *zeitgeist* within which each can be most legitimately understood.

Agency in Pre-Modern Settings

We begin with medieval town builders, for reasons of source material. The further back in time, the sparser is the historical record of who was responsible in what roles for which features of urban formation, especially those concerned with the layout and physical fabric of towns (which, in any age, can be notoriously anonymous). The more fragmentary and enigmatic the written sources, the greater the reliance that must be placed on the surviving evidence of the streets and structures themselves. However, here they are, in the language of statistical analysis, the "dependent variable"—the thing to be explained—and therefore not the most reliable source for specific agency, beyond the orbit of simple logic. For these reasons, the earliest eras of urban development, including those of the great Classical period in Europe during which so many regions saw the rise of the first cities in their midst, must remain beyond the scope of this study.

During the Middle Ages, the re-emergence of towns following the collapse of the Roman Empire was closely associated with the effort to provide material services, especially of trade and craft production, within otherwise rurally based, feudally organized societies. Amid the volatile flux of kingdoms and territorial competition, safety was a constant concern. Institutions powerful enough to offer security, and the essential privileges needed furthermore to encourage urban development, were thus paramount in the founding and nurturing of towns. Three institutions were seminal.

The first was the royal authority of kings. Claiming divine right to rule over their subjects, kings assumed ownership of all territory under their effective control, and within certain ultimate limits, their edicts were law. Though monarchs varied a great deal in their interest in and ability to understand urban development, many played critical roles in sponsoring and shaping towns. This is nowhere better illustrated than in the case of Edward I of England in the thirteenth century and his grasp of the value of towns, in addition to castles, in holding territory, especially newly won ground. In Chapter 2, Keith Lilley's study of Edward's town planning activities in north Wales articulates what can possibly be said about the specific role of kings in the complex sequence of events needed to create sustainable towns in new locations. Lilley shows how slender the direct references to these activities are in the written record. Yet he wrings meaning from the scant, curt, and oblique references in royal documents to site selection, surveying, construction of defensive works, and delegation of authority within the cadres of royal officials charged with executing royal orders.

Lilley offers a systematic model of the steps required to create a town on the ground and offers hypotheses about the likely hierarchy of responsibility in the delegation of tasks associated with each step. He illustrates this with excerpts from royal correspondence and seeks to fill in the copious gaps in the picture of agency by drawing out indications of agency embedded in the physical town plans themselves. Though much further research needs be done along these lines, Lilley's chapter begins to delineate the power and limits of royal prerogative and activism with respect to town founding in a turbulent era.

The second institution was the Church. Scholars have long recognized the role of the Christian church in Europe in administering towns during the chaotic period following the collapse of the Roman Empire. During the Middle Ages, the Church played a key role in sustaining urban life amid the shrunken ruins of surviving Roman towns, in founding new towns of its own on new sites, and in contributing powerfully to the shaping of towns in which it operated simply as one of several critical bastions of society. In Chapter 3, Terry Slater explores this theme with a special focus on the Church's impact on urban form, drawing on examples largely from Britain and continental Europe. He shows that ecclesiasts developed towns in much the same way as secular leaders, founding them as economic entities that produced rents but in such cases to underwrite the construction of church buildings for the glory of God rather than the territorial vanity of mere potentates. Consequently, the urban forms created specifically by and for the Church often gave medieval towns a distinctive character.

The third institution to emerge in the Middle Ages was a communal one seeking to represent the needs of the townspeople themselves and provide a measure of local government for the citizens residing in towns, embodied especially in the merchant burgesses and their leading body, the town council. In Chapter 4, Anngret Simms explores the struggles this group engaged in to rise as counterweights to the arbitrary control of the town lords, be they kings, bishops, or their vassals. Even though the power of town councils waned toward the end of the medieval period with the rise of the absolutist state, they had major and lasting impact on the morphology of towns. Armed with town-charters and through the creation of guilds, civic leaders were often instrumental in developing facilities such as market halls, assembly rooms, parish churches, weigh-stations, courts, schools, hospitals, and universities either complementary to the efforts of feudal lords or in the face of their disinterest. The emergence of systematic urban planning, including orthogonal street and plot layouts, can often be ascribed to the actions of medieval town-councils. It is impossible to grasp the far-reaching power of modern civil governments to shape cities without recognizing their roots in the medieval urban world.

Agency in Early Modern Settings

Bureaucratic and technological innovations during the late medieval and early Renaissance periods were instrumental in transforming many kingdoms and lesser political entities into absolutist states. With them came a new type of "authoritarian urban landscape," as Katharine Arntz Thomas describes it in Chapter 5. She outlines the dominant role of the potentate, illustrating this with the most extreme case—the court town—in which, for reasons of prestige and egotism, the ruler had maximum say in the design of the entire community and its built environment. Consequently, following the newest principles of architectural design, urban spaces were defined by the centrality of grand palaces and adjacent landscape parks, their supporting garrisons, official churches, and straight streets with regimented housing. Thomas lays out the complex and often troubled relationships between the potentate and those needed to carry out his vision by examining the example of Potsdam, the royal court town established outside Berlin in 1660 by Friedrich Wilhelm I of Prussia. She documents his detailed involvement in the plans for and early construction of the town and the creation of strict building regulations to govern subsequent growth and change. And yet even powerful rulers bowed to circumstances, because expectations, even when well defined, could run up against limits of the purse, peculiarities of site and available materials, the talent of architects and master-builders, and even, on occasion, the non-cooperation of the town's residents. Though there are more widely known models for the court town (e.g. Louis XIV's Versailles, begun 1664), and more visually spectacular layouts (Karlsruhe, founded in 1715), the records of Potsdam allow Thomas to delineate a particularly clear picture of multiple agency in the formation and development of such a distinctive urban type.

Potsdam, like Versailles, was a court town placed in a rural setting. A far more potent expression of imperial power on urban form and design is that of central Paris in the age of Napoléon III of France. It represented the retrofitting of a medieval city to conform to revolutionary ideas of urban modernity on a grand scale. It was the very opposite of green-field urban development: it involved the massive reconfiguration of the city's major street system, with all the disruption and redevelopment of property that entailed, which was utterly without precedent at the time.

Much has been written about Georges-Eugène Haussmann and his *Grands Travaux*, but in Chapter 6, Michaël Darin sketches out in the context of this book the intricacies of Haussmann's plan, amid all the bureaucratic ups and downs of his controversial administration. Darin also traces Haussmann's influence not only among his immediate planning successors well into the twentieth century but on his biographers and critics who would have their own influence on the course of urbanistic change in France's capital city. In doing so, Darin seeks to correct the slavish perception of Haussmann's overwhelming importance by stressing the value of a three-pronged approach, uniting a focus on the role of individuals with a concern for the social history of the time and a concern for the actual morphological products of the overall process that exerted their own reflexive influence on Paris's evolving urbanism. Unique to this case is also the complicating circumstance that Haussmann's *Mémoires*, written following the destruction by fire of most of the government's official files relating to the *Préfet's* grand project, have had their own powerful effect on subsequent scholarly assessment of his impact.

Though the chapters by Thomas and Darin provide a view of morphological agency at the very heart of empire, there is an alternative and no less useful perspective: Imperial urban development viewed at the very margins of empire. To examine agency under colonial conditions, one could cite cases of British town making in Australia, or the contrasting programs of urban establishment by the Spanish and Portuguese in the New World. For this collection, the example chosen is that of the Russian colonial effort on the North American continent and its subsequent fate after transfer in 1867 to American jurisdiction.

In Chapter 7, Michael Conzen examines the development of Novo-Arkhangel'sk (Sitka) as an operational base for Russia's marine fur trade in the North Pacific Ocean—which necessarily doubled as its colonial capital, flying the imperial flag atop the trading company's commanding citadel—and its inevitable but slow transformation under later ownership. Here, morphological agency involved a very different cast of players: trading company officials, minor military officers, contract employee residents, barely cooperative native Indians, and emphatically distant government bureaucrats (in St. Petersburg and Washington, DC). Though the morphological backdrop in this case is the natural deterioration of the wood in an all-log town and its delayed replacement with modern materials through essentially benign neglect on the part of remote officialdom, the verdict on morphological agency is one of extreme fracture. It reveals a situation in which external agents were often reluctant participants, and local agents fell into two groups: under-empowered public officials and frustrated businessmen. Sitka represents the opposite end of the spectrum of rapacious physical development and urban complexity to Paris and Berlin, yet in helping establish the bandwidth and something of the character of that spectrum, it is equally valuable to the book's theme.

Agency in Industrial-Era Settings

The Sitka case brings us into the nineteenth century. By then, in more metropolitan regions, industrialization was advancing with transformative rapidity. Aside from the large factories that typified the new urban landscapes of the era, there is no more potent or unifying symbol of the era than the steam railroad. In Chapter 8, Arthur Krim takes up what is arguably the most intriguing question about the relationship between railroads and cities: how the former were inserted within the already built-up areas of the latter, with special reference to their access to the commercial center. Krim offers a broad-scale comparison of early efforts in four large cities, two in Britain (Manchester and Liverpool) and two in the United States (Baltimore and Philadelphia). Though the earliest successful experiments with steam railroads belong to England, commercial interests in the United States were exceedingly quick to study and emulate the British experience and make innovations of their own. The comparison from a morphological point of view is an instructive one.

Krim shows how dense urban development in inner Manchester and Liverpool led from the outset to radical if expensive projects, such as tunnels and viaducts, to gain access to city centers, enshrining a clear separation of railroad traffic from other forms. In America's large East Coast cities, streets were generally wider than in Britain and therefore accommodated rail track within them for decades before being rerouted (except in the case of Boston, which found estuarine solutions to the railroad all its own). Though many of the social and economic factors underlying industrialization in the two countries were similar, physical conditions related to space and building traditions differed enough to presage the contrasting solutions that were adopted in introducing railroads to cities. These factors, more than politics or social habits, help to explain these contrasting solutions.

If railroads were the arteries that integrated new industrial production within a national and international network of exchange, it was the rise of the large-scale, purpose-built factory that forever changed the scale of manufacturing and created the consumer society. Factories sprang up in settlements of all sizes and many locations and took various forms, from peripheral additions to existing towns to concentrated clusters that themselves created new urban cores, but however much town leaders welcomed them for the economic vitality they brought, for which they sometimes felt compelled to offer incentives, factories appeared primarily through the investment decisions of risk-taking individual entrepreneurs. In Chapter 9, Marek Koter and Mariusz Kulesza explore a wide range of agents that came together to found and develop the industrial cities of Łódź and Zyrardów in central Poland during the nineteenth century. Here, the political climate favoring rapid industrialization was important, and therefore encouraged government incentives and an openness to foreign capital and the importation of new ideas about industrial organization. Koter and Kulesza present striking cases of large-scale industrial investments made in two different contexts, both involving elements of what came to be known as the "company town" model. In Łódź, the first mammoth textile factories came complete with workers' housing and owners' mansions from the beginning (built by the industrialist Karl Scheibler) but grafted onto the urban fringe of an existing manufacturing town based on artisan production. In the case of Zyrardów, the factories came at first without housing, but as the scale of the enterprise grew, a planned housing district was added, complete with extensive infrastructure and community amenities. As the scale of urbanization progressed in these cities, the unique role of the initial entrepreneurs—so crucial in the early stages—retreated as more actors joined the maelstrom of decisions that shaped the cities' urban environments.

In the flood-tide of nineteenth-century industrialization, the line between industrial developer and land speculator was often a thin one. As workers' housing districts sprang up all over large industrial cities, the new managerial class and the commercial middle class that benefitted from industrial growth created new demands for attractive residential environments. The "garden suburb" was one response to this rising social class, and it introduced a new morphology that would influence much urban development worldwide that came after. In Chapter 10, Michael Pacione looks at the landowners, builders, agents, and customers for one such case, Pollockshields in southwest Glasgow, Scotland's first garden suburb, and how they worked together or fought one another as the suburb took shape and expanded. He places the analysis within the context of Glasgow's growing residential segregation during its rapid industrialization, thus considering both the individual behavior of the actors involved and the structural factors operating at the larger scale that together shaped the suburb's destiny.

Yet the story of housing in modern industrial cities of the developed world is hardly one of large-scale enterprises and corporate interests alone. Indeed, industrialists for the most part shied away from the responsibility of providing shelter for their workers. In the end, the Scheiblers of Łódź, not to mention the likes of George Pullman of Chicago, were in the minority, and so the vast proportion of urban housing built in the nineteenth century was produced by small builders, and a good deal of it was actually "self-built" by their individual occupiers. It will never be known exactly how much housing was self-built, but the tradition has remained particularly strong in the United States, with its widespread tradition of "subdivision" development in which landowners sell building plots but leave construction entirely to the buyer or his or her contractor. In Chapter 11, Richard Harris explores this theme in depth at the scale of one industrial city in Illinois, Peoria, during the early-to-mid twentieth century. He focuses on modest residential neighborhoods during what he terms a crucial shift from "anarchic individualism" to "commercialized assistance," even as workingmen's families continued to construct their homes in the traditional way through sweat-equity. Significantly, self-built residential developments can look superficially little or no different from low-priced, speculative developments because their fabricators had access to the same house plans and materials, even though their agency was entirely different. The chapter casts a new light on the extent of this urban form and the nature of its underlying morphological agency.

Agency in Late Modern and Postmodern Settings

Up to this point in the present collection, the role of trained architects in creating urban form has been somewhat muted, although their presence in the "mix" as morphological agents has been clearly implicit throughout. The great castles, cathedrals, city walls, town halls, palaces, and other elaborate buildings that have studded cityscapes since the Middle Ages could not have been designed and constructed without their expertise. However, since the Renaissance, architects' identity and standing as a profession have only grown in public awareness, and by the twentieth century an increasing number would come to enjoy broad celebrity status on a par with great writers, musicians, painters, and other creative artists, and the most creative have become icons in mass culture. The Modernist Movement in world architecture, which began to forge a distinct identity by the 1920s and came into full force by the 1950s (Gold 1997, 2007), represents one of the greatest shifts ever in the historical development of architectural theory and ideology. It sought to adapt the basic principles of architectural design with the revolution in technology set in motion by the Industrial Revolution and with the attendant general "modernization" of society. Those who reacted against Modernism in architecture regarded it an outright rupture in the consistent if highly varied long-term evolution of the discipline. It produced a reaction late in the twentieth century known as "Postmodernism," against which "Neomodernism" has in turn arisen in further reaction.[5]

In perhaps no other country has the debate over the proper place of architectural Modernism in society been more fraught between its proponents and its detractors (committed to the value of historical continuity) than in Italy, where the unbroken lineage of a classical tradition is profoundly apparent. In Chapter 12, Nicola Marzot approaches this theme by examining the search for an alternative path in architectural evolution, one that explicitly acknowledges and incorporates the central role of precedent. It crystallized in the writings of Saverio Muratori and Gianfranco Caniggia, beginning in the 1950s. For these architects, the central concept is the architectural "type," and the steps by which one building type can lead to another. Building "typomorphology," therefore, concerns basic form relationships that go deeper than style and decoration. Marzot gives an account of the intellectual development of this historically based movement, and the struggles within the movement to articulate it and especially to demonstrate it through design commissions that express its ethos. Three celebrated examples provide illustration. The chapter stands, therefore, as a searching examination of the conceptual dynamics that motivate architects at a fundamental level, growing out of their cultural wellsprings and particularly when confronted with dissonant attitudes toward the future of the city within the profession and among many of its clients.

The period after the Second World War was characterized by other shifts in urban development. One of the most urgent was the postwar reconstruction of cities damaged during the war. In Britain, this necessitated the preparation of numerous plans for rebuilding, in a brief but intense period of activity culminating in the landmark Town and Country Planning Act of 1947. Peter Larkham in Chapter 13 traces the processes by which close to 200 reconstruction plans were prepared, arguing that they represent an unparalleled period of development in British planning, architecture, and urban design. It ushered in "technocentric," scientific modes of plan making based on surveys and formal analysis, during which public consultation became a standard part of the process. Most attention has previously been paid to prolific consultant planners, but more than half of the plans were produced by local authority employees. Larkham examines the intricate and diverse patterns of leadership behind the plans and points to outcomes that diverged from the intent of the new planning legislation. Despite the professionalization of urban plan making, many aspects of the process fell short of the elusive goal of objectivity.

Other important changes included the need to deal with urban overcrowding through renewed efforts to create "new towns" as antidotes to uncoordinated expansion. In such projects, neither architects nor planners by themselves, of course, determine the shape and course of urban redesign. In Chapter 14, John Gold places them within the wider circuit of actors in the drama and selects the "New Town" of Cumbernauld, in southern Scotland, as a prism through which to view their interactions. Here, in implementing and quickly modifying the "megastructure" town center that was the signal feature of this planning and design effort, the often troubled relations between national and local planning officials, politicians, design consultants, building contractors, and, last, new residents are revealed. The account is more than a cautionary tale, however, because it provides a means to evaluate how shifting ideologies, political control, fiscal realities, and personalities can influence outcomes in the built environment.

Rebuilding cities so that they can once again fulfill their previous roles within the economic networks of nations and the world, and building new towns as local fixes for overcrowding, represent urban strategies rooted in assumptions of returning somehow to the *status quo ante*. However, when fundamental shifts in global organization occur, whether through altered comparative advantage or technological change, urban communities can experience whole sectors of their economy and land use becoming redundant. The pressures to adjust and reinvent patterns of livelihood and revalorize urban assets (particularly land) rendered useless by these changes can cause massive changes in the morphology of cities. When it is no longer "business as usual," the alignments of urban stakeholders are bound to change and a new round of competition initiated to remodel the city. As cities in mature, industrialized countries have seen their manufacturing base savaged by overseas competition and "outsourcing" or, as mature commercial cities struggle to keep pace with ever bigger port facilities in new locations, the newly emerging "brown-fields" and obsolete waterfront districts become tax liabilities and a blight on the urban image. In Chapter 15, Kai Gu presents a case study of two major New Zealand port cities that have redeveloped former docklands into residential and entertainment districts more oriented to their likely post-industrial futures. Gu examines the dynamics between the agents of change in Auckland and Wellington and finds significant differences in their strategies and outcomes that reflect divergent community norms.

The extent to which urban imagery has been transformed in the developed world in the decades surrounding the millennium from a quaint cultural characteristic into a direct force for economic vitality is made clear by Tim Hall and Phil Hubbard in Chapter 16. In developing the place-promotion concept, they use variants of actor-network theory and regime theory to explore the contests that have raged in post-industrial Birmingham, United Kingdom, in the effort to reshape the city's international image as a "twenty-four-hour" city with a vibrant new center attracting tourism, conventions, and other sources of post-industrial income. In effect, city leaders and other interest groups have been busy transforming the city's landscapes from those of production to those of consumption. The picture presents a loose and ever-shifting network of actors united, even if transiently, by their common interest in facilitating the flow of capital through the city. Hall and Hubbard offer a diffused model of urban governance newly sensitive to external forces, which succeeds in regulating the amount, character, and location of critical regeneration within the city. The result is a radically reconfigured urban morphology.

Agency As a System of Behavior with a Morphological Outcome

The foregoing fifteen substantive chapters lay out a vast panorama of evolving human agency in the shaping of city morphologies, spread across several historical epochs and many geographical regions. Each has sought to focus on the human actors whose perceptions, preferences, and felt pressures have led to decisions and actions producing the myriad forms that comprise the built environment. Since each has been concerned to set the actors and their decision making in the context of a particular time, place, and outcome, the better to demonstrate how historico-geographical context affects agency, none have had the space to abstract and rigorously generalize the process by which intentions are translated into action in any systematic way.

This task has been reserved to the last chapter in the book. In Chapter 17, Karl Kropf delineates the communities of interest that form and mutually negotiate the process of arriving at collective decisions specifically focused on changes to urban form. The analysis is grounded in an empirical case of some planned extensions to the town of Leighton Buzzard in Bedfordshire, United Kingdom, but its significance lies in the overarching model of morphological agency that Kropf presents and in the derivation of several distinct types of agency and their reciprocal interrelations. The chapter is both a "worked example" of an intensive sequence of planning initiatives that led to acceptable plans for the town extensions and a derived model that could be applied in almost any case of decision making with direct impact on the morphological makeup of a town or city. The model's derivation from the Leighton Buzzard experience would be wholly incidental but for its demonstrable link to a real-world situation and potential applicability in many others.

This collection of chapters demonstrates fundamental principles of morphological agency revealed in real cases and their configuration in varied and interesting theoretical and conceptual paradigms. They stem from the individual and original research of their authors, but they have been brought together and edited in such a way as to provide a coherent and systematic introduction to the field. The volume also acknowledges the influence of one particular scholar, J. W. R. Whitehand, whose own contribution to urban morphological studies since the early 1970s has been innovative and substantial and who has done much to promote the development of the theme of morphological agency through his graduate students, meticulous editing, and tireless networking.

Notes

1 We deliberately use the term "urban landscape" rather than "townscape." "Townscape" has become a widely used term in the field of urban design and represents an approach to representing and perceiving the urban landscape developed and widely popularized by professionals such as Gordon Cullen and Thomas Sharp in the United Kingdom after the Second World War: see Bandini (1992) and Erten (2009). "Urban landscape" is a closer analogy to the German term *Stadtlandschaft*.

2 The development of urban morphological studies has been charted for numerous countries in a series of papers in *Urban Morphology*.

3 The dominance of Chicago School-derived land-use models under the headings of "urban form" or "urban morphology" persists in many school and undergraduate courses to this day (Larkham 2003; Kropf 2009: 108).

4 To reflect modern developments, a definition of "urban morphology" was advanced in the *Glossary of Urban Form* as "the study of the physical (or built) fabric of urban form, and the people and processes shaping it" (Larkham and Jones 1990: 55).

5 For a *précis* of such theories, see the extracts in Jencks and Kropf (2006).

References

Arnas, A., Arnott, R., and Small, K. A. (1998) Urban spatial structure. *Journal of Economic Literature*, 36: 1426-64.

Aston, M. and Bond, J. (1976) *The Landscape of Towns*. London: Dent.

Baker, N. and Holt, R. (2003) *Urban Growth and the Medieval Church: Gloucester and Worcester*. Aldershot: Ashgate Publishing.

Bandini, M. (1992) Some architectural approaches to urban form, in J. W. R. Whitehand and P. J. Larkham (eds.), *Urban Landscapes: International Perspectives*, 133–69. London: Routledge.

Barley, M. W. (ed.) (1976) *The Plans and Topography of Medieval Towns in England and Wales*, Research Paper 14. London: Council for British Archaeology.

Batty, M. (2005) *Cities and Complexity: Understanding Cities with Cellular Automata, Agent-Based Models, and Fractals*. Cambridge, MA: MIT Press.

Beresford, M. W. (1967) *New Towns of the Middle Ages*. London: Lutterworth.

Beresford, M. W. (1988) *East End, West End: The Face of Leeds during Urbanisation, 1684–1842*. Publications of the Thoresby Society 60/61. Leeds: Thoresby Society.

Bobek, H. (1927) Grundfragen der Stadtgeographie. *Geographischer Anzeiger*, 28: 213–24.

Boogaart, T. A. (2004) *An Ethnogeography of Late Medieval Bruges: Evolution of the Corporate Milieu, 1280–1349*. Lampeter, Wales: Edward Mellen Press.

Bowler, D. P. (ed.) (2004) *Perth: The Archaeology and Development of a Scottish Burgh*. Perth, Scotland: Tayside and Fife Archaeological Committee, monograph 3.

Carter, H. (1970) A decision-making approach to town plan analysis: a case study of Llandudno, in H. Carter and W. K. D. Davies (eds.), *Urban Essays: Studies in the Geography of Wales*, 66–78. London: Longman.

Chapin, F. S. (1964) Selected theories of urban growth and structure. *Journal of the American Institute of Planners*, 30: 51–58.

Christaller, W. (1933) *Die zentralen Orte in Süddeutschland*. Jena: Fischer.

Conzen, M. P. (1993) The historical impulse in geographical writing about the United States, 1850–1990, in M. P. Conzen, T. A. Rumney, and G. Wynn (eds.), *A Scholar's Guide to Geographical Writing on the American and Canadian Past*, 3–90. Chicago: University of Chicago Press.

Conzen, M. R. G. (1960) *Alnwick, Northumberland: A Study in Town-Plan Analysis*. London: George Philip, Institute of British Geographers Publication 27.

Conzen, M. R. G. (1962) The plan analysis of an English city centre (Newcastle upon Tyne), in K. Norborg (ed.), *Proceedings of the International Geographical Union Symposium on Urban Geography, Lund 1960*, 383–414. Lund, Sweden: C. W. Gleerup, Lund Studies in Geography, 24.

Conzen, M. R. G. (2004) A needed re-orientation in urban geography (considering the nature of geography), in M. P. Conzen (ed.), *Thinking about Urban Form: Papers on Urban Morphology*, 24–33. Oxford: Lang (a previously unpublished seminar paper given in 1970 at the Department of Geography, University of Glasgow).

Darby, H. C. (1953) On the relations of geography and history. *Transactions and Papers of the Institute of British Geographers*, 19: 1–11.

Davies, W. K. D. (1968) The morphology of central places: a case study. *Annals of the Association of American Geographers*, 58: 91–110.

Dickinson, R. E. (1934) The town plans of East Anglia. *Geography*, 19: 37–50.

Dickinson, R. E. (1945) The morphology of the medieval German town. *Geographical Review*, 35: 74–97.

Dickinson, R. E. (1951) *The West European City*. London: Routledge and Kegan Paul.

Domosh, M. (1998) *Invented Cities: The Creation of Landscape in Nineteenth-Century New York and Boston*. New Haven, CT: Yale University Press.

Dörries, H. (1930) Der gegenwärtige Stand der Stadtgeographie. *Petermanns Geographische Mitteilungen*, 209: 310–25.

Dyos, H. J. (1968) The speculative builders and developers of Victorian London. *Victorian Studies*, 11: 641–79.

Edwards, G. (2004) The morphological impact of ethnic minority ingress into an established suburban environment (unpublished MPhil thesis). Manchester: University of Manchester, School of Planning and Landscape.

Elsheshtawy, Y. (2010) *Dubai: Behind an Urban Spectacle*. Abingdon: Routledge.

Erten, E. (2009) Thomas Sharp's collaboration with H. De C. Hastings: the formulation of townscape as urban design pedagogy. *Planning Perspectives*, 24: 29–49.

Essex, S., and Brayshay, M. (2007) Vision, vested interest and pragmatism: who re-made Britain's blitzed cities? *Planning Perspectives*, 22: 417–41.

Fleure, H. J. (1931) City morphology of Europe. *Proceedings of the Royal Institution of Great Britain*, 27(1): 145–55.

Freeman, M. (1990) Commercial building development: the agents of change, in T. R. Slater (ed.), *The Built Form of Western Cities: Essays for M. R. G. Conzen on the Occasion of His Eightieth Birthday*, 253–76. Leicester: Leicester University Press.

Fritz, J. (1894) Deutsche Stadtanlangen. *Beilage zum Programm 520 des Lyzeums Strassburg*. Strassburg: J. H. E. Heitz.

Frölich, K. (1938) Zur Verfassungstopographie der deutschen Städte des Mittelalters. *Zeitschrift der Savigny-Stiftung fur Rechtsgeschichte, Germanistische Abteilung*, 58: 75–310.

Gad, G., and Holdsworth, D. (1987) Corporate capitalism and the emergence of the high-rise office building. *Urban Geography*, 8: 212–31.

Gaubatz, P. R. (1996) *Beyond the Great Wall: Urban Form and Transformation on the Chinese Frontiers*. Stanford, CA: Stanford University Press.

Geisler, W. (1924) *Die deutsche Stadt: ein Beitrag zur Morphologie der Kulturlandschaft*. Stuttgart: Engelhorn.

Giovannoni, G. (1931) *Veccie città ed edilizia nuova*. Turin: Unione Typografico-Editrice Torinese.

Gold, J. R. (1997) *The Experience of Modernism*. London: Spon.

Gold, J. R. (2007) *The Practice of Modernism*. Abingdon: Routledge.

Gordon, G. (1984) The shaping of urban morphology. *Urban History*, 11: 1–10.

Graham, B. J., and Proudfoot, L. (1992) Landlords, planning, and urban growth in eighteenth- and early nineteenth-century Ireland. *Journal of Urban History*, 18: 308–29.

Grimshaw, P. N., Shepherd, M. J., and Wilmott, A. J. (1970) An analysis of cluster analysis by computer to the study of urban morphology. *Transactions of the Institute of British Geographers*, 51: 143–62.

Groth, P. E. (1994) *Living Downtown: The History of Residential Hotels in the United States.* Berkeley, CA: University of California Press.

Guelke, L. (1982) *Historical Understanding in Geography.* Cambridge: Cambridge University Press.

Hooper, A. (1985) *The Role of Landed Property in the Production of the Built Environment*, Bartlett International Summer School, Paper 6. London: Bartlett School, University College London.

Hope, W. H. St. J. (1909) The ancient topography of Ludlow. *Archaeologia*, 61: 383–9.

Hoskins, W. G. (1955) *The Making of the English Landscape.* London: Hodder and Stoughton.

House, J. W., and Fullerton, B. (1955) City street: a half-century of change in Northumberland Street–Pilgrim Street, Newcastle-upon-Tyne, 1891–1955. *Planning Outlook*, 3 (4): 3–25.

Hughes, T. H., and Lamborn, E. A. G. (1923) *Towns and Town Planning Ancient and Modern.* Oxford: Clarendon Press.

Jencks, C., and Kropf, K. (2006) *Theories and Manifestoes of Contemporary Architecture*, 2nd ed. Chichester: Wiley.

Johnston, N. J. (1966) The caste and class of the urban form of historic Philadelphia. *Journal of the American Institute of Planners*, 32: 334–50.

Keyser, E. (1958) *Städtegründungen und Städtebau in Nordwestdeutschland im Mittelalter.* Remagen am Rhein: Bundesanstalt für Landeskunde.

King, A. D. (1984) The social production of building form: theory and research. *Environment and Planning D: Society and Space*, 3: 429–46.

King, H. W. H. (1962) Whither urban geography? Some signposts from the Australian scene, in K. Norborg (ed.), *Proceedings of the International Geographical Union Symposium on Urban Geography, Lund, 1960*, 275–84. Lund, Sweden: C.W.Gleerup, Lund Studies in Geography, 24.

Kirk, W. (1963) Problems of geography. *Geography*, 48: 357–71.

Knox, P. L. (1984) Symbolism, styles and settings: the built environment and the imperatives of urbanized capitalism. *Architecture et Comportement,* 2: 107–22.

Knox, P. L. (1987) The social production of the built environment: architects, architecture and the post-modern city. *Progress in Human Geography*, 11: 354–78.

Knox, P. L. (2011) *Cities and Design.* London: Routledge.

Kropf, K. S. (2009) Aspects of urban form. *Urban Morphology*, 13: 105–120.

Larkham, P. J. (1988a) Changing conservation areas in the English Midlands: evidence from local planning records. *Urban Geography*, 9: 445–65.

Larkham, P. J. (1988b) Agents and types of change in the conserved townscape. *Transactions of the Institute of British Geographers*, NS 13: 148–64.

Larkham, P. J. (2003) The teaching of urban form, in A. Petruccioli, M. Stella, and G. Strappa (eds.), *The Planned City*, vol. 3, 777–81. Bari: Uniongrafica Corcelli Editrice.

Larkham, P. J., and Jones, A. N. (1990) *A Glossary of Urban Form.* Norwich: GeoBooks, Institute of British Geographers Historical Geography Research Series 26.

Larsen, K., and Sinding-Larsen, A. (2001) *The Lhasa Atlas.* London: Serindia Publications.

Leighly, J. B. (1928) *The Towns of Mälardalen in Sweden: A Study in Urban Morphology*, Publications in Geography 3. Berkeley, Calif.: University of California.

Ley, D. (1988) From urban structure to urban landscape. *Urban Geography*, 9: 98–105.

Lilley, K. D. (1999) Urban landscapes and the cultural politics of territorial control in Anglo-Norman England. *Landscape Research*, 24: 5–23.

Lilley, K. D. (2001) Urban planning and the design of towns in the Middle Ages: the Earls of Devon and their new towns. *Planning Perspectives*, 16: 1–24.

Lu, D. (2006) *Remaking Chinese Urban Form: Modernity, Scarcity and Space, 1949–2005.* Abingdon, U.K.: Routledge.

McNamara, P. F. (1984) The role of estate agents in the residential development process. *Land Development Studies*, 1: 101–12.

McNeill, D. (2009) *The Global Architect: Firms, Fame and Urban Form.* New York: Routledge.

Martiny, R. (1928) *Die Grundrissgestaltung der deutschen Siedlungen.* Gotha: Justus Perthes.

Maumi, C. (2003) The will of a few men with common-sense: a few thoughts, in A. Petruccioli, M. Stella, and G. Strappa (eds.), *The Planned City*, vol. 3, 869–73. Bari: Uniongrafica Corcelli Editrice.

Meijers, E. (2007) From central place to network model: theory and evidence of a paradigm change. *Tijdschrift voor Economische en Sociale Geografie*, 98: 245–259.

Moudon, A. V. (1986) *Built for Change: Neighborhood Architecture in San Francisco.* Cambridge, MA: MIT Press.

Nasser, N. (2003) The challenge of ethnoscapes. *Urban Morphology*, 7: 45–8.

Nitz, H.-J. (2001) Medieval towns with grid plan and central market place in east-central Europe: origins and diffusion in the early-thirteenth century. *Urban Morphology*, 5: 81–97.

Pacione, M. (1991) Development pressure and the production of the built environment in the urban fringe. *Scottish Geographical Magazine*, 107: 162–9.

Palliser, D. M. (2008) Tall buildings in medieval London: precipitation, aspiration and thrills. *The London Journal*, 33: 201–15.

Palliser, D. M., Slater, T. R., and Dennison, P. (2000) The topography of towns 600–1300, in D. M. Palliser (ed.), *The Cambridge Urban History of Britain,* vol. 1, 153–86. Cambridge: Cambridge University Press.

Parr, J. B. (2002) The location of economic activity: central place theory and the wider urban system, in P. McGann (ed.), *Industrial Location Economics*, 32–82. Cheltenham, U.K.: Edward Elgar.

Preston, V., and Lo, L. (2000) "Asian theme" malls in suburban Toronto: land use conflict in Richmond Hill. *Canadian Geographer*, 44: 182–90.

Ratzel, F. (1882–99) *Anthropogeographie*. Stuttgart: J. Engelhorn.

Rego, R.L. and Meneguetti, K.S. (2008) British urban form in twentieth-century Brazil. *Urban Morphology*, 12: 25–36.

Reps, J. W. (1965) *The Making of Urban America: A History of City Planning in the United States.* Princeton, N. J.: Princeton University Press.

Reynaud, L. (1863) *Traité d'Architecture, II: Composition des Édifices*. Paris: Dunod.

Rietschel, S. (1897) *Markt und Stadt in ihrem rechtlichen Verhältnis: ein Beitrag zur Geschichte der deutschen Stadtverfassung*. Halle: Leipzig, Veit & Co.

Roger, R. G. (1981) Sources and methods of urban studies: the contribution of building records. *Area*, 13: 315-21.

Sandweiss, E. (2001) *St. Louis: The Evolution of an American Urban Landscape.* Philadelphia: Temple University Press.

Sargent, C. S., Jr. (1972) Toward a dynamic model of urban morphology. *Economic Geography*, 48: 357–74.

Schlüter, O. (1899a) Bemerkungen zur Siedlungsgeographie. *Geographische Zeitschrift,* 5: 65–84.

Schlüter, O. (1899b) Über der Grundriss der Städte. *Zeitschrift der Gesellschaft für Erdkunde zu Berlin*, 34: 446–62.

Schlüter, O. (1903) *Die Siedlungen im nordöstlichen Thüringen: ein Beispiel für die Behandlung siedlungsgeographischer Fragen.* Berlin: Costenoble.

Schöller, P. (1953) Aufgaben und Probleme der Stadtgeographie. *Erdkunde,* 7: 161–84.

Shaw, D. (2004) *City Building on the Eastern Frontier: Sorting the New Nineteenth-Century City*. Baltimore: Johns Hopkins University Press.

Siedler, E. J. (1914) *Märkischer Städtebau im Mittelalter.* Berlin: Julius Springer.

Slater, T. R. (1987) Ideal and reality in English episcopal medieval town planning. *Transactions of the Institute of British Geographers*, NS 12: 191–203.

Slater, T. R. (1996) Medieval town-founding on the estates of the Benedictine Order in England, in F.-E. Eliassen and G. A. Ersland (eds.), *Power, Profit and Urban Land*, 70–93. Aldershot: Ashgate.

Slater, T. R., and Rosser, G. (eds.) (1998) *The Church in the Medieval Town*. Aldershot: Ashgate.

Smailes, A. E. (1955) Some reflections on the geographical description and analysis of townscapes. *Transactions and Papers of the Institute of British Geographers*, 21: 99–115.

Smith, M. E. (2007) Form and meaning in the earliest cities: a new approach to ancient urban planning. *Journal of Planning History*, 6: 3–47.

Springett, J. (1982) Landowners and urban development: the Ramsden Estate and nineteenth-century Huddersfield. *Journal of Historical Geography*, 8: 129–44.

Stedman, M. B. (1958) The townscape of Birmingham in 1956. *Transactions and Papers of the Institute of British Geographers*, 25: 225–38.

Steel, R. W. (1984) *The Institute of British Geographers: The First Fifty Years*. London: Institute of British Geographers.

Stewart, D. J. (1999) Changing Cairo: the political economy of urban form. *International Journal of Urban and Regional Research*, 23: 103–27.

Tout, T. F. (1917) Mediaeval town planning: a lecture delivered at the John Rylands Library on the 13th December 1916. *Bulletin of the John Rylands Library*, 4(1): 3–35.

Tricart, J. (1954) *Cours de Geographie Humaine, II: l'habitat urbain*. Paris: Centre de Documentation Universitaire.

Trowell, F. (1985) Speculative housing development in Leeds and the involvement of local architects in the design process, 1866-1914. *Construction History,* 1: 13–24.

Unwin, T. (2000) A waste of space? Towards a critique of the social production of space. *Transactions of the Institute of British Geographers*, NS 25: 11–29.

Whitehand, J. W. R. (1977) The basis for an historico-geographical theory of urban form. *Transactions of the Institute of British Geographers*, NS 2: 400–16.

Whitehand, J. W. R. (1981) Background to the urban morphogenetic tradition, in J. W. R. Whitehand (ed.), *The Urban Landscape: Historical Development and Management: Papers by M. R. G. Conzen* (Institute of British Geographers, Special Publication 13), 1–24. London, Academic Press.

Whitehand, J. W. R. (1984) *Rebuilding Town Centres: Developers, Architects and Styles*, Occasional Publication 19. Birmingham: University of Birmingham Department of Geography.

Whitehand, J. W. R. (1987) Urban morphology, in M. Pacione (ed.) *Historical Geography: Progress and Prospect*, 250–76. London: Croom Helm.

Whitehand, J. W. R. (1992a) *The Making of the Urban Landscape.* Oxford: Blackwell, Institute of British Geographers Special Publication 26.

Whitehand, J. W. R. (1992b) The makers of British towns: architects, builders and property owners, *c.* 1850–1939. *Journal of Historical Geography*, 18: 417–38.

Whitehand, J. W. R. (2001) Changing suburban landscapes at the microscale. *Tijdschrift voor Economische en Sociale Geografie*, 92: 164–84.

Whitehand, J. W. R., and Arntz, K. (1999) Towards a theory of residential building form in Europe, in R. Corona and, G. L. Maffei (eds.), *Transformations of Urban Form: Sixth International Seminar on Urban Form*, W5–W8. Florence: Alinea Editrice.

Whitehand, J. W. R. and Carr, C. M. H. (2001) The creators of England's inter-war suburbs. *Urban History*, 28: 218–34.

Whitehand, J. W. R., and Whitehand, S. M. (1984) The physical fabric of town centres: the agents of change. *Transactions of the Institute of British Geographers*, NS 9: 231–47.

Whitehand, J. W. R., Gu, K., Whitehand, S. M., and Zhang, J. (2010) Urban morphology and conservation in China. *Cities*, 28: 171–85.

Witt, S. J. C., and Fleming, S. C. (1984) *Planning Councillors in an Area of Growth: Little Power but All the Blame?* Geographical Paper 85. Reading, U.K.: Department of Geography, University of Reading.

PART II

Agency in Pre-Modern Settings

2

ROYAL AUTHORITY AND URBAN FORMATION

King Edward I and the Making of His "New Towns"

Keith D. Lilley

Those responsible for shaping medieval urban landscapes are very rarely glimpsed. This can be a source of frustration for urban morphologists concerned with trying to unravel how a particular medieval town or city was shaped, especially when they see what abundant information is available for those dealing with later periods of urban formation. Yet contemporary records of the later Middle Ages, from the later-thirteenth century onward, begin to provide some clues about the processes involved in matters of urban design and planning, of who was doing what and when. This chapter draws upon these primary written sources and morphological evidence provided by town plans, to chart how new towns were brought into being under King Edward I (1272–1307). It is by necessity a preliminary enquiry into the relationship between royal authority and medieval urban formation, a starting point from which further exploration might lead in this relatively under-explored aspect of urban morphology.

Appreciation of the role played by agents in shaping built environments has gained greater depth in recent years in urban morphology. In Anglophone geography, for example, Jeremy Whitehand's contribution in particular has furthered our understanding of processes of decision making and decision makers at work in the formation and transformation of urban landscapes. Rather than simply mapping out how urban landscapes change over time, he has drawn attention to the myriad agents and agencies involved in urban morphogenesis, particularly the activities of institutions, landowners, architects, planners, and developers (see Whitehand 1991). For the modern, contemporary contexts with which Whitehand has been primarily concerned, there is always the possibility of gaining knowledge of these agents' roles by addressing questions to those groups—direct and indirect—involved in decision making and, if some historical perspective is required, then there is also the great volume of documentary material to draw upon spawned by urban planning during the twentieth century (Whitehand and Whitehand 1984).

What, though, for earlier times? Is it also possible, for instance, to begin to identify the decision making and decision makers that shaped urban landscapes of the Middle Ages? Whitehand's work provides a lead in this regard, as indeed does that of his mentor, M. R. G. Conzen. Conzen's interest in the formation of medieval towns and, in particular, his morphogenetic approach to mapping the spatial development of urban landscapes, provides a sound basis for looking at the often-unrecorded

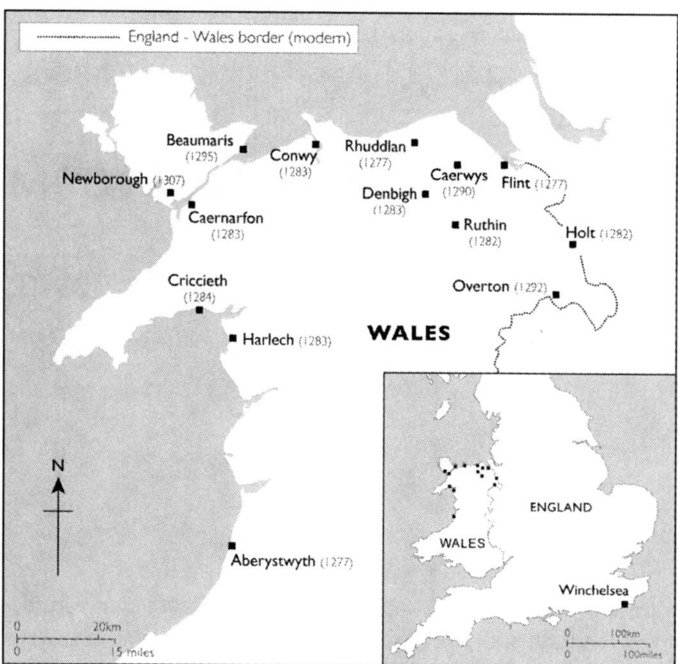

FIGURE 2.1 The location and distribution of Edward's new towns in England and Wales (dates reflect the time work began on the towns, and not necessarily when their charter was granted)

stages of medieval urban formation (Conzen 1960, 1968). Unrecorded in conventional historical records, that is, but preserved and fossilized in the vestiges of medieval street and plot patterns, but here lies the crux of the problem: we might be able to identify the stages by which a medieval urban landscape came into being, and perhaps even put dates to each phase of development, but finding out who was actually involved, who was responsible for conducting the physical formation of an urban landscape, usually is virtually impossible. This is simply because contemporaries so rarely recorded such matters, or if they did, their records have been lost (see Lilley 2001). There are, of course, exceptions: the new towns, for example, that were established by committee in the Florentine city republic in the late-thirteenth and early-fourteenth centuries (Friedman 1988) but, for earlier centuries and for other parts of medieval Europe, the picture is typically less clear (Lilley 2005). However, through combining what few records there are, together with study of the layouts of particular urban landscapes, some attempt can indeed be made to unravel which urban shapers were at work in medieval towns and cities.

The focus of this study is on new towns created under the authority of Edward I, one of medieval England's most remarkable monarchs (see Prestwich 1997; Fig. 2.1). His reign marked a boom in royal administration, and it is thanks to this bureaucracy and the records of his officials that we can today begin to piece together something of the processes that led to the formation of towns in his realm. It is not by any means a new topic of study. Edward's new towns were examined long ago by Tout (1934) and Beresford (1967), for example, and they continue to crop up as oft-cited examples in textbooks on urban form (Morris 1994; Schofield and Vince 2003). What is new, though, is the attempt made here to conceptualize the decision-making process that operated in Edward's realm and to examine in detail the various agents who were involved in creating Edward's new towns in the last three decades of the thirteenth century, in England, Wales, and Gascony.

To do this, the chapter examines in particular the individuals who were called upon to carry out various aspects of urban formation and puts forward a simple model of the stages that led to the realization of Edward's new towns. As there are comparatively few studies of medieval urban shapers, it is a working model, which, as such, should be adapted or perhaps refuted as further material is gathered from other parts of the cultural realm of medieval Europe. To this end, the chapter concludes on a comparative note, considering how Edward's new towns might be compared with those to be found elsewhere. However, to begin with, some discussion is appropriate on how medieval society was perceived at the time by those who were there, especially how royal authority itself was understood.

The Place of Royal Authority in Medieval Society

It was once fashionable to draw a distinction between the sacred and profane, the secular and the religious, in early societies, but the division is overly simplistic. In the Middle Ages, for example, religion—Christianity—pervaded all aspects of earthly life in Europe. This was reflected in medieval conceptions of society and, in particular, the idea that the king was divinely ordained, placed there by God to rule over earthly society (Gurevich 1985). He, and his society, were a microcosm of the wider cosmic body, over which God Himself ruled. This view of kingship, and the place of the king at the head of the state, has its origins in medieval Christian interpretations of neoplatonic sources that were widely circulated in the Latin West throughout the Middle Ages. One such text was the translation and commentary of Plato's *Timaeus* by Calcidius, made especially known in cloister and court by the many glosses and sermons that were based upon it (see Lilley 2009).

The importance of Calcidius's *Timaeus* for understanding medieval perceptions of royal authority lies in the prominence that it gives to the leader of the state, the view that the leader directs others beneath. An analogy was drawn between the order and hierarchy of the city and the cosmos and between the cosmos and the human body, where each are mutually organized and ordered through various parts that make up the whole, each part having its particular function to perform. Just as the head is that part of the body that governs, so the king, as figurehead of the "state," commands and directs those "beneath" him (Dutton 1983). This metaphorical city-cosmos-body that informed Christian thinking about the order and structure of society is to be seen, for example, in the writings of William of Conches, Alan of Lille, and Bernard Silvestris, all of whom reveal the influence of Calcidius's *Timaeus* in their work (Wetherbee 1988).

Such a view is, of course, of an imagined and idealized society, but it is revealing in that it justifies the place of royal authority in medieval society: the king as a lord, overseeing his "world," his people, on behalf of his Lord, the supreme architect of the universe, God Himself. All the paraphernalia and iconography of royal coronations and crowning legitimized and reinforced this divinely ordained position—the place of royal authority. In this respect, Edward's self-image, as ruler of an earthly realm, king of England and its dominions, was one derived from a Christian archetype, a fact that begins to erode those artificial distinctions drawn between the sacred and profane, religious and secular, at least in medieval times. It also posits a view of the king as the supreme being in the earthly state, as God Himself is the supreme being in the cosmos: an ordered and hierarchical idea of society.

This medieval Christian image of the king as directing those below him is one we should acknowledge when trying to conceptualize the decision-making process that formed new towns under royal authority. It suggests a top-down, hierarchical chain of command whereby a king issued orders to those beneath, who then carried them out. Recently, however, medieval historians have begun to look more closely at "top-down" versus "bottom-up" decision making, and social historians in particular, perhaps keen to give the "lower orders" their due, have made a case for the role of townspeople and country folk in matters concerning urban and rural decision making (see Giles and Dyer 2005). Indeed, what is beginning to emerge is a more complex picture of negotiation between social groups and individuals. The king, then, may have seen himself as directing and giving orders, and these orders may well have been passed on, but in the process—in reality—they were also resisted, challenged, and renegotiated along the way. The following part of this chapter explores this process in more detail by focusing on Edward's new towns and the stages of decision making—and the agents who were the decision makers—that created them.

Edward's New Towns and Their Formation

By the time of his death in 1307, Edward I's realm encompassed most of Britain and Ireland and parts of western France. Many of these lands were already well populated with towns and markets before his reign, but others, particularly along the frontier regions of Edward's dominion, where lands and people were to be brought closer under his control, were less so (see Prestwich 1997). Under Edward during the 1270s, 1280, and 1290s, it was these peripheral, marginal parts of his realm that saw the most intense urbanization through the founding of new towns, sometimes on "greenfield" sites, sometimes adjacent to existing settlements.

The new towns of Edward I were well studied by Beresford in his magisterial book *New Towns of the Middle Ages* (1967), still a standard reference work, in which he recognized the dual commercial and political motivation for creating new towns in areas at the edges of Edward's control. New towns encouraged new people to settle and trade to take place, which ultimately, of course, benefitted the monarch and his place in the world. Edward's main territorial concerns were in north Wales and in southern Scotland but also in Gascony in southwest France (Prestwich 1997). In seeking to secure his control and authority in these regions, Edward was quite prepared to take military action, but the formation of new towns was a more peaceful and no less strategic and rewarding means of achieving the same end. In the more settled lands, too, there was a need for new towns, exemplified in the founding of New Winchelsea on the south coast of England, following coastal erosion that had flooded the earlier town (Martin and Martin 2004). There was a set of processes that led to the formation of these new towns, and written records relating to the towns can be drawn on to elucidate them. From these sources, combined with morphological evidence, it is possible to identify the different stages necessary to create a medieval new town under royal authority and, on occasion, to identify who was involved at each stage. A five-stage model helps conceptualize the decision-making process (Fig. 2.2).

Forming a new town began with what may be termed strategic, "regional" planning involving the king and his senior advisors in timing the foundation of a town and deciding its location. After this, the next stages were concerned with the actual design and surveying work to create the town physically on the ground. Last, the final stage involved populating the town and ratifying its constitutional privileges through the grant of a charter. It is this latter stage upon which most historians of new towns, Beresford included, have tended to concentrate but, as we shall see, the bulk of the important planning work and decision making was done prior to chartering a town. That this was a lengthy and protracted process, from beginning to end, is exemplified by the case of Winchelsea (Martin and

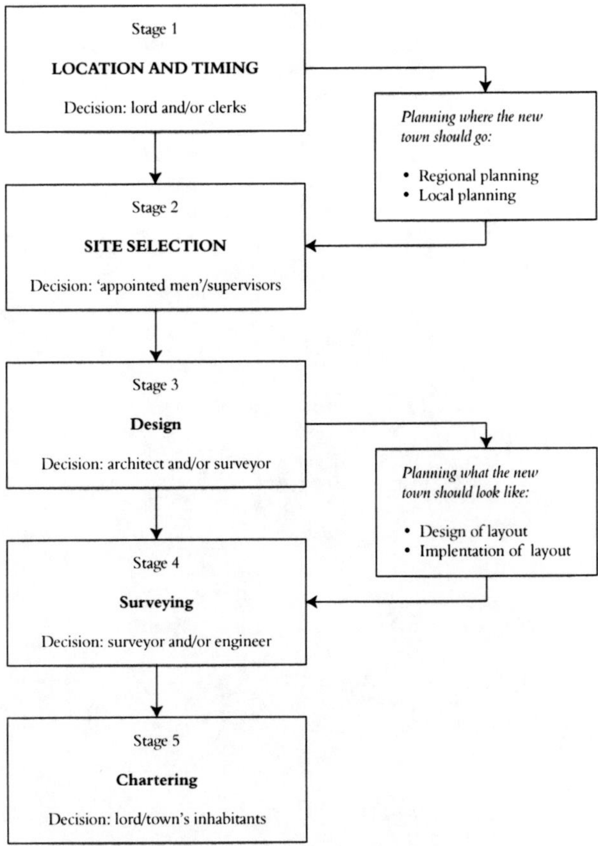

FIGURE 2.2 Diagram of the suggested relationships between key agents of change and the decision-making processes involved in founding a medieval 'new town'

Martin 2004; Fig. 2.3). Here negotiations began in 1280 to relocate the town and its people, but it was more than ten years later (by 1292) that townspeople were finally able to move from their old low-lying site and take up residence in their new town placed higher up, above the threat of flooding from the sea that had prompted the move in the first place. Who the agents were in such cases and what decisions they were taking will be discussed in relation to each of the five stages of the planning process as defined in the model. Written records relating to the planning of Edward's new towns will be examined first, and whatever evidence of decision making emerges from this will be checked for correspondence with the resulting forms of the towns themselves. It will be shown that such analysis helps to raise further questions about how decisions were made, particularly with regard to the more enigmatic stages of design and surveying.

Decisions about Timing and Locating a New Town

How far was Edward himself responsible for determining when and where a new town should be founded? It might be expected that he would act as the instigator, especially in the context of those areas of his realm where new towns directly followed military action, as was the case in north

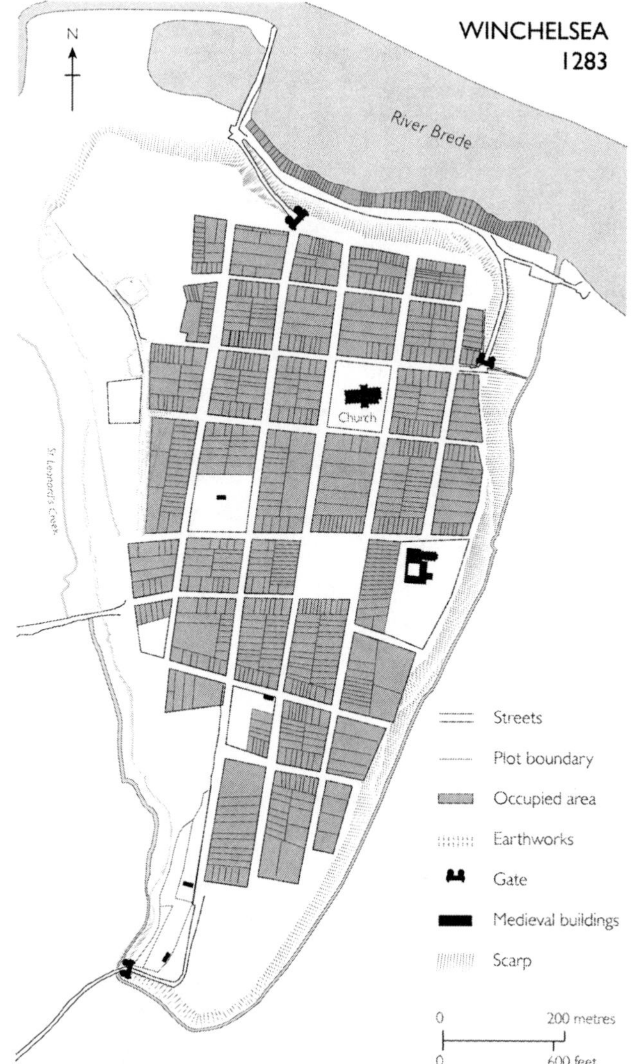

FIGURE 2.3 New Winchelsea, Sussex, England, reconstructed plan of town c.1300

Wales with the foundation of Aberystwyth, Flint, and Rhuddlan in 1277–8, which all came after the campaigns of 1276–7, and Caernarfon and Conwy in 1283–4 after the campaign of 1282–3 (Beresford 1967; Prestwich 1997). In these cases, too, the towns were created as adjuncts to a chain of new castles dotted along the coastline of Wales to provide a noose around the Welsh stronghold of Snowdonia (Lewis 1912; Lilley 2010; Fig. 2.4). Surely it would have been Edward's decision, first and foremost, to decide where the castle-towns should be sited and also when they should be built, perhaps in consultation with senior advisors such as Master James of St. George, to whom he had delegated the responsibility of building the castles (Taylor 1986). That Edward had such a strategic approach to thinking about the planning of new towns is suggested by his decision to call together a colloquium in 1297 to discuss how "to set out a new town at Berwick upon Tweed, lately

FIGURE 2.4 Conwy's historic townscape viewed from the westernmost corner of the Edwardian town walls, looking east across to the castle and Afon Conwy. Note that the causeway carrying road and rail is a modern intrusion

burned and damaged in the war with Scotland" (Beresford 1967: 4). This had followed an earlier royal writ, issued in September 1296, whereby "London was ordered to elect 'four wise men of the most knowing and most sufficient who know best how to devise, order and array a new town to the most profit of the king and of merchants,'" an order that was followed through in October when "the aldermen and four good men of each ward of the city" selected those they deemed to be most suitable for the king's request (Tout 1934: 27, citing Palgrave 1827: 49).

While the king himself therefore led the process, deciding when and where a new town should be founded, he took the advice of others and delegated to appropriately qualified individuals the task of doing the work. Away from the "hostile" territories of Wales and Scotland, such as in the more settled parts of southern England and southwest France, the king was sometimes petitioned to found a new town by locally interested parties. This occurred in the case of Winchelsea, for example, when the townspeople began to realize that their town would soon be washed away, and in Gascony, where some local lords dealt with the king's seneschal (agent) acting on his behalf (Martin and Martin 2004; Randolph 1995).

When it came to taking initial decisions about founding new towns, there can be no doubt that the king's role was fundamental. Whether the town was part of his overall strategic plan to dominate and control remote lands and people or whether it was suggested to him to meet some local need, Edward's decision was paramount, but at what level were decisions taken for the actual choice of site? Did the king take a direct interest in such matters or leave it for others to decide? In the case of Rhuddlan in north Wales, the king did not visit the site of the new town until work was already under way, and at the new bastide of Baa, close to Bordeaux, again Edward came to inspect what had previously been started and (as is so often reported) also bought drinks for those engaged on the job (Lilley et al. 2005a; Trabut-Cussac 1961).

Yet, of course, in the itinerant court of a medieval king, Edward would have had ample opportunity to consider and discuss suitable sites for his new towns beforehand, for instance in north Wales during his 1277 campaigns, where he traveled along the coast (see Fig. 2.1). Indeed, Flint seems to have been chosen as a site for a new castle-town directly after the king's encampment there (Soulsby 1983). In this regard, the decisions about which towns (and castles) to build first were also likely to have been made by the king, though again doubtless in consultation with his more senior advisors, his knights, or the clerks of his household. In Wales, the prominence of his clerks, such as William of March and William of Boston, is clear from contemporary accounts and from the earliest moment in cases such as Rhuddlan and Flint, when they were engaged as administrators on site (Lilley et al. 2005a).

Other new castle-towns in Wales came about through the actions (and decisions) of the king's closest vassals, such as, in the case of Holt in Flintshire, the Earl of Surrey (Pratt 1965). The pattern that emerges from this is one in which the first two stages of planning a new town—decisions over where and when to found towns—were dominated by the king but not made in isolation without taking advice or delegating to others. The third and fourth stages in the process are somewhat less clear in this respect.

Decisions about Designing and Surveying a New Town

How far was Edward responsible for devising the actual plans for his new towns? Historians tend to talk of Edward's new towns as if they were a product of his mind but, as we have already begun to appreciate, there were plenty of others involved in the decision-making process who could quite easily have exerted variable amounts of influence. This is evident in the case of the founding of New Winchelsea, an example that is frequently cited quite simply because the process of its formation is, by medieval standards, so well recorded. As noted earlier, the process began with petitions sent to the king by the inhabitants of what was soon to become "old" Winchelsea. The king dispatched certain appointed men to supervise the process of relocating the town, beginning in late 1280 when the king's steward was sent to Winchelsea to "extend and buy or obtain by exchange certain lands" (*Calendar of Patent Rolls* [hereafter CPR] 1272–81: 414). Three years later, in October 1283, and with the site of the town decided, three other men were appointed "to plan and give directions for streets and lanes necessary for the said new town, for places suitable for a market, and for two churches" (CPR 1281–92: 81–2). One interpretation of this statement is that these three men—Stephen Penecestre (warden of the Cinque Ports, of which Winchelsea was one), Henry le Waleys (mayor of London in 1273–4 and 1281–4; royal mayor of Bordeaux in 1275), and Gregory de Rokesley (mayor of London, 1274–81)—themselves drew up a plan appropriate for the new Winchelsea and then set about laying it out on the ground (see Fig. 2.3). However, an alternative view is also possible. Such senior men were administrators, two of whom were wealthy London merchant vintners (see Barron 2004). Should we really see them as the ones best equipped to design and survey a new town—

no mean task—or is it more likely they were appointed because of their contacts and experience in organizing others to do the work? The latter seems more plausible, not least because there is evidence for this from Baa, once again, for there a Master Gérard de la Tour was employed to carry out the ground-planning work (Trabut-Cussac 1961). With the Welsh castle-towns, too, a whole host of specialists were engaged in matters of design work, not least architect-masons and engineers (Taylor 1986; Coldstream 2003). These are more likely to be the sort of individuals whom Edward's appointed men called upon in the planning of the "new" Winchelsea.

Envisioning the process of medieval urban design and surveying is tantalizing, as it is so often obscure in contemporary records. It is not even clear whether design and surveying work was carried out separately by different individuals or all done by the same person. No doubt it varied from place to place. That towns were designed on parchment before work began on them is known, and architects of the Middle Ages certainly produced drawings of intended buildings (see Harvey 1984; Gimpel 1983). Skilled measurers and surveyors were also around and had the necessary expertise and capability to lay out new urban landscapes, as shown by evidence in thirteenth-century sources. These included civic records from the low countries and the *practica geometriae* texts circulating at this time that demonstrated, for example, ways of calculating how to measure land and construct buildings (see Lilley 2005). For the new towns being formed under Edward's authority, the actual urban designers and surveyors who were engaged remain, however, very shadowy characters. And yet, someone must have drawn up designs for the new towns and then laid them out on the ground. This is where the documentary trail begins to go cold. The king's household accounts mention clerks of the works involved with the castles and towns of Wales, some of whom were well educated before becoming royal officials, having attended school and university (Tout 1920). There they would have studied arithmetic and geometry as part of the *quadrivium*. These men thus had the intellectual capability to design towns, at least on parchment, but whether they were also sufficiently experienced in more earthy matters such as surveying and measuring out defenses, streets, and plots for a new town in the field is difficult to determine, when written sources alone are used. From such sources, we only very rarely glimpse a man such as Master Gérard (who, it might be noted, was overseen by a royal clerk, Richard de Escham; Trabut-Cussac 1961). To this end, the physical forms of the new towns themselves have to be examined as well, comparing them against the information yielded by the various written sources: as Beresford somewhat inelegantly put it, the town plan is "dumb witness" to the decision making of superficially anonymous urban shapers (Beresford 1967: 147).

Chartering and Populating a New Town

The final stage in making a new town was the granting of privileges enshrined in a charter. This was the impetus to bring people to settle in a town, offering special inducements to take up residence in those towns that were vulnerable to attack, as in the case of the Welsh towns. The charter itself was evidently drawn up as a kind of contract between lord and townspeople, providing each with mutual benefits and assurances (Lilley 2001). At Winchelsea, the townspeople simply kept the privileges they had previously held in their old town (see Martin and Martin 2004). The charter for the new town of Newton in Dorset, a commercial enterprise instigated by Edward in 1286, was granted after the town had been laid out, though in this particular case, the project was ultimately a failure, and the site of the new town today is lost beneath sandy heathland (Beresford and St. Joseph 1958). The same failures are to be found elsewhere, in Wales, for example, at Bere in Merionethshire, despite the inducement of a charter and borough privileges (Evans 1989).

At Rhuddlan, a town that Edward wished to become the seat of a bishopric and thus to attain regional importance, the process of populating the town is revealed by contemporary accounts of the royal household (see Taylor 1986). The first burgages had been granted in February 1278, before the charter of privileges issued in November of that year; after which, in 1279 and 1280, the inhabitants of Rhuddlan were recorded to be busy "building the town" ("Calendar of Welsh Rolls" [hereafter CWR]: 165, 188; *Calendar of Charter Rolls* [hereafter CChR], 1257–1300: 209). The chartering of a new town also had symbolic significance for the town's inhabitants, who had ventured perhaps some distance to settle and begin a new life. Randolph (1995) refers to a pole (*pau*) being raised in the market square of a newly formed bastide in France and the content of a charter being read out aloud to an assembled group. Such a custom was perhaps performed in Edward's towns in England and Wales. In February 1278, for example, an "order" was issued "to cause proclamation to be made that a market shall be held at Flint," suggesting that an announcement was made locally (CWR 1912: 165).

The five stages outlined here relate to stages in the decision-making process to create a new town. From what little evidence contemporaries have left us about those involved, it is possible to suggest in certain cases who the decision makers were. While the king had overall authority, the formation of a new town was by no means his responsibility alone. There were other agents involved, some commissioned by him and others by the clerks or advisors whom he appointed. Separating these individuals into the stages of urban formation shows how fluid their work was, with clerks in particular seemingly having input into the different stages of a town's planning. For urban morphologists interested in the actual shaping of the urban landscape, it is the third and fourth stages of the process that are perhaps most intriguing, and yet the agents involved and their decision making are the most vaguely recorded. To examine this stage of formation a little further, it is best to consider the evidence of the town plans themselves, for it might be expected that towns formed at around the same time, as Edward's new towns were, and in close proximity, and for similar reasons, would have similar morphological characteristics. If so, this might suggest the same individuals were responsible for shaping them. What emerges, however, is a complex picture.

The Forms of Edwardian Towns in Wales

Edward's new towns of north Wales are often described erroneously as *bastides*—a term that strictly applies to urban foundations in southwest France—and assumed to have broadly similar urban forms based upon a grid-pattern of streets (Morris 1994; Schofield and Vince 2003). On closer inspection, however, the only similarity between them and the bastides of southwest France is their shared variety in form. With recent studies of the morphology of the bastides, different types of plan have been identified, some with regional peculiarities (Lauret et al. 1988). For Edward's new towns in Wales, work has begun on trying to identify common characteristics in their physical forms that might indicate that they were a product of the same mind, or at least point towards a shared origin (Lilley et al. 2005a, 2007a). Analyzing and comparing the plans of these new towns is, perhaps surprisingly, a new endeavor; despite the quite considerable general historical attention the towns have received (Lilley et al. 2005b, 2007b). The following account is based on this recent work, and hence should be seen as a preliminary assessment at this stage. Even so, comparing the towns' plans is beginning to reveal some interesting similarities and contrasts, which help reveal something of the decision making and decision makers involved in shaping them.

The Edwardian new towns of north Wales fall into three groups, depending on when they were founded. Towns of the first group all date to 1277–8 and include Aberystwyth, Flint, and

Rhuddlan. The second group dates to 1284 and includes the castle-towns of Caernarfon, Conwy, Harlech, Criccieth, and Bere (these latter two based on earlier Welsh castles), while a third group dates rather later, to the 1290s (Caerwys, in 1290; Overton, in 1292; Beaumaris, in 1296), with one, Newborough, appearing as late as 1303 (for dates see Lewis 1912; Beresford 1967). Of these later towns, only Beaumaris was founded beside a castle; the others were simply market towns. It might be expected that this chronology had some bearing on the shapes and shaping of the new towns, with those belonging to one particular group having at least some similarity in their form. Plan analysis, however, does not present such a clear-cut picture. Indeed, towns that fall within the same group have different forms, and towns of different groups have identifiable similarities. This morphological evidence points to the activities of those involved in decision making in aspects of designing and surveying the layouts of the towns and perhaps provides some indication of who was involved in individual cases. To demonstrate this, Rhuddlan and Flint, despite belonging to the same group chronologically, show distinctly different urban forms. On the other hand, Conwy and Beaumaris display similar forms, although they do not belong to the same chronological group. An underlying assumption is that towns with similar plans were designed and surveyed by the same person or group of individuals, but this should, of course, be questioned (for example, one designer might come up with more than one design of a town). Hence there is a need to look not only at the morphological evidence but also at information from contemporary written sources, which in the case of Edward's Welsh towns provide particular potential. This is because the process of castle building—the most critical of the king's concerns—was so well documented by royal administrators and because the castles were so intimately connected to the new towns (see Taylor 1986).

In addition to being founded in the same year, Flint and Rhuddlan were also located only fifteen miles apart, and thus, in both time and space, were in close proximity to each other. Considering such common conditions, it is odd that their respective urban layouts are so different (Fig. 2.5). Flint's town plan is highly orthogonal, with straight streets intersecting at right angles laid out in front of the castle, the whole ensemble neatly contained within a rectangular defensive circuit. Rhuddlan, on the other hand, has an altogether different appearance. Here the plan is based on a skewed grid, although, with their common angles and alignments, the streets and plots making up the town look as if this skew was deliberate. Was it the towns' local sites that caused such morphological differences? Not in the case of Flint and Rhuddlan, as both towns share similarly flat terrain (see Lilley et al. 2007b). The different plans, then, suggest that different agents were responsible for shaping them—but who? Suggestions can be made by looking through those various individuals involved in setting up the castles and towns between 1277 and 1278 who are recorded in contemporary accounts. Here the focus is on who was doing precisely what and when within each of the towns, a process that began in both places during the summer of 1277. Notwithstanding the fact that Rhuddlan had already experienced urban development at the end of the eleventh century under Norman lordship and even earlier under the Anglo-Saxons in the tenth century, the Edwardian castle-town was in effect established on a "green-field" site (to the west of the sites of the two earlier towns; see Quinnell et al. 1994). Flint, of course, where no urban development had previously taken place, was clearly in this class (Edwards 1951).

Fossatores arrived at Flint on August 9, 1277 under the direction of William of March (Taylor 1986: 18). These diggers were presumably put to work on the outer defenses of the town and castle, the earthen ditch and embankment that surrounded them. This was the time at which the layout of Flint must have been decided, for the overall rectangular shape of the town was fixed by its defenses (not necessarily the internal orthogonal layout of streets and plots, but most likely so, as the three gates

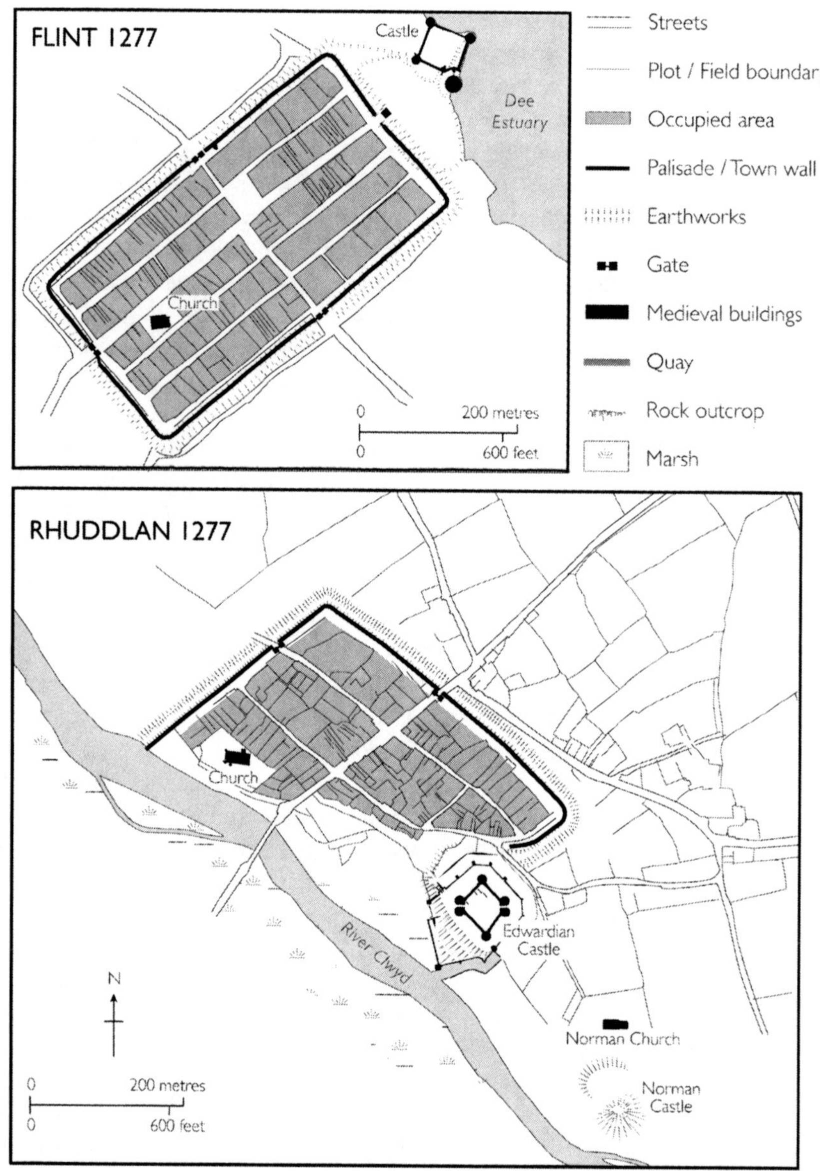

FIGURE 2.5 The new towns of Flint and Rhuddlan (founded 1277), reconstructed plans of the towns c.1300, to common scale

into the town would also have had to have been determined at the same time). William of March, as his name suggests, hailed from the fenlands of eastern England, as did many of his *fossatores*, where the need for diggers was especially great for making ditches and dykes to drain the land and reclaim it from the sea. William was later to become bishop of Bath and Wells, having served the king as an official of the wardrobe during the 1280s (Tout 1920). Meanwhile, at Rhuddlan, work had begun in June under William of Boston (another easterner) with the "new cut," to divert the River Clwyd to improve river access to the new castle and town (Taylor 1986: 27). The different plans of the two towns may thus reflect the influence of these two key individuals who, having to oversee the preparatory digging work—and presumably therefore the setting-out work—were perhaps drawing upon their knowledge as educated administrators.

During the autumn of 1277 the "keeper of works" was William Perton, and he dealt at the same time both with Rhuddlan and Flint; then in November, a Nicholas Bonel was appointed by the king to be "surveyor of works," again for both places (Taylor 1986: 19; CWR 1912: 160). So after the initial activity carried out under the two Williams, the two towns were then placed under the control of one single individual, suggesting once again that the towns' (different) plans had been decided earlier, during the summer of 1277. By February 1278, burgages were being granted in both places and being built upon soon after (see above). Later still, William of Louth, another wardrobe official of the king's household, came to Rhuddlan to survey these burgages for the king and report on those that were still vacant (CWR 1912: 178). The direct role of the king in the building work going on in the castle towns thus seems to have been minimal. He did pay a visit to Flint in November 1277 but, by this time, groundworks were in place, a situation similar to that of the founding of Baa (Taylor, 1986: 19; Trabut-Cussac 1961). Master James of St. George likewise arrived late on the scene, directing work at Flint castle in November 1280, and at Rhuddlan in April 1278, and thus he also presumably played no direct role in the shaping of the two towns (Taylor 1986: 20, 29).

It would seem, then, that the decisions regarding the design and surveying of the towns at Flint and Rhuddlan were being taken early on, possibly by two of the king's clerks, William of March and William of Boston. This could account for the differences in the forms of the two towns: two designs reflecting the work of two designers. Of course, it may be that the two Williams—as administrators rather than specialist experts themselves—sought advice on such matters. At Rhuddlan, two specialist individuals were employed, masters Peter and Bertram, both engineers (*ingeniatores*; Taylor 1986: 28–9). Their roles were, perhaps, akin to that of Simon "the builder," who was working at Ardres in Flanders in the early thirteenth century, rebuilding the town walls there. He was described by one contemporary observer as "master of geometrical work" supervising on site "the measurers and masters of the work who were always presiding and taking pains" (cited in Shopkow 2001: 190-1). Could it be that similar such specialist individuals, perhaps rarely recorded by the king's administrators (but more suited than they to do the practical work), were responsible for physically shaping the new towns? This question can be addressed by comparing the plans of the Edwardian new towns in Wales, for if certain similar design traits cross from one group of towns to another, might it not indicate that there were others responsible for creating them?

The layout of Flint, some have suggested, has certain similarities to the town of Aigues Mortes in southern France, a port through which Edward himself had passed on his way to the Crusades (Tout 1934; Prestwich 1997). As an outside influence is known to have operated in the building of the castles in Wales—through the work of Savoyard masons such as master James (see Taylor 1986; cf. Coldstream 2003)—the new towns, too, are often looked upon as reflecting an overseas influence, perhaps coming from south-west France and the bastides, perhaps from Savoy (Morris 1994). While not denying that such external influences may have shaped the new towns, there are other less romantic possibilities, one of which is that there was a pool of individuals (like masters Gérard and Simon) who were called upon to carry out tasks such as designing and laying out defenses, streets, and plots. They might have been engineers, architects, measurers, or even diggers of varying backgrounds and experiences, each directed on site by a clerk of works (see

Turner 2010). Though, in certain cases, their personal worlds may well have encompassed distant parts of continental Europe, many were as likely to be drawn from closer to home, as records show was the case for the labor-force used in the castle-building enterprise itself (Taylor 1986). This pool of local "planners" might account for the presence of certain design traits across the Welsh towns.

Until further detailed morphological study is completed, these identifiable similarities are broad ones. For example, with Flint the orthogonal, elongated plan compares favorably with that of Holt, a small castle-town on the River Dee developed under the lordship of John de Warenne, Earl of Surrey, and chartered some seven years after Flint (Lilley et al. 2005a). The similar forms of the two towns suggest that one person was behind them both, but the later date of the creation of Holt seems to point away from William of March as their joint "planner," for by this time, he held a high position in Edward's administration and hence was surely too important and busy to be working on laying out such a small town in the Welsh March belonging to one of Edward's vassals. If this was the case, the design of both Flint and Holt was plausibly carried out lower down the bureaucratic hierarchy by someone whom William had appointed at Flint and who later also worked at Holt.

Similar traits of urban design are also evident in the layouts of Conwy and Beaumaris but, in the case of these two places, there is quite clear evidence that Edward's chief architect had a hand in their formation. Conwy was founded in 1283–4 as a new town on the site of an existing monastery, situated on the shores of the Afon Conwy (Lewis 1912; see Fig. 2.4). Beaumaris likewise occupies a waterfront location but was established some years later, in 1296, though again, like Conwy, it required the removal of existing townspeople, this time the thriving little Welsh town of Llanfaes and its inhabitants (Beresford 1967). Their two castles were the work of Master James of St. George, and he was there at the outset giving directions on their construction (Taylor 1986). The two towns have comparable aspects to their form (Fig. 2.6). This is clear from even a cursory glance at their layouts if they are placed side by side, but even more so if the plans of the two are analyzed in detail. Both basically contain a castle and a main street that leads up to it, the street itself running parallel to the shoreline (which in both places also formed the town's quay). Furthermore, both plans are based upon a T-shaped street-system, with the streets each set out in a straight line—noticeably straight if they are compared to the other Edwardian new towns established in Wales (see Lilley et al. 2007a). Looking at the layouts of the two towns with the benefit of a Geographical Information System (GIS; see Lilley et al. 2005b), it is possible to identify yet further similarities. By inverting the layout of Beaumaris (in effect viewing it in reverse), for example, the plans of the two towns appear even closer in design terms (see Lilley et al. 2007b). In relation to the T-shaped street-pattern, their castles and churches can be seen to occupy similar positions, and the position of their quays matches, too. Both also have a curious curved street, and the plot series, like the main streets, have a particularly regular form (Fig. 2.7).

So despite different dates in their foundation (some twelve years separate them), the forms of Conwy and Beaumaris share similarities. The most plausible explanation is that we are seeing here the work of one individual in both places, and as Master James was at both and there right from the start of work on their respective castles, it seems likely that the plans of the two towns were his. The precise geometrical forms of their streets and the alignment of these to the castle entrance might also hint at the role of the castles' master architect—someone with an overall design of both castle and town and who was present when the groundwork of both was being laid. In this particular case, it appears that a single, common "blueprint" was used. The towns'

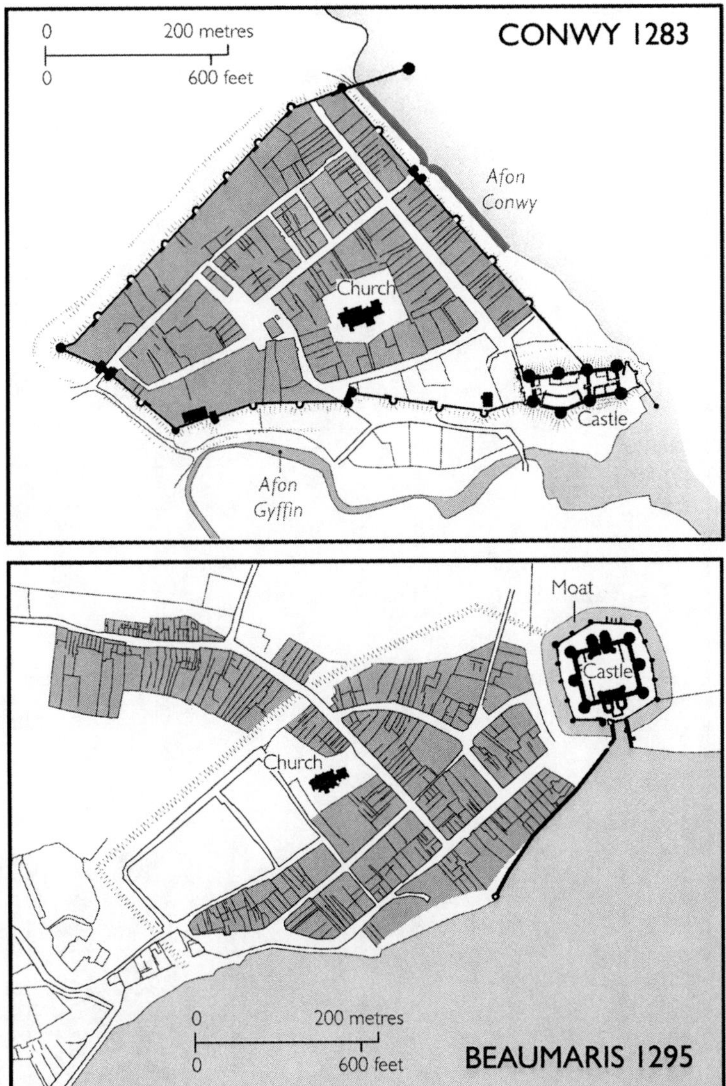

FIGURE 2.6 The new towns of Conwy (1283–4) and Beaumaris (1295–6), reconstructed plans of the towns c.1300, to common scale

shared morphologies point to this, but what is interesting is that to make the plan fit at Beaumaris (the later of the two towns), it had to be inverted—in effect, viewed from below. To do this easily would have required an intimate knowledge of the plan of Conwy and its local site features and an ability perhaps to manipulate its layout to fit the circumstances at Beaumaris. The easiest way to do this would have been to turn upside down a sketched plan of Conwy, just as was done using the GIS to analyze their layout. The shared layouts thus not only point to the work of the king's architect (in these cases) but to the strong possibility that the architect was working from a parchment plan.

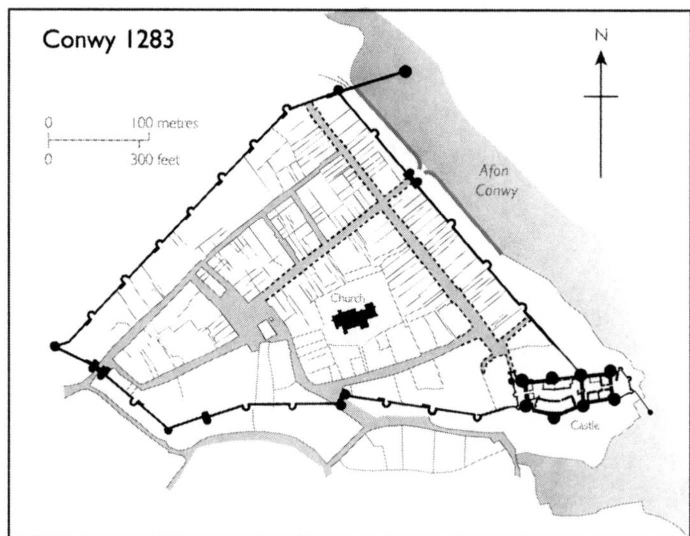

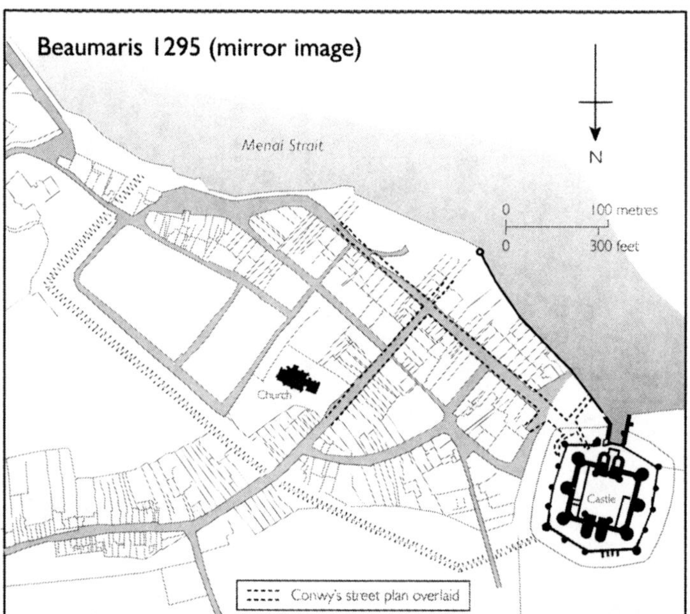

FIGURE 2.7 The plans of Conwy and Beaumaris compared. When overlaid, note how Conwy's T-shaped street plan (1283–4) matches exactly with the (inverted) plan of Beaumaris (1295–6) (see text)

Conclusion

Further study will, no doubt, reveal other more subtle similarities between Edward's towns in Wales and point to shared influences in their design and surveying. However, based upon these preliminary observations, it would appear that decisions about a town's layout involved a range of individuals, perhaps working locally and called upon to do the work by those higher up the social hierarchy and chain of command, such as Edward himself or (more likely) one of his appointed administrators. This does not preclude the possibility that in some cases there were external influences affecting urban design in the later Middle Ages, but the job itself would be carried out by people whose only apparent trace often lies in the layouts of the towns that they left behind. Until more morphological study is directed to these towns, their shapers will remain eclipsed by the higher level, better-documented agents of Edward's administrative hierarchy.

The aim of this chapter has been to begin to outline the processes through which medieval urban landscapes were brought into being. The focus has been on those new towns created under royal authority in England and Wales by Edward I, for which a model of decision making and decision makers has been proposed. The suggestion is that while the process of creating an urban landscape went through a series of quite well-defined stages, the agents involved in each were often overlapping and could encompass individuals from across the medieval social hierarchy, from the king to the *fossator* or *ingeniator* employed on the spot. How these agents interacted, how they were recruited, what networks they created, and how their knowledges were gained are all issues that have yet to be addressed as far as urban planning in the Middle Ages is concerned (see Lilley 2005).

Just because we are dealing with a "pre-modern" society does not mean that medieval urban design and planning were simple and straightforward; far from it. The processes and negotiations involved compare well with those of later centuries—a point that might cause us to pause and reflect on what actually makes modern urban planning "modern." To some extent, it is instructive to draw upon later parallels. Indeed, the decision making and decision makers shaping modern urban landscapes consciously and subconsciously inform our understanding of how earlier urban shapers worked. Of course, at the same time, it is also necessary to look carefully at the specific social and cultural contexts within which medieval urban shapers were working and the flows of people and ideas that were peculiar to that period of urban formation. There is the potential to develop this through the discussions about "top-down" versus "bottom-up" decision making already begun by historians. Here it seems that as far as Edward I's realm is concerned, royal authority and urban formation were intricately and elaborately linked. It was not the case that the king's new towns were themselves created by the king but rather that they were formed through various connected agents who were working in and for the royal administration and household. Yet, all the time we are—as regards England and Wales—confronted with the issue of how to uncover the actions and activities of those individuals whose work went largely unrecorded by such administration. By and large, it is the king and his higher officials who are well-recorded in written accounts of the time, but they were not necessarily those directly, nor solely, responsible for physically shaping urban landscapes on the ground, even though these are the very agents whom historians in the past have tended to regard as the most influential.

Comparative work at the European scale is required to expand the arguments made here and to clarify how urban landscapes were shaped in the Middle Ages. The later thirteenth and fourteenth centuries probably provide the best scope for doing this, as it is a reasonably well-documented period and yet still falls within the main period of medieval new town foundation in Europe. To this end, there remains much still to be done in comparing the morphologies of these towns, and doing so within the context of their documented histories. More thought also needs to be given to what the observable similarities and differences in urban forms might actually mean—how exactly are they to be interpreted as evidence for the ideas and ideals of those who created them? To answer this, parallels may be drawn between studies of medieval architectural form and built form, using common design traits to look for and understand the social processes shaping built environments in the Middle Ages (see Taylor 1986). How medieval urban landscapes were formed under different agents and authorities—royal, civic, secular, ecclesiastical—is also something yet to be explored, although the process may not actually be that dissimilar for each. After all, men such as William of March, clerks who were working for the king in Wales, had been educated by the clergy and, in some instance, in later life became ecclesiastical authorities themselves.

In a Christian world in which boundaries between secular and ecclesiastical were, perhaps, less defined than they are today (in Europe), such fluidity should not be surprising (Lilley 2009). The implications of this are still to be worked out for urban morphology in particular, and in this respect there is much to be said for placing urban shapers in their particular intellectual and social contexts. This is exactly what Whitehand and others (e.g. Whitehand and Larkham 1992) have done in their work on urban shapers, and it is a lead that those concerned with earlier periods of urban formation may wish to heed. In so doing, such a volume as this offers the potential to look across different historical periods of urban formation and thus help begin to identify those aspects of the process that are either different or common. To this end, further empirical work is undoubtedly required but not without some conceptualization of the ways in which "actors" and "networks" interact in the shaping of past and present urban landscapes.

Acknowledgments

The research on which this chapter is based derives largely from an Arts and Humanities Research Council (award B/RG/AN3206/APN14501) project called *Mapping the Medieval Urban Landscape* that ran from September 2003 to June 2005 (see http://www.qub.ac.uk/urban_mapping/). A Leverhulme Research Fellowship also enabled additional study on Edward I's urban policies thanks to funding received from The Leverhulme Trust (2006–2007). The author thanks both of these funding bodies for their generous research support and Gill Alexander for drawing the illustrations that appear here.

References

Barron, C. (2004) *London in the Middle Ages: Government and People 1200–1500.* Cambridge: Cambridge University Press.

Beresford, M. W. (1967) *New Towns of the Middle Ages: Town Plantation in England, Wales and Gascony.* London: Lutterworth.

Beresford, M. W., and St. Joseph, J. K. S. (1958) *Medieval England: An Aerial Survey*. Cambridge: Cambridge University Press.

Calendar of Charter Rolls (CChR) (1903–27). London: HMSO.

Calendar of Patent Rolls (CPR) (1893–1901). London: HMSO.

Calendar of Welsh Rolls (CWR) (1912) *Calendar of Various Chancery Rolls.* London: HMSO, 157–362.

Coldstream, N. (2003) Architects, advisers and design at Edward I's castles in Wales. *Architectural History*, 46: 19–36.

Conzen, M. R. G. (1960) *Alnwick, Northumberland: A Study in Town-Plan Analysis.* London: George Philip, Institute of British Geographers Publication 27.

Conzen, M. R. G. (1968) The use of town plans in the study of urban history, in H. J. Dyos (ed.), *The Study of Urban History: The Proceedings of an International Round-Table Conference at Gilbert Murray Hall, University of Leicester on 23–26 September 1966*, 113–30. London: Edward Arnold.

Dutton, P. E. (1983) *Illustre civitatis et populi exemplum*: Plato's *Timaeus* and the transmission from Calcidius to the end of the twelfth century of a tripartite scheme of society. *Mediaeval Studies*, 45: 79–119.

Edwards, J. G. (1951) The building of Flint. *Journal of the Flintshire Historical Society*, 12: 5–20.

Evans, E. D. (1989) Was there a borough of Bere? *Journal of the Merioneth Historical and Record Society*, 10: 290–8.

Friedman, D. (1988) *Florentine New Towns: Urban Design in the Late Middle Ages.* Cambridge, MA: MIT Press.

Giles, K., and Dyer, C. (eds.) (2005) *Town and Country in the Middle Ages: Contrasts, Contacts and Interconnections, 1100–1500.* Leeds, U.K.: Maney.

Gimpel, J. (1983) *The Cathedral Builders*, trans. T. Waugh. Salisbury, U.K.: Michael Russel.

Gurevich, A. J. (1985) *Categories of Medieval Culture*, trans. G. L. Campbell. London: Routledge and Kegan Paul.

Harvey, J. (1984) *English Mediaeval Architects: A Biographical Dictionary Down to 1550*. Gloucester, U.K.: Sutton.

Lauret, A., Malebranche, R., and Séraphin, G. (1988) *Bastides: Villes Nouvelles du Moyen Age*. Toulouse: Éd. Milan.

Lewis, E. A. (1912) *The Mediaeval Boroughs of Snowdonia*. London: Henry Sotheran.

Lilley, K. D. (2001) Urban planning and the design of towns in the Middle Ages: the Earls of Devon and their "new towns." *Planning Perspectives*, 16: 1–24.

Lilley, K. D. (2005) Urban landscapes and their design: creating town from country in the Middle Ages, in K. Giles and C. Dyer (eds.), *Town and Country in the Middle Ages: Contrasts, Contacts and Interconnections, 1100–1500*, 229–49. Leeds, U.K.: Maney.

Lilley, K. D. (2009) *City and Cosmos: The Medieval World in Urban Form*. London: Reaktion Books.

Lilley, K. D. (2010) The landscapes of Edward's new towns: their planning and design, in D. Williams and J. Kenyon (eds.), *The Impact of the Edwardian Castles on Wales*, 99–113. Oxford: Oxbow.

Lilley, K. D., Lloyd, C., and Trick, S. (2005a) *Mapping Medieval Townscapes: A Digital Atlas of the New Towns of Edward I*. York: University of York, AHDS Archaeology Data Service. Online. Available: <http://archaeologydataservice.ac.uk/archives/view/atlas_ahrb_2005/> (accessed 5 October 2012).

Lilley, K. D., Lloyd, C. D., Trick, S., and Graham, C. (2005b) Mapping and analysing medieval built form using GPS and GIS. *Urban Morphology*, 9 (1): 5–15.

Lilley, K. D., Lloyd, C., and Trick, S. (2007a) Designs and designers of medieval "new towns" in Wales. *Antiquity*, 81 (312): 279–93.

Lilley, K. D., Lloyd, C., and Trick, S. (2007b) Mapping medieval townscapes: GIS applications in landscape history and settlement study, in M. Gardiner and S. Rippon (eds.), *Medieval Landscapes*, 27–42. Macclesfield, U.K.: Windgather Press.

Martin, D., and Martin, B. (2004) *New Winchelsea, Sussex: A Medieval Port Town*. King's Lynn, U.K.: Heritage Marketing and Publications.

Morris, A. E. J. (1994) *History of Urban Form: Before the Industrial Revolutions*, 3rd ed. London: Prentice Hall.

Palgrave, F. (1827–34) *The Parliamentary Writs and Writs of Military Summons*. London: Record Commission.

Pratt, D. (1965) The medieval borough of Holt. *Denbighshire Historical Society Transactions*, 14: 9–74.

Prestwich, M. (1997) *Edward I*. New Haven: Yale University Press.

Quinnell, H., Blockley, M. R., and Berridge, P. (1994) *Excavations at Rhuddlan, Clwyd 1969–73, Mesolithic to Medieval*. York: Council for British Archaeology, CBA Research Report 95.

Randolph, A. (1995) Bastides of south-west France. *Art Bulletin*, 77: 290–307.

Schofield, J., and Vince, A. G. (2003) *Medieval Towns: The Archaeology of British Towns in Their European Setting*, 2nd ed. London: Continuum.

Shopkow, L. (ed.) (2001) *Lambert of Ardres: The History of the Counts of Guines and Lords of Ardres*. Philadelphia: University of Pennsylvania Press.

Soulsby, I. (1983) *The Towns of Medieval Wales: A Study of Their History, Archaeology and Early Topography*. Chichester, U.K.: Phillimore.

Taylor, A. J. (1986) *The Welsh Castles of Edward I*. London: Ronceverte.

Tout, T. F. (1920) *Chapters in the Administrative History of Mediaeval England: The Wardrobe, the Chamber and the Small Seals*, vol. 2. London: Longmans, Green & Co.

Tout, T. F. (1934) *Mediaeval Town Planning: A Lecture*. Manchester, U.K.: Manchester University Press.

Trabut-Cussac, J. P. (1961) Date, fondation et identification de la bastide de Baa. *Revue Historique de Bordeaux*, 10: 133–44.

Turner, R. (2010) The life and career of Richard the Engineer, in D. Williams and J. Kenyon (eds.), *The Impact of the Edwardian Castles on Wales*, 46–58. Oxford: Oxbow.

Wetherbee, W. (1988) Philosophy, cosmology, and the twelfth-century Renaissance, in P. Dronke (ed.), *A History of Twelfth-Century Western Philosophy*, 21–53. Cambridge: Cambridge University Press.

Whitehand, J. W. R. (1991) *The Making of the Urban Landscape*. Oxford: Blackwell.

Whitehand, J. W. R., and Larkham, P. J. (eds.) (1992) *Urban Landscapes: International Perspectives*. London: Routledge.

Whitehand, J. W. R., and Whitehand, S. M. (1984) The physical fabric of town centres: the agents of change. *Transactions of the Institute of British Geographers*, NS 9: 231–47.

3

ECCLESIASTICAL AUTHORITIES AND THE FORM OF MEDIEVAL TOWNS

Terry R. Slater

From the beginning of the revival of towns and urban life in the West, the Christian Church played a major role in the governance, planning, and built forms that characterized a high proportion of medieval towns. In the early medieval period, before the millennium, the Church, and most particularly church buildings, were important as "central places" stimulating the cohering of other central-place functions at a particular site. In other words, the Church was often one of the originating forces of town formation (Blair 1988; Morris 1989). In the later Middle Ages, the Church shared with other agencies both the continued development of early towns and the planned development of new towns as population and economy expanded in the period up to 1350 and as the bounds of western Christendom widened across eastern Europe and Iberia. It was less inclined than other lordships to share wholeheartedly in urban social development, however, especially in freeing town-dwellers from feudal ties. Town air might make people free, but they were usually less free if their lord was ecclesiastical! (Lobel 1933; Trenholme 1927).

Across much of the late-Roman Empire, particularly following the Constantinian declaration of Christianity as the official religion of the state in AD 312, the Church began to establish an administrative structure that paralleled that of the state. Consequently, it had an urban-based administration with dioceses centered on Roman towns where the cathedral church would normally be located. As the Western Empire disintegrated in the fifth century, it was the Church that preserved some semblance of administrative order and, in all but the northern and eastern reaches of the Empire, it was the Church, with its in-built centralizing functions, which stimulated the beginnings of urban revival. In most of Italy, Gaul, and Iberia, through the difficult times of the fifth and sixth centuries, the Roman *civitas* capitals became diocesan see towns and, with that function, preserved some semblance of urban life through to their first appearance in documents of the medieval period, usually in the seventh century (Loseby 2000). Even in the border province of Britannia, the excavators of Roman Wroxeter speculate that it was the bishop there who was responsible for the carefully planned construction of the great timber-framed buildings on well-made stone platforms, all laid out to Roman measurement systems, around the ruins of the baths-basilica (White 2000). It might be expected that churches would, therefore, be significant urban buildings in the late-Antique and early-medieval periods, but this is not so. Early church gatherings took place in domestic buildings, which were sometimes adapted as congregations grew. The earliest specialized churches were outside the walls, marking the burial places of Christian martyrs (San Salvatore in Spoleto, Italy is an upstanding example, still surrounded by its cemetery). If churches were not subsequently established within the walls then, as urban life was stimulated in the eighth or ninth centuries, towns were refocused on the suburban site. This occurred most famously at Xanten (literally "the saints") in the northern Rhineland (Knoll 1991), and at St. Albans, where a medieval abbey enclosed England's proto-martyr's tomb and led to the planned development of a town in the tenth century (Slater 1998).

Late-Antique churches within Roman towns are notable for their reuse of building material from disused or ruined buildings, so-called *spolia* (Christie 2000), particularly the re-use of columns, capitals and marble flooring. Roman towns continued to make good quarries for church building materials through to the tenth century throughout the West. Examples can be cited from the northern reaches of the Empire, where the archbishops of York presented materials for church building to places within reasonable reach of the city (Buckland and Sadler 1990; Eaton 2000), to the heart of the Empire, where the great Norman church of Trani, in southern Italy, boasts a fine collection of columns and capitals taken from the underlying Roman town (Strappa et al. 2003). Occasionally, whole buildings with a basilican form were reused, perhaps most famously in the town center at Assisi, where the church of Santa Maria took over the Roman temple of Minerva, the façade of which still stands today. However, other buildings could be adapted, including the possible use of the *frigidarium* of the baths at Wroxeter, and the reuse of the Roman basilicas at Chester and at Trier, among other examples. At the latter city, the preservation of the spectacular Porta Nigra (black gate) of the Roman city was assured through its use as a monastery in the early medieval period. It is difficult to assess precisely who was responsible for such decision making, but it seems unlikely that the diocesan bishop was not involved to a greater or lesser extent.

The *Urbs-Suburbium* Model

Despite the fact that much recent archaeological work has begun to undermine the *urbs-suburbium* model of medieval urban development, the model continues to hold sway as a convenient way of conceptualizing the interaction of people and townscape. It has particularly underpinned central European (especially German) historical ideas of the social, economic, and morphological development of medieval towns (Ennen 1978). In the model, churches, cathedrals, monasteries, and secular defensible structures of one sort or another are viewed as the built forms representing the centers of power of medieval towns. Spatially, they are the *urbs, burg*, or *cité*, to use the terminology of Latin, German, and French, respectively. Morphologically, this spatial unit of the medieval town normally had its own legal status, was located on the highest part of the site, and was often separately defended; its function was the secular and ecclesiastical governance of city and territory. The theory proposes that these centers of power then attract a community of craftsmen and traders to serve the residents of the *urbs* institution and the many visitors to it. This leads, in turn, to the development of further urban areas dominated by these service and trading functions: the *suburbium, stadt*, or *bourg*, respectively, but which were under the governance, at least initially, of the *urbs* institution (personified in the bishop, abbot, or castellan and their courts). Subsequently, these craft and trading areas often gained independent administrative, parochial, and legal status as they began to serve a local region as well as the institution.

The morphological outcome of such developments can be seen in many regions of Europe. It is clearest, perhaps, at the margins: in Poland's ninth/tenth-century Piast kingdom fortress (*gród* in Polish) and, from *c.* 1000, archiepiscopal cathedral city at Gniezno, for example. Here, each of the four urban

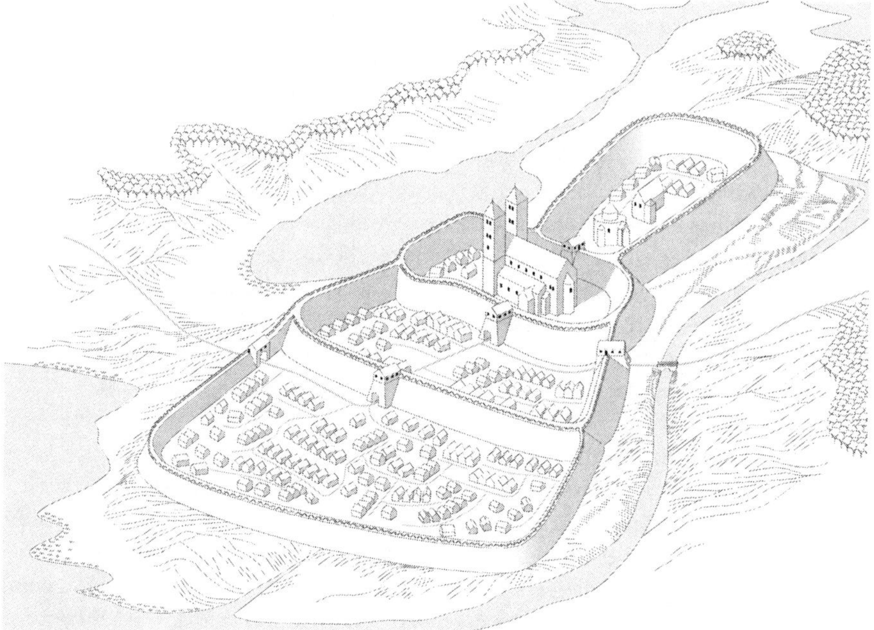

FIGURE 3.1 Reconstruction of the archiepiscopal city of Gniezno, Poland, *c.*1000. The defenses are timber-laced earthworks. The cathedral enclosure, and the bishop's palace and chapel beyond, represent the *urbs*, the trader and craftspeople's enclosures in front the *suburbium*

elements—secular castle, stone-built cathedral, the living quarters of the clergy, and the workshops and homes of the craftspeople—were each surrounded by impressive timber-laced ramparts by the eleventh century, while the market place (*targ* in Polish) was outside these defenses (Kalinowski 1972; Fig. 3.1). At the western extremity of Europe, the "monastic towns" of Ireland have been perceived as a distinctively Irish form of urbanism, but Brian Graham (1998) has suggested that they are no more than a variant of the *urbs-suburbium* model. The inner, usually circular, monastic enclosure of places such as Armagh and Kells (Simms and Simms 1990) functioned as the *urbs*, while the outer enclosure of craftspeople and others was the *suburbium*, with a later market space usually developing on the western edge at the entrance to the enclosures. Such a developmental sequence can be exemplified, too, in north-central Europe, at Münster, a city that takes name from the monastic cathedral at its heart. Bomb damage in the 1939–45 war has enabled archaeologists to work out much more precise chronologies of the monastic housing and church in the defended circular enclosure at the heart of the city and in the developing town of traders and craftspeople at the western entrance of the enclosure, which was to spread along the extramural road in both directions (Fig. 3.2). In southern Europe, the French town of Vaison-la-Romaine illuminates this sequential development in a very different topographical context and within the ruins of a Roman town. The Roman town, on the banks of the river L'Ouvèze, has a quite recently discovered late-Antique peripheral cemetery church, but its gem-like Romanesque cathedral is closer to the heart of the Roman town, celebrating its *Romanitas* (Brooks 2000) in its centrality, rather than locating on one of the nearby hilltops, as do so many French episcopal *cités*. Unusually, it is the commercial *bourg* that has colonized the hilltop, while a second planned "castle town" was established by the Count of Toulouse in the later medieval period on an adjacent hilltop across the river (Bellet 1992).

FIGURE 3.2 Model of the ecclesiastical enclosure of St. Peter's Abbey, Münster, Germany, seen from the south. The town hall was established immediately outside the enclosure entrance in the south-east and the market place extends from the town hall to St. Lambert's parish church (center right)

Ecclesiastical Precincts

Most large towns and cities of the period before *c.*1100, at least in the northern half of Europe, are characterized by a multiplicity of churches of different status levels. At the top of the hierarchy was the foundational minster, which frequently evolved later into a Benedictine abbey or a cathedral institution. During the course of that evolution, substantial walled precincts were created to enclose the church, domestic and monastic buildings, and the cemetery of the settlement, over which the foundation minster often had exclusive jurisdiction. In England, the majority of these early churches, but not all, were located in former Roman towns, including Canterbury, London, Winchester, Chichester, Exeter, Gloucester, and Worcester. It is often difficult to establish whether the king, who necessarily granted the site, or the bishop, possibly attracted to the *Romanitas* of the site, was the more essential individual. However, there can be no doubt that, thereafter, the ecclesiastical authorities had a significant influence on the development of both precinct and town.

In Winchester, for example, the whole south-east quadrant of the city, after its re-foundation by King Alfred, was dominated by a series of precincts enclosing ecclesiastical institutions (Fig. 3.3). The Old Minster had been founded *c.* 648, possibly as a mausoleum for the royal house of Wessex, but it soon became the cathedral church of the Wessex diocese. It was re-founded as a Benedictine monastery in 963 and very considerably enlarged thereafter (Biddle 1976). Immediately to the north, in a separate precinct, was the New Minster, founded in 901 on a constricted site between urban properties on the High Street of the town and the Old Minster, from both of which land had to be purchased at great expense. This institution was eventually to be moved to Hyde, beyond the town to the north, on the initiative of King Henry I in 1110, no doubt to improve the setting of the great new

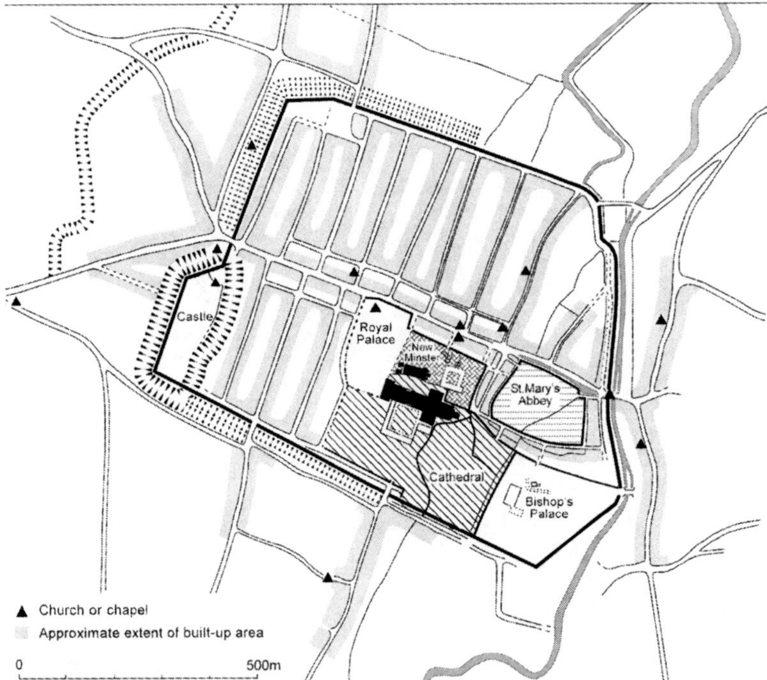

FIGURE 3.3 Ecclesiastical precincts in Winchester, England, *c.*1000

Norman cathedral built to the south of the Old Minster and approaching completion in that year. Besides the minster church, claustral buildings, and cemeteries, there were at least four other parish churches or chapels within, or on the bounds of, the New Minster precinct. To the east of the New Minster was a third monastery, also founded soon after 900 but for nuns. The Nunnaminster, or St. Mary's Abbey, was also alongside High Street, and further houses were purchased and demolished for the enclosure of its precinct. In the 960s, Bishop Aethelwold reorganized the boundaries between the three monastic precincts to try to prevent friction between the communities (Biddle 1976). Finally, in the southeast angle of the city defenses stood the bishop's palace, occupying another large enclosure contiguous with the cathedral precinct. Archaeological excavations show that the earliest building here dates to *c.*1000, and its enclosing wall was built on the orders of Bishop Aethelwold. Winchester is perhaps exceptional in having four large and contiguous ecclesiastical precincts, but at Gloucester, for example, two large monastic precincts adjoined one another in the same way and dominated the north-west quadrant of the city (Baker and Holt 2004).

It is important to understand that these precincts were normally jurisdictionally separate from the towns in which they were located and, in later medieval times, as towns became self-governing communities, they were a cause of considerable tension between town and church. Rosser (1998) has documented the ways in which the cathedral clergy and townspeople in Hereford sometimes contained conflict in urban rituals and processions, but at other times how such conflict broke out into violence. A similar picture can be drawn in Exeter, where there were no fewer than seven church jurisdictional fees that were not under the mayor's governance. Morphologically, socially, and legally, it is the boundaries of these fees that were of significance, and it is not surprising that they were carefully marked with walls and gates, stone crosses, and annual processions to ensure that bounds were fixed in minds as well as on the ground.

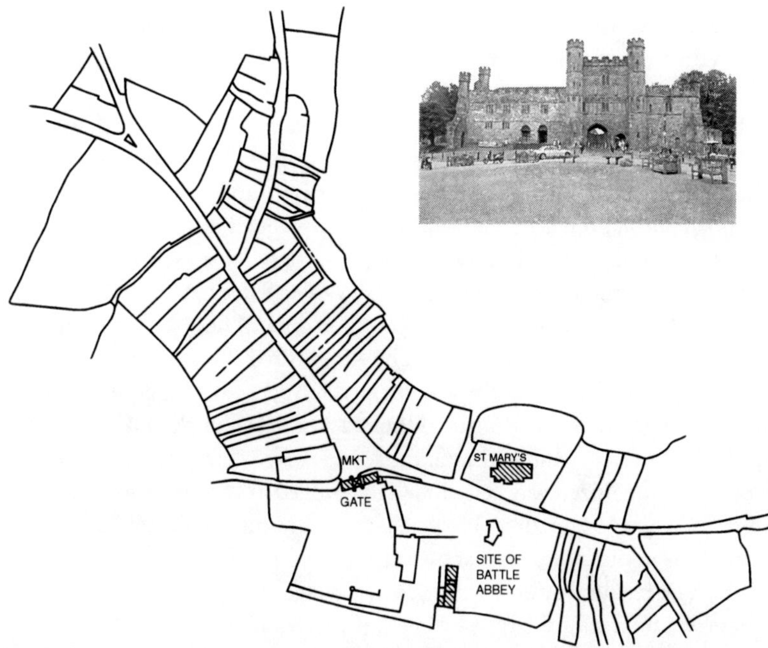

FIGURE 3.4 Plan of the new town of Battle, Sussex, England, established by William I to celebrate his victory at the battle of Hastings in 1066. The spectacular abbey gateway (inset) still stands looking down over the market place

In smaller towns, of course, (as well as some larger ones) townspeople were not self-governing communities; they remained the tenants of their ecclesiastical lord and, in many late-medieval monastic towns, there were expensive lawsuits between the parties and periodic bouts of violence. Precinct walls and fortified gates thus had practical as well as theological significance. However, they also had architectural and iconic significance, especially where they had been deliberately designed to front onto urban market places or where streets had been aligned on them. The "New Street" in Burton-upon-Trent was aligned on the abbey gate, for example, and both the old, pre-Norman market place and the new street market in Evesham were aligned on successive gateways into the abbey precinct there (Slater 1996). It is spectacularly evident in the vast abbey gateway fronting the southeast side of the market place in Battle (Sussex), where William I established a new monastery on the site of his famous victory over Harold and the English in 1066 (Fig. 3.4).

Town Planning in the Tenth and Eleventh Centuries

In the period following the English Benedictine revival, stimulated by abbots Dunstan (of Glastonbury), Aethelwold (of Abingdon), and Oswald (of Worcester), and encouraged by King Edgar of Wessex (957–73), there was created a network of powerful monasteries and nunneries under royal protection, as a bulwark of royal statecraft against the nobility (Burton 1994). This drive to found new monasteries was also closely linked with the development of existing markets into towns or with the creation of new towns, where the functions of trade, administration and defense were concentrated. Such places also enabled the king to control the minting of the coinage and to levy taxes more effectively. There were more than forty of these new reformed monasteries, most of them in southern and eastern England, and almost all of them had adjacent towns. The details of the processes, and even the timing of urban development, are still far from clear in many of these towns, but in several of them, recent research has begun to clarify the process.

Worcester was the location of the monastery of abbot Oswald. It was the shire town, and its monastic church had had cathedral status from the founding of the see in AD 680. In Worcester, the cooperation of king and bishop/abbot is, unusually, quite well documented, and recent research has enabled us to understand the topographical outcomes, in terms of a new planned townscape, as it was laid out in the tenth century. The king, in the guise of his *ealdorman* (earl) for Mercia, Aethelred, helped the bishop in the development of the settlement by providing, in the 880s or 890s, new earth and timber defenses for an extended settlement to the north of the Roman bank and ditch. These took the same form as found in the *burh* settlements of southern England founded by King Alfred (Hill 1981: 133–42). Such defensible towns were one of the means by which the king helped to secure his kingdom. In return, within the new *burh*, in 904, the bishop granted *ealdorman* Aethelred a valuable block of land on the western side of the town down beside the river, which became the town's quay (Sawyer 1968; Whitelock 1958: 451). This was developed in an organized way. It included the provision of a new parish church, St. Andrew's, for those who came to live and trade there. However, there is nothing rectangular or regular in the street and plot pattern in this plan unit. The plots are small and irregular, facing onto a rough cross of through streets (see Fig. 3.3). The residents were traders, for whom access to the river and the town quay were all important. There was no need for large plots with gardens and orchards.

The bishop's part of the *burh* had a broad High Street with very large blocks of land on each side for the subsequent use of what, in modern terminology, we would call property developers. These plots are referred to in the documents as "*hagas*," a word that derives from the Anglo-Saxon for "hedge," so we might imagine each of these blocks of land defined by a hedgerow boundary (Hooke 1981: 247–8). However, they were quite quickly subdivided into smaller lots so that they took on the more characteristic long, narrow, rectangular plot form familiar in towns all over northern Europe. Outside the defenses were two open areas that acted as the growing settlement's market place (Fig. 3.5).

The last of the planned outcomes was a feat of civil engineering on a grand scale. Such works are not normally considered when medieval town planning is discussed, with its concentration on street grids and rectangularity. However, at Worcester, in order to develop and extend the settlement gathered around the cathedral monastery, which was located within the massive sub-circular earthen embankments of the former Roman defenses, those earthen embankments were used to infill the equally massive exterior ditch (Baker et al. 1992). This enabled a new urban area (a plan-unit in the terminology of urban morphology; Conzen 1969) to be laid out to the north of the cathedral. In Worcester, then, the king and his *ealdorman* and the bishop/abbot of an important cathedral monastery worked together in a planned way to develop the economic, defensive, and social functions of the settlement so that it was irrefutably urban by the eleventh century. Successive bishops continued to lay out new areas for property development into the twelfth and thirteenth centuries, notably the linear suburb of Foregate and The Tything, along the ridge road running north of the cathedral and *burh*.

St. Albans is another example of early planned development where some of the individuals responsible can be named. In this case, the urban development and the planning of the new town seem to be wholly due to the second Benedictine abbot, Wulsin. In AD 948, the later evidence of the abbey's thirteenth-century chronicle suggests that Wulsin was responsible for developing the abbey estates economically by founding a new market outside the abbey precinct. The *Chronicle*

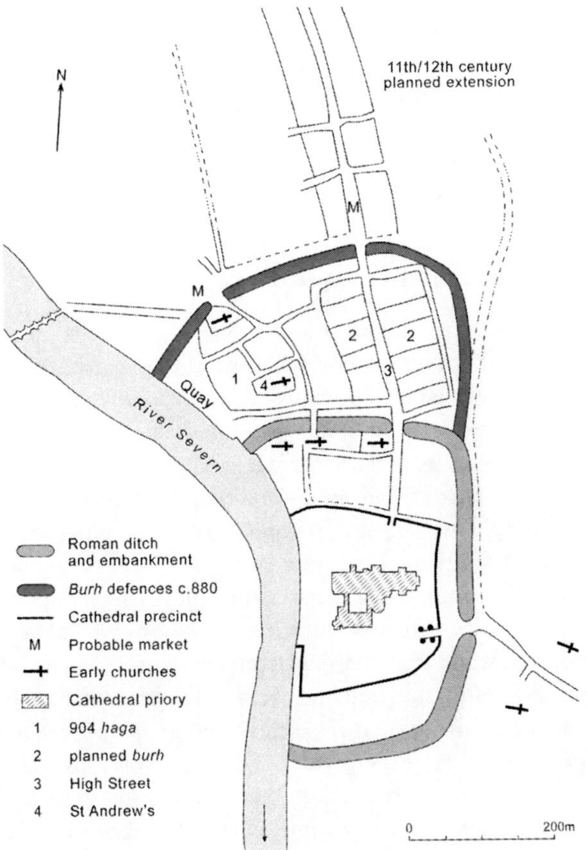

FIGURE 3.5 The planning of tenth- and eleventh-century Worcester, England: *haga*, *burh*, markets and suburb

tells of the monks providing timber and other materials for building the houses of new settlers and of Wulsin diverting the Roman roads aligned on *Verulamium* from the ruins of the city so that they went through the new market place (Riley 1867). It further tells of the founding of three churches at the points of diversion to mark the extremities of the town. If the *Chronicle* can be trusted—and the topographical and architectural evidence suggests that it can (the churches still stand and are late-Saxon in style; Taylor and Taylor 1965: 528–31)—then this is very early evidence for complex and large-scale urban planning.

The plan of this new settlement consists of a broad, very long, rectangular market space widening to a triangle north of the abbey precinct. On either side of this market place, and on down Holywell Hill, to the east of the precinct, were extremely long rectangular plots with the appearance of agricultural strip holdings. It may be that these plots were derived from field strips—certainly we know this was one form of development in later medieval new towns—but their length is quite exceptional in an urban context. They were some 311 meters long (Slater 1998). Later archaeological evidence shows that that many of them were divided transversely to increase the number of holdings. This happened in both the twelfth century and, again, in the early fifteenth century (Niblett and Thompson 2005). Notable in the planning of St. Albans is the marking of the town as a place of special holiness, belonging to God and the Church, through the building of new churches to mark its extremities. Many towns had stone crosses at their boundaries, but few others in Britain have fully developed parish churches, especially ones that retain elements of their stone-built, Anglo-Saxon, Romanesque architecture. The golden age of monastic new towns in Britain was the late-tenth and eleventh centuries. Clearly, the examples used so far show that this was not a period in which strict rectangularity of plan was a dominant characteristic. Nonetheless, this was a period in which town planning was important so long as we understand the term in its wider connotation.

Town Planning after the Norman Conquest

After the Norman Conquest in 1066, abbots, priors, bishops, and cathedral communities continued to found new market towns and extend existing towns so as to improve the economic returns from their estates, but their planning was generally small scale, utilitarian, and practical. However, the first effect of the Conquest was usually on the monasteries, cathedrals, and churches themselves. The late-eleventh and early-twelfth centuries were marked by an orgy of rebuilding of ecclesiastical structures by the new Norman élite in the style of their homeland that, in its own right, must have done much to increase the number of people working and trading in adjacent settlements. Many new monastic institutions were also founded in this period; more than 200 in the period between 1070 and 1130. Architectural historians have determined that many of these new, large-scale churches, cathedrals, and monasteries were initially built by Norman-French master masons who almost certainly used skilled craftsmen (glaziers, woodcarvers, and stonemasons) from France, too, but even with the large number of new buildings, the numbers of master craftsmen remained quite small (Morris 1989: 303–7). It is not until much later in the medieval period that we can begin to name some of these specialists.

Such building enterprises were very expensive, of course, and bishops and abbots were, therefore, keen to increase the revenues from their estates. This could be done by bringing more land into cultivation (a solution at Peterborough, for example, where the adjacent fenland was reclaimed); by exploiting land more intensively; by appropriating the revenues of parish churches; and by developing the market potential of particular settlements in strategic locations. Burton-upon-Trent is a particularly interesting monastic town to examine in this last respect. Superficially, it appears to have a roughly gridded town plan, though with little semblance of either regularity or rectangularity. As the founding of the town is especially well recorded in the abbey chronicles, however, it is possible to show that it was expanded in no fewer than five developmental phases between 1150 and 1260 by successive abbots. Each phase of development consisted only of a single street and its associated plots with each adding to the urban revenues of the abbey. There might appear to be little more to say about Burton, but the detailed analysis of the plan demonstrates other interesting byways in the practicalities of medieval planning in the twelfth and thirteenth centuries. It is clear, for example, how the abbot's surveyor adapted the underlying agricultural field patterns to his new urban plots, especially in the central part of the town where a cattle driftway is still evident (Slater 1996). This was a pastoral countryside, whereas at Stratford-upon-Avon (Warwickshire) it was an arable landscape of strip holdings that was adapted by the bishop of Worcester's surveyor (Slater 1997). The new urban holdings had precise dimensions, which are often stipulated in the founding charter, as they are in both Stratford and for one of the phases of Burton. Such records make it possible to show by metrological analysis of plans and the present townscape, that these dimensions continued to determine a large part of the layout of plots in these places through to the nineteenth century and, in some cases, to the present day. Sometimes they were specified by the areal measure of acres (0.4 hectares); more frequently, length and breadth measures were used, specified in English statute rods (16.5 feet; 5.03 meters; Slater 1980).

At the same time as some ecclesiastical institutions were founding new towns at their gates in the twelfth and thirteenth centuries, others were founding small new market towns on distant parts of their estates. Again, these places are obviously planned, but there is little to distinguish them from any of the other small towns being founded in large numbers by other lords, both secular and ecclesiastical, in all parts of the British Isles in the thirteenth century. Most were single street plans laid out along a main road with plots on either side. The widening of the street was usually sufficient for a market place; the community's chapel was well away from the valuable commercial space of the market place; and there were no defenses unless the town was founded in the less secure lands of Wales or Ireland. Stone or wooden crosses and a hedge or ditch marked the borough bounds. There are few examples of more complex grids (Slater 1987).

It is also worth noting here that in larger towns, new urban monasteries, convents, and friaries were being founded in the same period (twelfth to fourteenth centuries). As such institutions required large plots of land to build the necessary church, living accommodation, cloister, and kitchen and to establish gardens for growing food, they could normally be established only on the fringe of the built-up area. Where they were numerous, they often form a distinctive fringe-belt that, even when these institutions were dissolved (in the 1530s in England and Wales), continued to exert a strong influence on the formation of the inner fringe-belt of early modern towns. Keith Lilley's recent work (2012) on medieval Chester demonstrates this process was happening just inside the wall of the southwestern part of the city, while visitors to modern day Bergamo, Siena (Fig. 3.6), or Segovia, for example, can see numerous surviving examples of upstanding monasteries on the fringe of the medieval city.

Geometrical Knowledge and Orthogonal Planning

There were, nonetheless, some grid-plan towns established in England and Wales, and some of those were monastic or episcopal in origin. Perhaps the earliest and most spectacular is the great new town developed in front of the abbey at Bury St. Edmunds (Suffolk) in eastern England. The town was being developed and enlarged in the mid-eleventh century by its first Norman abbot, Baldwin (Gottfried 1982; Rowley 1983: 74–8). The plan of his new town is an extensive, quasi-rectilinear grid of streets to the west of the enlarged abbey precinct. It has short rectangular building plots and a large rectangular market place in its northwest quarter. Of most interest is the fact that two of the streets in the grid, Whiting Street and Churchgate Street, are laid out with geometrical precision at right angles to one another and that the latter is aligned on one of the abbey gateways, which thereby forms an architectural end point to the vista along the street (Slater 2000). Such geometrical precision at such an early date is unusual in a town plan in northwest Europe, and it is perhaps worth exploring in a little more detail how and when the knowledge necessary to undertake the laying out of such a plan was acquired, since the Classical knowledge of geometry had been lost over much of Europe in the Migration, or Dark Age, period.

In Britain, it is reasonably clear that it was, again, the Benedictine reform movement of the later tenth century that revitalized education and that it was the monasteries and their teachers who were responsible for increasing the knowledge of practical geometry. One of the two frameworks of monastic education was the *quadrivium*, consisting of arithmetic, geometry, astronomy and music. Charles Burnett (1997) has shown that it was the aim of the *quadrivium* to demonstrate by practice the ability of three-dimensional objects "to represent the work of God, who created the world by number, measure and proportion." It is also clear that this was not a static knowledge; teachers traveled between monasteries to gain access to the latest ideas and manuscripts, especially those

FIGURE 3.6 Siena, Italy: the contrada di Valdimonte centerd on the fringe-belt monastery of Santa Maria dei Servi with its extensive courts of accommodation. There are four other churches in the suburb together with the Palazzo Bianchi

derived from the contacts between Mediterranean monastic schools and the Islamic world. It was, however, an exclusive knowledge, limited largely to the monastic schools and to the masonic fraternities responsible for the construction of high-status buildings in stone.

Thanks to recent research, we have begun to trace the way in which mathematical (especially geometrical) knowledge was transferred from the Islamic world, through the monasteries of the Mediterranean, to northern Europe. Here the key center was the cathedral *scolasticus* at Liège, in the Lotharingian heartland of Charlemagne's Holy Roman Empire. In the eleventh century, a number of clerics trained at Liège were appointed to bishoprics and abbacies in England where they became centers for the diffusion of this new knowledge of astronomy, medicine, astrology, and geometry. One of these Lotharingian clerics was Giso, Bishop of Bath and Wells, and one of his wealthy tenants, Fastrad, perhaps himself a Lotharingian, was the father of Adelard of Bath. Adelard was to become one of the greatest scholars of the twelfth century (as well as tutor to King Henry II) being responsible, among many other things, for the translation of surviving Arab versions of Euclid's *Elements* into Latin in *c.* 1140 and, thereby, for the rediscovery of the principles of Euclidian geometry.

Now, to return to the layouts of new-planned towns, it would be surprising if this new mathematical and geometrical knowledge were not to have affected the practice of masons and surveyors. To begin with, we might expect it to be reflected in the architecture of churches and monastic buildings, particularly as so many of them were being rebuilt and enlarged in this period; where those same masons and surveyors were commissioned to lay out new towns, then that same knowledge was used to inform their plans. To this must be added the increasingly sophisticated way of "seeing" the world through the Neo-Platonist philosophies of many of the monks in monastic schools and the new universities of the thirteenth century (Lilley 2004). We should expect that the most sophisticated plans, in terms of the precision of their plan geometry, should be found where high-status lordship and contact with monastic or cathedral schools coincided in some way. At Bury St. Edmunds, therefore, it is significant that Burnett (1997) shows that many of the surviving manuscripts of Adelard's texts, and their predecessors, derive from the abbey library. It may have been precisely because the abbey was a major center of the most recent European learning that the new town laid out at its gate by the monastic community had such a sophisticated plan in terms of the accuracy of the iconic cross of streets at its core (Slater 2000).

Clearly, grid planning is not just an idea; there is also the practical problem of laying out streets and plots at right angles to one another. Lilley (1998) has suggested that there is a clear temporal divide between towns laid out with quasi-rectangular plans and those with strictly orthogonal plans in which true right angles characterize the plan elements of streets and plot pattern. The latter requires a knowledge of basic geometry. Given the scale of new church building in England at every level from cathedral and monastery, to parish churches and chapels, in the century after 1066, it is perhaps less surprising than it might otherwise be to find that the principles of setting out right angles was well understood, as such geometry was important in building those new churches (Bulmer-Thomas 1979). From about 1200, it also became important in laying out new towns, though comparatively rarely in Britain. The exceptions are some of the late thirteenth-century towns founded by King Edward I, most notably Flint and New Winchelsea, and the episcopal city of Salisbury. Edward I had summoned a group of men to advise him on laying out and developing new towns in 1296. Significantly, they met in Bury St. Edmunds and, the following year, in Salisbury (Beresford 1967: 3–13). Winchelsea has been the subject of much recent research, and the details of its plan, surviving wine merchant's cellars and rapid decline (thanks to coastal deposition cutting the town off from the sea) are now much better understood (Martin and Martin 2004). The huge parish church, dedicated to the newly fashionable St. Thomas of Canterbury and located in the center of the grid plan, today stands witness to these changing fortunes. The nave and aisles were demolished long ago (Fig. 3.7), and three friaries and two hospitals have disappeared entirely.

Planning Salisbury

New Salisbury was the largest new-planned medieval town in England. Given that it was developed by the bishop and the cathedral community, with their predilection for written records, and that it grew very rapidly in the thirteenth and fourteenth centuries to become the twelfth richest and seventh most populous town in England by the 1370s, its medieval development is comparatively well documented compared with many other cities. However, if we are searching for the people who made it happen, the evidence is much clearer for the new cathedral than for the town. Any analysis of the new town plan must, therefore, begin with the cathedral and the cathedral close, which, in any case, were planned well before the urban building campaign got underway (RCHME 1980, 1993a, 1993b).

FIGURE 3.7 The parish church of St. Thomas of Canterbury, Winchelsea, England, with the ruins of the north and south transepts, with the replacement west entrance and blank wall blocking the surviving chancel

The intention to remove the cathedral from the Iron-Age hillfort of Old Sarum a mile or so to the north dates from the early 1190s, only a century after its original construction. The reasons adduced for this desire can be discerned from contemporary documentation and through the insights of phenomenology. By trying to imagine how bishop and clergy reacted to their situation at Old Sarum we are in a better position to try to understand why they did what they did in New Salisbury, which might be seen as a desire for the antithesis of their existing situation (RCHME 1993a: 2). Old Sarum was cramped and constricting in its physical site so that there was no room to extend the cathedral church or provide suitable housing for the canons, so the new close was to be as spacious as possible. Old Sarum was dominated by military necessities as it was a royal castle and clergy often needed the permission of the guard to enter their own cathedral, so the new close was to be controlled by religious need, not military necessity. Old Sarum was climatologically exposed to winter gales and blizzards and to summer storms from all directions (the cathedral tower roof, for example, had been destroyed in a storm only five days after its dedication in 1092!) (Crittall 1962: 60); the new close was to be constructed in the warmth and shelter of the valley bottom. Old Sarum was extraordinarily short of water on its high chalk hilltop; it was unsuitable for any kind of settlement; it was a dry and dusty place for much of the year. The new close was to be surrounded with water on all sides, which could be managed, controlled, and used for a multiplicity of purposes; it also enabled a lush greensward of meadow grass to be an important part of the close landscape.

There is only modest evidence that such thoughts entered the minds of the Dean and Chapter and the Bishop, who planned New Salisbury, but it is sufficient, most notably in the wording of the appeal by the Dean and Chapter to the Pope in 1217 for permission to move the cathedral to the valley (RCHME 1993a: 2), and there is the surviving evidence of the two landscapes. Those landscapes contrast so significantly that it is difficult not to believe that these perceptions played no small part in the medieval decision-making process. Recently, Christian Frost has endeavored to show the ways in which the Dean and Chapter maintained the traditions of the cathedral by replicating processional routes within and around the old and the new cathedrals (Frost 2009) so that there were continuities through the process of change.

There is also sufficient evidence to be confident of the principal protagonists in that decision-making process: the brothers Henry and Richard Poore, who were two of the principal ecclesiastics of late-twelfth century England. Henry had become Bishop of Salisbury in 1194, while Richard was appointed Dean of the cathedral in 1199 (Crittall 1962: 61). The troubled years of King John's reign seems to have delayed the project, which was first discussed in 1194 (RCHME 1993b: 37), but plans for the new close were under detailed consideration by the chapter in 1213, and building materials were probably being assembled, though nothing more seems to have been done. King John died in 1216 and Bishop Henry in 1217. He was succeeded by his brother, who had spent two years away from Salisbury as Bishop of Chichester (RCHME 1993b: 40). Soon after, in 1218, the Papal license to move the cathedral was granted after an enquiry by the Papal legate. A new churchyard was at once consecrated on the site and a wooden chapel provided; work began in earnest in 1220. This commencement included the carefully choreographed laying of foundation stones in the presence of as many dignitaries as could be assembled and a fund-raising campaign across the kingdom. It is thought that Elias of Dereham, who had been involved in many major building campaigns, was brought to Salisbury by Poore in 1220 specifically to manage the finances of this huge project, though some earlier scholarship has seen him as the architect of the cathedral (RCHME 1993b: 52). Modern scholarship suggests that Robert of Ely was the architect. The eastern chapels of the cathedral were completed in 1225 and the tombs of the principal bishops removed from Old Sarum to the new cathedral the following year. The cathedral was consecrated in 1258 and was finished, including the cloisters and the massive detached bell tower with a 100-foot spire, by 1266. Only the upper stages of the central tower and its famous spire, the highest in the kingdom, remained to be added in the first half of the fourteenth century.

Given that Salisbury is the most geometrically perfect of all English cathedrals (RCHME 1993b: 62–3), it is surprising that the huge cathedral close and the extensive town are not also geometrically perfect, but they are not. The close was originally defined by a very deep drainage ditch enclosing the Myrfield, and it seems likely that it had existed for a long time before building operations started on the cathedral (Fig. 3.8). It was the morphological frame provided by this ditch, and by the existing road system descending the hill from Old Sarum, that determined the orientation of the grid of streets, distorted to parallelograms, that formed the frame for the first part of the town. There is some evidence (too complex to be described here) that suggests that the geometrically knowledgeable architects and stonemasons working on the cathedral applied their knowledge to the laying out of the streets and plots of the town as well as its complex of water channels. However, they were not sufficiently bound by the rules of geometry as to realign important drainage ditches or existing roadways. A further area of the city was begun in the 1260s, centered on the collegiate church of St. Edmund's (see Fig. 3.8). This new northern area has a street plan that is truly orthogonal to a base line provided by Endless Street. It seems likely that church and street plan are contemporaneous and that the streets and plots in this area should also be dated to 1269. New Salisbury is, thus, the first datable plan in the British Isles in which more than two streets are laid out with perfect orthogonal geometry.

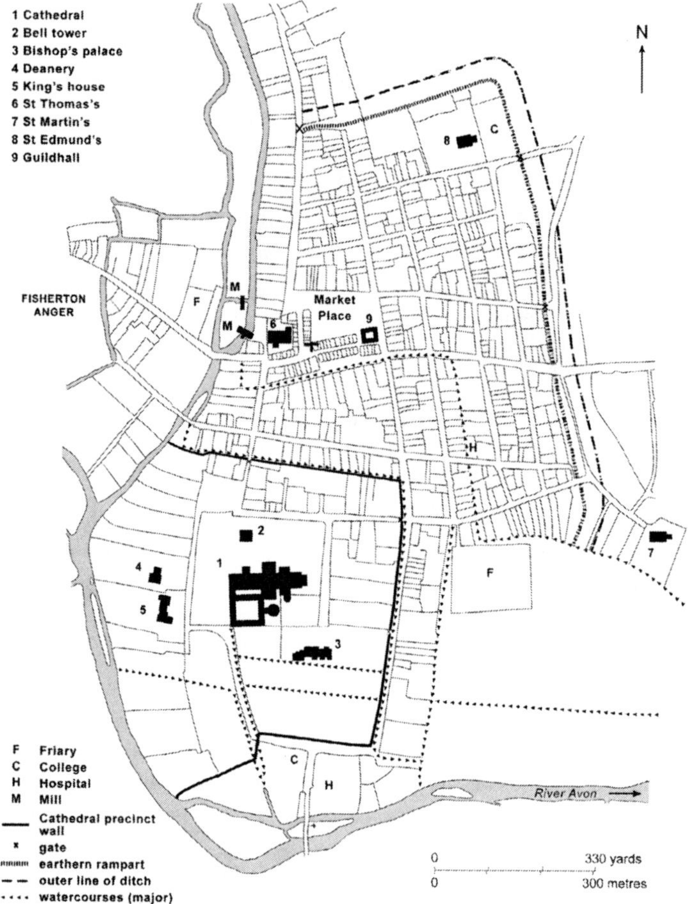

FIGURE 3.8 The plan of thirteenth-century New Salisbury, England. The orthogonally planned streets are in the north-east of the town

Conclusions

Seeking the men whose decision making, knowledge, or particular skills led to the development of towns across Europe is a difficult task for the medieval period. For the most part, we can talk only of the offices that they held; only rarely can we put names to them. Nonetheless, it is clear that at the decision-making level, it was bishops and abbots who held sway in most places and at most times. They can often be named, even in the early medieval centuries before the millennium. Equally important, however, were the most skillful masons and carpenters whose trade required knowledge of basic geometry if they were to successfully translate design ideas into the practical reality of cathedrals, abbey churches, and towns. That geometrical knowledge in its turn was derived from the schools of the great monasteries of Europe, which were the predecessors of the universities of later medieval centuries.

Though some towns might well have had symbolic attributes where they were owned by Church institutions, the vast majority of towns owned and developed by the Church were economic speculations. Their primary function was to provide the money that enabled post-millennial ecclesiastics to build churches anew to the glory of God in the latest architectural, iconographical, and liturgical fashion. It was the market place that was at the core of these towns, even where that market space was under the surveillance of ecclesiastical officials or provided the space to view the entrance gates to church precincts. Market tolls and fines provided cash. Similarly, urban properties provided rents, and decisions as to whether plots should be large or small in particular towns depended upon the perceived and actual demand for those plots in the early years of urban development. In sum, it is difficult to discern that there were large-scale differences between ecclesiastical and secular development processes in medieval Europe.

References

Baker, N. and Holt, R. (2004) *Urban Growth and the Medieval Church: Gloucester and Worcester.* Aldershot, U.K.: Ashgate.

Baker, N., Dalwood, H., Holt, R., Mundy, C., and Taylor, G. (1992) From Roman to medieval Worcester: development and planning in the Anglo-Saxon city. *Antiquity*, 66 (250): 65–74.

Bellet, M.-É. (ed.) (1992) *Recherches Archéologiques Récentes à Vaison-la-Romaine et aux Environs.* Avignon: Service d'Archéologie de Vaucluse, diff. Association pour la Promotion de la Recherche Archéologique en Vaucluse, Notices d'Archéologie Vauclusienne 2.

Beresford, M. W. (1967) *New Towns of the Middle Ages: Town Plantation in England, Wales and Gascony*. London: Lutterworth.

Biddle, M. (ed.) (1976) *Winchester in the Early Middle Ages.* Oxford: Oxford University Press.

Blair, J. (1988) Minster churches in the landscape, in D. Hooke (ed.), *Anglo-Saxon Settlements*, 35–58. Oxford: Blackwell.

Brooks, N. P. (2000) Rome, Canterbury and the construction of English identity, in J. M. H. Smith (ed.), *Early Medieval Rome and the Christian West: Essays in Honour of D. A. Bu*llough, 221–47. Leiden, Netherlands: Brill.

Buckland, P. C., and Sadler, J. (1990) Ballast and building stone: a discussion, in D. Parsons (ed.), *Stone: Quarrying and Building in England, A.D. 43–1525*, 114–25. Chichester, U.K.: Phillimore.

Bulmer-Thomas, I. (1979) Euclid and medieval architecture. *Archaeological Journal*, 136: 136–50.

Burnett, C. S. F. (1997) *The Introduction of Arabic Learning into England*. London: British Library.

Burton, J. E. (1994) *Monastic and Religious Orders in Britain, 1000–1300*. Cambridge: Cambridge University Press.

Christie, N. (2000) Construction and deconstruction: reconstructing the late-Roman townscape, in T. R. Slater (ed.), *Towns in Decline, A.D. 100–1600*, 51–71. Aldershot, U.K.: Ashgate.

Conzen, M. R. G. (1969) *Alnwick, Northumberland: A Study in Town-Plan Analysis*, 2nd ed. London: Publications of the Institute of British Geographers 12.

Crittall, E. (1962) *The Victoria County History of Wiltshire VI.* London: Oxford University Press.

Eaton, T. (2000) *Plundering the Past: Roman Stonework in Medieval Britain*. Stroud, U.K.: Tempus.

Ennen, E. (1978) *The Medieval Town*. Amsterdam: North Holland Publishing.

Frost, C. (2009) *Time, Space and Order: The Making of Medieval Salisbury.* Bern: Peter Lang.

Gottfried, R. S. (1982) *Bury St. Edmunds and the Urban Crisis, 1290–1539*. Princeton: Princeton University Press.

Graham, B. J. (1998) The town and the monastery: early medieval urbanization in Ireland, AD 800–1150, in T. R. Slater and G. Rosser (eds.), *The Church in the Medieval Town*, 131–54. Aldershot, U.K.: Ashgate.

Hill, D. (1981) *An Atlas of Anglo-Saxon England.* Oxford: Blackwell.

Hooke, D. (1981) *Anglo-Saxon Landscape of the West Midlands: The Charter Evidence*. Oxford: British Archaeological Reports British Series 95.

Kalinowski, W. (1972) City development in Poland, in E. A. Gutkind (ed.), *Urban Development in East-Central Europe: Poland, Czechoslovakia and Hungary*, 1–108. New York: Free Press.

Knoll, G. M. (1991) *Stadtführer am Niederrhein: Xanten*. Kleve: Boss-Verlag.

Lilley, K. D. (1998) Taking measures across the medieval landscape: aspects of urban design before the Renaissance. *Urban Morphology*, 2 (2): 82–92.

Lilley, K. D. (2004) Cities of God? Medieval urban forms and their Christian symbolism. *Transactions of the Institute of British Geographers*, NS 29 (3): 296–313.

Lilley, K. D. (2012) Imagined landscapes? Mapping medieval Chester through literature, cartography and information technology, in S. Lavaud (ed.), *Représenter la Ville*, 227–242. Bordeaux: Ausonius Éditions.

Lobel, M. D. (1933) *The Borough of Bury St. Edmunds: A Study in the Government and Development of a Medieval Town*, Oxford: Clarendon Press.

Loseby, S. T. (2000) Urban failures in late-Antique Gaul, in T. R. Slater (ed.), *Towns in Decline, A.D. 100–1600*, 72–95. Aldershot, U.K.: Ashgate.

Martin, D., and Martin, B. (2004) *New Winchelsea, Sussex: A Medieval Port Town*. Kings Lynn, U.K.: English Heritage.

Morris, R. (1989) *Churches in the Landscape*. London: Dent.

Nibblett, R., and Thompson, I. (2005) *Alban's Buried Towns: An Assessment of St. Albans' Archaeology up to AD 1600*. Oxford: Oxbow Books.

Riley, T. (ed.) (1867) *Gesta Abbatum Monasterii Sancti Albani: A Thoma Walsingham, regnante Ricardo Secundo, ejusdem ecclesiæ præcentore, compilata*, vol. 1. London: Longmans, Green.

Rosser, G. (1998) Conflict and political community in the medieval town: disputes between clergy and laity in Hereford, in T. R. Slater and G. Rosser (eds.), *The Church in the Medieval Town*, 20–42. Aldershot, U.K.: Ashgate.

Rowley, T. (1983) *The Norman Heritage, 1055–1200*. London: Routledge and Kegan Paul.

Royal Commission on the Historical Monuments of England (RCHME) (1980) *Ancient and Historical Monuments in the City of Salisbury I*. London: HMSO.

Royal Commission on the Historical Monuments of England (RCHME) (1993a) *Salisbury: The Houses of the Close*. London: HMSO.

Royal Commission on the Historical Monuments of England (RCHME) (1993b) *Salisbury Cathedral: Perspectives on the Architectural History*. London: HMSO.

Sawyer, P. H. (1968) *Anglo-Saxon Charters: An Annotated List and Bibliography*. London: Royal Historical Society, no. 1280.

Simms, A., and Simms, K. (1990) *Irish Historic Towns Atlas 4. Kells*. Dublin: Royal Irish Academy.

Slater, T. R. (1980) The analysis of burgage patterns in medieval towns. *Area*, 13 (3): 211–6.

Slater, T. R. (1987) Ideal and reality in English episcopal medieval town planning. *Transactions of the Institute of British Geographers*, NS 12 (2): 191–203.

Slater, T. R. (1996) Medieval town-founding on the estates of the Benedictine Order in England, in F.-E. Eliassen and G. A. Ersland (eds.), *Power, Profit and Urban Land: Landownership in Medieval and Early Modern Northern European Towns*, 70–92. Aldershot, U.K.: Scolar.

Slater, T. R. (1997) Domesday village to medieval town: the topography of medieval Stratford-upon-Avon, in R. Beareman (ed.), *The History of an English Borough: Stratford-upon-Avon, 1196–1996*, 30–42. Stroud, U.K.: Sutton Publishing.

Slater, T. R. (1998) Benedictine town planning in medieval England: evidence from St. Albans, in T. R. Slater and G. Rosser (eds.), *The Church in the Medieval Town*, 155–76. Aldershot, U.K.: Ashgate.

Slater, T. R. (2000) Medieval town planning: on facts and story-telling. *Urban Morphology*, 4 (2): 104–6.

Strappa, G., Ieva, M., and Dimatteo, M. A. (2003) *La Città come Organismo: lettura di trani alle diverse scale*. Bari: Adda Editore.

Taylor, H. M., and Taylor, J. (1965) *Anglo-Saxon Architecture*. Cambridge: Cambridge University Press.

Trenholme, N. M. (1927) *The English Monastic Boroughs: A Study in Medieval History*. Columbia, MO: University of Missouri.

White, R. (2000) Wroxeter and the transformation of late-Roman urbanism, in T. R. Slater (ed.), *Towns in Decline, A.D. 100–1600*, 96–119. Aldershot, U.K.: Ashgate.

Whitelock, D. (ed.) (1958) *English Historical Documents*, vol. I. Oxford: Oxford University Press.

Widawski, J. (1973) *Miejskie Mury Obronne w Panstwie Polskim do Poczatku XV Wieku*. Warsaw: Wydawnictwo Ministerstwa Obrony Narodowej, for the Instytut Sztuki Polskiej Akademii Nauk.

4

URBAN CORPORATE GOVERNANCE AND THE SHAPING OF MEDIEVAL TOWNS

Anngret Simms

Who were the morphological agents behind the formation of medieval towns? We owe the emphasis on the concept of morphological agents to Jeremy Whitehand (1977), who, working in M. R. G. Conzen's urban morphological tradition, helped us to look beyond town-plan analysis to the socioeconomic dynamic forces that have shaped urban space through time. This chapter follows this line of inquiry. The two powerful influences on medieval towns were, on the one hand, the town lords and, on the other, the town councils. We begin with an early-thirteenth-century text that illustrates how the king through his representatives attempted to keep control over towns:

> You may not without the permission of the country's judge (the king's representative) build a castle nor may you fortify a town with walls, nor with planks... You may without the permission of the judge build in wood or in stone three stories high, as long as one is underground with a door to the outside and the other two above.[1]

This is a quotation from the Saxon Mirror (*Sachsenspiegel*) that was compiled between 1220 and 1230. It is the oldest set of customary law in the German language. The document implies that, in the early thirteenth century, towns in Saxony were the property of lords who, in a perfect example of early planning, defined the framework within which the inhabitants were allowed to develop their own place. The dialectic between lords and townspeople runs right through the history of medieval towns.

Possible Viking Origin of Early Medieval Regularly Laid out Urban Plots

Hedeby, Birka, Kaupang, and Ribe were towns in the Viking period. These places and many of the contemporary emporia (seasonal trading places) were located at sites that on the one hand had sacred character going back into pagan times and, on the other hand, had central place functions associated with the military power of the local leader, who would provide a secure setting for trading. Individual property in these Viking age towns was divided into plots with a dwelling-house bordering the street, normally measuring five to eight meters wide (Skre 2007: 454). The length of the plots varied considerably. Plot divisions like this have not been discovered at any of the seasonal market places.

These plot patterns are interpreted as evidence of royal involvement, but this involvement does not imply absolute authority in this matter, because kings simply would not have had sufficient control over the economy and individuals in their kingdoms to create a town for which there was no economic basis. Therefore, the trading that a particular site was able to facilitate would have been just as crucial as royal patronage to its continued success.

Before the Birka excavations were undertaken, historians believed that the impulse for the creation of towns in Scandinavia came in the ninth century from the exposure of the Vikings to Western European urbanism, but Birka was an urban site nearly fifty years before the first documented Viking raids upon Western Europe. There is, therefore, a possibility of a Scandinavian origin for regularly laid out early-medieval plots quite independent of that which the Romans had practiced in their towns along the Rhine and Danube at the time of the late Roman Empire.

In Ireland the first mention of the Vikings of Åth Cliath (later Dublin) dates to AD 841. During excavations in the oldest part of the Viking town, seven plots were identified, but they were not yet regularly orientated (Simpson 2000: 21).When the Viking leaders returned to Dublin in AD 917, after a short period of enforced exile in England and Scotland, they came back under dynastic leadership. Trade would have been their primary aim and, therefore, proximity of settlement to the river bank was desirable. It made the task of the tax collector easier if plots were laid out in a regular fashion. Not surprisingly, therefore, after AD 917, Dublin continued to grow with regular streets bordered by regularly laid out plots. In Fishamble Street near the river Liffey, fourteen trapezoidal property plots fronting the street were found (Wallace 1992, pt 2: 42). Each of the plots was marked out by post-and-wattle boundary fences. Each plot consisted of a domestic house, outhouses, and paths. There appears to have been considerable stability of landholding in tenth- and eleventh-century Dublin (Fig. 4.1). P. F. Wallace (2000: 264) refers to the first use of the word *garrda* for a plot of land in Dublin, which occurred in 989, when the Irish High King Maelsechnail, claimed "an ounce of gold for every garden to be paid each Christmas Night forever." The evolution of Dublin into a flourishing Viking town coincided with the reign of Óláfr Cúarán (945–80), a former king of York, who became king of Dublin (Clarke 2002: 3). The importance of the interaction between lordship and townspeople in the early phases of urban growth is again apparent.

The Organization of Space and the Fabric of Medieval Towns As a Reflection of Their Corporate Character

In the twelfth century, existing towns underwent an important qualitative change by the grant of town charters. A large number of new towns were also created during this century, many in the context of medieval internal or external colonization. For example, the Dukes of Zähringen founded the town of Bern in Switzerland in 1191. The picture chronicle of the late fifteenth century shows the Duke visiting the building site underneath his castle, where stone masons were at work and carpenters cut down trees (Fig. 4.2).

Charters were granted by feudal lords according to existing models. In Ireland, the Anglo-Normans introduced the Law of Bristol to larger towns and that of Breteuil (Normandy) to smaller towns. Along the Baltic, it was Lübeck Law; in the territories east of the River Elbe, it was Magdeburg Law; and in the territories of the Slavic princes in East Central Europe, it was *ius teutonicum*. Town charters granted townspeople individual plots, called *burgage plots*, and fixed a permanent rent. Charters linked the grant of individual plots to freedom from toll and services to a lord and to the right to be tried by a court of equals. It would be tempting to assume that the concept

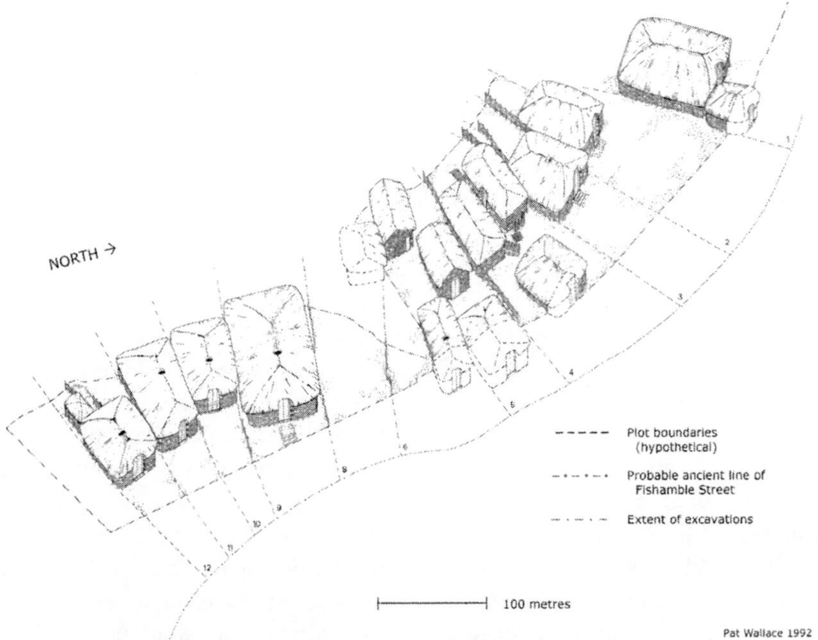

FIGURE 4.1 Reconstruction of Viking houses and house-plots in Fishamble Street, Dublin

FIGURE 4.2 The foundation of Bern, Switzerland, in 1191, picture chronicle of Spiez, 1484–1485

of a burgage plot came into existence with the charter but, as we have seen, house plots of regular size and rectangular shape already existed in Viking towns by the eleventh century.

Town charters provided the basis for the formation of urban communities with emphasis on horizontal bonds as they were found in the merchant and craft guilds. These were originally established to protect their members, who would bond together in feasting, religious ceremonies, and oath taking. Guilds were the first legal recognition of the rights of citizens to be organized in corporate bodies. They were a first step toward self-administration in a developing urban community. The élite among the burgesses were the urban patricians of the twelfth century. They were descended from seigniorial officials and small landowners. At first, urban property would have been as important a source of their wealth as trade but, with the growth of the medieval town based on local, regional, and long-distance trade came the status change from wealth through land holding to wealth from trade, a precondition for anyone wishing to sit on town councils. Only a restricted number of town inhabitants were burgesses. For example, clerics, Jews, and people without property were not. Craftsmen fought bitter battles for representation on council. There were successful craft revolts in the early fourteenth century. In fact, inner urban harmony was rare in medieval towns.

In the Rhinelands, episcopal cities had a particularly hard time in their effort to gain autonomy. In Cologne, in 1074, Archbishop Anno II confiscated a merchant ship to make it available to the bishop of Münster to enable him to return home with goods he had purchased. This intervention in private property met with the resistance of merchants in the town, who were supported by the young King Henry IV. The bishop's castle in Cologne was stormed, and it took the bishop some time to quell the protest. Two hundred years later, in 1288, Cologne succeeded in setting itself free of their local lord-bishop, who took up residence in nearby Bonn (Engel 1993: 38–54).[2] In Trier, the archbishop yielded power only in the middle of the fourteenth century.

It took a long time before town councils became autonomous local governments, which they achieved to a greater degree in the German lands than, for example, in England and Ireland. The first city council in the German Empire that became independent of a lord's tribunal was established at Utrecht in 1196, followed by Lübeck in 1201 and Cologne in 1216 (Nicholas 1997: 234). Even so, lords kept some rights of appointment, particularly in relation to policing and criminal courts and nominating some council members. By the fourteenth century, large cities like Cologne, with *c.* 40,000 inhabitants, had fought successfully for their independence, while others, such as Lübeck, Rostock, and Hamburg with between 10,000 and 20,000 inhabitants, had relative independence, but *c.* 95 percent of all urban dwellers lived in small towns between 2,000 and 10,000 inhabitants, and their lords would have kept closer control.

Sometimes, towns were able to exploit the financial difficulties in which city lords found themselves. For example, Augsburg was a town that by 1257 had a seal, city walls, council, and burgomaster but was granted a law code only in 1276 in return for paying an outstanding debt for the emperor (Nicholas 1997: 207). In 1292, Magdeburg supplied the military needs of its archbishop on the condition that he took taxes only with their agreement and that of the cathedral chapter. Town halls became the expression of the power of the town council and of municipal pride and accordingly constituted a threat to town lords. When, in 1232, the emperor Frederick II abolished the independent town council of Worms, he also pulled down the town hall (Nicholas 1997: 196).

The publication of the European Historic Towns Atlas project allows us to look at the spatial organization of towns and their institutions across Europe and to relate the particular to the general (Conzen 2008; Whitehand 2012: 60).[3] A comparison of three towns, one each from Ireland, Germany, and Hungary, respectively, during the thirteenth century shows how common concepts of town-charters, individual property plots, parish churches, religious houses, market-places, and town walls contributed to making Europe a coherent culture zone in the medieval period (see Table 4.1 for details; also Simms 2013).

Though the comparison shows astonishing similarities over great geographical distances, there are also some intriguing differences. Religious houses were numerous in Kilkenny, and they were founded by aristocratic families, whereas in Kalkar they were less numerous and, of those that were there, some were founded by townspeople whereas those of the Franciscans, later Benedictines, in Sopron were founded by royal edict.

Planning in Medieval Towns

With the grant of a charter by a lord, townspeople officially became partners in the creation of a town (diagram in Lilley 2009: 83). Town lords initiated the layout of a new town with a regular pattern. On very few occasions, we learn from charters or chronicles how townspeople constructed their town. A charter issued in 1120 for the foundation of the market in Freiburg in Germany refers to the space of the market place and to *areae*, building plots on the market, streets and to the fortification of the settlement. The construction of new towns usually involved the reorganization of existing settlement structures. We get evidence of burgesses as planners only in the second half of the thirteenth century, when the influence of the town-lords diminished. In Bern, the transition to communal planning was marked by building the bridge, establishing mendicant friars, pulling down the lord's castle, improving the drinking water, and banishing certain occupations such as curing leather into restricted corners of the town (Stercken 2006: 30).

Townspeople built town halls and parish churches as well as bridges and town walls. The finance for these works came partly from grants and partly from levies the townspeople imposed on themselves. For example, in Dresden in the thirteenth century, everyone who had a booth in the "Cloth-Hall" had to pay a fee for the maintenance of the bridge. The chronicler Vicke Schorler wrote in 1611 about Rostock:

> The building of the bridge outside the Steintor has been started ... In order to finance this bridge the citizens in possession of a house had twice to pay three guilders, those living in *Buden* (very small houses) half that and those living in cellars a quarter.
>
> (Schorler 1939)

Parts of Italy, Tuscany, for example, seem to have had written planning regulations already in the thirteenth century (Braunfels 1982). Documents from Siena dating to 1297 provide regulations for the building trade. They include guidelines on how to achieve regularity of windows in the palaces around the Campo of Siena and how to treat porches and balconies around the square. In relation to Florence, documents dating to 1299 mention the appointment of six officials to oversee the building and repair of streets. In 1339, regulations were issued prescribing limited building activities along the streets leading to the Cathedral of Florence in an attempt not to spoil the fine views. In 1363, there is a submission from the association of the merchants of Florence containing guidelines for the regular formation of houses around the Piazza San Giovanni. Intriguingly, in the first half of the fourteenth century, there is a communication from the Office for Beauty in Siena with the request to offer a particular citizen a job so that he would earn enough money to replace his present façade with a more attractive one. In 1466, the Office for Beauty received an application from a citizen with the request to be allowed to build an arch across the street and, in return, he offered to build a façade with two stories of triforium windows on little pillars.

TABLE 4.1 Morphological agents and components in thirteenth-century Kilkenny (Bradley 2000), Kalkar (Wensky and Weiss 2001) and Sopron (Janko et al. 2010)

	Kilkenny (Ireland)	*Kalkar (Rhineland)*	*Sopron (Hungary)*
Founder	Richard fitz Gilbert de Clare (Strongbow) built an earthwork castle in Kilkenny in 1173 south of the early-Christian Cathedral.	Duke Dietrich VI von Kleve founded the town in 1230 on tabula rasa (with permission of the Archbishop of Cologne).	King Béla IV founded the town in *c.* 1247 on the site of a former Roman town (no settlement continuity but preservation of Roman walls) succeeded by an ispán castle.
Charter	Charter by William Marshal, in 1207.	Oldest surviving Privilege (charter) from 1347.	Charter by Ladislas IV in 1277 referring to privileges granted by Béla IV and Stephen V.
Street-pattern	Linear, north-south main street with connecting side-street across the river	Linear north-south main street crossed by west-east street.	Three parallel streets plus suburbs following communication routes.
Burgage-plot	20 feet wide (charter, 1207).	44 feet wide and 140 feet in length (charter, 1347).	No contemporary written evidence.
Market place	Widening of main street in order to make space for the market, 1335 market cross erected.	A market square, first recorded 1326, later enlarged.	Main Square, thirteenth century, irregular, in front of town-hall, for expensive goods. Meat sold on salt market; fish, poultry, and vegetables at the gates and along the town walls, bulky commodities sold in suburban markets outside the town walls.
Town walls	Murage-grants *c.* 1248, town wall completed by *c.* 1300. Enclosed area 28 hectares.	Since fourteenth century town surrounded by double banks and ditches, first stone wall recorded in 1349. Enclosed area *c.* 25 hectares.	Medieval town walls built between 1297–1340 on remains of Roman town walls and the walls of the ispán castle. Enclosed area *c.* 8.7 hectares, extensive suburbs.
Parish church	St Mary's in existence *c.* 1205 (closed in 1960).	St Nicolai, recorded 1273, rebuilt after fire in 1409. Still in use as parish church.	St Michaelis, built before 1278 outside the walls to the north of the town. Still in use as parish church.

Religious houses, hospitals and synagogues	St Canice's Cathedral built *c.* 1205–85 (on site of Romanesque church). Round Tower built *c.* 1100. St John's Abbey, Augustinian Priory, founded by William Marshal the Elder in 1211, dissolved in 1540. In ruins. Black Abbey Church, Holy Trinity Priory (Dominicans), founded by William Marshal the Younger, in *c.* 1225, dissolved in 1540, reopened to Catholic worship since 1816. St Francis' Abbey, Franciscan Friary, founded by Richard Marshal between *c.* 1231–34, dissolved in 1540. In ruins. St John the Evangelist Hospital established by 1202, replaced by St John's Abbey in 1211, closed probably in fourteenth century. St John the Baptist's Hospital (Knights of St Thomas the Martyr of Acan) founded by 1219, closed probably in fourteenth century. St Mary Magdalen's Hospital. Leper hospital 1327, ruined in 1541.	Gasthauskirche (Guest-house Church), hospital, recorded in 1358. St Cäcilie, Kleiner Beginenkonvent (Small Beguines House), founded in 1413 by Albert Paepe and his wife Eva. In 1465 adoption of Augustinian rule. St Ursula, Grosser Beguinenkonvent (Big Beguines House), built before 1430 by Arnd Snoick. In 1578 merger of the two Beguines Houses. Dissolved 1802. Dominican Abbey, founded by Duke Johann I after his return from the Holy Land in 1455. Dissolved 1802. Building demolished.	St. Johanniskirche und Konvent der Johanniter with hospital (at different location), built 1247. Church functions as a chapel. Monastic building replaced in the 19th century, used as orphanage, currently under rebuilding. Hospital demolished in 1797. Franziskanerkirche and -kloster, later Benedictines, built 1278 by royal order, still in use as a church, former priory buildings used as old people's home. Gothic Synagogue, built at the turn of the thirteenth to the fourteenth centuries, probably by royal endorsement. Building now a Jewish museum.
Townhall	Tholsel on High Street in thirteenth century, demolished *c.* 1795	Old town-hall replaced by new representative building between 1438–1446	First town-hall recorded in 1422, moved to new site in 1459, to a third site on Main Square in 1496, still in use as town-hall.
Population	*c.* 2800 people in late-twelfth century (2006 (borough and environs): *c.* 22,000)	*c.* 1,000 people during Middle Ages *c.* 5,000 people at the end of Middle Ages (2009: *c.* 1400)	4,200 people in the early 1440s (at present *c.* 59,000 people)

The same person was always appointed to be both the master builder of the Cathedral and to direct building matters within the town. In 1310 Lorenzo Maitanis was appointed as such for Orvieto. Giotto was appointed in 1334 to be the master builder of the Cathedral and to direct building matters in the town. He was very preoccupied with regulations about windows and porches (Braunfels 1982: 249). In the thirteenth century, the "*mâitre d'oeuvre* de la Cathédrale Saint-Jean" was the highest authority in building matters in Rouen. Architectural harmony in certain quarters of medieval towns was due to building rules rather than to general cultural homogeneity. In smaller country towns, local lords took an active part in shaping their towns. For example, in Kalkar, the Duke of Kleve presented his cook and his wife in 1326 with a house-plot (*area*) with the instruction that they had to build a street paved with stones to meet the next stretch of paved street (Wensky and Weiss 2001).

As we see from the layout of the great medieval monastic houses, medieval people appreciated the beauty of geometrically perfect forms. To implement those concepts, they needed surveyors. In the thirteenth century, the theoretical geometry of Euclid filtered into the widely circulated "practical geometries" of the Middle Ages and would have informed the building of cathedrals and the layout of towns. By the end of the thirteenth century, surveyors had access to methods of accurate ground-measurement techniques based on abstract geometrical principles. Without the practical art of geometry, the new regular layout of town-plans that are particularly evident in East-Central Europe would not have been possible. The underlying motivation for this regularity was the conviction that beauty was based on "due proportion" and that one way in which proportional arrangements were perfected was through symmetry (Lilley 2009: 71). In the *Geometria Culmensis*, written *c.* 1400 to facilitate correct surveys in the territory of the Teutonic Knights, we find a difference between the professional surveyors and those who laid out towns by custom.

In Vienna, the town and the church of St Stephen's were planned simultaneously. The local lord supplied the site for the new town or at least gave his blessing. Somewhere near the center of the newly planned settlement, a pole would have been run into the ground from whence surveying would have been carried out (Opll 2010: 227). Planning needed to take account of existing topographical factors, as for example the river Danube and of the remains of the Roman town. In 1137, the documents refer to the *civitas* of Vienna on the site of the former Roman settlement. Building activity followed, and the erection of the town-wall with its four gates started in the 1190s. Analysis of property rights shows that rich merchants owned property within the old *civitas* but also in the area between the *civitas* and the later city-walls (Opll 2010: 240). It is likely that the territorial lord granted land in return for duties at one of the city's gates or for services in the defense of the town or for developing areas within the walled town. Elite citizens cooperated closely with the Habsburg princes, for example, by administering their finances. Vienna is a good example of the constant interplay between the aristocracy and the élite among the burgesses.

In the late-medieval period, in the second half of the fifteenth century, an internal urbanization process took place that often led to new town extensions or to suburbs. This process was brought about by urban leadership initiated by town councils. New mental attitudes began to dominate the town councils, where members took on the air of noble lords. This attitude went along with social exclusion on the one hand and an emphasis on the symbolism of government and power on the other. New town halls were built with the main aim of projecting power (Fouquet 1999: 433). Town councils tried to improve the infrastructure of their towns. They regulated the amount of wood that individual burgesses were allowed to take from the forests for building and burning and by issuing more regulations designed to avoid the outbreak of fire. Town councils increased taxes, improved the quality of streets by paving, set up regulations dealing with waste, and organized a steady supply of food. Major innovations included artfully decorated fountains, drainage pipes, and an improvement in hygiene by preventing chamber pots from being emptied from upper windows into the streets.

Contemporary Representation of Medieval Towns: Evidence from the Sixteenth Century Vicke Schorler Picture Chronicle of Rostock

Rostock on the German Baltic coast was granted Lübeck Law in 1218. In the fourteenth century as a member of the Hanseatic League, it was a powerful seaport town with *c.*12,000 inhabitants. Vicke Schorler produced his pictorial chronicle of Rostock between 1578 and 1586, just in time before major changes were made to the medieval building fabric during the Baroque and the Renaissance period. The original manuscript lies in the municipal archives of Rostock. The roll measures 18.70 meters in length and 60 cm in height. Buildings are shown in a kind of bird's-eye view. Schorler drew his buildings by pen and then colored them with watercolor. Within the walled town of Rostock, he shows 325 private houses, most built of brick with stepped gables in the Gothic style. His presentation shows the beauty of the uniformity in building style while allowing for a lot of detailed decorations of the brick-built gable fronts (Fig. 4.3). The city-walls and the gate-houses were also built of brick. Medieval Rostock had four parish-churches.[4] The largest was St. Mary's Church on the New Market (Fig. 4.4). St. Mary's, built in the thirteenth century, was the church of the townspeople, representing their wealth and power. There were once five religious houses within the walled medieval town, all but one of which were either destroyed by fire or were pulled down after the Reformation. For example, the stones of the Dominican Friary of St John's were used by Count Johan Albrecht von Mecklenburg-Schwerin in 1566 for the construction of the fortifications outside the Steintor. This is a useful reminder that, in the early-modern period, much of the power that the citizens had possessed in medieval times was taken back into the hands of the local lords.

The most important public building in the town was the town hall and court on the New Market Square in the center of the town, which in 1265, by a decision of the town council, replaced

FIGURE 4.3 Houses in Rostock, Germany, with stepped gables built in brick Gothic style

FIGURE 4.4 Medieval parish church of St. Mary's in Rostock

FIGURE 4.5 Medieval town-hall on the new Market Square in Rostock

two previous smaller town halls (Fig. 4.5). The new town hall with its seven turrets on top of the decorative Gothic gable, seven corresponding archways on the ground floor, and seven large windows on the first floor, was modeled on the town hall of Lübeck, whose town law it had been granted. This town hall is a good example of the importance of symmetry in architectural styles in the thirteenth century. There is a poster on the right-hand side of the front of the building showing how to fence, and there are wreaths hanging from poles indicating the availability of fresh beer.

The town hall was closely connected to the market square where major commercial transactions were carried out and where goods could be taxed and checked for quality. In our chronicle, the market is portrayed as a very lively institution for local products. Food seems to have been the main commodity. It was sold from prefabricated portable benches or hung from bars while pigs roamed around freely. Dried fish hung down from wooden frames, and pottery and pots were also on offer. Oxen are shown in the chronicle pulling sledges on their way to the fountain that is covered by an impressive roof. In

FIGURE 4.6 Medieval weighing-station in Rostock

the middle of the market square are stocks set up under a high roof where minor civic crimes were punished. The swords and chains that hang out of the little tower on top of this building are emblems of the court. The prison was kept in the cellar-rooms of the town hall. The image also shows sailing boats as they were used at the time of the Hanseatic League anchored parallel to the banks of the river Warnow.

A building called the Weighing Station is of great interest, because it illustrates how the town-council kept control over selling and buying. The chronicle shows a two-story house where horses enter at the ground floor, possibly with sacks of grain to be checked whether they conformed to the proper weight (Fig. 4.6).

Civic institutions were an important aspect of medieval towns. Among those were hospitals run by the town council, religious institutions or on the initiative of private benefactors. In Rostock, the Hospital of the Holy Spirit from the late thirteenth century was an impressive building with five gables over five naves. In the middle of the façade, between two large entrances, was the rain-room that allowed shelter on wet days (Fig. 4.7). The hospital became wealthy by way of donations and legacies from rich burgesses. It was a place that looked after people in need: the sick, the poor, and deserted children, but it was also a place where wealthy people without family retired in their old age in return for donations.

Another important institution for medieval Rostock was its university, founded in AD 1419 by the town with the approval of the Pope. It was one of the oldest universities in Northern Europe. The university consisted of a number of buildings. The *Lectorium* (*Auditorium Magnum*) was a large brick gabled house that was originally the town-hall of the New Town (Fig. 4.8). On its ground floor is a well. To the left of the building stands the *Wasserburg*, a roofed well. The chronicle shows a parade of 57 students with épées marching with music toward the town center after having successfully completed their doctoral exams. To the left of the Wasserburg stand five houses, individually named, that served the university in different ways. Four of these houses were gable-ended, and one had its roof ridge parallel to the street. The one on the outer left of the row of five houses was The New Houses, where students held celebrations after their exams were passed. The smallest house with the simple gothic gable belonged to Davidus Chytraeus, who was the resident theologian. His house had two entrances to cellar apartments. The house with the gable parallel to the street was used as *Auditorium medicum*. The house with the smooth gable was the *Collegium juris*. The chronicle also shows a large building,

FIGURE 4.7 Medieval Hospital of the Holy Spirit in Rostock

FIGURE 4.8 Medieval university building in Rostock in former town-hall

not reproduced here, designated as Collegium in 1582. Its full title was *Collegium facultatis artium, domus collegii*. It served as residence for eight professors and their students, many of whom were Swedish.

Another dominant feature in the medieval townscape would have been the residences of aristocratic families or of abbots of big monastic houses that held land in the countryside and who resided periodically in town. Since 1263, there is evidence in Rostock for the residence of the Abbot of the Cistercians of Bad Doberan. In our chronicle, this building is called Doberaner Hof. It is a gothic building with a large stepped gable in the roof and big chimneys that reach out of the roof (Fig. 4.9). At the dissolution of the monastery at Doberan in 1552, the building passed into secular hands and became a riding school for the university.

Near the town hall stand a number of houses, with their richly decorated gables facing the market; they were bigger than the average Rostock town-house. Schorler tells us in his handwritten chronicle that this is where aristocratic families came to stay (Schorler 1583–1625). At the other end of the scale there were the smaller houses referred to as *Buden*, half-houses of *c.* twenty feet width to the street; and then there were the cellar apartments for renting out. In a register of 1617 mentioned by Schorler, the following figures are given for Rostock: 755 houses, 1,302 *Buden*, and 326 cellar apartments, for a total population of 14,000 people. That is to say, over half of the population of

FIGURE 4.9 Medieval town-house in Rostock of the Cistercian monastery at Doberan

Rostock at the end of the Middle Ages did not live in the portions of the beautiful buildings presented in Schorler's chronicle but rather in their cellars or in larger numbers in more modest *Buden*.

Urban Landownership and Social Topography

How much do we know about urban landownership in the medieval period? Lübeck on the western edge of the Baltic in Germany is one of the towns where this question has been researched on an interdisciplinary basis.[5] In the middle of the twelfth century, at the foundation of the town by Duke Henry the Lion, the duke owned all the land in the town. It is believed that he then sold land to merchants, *ministeriales* (a specific group of people owing qualified services to their lord), noblemen, and religious institutions under the concept of *ius hereditarium* (hereditary rights) (Hammel-Kiesow 1996: 48). For a long time, historians believed that all property plots in Lübeck had the same narrow shape from the very beginning. In German, they were called *Gründungsparzellen* (plots at the time of foundation). However, thanks to more work on archival sources and mainly because of the results of archaeological excavations, we now know that the earliest property units in the town, referred to as *hereditates* in contemporary leases written in Latin, could be quite large.

However, because of an increase in population during the thirteenth century and because many merchants and craftsmen had accumulated wealth and could afford to buy property that they had until then only rented, there was an increasingly strong demand to subdivide the existing large property units. After 1276, this move was facilitated in Lübeck by a decree issued by the city council allowing all residents to buy their properties according to a list of agreed prices (Hammel-Kiesow 1996: 53). This move was supported by the fact that the most important asset a family would have wanted was ownership of their own house, because that enabled them to take on credit. And so, by the fourteenth century, most of the larger property units were subdivided into smaller ones, either for more owner occupiers or for rent. An astonishing map showing the reconstructed property pattern of Lübeck from the late thirteenth/early fourteenth century contains 1,664 property units but, lest we give the wrong impression, we must remember that most of the inhabitants of medieval Lübeck, as indeed of other medieval towns, lived in rented accommodation. For example, apprentices would have lived in with their masters.

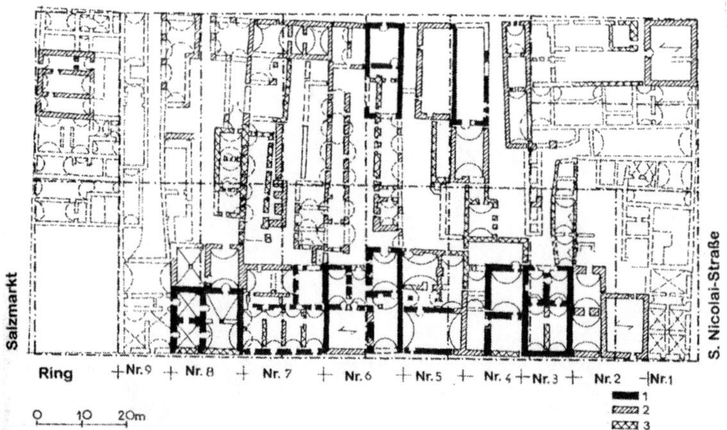

FIGURE 4.10 Changes in medieval plot-patterns around the market square in Wrocław. 1. Thirteenth century. 2. Fourteenth century and two-thirds of fifteenth century. 3. End of fifteenth century to beginning of sixteenth century

In Prague archaeologists discovered that a similar process of subdivision of the originally large property plots must have occurred. During the thirteenth century the street frontages in the neighborhood of the Old Town Square stabilized. According to written sources aristocratic families and high-ranking burgesses lived around the square. From the mid-thirteenth century onwards, under pressure from an increasing number of wealthy merchants for more prestigious house-sites on or near the market square, the original plots were narrowed down (Bureš *et al.* 1997). On the basis of archaeological excavations it has been shown how in Wrocław (Breslau) the pressure for more prestigious residential sites in the thirteenth century caused the subdivision of the originally large plots around the market square (Ring) into smaller units (Czaja 2010, p. 206) (Fig. 4.10). In the fourteenth century the process was reversed. Plots were amalgamated in order to obtain more space for the residential requirements of the urban élite. Only when fire-walls were introduced in the fourteenth century did plot patterns stabilize.[6]

A map showing the topography of different occupations in medieval Göttingen shows the clustering of certain occupations (Denecke 1987: 203; Fig. 4.11).[7] In 1458, there were fifty-four members of the merchant guild in Göttingen who lived around the market and the adjoining streets. Some merchants lived near the city gates or on marginal streets, but they did not represent rich merchant families. Another well-defined group was the wool weavers, who lived in the southern quarter of the town, where they had access to running water. The linen weavers, not as highly regarded as the wool weavers and paying very little tax, are found on the margins of the town. The number of shoemakers in a couple of streets is noteworthy. The bakers rose to become a strong group in the fourteenth to fifteenth century when immigration from the surrounding countryside increased. Craftsmen sold their products from their workshops, except for the butchers who had their own stalls on the market square. Smithies and workshops of carpenters and tailors were not concentrated in any particular location.

The social stratification of the town follows a center-periphery pattern, with the wealthiest families around the market. Indeed, by the end of the fourteenth century, 74 percent of all taxes collected in Göttingen came from that locality. The pattern gets more complicated when we look at the inhabitants of a single house, where a merchant would have lived with others who rented part of his house or worked in his house as servants. The quality of buildings was highest around the market square and adjoining streets. In the center of present-day Göttingen, one can still find medieval cross vaults that

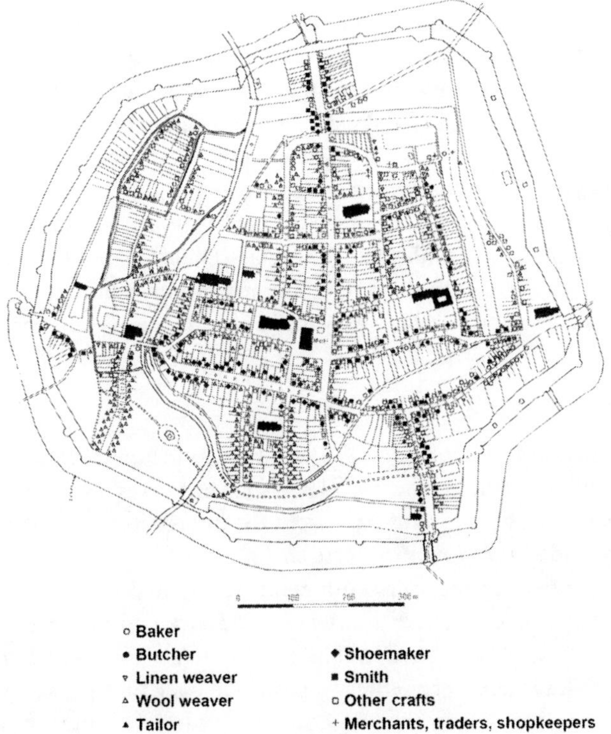

FIGURE 4.11 Location of different occupational groups in medieval Göttingen, Germany

would have carried large stone or half-timbered houses from the thirteenth to fifteenth centuries. The foundation walls of smaller half-timbered houses were excavated on the periphery of the town near the town-wall.

Cultural Leitmotivs *in Medieval Merchant Towns*

The dedication of parish churches to St. Nicholas in a great number of medieval towns in Central, East-Central, and Northern Europe and in Ireland can be interpreted as a *leitmotif* of merchant settlements (Blaschke 2003). A good example for church dedications built in sequence with the different stages of plan-development is the town of Rostock that we encountered in Schorler's sixteenth-century picture chronicle. The earliest part of the walled town is its northeastern quarter, where the oldest church in Rostock is dedicated to St. Peter. South of St. Peter's stands the very large Gothic church dedicated to St. Nicholas. It was built by long-distance merchants on the site where the long-distance road entered the town. In 1218, both churches were integrated into the Old Town (*Altstadt*). In 1232, the present central part of the old town was added, and the new parish church was dedicated to St. Mary. A short time later, in 1250, St. Jacob's was built in a western extension but still within the town walls. In Stralsund, another city on the Baltic about eighty km east of Rostock, one finds exactly the same chronological sequence of church dedications. In our context, this is an interesting detail because it indicates that there were accepted patterns of church dedications that were followed without either a lord or a town-council having to make any decisions.

The introduction of universities that were founded in the late-medieval period in German towns was almost always based on the initiative of aristocratic families but, in the case of Rostock, it was, as noted earlier, the town council. The establishment of hospitals frequently came from the initiative of medieval townspeople, often of husband and wife. The foundation of religious houses was usually the prerogative of aristocratic families. The building style, in stone or brick, both for churches and private houses, was in Romanesque or Gothic, which would have been used all over medieval Europe. Since the thirteenth century, Mendicant Orders set up in towns: Dominicans, Franciscans, and Augustinians. They represented the theology and philosophy of towns. Their organization was international. With the formation of urban religious orders and the founding of universities, religious life in towns was strengthened, which became outwardly visible by the large number of churches within the town walls.

Conclusions

In our effort to understand the morphological agents that contributed to the formation of medieval towns, we have sought to examine the broader social processes that influenced their physical character. These are complex because they represent the interaction of different forces. In the early Middle Ages, lords provided the necessary security for trading settlements. The granting of Latin town charters in the late twelfth and thirteenth centuries created a common urban constitutional framework for medieval Europe. These charters provided a contract between the lord and his townspeople for the benefit of both parties. The subdivision of the space within medieval towns into individual narrow plots facing a street was repeated all over Europe, as it was a convenient way to collect taxes and provide access to the street for the greatest number of inhabitants. With few exceptions in colonial settlement areas, lords did not found towns by granting a charter but granted a charter to settlements that were already economically productive. In the old settled areas, lords (and in particular bishops) yielded a larger degree of self-government to towns only when they were forced to do so. Lords succeeded in keeping a tighter rein on small country towns but, on the whole, they lost control over the larger towns during the thirteenth and fourteenth centuries. The guilds were the mechanism by which townspeople moved toward greater administrative independence. The institutions of Christianity, parish churches, and religious houses provided the cultural and spiritual foundation of medieval towns. Within this framework many behavioral patterns followed tradition, as, for example, in the naming of parish churches. Town councils in larger towns set up their own planning guidelines, as they did most successfully in Tuscany.

Though in the thirteenth century the struggle for independence from feudal lords who claimed control over their towns occupied the town councils, in the fourteenth century, the struggle became internal to the towns, when occupational guilds attempted to join the ranks of the old merchant élites and urban landowners on the town councils. Whether this shift affected the form of late-medieval towns in any way would be an interesting question to explore.

For the early period of urban foundations, however, there is no uncertainty as to the influence of the lords on the topographical layout of towns. Towns in Germany that originated in the Carolingian period around a manorial church, whose graveyard would in time turn into the market place of a growing settlement, have town plans where streets grew in concentric rings around the original church site, as, for example, in Wetzlar. By contrast, in the planned medieval towns east of the Elbe, the focus is on the market, representing the interest of the merchants and craftsmen, and the parish church was almost always placed slightly off the market square (Simms 2006, 2007).

The topographical identity of medieval towns was rooted on the one hand in their constitutional history and on the other—dare one say so—in fashion. How otherwise would we explain the medieval preference for orthogonally laid out town plans with regular plots, as in the bastide towns of Southern France and in East-Central Europe in contrast to castle-towns with a single main street fronted with plots, as built by Anglo-Norman feudal lords in the wake of their colonization of Britain and Ireland? Orthogonally laid out town plans reflect the idea of planning urban space. This approach constituted an innovation in the medieval period that might have been introduced by feudal lords in a drive for modernization but, on the other hand, it might also have been encouraged by the emerging merchant communities in an attempt to put order on the land. With the growth of towns and the development of urban self-government, the influence of the lords, secular or ecclesiastical, grew less, but it was never totally relinquished. The debate about who played the most important role in the formation of medieval towns goes on, but there is no doubt the townspeople, governed by their town councils in various manifestations, were a creative force.

Acknowledgments

I thank Felix Larkin, MA (Dublin), Professor Ferdinand Opll (Vienna), and Dr. Patrick Wallace (Dublin) for improving my text, and I thank Jennifer Moore for help with the scanning of the images. I also thank Keith Lilley, David Nicholas, and Susan Reynolds for their inspiration.

Notes

1 Sachsenspiegel, third book, section 66, text translated from German by the author of this chapter.

2 The bishop's seventeenth-century Schloss in Bonn became the core buildings for the present university in Bonn.

3 A wider discussion of this issue can be found in Clarke and Simms (1985 part II: 669–703). For a complete list of publications see: http://www.wien.gv.at/kultur/archiv/kooperationen/lbi/staedteatlas/bibliographie/index.html; for an English version of this list see: http://www.ria.ie/research/ihta/european-project.aspx.

4 Of the four parish churches, three were rebuilt after the end of WWII, but the old basilica of St. Jacob's was demolished under the Communist regime and is now a memorial site.

5 The archaeological evidence allows the reconstruction of the property pattern for Lübeck in the first 150 years of its existence. By means of land registers, the transformation of these plots could be followed from the late thirteenth century onward. The following registers were used: Oberstadtbücher, 1284–1879; Bücher des Hypothekenamts, 1879–1900; Grundbuch, 1900 to present (Hammel-Kiesow 1996: 49). Hammel-Kiesow discusses the methodological difficulties of pairing information from early registers with archaeological evidence.

6 The evidence for these dynamic processes comes from archaeological work on plot boundaries and from written sources.

7 This map was compiled on the basis of the superimposition of lists containing the names and occupational data of members of different guilds as well as from tax registers on early town-plans showing property units. Apprentices and servants as well as aristocracy and clergy who did not pay any taxes are not included in the reconstruction map.

References

Blaschke, K. (2003) Stadtplanforschung. Neue Methoden und Erkenntnisse zur Entstehung des hochmittelalterlichen Städtewesens in Mittel-, Ost- und Nodeuropa. *Sitzungsberichte der Sächsischen Akademie der Wissenschaften zu Leipzig*, Philologisch-historische Klasse, 138 (4): 3–42.

Bradley, J. (2000) *Irish Historic Towns Atlas No. 10*. Kilkenny, Dublin: O'Brien Press.

Braunfels, W. (1982) *Mittelalterliche Stadtbaukunst in der Toskana*. Berlin: Gebrüder Mann Studio Reihe.

Bureš, M., Voltech, K., and Vareka, P. (1997) The formation of high medieval tenements along the Old Town Square in Prague, in G. De Boe and F. Verhaeghe (eds.), *Urbanism in Medieval Europe: Papers of the Medieval Europe Brugge 1997 Conference* 1: 205–10. Zellik: Instituut voor het Archeologisch Patrimonium.

Clarke, H. B. (2002) *Dublin, Part 1, To 1610*, Irish Historic Towns Atlas No. 11. Dublin: Royal Irish Academy.

Clarke, H. B., and Simms, A. (eds.) (1985) *The Comparative History of Urban Origins in Non-Roman Europe*, parts I and II. Oxford: British Archaeological Reports.

Conzen, M. (2008) Retrieving the pre-industrial built environments of Europe: the Historic Towns Atlas programme and comparative morphological study. *Urban Morphology*, 12 (2): 143–56.

Czaja, R. (2010) Die Gestaltung des Sozialgefüges mittelalterlicher Städte am Beispiel Polens, in F. Opll and Ch. Sonnlechner (eds.), *Europäische Städte im Mittelalter*, Forschungen und Beiträge zur Wiener Stadtgeschichte 52: 203–216. Innsbruck: Studien Verlag.

Denecke, D. (1987) 'Sozialtopographie der mittelalterlichen Stadt Göttingen', in D. Denecke and H. M. Kühn (eds.), *Göttingen. Geschichte einer Universitätsstadt* 1: 199–210. Göttingen: Vandenhoeck & Ruprecht.

Engel, E. (1993) *Die deutsche Stadt des Mittelalters*. Munich: Beck.

Fouquet, G. (1999) *Bauen für die Stadt: Finanzen, Organisation und Arbeit in Kommunalen Baubetrieben des Spätmittelalters*, Städteforschung A/48. Cologne: Böhlau.

Hammel-Kiesow, R. (1996) Property patterns, buildings and the social structure of urban society. Some reflections on Ghent, Lübeck and Nowgorod, in F. E. Eliassen and G. A. Ersland (eds.), *Power, Profit and Urban Land: Land Ownership in Medieval and Early Modern Northern European Towns*, Historical Urban Studies, 37–60. Aldershot, U.K.: Scolar Press.

Janko, F., Kücsán, J. and Szende, K. (eds) (2010) *Hungarian Atlas of Historic Towns*. Budapest: Sopron.

Lilley, K. D. (2009) *City and Cosmos: The Medieval World in Urban Form*. London: Reaktion Books.

Nicholas, D. (1997) *The Growth of the Medieval City: From Late Antiquity to the Early Fourteenth Century*. London: Longman.

Opll, F. (2010) Planung oder Genese? Zur städtischen Entwicklung Wiens bis zum Ende des 13. Jahrhunderts, in F. Opll and Ch. Sonnlechner (eds.), *Europäische Städte im Mittelalter*, Forschungen und Beiträge zur Wiener Stadtgeschichte, 52: 217–52. Innsbruck: Studien Verlag.

Sachsenspiegel (Saxon Mirror) (1220–1230) Transl. Maria Dobozy. Philadelphia: University of Pennsylvania Press, 1999.

Schorler, V. (1583–1625) Handwritten chronicle of Rostock, Municipal Archives of Rostock.

Schorler, V., (1939) *Wahrhaftige Abcontrafactur der hoch loblichen und weitberumten alten See-und Hensestadt Rostock, Heubtstadt im Lande zu Mecklenburg 1578–1586* (original in watercolours), Municipal Archives of Rostock. Rostock: Carl Hinstorffs Verlag.

Simms, A. (2006) Interlocking spaces: the relative location of medieval parish churches, churchyards, marketplaces and town-halls, in H. B. Clarke and S. Philips (eds.), *Ireland, England and the Continent in the Middle Ages and Beyond: essays in memory of a turbulent friar, F. X. Martin, O.S.A.*, 222–32. Dublin: University College Dublin Press.

Simms, A. (2007) Mittelalterliche Gründungsstädte als Ausdruck regionaler Identität, in G. H. Jeute, J. Schmeeweiss, and C. Theune, *Aedificatio Terrae: Beiträge zur Umwelt und Siedlungsarchäologie Mitteleuropas. Festscrift für Eike Gringmuth-Dallmer zum 65 Geburtstag*, 347–54. Rahden, Westfalen: M. Leidorf.

Simms, A. (2013) Unity in diversity: a comparative analysis of the morphological agents creating medieval towns across Europe: Kilkenny, Kalkar and Sopron (based on the European Historic Towns Atlas), in S. Duffy (ed.), *Princes, Prelates and Poets: Essays on Medieval Ireland in Honour of Katherine Simms*, 107–23. Dublin: Four Courts Press.

Simpson, L. (2000) Forty years a-digging: a preliminary synthesis of archaeological investigations in medieval Dublin, in S. Duffy (ed.), *Medieval Dublin I: Proceedings of the Friends of Medieval Dublin Symposium*, 11–68. Dublin: Four Courts Press.

Skre, D. (ed.) (2007) *Kaupang in Skiringssal*, Kaupang Excavation Project Publication Series 1, Norske Oldfunn 22. Oslo: Museum of Cultural History, University of Oslo.

Stercken, M. (2006) Gebaute Ordnung, Stadtvorstellungen und Planung im Mittelalter, in B. Fritzsche, H.-J. Gilomen, and M. Stercken (eds.), *Städteplanung-Planungsstädte*, 15–23. Zürich: Chronos Verlag.

Wallace, P. F. (1992) *The Viking Age Buildings of Dublin*, Medieval Dublin Excavations 1962–81, Ser. A 1. Dublin: Royal Irish Academy for the National Museum of Ireland.

Wallace, P. F. (2000) Garrda and airbeada: the plot thickens in Viking Dublin, in A. P. Smyth (ed.) *Seanchas: Studies in Early and Medieval Irish Archaeology, History and Literature in Honour of Francis J. Byrne*: 261–74. Dublin: Four Courts Press.

Wensky, M., and Weiss, E. (eds.) (2001) *Kalkar*, Rheinischer Städteatlas, 14 (76). Cologne: Böhlau.

Whitehand, J. W. R. (1977) The basis for an historico-geographical theory of urban form. *Transactions of the Institute of British Geographers*, 2 (3): 231–47.

Whitehand, J. W. R. (2012) Issues in urban morphology. *Urban Morphology*, 16 (1): 55–65.

PART III

Agency in Early Modern Settings

5

ABSOLUTE DECISIONS

Towns Fit for a King

Katharine Arntz Thomas

It is common to portray absolutist rulers such as Friedrich II and Peter the Great as driving and determining the development of their chosen court-towns. However, few attempts have been made to tease out the detail of interactions between such rulers and other important actors to determine the extent to which these powerful potentates were able to impose their own visions, or were influenced—or indeed thwarted—by circumstances beyond their control. This issue is addressed using evidence from a number of court-towns, most particularly from Potsdam, Germany to examine development processes and to assess how consistently decisions, once made, were translated into reality. The extent to which the development of such towns can be described as the products of absolutist urban design is thus considered.

Motivation for Developing the Court-Town

Rulers were involved in town planning long before the creation of the unfortified court-towns of the seventeenth and eighteenth centuries. In varying circumstances, they regulated the right of individuals to build (Buff 1971), they encouraged construction through the provision of materials and finance (see, for instance, Kratzsch 1972), and they became involved in the design of ensembles or even town plans (see Braunfels 1987 for various examples). However, in the court-towns, a new level of achievement was reached. Here, potentates pursued their most ambitious visions and invested most time, energy and, above all, money.

Versailles was the first example of such a court-town. From 1682, the original hunting lodge was gradually transformed until it was fit to become the royal residence of Louis XIV. The palace dominated all other built structures and stood open to the town without defenses, while roads—including the rides within the landscaped park—and houses were arranged to focus on the palace, reflecting the relationship between subjects and monarch. Palace, park, and town were thus harmoniously designed to represent the glory of the king and his absolutist power (Braunfels 1987: 154–66, 228; Gerlach 1990: 18–49).

There is no doubt that Versailles was an important model for European rulers. The Austrian ambassador Freiherr von Ried suggested in 1763 that the Prussian King Friedrich II was "following the example of Louis XIV and Versailles and is building a palace that ... will be even larger than the royal palace in Berlin" (Volz 1901: vol. 2, 209). Equally clear is the influence of Versailles on Tsar Peter of Russia. He returned from his 1717 visit to France with an album of views of the palace and gardens at Versailles, which he kept in his study, and his plans to build a palace outside St. Petersburg that was to "vie with Versailles" were interrupted only by his death in 1725 (Hughes 1998: 218). The impact of Versailles on the German-speaking nobility was particularly great, because architectural theory had for so long concentrated on fortified settlements that there was virtually no German-language literature dealing with the unfortified town. Versailles filled this gap and, by 1690, knowledge of it had been widely disseminated among the European nobility: Many visited the French court-town themselves, while others were made aware of it through foreign architects or various copperplate prints (Fehl 1999: 6–18). Versailles provided potentates throughout Europe with a powerful vision.

Louis XIV's inspiring example would, however, have had little impact had it not coincided with specific economic and social conditions that acted as a motivation for, and enabled, change. Particularly in the German-speaking countries, the Thirty Years War (1618–48) caused great devastation. The population of the countryside is estimated to have shrunk by 35 percent to 40 percent and that of the towns by 25 percent to 30 percent, so it was fairly easy for rulers to find land—either from their own domains or through appropriation—on which to found their new court-towns. Large numbers of refugees, vagrants, and ex-soldiers provided a ready supply of labor for building work. The projects were also facilitated by the weakening of social structures, such as the guilds (Merkel 1990: 249; Müller 1990: 263–75).

Once equipped with a vision for a court-town and the opportunity of realizing that vision, the actual decision by rulers to move their seat of residence was prompted by a variety of reasons, often personal and not necessarily strictly rational. Braunfels (1987: 224) suggests that the political situation in France following the mid–seventeenth century war of the Fronde and the news of the beheading of the English king encouraged Louis XIV to build Versailles, allowing the king to distance himself from the people while remaining most glamorously visible. The choice of Potsdam by Friedrich Wilhelm I was fueled by his wish to accommodate his standing army in his immediate vicinity, and both he and Friedrich II were further influenced by their dislike of Berlin with its formality and society (Arntz 2001: 13, 17). Peter the Great's desire to open Russia to the sea and the West encouraged the transfer of his court from Moscow to St. Petersburg.

Perhaps the most obvious motivation for the growing popularity of court-towns was, however, the wish of rulers to build a monument to their own glory, often revealed by their naming the towns after themselves: Examples include St. Petersburg, Karlsruhe, and Christian-Erlang. A newly founded, or small and politically weak, town offered more scope for creative freedom than the existing capital cities (Schroeteler–von Brandt 2008: 80). Indeed, foreshadowing later developments, the extent to which the urban landscape of the capital could be molded to suit the ruler had often been tested before commencing the construction of a new court-town. Thus, late–seventeenth-century developments in Berlin linked the town palace and administrative center around Unter den Linden with surrounding parkland, woods, and summer palaces, as would later be the case in Potsdam. Various planned extensions were also laid out through the late seventeenth century, and groups of immigrants were encouraged to settle in the city. Many of the houses built in these extensions were heavily subsidized, and streetscapes were kept orderly through the implementation of building regulations governing the height of houses, enforcing uniform building lines, and restricting overhangs (Fischer and Bodenschatz 1992; Gerlach 1990: 17–41). Similarly, many of the regulations and fines used to bring regularity to St. Petersburg were first introduced in Moscow. For example, an insistence on masonry construction in Moscow predated the founding of St. Petersburg, and the concern for uniform building lines and façades that characterized building in St. Petersburg was first seen in 1704 when Moscow residents of the Kremlin and Kitaigorod were ordered to build along the streets, not in the middle of plots (Hughes 1998: 205).

Building the Court-Town: A Piecemeal and Often Pragmatic Process

Although the ruler concerned may have had grand visions for his court-town, initial building was often relatively modest. Money was usually limited, and the preliminary aim was simply to attract settlers who would build. Thus, the first planned extension of Potsdam (Fig. 5.1), begun in 1721, was characterized by simple timber-framed buildings that were cheaply and quickly built to relieve the worst pressure on accommodation caused by the quartering of Friedrich Wilhelm I's standing army in the town.

The second extension of 1733 was somewhat more ambitious. Terraces of two-story plastered timber-framed houses, often with solid front walls, were built according to prescribed models and arranged to produce rhythmic interchanges of forms (Fig. 5.2) (Gegenbauer 1991: 8). Yet compromises had to be made here, too. It is said that whole forests were sunk in the marshes of Potsdam as foundations (Mielke 1960: 10) and, even so, open squares had to be introduced into the town plan to accommodate extremely marshy areas that could not be built upon (see Fig. 5.1).

The Potsdam that Friedrich Wilhelm I left behind at his death in 1740 was altogether modest. His successor, Friedrich II, set about rebuilding the town on a grander scale. The town palace was

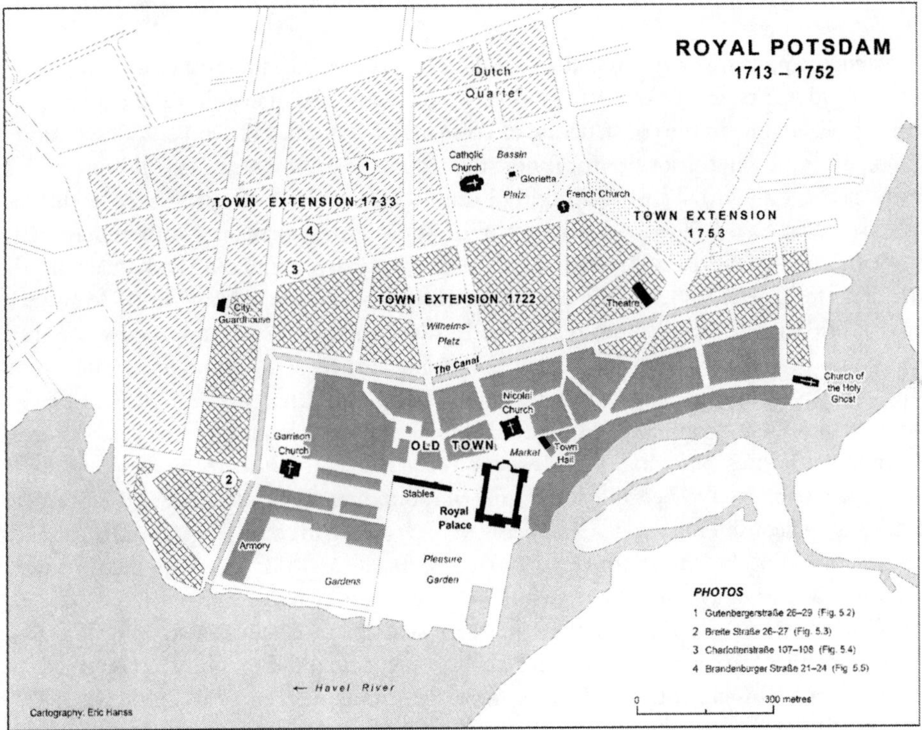

FIGURE 5.1 The town extensions of Potsdam, Germany

FIGURE 5.2 Gutenbergerstraße 26–29, Potsdam. The rhythmic interchange of forms characterizing the original streetscape of the second town extension can be recognized

reconstructed, the pleasure garden replanted, and prospects created, and most of the simple houses of the old town and its first extension were gradually replaced by elaborate villas and palaces (Fig. 5.3).

The piecemeal nature of the construction of Potsdam was typical. Even in Versailles, building work had to compete with other priorities for funds; thus, the figures for annual expenditure rose sharply in times of peace, only to fall just as abruptly in times of war (Braunfels 1987: 224). In Karlsruhe, pressures to contain costs were such that many of the initial houses were built with unseasoned timber and without adequate foundations so that, by the 1750s, extensive rebuilding and repairs had become necessary. This took place under Margrave Karl Friedrich, who came to power in 1746 and who, like the Prussian Friedrich II, was keen to render both palace and town more impressive. Attention was no longer concentrated only on the façades of houses but turned to the entire house, which was now to be built exclusively of stone and to be at least two stories high. Later, in the 1770s and 1780s, streets were surfaced and the market place redesigned. However, progress was piecemeal, with some of the old timber-frame houses surviving, while others were replaced by stone houses taking the form of whatever model happened to be valid at the time of rebuilding. Typically, neither the Margraves nor their architects had considered the process involved in changing the streetscape, but had concentrated only on their vision of the end result (Fehl 2007: 40). As late as 1811, a new model for townhouses was introduced as part of a comprehensive building regulation (Merkel 1990).

In St. Petersburg, development was perhaps most haphazard and drawn out. The town was officially founded in 1703 and, within a year, the fort protecting the harbor was complete; but Tsar Peter began to move his court from Moscow to St. Petersburg only in 1711, and it was 1727 before the building of houses became the focus of attention. All initial building work was in wood, which was later replaced at great cost with stone. Peter changed his mind several times about where the

FIGURE 5.3 Breite Straße 26–27, Potsdam (1769), designed by Unger. The façade was based on Inigo Jones's plan for the Palace of Whitehall in London

focus of the city should be and, as he was dissatisfied with the master development plans produced by Le Blond, he maintained a piecemeal approach throughout his reign, giving different projects to different architects. Flooding and marshland hindered progress even more than in Potsdam. All buildings had to be constructed on posts and, in 1703, only one year after the founding of the town, the flooding of the River Newa was so severe that 2,000 people were drowned. It was only under Empress Elisabeth in the early 1740s that the waters began to be controlled and used to enhance the architecture (Braunfels 1987: 234–8; Dannert 1984: 148–50; Hughes 1998: 216).

Creative Forces: Rulers and Architects

The driving force behind the creation of the court-town was the absolutist potentate searching for, among other things, fame and glory. Yet, while many of the rulers who founded court-towns tinkered with architecture, they necessarily had other commitments. The extent to which they were personally involved in the design and execution of plans varied greatly, both over time and between rulers. They all employed a number of architects, usually foreigners or those with experience abroad, who then enjoyed an often-turbulent relationship with their employer, falling in and out of favor and able to work with a greatly fluctuating degree of independence.

Examining the role of the two Prussian kings responsible for the creation of Potsdam sheds light on the complicated network of influence that produced the urban landscape of the court-town. Friedrich Wilhelm I's preoccupation with his army meant that he was most closely involved in building work that concerned military matters, such as the building of the town walls. He also chose sites for the public buildings and was involved in staking out the street lines and building blocks for the second extension of 1733, but—in keeping with his general parsimonious tendencies (Armbruster 1910: 64)—he was primarily interested in construction costs. A request for building permission had to be accompanied not by a detailed building plan or façade design but by a general plan of the proposal and an estimate of the volume of building and hence the building materials required (Mielke 1972: 102). The king was not wholly indifferent to the appearance of the town, as is shown by the wording of his response to a resident's request for financial help in the construction of a side-building in 1738: this "will not adorn the town, is only for his own use, he should pay" (Förster 1834: vol. 3, 35). Nonetheless, his main aim was to provide economical accommodation for his soldiers and he seems to have left actual design to his architects (Zieler 1913: 13). While able, these architects were seldom at the top of their profession, as Friedrich Wilhelm's concern with replenishing the treasury after the excesses of his father restricted the wages he was willing to pay (Mielke 1981: 26).

Contemporaries suggested that the rhythmic interchanges of the various house types characteristic of the second town extension of Potsdam (see Fig. 5.2) produced a streetscape suited to Friedrich Wilhelm's taste:

> the eye of the king was so indulged by his continuous preoccupation with his bodyguard regiment, which consisted of the best-looking and largest men from all over the earth, that on the newly laid out streets he wanted nothing other than houses representing soldiers standing in a row, with the dormer windows above the second floor resembling the pointed Grenadier hats.
>
> (Manger 1789: 19)

Yet the French architect and master builder, Peter v. Gayette, who was responsible for directing the building of the second plan extension, was undoubtedly aware that such an arrangement was also in keeping with international fashions, particularly the Palladian that was popular in German-speaking Europe at this time. Equally, the use of prescribed models was itself becoming an increasingly common method of ordering and regulating the streetscape: It had been used with success in Cologne (1619), Mannheim (1656), Düsseldorf (1669), and then later in Krefeld, Saarbrücken, Baden, and Karlsruhe. The final four blocks of the second extension of Potsdam were constructed a few years later than the rest of the plan extension—from 1737 onward. House types here were also arranged to produce harmonious streetscapes, but the style was Dutch (i.e. façades of red brick with wooden decorations around the door, visible window frames, and wind shutters on the lower windows of the ground floor). This choice of style can be interpreted as reflecting Friedrich Wilhelm's predilection for Dutch architecture and builders (Manger 1789: 10; Hinrichs 1964: 43), but it also satisfied the demands of the numerous Dutch immigrants whom the king had recruited on his trip to Amsterdam in the spring of 1732. It seems likely that the urban landscape created under Friedrich Wilhelm I represented the happy intersection of the king's taste and interests, architectural trends, and residents' wishes.

As Friedrich II was altogether more ambitious in his plans for Potsdam, his involvement in the design and building of the town was more intensive than that of his father. It is also better documented. Manger (1789: 542), who worked for Friedrich II in the Potsdam building office for thirty-seven years, commented that "here everything occurred according to His direct orders, supervision and execution." The detail of Manger's report makes it clear that the king was closely involved in all aspects of the building work, especially until the late 1770s. Friedrich insisted on seeing a plan and cost estimate for every proposed building; only after his approval could work begin. Every September, the king would fix the building program and budget, choosing from façade designs produced by the building office and scrutinizing the costing attached to them. The king would then order the allocation of money to the head of the building office, who was responsible for its distribution among master builders and owners. All receipts for money received were returned to Friedrich, who held those in charge of the building work accountable for any discrepancies. As an average of one-sixth of the building materials brought into Potsdam were stolen and, in some years, an equal amount was damaged (Manger 1789: 501), various architects and master builders including Büring, Hildebrandt, Gontard, and Manger himself were at different times arrested and imprisoned (Giersberg 1986: 26–8).

Friedrich II was not interested only in controlling expenditure, nor did he restrict himself to approving designs submitted to him by others. He also initiated the planning of particular buildings. He owned copies of most of the important architectural works of the time and corresponded with various architects (including Algarotti and Lord Burlington). From this material, he chose particular models that were to be adapted, so that copies of villas and palaces from Rome, Venice, London, Paris, and Amsterdam were constructed in the proximity of the palace and at visible sites around the town (see Fig. 5.3). As well as ordering his architects to copy models from all over Europe, Friedrich himself designed façades or sketched copies of façades from books (five pages with nine of Friedrich's sketches of house façades still exist in the town archives). Furthermore, he chose the color in which the houses were to be painted and the material for the decorative façade elements, decided where the houses were to be built, and usually chose the future owners to whom the houses were to be given, a gift of dubious worth owing to the impracticality of the houses and the expense of their maintenance (Giersberg 1986: 34–8, 144–53; Mielke 1972: 314–30).

Though the inspiration for these villas and palaces came from the king, it was his architects who produced the building plans from which they were constructed. Friedrich II's relationships with his architects were volatile, as Manger (1789: 45) recalls: "none of these master builders made the king happy, indeed as far as I know none of them enjoyed his lifelong favour." Mielke (1972: 106) suggests that this was, at least partly, because of the fact that Friedrich's architectural ambitions were not matched by his abilities. His sketches were so vague that it was mere chance if the architect entrusted with their transformation into building plans interpreted them according to the king's wishes.

Knobelsdorff was Friedrich's guide in architectural matters even before the latter became king—they first worked together on the Crown Prince Palace in Rheinsberg—and, in the year of his accession, 1740, Friedrich entrusted his friend with his most important building plans, following this in 1742 with an appointment as superintendent of all the royal palaces, houses, and gardens and as director-in-chief of building work in all provinces. However, the relationship between the two cooled as Friedrich became more independent in his architectural taste. By 1745, the Dutchman Boumann was the king's new favorite. Boumann led the refurbishment of the town palace in Potsdam and, by the early 1750s, was not only in charge of the actual building of Knobelsdorff's designs, adapting them considerably, but also bore the main responsibility for transforming Friedrich's own sketches into building plans (Giersberg 1986: 163). Büring succeeded Boumann, but neither he nor his predecessors were allowed any great degree of independence. Manger (1789: 201) mentions a typical example of Friedrich's behavior, recalling how in 1755 Büring's designs for seven factory buildings went back and forth between king and architect, with Friedrich correcting and altering Büring's plans many times before he was finally satisfied.

FIGURE 5.4 Charlottenstraße 107–108, Potsdam (1783), designed by Unger as one façade fronting two houses

Later in his reign, Friedrich's interest in architecture seems to have waned and, from the 1770s onward, there is no evidence of his having sketched any more houses as models. Gontard, head of the building office from 1765 until Friedrich's death in 1786, was able to gather around him architects such as Unger, Kruger, and Schulze and with them to work somewhat more independently than his predecessors. Gontard and his pupils primarily designed two-story town houses whose façade and layout corresponded better than in the palace copies so beloved by Friedrich II (Fig. 5.4). This did much to ensure the uniformity of the urban landscape as, by the time of Friedrich's death, such houses made up a majority of those that had been built during his reign (Mielke 1981: 41–4; Pehle 1938: 182).

Although Friedrich II was not solely responsible for the design of Potsdam's urban landscape, the building work was clearly one of his great passions. He spent about ten times more per house than had his father, using money from various sources including substantial annual revenue derived from his East Friesian inheritance (Mielke 1972). He is said to have answered all queries involving building issues on the same day that he received them, either in his own hand or through signing a cabinet statement (Manger 1789: 604). Even when he was out of the country, he liked to be kept informed of progress, as a letter written in 1742 to a member of his court clearly shows. "Tell Knobelsdorff that he is to write and tell me about my buildings, my furniture, my gardens and my opera house, so as to divert me'" (Seidel 1922: 127). Perhaps the greatest indication of his personal significance in the development of Potsdam was the dramatic fall in construction figures after his death in 1786. In that year, forty houses were built in the town, yet the very next year only four were constructed and, thereafter, similarly low annual figures remained the norm (Mielke 1972: 74).

The level of Friedrich's personal involvement in the building work of Potsdam was extreme, but echoes of something similar are found elsewhere. In the early years of the construction of Karlsruhe, Margrave Karl Wilhelm personally commented on every request for building permission (Merkel

1990: 248). In Stuttgart in the first half of the nineteenth century, Kings Friedrich and Wilhelm I both examined every request for building permission and often commented in detail on the attached plans. The king had the final decision, and often Wilhelm especially criticized the style of the façades, describing them as "very ugly" or as having "a very nasty appearance" (Hagel 1996: 18–21). Tsar Peter the Great's involvement in the creation of St. Petersburg resembled that of Friedrich in Potsdam even more closely. Every year the Tsar produced a list of projects for the next building season, and he also supplied rough sketches for some of the buildings, including the Mon Plaisir pavilion. Like Friedrich, he insisted on being kept closely informed about developments in his court-town while away at war and referred to St. Petersburg as "paradise," in direct contrast to the various "Hell-holes" in which he found himself (Hughes 1998: 213–25). And he, too, expended immense resources in building his court-town. Indeed, Peter's critics complained that while the new capital was shod in gold, the old capital Moscow had to make do with straw shoes (Dannert 1984: 152). After Peter's death in 1725, more than 100 of his handwritten orders and plans pertaining to building work were found among his papers, and the effect of his death on St. Petersburg was even more dramatic than that of Friedrich's death on Potsdam: The whole undertaking collapsed, half the population and all the nobles fled the town, and the young Peter II was taken to Moscow. It was 1732 before Anna Iwanowna returned and ordered building to recommence (Braunfels 1987: 237).

The Residents: A Frequently Forgotten Factor

Peter the Great, in seventeenth-century Russia, could allow himself the most autocratic approach of all of the founders of court towns. He ordered not only nobles on military and government service to move to St. Petersburg, but the masters of various handicrafts were also compulsorily transferred from Moscow to the new capital, and thousands of building workers were press-ganged and marched to St. Petersburg under armed guard (Hughes 1998: 213). Yet even Peter was troubled by a lack of cooperation from residents. There were problems of so-called "rural disorder": livestock wandered the streets damaging roads and trees, and behind the splendid buildings on the embankments was a jumble of log buildings and squalor. Inhabitants further disrupted the Tsar's notion of the town by building in the wrong place, so that Peter ended up threatening residents not employed in the military or fleet with the demolition of their residences if they persisted in disobeying his orders to move to Vasil'evsky Island (Hughes 1998: 216–22).

Elsewhere, the situation was somewhat different. To secure their growing power after the Thirty Years War, it was vital for rulers to attract settlers who would pay taxes and drive the economy. Indeed, the initial feasibility of any court-town depended on attracting enough people to populate and build the town. Offers of freedom from taxes and free building materials were therefore made to encourage immigrants to move to Versailles (Fehl 1999: 14), Stuttgart (Hagel 1996: 243), Karlsruhe, Ludwigsburg, Rastatt, and Mannheim (Müller 1990: 262–5). Guarantees of religious freedom were often also used to encourage the immigration of religious refugees. Thus, more than 1,500 Protestant Austrians settled in Berlin and the surrounding area in 1732; these were joined by a considerable number from Bohemia. It seems likely that some of these Protestant refugees ended up in Potsdam, where settlers were given particularly generous subsidies for the construction of houses: Rather than the 4 percent or 8 percent of costs usual in Prussia, citizens received 10 percent or 15 percent and, in later years, even fully constructed houses (Mielke 1972: 6, 142). In Christian-Erlang, later known as Erlangen, Margrave Christian Ernst went further to attract and keep settlers. In 1687, Huguenot refugees were granted freedom from taxes for ten years, were given a church and building materials for a seminary and a hospital, promised free choice and practice of religion, and given permission for the establishment of a court with three German and three French judges. The Margrave even sanctioned advertising intended to attract desirable settlers to the town. Brochures praised state investment, the wonderful surroundings, the proximity of Nürnberg, the importance of the two nearby rivers, the convenient road and water communications, the low costs of living, and the quality of the food (Berve 1975: 160–1). Such was the competition for skilled or relatively well-off refugees that rulers even accused their neighbors of unfairly keeping or attracting craftsmen while throwing poorer refugees on the mercy of others (Jakob 1990: 187). Yet, having once courted these residents in these ways, it later proved difficult to ensure that they played the role in the town's development that the ruler had envisaged.

In Potsdam, all residents were free to build on the back of their plots as they liked, restricted only by fire regulations. This resulted in a jumble of workshops, washrooms, additional accommodation and stables and in a wide variety of plot sizes and subdivisions, each house owner acquiring land and building according to individual needs and means. Inhabitants also influenced the urban landscape in ways more directly visible from the street. Records exist of various cases where individuals were able to persuade Friedrich II to rebuild their houses though they occupied sites that were neither particularly prominent nor were in the proximity of the palace (Mielke 1981: 52). After taking possession of their new houses, residents continued to make their mark on the urban landscape. Friedrich II granted houses to appropriate residents on the condition that they would be cared for and preserved, as is recorded in the gifting documents. For instance, in 1765, the silk-dyer Thomas Persani received his house Am Alten Markt 12 on the understanding that it would be preserved in an honorable condition, used in an orderly fashion, and kept in a state worthy of the great generosity of the king (Potsdam Stadtarchiv, *Schenkungsurkunde* of 24 April, 1765). Nonetheless, it is clear that such houses were neglected, and even altered, by their inhabitants both during Friedrich's reign and shortly afterward. In a cabinet order of December 8, 1776, Friedrich ordered the authorities to pay more attention to the upkeep and care of newly built houses, because he had noticed that "the citizens do not keep their new houses in anything approaching a good condition and order, but let them spoil completely" (Cabinets-Ordres-Buch Friedrich des Grossen 1776–1786). A further declaration was made by Friedrich Wilhelm II in 1787, forbidding residents of houses that had been built with the financial support of the monarch to alter the façades. The reason for the declaration is made clear by an account given by Manger (1789: 337) of the houses on the east side of Wilhelmplatz. He describes the ways in which the houses had been altered, mentioning particularly the removal of the original façade moldings and their replacement with heaps of unnecessary decoration, which rendered it possible only to recognize the bare bones of the architecture. Clearly, although residents had no say in the original design of their new houses, once they had taken possession of their homes, their influence on the urban landscape was decidedly increased. The cumulative effect of the piecemeal individual changes that were made is indicated in Fig. 5.5. These houses originally formed a harmonious streetscape similar to that shown in Fig. 5.2, but as the prosperity and independence of the residents increased, so they adapted the buildings to suit their own needs and preferences. The shop windows seen today are the culmination of a process begun in the mid-1800s; the added stories and attic conversions were also common, and occasionally residents even completely rebuilt their houses, as in the case of Brandenburger Straße 24 (on the left in Fig. 5.5), rebuilt in 1892 (*Acta specialia betr. Bau-Sachen*).

In Karlsruhe, founded in 1715, thirty-two streets radiate from the palace and its tower, which are the focus of a town plan generally accepted as being the purest embodiment of ideal town concepts of all of the German court-towns (Braunfels 1987: 153; Merkel 1990; Fig. 5.6). The houses in Karlsruhe were designed according to models of various sizes and standards but, as in Potsdam,

FIGURE 5.5 Brandenburger Straße 21–24

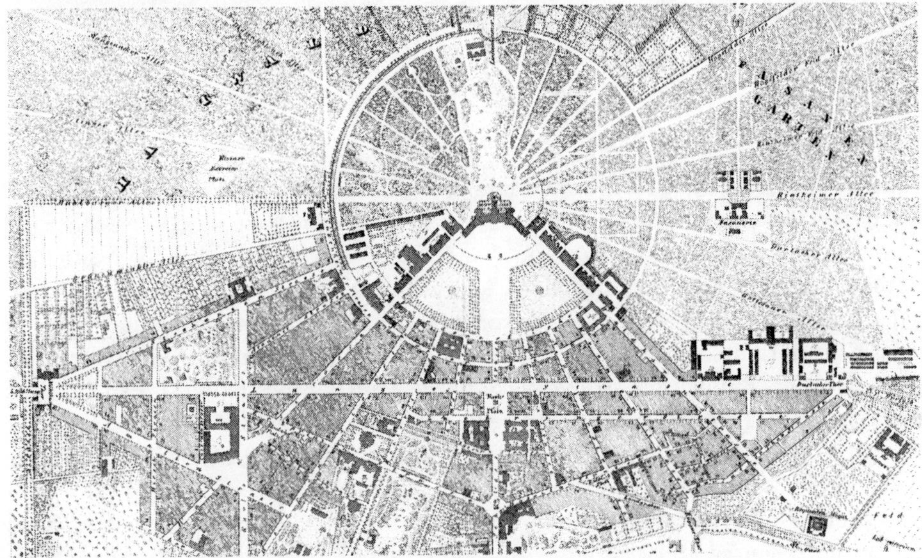

FIGURE 5.6 Town plan of Karlsruhe, as it had developed to 1843

usually only the façades were built according to the models: the backyards, gardens, interior plans and—on occasion—even the width of the houses varied considerably according to inhabitants' wishes. Indeed, in one area of the town, known as "Dörfle," all attempts at controlling the building activities of residents were actually abandoned. Single-story, irregular, and simple earth and wood huts were built along unplanned streets by those unable to afford to build and live in the planned

Karlsruhe: construction workers, lowly servants of the court, and soldiers. In the main part of the town, residents were also able to further mark their own priorities on the urban landscape. Margrave Karl Wilhelm intended that the various house types, and hence social groups, should be distributed through the town to result in a social structuring focused on the palace. However, economic factors were more important to residents than the wishes of the margrave. Not even the nobles chose to live exclusively in the area envisioned for them, while especially for those running a business a desirable location was not defined by proximity to the palace. Indeed, for many residents the market-place, rather than the palace, was the focus of the town. As early as the 1720s, citizens campaigned for a town hall to be located on the market place. They effectively overcame opposition from both the clergy and Margrave Karl Wilhelm by refusing to contribute to the costs of the hall if it were not built on their chosen site (Leiber 1990: 301–3; Merkel 1990: 248–9; Müller 1990: 272–5).

In early eighteenth-century Dresden, the burghers also hindered the rebuilding plans of the ruler. Marx (2008) cites examples of their successful resistance to various projects intended to enhance the regularity and symmetry of the townscape. In at least one case, when opposing demolition of part of the city walls, residents went as far as protest and sabotage (Marx 2008: 145).

The example of Stuttgart in the early nineteenth century again shows the influence that residents could have on the urban landscape. A royal declaration from 1843 states that deviations from the regulations or terms of building permission occurred daily, and a detailed analysis by Hagel (1996) shows that such misdemeanors often went unpunished. This state of affairs was a reflection of flaws and inconsistencies in the regulations, a point that the citizens of the town clearly recognized. In 1844, more than 1,000 citizens met to debate such issues and later sent a report of their conclusions to the king. This seems to have triggered discussion between the king and his officials about the drafting of a new State building regulation (Hagel 1996: 344–52).

Conclusion

Whitehand (1992: 5) identified three important dimensions in the role of agents and their influence on the development of the urban landscape. First, there is a distinction between the activities of public bodies and corporate entities on the one hand and, on the other, private or individual activities. Second, there is the degree of concentration of decision making. Finally, the roles of agents can be classified according to the functions they perform. Applying these considerations to the context of authoritarian urban landscapes underlines the dominant role of the potentate. The court-towns were laid out and developed under the strict control of the royal administration, at many times closely monitored and steered by the potentate himself. The records show the way in which rulers were personally involved in providing and controlling money, land, and materials; attracting residents; selecting architects; scrutinizing building plans; issuing building regulations; and even dabbling in architectural design. They thus, at varying times and to varying degrees, took on the functions of legislator, owner, financier, initiator, and housing officer. Decision making was, to an unprecedented and striking degree, concentrated in the hand of the potentate.

However, decisions are always contingent upon circumstances. Even authoritarian rulers were reliant on, and influenced by, factors and actions beyond their control. Any notion of a court-town directly reflecting the vision of its founder would be misplaced. None of these towns was created in one grand gesture but rather grew out of a long and largely pragmatic and piecemeal process that was seldom completed within the lifetime of the initiating ruler. Even if the potentate in question possessed a clear vision of what he wished to achieve (which was not always the case), the transformation of that vision into reality was influenced and restricted by various factors. Despite the vast sums spent on the court-towns, money was never unlimited; and this, along with the characteristics of the site and materials, often acted as a brake on more grandiose plans. Even the most enthusiastic among the town founders were reliant on the expertise and talent of architects and master builders and were handicapped in their own contribution by their lack of training—and perhaps talent—and by the demands placed upon them by other commitments. Finally, while rulers could usually rely on the cooperation of their dependent architects, they often faced opposition—or at least a lack of active cooperation—from other quarters: most notably from the residents of the towns. Thus, though absolutist urban design was driven by the will of the potentate, the nature of the urban landscape created was derived from a complex network of decision making and negotiation involving a large number of actors.

References

Armbruster, J. (1910) *Eine preußische Königstochter: Denkwürdigkeiten der Markgräfin von Bayreuth, Schwester Friedrichs des Großen*. Ebenhausen: Langenwiesche-Brandt.

Arntz, K. (2001) The garrison behind the façades: the development of Potsdam as the second residence of the Prussian monarchy. *Planning History*, 23: 13–19.

Berve, R. (1975) *Stadterweiterungen der fränkischen Residenzstädte Ansbach, Bayreuth und Erlangen im 17. und 18. Jahrhundert*. Düsseldorf: VDI Verlag.

Braunfels, W. (1987) *Abendländische Stadtbaukunst*. Köln: DuMont.

Buff, A. (1971) *Bauordnung im Wandel: historisch-politische, soziologische und technische Aspekte*. München: Callwey.

Cabinets-Ordres-Buch Friedrich des Grossen 1776–1786. *Mitteilungen des Vereins für die Geschichte Potsdams*, 11. Sitzung, 1863: 1–14.

Dannert, E. (1984) *Russland im Zeitalter der Aufklärung*. Wien: Hermann Böhlaus Nachf.

Fehl, G. (1999) Versailles as an urban model: new court-towns in Germany circa 1700. *Urban Morphology*, 3: 3–20.

Fehl, G. (2007) Perspektivischer Stadtraum—Modellmäßiger Hausbau, in T. Harlander (ed.), *Stadtwohnen: Geschichte Städtebau Perspektiven*, 19–45. Ludwigsburg: Wüstenrot Stiftung.

Fischer, F., and Bodenschatz, H. (1992) *Hauptstadt Berlin: zur Geschichte der Regierungsstandorte*. Berlin: Senatsverwaltung für Bau und Wohnungswesen.

Förster, F. (1834) *Friedrich Wilhelm I: König von Preußen*. Potsdam: Ferdinand Riegel.

Gegenbauer, C. (1991) Die zweite barocke Stadterweiterung. *Kulturbauten und Denkmale*, 2: 8–10.

Gerlach, S. (1990) *Die deutsche Stadt des Absolutismus im Spiegel barocker Veduten und zeitgenössischer Pläne*. Stuttgart: Steiner.

Giersberg, H.-J. (1986) *Friedrich als Bauherr*. Berlin: Siedler Verlag.

Hagel, J. (1996) *So soll es seyn: Königliche Randbemerkungen u. Befehle zur Stadtgestaltung in Stuttgart u. Cannstatt in der ersten Hälfte des 19. Jahrhunderts*. Stuttgart: Verlag Klett-Cotta, Veröffentlichungen des Archivs der Stadt Stuttgart 70.

Hinrichs, C. (1964) Friederich Wilhelm I: König von Preußen, in C. Hinrichs (ed.), *Preußen als historisches Problem: gesammelte Abhandlungen*. Berlin: G. Oestreich, 253–71. Veröffentlichungen der Historischen Kommission zu Berlin 10.

Hughes, L. (1998) *Russia in the Eyes of Peter the Great*. New Haven: Yale University Press.

Jakob, A. (1990) Die Legende von den "Hugenottenstädten": Deutsche Planstädte des 16. und 17. Jahrhunderts, in M. Maaß et al. (eds.), *Klar und lichtvoll, wie eine Regel*, 181–99. Karlsruhe: Braun.

Kratzsch, K. (1972) *Bergstädte des Erzgebirges*. München: Schnell & Steiner.

Leiber, G. (1990) Vom Jagdsitz zur Stadtanlage: die städtebauliche Entwicklung Karlsruhes bis zum Ende des 18. Jahrhunderts, in M. Maaß et al. (eds.), *Klar und lichtvoll, wie eine Regel*, 297–312. Karlsruhe: Braun.

Manger, H. L. (1789) *Baugeschichte von Potsdam*. Berlin/Stettin: Friedrich Nicolai.

Marx, B. (2008) From Protestant fortress to baroque apotheosis: Dresden from the sixteenth to the eighteenth century, in G. B. Cohen and F. A. J. Szabo (eds.), *Embodiments of Power: Building Baroque Cities*, 120–63. New York and Oxford: Berghahn Books.
Merkel, U. (1990) "Zu mehrerer Zierde und Gleichheit des Orths": der Modellhausbau des 18. Jahrhunderts in Karlsruhe, in M. Maaß et al. (eds.), *Klar und lichtvoll, wie eine Regel*, 243–58. Karlsruhe: Braun.
Mielke, F. (1960) *Das Holländische Viertel in Potsdam*. Berlin: Gebr. Mann.
Mielke, F. (1972) *Das Bürgerhaus in Potsdam*. Tübingen: Ernst Wasmuth.
Mielke, F. (1981) *Potsdamer Baukunst*. Frankfurt am Main: Propyläen.
Müller, C. (1990) Peuplierung, in M. Maaß et al. (eds.), *Klar und lichtvoll, wie eine Regel*, 259–78. Karlsruhe: Braun.
Pehle, M. (1938) *Potsdam: ein Heimatbuch*. Potsdam: Ludwig Voggenreiter.
Potsdam Stadtarchiv, Potsdam, Germany, *Schenkungsurkunde*, 24 April 1765, Sondersachen IV/299.
Schroeteler–von Brandt, H. (2008) *Stadtbau- und Stadtplanungsgeschichte*. Stuttgart: Kohlhammer.
Seidel, P. (1922) *Friedrich der Große und die bildende Kunst*. Leipzig/Berlin: Giesecke & Devrient.
Volz, G. B. (1901) *Friederich der Große im Spiegel seiner Zeit*. Berlin: Hobbing.
Whitehand, J. W. R. (1992) *The Making of the Urban Landscape*. Oxford: Blackwell.
Zieler, O. (1913) *Potsdam: ein Stadtbild des 18. Jahrhunderts*. Berlin: Weise.

6

HAUSSMANN

Reconsidering His Role in the Transformation of Paris

Michaël Darin

The Trade Name

It is 1991. An exhibition is held in Paris. The title is *Paris-Haussmann*; the work and the man. Or, more likely, the man and his work: *le pari d'Haussmann* (Haussmann's bet) is the subtitle of the catalog, and 1991 is the centenary of the death of Georges-Eugène Haussmann. The book of the exhibition sums up a long series of publications on the subject that seems thus to be closed for some time to come (des Car and Pinon 1991).[1] More than two decades later, however, the great number of new publications shows that the man and his work continue to attract great attention.[2]

Naming the transformations of Paris during the second half of the nineteenth century after Haussmann is not a recent invention. What later became a habit was first put into use during the Second Empire, when authors criticizing these works used to refer to them as *entreprises d'Haussmann* (Horn 1869) or *comptes d'Haussmann* (Ferry 1868). The family name later became an adjective, as is attested by the much-used terms *boulevards haussmanniens* and *immeubles haussmanniens*[3] and by the more specialized *style haussmannien* (see Larbodière 2000[4]) or *îlot haussmannien* (Castex et al. 1977) and, the most encompassing of all, Paris *haussmannien*. Apart from the specific physical elements, there is the general concept: *haussmannisme, haussmannisation* or *modèle haussmannien* all designate a kind of urban fabric or a type of massive urban renewal based on cutting new streets through dense centers of old cities.[5] By extension, there is also *neo-haussmannisme*, a term applied to projects carried out in Paris during the 1980s and 1990s, which tried to reproduce some of the physical characteristics of the urban landscape of the nineteenth century.[6]

The *Préfet*'s or Prefect's shadow spreads even further than Paris to cover all similar urban transformations of other French cities (de Moncan and Claude Heurteux 2002), and even the whole history of town planning during the nineteenth century. There are, for example, historians of architecture, inspired by Sigfried Giedion, who introduce the history of modern architecture by referring to some developments of the nineteenth century and give utmost importance to the accomplishments of Haussmann (for example, Benevolo 1977: 61–95; Frampton 1985: 23–5). Even more striking is the honor given to the *Préfet* by French historians interested in larger urban phenomena. The fourth volume of the *Histoire de la France Urbaine*, the synthesis of French urban history, is entitled *La Ville de l'Âge Industriel: le Cycle Haussmannien (1840–1940)* (Duby 1980–5). With this adjective, Haussmann becomes a kind of patron saint of French urban history of the period, if not of the whole.[7]

Sources

The name or word *Haussmann* and its different uses constitute a short-cut. Scholars know the approximation of this term and use it surrounded with mental quotation marks.[8] The words have, however, their own weight and, for the general public, the different "*Haussmannian*" entities reflect reality. They seem to correspond to different aspects of the transformations of Paris during the second half of the nineteenth century, works that fascinated their contemporaries and continue to fascinate today.

At the end of the 1860s, when Haussmann was still in power, many articles and brochures criticized the *Grands Travaux*, the Grand Works of Paris: the most well-known of which is by Ferry (1868). After the fall of the Second Empire, three important contributions were written by significant persons in charge of these works. First was *Les Promenades de Paris* (Adolph Alphand 1867–73), then *Les Travaux Souterrains de Paris* (Eugène Belgrand 1873–87) and finally Haussmann's own *Mémoires du Baron Haussmann*, the first two volumes of which were published in 1890 and the third in 1893, two years after the death of the author.

Haussmann knew that his book had a particular importance because all municipal documents dealing with the *Grands Travaux* had disappeared in 1871 in a fire that burned down the town hall and the adjoining building where the archives were deposited. Very little material was left capable of challenging his version of events. On all points, the authors who were later to be interested in Haussmann and "his" work reproduce his account. They must, surely, recognize that his book is a plea against criticism leveled at him. They must all know that they cannot trust all of the arguments that he put forward. They obviously have reservations about this or that statement or about his style in general.[9] They compare some of his details to those put forward by other contemporary authors such as Charles Merruau (1875), Henri de Laire (1896), and Emile Ollivier (1961). They find one or two minor letters in one or other archive. They summarize one or two sessions of the *Corps Législatif* (the parliament under the Second Empire) dealing with some aspect of the Works, but all these supplementary sources are arid compared with the richness of the *Mémoires*.[10] Although his biographers[11] try to convey their independence, they depend in fact on Haussmann for all the basic information and the structure of their own *exposés*.[12] They all have to be content with simply adding their personal sauce to Haussmann's dish, to take an image used by Chaudun (2000).

Paternity

In condensing the usual accounts, it is possible to start on June 27, 1853, the day on which the Paris-born Haussmann—who began his administrative career in different provincial prefectures in May 1831 at the age of 22—returned to the capital as the newly appointed *préfet* of the *département de la Seine* (the region of Paris and the adjacent suburbs). The previous *préfet*, Jean-Jacques Berger, who apparently did not share the Emperor's view on the future transformations of Paris, was to be replaced. Napoléon III, impressed with the reforms carried out in London, where he had been in exile, wanted to reshape the French capital and, to carry out his ambitious policy, he needed a new

FIGURE 6.1 Baron Haussmann (left) and Emperor Napoléon III (right)

préfet capable of realizing his ideas. Haussmann himself advanced this version, refusing all paternity for the works of which he was to be in charge: "I was only the one who put the idea into practice" (Fig. 6.1; Haussmann 2000: vol. II, 59).

This clear-cut division of labor, between idea and realization, begs a question: if the idea belonged to the Emperor and only the execution to the *Préfet*, why does the glory go to the latter? The city of Washington, DC is well associated with the name of Pierre L'Enfant, the extension of Barcelona with Ildefons Cerdà and Chandigarh with Le Corbusier (Charles-Éduard Jeanneret). So why Paris with Haussmann? It is as if, for once, it was understood that the importance in city building is not so much a general idea, nor even its translation into lines drawn on paper, but the long labor needed for executing a plan.

This would be too good to be true. Historically, things are somehow different. The *Grands Travaux* were already dissociated from the name of Napoléon III during the Second Empire. Attributing the *Grands Travaux* to the *Préfet* was, then, a means to express criticism by those who were supporting the Emperor but who opposed his urban policy. Those who were politically opposed to the regime also used this tactic because, in a regime that practiced censorship, criticizing the urban policy associated with the Emperor was a way to oppose the monarch. However, after the Empire's downfall, when the old opponents adopted the same attitudes toward urban affairs, they still ensured that they dissociated their urban policies from the name of Napoléon III. Jules Simon, who was once a fierce opponent of the *Grands Travaux* and who later—in the period 1870–7—was a minister several times (and once a prime minister), called in 1882 for the completion "by liberty the works which were started by despotism" (*Le Gaulois*, quoted by Haussmann 2000: vol. II, ix). The former critic of Haussmann was now his eulogist. For Simon, in the 1880s, enhancing the importance of the *Préfet* was a means to avoid glorifying the Emperor.

Fifty years later, the same attitudes persisted. In 1932, an important book by André Morizet was published. Morizet was an active socialist mayor of Boulogne Billancourt (a suburb of Paris) and a member of the senate representing the *département de la Seine*. For him, the transformations of

Paris were a splendid example of what town planning could achieve. He totally approved these works and posed one clear question: "Should the justified anti-Bonapartist passion of our parents obsess indefinitely our judgments about the *Grand Préfet*?" (Morizet 1932: 319). In the same year, Georges Laronze published the first biography of Haussmann, ending with two short sentences: "Haussmann could work for the dictatorship. He had France mainly in mind" (Laronze 1932: 258). In the 1930s, *Haussmannism* was a means to get around the rehabilitation of *Bonapartism*, even in relation to urban policy. From then on, writers continued to designate the *Grands Travaux* in the same way. Today, it is mere inertia that avoids creating the term *Napoleonian Paris*, which would have been more respectful of tradition. Will this trend continue in the future? One thing is certain: even if the habit to attribute the transformation semantically to Haussmann is still in vogue, "contemporary historiography mentions, after a long period of negation, the important role of the Emperor himself" (Bourillon 2001: 151).

Outside France, authors generally follow old French habits and attribute the transformations of Paris to Haussmann (for example, Londei 1982). There are, however, a few Anglophone authors who show great interest in the romantic figure of Louis Napoléon, but these biographers, such as William Smith (1972) or Fenton Bresler (1999), leave aside the transformations of Paris; although Smith's book has a few interesting paragraphs about the Emperor's method of governing. More important is David H. Pinkney's *Napoléon III and the Rebuilding of Paris* (1958). As with all the other books on the subject, it is mainly based on the *Mémoires* of Haussmann. Pinkney, however, gives an important role to the Emperor and shows it by his book's title. Moreover, he stresses the importance of the ideas of the future Napoléon III upon his arrival in Paris. He also underlines the closeness of the Emperor with the works: for instance, his participation in the ceremonies of the inauguration of major streets and the fact that these days were declared as public holidays. This book has never been translated into French.

Qualities of a Great Administrator

No one likes Georges-Eugène Haussmann as a person. It is his role as a *grand commis de l'État*, a Great State Administrator, that attracts biographers. His qualities were already underlined by Fialin duc de Persigny, the Minister of the Interior—the person who recommended Haussmann to Napoléon III. He was, first, impressed by Haussmann's appearance: "He was big, strong vigorous and full of energy ...".[13] Then came his mental makeup: "he was subtle, sly, resourceful" and endowed with "a kind of brutal cynicism." Such a person was capable, according to Persigny, to tame the persons of ill-will who supported the regime but were opposed to the urban measures envisaged by the Emperor (de Laire 1896: 253). They were numerous in economic as well as political spheres: many bankers and ministers, among others, did not approve of all that was done for Paris. The person in charge of the program had to be capable of defending the envisaged works against this kind of harmful internal opposition. In a frequently-quoted passage, Persigny wrote: "I was delighted in advance at the idea of throwing this animal of the feline race of large size amidst the pack of foxes and wolves incited against all the generous inspirations of the Empire" (de Laire 1896: 255).

Haussmann himself underlined his efficient use of the administrative machine he was heading. First was his choice of men. He summoned to Paris Belgrand and Alphand, two engineers of the *Ponts et Chaussées*, the prestigious State corps, whom he had met earlier in his career. He appointed them as the heads of two important departments of the Prefecture of the Seine: the Department of Water and Sewage and the Department of Plantations and Promenades. Haussmann also stressed the fact that, within the Prefecture, he knew whom to trust and promote: for instance Eugène Deschamps, the future head of the important Department of the Plan of Paris.

Apart from the individuals, Haussman reshuffled the whole organization of the Prefecture, changing the existing departments and creating new ones. A major innovation consisted in breaking down the walls between different departments and creating "multi-disciplinary teams permanently in charge of particular areas of the city, or grouped temporarily in order to carry out a project" (Dudilieu 2002: 228). This concern with coordination led him to set up a weekly meeting of all the directors and the chief engineers through which a team spirit was shaped (Landau and Gauthier 2000: 45).

The Financial Wizard

Haussmann's main reputation is, however, related to his approach to financial problems. The enormous cost of the Works of Paris was the major criticism thrown at him. He admitted that the program absorbed colossal sums of money but insisted on the idea that what had been invested in bettering the functioning of Paris would yield its returns by creating a much greater revenue for the City. According to him, the money borrowed was to be paid by growing sums of municipal taxes from a growing population, which went hand in hand with the growth in goods entering the city (which were taxed at the time) and in property values. This theory of "productive expenditure" is not solely Haussmann's, although he put it forward as a personal invention.[14] Nevertheless, it was Haussmann who took it upon himself to carry out this audacious policy, which progressively became more adventurous.

At the beginning, in the 1850s, the capital needed for public works was provided partly by the state and partly by loans voted by the *Corps Législatif*. At the time, Haussmann planned to cover a great part of the costs of the transformations by the surplus value created by them. The idea was to expropriate land and buildings at their value before the creation of new streets and sell the land adjacent to the newly created streets at the new value, much higher than the old one. This expectation soon proved unattainable when the juries of expropriation, created to bridge conflicts between public authorities and individual landlords, systematically found for the latter, who estimated the worth of their property according to the expected future value.

Haussman thus lost a most valuable source of revenue, but this setback did not stop him. On the contrary, during the 1860s, he behaved like any speculator having faith in his chance and created all sorts of mechanisms enabling him to borrow more and more money to cover an ever-spreading program and growing debts. He was issuing different kinds of municipal bonds, an uncommon practice that attracted much criticism from several state agencies, which argued that the *Préfet* was operating independently of all institutional controls. In 1860, the commission of budget had already expressed "its discontent with the issuing of bonds worth 15 million Francs by the *Caisse des travaux* according to a decree of 6 January 1859" (cf. Girard 1952: 170), but, as long as the Emperor supported him, he was unmovable, even if the opposition turned more and more against him personally, accusing him of fraudulent maneuvers and even of profiting personally from the Works.

The growing criticism led to Haussmann's dismissal in January 1870 and, twenty years later, to the publishing of the *Mémoires*, the main aim of which was to defend Haussmann from such charges. Haussmann went into much detail to explain the different loans contracted and bonds issued. He defended his reputation with much vigor, which is quite moving. But can we trust him? His arguments are based on his own official reports made when he was still *Préfet*, but what is the worth of such documents when the author himself is proud to explain his ability to juggle with numbers, hiding one expenditure behind another? In the first volume of his *Mémoires*, long before going into details about the accounts of the Works of Paris, Haussmann recalls a most telling episode. In August 1853, the Emperor asked him to provide more money for the remodeling of the Bois de Boulogne. Knowing that the Municipal Council would not let him use in advance money included in the 1854 budget, Haussmann decided to hide the supplementary expenditures by including them in those available for another project planned for the end of 1853, the purchase of land to increase the Bois de Boulogne (Haussmann 2000: vol. I, 409). Geneviève Massa-Gilles, in a most interesting and well-documented book on the subject, clearly explains the different means used by Haussmann to finance the Grand Works but is careful enough not to pass judgment on the balance sheet produced by Haussmann, repeating time and again that it impossible to verify his figures (Massa-Gilles 1973).

Incarnation of a Prestigious Social Type

The biographers are not disturbed by this question. They all agree that the great merit of the *Préfet* was to find all sorts of ways to bypass the inherent inefficiencies of the administration. They all suggest that he did not abide by the rules in financial matters, but they do not know how far he had pushed it. In fact, they do not much care to know. For them, what counts are the results: the transformations of Paris, his work.

For those who write about Haussmann, he is a "*grand commis de l'État*" (Lameyre 1958: 87; Choay, in Haussmann 2000: 21), an "incomparable administrator" (Hallays 1910), "an inspired executor" (Morizet 1932: 129). He is a particular exemplar of a French social type—*le grand commis de l'État*—which was personified through history by individuals such as Sully, Fouquet, Colbert, and Vauban. Haussmann is portraying himself as giving the impression "of our men of the State of bygone days" (Haussmann 1885: v)[15] and cites as an example Louis-Urbain-Aubert de Tourny, the eighteenth-century *intendant* (regional governor) responsible for prestigious public works in Bordeaux and several other neighboring towns.[16] When, at the end of his book, Chaudun (2000: 220) proceeds to a final appraisal of Haussmann, he compares him—somewhat negatively—to Fouquet and Colbert. The *grand commis de l'État* is a central figure of the French state culture. Other states do not all produce such a figure; they surely have worthy public servants, but these persons do not become cultural heroes, they do not incarnate a prestigious social figure. Outside France, people are often surprised to learn that the famous Haussmann was "only" a *préfet*, only an administrator. As for Haussmann, he gives an imperial tint to this particular social type. By defining his role as an "executing agent" (Haussmann 2000: vol. II, xiii), his modesty is not egregious; in fact, he aimed at the core of the Napoleonic ideal, defined already in 1840 by the future Emperor: "The Napoleonic idea gives importance only to things; it hates pointless words. The measures others discuss during ten years, it executes in only one year" (quoted by Lameyre 1958: 97). Being an "executing agent" in this kind of regime is a particular distinction that strengthens the role of a great administrator, already prestigious in the French social drama.

Haussmann personifies the social type many find necessary for French society. He is a figurehead for those who advocate strong town planning. One of the first to say so was Le Corbusier, for whom Haussmann was "a daring and courageous person."[17] It is Morizet, however, who makes the point much more clearly in his book, which is both a hymn to the glory of the *Préfet*, and a plea for modern regional planning (Morizet 1932). Paradoxically, fifty years later, the name of Haussmann attracted those who criticized modernistic town planning. In the meantime, during the 1960s and

1970s, Paris of the nineteenth century (more specifically the area around the Opera house) became a kind of ideal city for those who were repelled by the then-current urban renovation or by the huge new public housing estates. At the same time, the idea that Haussmann was the author of the "Transformations of Paris" was taken for granted. As a result, Haussmann began to be considered as a great town-planner. This is the way in which he is described today.[18]

Starting Afresh with Halbwachs

Fortunately, there is one author who was not obsessed by Haussmann and who attributed to him neither all the glory of the Great Works nor all their misfortunes. This is the young Maurice Halbwachs[19] who, at the age of thirty-four, wrote his meticulous *Les Expropriations et les Prix des Terrains à Paris* (Halbwachs 1909). This book is well known by all authors interested in the transformations of Paris during the second half of the nineteenth century. Haussmann's biographers, however, do not take it into account. It is true that this book must seem strange for those who start with the idea that these prestigious urban transformations are the work of one person, perhaps two. With this kind of perspective on human affairs, it is difficult to take seriously someone who stated that

> The individuals who were in charge of executing new streets, despite their authoritarian approach and their probable desire to leave their personal mark on these works, had to submit to the social needs manifested in the city ... Their own intervention touched only modalities, only details, but did not modify nor contradict the play of collective forces.
>
> (Halbwachs 1909: 377)

And, as if this statement were not enough, Halbwachs insisted on and emphasized the importance of the scale of intervention: "The larger the transformation aimed at, the more it has to prolong in a way the natural movement of the evolution of the city in order to succeed. In consequence, one has to submit to circumstances instead of commanding them" (Halbwachs 1909: 11).

Let us take one example. It is by now a commonly accepted idea that the debate that was to lead to the *Grands Travaux* had already begun in the 1840s, when some people were alerted by the fact that Paris was "moving" in a northwesterly direction. These people argued that prestigious activities and dwellings of the rich were migrating toward the *Grands Boulevards* (ancient limit of the city) and even to the *faubourgs* situated beyond.[20] These people pleaded for drastic measures to be taken and suggested opening all sorts of new streets through the historic parts of city or even a complete renewal of the *Ile de la Cité*, the heart of old Paris. The basic idea was to bring prestigious activities and dwellings back to the center of town by bettering conditions there and enhancing its image, thus increasing the value of its land, which was by then declining.

However, the *Grands Travaux* accomplished just the opposite, as they mainly strengthened the movement toward the west. The movement to the northwest changed its direction as a result, among other factors, of the creation of the Saint-Lazare railway station. It is in this direction, just beyond the *Grands Boulevards*, that the most symbolic public building of the time, the Opera House, was built. It is toward this building that the most emblematic of all new streets of Paris, the *Avenue de l'Opéra*, was opened up. It is in the west of Paris where the majestic *Avenue de l'Impératrice* was created; starting at the newly designed *Place de l'Étoile* (toward which were opened several impressive avenues) and leading toward the newly laid out leisure grounds for the well-to-do, the *Bois de Boulogne*. It is in these parts of the city that the area adjacent to the *Parc Monceaux* was developed, which attracted many wealthy people; it is there that the *Boulevard Haussmann* was opened—what a symbol—beside which were built two most prestigious department stores and the headquarters of major banks. The area around the Opera House and the *Boulevard Haussmann* attracted luxurious apartment houses, grand cafés, and elegant shops. It became the center of modern bourgeois life that gave to Paris the title of the "capital of the nineteenth century."

The rest of the city did not follow suit. Although *Ile de la Cité* was totally renovated to become a kind of administrative center endowed with a huge hospital, it completely lost the dense urban life that once took place there. The new streets of the center—the *Boulevard de Sébastopol* or that part of *Rue du Rivoli* east of the Louvre—are dull compared to their western counterparts. Similarly, the hustle and bustle of the *Place de la République* or the *Place de la Bastille* (the two other large squares connected to the *Grands Boulevards*) has little to do with the kind of activities related to the *Place de l'Opéra*. And what should we say about the *Place de la Nation* compared to the *Place de l'Étoile*? In fact, the *Grands Travaux* accentuated the split between the western and eastern parts of Paris.

Manners of City Making

The evolution of the *Grands Travaux,* which started with the ambition to save the center of Paris and ended with the strengthening of the west of the city, underlines the good sense of Halbwachs's thesis. The transformations of Paris result from general urban dynamics and not from the will of a small number of individuals. Halbwachs, however, pushed his ideas too far. According to him, new streets were created as a quasi-natural reaction to the growth in population. Halbwachs was hampered by his reaction against those who exaggerate the role of individuals in the making of cities. He was also limited by the fact that he was considering Paris during the years 1860–1900, independently of different developments elsewhere in France and abroad. More generally, he gave the impression that the functioning of a city is only a matter of the circulation of persons and goods. Halbwachs, who would later stress the importance of notions such as "collective memory," seems here to simplify the making of cities, a complex human activity that could figure as one of Ernst Cassirer's symbolic forms (Cassirer 1944).

Societies do not produce their cities in direct reaction to new material necessities. The representation of social needs is not derived directly from demographic or technical changes. Neither are the solutions that are meant to satisfy those needs. Moreover, the relationships between needs and solutions are not very simple. Solutions forged for old needs are sometimes applied to new ones; in a way, they can precede them. Means count as well: financial possibilities, legal measures, administrative structures, and other social frameworks also shape ideas and realizations. To render things even more complicated, time influences the making of cities. On the one hand, solutions, needs, means, and ideas do not evolve with the same rhythms. On the other, each intervention takes a long time, a factor that often causes many modifications and, sometimes, changes the meaning of programs. This is why the same kinds of demographic developments do not always lead to the same kinds of urban transformations in all societies, at all periods. Each culture, at each period, develops its own manners of making cities. Not all growing cities cut streets through the dense center of their towns.

The Role of Singular Agents

The different manners of making cities evolve slowly because they are shaped by the interaction of many social forces. This is why they are different from scientific paradigms, which describe the evolution of habits and conventions within narrower circles. This is why there is no revolution in town-making manners but rather uneven "evolutions," which result from uncoordinated developments taking place in different social spheres, which are only partly synchronic. The role of individuals is not negligible in this complex process.

Halbwachs demanded, as the proof of the decisive role of an individual in the act of opening a street, that "his initiative should be taken independently of social tendencies existing already or against them" (Halbwachs 1909: 12). It was—and is—an impossible demand; it is only a good polemical argument addressed at all the worshippers of Great Men, who assign to these exceptional individuals a kind of extra-social position. It goes without saying that every individual is a product of history and of society; for each of his or her acts, we can find a historical cause or an appropriate social current, to paraphrase Halbwachs himself (1909: 67). It is true, however, that a historically and socially made individual can in return weigh on his formative framework.

In France, the history of opening streets through cities goes back to the middle of the eighteenth century. It culminated in the period *c.*1850–80, when it became the dominating urbanistic manner that created the emblematic urbanistic figure of the period, the *percée* (known, mainly in English, as the "Haussmannian boulevard"; Darin 1987). It lasted until the 1960s.[21] In this long history, Napoléon III and Haussmann are not as insignificant as Halbwachs would suggest. Obviously, both do not invent the idea of opening new streets through Paris. Even the plan that Napoléon III is supposed to have given to Haussmann in 1853 cannot be considered as a personal masterpiece. In fact, it brought together all sorts of ideas that were circulating at the time in the circles interested in such matters; it was also closely followed by another document, the report of the commission head by Count Siméon (see Casselle 2000) which, in turn, was only a step in the ongoing process of the definition of the *Grands Travaux*. We know today that the plan presented to Haussmann on June 29, 1853 was only a step in a long process. It was preceded by a few others and was followed by the report of the Commission des Embellissements de Paris signed by Count Siméon on December 20. Later, ideas about opening streets continued to change during the 1850s and more so during the 1860s (Casselle 2000; Gaillard 1997; Pinon 2002; van Zanten 2001). The real issue with the mythical plan of June 29, 1853 is the status of any town plan. One often refers to this kind of document as if it were an architectural blueprint. Or is an urbanistic plan of a different nature? The stock of ideas presented on such a document is often only a milestone in a long social process. The definition and execution of an urbanistic project being a long collective work, it is punctuated by many plans, among which only the last is—*a posteriori*—proven to be the definitive one (Fig. 6.2).

Neither Napoléon III nor Haussmann created all the instruments of the 1853 plan, without which it would have been impossible to proceed to wide-ranging expropriations: cadastral plans, expropriation laws, competent state and municipal services, and so on. They did not create the demand for new housing in the center of Paris, nor were they responsible for the economic cycle, which made construction possible.

The Emperor and the *Préfet* could, however, reap the results of a wide range of developments concerning different aspects of city building. Both were social conductors who helped to accelerate a social movement while giving it a somehow personal touch. Napoléon III insisted on the role of Paris as a capital. In a regime obsessed with the glory of France, such a consideration led to the reshaping of the city. As the head of the state, some of the Emperor's decisions influenced the chain of events. He decided to appoint a new *préfet*. He participated in the public ceremonies, which were held for the opening of major new streets. These ceremonies were declared to be public holidays. All these details, as Halbwachs would say, amounted to the creation of a political atmosphere, which

FIGURE 6.2 *Les grandes percées*, Paris, France, 1848–1870

weakened the resistance against the opening of streets. This atmosphere influenced events outside Paris where, in many cities, streets were cut through the center without much necessity—in Nantes, for example (Darin 1994). Without the Emperor's personal touch, would Paris have reshaped existing "green spaces" and created new ones in the second half of the nineteenth century?

Haussmann also influenced the transformations of Paris. He interpreted the role of *Préfet* of the Seine *départment* differently than would a Vaïsse or a Le Roy. Before appointing Haussmann, Persigny had thought that these two other *préfets* could equally well have become the *préfet* of the *département de la Seine*. Claude-Marius Vaïsse later brilliantly carried out the task of renovating Lyon, and Ernest Hilaire Le Roy did the same regarding Rouen. At the beginning, in the early 1850s, when a consensual program was executed, his personal involvement is probably less tangible. The extension of the Rue de Rivoli, the creation of the Boulevard de Strasbourg et de Sébastopol, the opening up of the boulevard Malesherbes, and the creation of an east–west axis through the left Bank would all have been executed in any event. At the time, most of those who were interested in urban affairs approved of the works carried out. There was, as in all cities, an opposition against the opening of new arteries organized by landlords, merchants, and artisans whose interests were related to the existing arteries (the old "high" streets) and who were afraid to suffer from the competition of the new streets, but a Vaïsse or a Le Roy would not be very disturbed by it, as they were not disturbed by opposition in Lyon[22] or Rouen. They would probably also help in creating efficient water and sewage systems. Haussmann was very proud of the accomplishments under the leadership of Belgrand, and was, perhaps, personally responsible for some important decisions taken. However, these kinds of systems were created in all cities regardless of whether exceptional persons were in charge of affairs. In Rouen, Belgrand helped LeRoy install such a system.

Discord

The personal imprint of Haussmann becomes more tangible when he was operating outside shared opinions. This happened in the 1860s when the process for many of the streets being opened up was far from being consensual, when there was less public money for the *Grands Travaux*, and when Haussmann was becoming more and more adventurous in his way of conducting financial affairs.

Jeanne Gaillard (1997) insists on the point that, in the 1860s, the nature of the *Grands Travaux* was changing. According to her, the opening up of the congested center was no longer an issue.[23] The main issue then, she insists, was the industrial nature of the capital. On the one hand, there were industrialists whose businesses were in the annexed *arrondissements*; on the other hand, those who opposed the idea of Paris as an industrial center. Haussmann took sides with the latter and decided to withhold tax exemption, from which these industries benefited after the annexation. Gaillard (1997: 47–60) argues that the opening up of many new streets in the peripheral *arrondissements* was also done to encourage the transformation of industrial areas into residential neighborhoods. The question of the expansion of Paris is very important. For Lavedan, Haussmann was somehow behind his times, as he ignored this most important issue. In terms of expansion, the *Grands Travaux*, according to Lavedan, suffer from the comparison to the plans of New York of 1811 and of Barcelona of 1856.[24]

> In 1850 the Commission départementale de la Seine demanded that an overall plan should coordinate the direction of all the streets of Paris with the main roads existing outside the city. The *Préfet*, from 1853 to 1860, conducted the interventions with practically no consideration for the roads going through the neighbouring boroughs. After the annexation of the latter to Paris, he never thought about the areas situated beyond the fortifications.
>
> (Lavedan 1954: 76)

Less important perhaps—it was only a detail for Halbwachs—but much clearer (as so much was written about it) is the issue of demolition. A great number of engravings, paintings, photographs, and writings emphasized the incredible sacrifice of old Paris. For once, it was not water, earth, fire, or arms that reduced a city to ruins. It was, rather, hand tools and wheelbarrows that carried away buildings, streets, and souvenirs. Here again, in spite of the stupefaction about the scale of operations, there was much agreement. There was, then, a shared belief, among those who had a say in public affairs, in the worthlessness of the ordinary urban fabric; all minor streets and buildings were believed to deserve demolition for the sake of hygiene. In the mid-nineteenth century, consensus about conservation concerned only major monuments. No one thought of demolishing them. On the contrary: all new streets respected these buildings, many were opened up in the direction of monument, and others passed by as many major buildings as possible. It was a question of mutual valorization, of monuments, and of the new streets.

There was, however, an area of discord. The attitudes of those interested in urban affairs were changing. Some buildings, without being considered as monuments, started to be defended for the sake of art or in the name of historical souvenirs. It was mainly a question of relatively minor churches and some aristocratic *Hôtels*. A change of attitudes also concerned the shape of streets. Until then, it was widely admitted that a new street had to be as straight as possible, in opposition to winding streets, perceived as the horrendous legacy of the medieval period. However, in the mid-nineteenth century, some began to think that it was possible to break a straight line if it meant the conservation of what they considered a worthy building. Siméon's commission, for instance, mentioned such a solution, which was in accordance with the Emperor's wishes. The third "rule" of the seven defined by the *Commission des embellissements de Paris* according to "the desires of the Emperor" stated that

> important streets will follow as many lines as judged necessary by the architects in order to avoid demolishing either monuments or beautiful houses while keeping the same width of the streets; in this manner one would not be slave to the exclusively straight line.
>
> (Casselle 2000: 47)

Apparently however, Haussmann and those working with him had quite a pronounced classical taste and preferred a good old perfectly straight line—preferably with a monument at its end—to any other solution. With this idea in mind, his team caused the destruction of many buildings and earned him the title of Vandal (cf. Raval 1943; Pillement 1941, 1943; Réau 1959).

This is an example showing that the personal preference of an agent—the *préfet* or other people occupying major posts at the time—can count. It happens when the existing social tendencies, to take Halbwach's term, permit different lines of action. Single agents thus have a greater personal influence on events when an old consensus is breaking down and a new one has not yet emerged (Darin 2009: 357–402).

Semantic Overflows

Those who criticize what, for them, is a dull aspect of the new streets created in Paris in the second half of the nineteenth century turn against Haussmann as if he were responsible for them. It is true that Haussmann, in his *Mémoires*, shows a preference for uniform architecture (Haussmann 2000). It is also true that, as a result of a document he signed on October 5, 1855, all contracts for the sale of land by the municipality included precise instructions: "The façade will be constructed from cut stone with balcony, cornices and mouldings. The purchasers [of land] and their neighbours could agree to have the same height of floors thus creating continuing horizontal lines making the city block one architectural unit" (see Darin 1986: 26). Such a document proves that there was an idea of the desirable appearance of buildings, but the imprecise phrasing of this document ("could agree," for instance) also demonstrates that the administration did not wish to go too far and scare future buyers by imposing too many constraints. Thus the appearance of the streets, which are, for us, a synonym of uniformity, is due less to Haussmann's ideas and his way of operating than to the shared architectural culture of the time, common to landlords, architects, and builders.[25]

This is why it is far too much of an exaggeration to name the style of buildings constructed during the Second Empire as "Haussmannian." One could think that this way of naming a style corresponds to old habits, those who gave other labels such as *Style Louis XIV*. However, beside the fact that Haussmann was a *préfet* and not a monarch, it is interesting to note that, this time, the usage becomes original because it extends beyond the period of the Second Empire and covers the next fifty years. David van Zanten argues this point nicely:

> Contemporary photographs make it evident that such characteristically "Haussmannian" passages as the Châtelet or the Place de l'Opéra were clearly islands of new construction afloat in a then-considered sea of older buildings, and that Haussmann's cornice line was less a limit to cut construction down than a goal to tempt building up.
>
> (van Zanten 2001: 202)

This kind of exaggeration covers not merely exterior appearance, because the term "Haussmannian apartment houses" now tends to be used to identify all apartment houses constructed between 1840 and the First World War. Once again, many know that this name is "abusive," but it is now part of everyday language. The same is true of "Haussmannian boulevards" or the "Haussmannian block," the latter used today by architects in a much wider sense than when it was first introduced—and which was by then already misused—to the point that it currently means "traditional block," as if such an entity existed. The triangular "Haussmannian block" has nothing to do with blocks related to streets opened through the center of the city. It is a block resulting from street configuration in the peripheral areas; it had already appeared in a few layouts created outside the center of Paris in the 1820s.

Singular Agents and the Evolution of Cities

Haussmannian styles, Haussmannian apartment houses, Haussmannian blocs, Haussmannian boulevards, and Haussmannian Paris are short-cuts we use to indicate what became a planner's desired city since the 1970s. This designation prolongs habits already begun under the Second Empire and continued into the 1930s by those who were then calling for drastic urbanistic measures and for whom the transformations of Paris during the second half of the nineteenth century were the example of what planning could do. In extension, biographers were interested in the career of the *Préfet* as a model of the *grand commis de l'État*. In all these cases, the interest taken in Haussmann and "his" work combine history and the will for action.

It is out of this interaction that the history of urbanism was born: history that was used to legitimize the activity it was studying. This history, however, tends to focus too much on the role of individuals, even when mentioning the need to understand the role of such persons in wider context. It is, therefore, important to combine works issuing from this tradition with the readings of the *Grands Travaux* coming from social urban history; even though these latter authors, for whom the city is mainly a social organism, are less interested in the ways by which the physical environment is created and thus do not confront directly the tradition that assigns an overwhelming importance to the *Préfet* in the changes that took place in Paris during the second half of the nineteenth century.[26] A third important approach is morphological history, which is interested in the physical evolution of urban fabric over long spans of time. It examines the evolution of a plan of a city during the centuries; it focuses on the processes by which building typologies develop, either by internal mechanisms or by import of foreign elements. This approach is less concerned in "Great Men" and thus permits us to better understand the contribution of singular agents to the evolution of cities.[27]

It is by combining these three approaches that this chapter has attempted to sketch a framework that could help to understand the relationship between an individual and the general social dynamics that shape the evolution of a city. Leaving aside important issues (the idea that streets were opened for military reasons and that poorer populations were exiled out of Paris, for instance), it has tried to show that within the limits of a period, each person interprets his social role in a particular way and that his interpretation is more clearly evident where the limits in question—which are not fixed forever—are blurred because they are changing.[28] At the same time, it has been suggested throughout this chapter that there is a major handicap in arriving at a satisfying account concerning the role of Haussmann in the transformations of Paris during the second half of the nineteenth century: the importance of the *Préfet*'s *Mémoires* in all the historical accounts of this process. No one manages to forget this book. And in this sense, and only in this sense, Haussmann is, and will remain (perhaps forever), the absolute author of the *Grands travaux de Paris*.

Notes

1 Jean des Car, who thirteen years earlier had written *Haussmann: la gloire du Second Empire*, takes up some aspects of the life of the *Préfet*. Pierre Pinon summarizes existing knowledge on the Works. Seventeen other authors contribute short articles on different points of the Transformations of Paris.

2 Publications were particularly abundant in 2000: Nicolas Chaudun, *Haussmann au Crible*; Georges Valance, *Haussmann le Grand*; Michel Carmona, *Haussmann*; and Françoise Choay's edition of Haussmann's *Mémoires*. Two years later, two further books were published: Pinon's *Atlas du Paris Haussmannien,*and a finely illustrated book by Patrice de Moncan and Claude Heurteux, *Le Paris d'Haussmann*.

3 This term is used, for instance, in real estate advertisements.

4 Jean Marc Larbodière's *Reconnaître les Façades* (2000) names the different styles of the façades of Parisian apartment houses by referring to periods (such as Middle-Ages, sixteenth century, 1930–9), to kings (Louis XIII, Louis Philippe, etc.), and to accepted stylistic terms (*Art Nouveau* and *Art Déco*). In this context, Haussmann is an exception: He is the only non-royal person who is used to qualify a style, and his is the only name used to qualify more than one style: "*Le style Haussmannien* (1850–70)", "*L'immeuble post-Haussmannien* (1870–95)" and "*Derniers feux* [last glows of] *Haussmanniens* (1895–1914)"!

5 The most eloquent account of the Parisian urban fabric of the nineteenth century is given by François Loyer (1987), whose book can be seen as the *a posteriori* theory of *Haussmannisme*, the one element that, according to the author, was missing for the glory of this manner of city making. Loyer writes: "*Haussmannisme* missed theoreticians: it this absence of intellectual dignity which undermined its reputation mainly in France where the value of artistic production is very often judged by the intelligence of the discourse which accompanies it" (Loyer 1987: 471). In this sense, the *Haussmannisme* of Loyer is quite similar to the Manhattanism of Rem Koolhaas; the difference between the two—and it is not negligible—is that, in the one case, it is the name of a state administrator that is used to designate an overall social phenomenon and, in the other, the name of a place.

6 This term was created by those who advocated this kind of policy and is used today mainly by its critics.

7 It is noteworthy that only one other title in this series of five volumes refers to a personal name: It is the second, *La Ville Médiévale: des Carolingiens à la Renaissance*, in which appears the name of the Carolingians; however, this is a dynasty and not an individual.

8 The quotation marks are even used with some kind of irony, as in the title of a symposium held in Paris in 1999, the proceedings of which were published two years later (Bowie 2001).

9 Chaudun, for instance, states that "Haussmann gathered all his speeches, notes and drafts of letters he had in his possession and prepared these ingredients with heavy and lumpy sauce. The sharp pen that was once used to whip his opponents now left him as well. Presumptuousness and lies weaken much of his defense speech" (author's translation: Chaudun 2000: 218).

10 The fidelity to the *Mémoires* is mainly a result of the scarcity of other sources. The fire that burned down the town hall and its annexes has been mentioned; but Haussmann's personal archives also disappeared. David P. Jordan, who had the ambition—as he tells it—of writing an Anglo-Saxon-style biography based on as many documents as possible, came back after many pleasant trips through France ("the best part of the undertaking") with very few findings (Jordan 1995: xix).

11 Haussmann's biographers are, by now, numerous and include Georges Laronze 1932; Gérard Lameyre 1958; Pierre-André Touttain 1971; Henri Malet 1973; des Cars 1978; Chaudun 2000; Valance 2000; and Carmona 2000.

12 Chaudun (2000: 218), for instance, writes "it is tedious to read the *Mémoires* but they do give a faithful panorama of the administration of the time; they contain more information than any other thesis about the method and the means used then in Paris"; Choay goes much further by considering the *Mémoires* as a "*magistral discours de la méthode*" (Haussmann, ed. Choay 2000: 34). Even Pinon (2002), who shows the

shortcomings of his title *Paris Haussmannien* by his sub-title, *La ville en héritage du Second Empire à nos jours* (the city in heritage from the Second Empire until today) and who is aware of the collective dimension of the *Grands Travaux*, is resigned to giving the highest priority to the *Préfet* by the structure of the book, which is composed of seven chapters: (1) Paris before the Second Empire, (2) The project of Napoléon III and Haussmann for Paris, (3) The *Grands Travaux* of Paris, (4) The Haussmannian system and the persons, (5) The Haussmannian landscape, (6) The urban projects carried out by Haussmann, (7) The effects of the *transformation de Paris* and Haussmannian posterity.

13 The physical aspects of the *Préfet* are significant. Bernard Le Clère and Vincent Wright (1973: 163) quote an article by Emmanuel Arène who criticizes the *préfets* of the Third Republic: "They no longer have this beautiful and imposing bearing, this admirable appearance which made the *préfets* of the Empire resemble a corps of administrative *cent-gardes* [Napoléon III's honorary guards]."

14 Persigny (de Laire 1896: 244) says that he suggested it to Haussmann. Pinon (2002: 58) argues that Hippolyte Meynadier had already advanced this idea in 1843; and de Moncan, P. and Heurteux (2002: 66) mention that Pierre Magne developed this theme in 1846. In fact, the concept of "productive expenditures" applies to Parisian ideas in vogue in the Saint Simonian circles.

15 Haussmann, *Joli Sentier*, 1885: a poem Haussmann wrote and published himself.

16 "In his speech in the Senate on 6 June 1861, Haussmann makes a parallel between the *intendant* Tourny and himself" (Lameyre 1958: 96).

17 Le Corbusier, as an attentive reader, drew out of the *Mémoires* the lesson which was important for him: "What Haussmann did is really impressive. And while destroying chaos he fortified the Emperor"s finances." For Le Corbusier, such an example was most important because it helped him to argue that "Urbanism does not cost, it creates wealth" (Le Corbusier 1966: 149).

18 The title of *urbaniste* is given to him at the present. Choay (in Haussmann 2000: 10) goes further, explaining that Haussmann was, without knowing it, one of the founders of town planning, a discipline whose real founder, according to her, was Cerdà.

19 Halbwachs was later to become, and remains to the present day, regarded as one of the main French sociologists.

20 The first historical work on this subject is Pierre Lavedan (1969).

21 The main streets in reconstructed cities such as Royan and Saint-Dié are the embodiment of an aesthetic ideal going back to the Rue Royale created in both Orleans and Paris during 1750 and to the model in this matter: the Rue de Rivoli, designed in 1802. The last *percée* was executed during the 1960s in Le Mans and is named Avenue Charles de Gaulle.

22 Ollivier (1895–1915: vol. III, 87) notes that Vaïsse was a distinguished administrator; with opposite qualities (measure, tact, and moderation), he obtained the same success in Lyon as did Haussmann in Paris.

23 It would continue, however, in the 1870s and 1880s with the opening up of most of the Avenue de l'Opera, half of the Boulevard Saint-Germain, and the creation of the Rue de Quatre Septembre and Rue Etienne Marcel.

24 The same argument had already been used by Lavedan (1952: 123). Twenty years later, however, Lavedan, in a seventy-page description of the *Grands Travaux*, did not bring it up (Lavedan 1975).

25 Today, the same kind of document would in no way assist in creating the same kind of homogeneous urban landscape; the present architectural culture favors efforts aiming at individual distinction, and any self-respecting architect would expend much effort to bypass such instructions.

26 Jeanne Gaillard (1997) disagrees with this or that interpretation given to this or that act and stresses the fact that the nature of the works changed after the annexation of 1860, and so on and gives obvious importance to general urban dynamics; but she does not challenge the personal importance given to the *Préfet* and the Emperor in the transformations of Paris. Florence Bourillon (1992, 2002) continues within the same tradition and shows how complex the transformations were and suggests that the role of Haussmann is often overestimated.

27 To mention only two examples: No "Great Man" is present in the long evolution of Alnwick (Conzen 1960) and, even in Florence, the role of exceptional individuals is minimized (Caniggia 1986).

28 For the notion of a limit:

> Is there not a limit, a ceiling, which borders the entire life of men, envelops it like a more or less large frontier, which is difficult to reach and even more to get over? It is the limit which is established in every period, even ours, between the *possible* and the *impossible*, between that which can be achieved, not without difficulty, and that which remains refused to men ... (Braudel 1979: 11).

References

Alphand, A. (1867–73) *Les Promenades de Paris*. Paris: J. Rothschild.
Belgrand, E. (1873–87) *Les Travaux Souterrain de Paris*. Paris: Ch. Dunod.
Beneveolo, L. (1960) *Storia dell'archittetura Moderna*, transl. as *History of Modern Architecture*. Cambridge, MA: MIT Press (1977).
Benevolo, L. (1977) *History of Modern Architecture vol. 1: The Tradition of Modern Architecture*. Cambridge, MA: MIT Press.
Bourillon, F. (1992) *Les Villes en France au XIXe Siècle*. Paris: Ophrys.
Bourillon, F. (2001) À propos de la commission des embellissements, in K. Bowie (ed.), *La Modernité Avant Haussmann*, 139–51. Paris: Éditions Recherches.
Bourillon, F. (2002) Des relectures d'Haussmann. *Histoire Urbaine*, 5: 189–99.
Bowie, K. (ed.) (2001) *La Modernité avant Haussmann*. Paris: Éditions Recherches.
Braudel, F. (1979) *Civilsation Matérielle, Économie et Capitalisme, XVe—XVIIIe Siècle; Vol I: Les Strucutures du Quotidien*. Paris: Armand Colin.
Bresler, F. (1999) *Napoleon III: A Life*. London: HarperCollins.
Caniggia, G. (1986) *Lecture de Florence*. Brussels: Insitut Supérior d'Architecture Saint-Luc.
des Cars, J. (1978) *Haussmann: La Gloire du Second Empire*. Paris: Librairie Académique Perrin.
des Cars, J., and Pinon, P. (1991) *Paris-Haussmann*. Paris: Picard.
Carmona, M. (2000) *Haussmann*. Paris: Fayard.
Casselle, P. (ed.) (2000) Commission des embellissements de Paris: rapport à l'Empereur Napoléon III. *Cahiers de la Rotonde* [special issue], 23.
Cassirer, E. (1944) *An Essay on Man*. New Haven: Yale University Press.
Castex, J., Depaule, J.-Ch., and Panerai, P. (1977) *Formes Urbaines: De l'Ilot à la Barre*. Paris: Dunod; transl. with I. Samuels, *Urban Forms: The Death and Life of the Urban Block*. Oxford: Architectural Press (2004).
Chaudun, N. (2000) *Haussmann au Crible*. Paris: Éditions des Syrthes.
le Clère, B., and Wright, V. (1973) *Les Préfets du Second Empire*. Paris: Armand Colin, for the Fondation Nationale des Sciences Politiques.
Conzen, M. R. G. (1960) *Alnwick, Northumberland: A Study in Town-Plan Analysis*. London: George Philip, Institute of British Geographers Publication 27.
Le Corbusier (1966) *Urbanisme*. Paris: V. Fréal (first published 1924 by G. Grès, Paris).
Darin, M. (1986) *Immeubles du Boulevard Saint Germain*. Nantes: Ville Recherche Diffusion.
Darin, M. (1987) *La Grande Percée*. Paris: Bureau de la Recherche Architecturale.
Darin, M. (1994) La rue de Strasbourg à Nantes. *Revue de l'Art*, 106: 59–66.
Darin, M. (2009) *La Comédie Urbaine: Voir la Ville Autrement*. Gallion: Infolio Éditions.
Duby, G. (ed.) (1980–5) *Histoire de la France Urbaine*. Paris: Seuil.
Dudilieu, J.-J. (2002) Les concessions à l'époque d'Haussmann, in J. des Cars and P. Pinon (eds.), *Paris-Haussmann*, 226–30. Paris: Picard.
Ferry, J. (1868) *Les Comptes Fantastiques d'Haussmann*. Paris: Armand Le Chevalier.
Frampton, K. (1985) *Modern Architecture: A Critical History*. London: Thames and Hudson.
Gaillard, J. (1997) *Paris: La Ville, 1850–1870*. Paris: L'Harmattan (originally a thesis, 1975).
Girard, L. (1952) *La Politique des Travaux Publics du Second Empire*. Paris: Armand Colin.
Halbwachs, M. (1909) *Les Expropriations et les Prix des Terrains à Paris, 1860–1900*. Paris: E. Cornély et Cie.
Hallays, A. (1910) Haussmann et les travaux de Paris sous le second Empire, *Le Revue Hébdomadaire*, 5 February: 31–51.
Haussmann, G.-E. (1885) *Joli Sentier*. Clagney: Haussmann (self-published).
Haussmann, G.-E. (2000) *Mémoires du Baron Haussmann* [ed. prepared by F. Choay]. Paris: Éditions du Seuil (first published 1890–3).
Horn, J. E. (1869) *Les Finances de l'Hôtel de Ville*. Paris: E. Dentu.
Jordan, D. P. (1995) *Transforming Paris: The Life and Labors of Baron Haussmann*. New York: The Free Press.
de Laire, H. (ed.) (1896) *Mémoires du Duc de Persigny*. Paris: E. Plon, Nourrit & Cie.

Landau, B., and Gauthier, V. S.-M. (2000) Actualité de l'œuvre haussmannienne, in G.-E. Haussmann, *Mémoires du Baron Haussmann* [ed. prepared by F. Choay], 41–61. Paris: Éditions du Seuil.

Lameyre, G. (1958) *Haussmann: Préfet de Paris*. Paris: Flammarion Editeur.

Larbodière, J.-M. (2000) *Reconnaître les Façades: Du Moyen Âge à nos Jours, à Paris*. Paris: Massin.

Laronze, G. (1932) *Le Baron Haussmann*. Paris: Librairie Félix Alcan.

Lavedan, P. (1952) *Histoire de l'Urbanisme: Époque Contemporaine*. Paris: Henri Laurens.

Lavedan, P. (1954) Mérites et torts d'Haussmann urbaniste, in L. Réau, P. Lavedan, R. Plouin, J. Hugueney, and R. Auzelle, *L'Œuvre du Baron Haussmann*, 74–80. Paris: Presses Universitaires de France.

Lavedan, P. (1969) *La Question du Déplacement de Paris et du Transfert des Halles au Conseil Municipal sou la Monarchie de Juillet*. Paris: Ville de Paris, Sous-Commission de Recherches d'Histoire Municipale Contemporaine.

Lavedan, P. (1975) *Histoire de l'Urbanisme de Paris*. Paris: Diffusion Hachette.

Londei, E. F. (1982) *La Parigi di Haussmann: La Trasformazione Urbanistica di Parigi Durante il Secondo Impero*. Rome: Edizioni Kappa.

Loyer, F. (1987) *Paris XIXe Siècle: l'Immeuble et la Rue*. Paris: Hazan.

Malet, H. (1973) *Le Baron Haussmann et la Rénovation de Paris*. Paris: Les Éditions Municipales.

Massa-Gilles, G. (1973) *Histoire des Emprunts de la Ville de Paris, 1814–1875*. Paris: Ville de Paris, Commission des Travaux Historiques.

Merruau, C. (1875) *Souvenirs de l'Hôtel de Ville, 1848–1852*. Paris: Plon.

de Moncan, P., and Heurteux, C. (2002) *Le Paris d'Haussmann*. Paris: Les Éditions du Mécène.

de Moncan, P., and Heurteux, C. (eds.) (2003) *Villes Haussmannienne: Bordeaux, Lilles, Lyon, Marseille*. Paris: Les Éditions du Mécène.

Morizet, A. (1932) *Du Vieux Paris au Paris Moderne: Haussmann et ses Prédécesseurs*. Paris: Hachette.

Ollivier, E. (1895–1915) *L'Empire Libérale: Études, Réits, Souvenirs*. Paris: Garnier Frères.

Ollivier, E. (1961) *Journal 1846–1869*. Paris: R. Julliard.

Pillement, G. (1941) *Destruction de Paris*. Paris: Grasset.

Pillement, G. (1943) Démolitions présentes et futures, in B. Champigneulle et al. (collected volume) *Destinée de Paris*, 79–108. Paris: Les Éditions du Chêne.

Pinkney, D. H. (1958) *Napoléon III and the Rebuilding of Paris*. Princeton: Princeton University Press.

Pinon, P. (2002) *Atlas du Paris Haussmannien: La Ville en Héritage du Second Empire à nos Jours*. Paris: Parigramme.

Raval, M. (1943) Haussmann contre Paris, in B. Champigneulle et al. (collected volume) *Destinée de Paris*, 43–78. Paris: Les Éditions du Chêne.

Réau, L. (1959) *Histoire du Vandalisme: Les Monuments Détruits de l'Art Français*. Paris: Hachette (reprinted 1994, Paris: Robert Lafont).

Smith, W. H. C. (1972) *Napoléon III*. London: Wayland.

Touttain, P.-A. (1971) *Haussmann: Artisan du Second Empire, Créateur du Paris Moderne*. Paris: Libraire Gründ.

Valance, G. (2000) *Haussmann le Grand*. Paris: Flammarion.

van Zanten, D. (2001) How much Haussmann was there in Haussmannisation, in B. C. Scheer and K. Stanilov (eds.), *Proceedings of the International Seminar on Urban Form*, 201–3. Cincinnati, OH: University of Cincinnati.

7

COLONIAL REGIME CHANGE AND URBAN FORM

How Russian Novo-Arkhangel'sk Became American Sitka

Michael P. Conzen

> The town of Sitka, founded in 1799, contained at the time of transfer less than a thousand inhabitants, and, in its every appearance and arrangement, was totally un-American...
>
> C. Delevan Bloodgood (1869)

> Sitka in 1865:— The houses were all of logs, but painted a dull yellow, the metal roofs were red and with the emerald green spire of the church, projected against the dark evergreen of the adjacent hills, presented an extremely picturesque appearance. It was quite unlike anything else in America, and seemed to belong to a world of its own.
>
> William H. Dall (1870: 255)

In all but dynastic civilizations, urban form throughout history has been to some degree in flux. The rates of change have varied by region and historical period, but changes to the built environment at whatever pace have usually come through evolution rather than revolution. Changing requirements of urban populations, however imperfectly and with whatever delay, have inevitably brought pressure on the physical fabric to adjust. It is commonplace to assume a time lag between pressing social needs and actual reconstruction, because of cost and organization. It is also common to assume that such overall change is relatively routine in the case of mature cities, quite rapid in the case of new cities, and perhaps even radical in the case of cities overtaken by wars, natural catastrophes, or revolutionary changes in political regimes.

History is replete with examples of cities that have passed from the domination of one political power to another, in which the triumphant authority compels changes to the central institutions of the society and their buildings to reflect the new order. Depending on the character of the ascendant power, colonial regime change can mean either catastrophic ruin and rebuilding, even abandonment, or perhaps little or no immediate change. The literature of urban morphology, with its central focus on the complex composition and dynamics of the physical fabric of cities, has yet to develop a broad theoretical approach to urban transformation under conditions of colonial regime change. This chapter, therefore, seeks to contribute to such a conceptual framework by exploring the dynamics of one case with special characteristics and with an emphasis on the multiple agency behind the transformation that attended the shift in governing power.

The case concerns the only overseas colonial capital ever established by the Russian Empire: Novo-Arkhangel'sk (New Archangel), or Sitka as it later became known. It was created to coordinate the hugely profitable exploitation of marine resources in the northern Pacific Ocean at the end of the eighteenth century. The town perched awkwardly on the extreme northwestern edge of the North American continent, in what is today southeastern Alaska, ideal for immediate purposes at the time but unsustainable in the long term. The history of its construction, maintenance, and ultimate transfer, by sale in 1867, to a competing "colonial" regime (the United States is considered here as an expansionist state that acquired territories that were initially in a directly "colonial" relation to it) is contained within the comparatively short period of seventy-five years (Black 2004: xiv). Its physical fabric was utterly different from that of any towns and cities in the rest of North America, so that an account of its transformation from imperial Russian resource depot to minor American regional administrative outpost is one of almost total reinvention but one stretched out over a further two-thirds of a century. The driving forces behind the transition were neither war, aggressive political subjugation, nor violent ethnic strife. Rather, they involved more subtle differences, such as the fundamental urban way of life, social assumptions, effects of geographic isolation, and governmental attention. They help explain the unusually prolonged gestation of this process. Though Sitka's destiny in the annals of the world's cities was not one of high glory, its experience nevertheless reveals much that can inform conceptual models of morphological change under diverse conditions.

The theoretical questions in this case might be grouped under three headings. First of all, what happens to urban form when a town or city is transferred from one empire to another? The most likely outcome would be some type of cultural collision, reflected possibly in a sharp change in governing style, religious privilege, or existential social relations, or some combination of these factors. Consequently, there might be a substantial succession of physical forms resulting in a notably altered urban landscape. The severity and velocity of change would most likely be tied to the pace of general economic growth. The Sitka case shows all of these symptoms but in varying configurations. Second, one can ask how does urban form change in a remote place far from the immediate reach of central government? One could posit confusion of authority, the persistence of old habits among the continuing population, and general stagnation, cultural as well as economic. In this respect, Sitka displayed these features, too, some to an extreme degree. And, third, what interactions might be expected among the agents shaping urban form under such conditions? Three types of interaction suggest themselves: contest between government officials and entrepreneurs seeking to benefit from an altered political environment; the emergence of energetic self-help on the part of residents, especially in the absence of regulation; and, consequently, a broad lack of planning at all levels of urban society, resulting in piecemeal transformation of the physical fabric through the scarcity and arbitrariness of government edicts and deterioration brought on with the passage of time. In Sitka's case, the interactions among the agents of urban transformation can be measured with respect to five distinct categories of actors: central government officials (temporary colonial diplomatic corps at first, resident representatives of the national government later), the designated local government authorities, the merchants, church leaders, and ordinary residents.

Novo-Arkhangel'sk's urban reinvention as Sitka did involve a massive cultural shift in which the strongly communal foundation of urban development under Russian auspices (as essentially a government-chartered company town) faced systematic destruction by the intensely privatistic property precepts prevailing under American control. With such altered urban dynamics, the townscape was transmogrified from one of ubiquitous, massive log construction and many large community buildings arranged somewhat loosely in space to a townscape of lightweight frame structures disciplined by precise parcelization and limited public space. At the time of Transfer (a truly "watershed" event), the little city fitted the description of visitors such as Delevan Bloodgood and William Dall, quoted above; by the late 1920s, Sitka was a thoroughly American small town, the character of which time would only intensify. What role did the actors and agents of change in this critical period play in such a significant urban reinvention? The narrative that follows outlines the essential design of the Russian town; the formalistic changes imposed by American government policy, and the often sharp divergence between American precept and practice that followed; and it concludes with an assessment of the role of the key actors in the drama of Sitka's urban reinvention.

Russian Urbanism in North America

Russian harvesting of animal furs along the coasts of Alaska, particularly of the sea otter, required little in the way of elaborate urban development, but it did require a staging ground and administrative center. Organized as the Russian–American Company with a monopoly charter from the tsar, the operation in 1799 established a settlement at Novo-Arkhangel'sk on Chicagou Island in southeastern Alaska, which, after a re-founding in 1804 following native Tlingit resistance, became the colony's capital in 1808. The charter specified responsibilities well beyond those of simply pursuing commercial gain: as the tsar's corporate representative, the company was commanded to assert and defend the territorial and broad colonial interests of the imperial government of Russia, and it was also obliged to provide facilities for the Greco–Russian Orthodox Church in Alaska. Besides providing the necessities of commerce (warehouses, clerical offices, port facilities, including boat building and repair), the settlement supported company services such as a school, a hospital, and the stationing of an imperial military detachment for protection. To this were added ecclesiastical functions such as churches (and, after 1848, a cathedral), a bishop's palace, a seminary for the training of priests, and a church for the Indians. Rounding out these services were corollaries such as a sawmill, foundry, icehouse, fish-houses, bathhouses, and a laundry. All these urban functions were guaranteed by an emperor and a company headquartered in St. Petersburg—an astounding 8,000 sea and land miles away, across the Aleutian archipelago, the Bering Straits, Kamchatka, and the entire length of Siberia and European Russia (Gibson 1976, 1980: 135).

Novo-Arkhangel'sk's community maintained a clear segmentation: the Company hierarchy (governor, a small managerial corps, artisans, and *promyshlenniki*—mainly Siberian contract workers drawn from the state serf and townsman classes), the military, the church, and the Indians. The latter, at first banished from the site for their enmity, were allowed after 1820 to settle outside the Russian stockade along a beach north of the town, by which time their value as additional labor and as a vital source of fresh food through barter had became all too apparent.

The resulting spatial form of the town organized these social classes into five distinct districts (one could almost say "plan-units"), well reflected on a company map from 1845 (Fig. 7.1, from Russian–American Company, 1845). At the western end, surrounding a small promontory jutting into Sitka Bay was the port/citadel complex, a cluster of large buildings comprising the governor's house, a veritable citadel (popularly known as Baranof Castle) atop a small volcanic plug, offices, warehouses, barracks, commissary, and the admiralty (Fig. 7.2). Immediately east of this was the central district of the town—the residential district of the *promyshlenniki*—together with some fish-houses, the officers' club (away from officialdom), and a Russian tea garden and, completed in 1848,

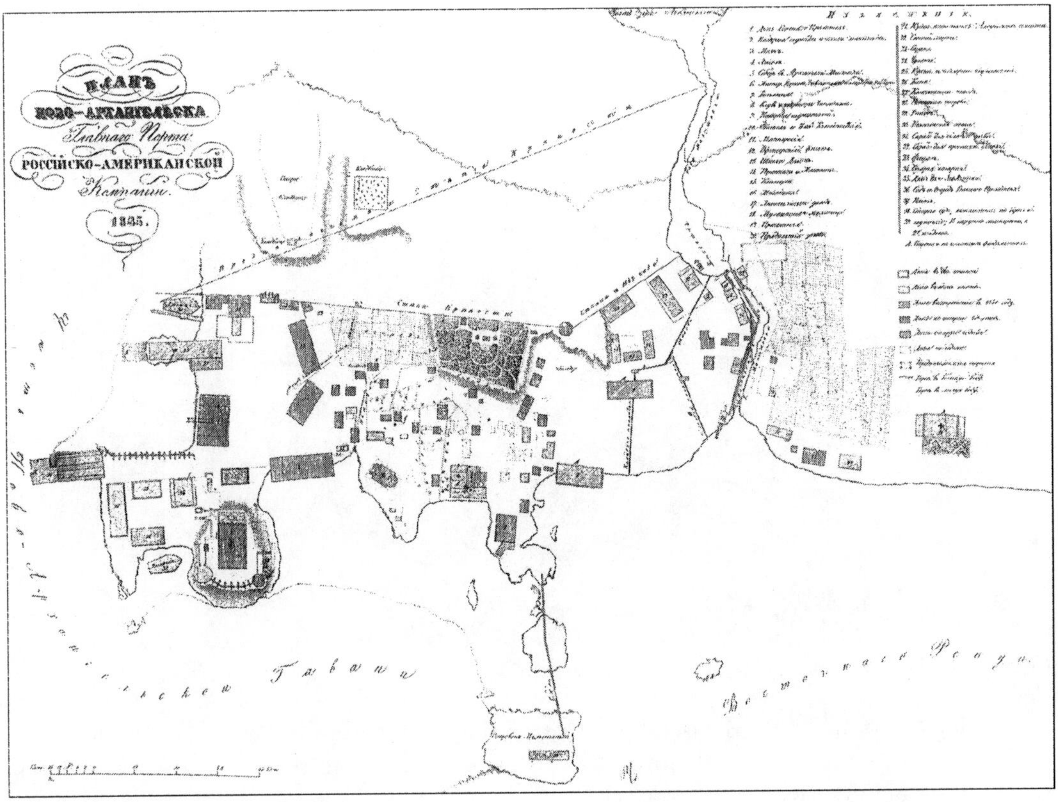

FIGURE 7.1 Plan of Sitka in 1845, produced by the Russian–American Company

FIGURE 7.2 Sitka's Russian townscape: the view from the harbor, looking east

FIGURE 7.3 Sitka's Russian townscape: the view from Castle Hill, looking east

the striking Cathedral of St. Michael the Archangel (Fig. 7.3). East of this as far as a ravine was an open zone containing many of the town's industrial premises, with flume and sluices providing water power and drainage from Swan Lake to the north. East of the ravine was the ecclesiastical precinct, with the bishop's house, hospital, and numerous vegetable gardens essential to the town's precarious health (see Fig. 7.1). The first three districts were sheltered by a high stockade with watchtowers on their northern edge, overlooking the ribbon-like Tlingit village skirting the bay northward. Speaking volumes, the Company's official map fails to acknowledge the Indian village, placing the map's cartouche conveniently over its location.

Thus, Novo-Arkhangel'sk in the Russian era consisted of two macro-morphological units: the Russian log town and the Indian log village north of the stockade. Traditional Tlingit houses were large, one-story structures housing entire families in a single, communal room. Both districts were spatially loose assemblages of structures spread along the east and west margins of Sitka Bay (Fig. 7.4). The Indian village literally bordered the water's edge at high tide. The Russian town also possessed no streets; there were only pathways through the undulating strand, which often became muddy channels in the damp climate. Later, planked footways replaced them, but they easily wore out. The only quasi-street, called "Governor's Walk" (because the colony's first governor took Sunday strolls to a rocky spot on the bay east of town) had no defined margins, save in part along the stretch between the dockside warehouse and the long commissary building that marked the limit of the harbor complex. There was, of course, no private land, the whole settlement being "company land" by act of colonization and imperial charter. Eventually, the *promyshlenniki* were allowed to build cabins on open ground on their own time, but the land under them remained the company's. The informal layout of this Russian colonial capital resulted from its purpose and its site. The colony's lifeblood was the action out at sea, catching otters in small boats. The town was an appendage to this, hugging the mountainous coast practically devoid of cultivable land and with no other settlements with which to connect by land. Who needed streets?

On the other hand, there was a certain overall spatial coherence to the town's morphology. The heartbeat of the colony was the port/citadel area, as close to a "downtown" as Novo-Arkhangel'sk would have, right at the angle of the bay formed by the protruding rock that provided a strategic topographical eminence. Within the fortified town, the workers' residential district formed the first "ring" followed by an industrial fringe belt ("*intra muros*"), with an "extramural" extension beyond the stockade that contained the gardens of the ecclesiastical precinct, the Russian cemetery, and elements of the Tlingit village. If the informality of this walled town bore any vague and belated resemblance to the general irregularity of a European medieval town, one might suggest the Bishop's church precinct formed a perfect "distal extramural" element within the town's eastern fringe belt reminiscent of the many "*conventi*" or religious houses surrounding Italian medieval towns (Conzen 2010: 163; Conzen et al. 2012: 32).

All structures, from the humblest cabins to the grandest edifices, were built of logs cut from the abundant Sitka spruce forests that covered the region. Ordinary buildings contained logs hewn in the horizontal plane and left round in the vertical plane; official buildings were built of logs squared on all sides, often a foot thick in both dimensions, and carefully dovetailed at the corners. Many such buildings were designed in a simplified neoclassical style, with elegant lunette windows set within the log walls of the upper gables. In large buildings with few windows, such as warehouses, single logs could measure up to sixty-nine feet (twenty-one meters) in length (Arndt and Pierce 2003: 42). Given the weather, log structures deteriorated relatively fast; officials regarded the lifespan of the average log building to be between twelve and twenty years (Arndt and Pierce 2003: 138–139). With wood limitless, bricks prohibitively expensive to import, and quarried stone out of the question in this wilderness, Novo-Arkhangel'sk by the 1860s grew into the largest all-log town anywhere on the North American continent.

The Sitka Provisions in the 1867 Treaty for the Sale of Alaska

Few people outside diplomatic circles had any inkling that the vast territory of Alaska would change political hands two years after the close of the American Civil War. After its own disastrous naval losses during the Crimean War, Russia's anxiety over the potential loss of Alaska without compensation, most especially to Great Britain, prompted the tsar to offer this indefensible territory to the United States. After a price was negotiated, the treaty was signed on March 20, 1867 and ratified by the U.S. Congress on May 28, and copies of the treaty were exchanged between the nations at Novo-Arkhangel'sk (quickly renamed Sitka) on June 20. Several key provisions directly affected Sitka's existing and future urban morphology.

Most significantly, the right of individuals to own real estate—land as well as buildings—became immediately operative. Therefore, an open property market could henceforth develop, and future buildings could be added to the building stock through impersonal market forces rather than managerial decision-making. Furthermore, while all buildings formerly belonging to the Russian–American Company would pass to the United States as "public property" to be administered by the U.S. federal government, there were two exceptions. First, the buildings and grounds formerly held by the Russian Orthodox Church, which would now operate as a disestablished but free church community, would pass into its ownership in fee simple and, second, the dwellings occupied by individuals, and the ground they stood on, would be conveyed prior to the treaty by the Company to them (mostly Russians choosing to stay and, in effect, become American citizens) and would be recognized as theirs by American law. Included in the transfer to U.S. federal authorities, not surprisingly, of course, were Sitka's fortifications and other military structures. Strikingly, these consisted of defenses—town stockade, blockhouses with cannon, barracks, and a dockside battery with cannon—all designed for defense against the local Indian villagers rather than any foreign enemy arriving by sea (U.S. Congress 1868: 5–9).

Critical to the treaty was a detailed accounting of urban property and facilities in the form of a fairly accurate cadastral map of the town prepared by U.S. naval engineers (known as the "Transfer Map," which formed the basis for Fig. 7.4). It was more nearly planimetrically precise than any prior map prepared by Russian cartographers, reflecting perhaps the American concern for exact property delineation, laying the groundwork, so to speak, for the future uniform enjoyment of individual property rights (U.S. Congress 1867).

Fundamental to the theme of this study, the treaty provisions replaced the former imperial authority and its surrogate, the Russian–American Company, with the U.S. federal government but without the latter possessing any commercial involvement remotely comparable to that which had prompted Sitka's colonization in the first place. The Russian Orthodox Church, now shorn of its government support, would nevertheless enjoy the protections afforded any corporate religious institution under the American Constitution, and as the dominant denomination in town could adopt, if anything, a freer role in helping shape the city than it had hitherto done. Newly empowered as shapers of future urban form was the new class of freeholders, whether independent merchants, service providers, or ordinary working residents in what would continue for some time to be the capital city of Alaska. How the new chemistry would work, however, would depend on the forms that local governance took and the prospects for economic growth, once freed from the limited vision of a chartered fur trading organization.

In the rather hectic and chaotic run-up to the handover, the resident Russian governor, Prince Dmitrii Petrovich Maksoutoff, took some actions that influenced the future course of Sitka's built environment. Company policy toward its "old servants" had for some considerable time been to grant them dwellings at the Company's cost, but "there were no particular regulations, restrictions, or formalities," wrote S. N. Buynitsky in a Russian memorandum (U.S. Congress 1868: 23). The chief administrator selected

> a place for the new settlement [i.e., dwelling] according to his own better understanding; and this simple designation of whereabouts gave the settler a right to occupy and use such area of land and trading grounds as he could or thought it necessary to occupy for his housekeeping and fishing requirements.

In other words, there were no fixed property boundaries on the ground for what by treaty would now become full, private, freehold tenements for those Russians deciding to remain at Sitka, but American rules required such boundaries and documentation authenticating them. So the prince made out a substantial number of certificates granting homestead parcels to the individuals who had settled on them, and the configuration of these parcels on the map simply formalized the idiosyncratic pattern of scattered house locations, without streets. Though understandable in the circumstances, this action contributed to decades of uncertainty over the town's future rational development.

General Lovell Rousseau, the American transfer commissioner, spent "days completing the transfer of properties and attempting with [Russian commissioner Captain Alexis] Pestchouroff and Maksoutoff to categorize all buildings in Sitka as either public or private" (Hughes and Whitney

2002: 370). Both just before and immediately after the transfer, non-Russian adventurers arrived from British Columbia and California hoping for quick pickings (which included the sell-off of vast stores of valuable otter furs in the former Company harbor-side warehouses) and, in the process, squatted in vacant houses or on open land seemingly belonging to no one. Quite a few squatters filed claims for purchase, which Maksoutoff honored with deeds upon payment. Deeds to parcels without houses upon them caused numerous problems later on, and many claims to title became thoroughly clouded (DeArmond 1995: 184, 213).

The Long Era of Military Government and Inadequate Civil Administration

Alaska's acquisition by the United States was on a grand scale opportunistic, seen by many as an expensive diplomatic folly. It had little contemporary strategic or economic value, although later, in retrospect, it turned out to have been an extraordinary geopolitical and economic bargain. In 1867 and the years following, the U.S. government faced daunting problems of knitting back together a nation torn asunder by civil war. As a result, Alaska and Sitka languished in deep neglect, administered by a skeletal military post with woefully insufficient resources, 4,500 miles distant from the seat of American power in Washington, DC. From 1867 to 1877, Sitka was governed by a detachment of the U.S. Army (under Gen. Jefferson C. Davis for two years, and thereafter by two company captains and a major). From 1877 to 1879, the lone federal official in Sitka—theoretically responsible for all matters that could not be settled by town leaders—was the U.S. Customs Collector. From 1879 to 1884, Sitka was administered by the U.S. Navy (under captains and commanders who rarely served in their posts for more than a few months). In 1884, Alaska was created as a "land district" with a District Organic Act setting up a civil government, consisting of a land sales office. Notwithstanding the belated appointment of a Surveyor-General for the District of Alaska thirteen years later, based in Sitka, the town itself remained un-surveyed until 1924, meaning that land sales had no legal standing until then. In 1900, Sitka lost its status as capital of Alaska to Juneau, a booming goldfield town on a mainland fjord. Finally, in 1912, the U.S. Marines, who had followed the Navy at the Sitka military base, departed. Only in 1913 did Sitka achieve municipal incorporation as a "second-class city." Coincident with this long period of governmental minimalism was a protracted economic depression that severely stunted Sitka's development (DeArmond 1993: 40–41). From a high in 1870 of 1,851 residents, reflecting the temporary bubble of post-Transfer faith in Sitka's future, the town's population slid down to a low of 1,056 in 1930 (before rising significantly thereafter when American fears of war and Communism gave Sitka a renewed military underpinning). What consequences did such a political and economic experience have for Sitka's physical development under American jurisdiction?

As log structures deteriorate over time, more quickly than otherwise in a damp climate, Sitka's building fabric, entirely of log construction before 1867, continued after Transfer to rot away, slowly but surely. No American had any interest in replacing buildings using massive Russian hewn-log, post-and-beam technology. By the late 1860s, all Americans were familiar with balloon-frame construction sheathed with clapboard (Sprague 1981). Patrick O'Dwyer, a Canadian adventurer from Victoria, BC, who opened a store in Sitka even before the treaty, "complained that timber workers, builders of log houses, were plentiful but that none of the local workmen knew how to put up a frame building" (DeArmond 1995: 211). Sitka embarked upon an uncoordinated program of wholesale replacement of log structures with frame ones, precipitating a profound transformation of the urban landscape, but the process would take decades.

From the point of view of agency in the built environment, the post-Transfer period of extremely weak government and equally weak economic stimulus is interesting for the attempts made by officials to regulate the transition from log to frame construction and related issues in upgrading the town's urban form and for the means ordinary residents used to circumvent or accelerate the transformation. Most residents, of course, would have to view Sitka's physical evolution in terms of what profits might be made from expansion and redevelopment. Newcomers brought with them a business model based on real estate turnover. The old Russians had to learn the power of making replacement profitable.

Sitka received a municipal charter on November 14, 1867, which gave the mayor purely local power to "recognize property title records and real estate transfers, once they had paid taxes and assuming they did not contravene "Acts of the Military and Naval authorities of the U.S." So eager were some new residents to profit from buying and selling property, hoping to cash in on rises in its value, that the charter stipulated "all claims, preemptions, mortgages, deeds, bonds, leases and other instruments" be recorded with "the *minute* [present author's emphasis], hour, day, month, and year when the same was filed." Two "Street Commissioners" were created, "who shall act as Assessors" to levy a tax on property "for the improvement of streets, roads, and wharves of the city," while exempting U.S. property (Lautaret 1989: 13–14). Thus, a beginning was made to enable urban improvements, but this occurred in a vacuum of legal finality: Sitka had no county courthouse in which property transfers could be routinely registered and resist challenge in a court of law. The town charter itself was technically illegal because no federal law had been passed that could have authorized it, but it served in effect as the local law from late 1867 until the demise of the city Council in 1873. Technically, all Sitka property claims made after Transfer until well into the twentieth century were squatters' claims and subject to removal, by force if necessary. "The mayor exercises what little power is allowed him by the military rule," noted Lady Franklin, a perceptive British visitor to Sitka in 1870 (Cracroft 1981: 13).

Beyond the issue of property transfers lay the even more fundamental problem of property demarcation on the ground. The city charter attempted a unique solution in the case of buildings erected during Russian times without a surrounding plot.

> That [private property] which is improved and enclosed shall be entered with metes and bounds in accordance with the enclosure. That which is not enclosed shall be entitled to a frontage of not more than ten feet on each side of the building and a depth of not more than one hundred and twenty feet from the street line. Provided that when a smaller space than twenty feet exists between two houses it shall be divided equally.
>
> (Lautaret 1989: 14)

This helps account for additional irregularities that would develop in the old town's plot pattern following Transfer.

What follows are some examples of the occasional military edicts and municipal experiments that characterized urban change during the next half century of underdeveloped government.

Within two weeks of the charter's proclamation, the mayor and council designated the creation of seven streets: Lincoln (the old Governor's Walk), American, Club, Lake, Bishop (later Monastery), Hospital (later Baranoff [*sic*]), and Alaska streets. They were to be eighty feet wide. However, the ragged pattern of existing buildings did not permit such streets to be laid out, and no further attempt to formally survey streets was made until the early years of the twentieth century. It is clear that the street commissioners did little.

> Attempts to Americanize the building stock of Sitka also began soon after Transfer. "Disregarding our frequent warnings that Sitka lacks available houses," Capt. Pestchurov reported in mid-November to the Russian Ambassador in Washington, the Americans sent over a great number of officials, and to date have not started to put up the new buildings which they brought from San Francisco and which they affirmed, would eliminate all difficulties in accommodating the newcomers in Sitka ... The buildings which the Americans planned to erect during the first days after their arrival are only projects still.
>
> (Miller 1981: 141)

Economic complications or lethargy ruled the day.

Sitka during the early 1870s was a rough place. The army detachment stationed there comprised many soldiers the commandant in San Francisco most wanted out of the way, and Gen. Davis had as much trouble from his men in the town as from its resident rowdies. After the Russian–American Company wound up its business, commercial interests were slow to replace its community services. In October 1867, there were a mere handful of retail shops, two bowling alleys, two saloons, and a restaurant (Hughes and Whitney 2002: 370). By 1870, there were eleven shops, eleven saloons, and assorted artisans but still no hotel; by 1872, the saloons had grown to nineteen, the Collector of Customs reported to his superior (Cracroft 1981: xxvii; DeArmond 1993: 6). The Army was ordered out of Sitka, and all Alaska, in 1877. This emboldened the Indians, who tore down portions of the stockade and burned down the army officers' quarters on the parade ground. With the departure of the Army, the "citadel" was abandoned as a residence and command post because physical decay had set in. Yet a visitor to Sitka the following year noted,

> the place is not nearly as much reduced in property as reports would make us believe. The houses of the Russian mechanics have been improved in appearance and they are very clean. Potatoes, turnips, cauliflower and cabbage are growing in every garden. [But] In the Indian village everything betokens a retrograde movement. A few houses have been provided with a painted or whitewashed front, but inside there is not the slightest change.
>
> (Petroff 1966: 47)

Nevertheless, there were empty buildings everywhere, especially along the "chaotic" Indian waterfront, which reminded Alaska's future civilian governor, John G. Brady, of eastern slums (Hinckley 1982: 35). Anxiety over the aggressiveness of the Indians drove Sitka's leaders to request British help, and for about five months in 1879, the town was actually under the protection of HMS *Osprey*, sent up from Victoria, Canada.

Prompted to end this embarrassment, the U.S. government instituted a five-year period of urban control by the U.S. Navy, whose ships in the bay intimidated the Tlingit villagers enough to pacify them. In 1881, the able Commander Henry Glass ordered them to clean up their village and reposition some of their houses to create a straighter line along the shore and gave the structures house numbers. This set up the preconditions for what would become, decades later, Katlian Street. The commander went further and issued an order that the old log clan houses should be replaced as soon as possible with frame houses. Though such replacement did not happen overnight, it connoted a fundamental shift in the nature of domestic space in the Indian village from structures with large communal living areas to buildings with many rooms for individualized use (Cracroft 1981: xx). This aspect of an emerging Americanization for the Tlingit was instituted, in effect, under the threat of Navy guns.

In the Russian district, the sanitary theme was even more thorough: walks were planked, street spaces graveled and curbed, and old houses repainted. However, for the most part, the town's building stock hardly changed:

> Twenty years ago [i.e., *c.*1867] there were one hundred and twenty-five buildings in the town proper, and it is doubtful if a dozen have been erected since ... The buildings on the main street are all heavy log houses, some of them clapboarded over, and a few of them whitewashed, but decay has seized upon many, and their roofs are sinking under the weight of moss.
>
> (Scidmore 1885: 218, 154)

This account fits perfectly with the contemporaneous photograph shown in Figure 7.3, but during the 1880s, clapboarded frame buildings began to appear in more than token fashion, often with squared-off "false-front" façades that hid the pitched roofs behind. They slowly colonized gaps between existing structures or replaced log ones that had decayed to the point of collapse. And those owners of log buildings who sought to keep up with the times, or give the impression of doing so, covered them with neat clapboard skins in mimicry of the real thing. This undoubtedly prolonged the life of those structures for a time.

From 1884 on, Sitka was under civil jurisdiction, principally in the person of a governor, presiding over Alaska as a land district. Foreseeing that future private development might fill up the town without adequate provision for public space, Gov. Lyman Knapp in 1887 drew up a list of sites that he felt should be reserved for public facilities, many necessarily on the town's periphery but several within the old Russian quarter. Powerless himself to implement these recommendations, he petitioned President Benjamin Harrison to act, and on June 21, 1890, an Executive Order reserved many of the lands on Knapp's list. In the old town, these included formal designation of a reserve for military barracks and a parade ground (which formalized the future use of the old admiralty area), a school plot near the Bishop's palace, a tract from the town wharf along Lincoln Street (including Castle Hill) for government buildings, and a knoll on Seward Street for a future governor's mansion. Within the town's now emerging outer fringe belt, large sites were reserved for a public park (at the east end), a military cemetery (on the slopes east of Swan Lake), and the whole of Japonski Island (in Sitka Bay to the west of town) for future military purposes (DeArmond 1995: 185). This action, born of local observation by a thoughtful federal official, required the direct intervention of the United States president himself in the absence of adequate local and regional decision-making authority, owing to Alaska's primitive legal status as, in effect, a colonial territory. These reserves proved highly beneficial to the town's future functioning.

Sitka's urban morphology in the early-twentieth century bore undeniable signs of creeping Americanization (Fig. 7.5). Long gone was the town palisade defending it against the Indians, although the Tlingit village remained, as ever, spatially segregated from the town's Euro-American population. Shifts in government needs had transformed the old port/citadel district adjacent to Castle Hill. Fire had consumed Baranof Castle in 1894 and, by 1914, the military presence gave way to a fish-processing pier and plant and several U.S. federal facilities, such as a post office, court, jail, and agricultural station offices. In the central and eastern portions of the town, street lines were becoming established, even though they still had tenuous legal standing (the lines in Fig. 7.5 are based on Sanborn fire insurance plan delineations that, though strictly unofficial, recorded what was evident on the ground). For the most part, in the dense central area, street definition made the best of available space, given the tenacity of private owners in resisting any rationalization that

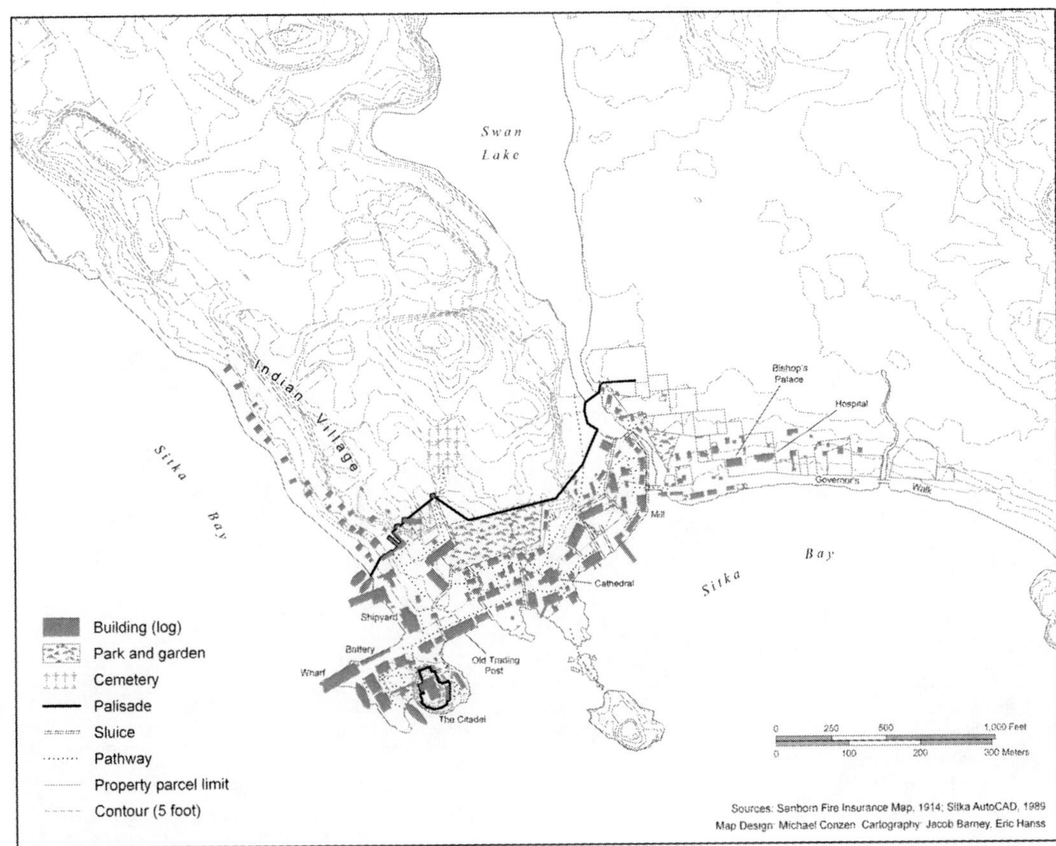

FIGURE 7.4 Plan of Russian Sitka at transfer, 1867

impinged on their ground. Sitka's east end showed most clearly the effects of modest urban growth. By 1914, numerous new homes and several businesses had sprung up in a loose pattern that, one street segment at a time, acquired a rudimentary circulation network.

Not explicit on the map were the inevitable changes that came to the log townscape, except that it did reflect the decrease in the number of buildings with very large footprints (compare Figs. 7.4 and 7.5). As long as their upkeep was practical, many log buildings, especially those of general significance to the community, were "re-purposed"—a school near the cathedral became a fire station and mayor's office (1867), a church hospital became a school (*c*. 1883), a log saloon was turned into the town's first Catholic church (1885), and a large fish-house on the southern bay front was converted into a Navy hospital (1888). Many acquired clapboard sheathing that masked their antiquity. More dramatic were the outright losses of significant log structures to fire or demolition—for example, the Ice House (1867), the "Double-Decker" tenement (1881), the Russian hospital (1882), the Governor's bathhouse (1893), Baranof Castle (1894), the Russian Club House (demolished 1900), the great dockside warehouse (1916), the Russian schoolhouse and the Russian barracks (1921), the Customs House (1883, 1936), the Millmore Hotel (1944) and, most sadly, the original fabric of St. Michael's Cathedral (1966, rebuilt almost immediately for symbolic reasons).

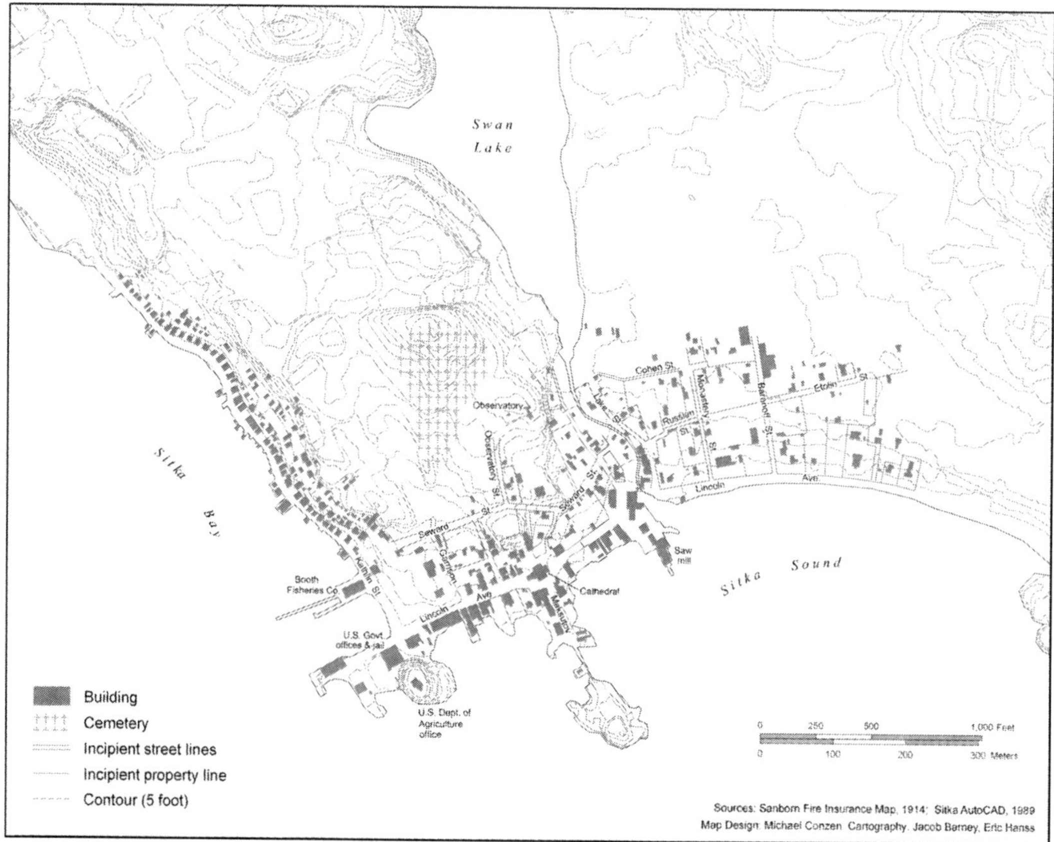

FIGURE 7.5 Plan of Sitka in 1914

At Long Last: Townsite Surveys

Sitka's plodding march toward modernity was not helped by the loss of its historic regional capital status to the jumped-up gold-rush camp, Juneau, on the mainland. Nevertheless, Sitka remained a stopping-point for coastal traffic between Portland and San Francisco to the south and the rest of Alaska to the northwest, and it developed a solid fishing and fish-processing industry. There were various improvements to the town's physical infrastructure by the turn of the century. The federal government brought limited improvements to its facilities, including the construction of a large water tank on Castle Hill in 1895 to supply running water to various offices, but it was up to private business to decide when demand was enough to repay investment in new services. The W. P. Mills family came to Sitka in the 1880s and soon became a leading mercantile business in town. The company improved the town wharf, which it came to own outright (a classic case of creeping privatization); organized the Sitka Water Company in 1904 to bring running water to households; brought the first petroleum products to Sitka; and in 1928 began producing and distributing electric power to the community. In 1912, Alaska became a U.S. Territory, and the following year Sitka achieved proper municipal self-government (DeArmond 1995: 41). The first concrete sidewalk was laid in 1921.

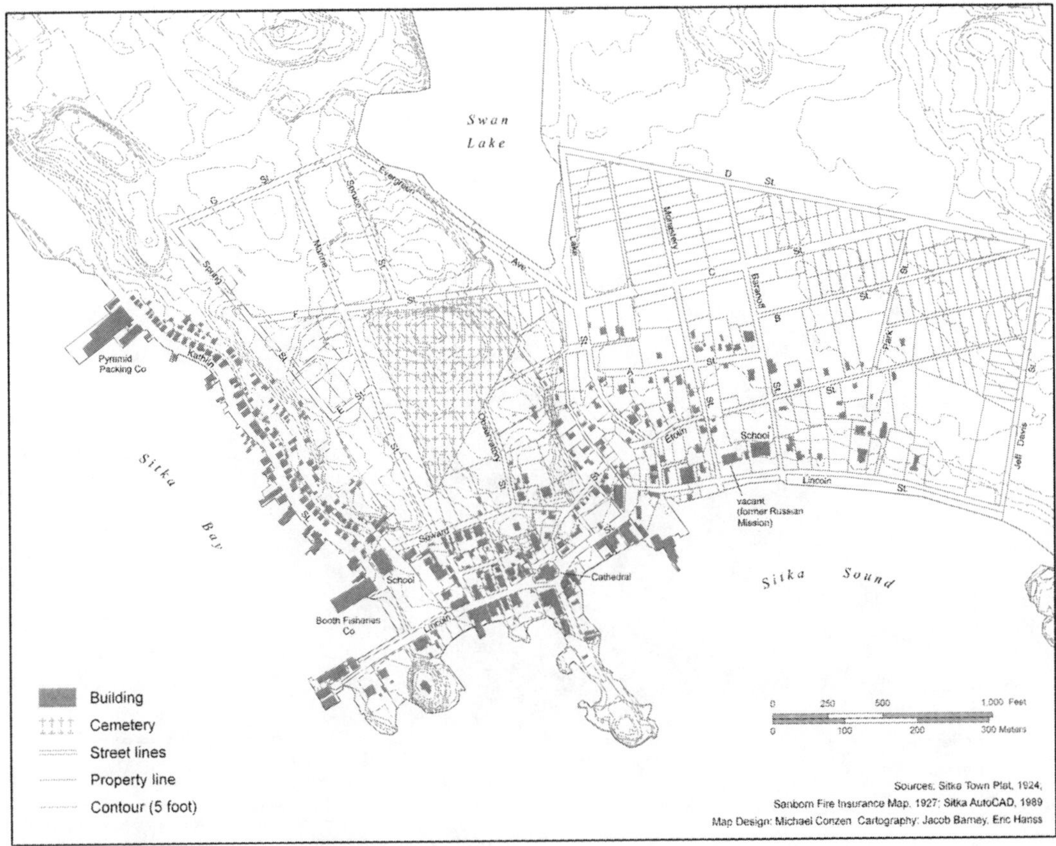

FIGURE 7.6 Plan of Sitka in 1927

The early 1920s was a period of new urban awakening and, finally, in 1923, the federal government sent a surveyor to officially "plat," that is, lay out the townsite of Sitka. This meant tackling the irregular Russian districts and preparing some new land for urban growth. Fred Dahlquist, the General Land Office surveyor who ran the lines, had to accomplish several goals: (1) to fix once and for all the street lines in the old downtown area; (2) rationalize the haphazard streets of comparatively recent origin in the district behind the Bishop's palace; (3) extend the street and plot system into new territory for immediate urban expansion; and (4) put in a skeletal street system in the town's northern sector between the community cemetery and Swan Lake for further growth. Obliged to respect existing property claims as much as possible, the morphological compromises he made are exquisitely displayed in the city map of 1927 (Fig. 7.6). This map is a composite of the U.S. Survey Map of 1924, which shows official street and plot boundaries but not structures and the 1927 Sanborn fire insurance plan that does show buildings. Throughout the existing town, the irregular plot patterns are apparent. At the urban fringe, where the land still belonged to the federal government, the plot patterns are regular. New homeowners would buy plots directly from the United States Land Office or, where it had been bought up in blocks, from early-bird realtors. While the existing town proved resistant to much change, the nearly doubling of the city's platted area gave it an unmistakable appearance of adjustment to American planning norms.

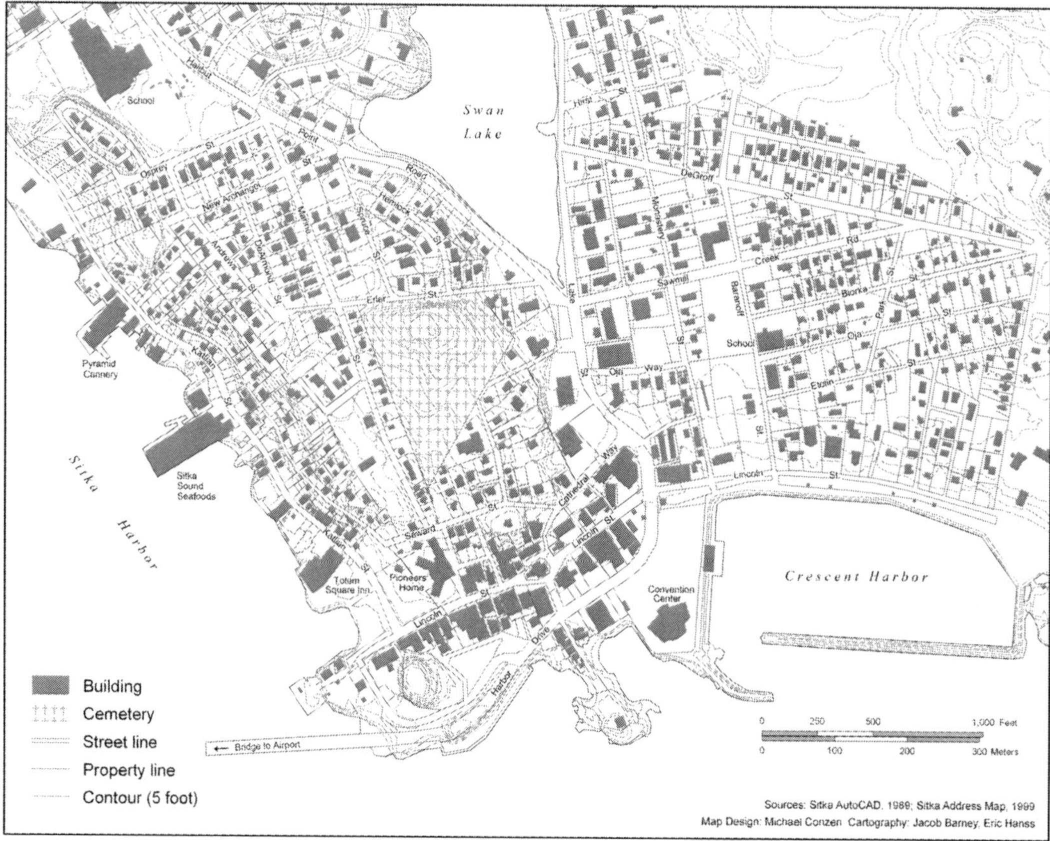

FIGURE 7.7 Plan of Sitka in 1999

Morphologically, the 1923–24 Townsite Survey represents a watershed in Sitka's morphological development. Mr. Dahlquist employed no theory or practice outside the routines of American townsite creation that had been common for more than three centuries. The gridiron principle sufficed and, admittedly, for the fairly level ground over which it was thrown, it served satisfactorily. What is striking is that the Indian district was omitted from the Townsite Survey. As wards of the national government, Indian tribes fell under different jurisdiction, and it was not until 1943 that a full professional survey of the Katlian Street district was carried out by F. W. Williamson. There was not much to be done with the now tightly packed housing of the village, except to widen Katlian Street where possible and introduce a narrow, parallel lane halfway up the hillside to give decent access to the houses perched on the slope. By this time, the comparatively deep water along the Indian village shore had attracted modest industrial waterfront development, complete with wharves and fish-processing plants. The workforce for these companies lived yards away, just across the street (see Fig. 7.6).

The remainder of the twentieth century saw the Dahlquist and Williamson plats fill up with housing and become extended (Fig. 7.7). World war in the Pacific region, followed by the Cold War with the Soviet Union, gave Sitka new strategic importance and, as a consequence, the city's population grew from just under 2,000 residents in 1940 to almost 8,000 in 1980 and 8,835 in 2000. The interrupted nature of the city's terrain made for small street and plan units and overall

FIGURE 7.8 Lincoln Street east of the cathedral, c.1885 and 2006

a modest pattern of residential housing. Most noticeable by the century's end, however, was the densification of the downtown spine along Lincoln Street, with much larger structures than ever before now dominant. Large industrial and institutional buildings around the inner and outer fringe belts, such as the canneries, schools, convention center, hotels, and the Pioneer Home, had also become numerous. The scale of Sitka now approximated that of many small and medium-sized American cities.

The transformation of Sitka's built environment from a largely single- and two-storied Russian townscape of "ponderous" log construction to the boxier but lightweight multi-storied American scene of today is best captured in a series of "then-and-now" comparisons. East Lincoln Street once looked not unlike a street in a Russian peasant village, notwithstanding the huge officers' club in the center of the photograph (Fig. 7.8). The false-front structure at right signaled that American-style buildings were beginning to infiltrate the area. Today, this stretch of street is part of Sitka's modern retail section. Similarly, the massive, once proud log buildings of the Russian admiralty (Fig. 7.9) contrast with the boxy, 1920s-era commercial and municipal buildings that replaced them on the same sites and which survive to this day. Most dramatic is the contrast between the "Double-Decker" log tenement building on a street behind the cathedral in Russian times and the district's modern appearance, dominated by a large hotel today (note the bell-tower and onion-dome cupola of the cathedral closing the vista) (Fig. 7.10).

FIGURE 7.9 Streetscape along the old admiralty, 1868 and 2006

Conclusion: A Struggle between Decay and Renewal, Hindered Entrepreneurship, and Fractured Agency

What evidence emerges from the Sitka case that might inform a model of morphological agency under conditions of colonial regime change? Most obviously, regime change at the fringes of empire offers a greater chance of transition without the bloodshed and violent upheavals more likely when vital interests and imperial status are at stake. Yet here, even in the absence of an imperative to stamp the victor's institutions crassly upon the urban landscape, a cultural shift was inevitably set in motion.

Sitka's morphological transformation between 1867 and the 1920s indeed reveals a stark clash of cultural values. The town bequeathed to the Americans was built on corporate and communal lines, expressed in the hierarchical building organization of Company compound, employees' district, industrial, and ecclesiastical areas on the fringe and a fenced-off Native village. American governance, in contrast, was predicated upon minimal top-down control of entrepreneurial activity but with a touch so light it failed for a long time to stimulate economic growth or provide much needed infrastructure. Religious privilege gave way to competitive freedom, but this in the end had little impact on the townscape, largely because the Russian Orthodox community was never subsequently refreshed by further immigration. The creative individualism that American precepts assumed took hold only as development opportunities materialized—which was slowly. Time softened these

FIGURE 7.10 District northeast of the cathedral, 1868 and 2006

distinctions and, as Russians, Euro-Americans, and Natives increasingly intermingled, a somewhat hybrid culture emerged but within the constraints of a tardy legal framework of strictly American character. The townscape reflected these changes in a glacial shift from log to clapboard design, set within a ground plan that ultimately placed the informal Russian town within a gridded girdle. The pace of this change was regulated entirely through limited growth prospects rather than government stimulus.

These observations also serve to answer the question about morphological change in a remote place far from the centers of political power. Without a compelling resource to exploit (the fur trade was in general decline), stagnation ruled, and replacement of buildings and infrastructure was minimal. This helps explain why the early spatial framework of the Russian urban core remained an enduring feature of the town. Only one high-rise building has ever been built in downtown Sitka—an apartment building placed inexcusably next door to the cathedral in 1951, robbing it of its prominence across the cityscape (compare Fig. 7.3 and Fig. 7.10; DeArmond 1993: 113).

Finally, these broader conditions shaped the interactions between actors who shaped Sitka's urban form. The imperial and federal officials who made decisions about the transfer of property profoundly shaped the limits of action later. Gen. Davis, the first post-Transfer American administrator, was keenly aware of the insufficiency of buildings assigned to the new government and of those, including quite a number of Russian company structures (such as offices, warehouses) that had been allowed in the course of the transfer to end up in private hands (Hughes and Whitney 2002: 372). In part this was inevitable, as there was no American commercial enterprise to step into the shoes of the Russian–American Company. Urban form and urban infrastructure would henceforth be subject to thousands of individual decisions, most made in the context of prevailing market pressures and substantial silence on the part of government regulation. Hence, when additional government installations were needed, it took a rare edict from the nation's president to secure land in the town for them.

Overall, it can be said interactions between the agents of change in Sitka's built environment were marred by periodic confusion over authority, occasional contest between handicapped officials and frustrated businessmen, frequent self-help in the absence of regulation, and a piecemeal approach to development and planning. Yet, in a general environment of relative scarcity and privation, the city survived Transfer, depression and loss of capital status and, in the process, saw its building stock converted from a pre-industrial form to an industrial one. If the transformation was painfully slow, it was at least incremental rather than disruptive and more or less within the means of its citizens. By the 1920s, Sitka had already become thoroughly American. If one can regret that more of the original, distinctively Russian log structures did not survive to bolster an emerging tourist economy in later times, at least Sitkans came to enjoy domestic running water, modern sewage, electricity, and the other material accoutrements of a modern economy. Sitka is no longer a colonial town, but its small-textured and oddity-filled morphology bears to this day some of the old scars of a remote urban pawn in the contest of empires.

Acknowledgments

The author acknowledges the special assistance given during the research for this study by Robert DeArmond, Sitka; David McMahon, Alaska State Archaeologist, Anchorage; Wells Williams, Planning Director of the City and Borough of Sitka; Katherine Arndt, University of Alaska at Fairbanks; and Karen Meizner, Isabel Miller Museum and Sitka Historical Society, Sitka, Alaska.

References

Arndt, K. L., and Pierce, R. A. (2003) *Sitka National Historical Park Historical Context Study: A Construction History of Sitka, Alaska, as Documented in the Records of the Russian–American Company*, 2nd ed. Sitka, AL: Sitka National Historical Park, National Park Service.

Black, L. T. (2004) *Russians in Alaska, 1732–1867*. Fairbanks: University of Alaska Fairbanks.

Bloodgood, C. D. (1869) Eight months at Sitka. *The Overland Monthly*, 2: 175–86.

Conzen, M. P. (2010) A cartographic analysis of Como's urban morphology, in C. Cerreti, L. Federzoni, and S. Salgaro (eds.), *Cartografia di Paesaggi, Paesaggi nella Cartografia*, 149–66. Bologna: Pàtron Editore. Geografia e organizzazione dello sviluppo territoriale, Studi regionali e monografici.

Conzen, M. P., Gu, K., and Whitehand, J. W. R. (2012) Comparing traditional urban form in China and Europe: a fringe-belt approach. *Urban Geography*, 33 (1): 22–45.

Cracroft, S. (1981) *Lady Franklin Visits Sitka, Alaska, 1870: The Journal of Sophia Cracroft, Sir John Franklin's Niece*, R. N. DeArmond (ed.). Anchorage: Alaska Historical Society.

Dall, W. H. (1870) *Alaska and Its Resources*. Boston: Lee and Shepard.

DeArmond, R. N. (1993) *Sitka Chronology: 1867–1987 with index*. Sitka, AL: Sitka Historical Society.

DeArmond, R. N. (1995) *From Sitka's Past*. Sitka, AL: Sitka Historical Society.

Gibson, J. R. (1976) *Imperial Russia in Colonial America*. New York: Oxford University Press: 3–31.

Gibson, J. R. (1980) Russian expansion in Siberia and Russia. *Geographical Review*, 70 (2): 127–36.

Hinckley, T. C. (1982) *Alaskan John G. Brady: Missionary, Businessman, Judge, and Governor, 1878–1918.* Columbus: Ohio State University Press, for Miami University.

Hughes, N. C., and Whitney, G. D. (2002) *Jefferson Davis in Blue: The Life of Sherman's Relentless Warrior.* Baton Rouge: Louisiana State University Press.

Lautaret, R. (1989) *Alaskan Historical Documents since 1867.* Jefferson, NC: McFarland.

Miller, D. H. (1981) *The Alaska Treaty.* Kingston, Ont.: Limestone Press.

Petroff, I. (1966) Journal of a trip to Alaska in search of information for the Bancroft Library, San Francisco. *Journal of the West,* 5 (1): 43–70.

Russian–American Company (1845) *Otchet Rossiisko-Amerikanskoi Kompanii Glavnago Pravleniia za odin god, po 1 ianvaria 1845* [Annual report of the Russian–American Company's Board of Directors for one year, to 1 January 1845]. St. Petersburg, Russia: Russian–American Company.

Scidmore, E. R. (1885) *Alaska: Its Southern Coast, and the Sitkan Archipelago.* Boston: D. Lothrop & Co.

Sprague, P. E. (1981) The origin of balloon framing. *Journal of the Society of Architectural Historians,* 40 (4): 311–19.

U.S. Congress, House of Representatives (1867) Alaska. Map of the Settlement at New Archangel, Sitka, accompanying a letter from Gen. L. H. Rousseau of Dec. 5, 1867, with inventories. Published in House Ex. Doc. No. 125, 40th Congress, 2d Sess. [Serial 1337]. [Handwritten title, in extreme top lefthand corner:] 'W.O.D.C.-SIT-9002'.

U.S. Congress, House of Representatives (1868) *Russian America. Message from the President of the United States, in Relation to the Transfer of Territory from Russia to the United States.* Washington, D. C.: Government Printing Office, House Exec. Doc. 177, 40th Congress, 2nd Sess., February 19.

PART IV

Agency in Industrial-Era Settings

8

SQUEEZING RAILROADS INTO CITIES

Creating Variable Solutions in Britain and the United States, 1820–1900

Arthur J. Krim

Time and technological change challenge cities to adapt at every turn. New modes of operation, new machines, new behaviors all put pressure on the physical fabric of the city to make way for rising necessities and to lose attachment to multiplying redundancies. This is nowhere more graphically illustrated than with the transport equipment of metropolitan areas. The advent of the steam railroad in the first half of the nineteenth century confronted existing cities of any size with usually significant crises of adjustment. Railroads required large, costly terminal spaces and wide curves on a scale not easily created in already dense environments, so the task of squeezing out space to permit steam trains to enter built-up areas could be daunting. For small places, the prospect was rarely difficult; merely placing railroad tracks at the urban fringe of a compact town solved the dilemma. Incorporating rail lines in newly established towns was even easier; they could be simply embedded within the plan from the outset. However, retrofitting rail facilities through dense and often serpentine street systems, across complex property holding patterns, and sometimes over uncompromising terrain raised unique and pressing problems. Given their potential for mass transport of both goods and people, steam railroads needed to reach close to—if not directly into—the core business centers of large cities. How was this done and with what consequences for the inevitable transformation of the spatial morphology of the built environment?

To approach these questions and to tease out different assessments of the problems and solutions employed in different economic and social contexts, this chapter examines four cases of large-city accommodation to the steam railroad on two continents: Liverpool and Manchester in the United Kingdom and Philadelphia and Baltimore in the United States. Greatest concern is given to decisions made in the earliest decades of urban railroad development, but attention will also be given to the longer-term evolution of metropolitan patterns and their bearing on the broad-scale urban morphology of the cities examined.

In the British case, the period between 1820 and 1830 represents the initial phase of urban railroad location, and the specific example of the Liverpool and Manchester Railway (L&M) and its termini will serve to introduce the theme. In the United States, the opening phase spanned the period 1828 to about 1840, exemplified by the Baltimore and Ohio Railroad (B&O) and the railroad terminals of Philadelphia. They provide revealing glimpses of contrasting preferences on opposite sides of the Atlantic Ocean. As case histories, they demonstrate the manner in which the early modern morphology of cities, both at the meso- and micro-scales, was adjusted to the new transport technology through complex sequences of decisions made by engineers, capitalists, and city officials. The period spans the original survey of these railroads and their inward extension to the urban cores of their respective cities by 1834.[1] By this time, different solutions had emerged in British and American practice, and they defined cultural choices made in specifying the spatial design of railroad incorporation in urban areas in Europe and America that would endure for a century or more.

In these examples, the interplay between urban agency and morphological consequence can be seen in some detail. In Europe, to this day, railroads continue their vital transport role within large urban areas, particularly with regard to passenger service. In the United States, the manic swing toward over-reliance on superhighways for bulk transit during the second half of the twentieth century in too many cases left countless railroad lines as empty corridors marooned within the urban mass, but even there, the earliest decisions made in placing railroads within heavily built-up areas have remained as confounding and challenging artifacts for citizens and planners alike.

Railroads and City Morphology

The study of railroad morphology within towns has a respectable lineage among urban geographers and historians. Stanley Beaver (1937) provided an early look at the major capital cities of pre-war Europe. He defined a radial pattern of urban commuter lines, linked by a circular beltline railroad connecting the marginally placed terminal stations. More direct observation was made by Robert Dickinson, who proposed three basic features of urban railroad location, namely: railroads that seek terminals "as near as possible to the city centre"; railroads that radiate to suburban districts from the inner-city terminals; and inner-city beltway lines developed to connect the central city stations (Dickinson 1947: 103). J. H. Appleton placed railroads in the landscape within an explicitly morphological context but dealt only incidentally with its urban aspects (Appleton 1965). Later American geographers extended the initial British observations regarding central urban terminal locations, including Harold M. Mayer (1944), Raymond E. Murphy (1966: 232–3), and James E. Vance, Jr. (1995). The historian John Kellett (1969: 8–9) noted that early railroads in British cities would "chisel their way to the fringe of the town centre," only through expensive urban land acquisition. In a more recent, wide-ranging study, Micheline Nilsen (2008) has extended such considerations to the capital cities of France, Belgium, and Germany. In such a context, this chapter will compare the process by which passenger terminal locations were inserted close to city centers in Britain and the United States and the solutions found by railroad surveyors so that freight terminals could be placed within waterfront industrial districts.

Pre-railroad Origins

The origin of the inter-city passenger railroad has been the subject of numerous historical studies, especially of the earliest English cases before 1830 (Lee 1937; Robbins 1962). These origins can be traced to medieval mining tramroads in Central Europe during the sixteenth century with wooden carts on wooden rails (Lewis 1970). Such medieval tramroads, or wagonways, are first documented in England by the mid-seventeenth century in the Northumberland coalfields along the River Tyne at Newcastle and Gateshead (Hoole 1986: 200–2). With the development of heavy locomotive engines, wooden rail technology was abandoned by 1820, and wrought iron rails anchored on stone "sleeper" blocks with cast iron "chairs" came into general use (Lee 1937: 46–55).

The Tyneside railroad technology of steam engine locomotives on iron rails encouraged the planning of regional railroad projects in the counties of Northumberland and Durham. Among the first was the Stockton and Darlington Railway connecting the coalfield north-west of Darlington to Stockton on the tidal River Tees. In 1816, Quaker merchants in Darlington began discussing a combination canal-and-railroad line to the coalfields, changing their proposal to a full railroad route in 1818. This innovation was supported through connections with Quaker associates in London. This resulted in a railroad charter obtained in March 1821, when George Stephenson was engaged as surveyor (Kirby 1993: 25–41). The projected route, approved in January 1822, connected Darlington and Stockton by twelve miles of iron railroad, extending another twelve miles northwest to the collieries at Wilton Park and Bishop Auckland. The Stockton and Darlington Railway opened in September 1825, using steam locomotives pulling a celebratory passenger train of coal wagons at eight miles per hour, a major achievement at the time. Yet for all its status as the first chartered intercity steam railroad in England, the Stockton and Darlington remained essentially a regional colliery wagonway that circumnavigated the towns without directly approaching their central areas, except for short spur tracks to the loading docks in Stockton (Rolt 1960: 60, 86; Kirby 1993: 54–6, Fig. 3). As with other early infrastructure projects, the impetus for railroads came from businessmen interested in the movement of goods, especially those with connections to water transport. The importance of building railroads that connected city centers for the convenience of passengers came slightly later.

Liverpool and Manchester

Before the success of the Stockton and Darlington Railway was assured, a more ambitious intercity passenger railroad was already under study by the textile merchants of Liverpool and Manchester in Lancashire. An early proposal for a railroad between these two industrial centers was made in 1820 by Thomas Gray in his *Observations for a General Iron Rail-way* and was further promoted by William James, a local colliery owner, who in addition envisioned a "rail-way or tram road" from the Lancashire coal fields to London (Marshall 1938, Fig. 8.2; Rolt 1960: 87–9; Carlson 1969: 37–42; Ferneyhough 1980: 14–15). With their cotton textile traffic tied to high-cost canals, Manchester and Liverpool merchants were especially eager for any solution that would reduce the cost of transport between the two towns (Jackman 1969: 519–21).

In the spring of 1821, James gained the attention of Manchester merchant Joseph Cowlishaw, who introduced James to the Liverpool investor, Joseph Sandars, who showed interest in a steam-powered railroad line in Manchester. Although earlier efforts for a horse-powered wagonway had been made by Liverpool businessmen, that summer James offered Sandars a detailed survey of a railroad route to Manchester (Rolt 1960: 90–1; Ferneyhough 1980: 14–15). A second survey was made in the spring of 1822, reportedly on a northerly line from Liverpool around the rocky prominence of Olive Mount and east over the bogland of Chat Moss to Manchester (Rolt 1960: 91; Carlson 1969: 40–6). With the James survey in hand, Sandars then formed a Provisional Committee for a "line of engine railroad from Liverpool to Manchester" in the summer of 1822 (Carlson 1969: 55). The primary concern with these initial surveys was to map the regional route between Manchester and Liverpool, while the specific location within the towns was deferred. In early 1823, James suffered a serious financial failure and resigned without publication of his surveys, although a later 1830 map indicates the original 1823 route (Donaghy 1972: 65). This appears to show a projected line entering Liverpool from the northwest along the Leeds and Liverpool Canal (Fig. 8.1). In Manchester, the railroad line appears to terminate on the west side of the River Irwell without access to the old town (see Fig. 8.2).

The Liverpool and Manchester railroad project was continued by Joseph Sandars who in June, 1824 took it upon himself to hire George Stephenson (following his work on the Stockton and Darlington railroad) to make a third survey (Rolt 1960: 92–9; Carlson 1969: 66–7). The Stephenson plan of October, 1824, has survived and shows that the railroad was to enter Liverpool from the northwest along the Leeds and Liverpool Canal, a route initially proposed by James, and was to enter Liverpool following Vauxhall Road to Prince's Dock on Merseyside. In Manchester, the route reached the southern edge of town by crossing the River Irwell and terminating at the Old Quay Timber Yard on Water Street (Baines 1852: 601–2; Fitzgerald 1980: see Fig. 1). With the survey announced in August 1824, objections were immediately raised by the Liverpool Common Council to the proposed use of steam engines along Vauxhall road to the Mersey Docks, while in Manchester, canal owners objected to the proposed railroad bridge over the River Irwell as a hindrance to barge navigation (Fitzgerald 1980: 103). Despite these local issues, the most intense opposition to the railroad route came from wealthy landowners northeast of Liverpool, who vigorously opposed any steam locomotive line set across their private estates (Ferneyhough 1980: 17–18).

With the Stephenson survey in hand, a bill for the "Liverpool and Manchester Railway Company" was presented to Parliament in February 1825. During the course of the proceedings, Stephenson was questioned intensely about his technical knowledge, but his testimony faltered under pressure of the opposition landowners. The result was a defeat of the Railway Bill in June 1825, and Stephenson's dismissal as principal engineer (Carlson 1969: 132–9). To regain momentum, the Liverpool and Manchester Company offered the position of chief engineer to John Rennie, a well-known canal builder, who in turn hired George Vignoles as chief surveyor (Carlson 1969: 143–4). To avoid the objections of estate owners, Vignoles selected a direct route into Liverpool from the east, without the circuitous northern loop along the Leeds and Liverpool Canal, or any street trackage along Vauxhall Road.

The Vignoles survey introduced two engineering innovations for gaining access to the town centers in Liverpool and Manchester. The first was to cut a line through the bedrock of Mount Olive, north of Liverpool at Edge Hill, and then to drive a tunnel through the red sandstone under Liverpool's town center to the Merseyside Docks at Wapping Road, avoiding all street operation (see Fig. 8.1). In Manchester, Vignoles proposed that the railroad keep to the west, or Salford, side of the River Irwell with a station at the New Bailey Prison. In Liverpool, the innovation of a railroad tunnel under the city to the Wapping docks was proposed for goods only, to be operated by winding cables without steam locomotives, while the passenger station was placed at Crown Street in the far eastern suburban fringe (see Fig. 8.1). The Vignoles tunnel route satisfied the Liverpool Borough Council, and approval was given in December 1825. With local support, a new Railway Bill passed Parliament in May 1826, to laudatory celebration in Manchester and Liverpool for "this great undertaking" (Baines 1852: 611–2; Carlson 1969: 144–5, 151–2, 168; Fitzgerald 1980: 7; see Fig. 8.2).

The success of the Liverpool and Manchester Railway Bill set in motion the immediate construction of the confirmed Vignoles route. However, local favor for Stephenson was still strong, and he was re-hired as chief engineer with his son Robert, to follow the Vignoles survey as accepted by Parliament (Baines 1852: 612; Carlson 1969: 184–7). Work on the Wapping Tunnel began in August 1826, under the direction of Joseph Locke, a Tyneside colliery engineer and associate of Stephenson. Construction of the tunnel proceeded up-grade from the Mersey shore for a mile and

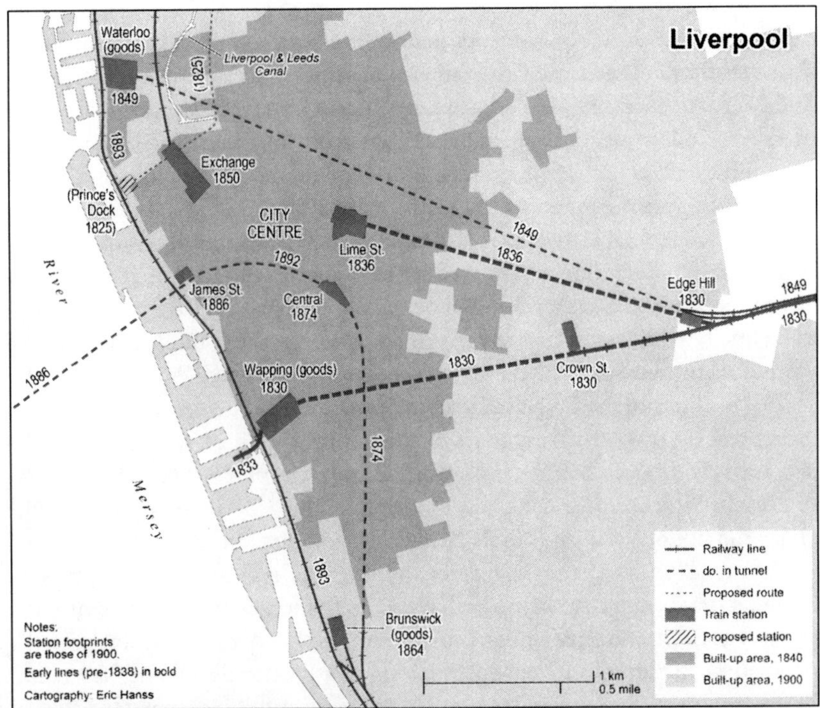

FIGURE 8.1 Railroad lines and stations in central Liverpool, 1825–1900

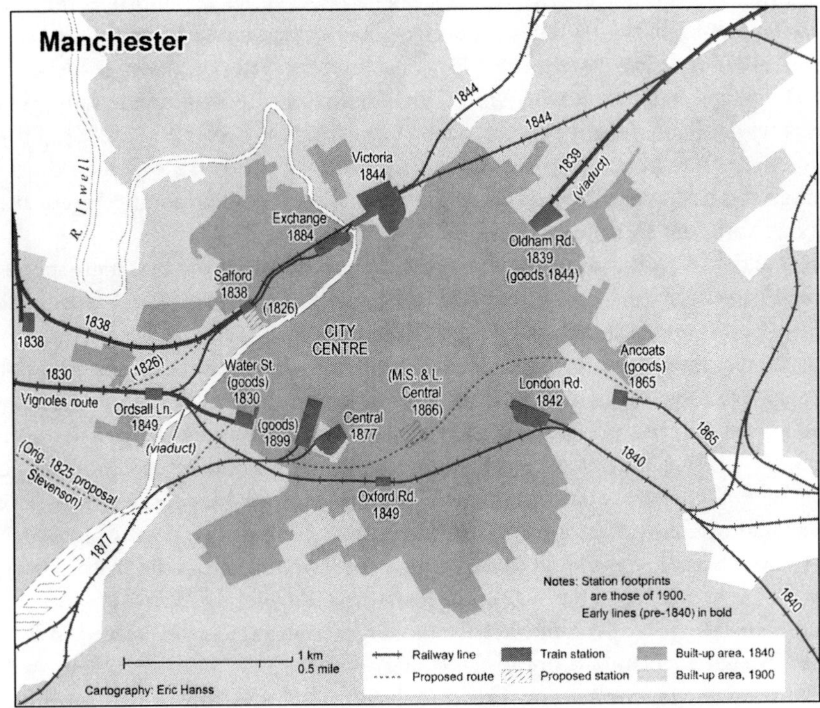

FIGURE 8.2 Railroad lines and stations in central Manchester and Salford, 1825–1900

a quarter (2,250 yards) to the Crown Street station and was completed without serious incident in June 1827. It was the first section of the railroad open for public inspection (Booth 1830: 48–9; Kellett 1969: 175–7). The Wapping Tunnel was a significant innovation in early railroad engineering. It established the precedent of locating railroad lines from the suburban fringe to the industrial waterfront by controlled-access rights-of-way, although the actual engineering effort was based upon traditional British mining practices (Sandstrom 1965: 87).

In Manchester, the terminal station was relocated at the last moment in February 1828, with an agreement by the canal owners for a high viaduct bridge across the River Irwell to a site at Water Street and Liverpool Road, as Stephenson had originally proposed (Fitzgerald 1980:10–12; see Fig. 1). This was essentially an elevated railroad terminating within the southwest fringe of Manchester, somewhat more directly accessible to the town center (Donaghy 1972: 119). Thus, by the end of 1828, the terminal facilities of the L&M railroad in both cities had been secured—after considerable debate and expense—by restricted routes from the suburban fringe to the edge of town centers either through tunnels or over bridges. The formal opening of the L&M Railroad with George Stephenson's "Rocket" locomotive took place on September 13, 1830, although fully scheduled passenger service did not begin until March 1832 (Ferneyhough: 1980: 81–3).

These developments spurred the realization among the public and entrepreneurs alike that railroads had a great future in transporting both passengers and goods. Consequently, the urgency of improving railroad access to the city center gained traction. In Manchester, the station's position in this respect was satisfactory, but in Liverpool, the long trek for travelers from the town center out to the Edge Hill station was unacceptable. In August 1831, a second cable-operated railroad tunnel was proposed from Edge Hill to the Old Cattle Market at Lime Street for passenger service to reach the very heart of Liverpool (Ferneyhough 1980: 102). The new tunnel was approved in May 1832 and completed in August 1836, with a handsome Neo-Classical station at Lime Street (*The Stranger in Liverpool* 1841: 118; *Picturesque Hand-Book* 1841: 72). A second effort was also made at the Wapping goods station to extend freight tracks to Kings Dock in October 1832 by laying rails across Wapping Street, apparently completed eight months later. (Gage 1836; Wheeler 1836: 295). Though only a few yards in length and operated by horses, the Kings Dock goods track was an early innovation in British urban rail design and offered a limited parallel with contemporary American practice in Baltimore, New York, and Philadelphia.

The success of the L&M Railway as a whole rested upon its role as the first high-speed interurban steam-operated passenger line, and, after 1830, it became, in many technical aspects, the primary model for British and American railroad design (Robbins 1962: 21).

To a large degree, early decisions regarding central city access governed later developments. In Liverpool, more extensive tunnels were built in the decades that followed, as additional railroad access to the waterfront was needed and as crucial links for new railroad corridors into the city became necessary (see Fig. 8.1). Waterloo Station established a second connection for goods traffic from Manchester. Brunswick Station, on the Cheshire Line to Manchester, was replaced as its passenger terminal by Central Station in 1874 to compete for patronage with Lime Street Station. Ultimately, Central Station was linked to Birkenhead by a tunnel across the River Mersey, opening up an effective connection for goods and commuters to and from the Wirral Peninsula. Before the century's end, the waterfront elevated electric railroad, completed in 1893, served to tie together all the vast and elongated docklands with the city center.

In Manchester, the Manchester and Leeds Railway in 1839 established its terminal passenger station at Oldham Road, at the northeast fringe of the city, with trains reaching it by viaduct, but the need for closer access to the city center brought an agreement with the L&M Railway to share a new station at Victoria Street, completed in 1844 (see Fig. 8.2). Following this, the Oldham station was confined to goods operations. Other stations, actual and only proposed, sought locations around the southern rim of the city (e.g. London Road, originally Store Street Station) from the 1840s to the 1870s, with only Central Station (1877) reaching really close to the city center. An abortive effort to run a line along the Rochdale Canal during the 1860s, proved too costly in property acquisition.

Baltimore and the B&O Railway Company

Developments on intercity steam railroads in Great Britain were carefully watched by American observers. The L&M Railway provided a blueprint of sorts for the charter of the Baltimore and Ohio Railroad, which incorporated novel features of urban terminal location. American railroad interest was initially linked to trans-Appalachian canal projects. Canals preceded railroads in North America by a much shorter time span than in Britain and thus soon received competition from the iron horse for the same pools of capital. Had there been a greater separation in time, canals would have made a greater impact on American urban morphology than was the case. Railroads, with their initially lighter impact on the structure of the built environment, soon proved spatially more versatile. Then, too, the vastly greater distance relationships between and within towns on opposite sides of the Atlantic also played into differences in timing, experience, and preferred solutions. Nevertheless, when railroads in Britain began to proliferate, American merchants were quick to spot their potential and, as in England, turned to canal engineers for advice.

In the summer of 1825, a Philadelphia architect and engineer, William Strickland, was sent to England to report on railroad operations for the Pennsylvania state canal (Dunbar 1915: 900; Dilts 1993: 26–7). This Philadelphia interest spurred merchants in rival Baltimore to consider a canal and railroad route over the Allegheny Mountains to the Ohio River at Wheeling. In the autumn of 1826, discussions among Baltimore investors regarding a railroad-canal project began in earnest. Crucial to the discussions was Quaker merchant Evan Thomas, who brought to them personal reports concerning the steam engine operations of the new Stockton and Darlington Railway. On the strength of these accounts, his brother Philip Thomas arranged a meeting of merchants in February 1827 for a Baltimore railroad project westward to Wheeling (Dilts 1993: 36–8). Within a fortnight, a committee was formed to organize the "Baltimore and Ohio Railway," and a state charter was quickly awarded by the end of the month (Hungerford 1928: 18, 25–7).

The initial route projected from Baltimore was discussed in general terms with the city terminal location—as in the British cases—left unresolved. During the spring of 1827, company officials visited several local railroad operations, including the horse-drawn colliery tramroad on the Lehigh Canal at Mauch Chunk, Pennsylvania, and the Quincy Granite Railway in suburban Boston, opened the previous year (Dilts 1993: 51). There, Baltimore officials were fascinated by the use of grooved granite rails at highway crossings, inset with iron straps for convenience of wagon traffic (Holly 1991: 3).

The location of a terminal station in Baltimore was still unresolved in the spring of 1828, when the state passed a law allowing the railroad terminus to be sited anywhere within the city of Baltimore, provided the mayor and City Council, as partial investors in the company, gave their consent. The original intent was to locate a terminal about three-quarters of a mile west of the city center, having crossed the suburban estate of one of the company's directors, James Carroll. Instead, Baltimore officials offered land for a terminal toward the southeast edge of the city at Fells

Point, requiring a projected street track through the city center (Dilts 1993: 65–6). Other company directors, unhappy with a secret arrangement by Carroll for a branch line to the waterfront on his property from Mount Clare, forced a slightly more northerly realignment of the B&O approach to the city, which intersected with Pratt Street, the city's main east–west thoroughfare (see Fig. 8.3). Without a firm decision on the terminal location, company officials, for the occasion of an inaugural stone-laying ceremony on 4 July 1828, located a temporary terminal at the western Pratt Street intersection (Stover 1987: 25) (Mt. Clare on Fig. 8.3).

The more pressing question was the matter of motive power—by horse or steam engine. To resolve the issue, the company sent its survey engineers to England in October 1828 to examine the Stockton and Darlington locomotive engines and the construction progress of the L&M Railway. Returning to Baltimore in March 1829, before the success of Stephenson's "Rocket" locomotive was assured, company directors opted for horse-powered trains when the railroad was opened to Ellicott City in May 1830 (Hungerford 1928: 93–4; Dilts 1993: 86–7).

Beyond matters of locomotion, the original question of a tidewater terminal in Baltimore Harbor remained unresolved. In January 1829, Carroll published a plan for a beltline railroad, which would run northeast under the city center through a tunnel, turn east near Monument Square along East Monument Street, and then proceed south along Canal Street to the City Dock at Fells Point. The plan had little support in City Council and, instead, company officials in March revived the plan to locate an extension from Mount Clare directly on local streets to the City Dock. During the summer, railroad surveyor Jonathan Knight mapped out a route directly east on Pratt Street from Mount Clare station. Meanwhile, railroad officials tested an experimental steam engine, "Tom Thumb," in August 1830, deciding that steam locomotives were in fact a practical method of motive power for the main line. The question of the tidewater extension rested again until September, when Knight proposed that a railroad track be located on Pratt Street to the Inner Basin. An intense debate followed, with a series of City Council votes in the early months of the following year. Finally on April 1, 1831, the Council approved the "City Extension" to the B&O Railroad, to operate their cars by horsepower as far as the City Dock at Fells Point (Smith 1853: 28, 98; Olson 1980: 74, 76; Stover 1987: 34–8; Dilts 1993: 141–3).

Once approved, the City Extension was under construction along Pratt Street during that summer, opened to Light Street at the head of the Inner Harbor, one mile east of Mount Clare station. The Pratt Street extension was built with grooved granite rails, much like those seen on the Quincy Granite Railway, permitting wagons and carriages to cross without obstruction. However, by December 1831, city officials objected to freight cars standing overnight blocking traffic, and the railroad agreed to chain the trains after dark. The final section of the City Extension was approved in August 1832, with the track opened in October the full two miles along Pratt Street, turning south on President Street to the City Dock (Olson 1980: 144; Dilts 1993: 144).

The Pratt Street extension in Baltimore proved to be a critical early development in American railroad design, with an immediate and long-term impact upon urban morphology. The use of grooved rail tracks on local city streets avoided the expense of British cable-operated tunnels or elevated viaducts to reach center terminals. However, it also established the pattern of permitting the new rail technology to mix dangerously with traditional pedestrian and horse-drawn wagon and carriage traffic in city streets. It was a decision that, with the growing scale and speed of trains, created sufficient fatalities and injuries over the next century in America's largest cities to force many costly and cumbersome forms of "grade separation" to be made—retrospectively, at least. Nevertheless, in the absence of foresight, the Pratt Street railroad route served as an immediate example to other American railroads for use of local streets to gain access to city center districts. Other eastern seaboard cities adopted the Baltimore "in-the-street" solution, most significantly Philadelphia and New York City.

In other respects, the addition of railroads to Baltimore followed another principle, one of locating deliberately at or beyond the edge of the built-up area to let the city's existing traffic find its way there and consequently to stimulate development at the urban margins, such was the—by then—ingrained expectation that city growth was inevitable and there was money to be made from it. Although the Baltimore and Port Deposit Railroad, entering the city from the east, connected directly with the City Dock, early rail lines from the north stopped well short of the urban edge at the time (such as the Baltimore and Susquehanna Railroad, 1852), confident that growth would engulf them before long. Eventually, the B&O Railroad required central facilities on a scale that brought a major realignment of its tracks and terminal location on the southwest corner of the business district (see Fig. 8.3). And later still, in 1895, corporate competition forced the B&O to construct the Howard Street tunnel, providing it with a dedicated railroad corridor northward under of the city and out toward Philadelphia.

Philadelphia and Railroads in the Street

In Philadelphia, railroad interest emerged in 1825, when William Strickland was sent to England to report on railroad operations in the Northumberland coalfields. Two early railroads were chartered, built and operating by 1833, approaching the city from the west and north, the chief directions by which to engage with the city's economic hinterland. The first, a state-sponsored railroad to Columbia on the Susquehanna, was chartered in 1826 and approved two years later to enter the city across the Schuylkill River as the Philadelphia and Columbia Railroad. The terminal station was located on the north edge of the city limits at Broad and Vine Streets in 1829 and became the operating terminus when the railroad opened in May 1832 (Fig. 8.4). Efforts to extend a railroad line through the city center to the Delaware River docks were initially opposed by civic officials and local teamsters. Finally, in January 1833, a charter for a "City Railroad" was approved by the City Council for operation of horse-drawn freight trains on Broad Street with grooved granite rails, and opened by December (Scharf and Westcott 1884: 2171–6; Roberts 1980: 28).

Similarly peripheral, by intent, the Philadelphia, Germantown, and Norristown Railroad (PG&N), which opened in 1832, approached from the north and terminated at Green and Ninth streets, then the edge of the city. Within six months, horses were replaced by locomotives. A year later, an extension was authorized to connect, via city streets, with the Columbia Railroad's station at Broad and Vine streets (Scharf and Westcott 1884: 2178).

Within another year, two further connecting freight lines were extended on city streets—the Southwark Railroad and the Northern Liberties Railroad—both operating by November 1834 (Scharf and Westcott 1884: 2180; Roberts 1980: 29). The result was a circumferential beltway network of rail lines linking two spots on the Delaware River docks with the city's western hinterland but largely avoiding the congested city center. In addition, these lines were used for informal "pleasure cars" to the suburbs, providing Philadelphia with a rudimentary urban transit system as early as 1834 (Ash 1837: 88; Krim 1983).

Meanwhile, the state legislature had authorized a City Railroad in 1831, but no construction occurred until the Broad Street line was built in 1833. Orthogonal lines were added along Market Street only in 1838 and 1839. These lines all used horses for motive power. The enabling legislation

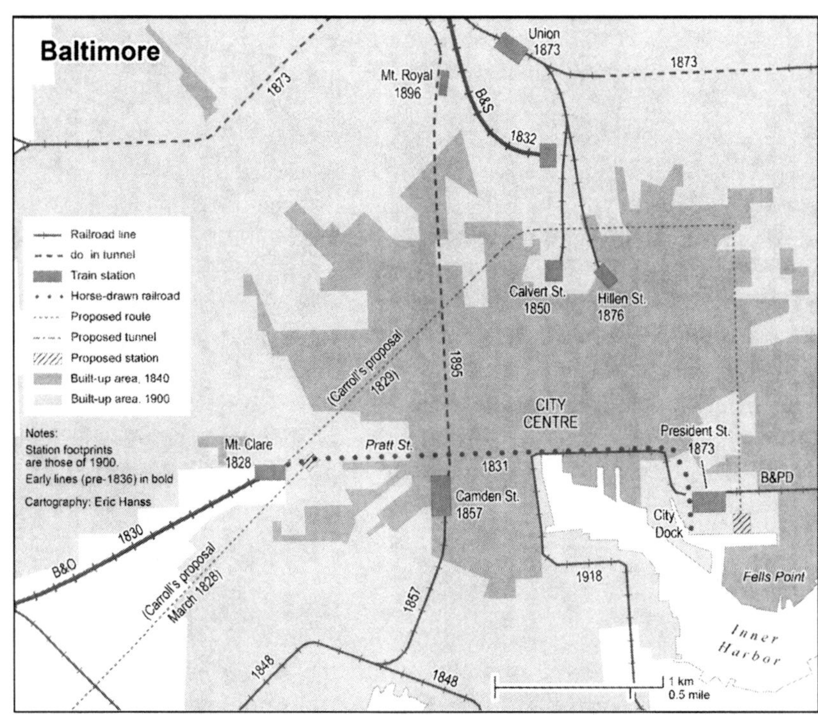

FIGURE 8.3 Railroad lines and stations in central Baltimore, 1828–1900

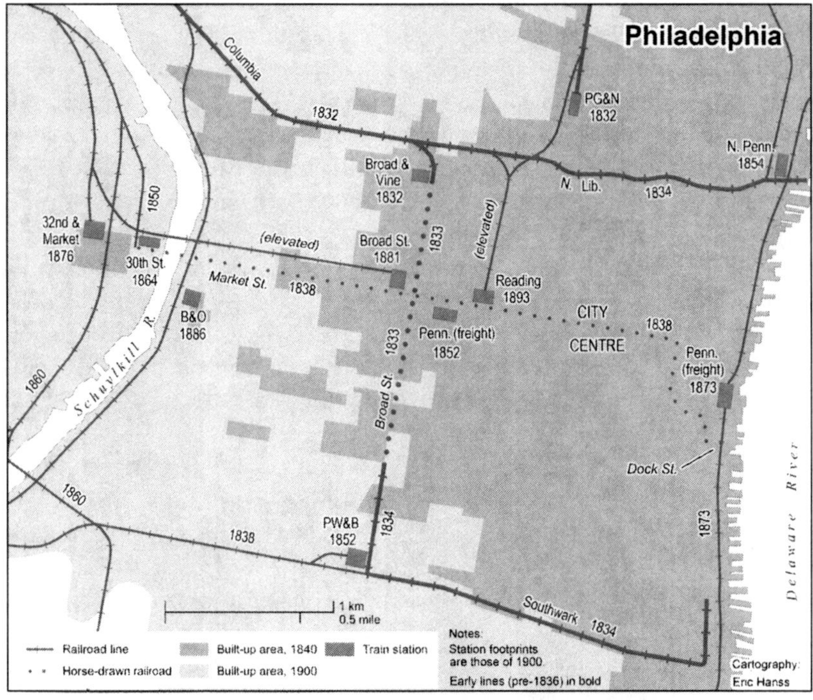

FIGURE 8.4 Railroad lines and stations in central Philadelphia, 1832–1900

had mandated that only animal power be used on city streets, so, from 1834 until the restriction ended in 1873, steam power was prohibited from city streets (Roberts 1980: 33). Strikingly, then, a large proportion of the city's built-up core remained remote from the steam-train terminals until late in the nineteenth century (see Fig. 8.4).

The pressure so created was relieved with a vengeance after 1880, when the Pennsylvania and the Reading railroads—by then with large, consolidated rail systems threading the city's hinterland—pushed deep into the heart of the expanded city's central business district with large arched terminal facilities and imposing head-houses at the end of lengthy viaducts in 1881 and 1893, respectively. In addition, the Delaware waterfront received a railroad running along Front Street in 1874, completed by the century's end, by which time it functioned as a dockside segment of a larger, metropolitan network of interconnecting beltways, as in Liverpool and Baltimore (compare Figs. 8.1, 8.3, and 8.4).

The development of rail facilities within inner Philadelphia during the nineteenth century followed the precedent set in Baltimore, of tracks in the streets but with more emphasis and greater spatial consequence. Only decades later—as the city's business center had migrated to the central cross-axis originally planned by William Penn, by then crowned with the imposing Philadelphia City Hall—did the railroads resort to expensive viaducts to emphatically penetrate the urban core.

Beltlines and the Metropolitan Context

If one compares the broader pattern of railroad development in and around the four cases examined, several features stand out. First, the extent of the respective built-up areas of Liverpool, Manchester, Baltimore, and Philadelphia varied much less around 1900 than did the cities' populations. Differences in central city proportions of metropolitan population need to be balanced in any comparison against the difficulty of generalizing the areas considered as "built-up," given their statistical and cartographic representations in Britain and the United States records. However, while Manchester and Philadelphia had approximately 1.5 million residents each in 1900–1901, Liverpool and Baltimore supported between one-half and two-thirds of a million residents each. Yet these differences hardly play out in terms of the extent of the built-up areas or the density and complexity of their railroad infrastructure (Fig. 8.5). Philadelphia's large area only highlighted the dispersed pattern of its railroad network, while Manchester's compactness emphasized its tightly woven system of inner railroads.

Second, railroad engineers and railroad officials in Liverpool and Baltimore solved city center access with tunnels, but this was done early in the former case and relatively late in the latter. Third, unsurprisingly, all cases displayed substantial beltline connections around their metropolitan fringes to ease goods movement through the regions, although none display strong coordination in their evolution. And, fourth, though there is evidence of some later simplification in the number and location of stations, the majority, once built, remained stubbornly rooted in the urban fabric over substantial periods of time—reflecting the high fixed costs of their placement.

Conclusion

The insertion of steam railroads into urban centers during the early decades of the nineteenth century promoted a radical morphological transformation that produced the modern industrial city. The development of the steam passenger railroad in Great Britain after 1820, particularly when the success of the L&M Railway was assured after 1830, provides examples of terminal railroad locations

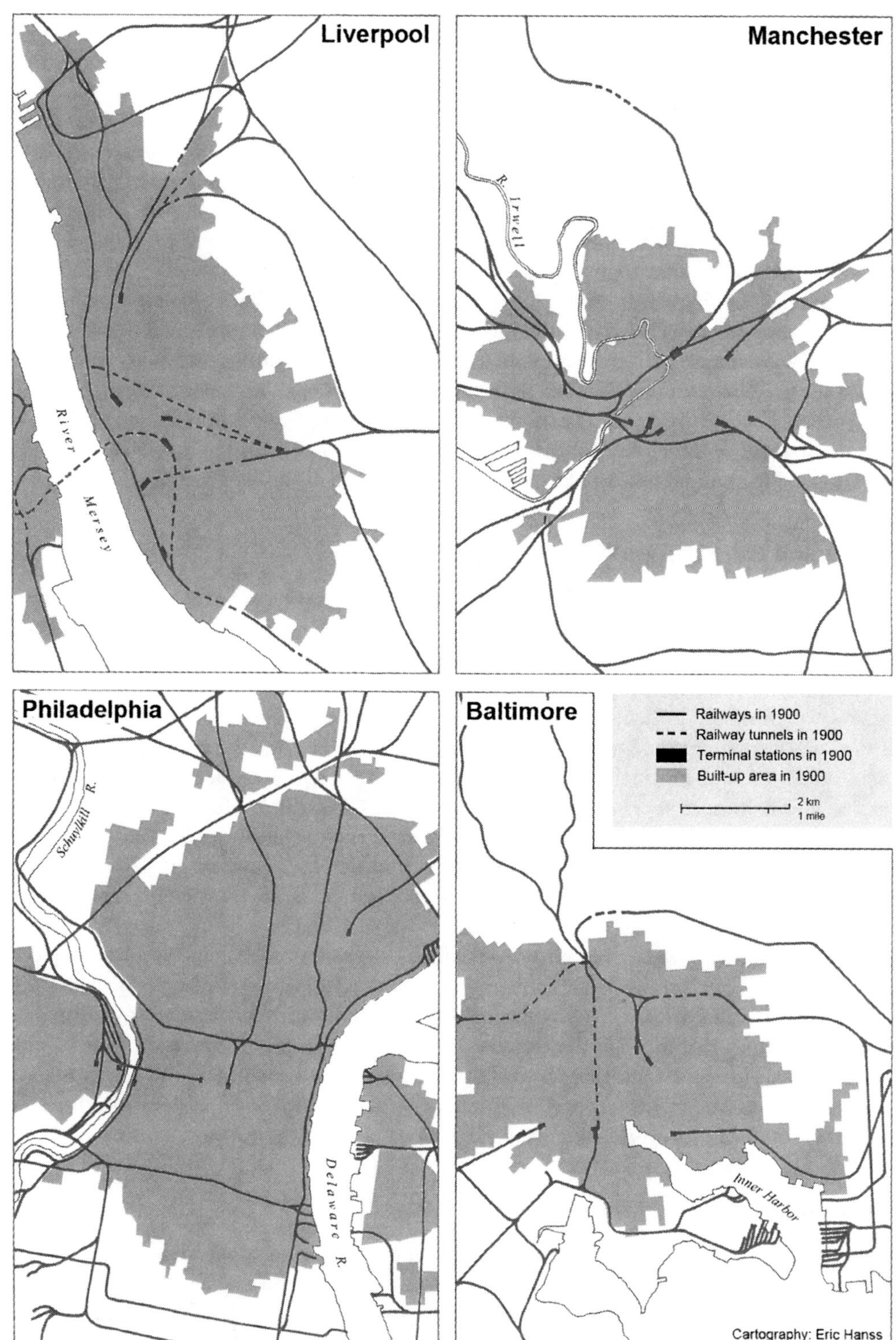

FIGURE 8.5 Terminal stations in relation to the metropolitan railroad patterns of the four cities in 1900

on the fringe of dense urban centers, using restricted rights of way and employing elevated viaducts and subway tunnels to reach the town center. The access achieved in this way was particularly close-in, often at large engineering and financial cost, and reflected the high volume of demand to be tapped.

By contrast, American railroads of the same period relied heavily on the street track railroad to gain access to central city locations, mixing trains and conventional street traffic. The case of the Pratt Street line of the B&O Railroad in 1831, initially with grooved granite rails that permitted easy crossing by wheeled vehicles, became the accepted model for other early American urban railroads. They were originally restricted to horse power to avoid the collision of locomotives and people. Whether steam railroad terminals were held at bay by legal restrictions or political will, their more distant relationship to the commercial core reflected an additional impulse. This was the expectation that the railroad terminals would act as development poles in themselves, as the large cities they were connecting proved the value of their macro-geographical positions within a resource-rich continent and hence were generating rapid urban growth. As metric space has always had a different value in wide-open America from that of long-settled, minutely owned Europe, this looser pattern created a more spread-out rail network.

The divergence between European and American urban railroad locations within cities appears to rest on the age and density differential of the two cultures. In England and Europe, established town centers kept railroad access to the suburban fringe by prohibitive restrictions of local civic authorities, except by such extraordinary means as cable subway tunnels. In the United States, the very youth of the cities allowed a flexibility of solution, though also restricted by civic authority, permitting surface street railroads under special charter to locate within the commercial core.

What is most striking, given the early date of development, is the rapid adoption of the railroad by 1830 in both Great Britain and the United States. Curiously, the innovative trigger appears to be the risk venture of Quaker merchants with the original Stockton and Darlington Railway, the Liverpool and Manchester, and the Baltimore and Ohio Railroad in the 1820s. These ventures were linked by a network of Friends in London, Liverpool, and Baltimore eager to test the technology of the new steam locomotive engines for regional passenger service. However, the differential between English and American investment is seen between the calculated expense of the Liverpool and Manchester line and the practical frugality of the Baltimore and Ohio route in seeking urban center terminal locations. In Liverpool, a deep-bore tunnel and, in Baltimore, a granite street track provided links to the waterfront dock districts. These alternative solutions mark a divide by 1831 between British and American practice.

From this point forward, the two urban cultures diverged to accommodate the steam railroad, one at a respectful suburban distance, the other inserted close to the city core. Less contrast can be seen in the economic and political agency that underlay railroad immersion in the cities. On both sides of the Atlantic, railroad matters were worked through by merchants, engineers, and government officials. National and state legislators eagerly enabled projects to improve intercity transport but gave ample leeway to city officials in shaping local conditions. Beyond that, competing commercial interests with investments in different city locations struggled against one another to gain advantage. The major national difference was the absence of a landed aristocracy in the United States and the more immediate presence of the national government in Britain.

The study of early railroad insertion within the nineteenth-century city can provide a detailed glimpse at the outcomes of such cultural differences, and it demonstrates how rapidly new transport technologies can be embedded within the morphology of the urban fabric. It took increasing central densities in large American cities much later in the century to force implementation of grade separation for safety purposes, thereby delaying morphological change through changing transport technology. In Britain, that separation was instituted from the beginning and remains substantially intact. The rapid decline of the railroad as a viable transport medium within American cities during the twentieth century, however, rendered large areas of former railroad property obsolete and, therefore, both ready for, and inviting to, the entrepreneurs behind large-scale redevelopment.

Note

1 The use of the terms "railway" and "railroad" were interchangeable at this time, although "railway" eventually became common usage in Great Britain for corporate charters, and "railroad" in the United States.

References

Appleton, J. (1965) *A Morphological Approach to the Geography of Transport*. Hull, U.K.: University of Hull, Occasional Papers in Geography 3.

Ash, T. (1837) *Guide to the Lions of Philadelphia*. Philadelphia: T. H. Ash.

Baines, T. (1852) *History of Liverpool*. London: Longman, Brown, Green and Longman.

Beaver, S. (1937) The railways of great cities. *Geography*, 22: 116–20.

Booth, H. (1830) *An Account of the Liverpool and Manchester Railway*. Liverpool: Wales and Baines.

Carlson, R. (1969) *The Liverpool & Manchester Railway Project, 1821–1831*. New York: Augustus M. Kelley.

Dickinson, R. (1947) *City Region and Regionalism: A Geographical Contribution to Human Ecology*. London: Kegan Paul, Rench, Trubner and Co.

Dilts, J. (1993) *The Great Road: The Building of the Baltimore and Ohio, 1828–1853*. Stanford: Stanford University Press.

Donaghy, T. (1972) *Liverpool & Manchester Railway Operations, 1831–1845*. Newton Abbott, U.K.: David and Charles.

Dunbar, S. (1915) *A History of Travel in America*. New York: Bobbs-Merrill Company.

Ferneyhough, F. (1980) *Liverpool & Manchester Railway, 1830–1980*. London: Robert Hale.

Fitzgerald, R. (1980) *Liverpool Road Station, Manchester: A Historical and Architectural Survey*. Manchester: Manchester University Press.

Gage, A. (1836) *Town and Port of Liverpool*. London: Thomas Starling.

Holly, H. (1991) The Granite Railway. *Quincy History*, 26: 1–4.

Hoole, K. (1986) *History of the Railways of Great Britain: the North East*. Newton Abbott, U.K.: David and Charles.

Hungerford, E. (1928) *The Story of the Baltimore & Ohio Railroad, 1827–1927*, vol. 1. New York: G. P. Putnam's Sons.

Jackman, A. (1969) *London's Termini*. New York: Augustus M. Kelly.

Kellett, J. (1969) *The Impact of Railways on Victorian Cities*. London: Routledge and Kegan Paul.

Kirby, M. (1993) *The Origins of Railway Enterprise: The Stockton and Darlington Railway, 1821–1863*. Cambridge: Cambridge University Press.

Krim, A. (1983) Early urban street railways, the graphic evidence, 1830–1860. Unpublished paper presented at the Eastern Historical Geography Association, Geneseo, New York.

Lee, C. (1937) *The Evolution of Railways*. London: The Railway Gazette.

Lewis, M. (1970) *Early Wooden Railways*. New York: Augustus M. Kelley.

Marshall, C. F. D. (1938) *A History of British Railways Down to the Year 1830*. London: Oxford University Press.

Mayer, H. (1944) Localization of railway facilities in metropolitan centers as typified by Chicago. *Journal of Land and Public Utility Economics*, 20: 299–315.

Murphy, R. (1966) *The American City: An Urban Geography*. New York: McGraw-Hill Book Company.

Nilsen, M. (2008) *Railways and the Western European Capitals: Studies of Implantation in London, Paris, Berlin, and Brussels*. New York: Palgrave Macmillan.

Olson, S. (1980) *Baltimore: The Building of an American City*. Baltimore: Johns Hopkins University Press.

Picturesque Hand-Book to Liverpool (1842) Liverpool: Wareing Webb.

Robbins, M. (1962) *The Railway Age in Britain*. London: Routledge and Kegan Paul.

Roberts, J. (1980) Railroads and the downtown: Philadelphia, 1830–1900, in W. Cutler and H. Gillette (eds.), *The Divided Metropolis: Social and Spatial Dimensions of Philadelphia, 1800–1975*, 27–55. Westport: Greenwood Press.

Rolt, L. (1960) *The Railway Revolution: George and Robert Stephenson*. New York: St. Martin's Press.

Sandstrom, G. (1965) *Tunnels*. New York: Holt, Rinehart and Winston.

Scharf, J. T., and Westcott, T. (1884) *History of Philadelphia*, vol. 3. Philadelphia: L. H. Everts and Co.

Smith, W. (1853) *History and Description of the Baltimore and Ohio Railroad*. Baltimore: John Murphy.

Stover, J. (1987) *History of the Baltimore & Ohio Railroad.* West Lafayette: Purdue University Press.

The Stranger in Liverpool (1841) Liverpool: Thos. Kaye.

Vance, J. (1995) *The North American Railroad.* Baltimore: Johns Hopkins University Press.

Wheeler, J. (1836) *Manchester: Its Political, Social and Commercial History*. London: Whittaker and Co.

9

SHAPING THE HOUSING OF INDUSTRIALISTS AND WORKERS

The Textile Settlements of Księży Młyn (Łódź) and Żyrardów in Poland

Marek Koter and Mariusz Kulesza

The impact of the Industrial Revolution on the form of cities was rarely orderly or coherent. It created entirely new urban places and profoundly transformed existing ones. It accelerated change, boosted or retarded urban growth by its geographical selectivity, and brought with it unprecedented construction forms and spatial configurations of land use. At the same time, it introduced entirely new actors to the urban drama and upended traditional types and combinations of agency in the production and management of urban form. This chapter will explore these themes in the context of a particular industry (the manufacture of textiles), in a particular regional setting (Poland), and during a particularly hectic historical epoch (the nineteenth century). It will demonstrate the interplay of forces that transformed the morphological character of Łódź, now the nation's second-largest city, and how that paralleled but also differed from that of Żyrardów, a new textile town between Warsaw and Łódź. Although archival data allowing the accurate attribution of individual buildings and urban layouts to specific architects and engineers is often missing, the influence of national industrial policy and the development of "industrial empires" by powerful individuals and families are especially significant factors.

A long-standing interpretation of the industrialization process emphasizes the role of surplus merchant capital in seeding the rise of industry on the factory principle and in encouraging the spread of technological innovations in manufacture. Such a view privileges the role of the entrepreneur as an energetic and imaginative actor in creating great new factories and the jobs that went with them and in stimulating the addition of urban facilities that serviced them. The actual picture is, of course, more complex, and while the new Industrial Age flourished in a business climate of substantial, and sometimes almost unfettered *laissez faire*, the role of government as both stimulus and regulator must also be recognized. This is emphatically true in cases where industrial development occurred in locations far from existing towns, in which government stimulus was critical to success. Furthermore, the sources of capital and labor were often non-local, so that the origins of industrialists, and the cultural baggage they brought with them, and the migrations of workers and their families figure significantly in the equation. All these factors contributed to the mixture of influences that produced the urban landscapes of the Industrial Revolution (Dumała 1974). In the case of Łódź and Żyrardów, such actors were often not native-born Poles but drawn to this region by a range of push and pull factors. The education and experience of the industrialists, and of the engineers and designers whom they employed, critically informed the layout and design of these towns, of the factories, of the workers' housing and related facilities, and of the villas built for the owners themselves. As often as not, the layout and buildings of the new factory complexes followed ideal models developed earlier and elsewhere but, inevitably, their application in the Polish settings examined here produced results with highly individual character.

The State as Initial Stimulus for Industrialization in Poland

The origin of textile towns such as Łódź and Żyrardów in central Poland stems from the situation produced by the partition of the country by Prussia, Russia, and Austria at the end of the eighteenth century and the subsequent border shifts caused by the edicts of the Congress of Vienna in 1815 (Ostrowski 1966: 36). The division of Polish lands was then revised in favor of Russia, ending in the establishment of the autonomous Congress Kingdom of Poland within the Russian Empire. The new territorial division brought about far-reaching changes in the economic situation of different segments of the fragmented Polish lands. Some became cut off from their traditional export markets; others lost their major industrial centers. This was the case for the Kingdom of Poland, as its sources of supply for textile products remained beyond the border with Prussia, whereas salt mines and other mineral resources were taken over by Austria. To make matters worse, these countries imposed customs restrictions, thus hindering trans-border trade.

Faced with this difficult situation, the government of the Kingdom of Poland in 1820 launched a policy of rapid industrialization of the hitherto largely agricultural country. Within a remarkably short period of time (until the abolition of autonomy in 1831), it succeeded in developing a mining industry based on coal and non-ferrous ores in the southern region, metallurgy in the Świętokrzyskie Mountain region, salt production at Ciechocinek, and several industrial textile settlements in its central region. In addition, a new, regular road network was created. The most spectacular of these achievements was the creation of new settlements for the industrial production of textiles. In this regard, Łódź, as Poland's largest cotton industry center, and Żyrardów, a linen-manufacturing town, offer particularly interesting cases by which to assess the role various forms of agency played in their gestation.

Early Government Planning for Industrial Diversity at Łódź

Łódź has enjoyed technical city status since 1423 but, for most of its history, it functioned as no more than an agricultural village in a remote transition zone between Western and Eastern Europe (Liszewski 1997: 11). In 1820, however, it was selected as a site for future industrial development by the government of the Kingdom of Poland, and a plan was drawn up under the supervision of Rajmund Rembieliński, president of the Commission of Mazowsze Region, organized in two phases. First, in 1821–3, a new "greenfield" settlement was grafted onto the historic core on its southern side, complete with octagonal market square, small house plots, and separate orchard plots, designed to attract clothiers, especially makers of cotton fabric. Second, in the years 1824–8, a cotton-linen settlement was added, a linear street-village laid out along a newly created arterial street, Piotrkowska Street, leading south. This contained deep but narrow-frontage lots for weavers' cottages, flanked by double-width lots behind (to east and west) for spinners to grow their own flax and spin yarn. At the same time, the valley of the Jasień River further to the south was reserved for large factory development and subdivided into very large parcels (Kossmann 1966; Koter 1980; Liszewski 1997: 15). The settlements were inhabited by craftsmen who came at the government's invitation from German countries and from Silesia (then part of the Habsburg portion of Bohemia), where the traditional textile industry had experienced a sharp decline in the face of serious competition from British mechanized manufacturing.

These settlers were attracted to the Kingdom of Poland by excellent conditions: in the settlements laid out by the government or the towns' owners, they found houses ready to be occupied, while special loans were offered to start businesses, and taxes were reduced. Moreover, a customs barrier was implemented to discourage foreign competition. In addition, residents were given the privilege of cutting timber in the surrounding state forests, important for production and living. Initially, the production was from handiwork, made mainly in private houses that contained spinning and weaving workshops. Only some finishing operations (bleaching, dying, and cotton spinning) were carried out in special manufacturing buildings utilizing water power. The first steam machinery, however, was installed in Łódź as early as 1838, and mechanized textile factories developed thereafter (Komar 1933). Łódź was unique in the history of European town planning in exemplifying the rational planning by central government of an industrial town in a way that anticipated both the needs of artisans and of large factories (Ostrowski 1966: 38; Koter 1969).

As a result, migrants flocked to the new settlements at Łódź, as did entrepreneurs bringing much-needed outside capital, such as Christian Friedrich Wendisch, Ludwig Geyer and David von Lande – all receiving credit and privileges on condition that they built factories there (Flatt 1853; Rynkowska 1951). Piotrkowska Street filled up with artisans and became increasingly overcrowded, even as it acquired status as the city's main street. The Jasień valley industrial corridor received several textile mills at intervals, determined by the sites designed to deliver water power, with abundant land in reserve for industrial expansion.

Despite these early developments, it was not until the 1860s that Łódź entered the most dynamic phase of transformation from a handicraft settlement to a large industrial city. After the emancipation of the serfs in 1864, Łódź was flooded by waves of migrants from the countryside who constituted a cheap labor supply. In this period, several affluent entrepreneurs set up their businesses in Łódź and, from 1865 on, the city was served by rail. Owing to this set of favorable circumstances in the second half of the nineteenth century, the city experienced an explosive rate of growth, comparable to that of many urban centers in the United States. The population multiplied from 800 inhabitants in 1820, to 15,500 in 1840, 40,000 in 1865, 108,000 in 1885, 283,000 in 1900, and to 478,000 in 1914. Within a few short decades, Łódź grew into the second largest city in the Kingdom of Poland and the largest industrial textile center in the Russian Empire (Koter et al. 2005).

As with other sizeable industrial towns in Europe, the cityscape of Łódź grew dense with commercial properties, small factories, and speculative housing, all fitting awkwardly within the tight frame of the established street and plot system—not designed with such extraordinary growth in mind (Stefański 2001; Koter 2009). The agency in this lay not in the abiding power of the municipality to force or guide such growth but rather in its virtual absence as a shaping force. Though there was an office of "town architect," the appointee mainly worked for private clients. The public authority that had produced the early additions to the old town, including the large factory reserves, had been the national state and, once it had triggered development, it withdrew in the face of free enterprise and liberal economic forces. Urban planning became simply what entrepreneurs individually desired (Popławska and Muthesius 1986: 151). By the end of the nineteenth century, Łódź boasted some 900 factories, the largest and most elaborate of which belonged to Karl Scheibler.

Karl Scheibler's Łódź

Karl Wilhelm Scheibler (1820–81), a German from a well-to-do textile manufacturing family in Monschau in the Eifel region, gained his professional experience in the famous Cockerill's manufactory in Belgium. In the political atmosphere of 1848, he came to the Kingdom of Poland and took the position of director at his uncle Schlösser's spinning mill at Ozorków, 25 kilometers north of Łódź. He moved to Łódź in 1854 to open—at age 28—a large cotton manufactory the following year. Scheibler made his fortune by clever speculations carried out during the so-called "cotton crisis" caused by the American Civil War (1861–65). As soon as he realized that the American conflict would likely starve the European textile industry of its raw material, he began to buy and store huge amounts of cotton. Later, while many textile entrepreneurs ran out of supplies, he was able to continue production and sell fabrics at very high prices. Growing rich, he bought out the manufactories of many who went bankrupt (although not the neighboring Grohmann company), thereby steadily expanding his business. From a small site on the edge of the designated industrial corridor, "Scheibler's Empire" eventually covered almost the entire area along the Jasień valley designated for industry according to the initial development plan (see Fig. 9.1). This included, after a corporate merger in 1921, the Grohmann complex as well. Extending over three kilometers, Scheibler property covered one-seventh of the city area (Stefański 2009: 13).

The gargantuan manufacturing establishment developed by Scheibler was distinguished by both its modern technology and excellent spatial arrangement (see Fig. 9.2). The central part of the complex, Księży Młyn (Priest's Mill), constructed in the 1870s, was composed of factories, workers' houses and a series of owner's residences. It represents one of the most interesting examples of industrial urban planning in Europe.

FIGURE 9.1 'Scheibler's Empire': panoramic view of the industrial complex of Księży Młyn, Łódź, in the 1880s

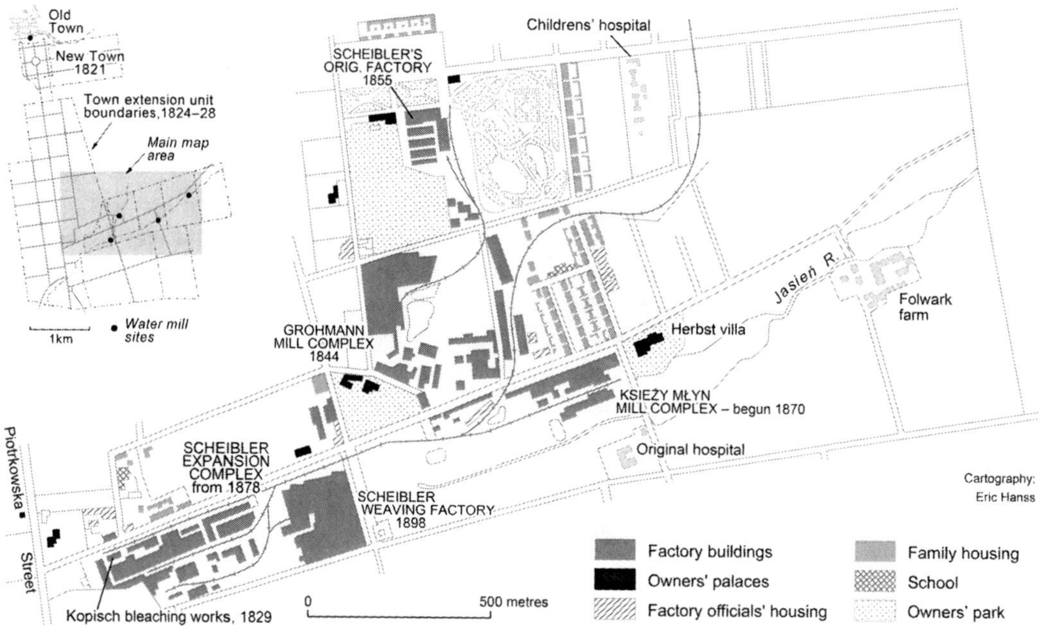

FIGURE 9.2 The early growth stages of Łódź (top left) and Scheibler's multi-factory industrial complex in the Księży Młyn district, as it had matured by the mid-twentieth century

Prior to 1870 the industrial evolution of the Księży Młyn site had been slow. Since 1822, two generations of spinning mills had flourished briefly under other ownership before succumbing to depression and destruction by fire. When Scheibler bought the site, the transformation of Księży Młyn began in earnest, with a monumental four-story building housing a spinning mill and a hall for preparing the raw material. Built in 1870–3, this huge quadrangular structure (207 meters long and 35.5 meters wide) was set out along St. Emily Street, named after Scheibler's wife. The building was made of red bricks and unplastered, patterned after German *rohbau* architecture. The spinning mill's eclectic style, neo-Gothic elements and monolithic proportions lent the building a fortress-like appearance. Its extremely long façade of fifty-five bays with modest decoration emphasized its extraordinary proportions. At the corners, octagonal castle-like towers, complete with crenellations, contained staircases or lifts (see Fig. 9.3). In the center of the building, projecting slightly from the façade, were main doorways with cast iron eaves embellished with floral and geometric motifs in an oriental style—somewhat surprising in this context. This part of the building was topped with a little turret containing a siren, which called the workers to work. Inside were vast halls with spinning machines, divided into "naves" by rows of iron columns supporting the roof (Popławska and Muthesius 1986: 152–3).

In 1877, another spinning mill was raised parallel to the first (see Fig. 9.4). Built in the same architectural style, this was also a massive structure. Between the two mills were located some service buildings, including boiler-houses with tall chimneys overlooking the entire complex and the first gashouse, erected in 1878 and adorned with some neo-Gothic features.

The spinning mills formed the core of the Księży Młyn complex. Such vast mechanized factories signaled the ultimate separation of work and living for the growing class of workers and the

FIGURE 9.3 The first cotton spinning mill at Księży Młyn, Łódź (1870–3)

FIGURE 9.4 The second cotton spinning mill at Księży Młyn, Łódź (1877)

appearance in the cityscape of purpose-built workers' tenement housing. Around 1875, Scheibler added a workers' housing estate to his production complex, directly facing the mill area itself. Had such housing been left to speculative builders or the workers themselves, the necessary housing would likely have been somewhat scattered throughout the city, but the industrialist had every reason to concentrate his tenements next to his factories—on land he controlled. The results in terms of changing the form of the city were unprecedented (Popławska 1992).

Workers' Housing

The housing estate was composed of three rows of two-and-a-half-story buildings built of red brick (see Figs. 9.1, 9.5). Austere in style, they resembled military barracks. Each house contained eighteen flats—eight on each floor and two in the garret situated adjacent to a long corridor. The floor area was either twenty-five square meters (one room) or forty square meters (two rooms). There were no sanitary facilities inside the flats. Behind the houses, parallel to them, were low bins for storing wood, coal, potatoes, cabbage, and so on, and toilets. The main *allée*, laid out between two western rows of houses, divided the housing estate into two unequal parts. This asymmetry was deliberate: The main axis of the estate was aligned with the main factory gate, thus joining the two parts of the complex. This broad tree-lined *allée* was flanked with two stone-paved access roads (see Fig. 9.2). A green strip with benches ran down the middle and was used for recreation. In addition, there were public wells with pumps providing water for the inhabitants. The third row of houses was located some distance away, along Przędzalniana (Spinning) Street. It was extended in the later phase of development in 1885–9 by another row of houses of similar architectural style but, at three storys, somewhat higher. The estate was fenced, and its gates closed at night (Pytlas et al. 1998).

FIGURE 9.5 Workers' housing at Księży Młyn, Łódź (1870–3)

Community Buildings

The housing estate was confined to the north by a row of community buildings, distinguishable by their functions, situated perpendicularly to the main axis. They included a school with teachers' flats, a workers' canteen, a clubhouse with a room for dancing and shows, and a small grocery store. To the west, adjacent to the housing estate, was a fire station—an original building built in 1878—with a high tower, a stable, and garages for vehicles. In the early 1880s, after a local railway branch serving the Scheibler industrial complex had been constructed, a freight railway terminal with three long storage houses was developed, closing the complex on the west side. The hospital of St. Ann, meant for workers and named after one of Scheibler's granddaughters who died prematurely, was built in 1882 and placed at the southern margin of the complex (see Fig. 9.2). Such institutional services were unusual in any industrial setting in Europe at this time, and their provision by a factory owner highlights the weakness of the municipal authority as a provider of social infrastructure. Łódź as a city had neither municipal water supply nor sewage system before 1914 (Smith 2000: 56).

The Księży Młyn housing estate was distinct from other workers' housing in Łódź, which consisted typically of the old weavers' cottages along Piotrkowska Street or the often cramped tenement buildings that had replaced them, often wedged on the plots behind them (Koter 1990). Księży Młyn occupants were provided with modest, but healthy and secure, living conditions, and their basic social needs were satisfied by substantial amenities uncommon in Łódź at the time (Popławska 1992). Living in Księży Młyn was greatly appreciated among members of the working class. Very strong neighborly ties developed among the inhabitants and, even today, many workers of the former Scheibler manufactory do not wish to move, although the housing conditions would be considered poor by modern standards.

Owners' Villas

An elegant villa was built in 1876 for Scheibler's daughter Matylda and her husband, Edward Herbst, who took over "Scheibler's Empire" after the death of its founder in 1881. Located to the east of the industrial and residential sectors, at the corner of St. Emily Street and Przędzalniana Street, the villa was situated such that the factory and the residential quarter were both visible from its windows (see Fig. 9.6). The siting of such residences next to industrial plants was characteristic of Łódź's entrepreneurs. Within the span of just one generation, they had risen from simple craftsmen to the status of well-to-do entrepreneurs. As was typical of the *nouveaux riches*, they were anxious to keep an eye on their businesses. It was the following generation of industrialists who began to build their residences in more attractive and agreeable surroundings away from centers of industrial production, but for half a century or more, industrial entrepreneurs and their architects fashioned "model" company town-sites—some in remote locations, others at the edges of existing cities—over which they had complete, unitary, and assertive control in shaping the spaces and appearance of their settlements. In this, Scheibler and his architect at the time, Jan Bojanowski, the first town architect of Łódź, followed in the mold of Robert Owen and his industrial village of New Lanark in Scotland and prefigured by just a few years the Cadbury brothers at Bournville, outside Birmingham in England, and George Pullman at Pullman, outside Chicago in the United States.

The Herbst villa was given an elegant late-Italian Renaissance style. Adjacent to this two-story edifice were a Swiss-style annex with timber-framed attic, a splendid ballroom in English Gothic style, and an orangery or winter garden. The interior was richly embellished with neo-Renaissance

FIGURE 9.6 The Herbst villa (1876) at Księży Młyn, Łódź

and neo-Rococo motifs. An elaborately arranged park with a pond surrounded the residence. To the rear were a gardener's house and a beautifully ornamented stable. Furthermore, there was a vast agricultural holding of 100 hectares with lakes, greenery, and service buildings and a couple of farms, all still within the city limits (see Fig. 9.2). There can be little doubt that in the case of this villa the architect sought to emulate the splendor of urban mansions of the nobility found in capital cities such as Warsaw. Little of its opulence, of course, filtered down to the workers' tenements, although they were not devoid of simple ornamentation. Such contrasts, by their very juxtaposition in space, emphasized social divisions (Popławska and Muthesius 1986: 160).

Księży Młyn, then, the first and ultimately the largest industrial complex established in Łódź, was thus composed of three morphological units serving different functions: manufacturing plants, workers' housing estate, and owner's residence. This complex was to a great extent a self-sufficient organism, largely autonomous in relation to the larger city; hence it was commonly referred to as "Scheibler's Empire," The social hierarchy was clearly expressed in the layout and design of the district (Turowski 1976; Smith 2000: 59).

Design Authorship

The authorship of Księży Młyn's layout and architecture as a whole remains in question. It is commonly believed to be a product of the city architect, Hilary Majewski (1838–92; Szram 1984).

Majewski graduated from the Fine Arts Academy in St. Petersburg in 1861 and then, on a government scholarship, continued his education in Italy (in Florence and Siena, among others) and France. Thanks to these early experiences, his works were predominantly inspired by mature Renaissance forms such as those found in Florence. Appointed as the city architect of Łódź in 1872, Majewski was charged with designing tenement houses, villas, palaces, sacred architecture of different denominations, public edifices, industrial plants, and other structures. Although more than 600 designs are signed with his name (Stefański 2009: 115–18), in all probability he was not personally the designer of them all. It is highly likely that, taking advantage of his position, he also signed works of other architects, Polish and German, who did not have Russian authorization to practice their profession. Scheibler, using his German connections, may have commissioned German architects to design industrial structures, as Majewski had little experience with such immense structures at that time. Nevertheless, the attribution of the housing estate at Księży Młyn to Majewski seems probable, and he was almost certainly the designer of the Herbst villa (Stefański 2009: 118). Nevertheless, Majewski would not have produced these designs without close and sustained consultations at all stages with Scheibler.

Fortunately, the Księży Młyn complex has survived almost intact. The former Scheibler manufactory houses several small firms, even after the bankruptcy of some of the large textile establishments in Łódź in the 1990s. The Herbst villa has become a branch of the Museum of Arts, and the workers' housing estate remains a living residential quarter to this day. The entire site has been registered as a historical district and thus enjoys certain legal protections.

Żyrardów: From Country Estate to Model Factory Town

Another significant modern industrial textile settlement in the Kingdom of Poland is Żyrardów, which sprang up after the establishment of a linen textile factory. A housing estate with modern community facilities was built to serve the needs of the workers employed in this factory. Unlike the Księży Młyn complex in Łódź, Żyrardów did not emerge rapidly on the fringe of an existing town as a result of the singular actions and energy of a Karl Scheibler. It developed from a completely rural site in several stages under several groups of stakeholders over a period of some seventy years (see Fig. 9.7).

Consortium of Landowners, Capitalists, and a Technician

The first stage consisted of preparatory works and the construction of an initial factory during the 1820s and 1830s. Żyrardów was part of the same program of industrialization put into operation by the government of the Kingdom of Poland at Łódź, with similar incentives to attract distinguished specialists from abroad. One of these specialists was Philippe de Girard (1775–1844), a French engineer famed for having invented a linen spinning machine in 1810. He came to Poland in 1825 to take the position of chief technician at the Department of Mining of the Governmental Committee for Revenue and Treasury. Three years later, he was commissioned to launch an experimental linen spinning mill at Marymont (today a district within the city of Warsaw) that would be supplied with locally grown flax. The ultimate goal, however, was to construct a large manufactory for linen fabrics.

The establishment of the manufactory and the settlement at Żyrardów originated with the activities of a group of influential people, including local landlords, industrial entrepreneurs, and

FIGURE 9.7 Panoramic view of the industrial complex of Żyrardów in 1899

bankers, all of whom had significant relationships with the state authorities. Looking to gain huge potential profits and to develop their lands, they decided to create a center for the linen industry between Warsaw and Łódź, which would experience a period of dynamic growth. The Łubieński brothers were the most prominent members of this group. They were from a well-connected family: Their father, Count Feliks Franciszek Łubieński, was a minister of justice in the government of the Grand Duchy of Warsaw, a state established by Napoléon. The Łubieński brothers were the owners of the agricultural estate of Guzów (the future site of Żyrardów), where they had introduced a modern agricultural management system. Furthermore, they also had influence in the newly created, Warsaw-based Polish Bank, which could loan capital. Here were the preconditions for industrial development.

The Society for Linen Production was founded in Warsaw on June 24, 1829, to promote flax culture and to construct a manufactory for linen fabrics that would use Girard's technical innovations. On March 1, 1830, the Governmental Committee for the Interior signed an agreement with the Society authorizing construction of a large linen spinning mill at Ruda Guzowska, a village of 150 inhabitants within the Łubieńskis' estate. The location was deemed superior for the cultivation of flax. The mill was officially established by Karol Scholtz & Co. on August 9, 1830. Its founders were Tomasz Łubieński (representing Łubieński Brothers & Co., a merchandise company), Henryk Łubieński (director of the Polish Bank), Jan Łubieński, Józef Lubowidzki (vice-president of the Polish Bank), and Karol Scholtz (trade counselor of the Bank). Philippe de Girard was appointed as technical director of the manufactory. The place name Żyrardów (a Polonized derivation of Girard) appeared in the notarial Act, serving to express the esteem in which the group held the French engineer's achievements. This was unusual as, in most cases, new settlements were named either after the localities in which they were placed, or after the owner's first name.

During the first stage of the industrial settlement's development (1830–46), when the factory was run by Scholtz, the Łubieński brothers and Girard, a spinning mill was erected on a rectangular site of seventeen hectares (see Fig. 9.8). It was situated on the main north–south road linking the local towns of Wiskitki and Mszczonów, fronted by a lavish formal garden. This road constituted the eastern boundary of the industrial complex. To the west, the factory complex was confined by the Pisia River, which supplied waterpower to the mill. Across the road from the spinning mill to the east, two brick dwelling houses for managers and clerks were built. These buildings (now

FIGURE 9.8 Linen spinning mill at Żyrardów (1833, enlarged later in the nineteenth century)

demolished) constituted the entirety of the early housing provision. Workers were drawn from the preexisting nearby village or from the surrounding district. Żyrardów was the first industrial settlement in the Kingdom of Poland to be accessible by rail, being served since 1845 by the Warsaw–Vienna railway (Dumała 1974: 282).

German Businessmen to the Rescue

As a result of debts built up by the K. Scholtz Company and the Łubieński brothers, the manufactory was taken over by the Polish Bank, coming under its direct administration. This period saw a slight enlargement of the factory and limited spatial growth of the settlement. In 1857, the Polish Bank, which had proved to be an unsuccessful manager, sold the factory to two German businessmen: Karl Theodor Hielle (1822–71) and Karl August Dittrich (1819–86). This event marks the beginning of the most dynamic development of Żyrardów, which was carried on after Dittrich's death by his son, Karl Dittrich, Jr. (1853–1918). During the 1860s, a linen weaving mill was constructed on the site of gardens formerly separating the spinning mill from the road to Wiskitki. In 1867 the new owners, seeking to expand the workforce, recognized the necessity of providing decent living conditions and initiated a large planned settlement of workers' housing.

Workers' Housing

The housing quarter was sited on the side of the road opposite the industrial plant (see Fig. 9.9). The main axis of the settlement, perpendicular to the main road, was aligned with the gate leading to the new weaving mill. Its first section had the form of an elongated rectangular market square, 200 meters long. Further down was a church square, followed by an 800-meter long and 45-meter wide *allée* bordering a 15-meter wide street, flanked by two rows of trees. The first workers' settlement, called "the New World," was set up either side of this central *allée*. The settlement at the time was

FIGURE 9.9 Plan (a), and spatial structure (b) of the historic core of Żyrardów

composed of detached two-story buildings arranged in quadrangles within the street blocks. Built of red brick, the buildings had an austere appearance with only few architectural details, such as moldings and angular pilasters (see Fig. 9.10). They were built on a rectangular plan with façades of seven bays and covered with a low gabled roof with large eaves. The building interiors were divided into two sections by a central corridor. Each floor contained four flats of two rooms each. They were intended to house the weavers working from home as contractors. Inside the quadrangular spaces between the houses were gardens and typical wooden bins with privies and external stairs leading to the upper floor.

The oldest of the houses in this section of the settlement date from 1867. The largest dwelling type in the entire settlement at this time was the so-called *familijniak* (family house). This was a four-story structure intended for seasonal workers, with large rooms and a façade of seven bays. The following year, Żyrardów's new housing was described in the magazine *Kłosy* with the following words:

FIGURE 9.10 Workers' housing at Żyrardów (1867–71), front and rear views

> Clean and cheap flats in 24 workers' houses provide a comfortable and healthy accommodation for the inhabitants. For transitory inhabitants there is a big barracks-like house with spacious and warm rooms where, for a moderate price, workers are offered iron beds with mattresses and free usage of a common kitchen heated and served at the expense of the factory. Every worker has the right to health service and medicines refunded by social security, as well as cost-free education for children in two elementary schools and one evening school. Soon a kindergarten will be opened for children whose parents are not able to take care of them during the workday.
>
> (authors' translation; originally quoted in Kołodziej 2001: 40)

This planned settlement subsequently developed in two stages: first in 1871–4 in connection with a rapid increase in employment in the factory, and then in 1885–1910, which marked the climax of its development.

The structures built in the settlement between 1871 and 1896 were characterized by the use of two types of building units—one standard and the other slightly larger—used in different combinations, depending on the required living area. The residential buildings continued to be built of brick, mostly two storys in elevation, on a rectangular plan without cellars and covered with a low gabled roof. The façades were still unplastered but had more ornamentation than did earlier buildings. The typical internal layout of the buildings consisted of two or three units on each floor. Two types of units were used: the first with four rooms (two flats of two rooms each) and the second with five rooms (one two-room flat and one three-room flat). In the years before 1896, a few similarly configured residential buildings were constructed; these, however, featured plastered façades. In the same period, two rows of one-unit, one-story houses with habitable timber-framed attics and plastered exteriors were built along Długa Street (now Limanowskiego, parallel to New World).

Spatial Structure Reflected Social Structure

The settlement's geographically differentiated architecture reflected the town's blunt social hierarchy and building functions (see Fig. 9.9b). There were houses for workers, foremen, middle and upper engineers, and administration staff and administration buildings and various community buildings (Szafer and Trzebiński 1954). The workers' houses were the most austere; those intended for the foremen exhibited a more richly decorated interior of a higher standard than that of the line workers. In contrast to both were the villas for high-ranking staff constructed in the 1880s. Situated near the landscape park, these were rectangular-plan two-story houses with cellars and habitable garrets, capped by high mansard roofs with dormer windows. Their red brick façades, punctuated with projections and horizontal bands, recalled the architecture of the French Renaissance. The villa for the general manager displayed a different flavor: its segmented form and richly embellished façade invoked a Swiss style.

At the top of the social hierarchy stood the owner's residence, known as "Karl Dittrich"s palace" (see Fig. 9.11), which represented a separate morphological unit within the settlement. Situated amid a vast landscape park and surrounded by arms of the Pisia River, this medium-size, one-story villa with a habitable garret was built in 1885–90 to a design by Władysław Hirshel. Eclectic in its style, it featured some elements of French Renaissance architecture. At a certain distance, near the factory, there was another residence called the "Tyrolean Palace." After its construction in the 1860s, it was used by Karl Dittrich's son-in-law.

The development of the settlement was stimulated by the growth of Żyrardów's industrial plant, which in the last quarter of the nineteenth century was among the largest linen manufactories in Europe and became the largest in the early twentieth century. In addition to linen, the enterprise also engaged in cotton and wool production. As early as 1870, a new factory for stocking manufacture was opened and extended in 1890–1910. In 1885, a counting house (administration building) was constructed and, in the early twentieth century, a new modern linen spinning mill was erected. The enlargement of the factory was followed by a steady increase in employment: from 780 employees in 1863 to 7,300 in 1882 and nearly 10,000 in 1915. As the settlement could not house all the workers, the surrounding rural fringe began to be parceled out for building sites. The majority of structures built on these were substandard houses, mostly of wood. In 1872, the population of the settlement

FIGURE 9.11 'Karl Dittrich's palace' (1885–90) at Żyrardów

was 6,300 but, by 1897, the settlement, together with these "spontaneous" extensions, totaled 25,500 people, including 2,530 Jews and 4,200 Protestants. Żyrardów as a whole held 33,000 people in 1913, although it did not receive the administrative status of a town until three years later.

Community Facilities

The large numbers of workers and their families had various needs regarding social life, education, health, and culture. In the spirit of the model communities that were beginning to appear elsewhere in Britain and Western Europe alluded to earlier, the company's owners accepted the responsibility to satisfy these needs through the provision of community buildings and social services—there was, of course, no public agency on the ground to do so, because until 1916 this was strictly a company town. It was an impressive project involving a significant array of services, which were seldom found in other Polish towns of that period, although the appearance of these services was staggered over decades (Gryciuk 1980: 117–22).

The amenities ranged across the fields of infant care, education, health, religion, socialization, and a few utilitarian necessities. After an 1885 extension, the kindergarten was attended by as many as 1,200 children divided into twenty classes and taught by thiry-five women who lived in an adjacent building. Three elementary schools were established in 1867, 1882, and 1892–6 (see Fig. 9.12), and a so-called *Kantoratschule* "for 40 boys" from German families only, was added in 1899 to prepare them to be accountants (Dumała 1974: 282–3). A Jewish school was in operation by 1910. Churches were provided by the company as the workforce became ethnically and religiously more diverse. Catholic devotions were initially provided for in a small structure placed centrally within the workers' housing district in 1891, but greater need led to a large and imposing church in 1903,

FIGURE 9.12 'New School' for workers' children (1892–6) at Żyrardów

which was located at the head of the open market square, facing the factory district, symbolically privileging the Catholic majority in the town (see Fig. 9.13). A Protestant church was added in 1898 and placed eccentrically on the outer fringe of the managerial district. In the early twentieth century a synagogue was built, also on the urban margin. A modern hospital with eighty beds was built in 1894, patterned after the famous Dresden Clinic, and the elderly people received a nursing house in 1913. While the managerial class received a social club, the *Resursa*, in the 1880s, the workers' social center came only in 1913. Basic services included a combined laundry and bath (in the 1880s), a slaughterhouse (about 1890), shops at the corners of the market square (1890s), a canteen (1906), and a post office (1910), all built by the company.

Most of the buildings for public use were placed close to the market square (see Fig. 9.9b). Distinguished by interesting, mostly neo-Gothic, architecture, these structures were characterized by a monochromatic appearance owing to their unplastered red brick façades. The only exception was the People's House, which was built in the modernist style and coated with plaster.

Design Authorship

The designers of the majority of these buildings remain in most cases unfortunately unknown; although the Dittrich villa is known to have been designed by Władysław Hirshel, the Evangelical church by Loessner, and the new Catholic church by Józef Dziekoński. These architects were either Polish or German. More significantly, however, the designer of the entire urban setting is also unknown. It can be presumed, however, that Karl Dittrich—the owner of the industrial settlement of Żyrardów—personally exerted major influence on its spatial configuration and that the scheme was laid out by a foreign architect or urban planner (Nazięblo 2001).

Some 95 percent of the original structures of the industrial settlement of Żyrardów have survived. These consist of 130 houses, 19 service buildings, and 60 related structures. With the exception of the wooden bins, the buildings are all built of brick and retain their original appearance of unplastered red brick walls. The housing is generally in a good state of conservation, and most of the factory

FIGURE 9.13 Market square and Catholic parish church (1900–3) at Żyrardów

buildings, having weathered a period of abandonment after closure of the mills in the 1990s, are slowly being reclaimed for modern, mixed use, some of it serving a rising tide of heritage tourism.

Conclusion

Established in the last three decades of the nineteenth century, the industrial settlements at Księży Młyn in Łódź and in Żyrardów rank among the most important achievements of European industrial architecture of the period. They embody several ideas of modern urban planning. In both cases, housing and industrial districts are detached, but their spatial connections have not been disrupted. The housing district was planned as a whole, in the form of detached blocks, pertinently placed amid greenery. Adhering to the concept of the ideal town, the settlements were supplied with a wide array of service amenities. Conforming to the idea of "social solidarity," these settlements also served to bind the employees to their workplace.

Both cases resulted from central government inducements for entrepreneurs to initiate manufacturing operations in previously rural environments. Both saw their greatest growth occur during a second or third generation of investors. The momentum thus developed produced the large-scale, uniformly planned housing districts that stand out so starkly as monuments to industrial integration. In both cases, the comparative uniformity of design reflected the agency of industrialist working with architect and engineer to create a built environment that expressed the power of capital to generate wealth. And it also etched upon the townscape the resulting social distinctions between owner, manager, and worker required by the system. The ultimate morphological differences between the two towns lay in the single strand of sequential decision making embodied in Żyrardów and the multiple strands of parallel and competing development decisions brought together only through corporate takeover and merger in Łódź. The greater extent of uniform housing seen in the former compared with the latter was balanced, however, by the similarities in the architectural diversity of buildings in both factory complexes.

Although there are many industrial complexes of this type in Western Europe, especially in Great Britain, France, and Germany, nevertheless the industrial settlements of Księży Młyn and Żyrardów are now exceptional in their historical integrity and recovered state of preservation. This has led to an application for their enrollment in the UNESCO World Heritage List. Preserved in almost unchanged form, these settlements offer the prospect of rich interpretation of Poland's—and Europe's—industrial history and the role of entrepreneurs in shaping a social reality indicative of their greatest historical era.

What is interesting in this examination from the perspective of the agency that produces urban form is the role that industrialists played in the context of all other potential actors. To the extent they defined the shape of whole town territories—at least until the path of development introduced a wider set of participants—they could act with the seeming freedom and authority of emperors, such was the power of capital to concentrate decision making. While they needed the technical expertise of architects and engineers for the design of structures, the entrepreneurs could control the crucial spatial arrangement of activities and, therefore, building types, according to their conceptions of mechanical efficiency and social position. Ideal models of industrial town design spread internationally among businessmen at the forefront of industrial mechanization during the late eighteenth and early nineteenth century—from New Lanark, to Saltaire, to Noisiel, to Pullman. Industrialists in Poland, many of them Germans finding opportunity in the Polish holdings of the Russian Tsar, were quick to adopt their essential planning principles (Ostrowski 1966: 36–7; Szyburska and Kubiak 1978).

Part of this power to determine the fundamental "look" of such industrial towns stemmed from the relative geographical isolation of the new factory sites, often in rural areas or grafted lopsidedly on the edge of quiescent dwarf towns, as in the case of Łódź. Part also stemmed from the frequent absence of other authorities capable of providing or enforcing alternative visions of industrial organization, such as historically mature municipalities with independent civic powers. What resulted, then, was the necessity for the capitalist to invest in social services and physical urban infrastructure for his workers, when an existing local public realm with taxing resources might have been able and willing to shoulder that burden.

The most distinctive morphological features of the planned manufacturing town of the high Industrial Revolution were the tripartite spatial structure of factory complex, workers' housing, and managerial precinct (with the owner's mansion as its most ostentatious emblem) and the choice of differential decorative styles and materials to reinforce the spatial distinctions. The uniformity of workers' housing may have put the residents firmly in their social place, but for many, of course, such housing represented far better accommodations than they had known before or could obtain elsewhere. While minimizing construction cost, such housing displayed a minimal level of architectural appeal, the better to bind their occupants to the workplace and to uphold the unity of the town's overall conception.

Meanwhile, the presence and prominence of industrialists' palaces and gardens within the industrial complexes is striking, imitating at some level the grandeur of the nobility. The connection of such new wealth to aesthetic refinement in the townscape bespeaks an emergent bourgeoisie patronizing the arts in emulation of the aristocracy (Szram 1984: 283). More fundamentally, the juxtaposition of mansion and factory, and the architectural gulf between them, reflected the awkward but necessary functional tie between the pretentious outcome of wealth and the pedestrian means of its accumulation (Smith 2000: 59).

Księży Młyn and Żyrardów, therefore, stand as symbols of a centralized design authority that stamped whole urban districts with the mark of a complex social and physical bargain: to revolutionize manufacturing, create new wealth, distribute it hierarchically, and form viable new communities with willing participants. Though topography may have defined the particular configurations in any given case, the tight yet disparate relation between factory, workers' housing, and owner's mansion remains the generalizing principle. Historically speaking, in no other urban setting—except perhaps the limited residential creations of absolute monarchs or absolute socialist planning—has centralized power had so marked an effect on urban form.

References

Dumała, K. (1974) *Przemiany Przestrzenne Miast i Rozwój Osiedli Przemysłowych w Królestwie Polskim w Latach 1831–1869* [Spatial Transformation of Cities and Industrial Development of Settlements in the Polish Kingdom in the Years 1831–1869]. Wrocław: Zakład Narodowy imienia Ossolińskich.

Flatt, O. (1853) *Opis Miasta Łodzi pod Względem Historycznym, Statystycznym i Przemysłowym* [A Historical, Statistical and Industrial Description of the City of Łódź]. Warsaw: W Drukarni Gazety Codziennej.

Gryciuk, A. (1980) Kształtowanie się osady fabrycznej [Development of the factory settlement], in I. Pietrzak-Pawłowska (ed.), *Żyrardów, 1829–1945: Praca Zbiorowa* [Żyrardów, 1829–1945: Collected Essays], 103–24. Warsaw: Państwowe Wydawnictwo Naukowe.

Kołodziej, J. (2001) Żyrardów jako unikalny zespół dziedzictwa przemysłowego [Żyrardów as a unique industrial heritage site], in A. Grudziński and J. Nazięblo (eds.), *Problemy Rewitalizacji Żyrardowa: Prawne Unormowanie Rewitalizacji* [Regeneration in Żyrardów: Legal Issues in Revitalization]. Żyrardów: Urząd Miasta.

Komar, M. (1933) Powstanie i rozwój zakładów przemysłowych Ludwika Geyera 1828–1847 [Origin and development of Ludwig Geyer's industrial enterprise, 1828–1847]. *Rocznik Łódzi: Poświęcony Historji Łodzi i Okolicy*, 3: 187–268.

Kossmann, E. O. (1966) *Lodz: Eine Historisch-Geographische Analyse*, Marburger Ostforschungen, no. 25 Würzburg: Holzner-Verlag.

Koter, M. (1969) *Geneza Układu Przestrzennego Łodzi Przemysłowej* [Origin of the Spatial Pattern of Industrial Łódź]. Warszawa: Państwowe Wydawnictwo Naukowe, Instytut Geografii Polskiej Akademii Nauk, Prace Geograficzne 79.

Koter, M. (1980) Rozwój przestrzenny i zabudowa miasta [Spatial development and city building], in R. Rosin (ed.), *Łódź: Dzieje Miasta, tom 1* [Łódź: History of the City, vol. 1], 148–91. Warsaw-Łódź: Państwowe Wydawnictwo Naukowe.

Koter, M. (1990) The morphological evolution of a nineteenth-century city centre: Łódź, Poland, 1825–1973, in T. R. Slater (ed.), *The Built Form of Western Cities: Essays for M. R. G. Conzen on the Occasion of his Eightieth Birthday*, 109–41. Leicester, U.K.: Leicester University Press.

Koter, M. (2009) Kształtowanie się tkanki miejskiej Łodzi do 1918 roku [Shaping of the urban tissue of Łódź until the year 1918], in S. Liszewski (ed.), *Łódź: Monografia Miasta* [Łódź: Monograph of the City], 62–97. Łódź: Łódzkie Towarzystwo Naukowe.

Koter, M., Kulesza, M., Puś, W., and Pytlas, S. (2005) *Wpływ Wielonarodowego Dziedzictwa Kulturowego Łodzi na Współczesne Oblicze Miasta* [The Influence of the Multi-ethnic Cultural Heritage of Łódź on the Present Face of the City]. Łódź: Wydawnictwo Uniwersytetu Łódzkiego.

Liszewski, S. (1997) The origins and stages of development of industrial Łódź and the Łódź urban region, in S. Liszewski and C. Young (eds.), *A Comparative Study of Łódź and Manchester: Geographies of European Cities in Transition*, 11–34. Łódź: Łódź University Press.

Nazięblo, J. (2001) Unikatowy układ urbanistyczny Żyrardowa: historia i problemy ochrony' [Żyrardów's unique urban layout: history and problems of conservation], in A. Grudziński and J. Nazięblo (eds.), *Problemy Rewitalizacji Żyrardowa: Prawne Unormowania Rewitalizacji* [Regeneration in Żyrardów: Legal Issues in Revitalization], 41–42. Żyrardów: Stowarzyszenie Forum Rewitalizacji.

Ostrowski, W. (1966) History of urban development and planning, in J. C. Fisher (ed.), *City and Regional Planning in Poland*, 3–55. Ithaca: Cornell University Press.

Popławska, I. (1992) *Architektura Mieszkaniowa Łodzi w XIX w.* [Residential Architecture in Nineteenth-Century Łódź]. Warsaw: Polska Akademia Nauk, Komitet Architektury i Urbanistyki.

Popławska, I., and Muthesius, S. (1986) Poland's Manchester: 19th-century industrial and domestic architecture. *Journal of the Society of Architectural Historians*, 45 (2): 148–60.

Pytlas, S., Salm, J., Berbelska, D., and Zielińska, A. (1998) *Księży Młyn*. Łódź: Wydział Strategii Miasta.

Rynkowska, A. (1951) *Działalnośc Gospodarcza Władz Królestwa Polskiego na Terenie Łodzi Przemysłowej w Latach 1821–1831* [The Development Activities of the Authorities of the Kingdom of Poland in the Łódź Industrial District 1821–1831]. Łódź: Łódzkie Towarzystwo Naukowe, Wydziału II, Prace, no. 5.

Smith, D. M. (2000) *Moral Geographies: Ethics in a World of Difference*. Edinburgh: Edinburgh University Press.

Stefański, K. (2001) *Jak Budowano Przemysłową Łódź: Architektura i Urbanistyka Miasta w Latach 1821–1914* [The Industrialization of Łódź: Architecture and Urban Planning of the City, 1821–1914]. Łódź: Regionalny Ośrodek Studiów i Ochrony Środowiska Kulturowego w Łodzi.

Stefański, K. (2009) *Ludzie Którzy Zbudowali Łodź: Leksykon Architektów i Budowniczych Miasta (do 1939 roku)* [The People Who Built Łódź: Dictionary of Architects and Builders of the City (to 1939)]. Łodź: Księży Młyn Dom Wydawniczy.

Szafer, P., and Trzebiński, W. (1954) Geneza układu przestrzennego Żyrardowa [Spatial evolution of Żyrardów]. *Biuletyn Instytutu Urbanistyki i Architektury*, 6, 1–2.

Szram, A. (1984) The impact of the investor on the work of the architect taking as examples the activities of factory owners. *Kwartalnik Architektury i Urbanistyki*, 29 (1–2): 281–7.

Szyburska, T., and Kubiak, J. (1978) Koncepcja urbanistyczna Żyrardowa' [The urbanistic concept of Żyrardów]. *Biuletyn Historii Sztuki*, 40: 341–50.

Turowski, A. (1976) Styl wzniosły i przestrzeń bogata (struktura przestrzenna założenia urbanistycznego Księży Młyn) [High style and rich space (the spatial structure of the urbanistic system of Księży Młyn)]. *Teksty*, 4–5 (28–9): 149–76.

10

RESIDENTIAL DIFFERENTIATION IN NINETEENTH-CENTURY GLASGOW

A Morphogenetic Study of Pollokshields Garden Suburb

Michael Pacione

The rise of industrial capitalism and the unprecedented growth of urban populations in nineteenth-century Britain were accompanied by social and spatial upheavals in the physical fabric of Britain's cities. The principal social change was a reconstruction of the meaning of status whereby new social classes founded on money replaced a social structure based on occupational clusters promoted by medieval craft guilds. The key spatial change was growing residential differentiation that reinforced the social distance between classes (Briggs 1963). As the nineteenth century advanced, increasing social segregation and social distance were translated into geographical distance and residential segregation as the upper classes, and—by the Edwardian period—the middle classes, engaged in a process of suburbanization (Lawton and Pooley 1976; Shaw 1977; Dennis 1984). The garden suburb was both a key agent of change and a distinctive product of this process of residential suburbanization and segregation.

Despite the importance of the garden suburb for the spread of middle-class housing in nineteenth-century Britain, most academic research into nineteenth-century and early-twentieth-century suburbanization has focused on the experience of garden city developments, including Victoria, 1849 (Buckingham 1849); Saltaire, 1853 (Reynolds 1983); Port Sunlight, 1888 (Hubbard and Shippobottom 1988); Bourneville, 1893 (Cadbury 1915); Letchworth, 1903 (Miller 1989); and Welwyn, 1920 (Howard 1902). In addition, most of the research has been undertaken with specific reference to developments in England. As Richard Rodger (1983: 71) has pointed out, "examples of early town planning invariably overlook the Scottish dimension." Limited attention has been afforded to the development of the planned garden suburb in Scotland (Smith 1998). This chapter seeks to redress this imbalance in our understanding of the garden suburb phenomenon by examining the genesis and development of the pioneering Scottish garden suburb of Pollokshields. The focus here is on the genesis and evolution of Pollokshields garden suburb, tracing the key elements of continuity and change in its development from the beginnings in the mid-nineteenth century to the contemporary socio-spatial geography of the modern suburb.

The chapter is organized in five main parts. In the first section, a necessary distinction is drawn between the concepts of garden city and garden suburb. The following section examines the lure of the garden suburb in nineteenth-century Britain. The subsequent section establishes the historical and conceptual context for middle-class suburbanization in Glasgow by identifying the key agents and processes underlying the socio-spatial development of the city in the nineteenth century, and the fourth and fifth sections build on this historical and conceptual base to examine the origins and development of Pollokshields from 1851 to 2001.

The Origins of the Garden Suburb

It is important, at the outset, to differentiate between the concepts of garden city and garden suburb, as the present focus is on the latter. The distinction is most apparent in the development of Letchworth Garden City and Hampstead Garden Suburb, both of which were designed by Barry Parker and Raymond Unwin. Though Letchworth was planned according to the principles of garden city purists such as Ebenezer Howard, Frederic Osborn and C. B. Purdom (Beevers 1988), Hampstead "had the appearance of a garden city and some of its community spirit, [but] was in every respect a pure commuter suburb...and was effectively separated from London only by Hampstead Heath" (Hall and Ward 1998: 41). Although both developments involved changing the physical arrangements for urban living, there was a notable shift in emphasis between Letchworth Garden City and Hampstead Garden Suburb from social reform (a hallmark of the garden city) to physical planning (the trademark of the garden suburb). In essence, garden cities were intended to be self-contained independent settlements, whereas garden suburbs were planned as residential environments without social idealism.

In practice, notwithstanding the success of Letchworth and Welwyn Garden City and the stimulus provided for the postwar new towns in Britain and elsewhere, Howard's vision of self-contained garden cities based on cooperative principles was never fully realized. The garden suburb concept, on the other hand, has had a major influence on the form of suburbanization across the globe. In the United States, the garden suburb ideal underlay the design of Radburn (1924–8), which became the template for

> virtually every American new town built until 1980, including the towns of the 1930s, the private new towns of Reston and Columbia in the 1960s, the federal new communities of the 1960s and 1970s, and the large-scale master planned communities in California such as Irvine, Valencia and Westlake Village.
>
> (Fulton 2002: 163)

The distinction between garden cities and garden suburbs is central to the debate over the origins of the garden suburb in Britain. A fundamental question is whether a garden suburb must share the philanthropic principles of the garden city. If the answer is in the affirmative, the origins of the garden suburb may be identified with Saltaire and Bournville. If, however, it is considered that a suburb planned and developed solely on a commercial basis meets the definition of a garden suburb, the origins of the British garden suburb are to be found elsewhere. The former interpretation conflates the concepts of garden suburb and garden city, whereas the later perspective differentiates between the two concepts and acknowledges private-sector planned garden suburbs as antecedents of the garden city movement. The distinction between garden city and garden suburb is not only of conceptual importance but provides a yardstick with which to examine the validity of various claims to be "Britain's first garden suburb."

There has been considerable debate over the origins of the garden suburb. David Lloyd (1984: 240), with reference to John Nash's plan for detached villas among the trees of Regent's Park and the clusters of houses in Park Village West and East (1824), maintains that "more particularly than anywhere else this is the prototype of the English low-density suburb." Alternatively, according to Stephen Ward (1994: 28) "the earliest garden suburbs appeared during the Edwardian period. ... Most famous was Hampstead Garden Suburb, in London, conceived in 1904." Affleck Greeves (1975) promotes Bedford Park in Chiswick, London started in 1875 as the "world's first garden suburb," whereas Aileen Reid (2000) refers to Brentham in Ealing, west London as "the pioneering garden suburb." Pollokshields garden suburb in Glasgow, which commenced development in 1851, can also make a legitimate claim to be "Britain's earliest planned garden suburb" (Glasgow City Council 2009). Though there is a lack of consensus over the location of the first garden suburb, the key distinction between garden suburbs and garden cities, discussed above, has been established. Achieving agreement on the location of the first garden suburb is probably not possible given the absence of consensus over definition of the concept. Of greater concern, however, is the dearth of research on garden suburb developments beyond the current corpus of knowledge focused on experience from England, a deficiency that includes the early garden suburb of Pollokshields in Glasgow.

Rus in urbe: The Lure of the Garden Suburb in the Nineteenth-Century British City

Residential segregation was the spatial expression of class-consciousness in the nineteenth-century British city. As will be apparent later in relation to Glasgow, socio-spatial segregation was a consequence of competition among a hierarchy of claimant land uses for any site. Industry was the most powerful element. It had no inhibitions about affecting the amenity of others. Once a firm had established itself, other land users tend to retreat because of the "external diseconomies" it imposed on them. This was especially true of the upper classes (the sponsors of industry) and their housing. "The middle class, especially the wealthier of them, come next. For though they retreated before their own industrial creations, they had a wide choice of alternatives: they could bear travel costs, and they could afford homes well outside the city" (Checkland 1964: 41). As Gerald Burke (1975: 131) observed,

> while the merchants, guildsmen, landowners and princes of medieval and renaissance towns identified themselves with the locality and manifested their own status and success by building proud buildings and implementing elegant and financially rewarding schemes of town improvement ... Not so the early-nineteenth-century industrialist or merchant, who seemed to regard the city as a workshop and emporium for all the citizens but as a home mainly for those who could not afford to live elsewhere

Other important factors of choice and constraint in residential decision making for the upper-middle class included the "powerful urge for people of like condition to want to live in the same neighbourhood with their kind [and] to decline to be mixed up with their social inferiors" (Thompson 1974: 241), and the desire of developers to satisfy these demands within a context of upsurges and downswings in land prices and building cycles that substantially influenced the scale and character of development. As Brian Dicks (1985) concluded, it is appropriate to view the high-class Victorian suburb as the manifestation of a complex of lofty ideals, desires, and decisions that were inevitably tempered by the financial tenets that governed supply and demand. Competition between housing speculators was fierce, for the middle-class house hunter could afford to choose between several rival developments. The middle class had to be enticed and convinced of the excellence, indeed superiority, of a residential site both in terms of the accommodation it provided and its general environmental setting.

The middle-class retreat to the suburbs was made possible by the developers and by the availability of estate land on the urban edge (Dyos 1961). The controlling influence of the landowner on the suburbanization process is generally viewed as a function of estate size, the contention being that the larger the land holding, the greater the monopoly of control exercised on development and the greater the prospect that the suburb would be comprehensively planned at the outset and to have its character maintained by the enforcement of covenants. Such estates were more likely to house middle-class residents (Olsen 1976). Though this is by no means a general law, with notable exceptions evident in the fragmented pattern of land ownership underlying the upper-middle-class suburbs of Hampstead (Thompson 1974; Miller and Gray 1992) and Glasgow's west end (Simpson 1977), the proposition does hold true for estate developments at Edgbaston in Birmingham (Cannadine 1980) and, as will be shown, Pollokshields in Glasgow.

In addition to their geographical location on the edge of the built-up area, suburbs were also characterized by a particular residential ambience. As F. M. L. Thompson (1982: 7) commented, "architectural historians are in no doubt that detached and semi-detached houses built for single family occupation are of the suburban essence, and that such houses did not exist before the nineteenth century." According to Geoffrey Best (1985: 35), "a villa, detached for preference in a private estate, became the rich mid-Victorian town dweller's ideal [while] semi-detached villas were the next best thing." It is clear that, while the development of residential suburbs was a feature of Victorian urban Britain, another was the widespread rejection by the middle classes of the terrace house as a desirable type of dwelling in favor of the detached or semi-detached villa, preferably in a garden setting. Citing the example of Nash's plan for Regent's Park, Thompson (1982) posits how the concept of a garden was transformed in the nineteenth century from the eighteenth-century stigma of a backward and hostile backdrop into a cultivated and admired part of a natural and virtuous home. Thus, the concept of *rus in urbe* was no longer the monopoly of the upper and aristocratic classes. It became not only a model for developers and builders of garden suburbs but a pattern for the ambitious middle class to emulate. As Lloyd (1984) explains, ideally each house in a villa suburb would be visually isolated from its neighbors, giving the illusion of total seclusion. Gardens were, characteristically, thickly planted on their perimeters with trees and shrubs, enclosing secluded lawns and flower beds. The villas might be glimpsed through contrived gaps in the planting, from the street outside. They were usually fronted by substantial garden walls or thick hedges with massive gateposts flanking the entrances. If the front garden were deep enough, the approach to the front door might be curving and indirect to enhance the effect of a secluded domain.

Because of the pressure on land around fast-growing towns, suburbs could not always be as spacious or secluded as their residents might wish.

> The semi-detached villa was an ingenious compromise. Early pairs of such houses were usually designed so as to appear at first sight as single dwellings, their entrances being at the sides, giving the occupants of each part a high degree of privacy from their neighbours, and their visitors the illusion that they lived in a house twice as large. Curving roads, carefully related to topography and landscaping, so that views along the roads were generally limited by the planting in the gardens on the outsides of the curves, with occasional glimpses of gables,

> rooftops or chimneys, could enhance the feel of suburban seclusion. There was a close analogy between the layouts of the more intricate suburbs and that of informal landscaped parks.
> (Lloyd 1984: 242)

This provided the ideal image to which developers and residents of nineteenth-century garden suburbs aspired. Before turning to examine how this vision was transformed into practice on the ground in Pollokshields, it is well first to establish the general socio-spatial framework of urban growth and residential segregation in nineteenth-century Glasgow.

Residential Segregation in Nineteenth-Century Glasgow

Though most visible in the Victorian city, a tendency toward greater residential segregation on class lines was apparent in Glasgow from the middle of the eighteenth century. The "tobacco lords" spearheaded the development of the Georgian city and the move westward away from the old center of Glasgow Cross. The spatial distances were not great, but the decision to separate residence and business broke with tradition and set in train a movement that gathered momentum as the city grew into an industrial metropolis. In the late eighteenth century, attempts were made to develop high-quality residential property to the east and south of High Street. Charlotte Street (1779) was cut from Gallowgate down to the open common or Green, and Montieth Row was laid out on land taken from the common. At first, both attracted wealthy residents, including David Dale but, within a generation, the district had gone "down market." In the same area, St. Andrew's Square, completed in 1787 (Fig. 10.1) initially attracted the upper classes but, within a generation, had been occupied by tradespeople including leather-merchants, tailors, pawnbrokers, and tobacconists. The failure to maintain the integrity of these high-class residential areas led to the abandonment of plans for two further east-side squares to be known as St. James Square and Graham Square. A similar fate befell an ambitious attempt by David and James Laurie to establish a quality residential development (Laurieston) south of the river on the Hutcheson lands between the two bridges just west of the small village of Bridgend or Gorbals (see Fig. 10.1). In the 1790s this area of agricultural land began to be broken up for development, and the Laurie brothers obtained forty-seven acres with the intention of laying out a high-class Regency suburb. Street names reflected the social pretensions of the scheme. Carlton Place, fronting the river, was named after the residence of the Prince of Wales, and other streets bore the names of English nobility, such as Cavendish, Portland, Salisbury, and Marlborough. The forty-seven-acre site was divided into 374 separate properties for feuing (a Scots' system of converting land rent paid in money instead of military service, much used in urban development). These ranged in value from £1,500 for sites on Carlton Place to £200 for less-prestigious interior sites. However, despite the rural ambience, grand design, and construction of an elegant footbridge to the city, properties were not taken up as rapidly as the Lauries had anticipated. The future of Laurieston was undermined by the developers' inability to prevent the encroachment of intensive industrial activities such as brick making and coal mining. As the whole area south of the river lay beyond the jurisdiction of the City Corporation, there was no authority capable of enforcing land use zoning. The hammer blow to Laurieston as a high-class residential area was struck by William Dixon—a local coal master and proprietor of an ironworks—who, around 1800, built a wagon way across the undeveloped main streets of Laurieston to supply coaling quays at Windmillcroft, Tradeston—having procured a temporary recall of an injunction obtained by James Laurie against such an event. Hundreds of smaller trades operating from yards and backstreet premises followed suit, and those genteel residents who had arrived soon

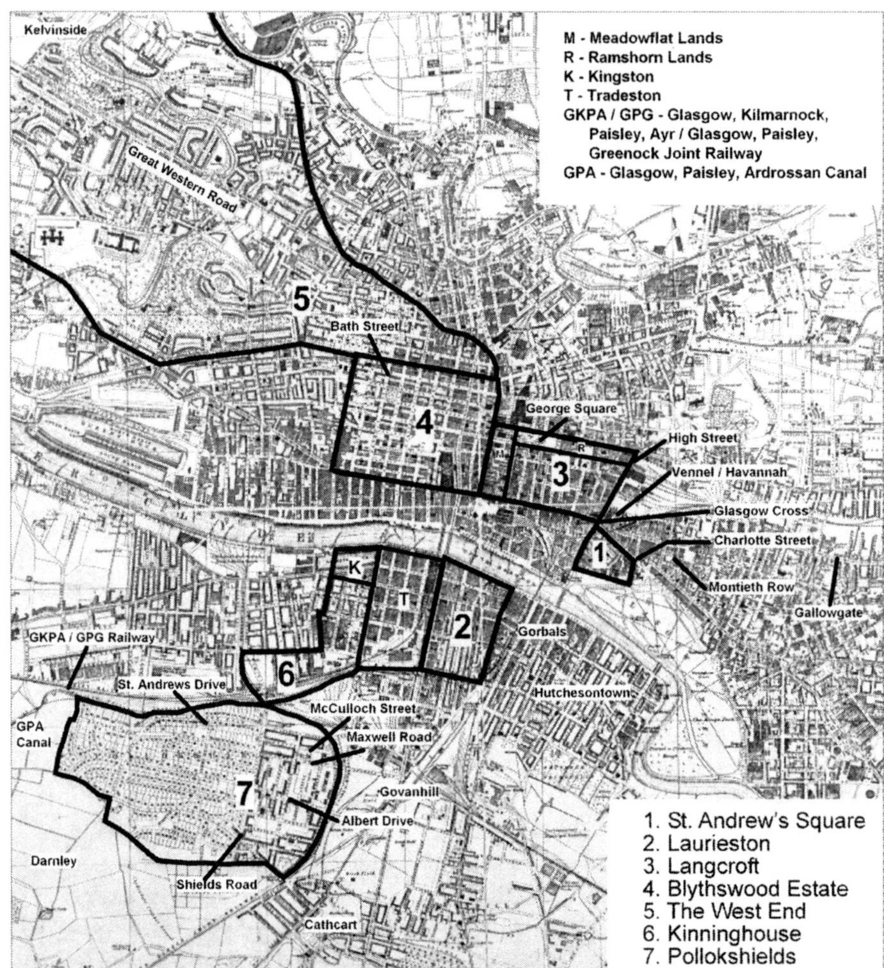

FIGURE 10.1 Glasgow, Scotland—map of locations mentioned in the text

decamped for the more assured exclusivity of the Blythswood estate and growing "west end" north of the river. The demise of Laurieston as a fashionable area was completed by the Glasgow, Paisley, Kilmarnock, and Ayr and the Glasgow, Paisley, and Greenock railway companies, which drove a joint line through the estate to the river (Kellet 1969a). The housing already built in Laurieston was left to decline into warrens of one- and two-roomed houses for casual laborers, and the area as a whole degenerated into a slum annex to Gorbals.

By the end of the eighteenth century, demand from the growing upper class for elegant houses on the urban fringe was inexorable. This was satisfied in part by expansion to the north and west of the Langcroft on the Ramshorn and Meadowflat lands (see Fig. 10.1). These were acquired by the Town Council in 1772 on the grounds that "the public demand for building purposes being no longer restrainable, the magistrates deemed it proper to relieve the hospital of their property" (McFarlane 1919: 200). Plans for a street layout and plot feuing were prepared by the town's surveyor, James Barry (Fig. 10.2). The resources needed to bring the schemes to fruition were provided by speculative builders such as Dugald Bannatyne, who founded the Glasgow Building Company in 1786. In 1800,

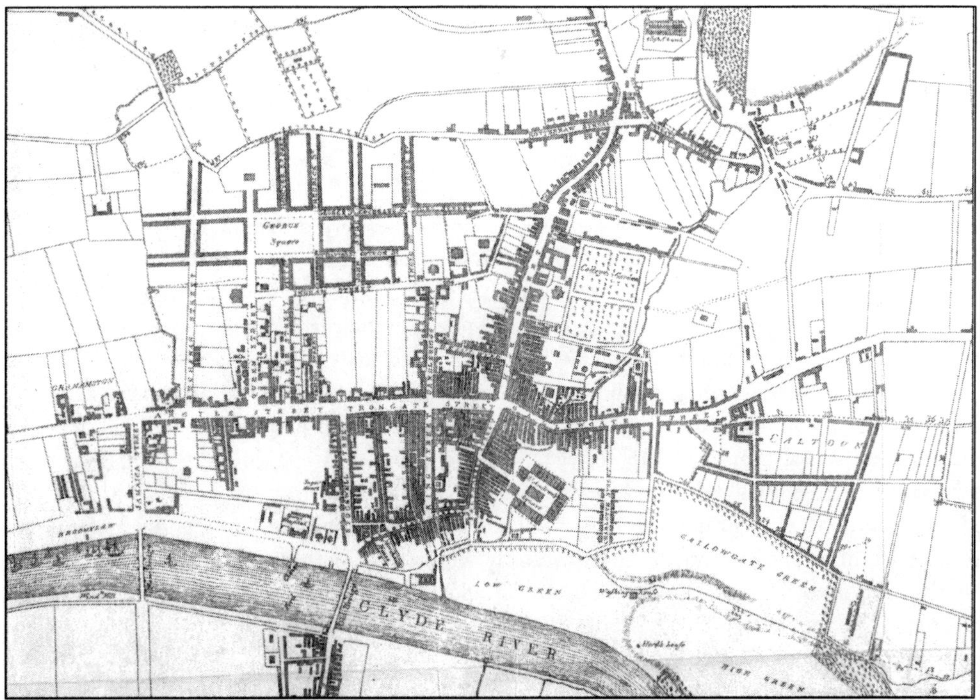

FIGURE 10.2 The City of Glasgow in 1782

the Glasgow Building Company opened a street (later known as Bath Street), but building proceeded slowly until William Harley, the principal speculator on the Blythswood lands, opened baths in 1804. Even in the expanding housing market of the early nineteenth century, however, property speculators entailed considerable financial risk as they were required to expend large sums to bring the land up to a standard that would attract house buyers. By 1814, even Harley, who spent £54,000 on his portion of the Blythswood estate, was in financial difficulty; and the trustees who took over his affairs in 1816 themselves went bankrupt. The fortunes of the Campbells of Blythswood, on the other hand, were augmented handsomely by the development of their estate (see Fig. 10.1). Income derived from the sale of the land for building at sums of between 200 and 300 times the agricultural rent and from the feu duties, which accrued to the landowner. Under the Scottish tradition of feuing, once a purchase price for a tract of land had been agreed, part of the price would be paid in a lump sum, with the remainder translated into a feu or perpetual rent. In the fifty years from 1799 to 1849, the Campbells' rent roll increased from £223 to £25,000 per annum (Senex 1884: 319), providing a clear indication of the profits to be made from successful residential developments.

By 1820, both the first new town around George Square (laid out in 1781) and the second grid development on the lands of Blythswood were under pressure from businesses encroaching from the expanding central area. Banks, legal services, and the new professions such as accountancy and stock broking were particularly strenuous in their attempts to colonize the former high-class residential area. The response of the upper-middle class was to look for another suburb. To satisfy this demand, the developers turned their attention further to the west. Commercial encroachment, however, was only one cause of the migration and segregation of the affluent classes. A further push factor was the deteriorating physical and social fabric of the old city. The dangers from crime and vice prevalent in the Vennel and Havannah slums were compounded by the threat of cholera, which, though originating in the slums, was no respecter of social class. In addition to these "push" factors, the social elite of nineteenth-century Glasgow had a clearly-defined set of "pull" criteria against which to judge a potential suburb. As discussed in the previous section, the social composition of a neighborhood was of the greatest importance, which had to be exclusively upper-middle class. This was the goal of the developers of the new west end (see Fig. 10.1). Despite the presence of rich deposits of coal, iron, brick clay, building sand, and freestone, the absence of statutory planning controls, and the fact that the areas to the north along the canal and south along the river had been committed to industrial use, the owners of all twenty-three properties comprising the west end reserved their land for high-quality housing. This land-use "zoning" consensus appears to have been reached not as a result of formal cooperation among developers but as a process of "growth by contagion" whereby the presence of buildings of a certain cost and quality encouraged later speculators to emulate the existing arrangement. The exclusiveness of the west end was also protected by restrictive clauses in feu charters, ground annuals (leaseholds), and dispositions (freeholds). The middle class was also attracted by a picturesque, "healthful and well-aired" environment, yet had no wish to leap-frog too far from the built-up area. The west end, with its rolling drumlin topography, prevailing westerly winds, and location above and to the west of the industrial areas and the insalubrious old town, fulfilled these requirements. A further attraction was the proximity of the west end to the central business district where the majority of Glasgow's leading citizens were engaged. The construction of the Great Western Road in 1841 reduced travel times to the city center even further and promoted feuing of land up to half a mile deep on either side of the new axis. A related advantage pointed out by Matthew Montgomerie, one of the major west-end developers, was that the Great Western Road made the west end "the only district from which access to town can be obtained without passing through an inferior district" (Kellett 1969b: 13). The west end dominated the spatial expansion of middle-class Glasgow in the nineteenth century, but attempts were made to attract the élite to other parts of the growing city. The most successful of these was the plan of 1849 to develop the southern portion of the lands belonging to the Maxwells of Pollok.

Pollokshields: Scotland's First Garden Suburb

M. A. Simpson and T. H. Lloyd (1977: 9), in highlighting the importance of middle-class housing developments in nineteenth-century urban Britain, observed that "only rarely was an estate developed as a whole, to a coherent plan." They point out that comprehensive large-scale planning of this kind took place on the Maryon Wilson estate in Hampstead, in the Duke of Newcastle's Park at Nottingham, and in Kelvinside in Glasgow. However, they fail to acknowledge the comprehensively planned development of Scotland's, if not Britain's, first garden suburb at Pollokshields on the city's south side.

Though the general pattern of estate development in Glasgow can be compared to that in English towns such as Sheffield (Dicks 1985), in terms of land ownership Glasgow lacked the aristocratic ownership that is typical of middle-class suburban developments found around London and Birmingham. The exception to this was the Pollok estate, which was controlled by the Maxwells. The Maxwell family, owners of the Pollok estate since the twelfth century, was the driving force behind the development of what has been described as Britain's first garden suburb.

Pollokshields was part of the larger Pollok estate that stretched from the south bank of the River Clyde to Darnley and Cathcart and from Pollokshaws Road west to Crookston (see Fig. 10.1). The first developments on the Pollok estate were along the bank of the Clyde in the early nineteenth century.

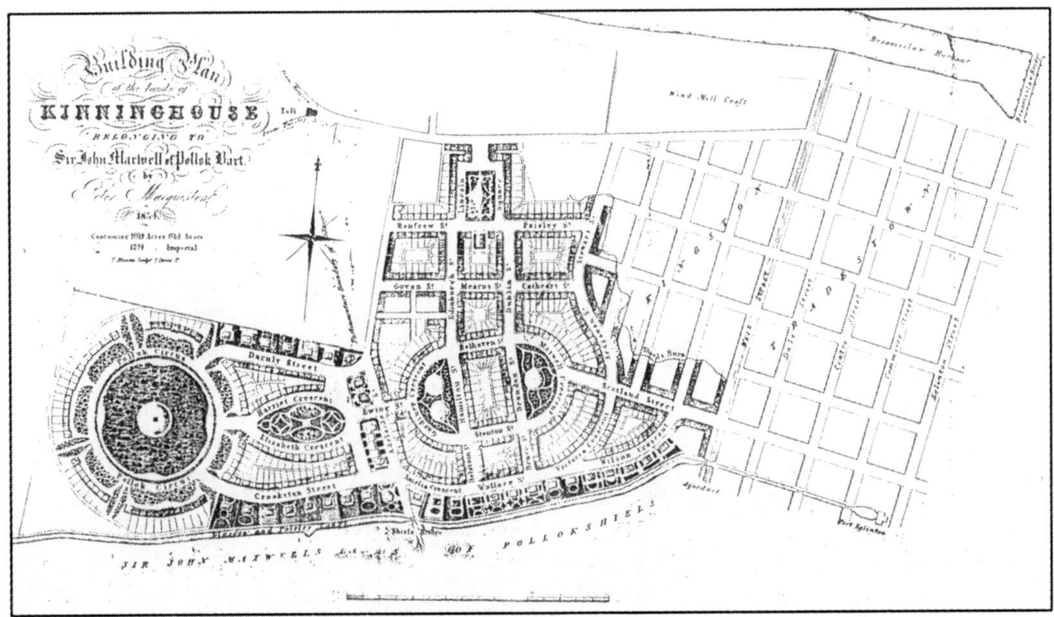

FIGURE 10.3 Design plan for Kinninghouse, 1834

The residential development of Pollokshields commenced later in the mid-century. This was preceded by an unsuccessful attempt by the Maxwell family to erect a garden suburb at Kinninghouse, between Pollokshields and the River Clyde. Encouraged by grid plan developments in adjacent Tradeston and Hutchesontown and undeterred by the failure of the Lauries' plan to the east, Sir John Maxwell in 1834 proposed a feuing plan based on a grand design that reflected the Lauries' ambitious scheme to develop an upper-class suburb south of the River Clyde (Fig. 10.3). The up-market development of squares, crescents and circuses was linked to the already built up area of Kingston. The Kinninghouse plan was not carried through, possibly due to a realization that, as the Lauries had found, industrial activities were a more natural use for land close to the river than a high-class residential suburb (McCallum 1921–2). Arguably, the Kinninghouse scheme was ahead of its time, but the setback did not dissuade Sir John Maxwell from pursuing his interest in speculative house building. In 1849, he selected another site at Pollokshields and commissioned an eminent Edinburgh architect, David Rhind, to prepare a feuing design plan for the Shields part of his estate (Fig. 10.4). There were clear similarities with the classical design elements of the abandoned Kinninghouse scheme. The eastern part comprised low rows of terraces (later revised to tenements), with an inner core laid out around a north-south axis of formal gardens. Similar formality is evident in the part to the west of the dividing line of Shields Road but, in this area, the greater part is laid out for villas arranged along curving roads that, as in Glasgow's west end, conformed to the rolling drumlin topography of the site. Landscaping was particularly important in West Pollokshields, where ample gardens set off the villas to best advantage. An eclectic range of building styles was intended to display the individuality of property owners. Architectural styles ranged from Classical to Italianate, "Glasgow Style" to Gothic, and from Scots baronial to "Old English" and included work by the innovative architect Alexander "Greek" Thomson. The more level east was mainly developed over the period 1855–1910 in a grid street pattern of up-market tenement flats, limited by feu contract to three stories in height rather than the more usual four-story Scottish tenement. The

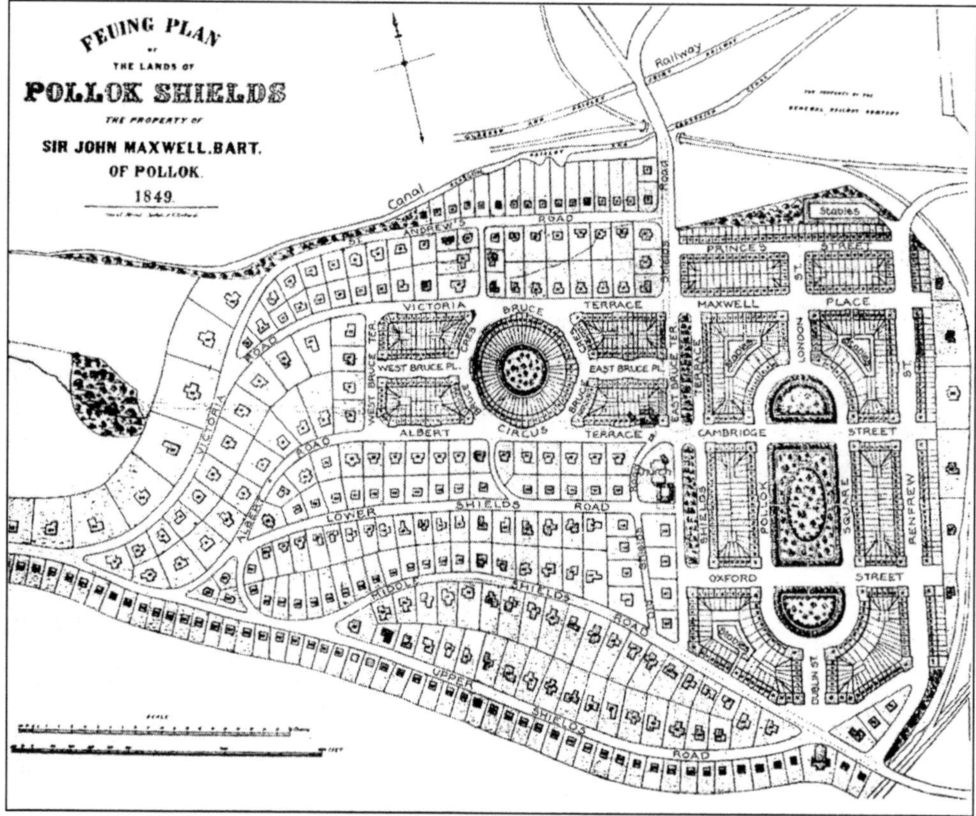

FIGURE 10.4 Feuing plan for Pollokshields, 1849

suburb had clearly demarcated boundaries with a canal and railway lines to the north and east and a long line of inward-facing villas on the south, leaving only four access routes to emphasize the area's exclusivity. The open land to the west also belonged to the Pollok estate and would eventually be transformed into the suburbs of Dumbreck and South Pollokshields.

Despite the grand design, by 1865 only a small part of the estate had been feued in the fifteen years since the scheme had been laid out. Around forty villas had been built along the Glasgow, Paisley, and Ardrossan canal edge of the estate, and there were signs of the beginnings of tenement construction in the eastern portion (Fig. 10.5). The careful planning, high quality, and desirability of the housing in Pollokshields were evident from the earliest development. MacDonald (1854: 21) describes,

> the picturesque little village of Pollokshields [that] has recently sprung into existence, with a degree of rapidity which fairly rivals the go-a-head Yankee system of town development. This miniature community is composed of elegant cottages and villas, each edifice having its own belt of garden-ground walled in, and tastefully planted in front with flowers and shrubs, and in the rear with kitchen vegetables. The greatest variety of architectural taste, moreover, seems to prevail in this rising suburban settlement. Some two score or so of houses are already erected, or are in process of erection, and scarcely two of them are similar in design or construction. Each individual proprietor seems to have had his own idea in stone and lime and every man's

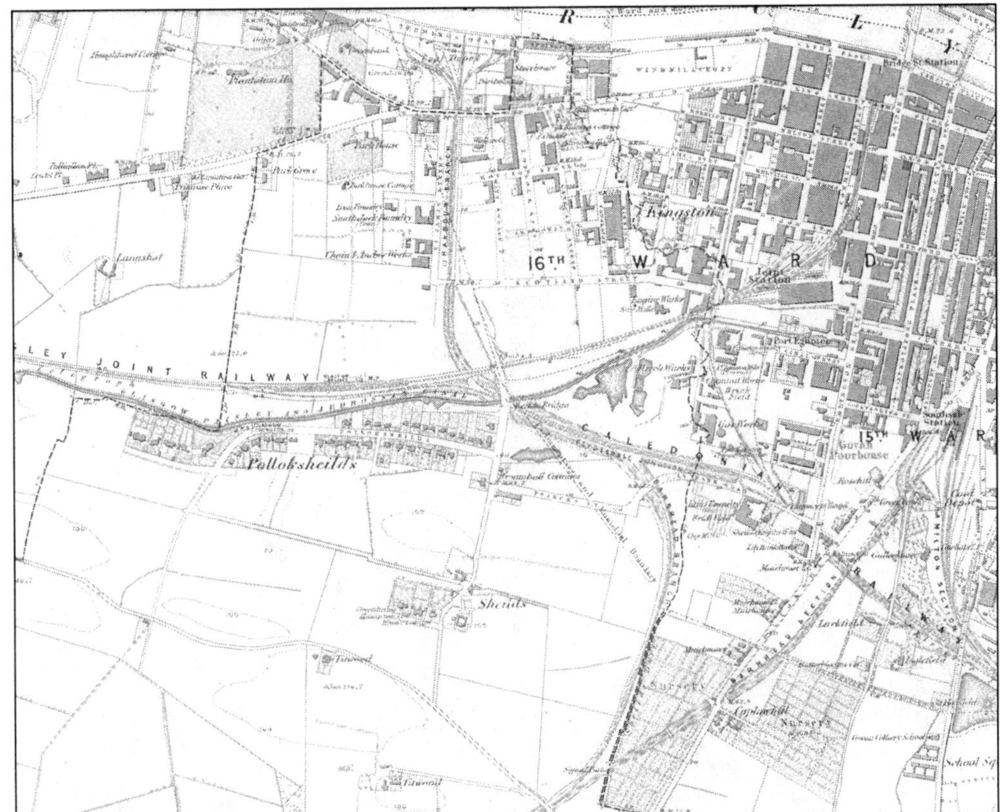

FIGURE 10.5 Pollokshields in 1865

> house is as unlike his neighbours as possible … so far as it has gone this variety has, on the whole, an exceedingly pleasing and picturesque effect, and we know few places in the vicinity of our City where we would more readily wish for a snug cottage home, if "the lamp of Alladin" were for a brief period ours.

Rhind's initial classical feuing design plan for Pollokshields was gradually revised over the years under the administration of the more pragmatic William Colledge, the estate factor. By 1867, the grand circus on the west side had been replaced by a grid and, similarly in the east, the formal classical layout was wholly replaced by a simple grid plan. The form of housing in the east section was now designated as tenements in preference to the original terraces in Rhind's plan (Fig. 10.6). In sympathy with the general standards of the suburb and in contrast to working-class tenements in nearby Govanhill, the flats were relatively large, varying in size from three to six rooms with considerable variety of exterior detail and elaborate plaster ceilings within. The original flats provided in the early tenements (built on the south side of McCulloch Street), were very spacious, some being two-story flats or maisonettes on the upper floors. The generous proportions of these flats—some with up to nine rooms—have made them vulnerable to subdivision during the twentieth century. The feu conditions prohibited sharing of outside toilets, and all flats were provided with baths from the outset in marked contrast to the standard of provision in most contemporary tenement housing elsewhere in the city (Worsdal 1979).

FIGURE 10.6 Pollokshields in 1883

As the experience of the development of Glasgow's west end confirms, a slow start to feuing and revision of initial grand designs were not unusual in such schemes, often being a necessary response to market conditions (Morgan 1996). In 1870, Colledge recommended construction of a bridge over the railway lines to the east to provide an impetus to the feuing at Pollokshields. By 1881, West Pollokshields had 2,104 inhabitants compared with 4,360 in East Pollokshields, although the west covered more than twice the territory. West Pollokshields was also exclusively residential, whereas relaxation of feu restrictions in East Pollokshields allowed shops to be located on the ground floor of tenements at focal points such as Albert Drive and Maxwell Road/Shields Road. Continuing demand for houses led to feuing of the southern part of the estate along with the neighboring estate of Dumbreck (also owned by the Maxwell family). The garden suburb ambience of West Pollokshields was enhanced further in 1878—by which time West Pollokshields had more than 400 villas—with the donation of Maxwell Park to local residents. The healthy and "well aired" environment and the general affluence of residents of West Pollokshields are indicated by the 1890 annual report of the Medical Officer of Health for the burgh. The report records an "extraordinarily low death rate of 4.2 per thousand, a mortality rate unexampled amongst burghs for its lowness" (Lythe 1990: 20). This, together with evidence from the 1881 Census of Population, indicates a young to middle-aged demographic. In terms of social class, according to R. Smith (1998: 10), the population of West Pollokshields comprised the

> denizens of trade and industry—iron founders and merchants, mantle makers, wholesalers, commission agents, ships' chandlers, hatters and confectioners as well as stockbrokers and even a pawnbroker. Prospering professionals, like lawyers and teachers, first resident in the tenement closes, often moved over to the villas.

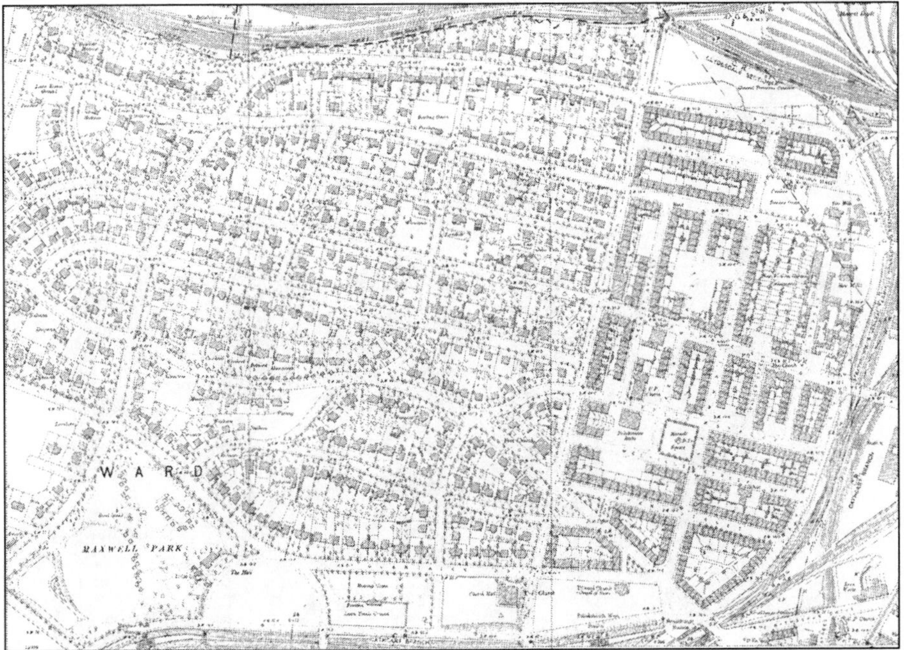

FIGURE 10.7 Plan of Pollokshields, 1894

By the end of the nineteenth century (Fig. 10.7), the built-up area of Pollokshields had largely assumed its present day characteristics with villas, tenements, and public buildings of sandstone—initially blonde sandstone from local quarries at Giffnock and later, as elsewhere in the city, red sandstone from Ballochmyle (Ayrshire) and Locharbriggs (Dumfriesshire). West Pollokshields was substantially completed by the construction of some of the largest and most opulent houses in the avenues on the western fringes. The final layout of the garden suburb was based on a strict division between the villas of West Pollokshields (Fig. 10.8) and the tenements of East Pollokshields (Fig. 10.9). The two areas were separated by Shields Road, a division so entrenched that two separate burghs had been formed in the 1870s prior to their incorporation into Glasgow in 1891. To the west of Shields Road, the villa development was extended beyond its original planned area in response to growing demand from the upper-middle class to create a south-side equivalent of the west end. To the east, the tenements attracted the working classes while a relaxation of feu restrictions allowed shops to be located on the ground floor of the tenements. Clearly, the east–west division entrenched in the original feu design plan for Pollokshields has conditioned the socio-spatial development of the suburb to the present day.

Pollokshields in the Twentieth Century

Both the villa and tenement areas of Pollokshields retained their up-market status in the early part of the twentieth century. During the inter-war period, however, there was a lull in development, with several substantial sites between villas dating from the turn of the century remaining vacant. In West Pollokshields, a slackening in demand for larger family housing, the unavailability of domestic staff, and high maintenance costs led to subdivision of villas or their conversion to such institutional uses as children's homes, religious orders, and nursing homes. As Shiela Ogilvie (1989: 21) notes,

FIGURE 10.8 Villa development in West Pollokshields

FIGURE 10.9 Tenements in East Pollokshields

> as early as 1936 a small revolution took place in No. 9 Maxwell Drive. The owner was desirous of having a single storey house with a garden, so he divided his detached villa into two flats by adding a new entrance door at the side of the house, giving access to the top half via the original stairwell. Thus was born The Conversion and after the end of the war such sub-division became increasingly popular and the population of the district increased in proportion.

At the same time, the remaining vacant sites on the western fringes of the area were gradually built up, partly with blocks of privately owned flats and latterly with speculative developments of standard English house types. East Pollokshields was also subject to a number of non-conforming infill developments using facing brick and concrete tile instead of the traditional sandstone.

The greatest impact on the character of the area was felt in the 1950s when the City Corporation began to acquire villas in Pollokshields through compulsory purchase to provide land for higher-density council house development. By 1969, 560 flat-roofed deck-access local authority flats in five- and eight-story blocks had replaced the original villas in St. Andrew's Drive, including four by Alexander "Greek" Thomson, leaving only eleven of the original villas *in situ* (Smith 1998). By the mid-1950s, postwar shortages of materials and a declining city population contributed to neglect of the urban fabric in parts of the suburb. Smoke from railways and domestic coal fires had also blackened and damaged many of the buildings. The declining environmental quality was addressed during the 1960s with the designation of Pollokshields as a smokeless zone under the Clean Air Act of 1962. The availability of housing improvement grants over subsequent decades also led to stone cleaning, back court improvements, and rehabilitation of property that greatly enhanced the area's appearance and revitalized interest from house-buyers. By 1965, local concern had been channeled into the formation of the Pollokshields Preservation and Development Association. This organization persuaded the Corporation to halt the villa acquisition program and to sell several derelict villas to the Association, which then resold them to private individuals. The Corporation also embraced the need to preserve the area's historic character and, in 1973, both the villa and tenement parts of the suburb were awarded conservation area status. The West Pollokshields conservation area was declared "outstanding" for the purpose of grant aid, and piecemeal infill development within the villa area became strictly controlled through statutory local plan policies with the aim of preserving building lines, regulating the use of appropriate building materials, and ensuring that house and plot sizes be in keeping with local tradition (Glasgow City Council 2009). The local plan also encouraged a reduction in the institutional use of properties to further restore the residential character of the area (City of Glasgow District Council 1979).

Socio-morphological Correlations in Pollokshields

Further detailed insight into the impact of these processes on the suburb can be gained through analysis of data from the 2001 Census of Population (Pacione 2011). To achieve this, a set of thirteen social, economic, and environmental indicators was extracted for each of the eighty-two census output areas in Pollokshields. The resulting data matrix was analyzed using univariate and multivariate statistical and cartographic methods to uncover the major socio-spatial characteristics of the area, and in particular the enduring legacy of the feuing plans for East and West Pollokshields. The significance of the socio-spatial divide along the line of Shields Road is clearly marked in terms of ethnicity, social class, housing tenure, and the type and quality of accommodation. Mapping of these data revealed the contemporary physical and social geographies of the suburb. Space, however, precludes presentation of all thirteen univarate maps here.

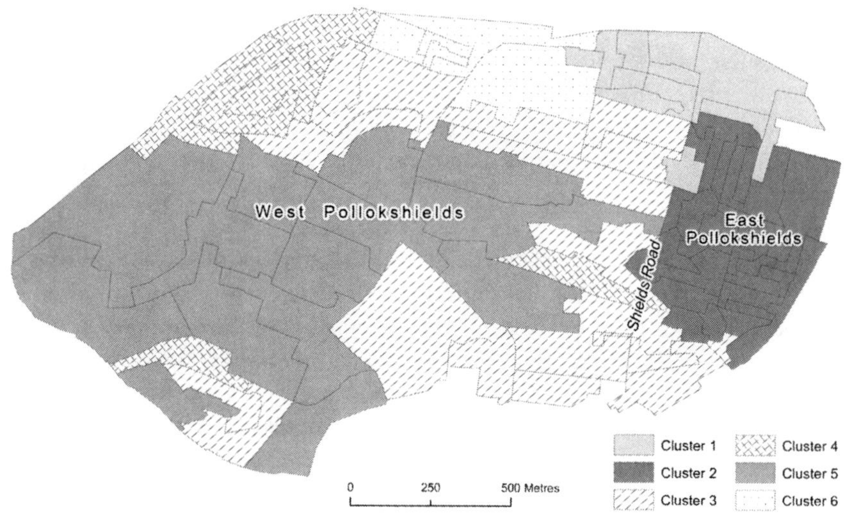

FIGURE 10.10 Mapping of six-cluster grouping of socio-morphological characteristics of Pollokshields, 2001

Univariate analysis also suggested a degree of statistical and geographical correlation among several of the independent variables. To identify the underlying commonalities in the data, the multivariate technique of cluster analysis was employed. A k-means cluster analysis produced six clusters, each of which could be labeled clearly by reference to the overall mean value for each variable. Mapping the six-cluster solution revealed the principal dimensions underlying the socio-spatial geography of Pollokshields. As Figure 10.10 shows, Cluster 1, located in the north-east of the suburb, is associated most strongly with apartments (96 percent of dwellings), of lower quality (20 percent without central heating), occupied by car-less working-class population (68 percent), predominantly white (78 percent) but with pockets of Pakistani residents. Cluster 2, with a spatial concentration in East Pollokshields, reveals an environment of lower-quality privately rented flatted accommodation occupied predominantly (58 percent of residents) by households of Pakistani origins (see also McGarrigle 2010). There is also an above-average incidence of overcrowded housing, (13 percent compared to the suburb mean of 7 percent), and of flats without central heating (29 percent compared to a suburb mean of 15 percent). In contrast, Cluster 3 is characterized by higher-quality owner-occupied apartments, with above-average space standards occupied primarily by white households. Cluster 4, located in the northwest corner of the suburb, is an area of higher-quality housing comprising a mix of owner-occupied detached and semi-detached (69 percent) and flatted (30 percent) properties, occupied by a middle class of Pakistani (39 percent) and white (49 percent) households. Cluster 5 covers the greatest spatial extent and embraces most of the area of West Pollokshields. This is the core area of affluent white residences. Two-thirds of the properties are detached or semi-detached, and one-third are flats, predominantly villa conversions. Most (94 percent) of properties are owner-occupied, with less than 1 percent social rented; 60 percent of households have two or more cars, and space standards are well above the average, with 79 percent, (compared to a mean of 35 percent) of households having an occupancy rating of +2 or more. Finally, Cluster 6 represents an area of mixed owner-occupied (47 percent) properties and social rented (41 percent) accommodation constructed by the city council as part of a strategy to diversify the tenure structure of the suburb.

Conclusion

The study of urban morphogenesis has a long and distinguished history in urban geography. In its more recent formulations, the approach has sought to advance from earlier description and classification of urban forms (Dickinson 1951) to analysis of the causal forces underlying changes in the pattern of urban land (Whitehand 1992). Much current research in the morphogenetic tradition stems from the seminal work of M. R. G. Conzen (1960), who divided the urban landscape into three main elements of town plan, building forms, and land use and demonstrated how each reacted at a different rate to the forces of change. Conzen also introduced the concept of the fringe belt to aid analysis of urban change. The existence of a fringe belt and associated fixation line reflects the fact that urban growth is cyclical rather than continuous, with periods of outward extension alternating with periods of standstill (often marked by a fixation line) due to a downturn in the building cycle. A succession of fringe belts can be identified around most towns, related to phases of active growth (Whitehand 1967).

Jeremy Whitehand (1992) has developed these concepts into an approach that seeks to identify the decision-making behavior underlying land-use zoning and change. This is based on the premise that the morphology of a town at any one time is the outcome of the perceptions, principles, and policies of individuals (e.g. landowners) or agencies (e.g. local planning departments) that exercise the necessary power. More recent evidence of the influence of landowners, developers, and planners on urban structure is provided by Whitehand's studies of residential infilling in Amersham in Berkshire (Whitehand 1992) and of the Edwardian fringe belt of Birmingham (Whitehand and Morton 2006), in which he explores the decision-making processes underlying urban change, focusing on negotiations between developers and the local planning authority. These attempts to explore the backgrounds, motivations, and actions of the major agents in the creation of townscapes at the local level represent a major advance on earlier interpretations of evolved town morphologies based largely on cartographic analysis. This chapter employs a similar focus on agents and agency to explain the processes of residential segregation and suburban development that underpinned the genesis and growth of Pollokshields garden suburb in Glasgow.

Several processes underlay the pattern of residential segregation in Victorian Glasgow. First, in terms of the physical growth of the city and the evolution of housing areas, much of the house building was undertaken by speculative builders, who were rarely interested in building for the lower end of the market. As a result, the demand for cheap housing remained high, especially after the influx of migrants from the Irish famine in the mid-nineteenth century. This demand was met by multiple-occupancy construction, leading to overcrowded conditions in the central slum areas of most cities. Second, the development of residential segregation was a result of individual locational decisions within the context of a rapidly expanding urban population. Few urban dwellers remained in the same house for long in the nineteenth century, and both migrants and established residents were continually reevaluating the suitability of their residential location (Pooley 1982). The main economic constraints on residential relocation were those of disposable income, the availability of employment in different areas, and access to accommodation in different sectors of the housing market. Social, demographic, and cultural characteristics and knowledge of the city also influenced residential location. Third, the process of residential differentiation was also influenced by the development of commercial and industrial areas within the city that imposed constraints on the nature of residential development. These constraints were exerted through pressure on land in certain districts, such as the invasion of inner-city housing areas by commercial development; through the provision of employment, in particular areas with associated working-class housing close by, and through industrial pollution that prompted those who could do so to move away. Fourth, although land-use planning did not exist in the Victorian city and institutional forces were weaker than they are today, national and local governments affected residential development in several ways. Local by-laws, together with national health and housing legislation, imposed some control over new housing development. The rate at which new houses were built and their tenure and form were also constrained by private-sector factors such as the problem of land-ownership and the prevailing rate of return on investment. Finally, residential differentiation was perpetuated through popular images of different urban areas. Certain parts of the city could gain a reputation as being of high status, unhealthy, or predominantly Irish (ethnic minority).

Residential differentiation was a characteristic of nineteenth-century Glasgow. In marked contrast to the slum areas were the status areas occupied by the elite who sought to distance themselves socially and spatially from the lower classes. This process of socio-spatial segregation was facilitated by the suburban residential schemes of large estate landowners and speculative developers, such as the Maxwells of Pollok, who sought to capitalize on the growing demand for upper-middle-class housing environments and the fortuitous location of their estate on the urban fringe.

In the twentieth century, the social and morphological development of Pollokshields garden suburb was influenced by a change in the balance of power between private sector agents, such as landowners and speculative builders, and public agency. This was marked especially in the postwar period with the growth of urban planning regulation. In Pollokshields, this shift was manifested in a number of ways as the century progressed. During the 1950s and 1960s, these changes included the public improvement of decaying properties and an ideological commitment by the local authority in the 1960s to "balanced communities" that saw the introduction of social housing on the edge of the garden suburb. These were followed in the 1970s by cooperation with local private householders, leading to conferment of conservation area status on Pollokshields.

In the study of urban morphogenesis, change is a constant. In Pollokshields, however, there is also a remarkable degree of continuity—particularly of physical layout—that stems directly from the original feuing decisions of the estate owner to develop a high-class south-side garden suburb as an alternative to the west end north of the river. In the case of Pollokshields, we see clear evidence of how the different motives and changing influences of a host of private and public actors have conditioned the social and morphological development of the garden suburb over the course of the past 150 years.

Note

This chapter is in part an abridged version of an article published in *Urban Geography*, 32 (1), 2011 (see Pacione 2011) but with new material added.

References

Beevers, R. (1988) *The Garden City Utopia: A Critical Biography of Ebenezer Howard.* Basingstoke: Macmillan.
Best, G. (1985) *Mid-Victorian Britain, 1851–1875.* London: Flamingo.
Briggs, A. (1963) *Victorian Cities.* London: Oldhams.
Buckingham, J. (1849) *National Evils and Practical Remedies.* London: Peter Jackson.
Burke, G. L. (1975) *Towns in the Making.* London: Arnold.
Cadbury, G. (1915) *Town Planning with Special Reference to the Birmingham Schemes.* London: Longman Green.
Cannadine, D. (1980) *Lords and Landlords: The Aristocracy and the Towns, 1774–1967.* Leicester: Leicester University Press.
Checkland, S. (1964) The British industrial city as history: the Glasgow case. *Urban Studies*, 1: 34–54.

City of Glasgow District Council (1979) *Pollokshields-Dumbreck Local Plan*. Glasgow: City of Glasgow District Council.

Conzen, M. R. G. (1960) *Alnwick, Northumberland: A Study in Town-Plan Analysis*. London: George Philip, Institute of British Geographers Publication 27.

Dennis, R. (1984) *English Industrial Cities of the Nineteenth Century: A Social Geography*. Cambridge: Cambridge University Press.

Dickinson, R. (1951) *The West European City: A Geographical Interpretation*. London: Routledge.

Dicks, B. (1985) Choice and constraint: further perspectives on socio-residential segregation in nineteenth century Glasgow with particular reference to its west end, in G. Gordon (ed.), *Perspectives of the Scottish City*, 91–124. Aberdeen: Aberdeen University Press.

Dyos, H. J. (1961) *Victorian Suburb: A Study of the Growth of Camberwell*. Leicester: Leicester University Press.

Fulton, W. (2002) The garden suburb and the new urbanism, in K. Parsons and D. Schuyler (eds.), *From Garden City to Green City: The Legacy of Ebenezer Howard*, 159–70. Baltimore: Johns Hopkins University Press.

Glasgow City Council (2009) *West Pollokshields Conservation Area Appraisal*. Glasgow: Glasgow City Council.

Greeves, T. A. (1975) *Bedford Park: The First Garden Suburb*. London: Anne Bingley.

Hall, P., and Ward, P. (1998) *Sociable Cities: The Legacy of Ebenezer Howard*. Chichester: Wiley.

Howard, E. (1902) *Garden Cities of To-Morrow*. London: Swan Sonnenschein.

Hubbard, E., and Shippobottom, M. (1988) *A Guide to Port Sunlight Village*. Liverpool: Liverpool University Press.

Kellett, J. (1969a) *The Impact of Railways on Victorian Cities*. London: Routledge and Kegan Paul.

Kellett, J. (1969b) Glasgow, in M. Lobel (ed.), *Historic Towns*, vol. 1, 1–13. Baltimore: Johns Hopkins Press.

Lawton, R., and Pooley, C. (1976) *The Social Geography of Merseyside in the Nineteenth Century*. Liverpool: University of Liverpool Press.

Lloyd, D. (1984) *The Making of English Towns: 2000 Years of Evolution*. London: Victor Gollancz.

Lythe, S. (1990) Suburban history: some questions from Pollokshields. *Scottish Local History*, 22: 20–1.

McCallum, A. (1921–2) Haggs, Titwood and Shields. *Old Glasgow Club Transactions*, 4: 61–7.

MacDonald, H. (1854) *Rambles Round Glasgow*. Glasgow: James Hedderwick.

McFarlane, J. (1919) Hutcheson's hospital. *Old Glasgow Club Transactions*, 3: 200–5.

McGarrigle, J. L. (2010) *Understanding Processes of Ethnic Concentration and Dispersal: South Asian Residential Preferences in Glasgow*. Amsterdam: Amsterdam University Press.

Miller, M. (1989) *Letchworth: The First Garden City*. Chichester: Phillimore.

Miller, M., and Gray, A. (1992) *Hampstead Garden Suburb*. Chichester: Phillimore.

Morgan, N. (1996) Building the city, in H. Fraser and I. Maver (eds.), *Glasgow 1830–1912*, 8–51. Manchester: Manchester University Press.

Ogilvie, S. (1989) *Pollokshields Pastiche*. Glasgow: Brown, Son and Ferguson Ltd.

Olsen, D. (1976) *The Growth of Victorian London*. London: Batsford.

Pacione, M. (2011) Continuity and change in Scotland's first garden suburb: the genesis and development of Pollokshields, Glasgow. *Urban Geography*, 32 (1): 23–49.

Pooley, C. (1982) Choice and constraint in the nineteenth-century city: a basis for residential differentiation, in J. Johnston and C. Pooley (eds.), *The Structure of Nineteenth-Century Cities*, 199–233. London: Croom Helm.

Reid, A. (2000) *Brentham: A History of the Pioneer Garden Suburb*. London: Brentham Heritage Society.

Reynolds, J. (1983) *The Great Paternalist: Titus Salt and the Growth of Nineteenth-Century Bradford*. London: Temple Smith.

Rodger, R. (1983) The evolution of Scottish town planning, in G. Gordon and B. Dicks (eds.), *Scottish Urban History*, 71–91. Aberdeen: Aberdeen University Press.

Senex (1884) *Glasgow Past and Present*. Glasgow: David Robertson and Company.

Shaw, M. (1977) The ecology of social change: Wolverhampton 1851–71. *Transactions of the Institute of British Geographers*, 2: 332–48.

Simpson, M. (1977) The west end of Glasgow, 1830–1914, in M. Simpson and T. Lloyd (eds.), *Middle Class Housing in Britain*, 44–85. Newton Abbot, U.K.: David and Charles.

Simpson, M., and Lloyd, T. (1977) *Middle Class Housing in Britain*. Newton Abbot, U.K.: David and Charles.

Smith, R. (1998) *Pollokshields: Historic Guide and Heritage Walk*. Glasgow: Glasgow City Council.

Thompson, F. M. L. (1974) *Hampstead: Building a Borough, 1650–1964.* London: Routledge and Kegan Paul.

Thompson, F. M. L. (1982) *The Rise of Suburbia*. Leicester: Leicester University Press.

Ward, S. V. (1994) *Planning and Urban Change*. London: Paul Chapman Publishing.

Whitehand, J. W. R. (1967) Fringe belts: a neglected concept of urban geography. *Transactions of the Institute of British Geographers*, 41: 223–33.

Whitehand, J. W. R. (1992) *The Making of the Urban Landscape.* Institute of British Geographers, Special Publication 16. Oxford: Blackwell.

Whitehand, J. W. R., and Morton, N. (2006) The fringe belt phenomenon and socio-economic change. *Urban Studies*, 43 (11): 2047–66.

Worsdall, F. (1979) *The Glasgow Tenement: A Way of Life*. Edinburgh: Chambers.

11

THE IMPRINT OF THE OWNER-BUILDER ON AMERICAN SUBURBS

Richard Harris

Builders are directly responsible for most of what we see in cities, but we know little about their distinct effect on the landscape. We often assume that they are mere agents, expressing a culture or perhaps the consumer's sovereignty and that it is land developers who matter, whether because they define street layouts and lot sizes or because they sometimes regulate what may be built. Only a few writers have considered the builders who translate such definings and regulations into a built environment. These writers have concentrated on the professionals who build for the anonymous buyer (Dyos 1961; Warner 1962; Whitehand and Carr 2001). In Britain this makes sense: speculative builders have long dominated the market for new homes. The same has not been as true in most other parts of the world. In North America until recently, general contractors and rank amateurs accounted for a good deal of house building, especially around smaller and medium-sized centers. Focusing on the amateur owner-builders, this chapter analyses their changing imprint on the American suburban scene from the 1920s to the late 1950s.

The impact of owner-builders on the landscape has varied according to how they were embedded in a process of development. In the early 1900s, their imprint was usually anarchic in form because they were unregulated and only loosely connected to land developers, suppliers and lenders (Harris 1996a), but there are other possible forms of owner-building, and the main purpose of this chapter is to explore these in a systematic fashion. These possibilities have a history. In a study of the cities of Oakland and Berkeley, California, Paul Groth (2004) has suggested that by the 1920s, professionals had largely displaced amateurs, even in the construction of workers' housing, but if the owner-built home had come and gone, it also came again. The context in which owner-builders operated has always been in flux but never more so than in the decade after 1945. In the suburbs, by contrast, new regulations shaped and limited the efforts of amateurs, while a brief boom in owner-building encouraged lenders and suppliers to offer unprecedented assistance. By the mid-1950s, amateurs were operating in very different ways, and with different results, than they had in the 1900s. Therefore, an incidental purpose of this chapter is to illustrate the nature of this change.

It would be possible to illustrate the argument with examples drawn from across Canada and the United States, for owner-builders were ubiquitous. In 1949, they accounted for 27 percent of all housing starts in the United States (U.S. Department of Labor 1954). The proportion was lower within metropolitan areas (14 percent) than beyond (58 percent) but, even in the New York area (8 percent), it was not trivial. Until at least the 1950s, however, regional and local differences mattered, made manifest in methods of financing and building as well as in house styles. This local and regional diversity was an important part of the American scene, in contrast, for example, to the more uniform character of development within England, but for analytical purposes, this continent-wide diversity may actually muddy our understanding of the possibilities of owner-building. To focus the examination, this chapter uses examples drawn from Peoria, Illinois. Broader patterns and implications are discussed in the conclusion.

The Case of Peoria, Illinois

Peoria is a peculiarly appropriate place in which to analyze the character of owner-building. From the 1920s to the 1950s, it was both typical and, in useful ways, unusual. Culturally, it was regarded as a "litmus test for American taste and mentality" (Teaford 1993: 253). With a metropolitan population of 250,000 in 1950, its housing market was deemed by the United States Federal Housing Administration (FHA) to exemplify the class of diversified, mid-sized cities that themselves exhibited no exceptional features (*Architectural Forum* 1934; U.S.A. FHA 1935: 5). Typically, too, by the inter-war years, most development was occurring in the suburbs. In the 1930s, 80 percent of population growth in the Peoria area occurred beyond city limits, in the industrial suburb of East Peoria, the residential suburbs of Creve Coeur or Peoria Heights, the suburban town of Bartonville, or the unincorporated portions of Peoria or Tazewell counties ("Building activity..." 1939; Fig. 11.1).[1]

Peoria was also typical in that much of the suburban development was unregulated and, at first, unserviced. Until the 1940s a "planning commission" controlled land subdivision for one-and-a-half miles beyond city limits but could not require improvements such as water, sewers, and sidewalks (Wittick 1939). Neither East Peoria, Creve Coeur, nor the unincorporated areas had any building regulations. The lack of regulation and services bothered mortgage lenders who redlined many fringe areas until they were established (Theobold 1974: 164). As this limited business, led by People's Federal Savings and Loan Association (hereafter "People's Federal"), the lenders organized a "development commission" (Theobold 1974: 191).[2] This body lobbied for county-wide zoning, which was enacted in 1948 for Peoria County, with land use and street setbacks being enforced through building permits ("Zoning idea moves out..." 1948). Servicing, however, remained problematic even here, while Tazewell County, across the Illinois River, was unregulated for many more years. Well into the 1950s, then, public regulation of suburban development was variable and generally weak. In that respect, too, this small Midwestern city was very American (cf. Hawley 1956).

Weak government attracted owner-builders. For this chapter, I undertook interviews with twenty-five people who had built at least one home for themselves in the Peoria area in the 1930s, 1940s, or 1950s.[3] Nineteen chose unincorporated areas, especially in Tazewell County, often because of the absence of building inspectors.[4] The same consideration drew people to incorporated places such as East Peoria, where Lloyd Johnson started his first home in 1940 and then built a second in the mid-1950s.[5] In this regulatory vacuum, a few subdividers imposed their own controls. These could be effective. An example was Knoll Crest, a "choice" postwar subdivision of serviced lots just north of the city where the developer built a few homes, then disposed of individual lots ("Drive out..." 1946). As these sold, he set up a residents' association that was responsible for approving plans and monitoring maintenance. Supported by an annual levy on each property, a five-person "building and street committee" exerted complete control. Its first chair, Mel Schmidt, recalls that, after 1948, the Peoria County Zoning

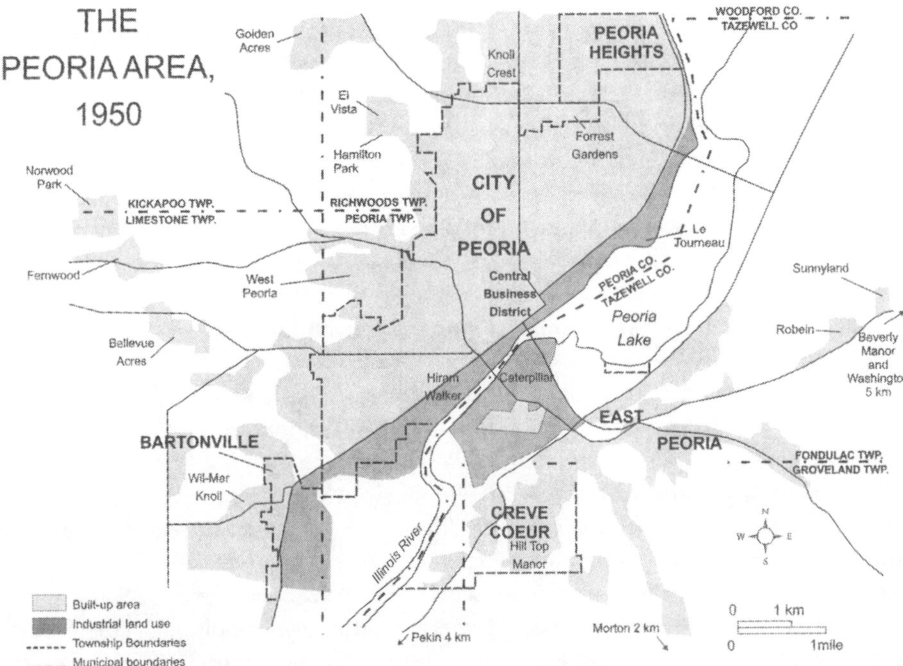

FIGURE 11.1 Peoria, Illinois, in 1950. By the 1930s most development was occurring in unincorporated fringe areas that lacked regulation or services

Commissioner rubber-stamped the committee's decisions.[6] Most subdividers, however, were more lax. In the Hill Top Manor district of Creve Coeur, for example, in the mid-1930s the developer prohibited buildings on the front of the lot worth less than $3,500, a substantial sum. (Anything could be built and occupied at the back.) Horace Mead, one of the first to build in the area, followed the guideline but recalls that "there was no real enforcement."[7] Lack of regulation was the norm.

The absence of services was handled individually and sometimes informally. For Christmas 1950, in their new home in El Vista, for example, the Speirs obtained electricity by stringing a wire from their neighbor's house.[8] Water was commonly obtained by sinking a well, as the Oedewalts did after employing a dowser.[9] Those with larger lots installed septic tanks. With an acre lot and a fifty-five-foot well, Dan Letizia built his own 1,000-gallon septic tank, with 250 feet of field tile.[10] In denser developments, subdividers sank large wells for collective use. In Ed Schlaffer's small subdivision, one well served thirty-one families; when the developer created another fifty-one lots, he sank a second.[11] In the Peoria area, then, owner-builders were attracted to an inexpensive fringe where regulations and services were limited and taxes were low. It was the same story around almost every North American city until the late 1950s.

In some ways, however, Peoria was unique. The quality of local leadership among the lending institutions was exceptional. Savings and loan companies—locally based like the early British building societies—were the major source of mortgage finance in the United States, and in Peoria they were preeminent. In 1934, they held 63 percent of the first mortgages in the city (Wickens 1937: xix). They remained dominant through the 1940s and 1950s because of the leadership of People's Federal. In 1935, control of the company passed to G. Hicks Fallin who, while in Washington DC in 1933–4, had helped to frame the charter that governed federal savings and loan associations. Under

Fallin, People's Federal rose from fourth to first place among savings and loan associations in the Peoria area. Then, in 1946, the company secured the services of A. D. Theobold, formerly director of the national U.S. Savings and Loan League and co-author of the standard textbook on savings and loan practice (Bodfish and Theobold 1938). By 1949, it held half the assets (share accounts) of all savings and loans in the Peoria area ("Assets of the Peoria..." 1949). Across the United States, savings and loans were more willing than other lenders to make construction loans on small homes. Fallin was committed to this policy; he commented that owner-builders were "the best moral risk a home financing institution can secure" (*Building Supply News* 1939; cf. *American Lumberman* 1946; *House Beautiful* 1946). Theobold agreed, and under their leadership, People's Federal pushed other local lenders in this direction. This was critical in assisting owner-builders.

Like everywhere else, Peoria was devastated by the Great Depression. Manufacturing employment in May 1933 was barely one-third as high as it had been in April 1930, but then the local economy rebounded. With the end of prohibition in 1933, Hiram Walker built the world's largest distillery in Peoria. Caterpillar Corporation, the city's largest employer, captured contracts for heavy equipment from the U.S. federal government and the Soviet Union. From May to December 1933, manufacturing employment doubled, and between 1933 and 1934, the number of marriages registered locally jumped by a third. Growth was sustained through the 1930s and 1940s, when Caterpillar made military tanks. In the Peoria area, the postwar suburban boom started twelve years early.

Peoria's early economic boom provided great scope for owner-building. During the 1930s, population growth overwhelmed the local building industry, as it did elsewhere after 1945, but Depression wages were low, and to acquire homes, families had to build their own. A trade journal estimated that 3,000 Peorians built themselves homes during the 1930s; if true, the rate of owner-building exceeded 60 percent (*Building Supply News* 1939). Moreover, the wave of owner-building lasted. The growth of suburban regulation in general gathered pace in the 1950, so that owner-builders had free reign for barely a decade. In Peoria, they had a long head-start. In the late 1940s, the rate of owner-building in the Peoria area reached 75 percent in unincorporated districts (U.S. FHA 1949: 8). For two decades, then, Peoria offered abundant opportunities for entrepreneurs and governments to explore ways of assisting the amateur builder. It provides examples of almost all of the logical possibilities.

The Elements of Owner-Building

The impact of owner-builders on the landscape depends upon how they are embedded in the larger development process: the more embedded, the less distinctive their imprint would be.

Building a house involves a sequence of tasks. A builder needs land; even the simplest structure must be conceived, or designed; materials must be produced before being assembled on site. Then, too, because land and materials cost so much, builders must save or borrow money. In each respect, owner-builders rely to some extent on others. At the extreme, they may do almost everything, searching out a site, sketching a plan, cutting and fashioning their own wood, and building in stages to eliminate the need for credit. Pioneering once existed in some suburban districts but was never the norm. By the early 1900s, services were available commercially. Unserviced lots were subdivided and marketed on "easy" terms; plan books were published; suppliers sold milled lumber and offered credit. Amateurs could save money by dispensing with one or other of these services, but all were linked in the local economy. The nature of those links—to the purveyors of land, plans, materials, technical assistance, and credit—determined how owner-builders operated and with what effects upon the landscape.

Land

Owner-builders can produce different types of houses and landscapes, depending on how they acquire building lots. Sites may be widely scattered, and this became common in North America after the 1920s, when many workers acquired automobiles and when farmers catered to their demand by severing building lots along rural back roads. None of those whom I interviewed in the Peoria area had bought such a lot, but a number were, or had perceived themselves to be, geographically isolated. They resolved building issues on their own, and sometimes idiosyncratically. The characteristic result is a landscape where development is widely scattered and where rural roads on a broad grid provide the main element of regularity.

A common alternative is for amateurs to cluster loosely in specific suburban areas and subdivisions. Typically, these are unregulated and unserviced. Speculative builders avoid such areas because houses may be difficult to sell; amateurs are attracted because land is cheap, taxes are low, and they have free reign to learn through trial and error. The characteristic absence of subdivision controls, however, means that clustering is loose, producing blocks that boast gap-toothed development for many years. Such development is common where workers commute on foot or by public transport. For example, they were the typical context for owner-built development around Toronto in the early decades of the twentieth century (Harris 1996a). They were also common around Peoria, before and after World War II. In the 1930s, population growth was concentrated in Creve Coeur, within walking distance of Caterpillar's factory in East Peoria (Fig. 11.1). This suburb's population trebled between 1930 and

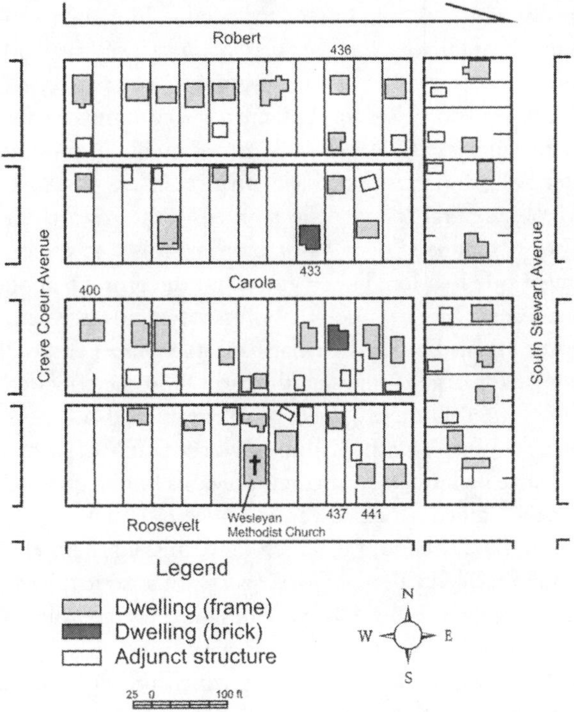

FIGURE 11.2 Anarchic development, Carola Avenue, Creve Coeur, Illinois, 1956. Here, from the 1930s, development was weakly regulated. Amateurs built in stages, often starting with garage homes at the rear of lots. They left an imprint of modest, one-story frame dwellings with varied street setbacks, interspersed with vacant lots

1936, when it reached 3,000 ("Fastest growing town..." 1936). Almost half of its labor force worked at Caterpillar. In new subdivisions, regulation was weak or absent; "there was not a sidewalk in town"; piped water and gas were installed only in 1938; and almost all homes were owner-built ("Fastest growing town..." 1936).[12] On the side of the block in Hill Top Manor where Horace Mead began a garage home in 1936, seven of ten homes were owner-built.[13] Contemporary photographs and insurance atlases show that the result was an anarchic landscape of small, single-story, frame houses with varied street setbacks ("Boom town with a future" 1937; Fig. 11.2). It was an imprint typical of subdivisions across the continent, from Toronto, Ontario, to South Gate, California (cf. Nicolaides 2002: 35–8).

The clustering of owner-construction was greatest where land subdividers actually targeted amateurs, which they did only when demand was assured. Hill Top Manor was advertised open-endedly to anyone who wished to buy a lot for $5 down and $5 a month. By 1939, however, a new Hill Top Extension was marketed specifically for owner-builders, as were other, scattered subdivisions accessible only by car ("Build in Hilltop Extension" 1939). In June, South Side Realty advertised lots in Bellevue Acres, a ten-minute drive due west of the city, where "141 splendid owner-built homes" had been completed with "32 under construction" ("Bellevue Acres" 1939). The area boasted electricity, gravel roads, and a four-room school. By September, it was maturing. One resident, Milo James, had "moved from his temporary house into the basement which he completed during the summer." Two hundred and forty-five houses had been completed, and the school enrollment had risen to 153, with 200 expected by Christmas (Alexander 1939). The appeal was obvious. As a newspaper article on another such area emphasized, owner-building in Norwood Park was easy because there were no regulations ("Every convenience..." 1940). In targeted subdivisions such as these, some houses must have been erected by general contractors, but the great majority were the work of the amateur.

Clustering was greatest where groups of owner-builders banded together to create their own subdivision. Temporarily, in the late 1940s, this became quite common across the United States (U.S. Housing and Home Finance Agency 1951). Veterans formed building co-ops to secure finance, acquire land, and trade labor. After 1949, the FHA helped with finance. At least two such developments occurred in Peoria. In the early 1950s, several friends who worked in the research department at Caterpillar started a cooperative. They bought land near Washington, Illinois, a town six miles east of Peoria, and each family was then given title to a lot. The engineers in the group laid out streets and contracted for services. Each family designed its own house and, in varying degrees, invested its own labor.[14] A variation on this theme was initiated by Cyril Schlarman, an engineer and Catholic priest. Concerned about the shortage of homes for large families, in the early 1950s he bought a small property, laid out a *cul-de-sac* and sixteen lots, and sold these subject to a restriction that buyers must have at least four children.[15] One of those to move in were the Kathuses, whose family of six had expanded more rapidly than they could accommodate by building onto their previous home; two other families had fourteen children. With the others, the Kathuses formed a co-op and corporation to enforce the restriction. Each employed a contractor to build a shell house, which they finished themselves and then extended as families grew.[16] Shell homes erected by professionals may seem to stretch beyond breaking the concept of owner-construction. However, these shells were designed by, and built under contract to, each owner; some consisted of no more than four walls and a roof; and all owners undertook a significant amount of physical labor. Shells are one common way in which amateurs can effectively build, whether as individuals or, as here, in a co-op (Shenkel 1967).

If owner-builders cluster from choice, most are also constrained to do so. People who build their own homes usually do so from economic necessity. They have low or moderate incomes and may be viewed by other homebuyers as undesirable. Subdividers who wish to target the affluent may impose

FIGURE 11.3 Controlled development, Knoll Crest, Peoria, Illinois, 1947. Unusually in this area, under privately enforced building regulations, owner-builders and general contractors were both active. The circled site was being developed by its owner

building restrictions that exclude those who wish to build modestly or in stages. In Peoria in 1940, for example, buyers of lots and architect-designed homes in Wildwood Park were assured that restrictions would prevent the construction of "shacks, garage homes, tents or similar abodes," even as temporary measures and on the back of lots ("Prize winning home..." 1940). In exceptional situations, however, owner-builders might be allowed to insert themselves into quite affluent subdivisions. In Peoria in 1947, for example, a real estate company was advertising 150 lots in Ravenwood Farm, a privately regulated subdivision five miles north of the city. It encouraged owner-builders to apply, as well as those who intended to hire general contractors ("Announce suburban homes..." 1946). This probably evolved in a similar manner as Knoll Crest (Fig. 11.3). There, Mel Schmidt and a group of co-workers at Caterpillar had the idea of buying individual lots and of employing builders to erect shell homes that they could finish. As they could not find a willing contractor, they built for themselves.

Such intermingling of amateur and professional builders has never been the norm, but for a few years after 1945, it was not unusual, especially in the Peoria area. Across North America, the war had been a social leveler: in its aftermath, young couples with decent incomes had limited savings and desperately wanted a private, detached home. They were willing to build for themselves, and such aspirations were widely viewed as acceptable. Especially in the smaller urban centers where many builders operated on contract rather than on speculation, owner-building could be more easily accommodated: builders did not have to worry about selling homes in "mixed" areas. In Peoria, especially, owner-building was so common that it was widely viewed as acceptable, but even there subdivisions such as Ravenwood Farms and Knoll Crest were the exception, not the rule. Whether because of careful marketing or the logic of the land market, those owner-builders who were not scattered across the exurban landscape were usually clustered into distinct areas.

Plans

If land development affects the metropolitan geography of owner-construction, house plans affect its imprint on a smaller scale. In the early 1900s, amateurs sketched rudimentary plans for themselves. For small houses, they produced acceptable variations on simple square or rectangular themes, usually with gabled roofs. As homes were expanded, however, do-it-yourself designs produced variety—and also problems. Floreine Harris recalled that, when her brother-in-law built in East Peoria after 1945, he did not have a floor plan "of any kind," and she commented that "this was not a good idea,"[17] Many houses evolved unpredictably. In 1936, Horace Mead bought materials for a twenty-by-forty-foot garage, which he erected and occupied on the back of his lot in Hill Top Manor. A year later, he built a smaller structure, twenty-by-twenty-four feet, as a real garage, and improved the original structure. In 1939, he decided to build a proper house at the front of the lot. Having dug a basement, he decided he had done enough to the original "garage" to justify relocating it. Once this was in place, he built additions—four by fourteen feet on the front and eight by fourteen feet at the back.[18] For amateurs such as Mead, and especially those without a steady income, improvisation was the order of the day.

Improvisation could be combined with an explicit plan at each stage. Some began with a vision. Joyce McLeod's husband built their Swiss Chalet home "in his mind" during the war.[19] Visions were usually translated into precise designs, often ones that amateurs had devised themselves. For example, observing her brother-in-law's problems, Mrs. Harris drew up plans for the house that her husband, brother, and brother-in-law built in East Peoria in 1953.[20] Some became ambitious. With a little drafting experience in high school and using small home guides published by the University of Illinois, Ed Schlaffer added distinctive touches, including a hinged bookcase that hid stairs to the attic.[21] A few could tap real expertise. Trained as a mechanical engineer, Lloyd Johnson designed the house he began in 1940. He received advice about the kitchen layout from his wife, Rosemae, ex-manager of the Tasting-Test kitchen for *Better Homes and Gardens* magazine.[22] These were exceptions. Most couples could not design a house unaided and sought guidance. One possibility was to find an expert who could translate into accurate plans of a livable design. Architects provided this service, but most people could not afford their fees. For modest homes, local lumber dealers served. In 1954, for example, Jason Hopkins took his ideas to Reinhard Lumber in Pekin, Illinois, a small town five miles south of Creve Coeur. Reinhard refined these and then sold him what he needed.[23]

Most commonly, owner-builders picked a plan. Dealers routinely carried a variety that suited local needs. In the Peoria area, all dealers probably carried plans by the 1920s, if not before ("The Mackemer Lumber Co." 1938). Some lenders did too, even before the Second World War. In Peoria, these included both the Farmers' Savings, Loan and Homestead Association and People's Federal ("Popular free…" 1939; "People"s Federal…" 1939). Often, this was a free service. Several, including the Commercial Travellers Loan and Homestead Association, set up "home libraries" where customers could come and browse (e.g. "Home plans" 1950). As they had done for many years, national companies such as Standard Homes and the Southern Pine Association sold plan books from which buyers could order blueprints (Southern Pine Association 1935). By 1950, Standard Homes claimed to have sold the plans for enough dwellings to house a million people (Standard Homes Company 1950). Plan services were advertised in local newspapers (e.g. "Now You Can Build…" 1945). Local and national businesses often found it convenient to cooperate. Dealers made arrangements with plan companies. In Peoria, Wahlfeld Lumber carried the designs of the National Plan Service. Local newspapers did the same thing. In the late 1930s, the Peoria *Journal-Transcript* ran a weekly feature that illustrated homes designed for the Southern Pine Association. Readers could buy plans from the paper's "Building Improvement Department," but checks were payable to the Association (e.g. “Inexpensive convenience” 1939). After 1945, national magazines also carried advertising while many featured homes designed by their own architects. These were modulated to their readership. Modest houses were illustrated in *Parents’ Magazine* or *Small Homes Guide*, more generous ones in *House Beautiful* and *Ladies Home Journal* (e.g. Livingstone 1946, 1949; Pratt 1950; *Small Homes Guide* 1951). With plans available cheaply from so many sources, there was no need for owners to design their own home unless they wanted something wholly unique.

In many cases, plans were specifically targeted at owner-builders. In the Peoria area, for example, by July 1939 Wahlfeld’s advertising was directed primarily at this group (e.g. “No matter what you earn…” 1940). Nationally, consumer magazines caught on to this market after 1945. Then, for example, every year *Parents Magazine* featured an “expandable home” suited to those who built in stages. Encouraged, a growing number of owner-builders bought plans, including most of those whom I interviewed in Peoria. They obtained these from every possible source, including dealers, magazines, and national catalog houses.[24] Even so, they often adapted them. Occasionally, the adaptation was planned. Walter Barnevolt, for example, reworked plans from the Sunday newspaper by adding a hallway (Fig. 11.4).[25] Mostly, plans were changed later, through piecemeal additions. For their 1950 Cape Cod house in El Vista, the Speirs obtained blueprints and materials from Wahlfeld. In 1956, their first daughter was

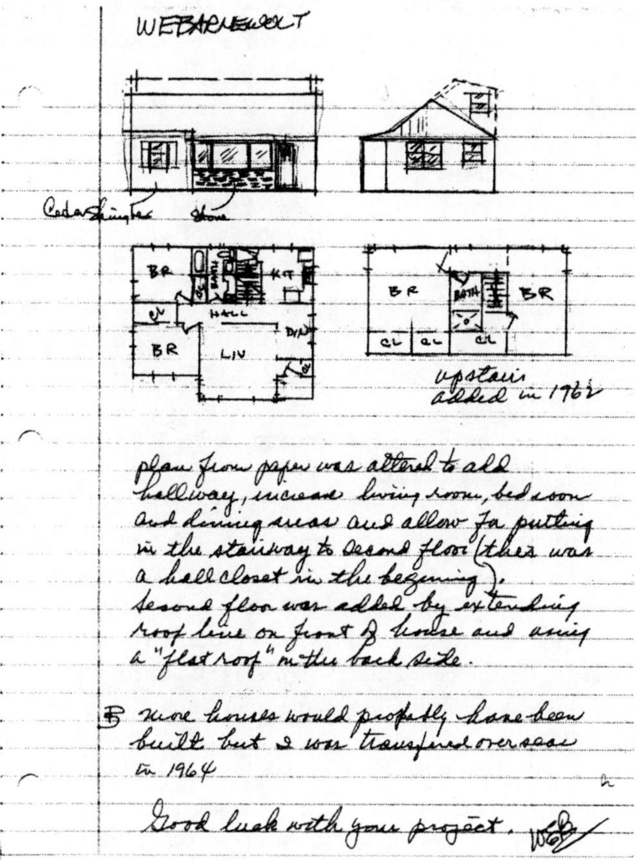

FIGURE 11.4 Sketch of the Barnevolt house, Peoria, Illinois, 1996. In 1950, Walter Barnevolt, like many amateur builders, purchased a house plan that he then altered, initially by adding a hallway and later by raising the roof

born, and they built a nine-by-twelve-foot addition on the kitchen; when a second daughter arrived, they finished the attic.[26] The Wegners made changes to accommodate a growing family that became eight. Dormers were added to light a newly finished attic, and the master bedroom was subdivided to accommodate bunk beds.[27] Inside and out, adaptations and extensions made each house unique. In general, however, the growing use of purchased plans made houses more similar.

Materials

Standardization was also encouraged by the use of manufactured materials. Amateurs have often been happy to save money by scavenging, as they build slowly and often to a relaxed schedule. This was still being done in the Peoria area in the 1940s, where recyclable wood for joists, studs, sash, flooring, and sheathing were advertised (e.g. "Used building material…" 1940). The results were unpredictable in quality and appearance. To a lesser extent, the same is true where owners fashion their own materials. The easiest to make are concrete blocks, which are also easier to lay than smaller, clay bricks. During the local population boom of the 1930s, many builders in Creve Coeur saved money this way, as did several of those I interviewed. The Oedewalts, for example, established a routine of making twenty-one blocks every evening after work.[28] Dimensions varied. Hand-operated block-making machines were available, but many families made their own forms. For this reason, and because amateurs found it difficult to keep courses level, the results could be idiosyncratic.

Other materials, notably milled lumber, were purchased in standard dimensions. Looking for deals, some buyers, such as the Andrewses, shopped around.[29] Many, however, preferred the convenience of getting everything from one dealer, and dealers responded by diversifying their product lines and by offering better prices and credit to their regular customers. By the late 1930s, a number of dealers in the Peoria area, including Wahlfeld's, Proctor's, and Allen's, claimed to offer a complete line of materials (e.g. *American Lumberman* 1941; *Building Supply News* 1945; Schneider *c.*1991: 6; "Allen Lumber Co." 1938: 2). By the late 1940s, most of the remainder, including Lauterbach's, East Peoria Lumber, and Mid-Continental, were doing the same thing and had begun to feature showrooms (e.g. "Complete line…" 1950; "Basement homeowners!" 1952). As lumber came in standard dimensions, as did a growing range of new materials such as brand-name plasterboard, it did not make much difference whether customers shopped around. Either way, the product was likely to look standardized and professional.

The strongest force for standardization was when dealers combined plans and materials into house kits. In the early 1900s, a number of mail-order companies, including Aladdin, Van Tyne, and Sears, had done well selling kits (Schweitzer and Davis 1990). Their annual catalogs included endorsements from amateurs. A number of Van Tyne's kits were erected in and around Peoria during the 1930s alone.[30] Across the United States, however, most kits were produced by lumber dealers and distributed locally. Certainly this was true in the Peoria area, where several nearby dealers, including Reinhard in Pekin, Illinois, marketed this service. Wahlfeld became so prominent that it was featured nationally in *House Beautiful*, having built up its millwork operations to produce "precut parts" to go with its range of "stock plans" (*House Beautiful* 1946). By 1940 it was advertising "Wahlfeld owner-bilt homes" [*sic*] which included plans, instructions and all materials ("What we have done…" 1940; Fig. 11.5).

Whether distributed locally or nationally, the cheapest kits were the smallest and the most standardized. During the 1940s, with federal encouragement, dozens of new companies began to manufacture homes for regional or national markets. Many, including Raleigh Mastercraft, Strathmoor, P & H, Adirondack, Samson, National, Standard, and Midwest Homes, advertised in

FIGURE 11.5 Advertisement for owner-builder housing service offered by a leading Peoria lumber dealer

the Peoria newspaper.[31] In addition, the recycling of whole structures, whether obsolete railroad refrigerator cars or buildings from nearby Camp Ellis, was also promoted ("Refrigerator car homes…" 1946; "Build a home for yourself…" 1951). Aladdin and Sears also specifically advertised their most modest offerings ("Going to build..." 1940; "Sears—immediate delivery…" 1947).

In the Peoria area, the most successful kit manufacturer was W. G. Best, a contractor who had supervised the construction of Army prefabs during the war and who set up a local factory in 1947. As prefabricated houses had acquired a bad reputation, he marketed them as conventional structures that were pre-cut. He shipped within a 350-mile radius, but more than two-thirds were sold locally. The company produced several similar designs, but one, the "Security Home," accounted for four-fifths of all sales by 1950, and by the end of that year, sales had reached a cumulative total of about 1,000 ("Peorian still sold…" 1950). A contractor who worked for Best has estimated that about 85 percent of the company's homes were erected by professionals, but they were suited to amateurs, too (cf. Zweifel 1955: 3–4).[32]

Advertisements underlined the savings from doing your own assembly: In 1947 a basic model cost $3,462 erected, but $2,732 as a kit delivered to the site ("Build your own…" 1947). Assembled units still required plumbing, plasterwork (or wallboard) and painting, and many employed a contractor to erect only the shell. The "Security Home," then, became the most common owner-built home around Peoria by the early 1950s. Most of Best's houses were erected in three large subdivisions, Forrest Gardens (from 1947), Hamilton Park (from 1951), and Rolling Acres (from 1955; "Big subdivision planned…" 1951). They helped to constitute an unusually uniform landscape, one of the most uniform that could be imagined.

Tools, Knowledge, and Advice

To build successfully, amateurs need tools and a basic knowledge of construction. Dealers and hardware and department stores used to carry the goods and offered tips. The latter service became more important after 1945 as new materials and tools became available (Harris 2000). Most of these made amateur construction easier. "Cemesto," for example, a proprietary wall material, was advertised in Peoria as a labor-saver that served as siding, sheathing, building paper, insulation, lath, and plaster all in one ("Cemesto house…" 1949). Power tools eased the tasks of cutting, planing, sanding, and even nailing, but if they made physical tasks easier, these materials and tools also multiplied choice, and information became more important than ever. Publishers thus obliged with a stream of "how-to" advice that became a flood after 1945. Home magazines included regular columns of building tips. Books led owner-builders through the process, from buying a lot to landscaping the front yard, one of the more popular authors being Douglas Tuomey (1949; see also Cobb 1950; Corey 1946; and Leckey 1947). These were brought to the attention of readers of local newspapers, perhaps most effectively through reviews such as the one the Peoria *Journal-Transcript* ran of Tuomey's new book in 1949 ("Build new house?" 1949). One of the owner-builders whom I interviewed "learned everything" from such books; another found them very useful.[33] Amateurs could also rely on local newspapers, which in Peoria in 1939–40 and then again after 1945 ran a weekly column on topics such as the appropriate spacing of studs for framing (e.g. "Correct construction" 1939; Whitman 1945). The home design "libraries" run by dealers and some lenders included building advice and house plans. More practical were demonstrations such as those organized in Peoria by the Central Illinois Light Company ("Home wiring…" 1948), and from the late 1940s as part of an annual local home show (e.g. "Home show to feature builders…" 1949). Better still were courses in construction and home planning. While some, such as the Apprentice Training School, were directed at those who were entering the trades ("Veterans learn secrets…" 1946), others, notably those organized by the Peoria Chamber of Commerce and local lumber dealers, were for all-comers. They consisted of about a dozen sessions that ran weekly, offering step-by-step, hands-on training at nominal cost to rank amateurs (e.g. "Home Planners Institute…" 1945).

The most useful advice was both practical and timely. Few amateurs can build a home in twelve weeks. What they need above all is on-site supervision and assistance. A few are able to call on informal assistance from friends and family in the building trades. At least five of those interviewed in Peoria tapped help of this kind. Rick Post was assisted by his brother-in-law, a plumber; John Harris's father was a carpenter and his brother an electrician; Lloid Brugger was apprenticing as a carpenter, and his supervisor helped frame his house; Ken Wegner could sometimes call on his brother, a contractor in a nearby town; Frank Elam, himself a carpenter, traded labor with a plasterer who was also building a house.[34] Most, however, had no special skills or connections. At most, like Dan McLeod, they had taken woodworking in high school and were willing to learn by "trial and error."[35]

Amateurs like McLeod needed steady guidance, and dealers were in the best position to offer it. They routinely visited building sites at regular intervals to deliver materials and so could monitor progress. As they provided short-term credit, they were interested to ensure that the materials they sold were used wisely. To the extent that they successfully guided construction by amateurs, they ensured the adoption of professional techniques and standards. In the Peoria area, a number of dealers employed people to provide on-site assistance. Horace Mead recalls that Frank Hartsock, the yard foreman at Wahlfeld in 1936, came out to their lot and "showed us how things should be done."[36] Echoing Mead's comment, Mel Schmidt praised the way that in the late 1940s, Jim Pike of H. E. Lauterbach Lumber often provided "an extra pair of hands."[37] Some companies eventually formalized such assistance into a service, employing a full-time "runner." As early as 1940, Wahlfeld had a scheme whereby the company undertook to provide a "complete consultation service" during construction, which involved frequent site visits ("No matter what you earn…" 1940).

Perhaps the most complete service was that offered by Reinhard Lumber in Pekin. There, the runner in the early 1950s was Jack Bolam, the yard manager's son. Bolam recalls that he routinely helped survey and stake out foundations, demonstrated how to lay blocks and bricks, and took amateurs through the elements of framing. He would visit sites up to four times a week, a job made easier by the fact that the company laid out two of its own subdivisions.[38] One of his clients, Jason Hopkins, agrees with his account and has commented that through Bolam he "learned many things" about how to build.[39] In fact, Reinhard took on the role of contractor, supervising not only the work of their own customers but that of any subcontractors. The purchase agreement that Hopkins signed was a standard builder's contract except that he was allowed a substantial credit for owner-labor. Wahlfeld's plan evolved in a similar direction (Zweifel 1955: 3). In such ways, advice shaded into close supervision. Through the dissemination of professional building practices, the result was not only a higher standard of construction but the adoption by amateurs of methods that themselves were the industry's standard (Fig. 11.6).

FIGURE 11.6 Privately-assisted self-help housing in the Reinhard Addition, Pekin, Illinois, 1995. Here a lumber dealer and lender provided plans, materials, advice and credit to owner-builders who sometimes added their own touches

FIGURE 11.7 The basement of the Andrews' house, Peoria Heights, Illinois, 1947. Following traditional practice, the Andrews minimized the use of credit by building in stages and by occupying the basement as soon as it was covered

Credit

The least visible, but the most important, agent of standardization was credit. Until the 1940s, amateur builders had neither the ability nor the inclination to use much credit during construction. They saved and bought what and as they could. This procedure resisted standardization. The Andrews, for example, who started building in Peoria Heights in 1947, had been raised never to go into debt, saved weekly, bought tools and materials as needed, began without house plans, and mixed their own concrete for the basement, which they occupied when they had covered it with tar paper (Fig. 11.7).[40] Similarly, because the Bruggers "never considered" going into debt, they began in a similar fashion. Necessity then compelled them to seek a construction loan, which they obtained because Mr. Brugger had shown commitment by digging out the basement with a shovel (it took three months).[41] Others were willing to accept credit and turned to their parents. Millie Wegner's father loaned $1,000 and proved "very patient" about the repayments.[42] Walter Speir's mother took out a second mortgage so that the young couple could start their own house in El Vista.[43] This was repaid, and the house refinanced with People's Federal, when building was complete. Amateurs required credit, especially during the building process, and building supply dealers were acutely sensitive to this need. They routinely provided sixty-day credit to regular customers, chiefly contractors, and thirty-day credit to almost everyone. This was helpful but insufficient, and lumber dealers had an incentive to go further. Many did. Horace Mead, for example, was not a good credit risk in 1936 and was turned down by two dealers before being able to obtain a standing $300 line of credit from Wahlfeld.[44] In the mid-1940s, the Boatmans tried hard to pay on a cash-and-carry basis but were offered credit from Lauterbach Lumber, initially for thirty days but later for longer periods. Eventually, even some of the charges for heating and electrical contractors, which Lauterbach helped to supervise, were added to the bill.[45] Eager to make sales, dealers drew amateurs into debt.

Lumber dealers carried short-term debt but only from necessity. It was a means to an end—and a source of aggravation. Local mortgage lenders had more extensive funds and were equipped to monitor the repayment of debt. In the United States, local savings and loan companies have been the main source of construction loans and, if only because of their local dominance of the mortgage scene, this was certainly true in Peoria. Many of those builders whom I interviewed relied heavily on construction finance from local lenders. The latter included some banks, such as the Bartonville Bank and the South Side Bank,[46] but more prominently savings and loans, including the Farmers,' Commercial Travellers,' and Morton Federal (cf. "We built our own" 1947).[47] The most important was People's Federal. It is also the best documented. In the mid-1950s, George Zweifel, who had worked in the loan division of People's Federal in the late 1940s and who rose to senior vice president, undertook a study of his company's construction loan policy for owner-builders. He found that the company had begun the practice during the 1930s, when procedures were informal. Loans were usually staged to correspond to steps in the construction process, and at first, the site inspections that this process entailed were undertaken by office staff before or after work (Zweifel 1955: 1). After 1945, however, the number of loans increased, justifying the establishment of a separate construction loan department that was responsible for examining plans, offering advice, and disbursing funds. This meant a full-time field staff. Three of those whom I interviewed had used this full, postwar construction loan service. All praised it, and one (Post) commented that People's Federal was the lender that was best attuned to the needs of amateur builders, especially those settling in unserviced fringe areas.[48] This was a field where there was room for considerable differences in corporate policy and administrative discretion.

The use of credit exerted an inexorable pressure for amateurs to build in standard ways. Even patient fathers were likely to encourage young couples to buy lots in respectable subdivisions and to use conventional designs and materials. Dealers offered credit only on what they themselves sold, which, increasingly, included nationally branded materials. Lending institutions knew that houses must offer security for their loans by being well built and easily marketable. Idiosyncrasies of style, design, workmanship, and materials were to be discouraged. When amateurs obtained credit, they were directed to produce the same sorts of houses as professionals. When they followed this directive, the distinctiveness of their imprint faded.

A Continuum

Although there has been room only to sketch the main ways in which owner-builders operated, it might seem that the possible combinations of site, design, materials, and finance were almost limitless. In practice, two combinations were especially common, forming clusters on a continuum that extended from individualistic anarchy to constrained uniformity.

Normally, at one end of the spectrum was the individualistic process and anarchic pattern described in detail elsewhere (Harris 1996a, 1997). Families acquired scattered sites, lacked credit, collected materials as they could, and erected shacks or basements that, with luck, they eventually improved. Of those interviewed in Peoria, the Wegners fit this model as closely as any. In 1946, while living in a small apartment, they bought a lot in West Peoria, borrowed money from Millie's father, and began work. Ken worked at Caterpillar while Millie stayed home. After his shift ended at 4:30 p.m., they would each take a bus to their lot, with Millie bringing a hot casserole for their supper. In the evening, they laid blocks for the basement, mixing mortar in the box that Ken made. When it got dark, Millie held the extension light; they knocked off in time to walk three blocks to catch the last bus home at 11:30 p.m. Later, they called on Ken's brother, a contractor, who helped them frame a structure and built the stairs. After their daughter was born in January 1947, they left her with Ken's mother or brought her to the building site, swaddling her in a blanket under the second floor dormer window while they nailed the sub-flooring. Soon they moved in, finishing floors and rooms one by one.[49] This individualistic process, perhaps aided by family, was common everywhere until at least the 1940s.

The constrained extreme was always rarer. It emerged not only where owner-builders had access to advice and finance but where they were compelled to use standard designs and materials in specific subdivisions. The best-documented example is the program of publicly assisted self-help developed by the City of Stockholm, Sweden, in the late 1920s, which ran until the 1980s (Harris 1999: 289–90, 295–6). Builders used locally manufactured kits, and subdivisions were very uniform, especially in the early years. There was no equivalent to this in North America, but Peoria offers an illustration of a parallel possibility within the private sector. Between 1947 and 1955, three registered subdivisions received only houses that were being manufactured by W. G. Best. Some of Best's homes were erected in scattered locations, but the majority was sold as part of a package that included finance and a site in one of these subdivisions. People's Federal played a key role. It laid out the first survey, Forrest Gardens, and because the area then lay just beyond city limits, it also installed services. After Best set up his factory, People's agreed to provide a financial package for buyers, promoting this for lots in their own subdivision. The success of this arrangement encouraged the two companies to cooperate in establishing Hamilton Park (1951) and Rolling Acres (1955). Buyers had a limited choice of designs, and none of these areas was as uniform as the early projects in Stockholm, but the development process was tightly constrained, and to this day its imprint on the landscape is clear (Fig. 11.8).

The three joint projects of W. G. Best and People's Federal attracted attention because they were unusual. Such projects were less common elsewhere, as they required close cooperation between a lender and a kit manufacturer and a willingness to accommodate the owner-builder. This, in turn, depended upon a large, predictable demand from this type of buyer. More typical was a looser model of assistance. In recent decades, the idea of publicly assisted self-help housing has been widely discussed, usually in the context of the developing world. Assistance usually takes the form of the subsidized production of serviced sites, coupled with varying amounts of technical and financial support. In the mid-twentieth century, two Canadian programs offered slightly different versions of this type of scheme (Harris 2001; Shulist and Harris 2002). No equivalent scheme was developed in the continental United States, but a close approximation was developed on the initiative of a lumber dealer in the Peoria area. Wilbur Lauterbach, owner of one of the two Lauterbach dealerships and chairman of the Peoria County Housing Authority, persuaded the Authority to lay out and service lots in "Wil-Mar Knoll," a small subdivision in Bartonville. Most buyers made arrangements with general contractors, including Lauterbach, but a few, like the Griffins, built their own houses ("Wil-Mar Knoll subdivision…" 1949).[50] Lots were large, and designs were varied; the result was a diverse landscape that ranged from compact brick-clad bungalows to sprawling ranch-style homes, some with picture windows and flat roofs (*Journal of Housing* 1952; Fig. 11.9). The Housing Authority did not provide plans, technical assistance, or finance. Instead, buyers were encouraged to turn for assistance to Lauterbach. Although nominally a public development, then, Wil-Mar Knoll owed much to the private sector.

In Peoria, and across North America, assisted self-help usually took a wholly private form. Several variations on the theme were most likely. The minimal possibility, already discussed, was for lenders

FIGURE 11.8 Constrained owner-building: two versions of W.G. Best's 'Security Home' in Hamilton Park, Peoria, Illinois, 1995. Precuts of this dwelling type were erected in the early 1950s in planned subdivisions where they helped define a standardized landscape

to offer credit to families who could then buy land and materials wherever they saw fit. In Peoria, People's Federal was willing to operate this way, but it required careful supervision (Zweifel 1955: 5). A preferable option was for borrowers to rely on one supplier, ideally one with whom the lender had an established relationship. In this manner, a supplier's short-term finance could easily be folded into a construction loan, while a reliable dealer might supervise construction, reducing the need for a lender's vigilance. Where dealers were willing to reciprocate by referring their customers on a

FIGURE 11.9 State-assisted self-help housing in Wil-Mar Knoll, Bartonville, Illinois, 1995. Subdivided by the County Housing Authority, this area contained a minority of houses such as this that were erected by owner-builders.

more or less exclusive basis, the advantage of forming arrangements with particular dealers could be considerable. When Wahlfeld advertised that its services included financing plans it was, in effect, creating business for People's Federal ("You select the design..." 1939). For all of these reasons, People's Federal favored Wahlfeld in Peoria and Reinhard in Pekin, in effect forming partnerships. The companies became closely attuned. People's Federal routinely approved house plans that were provided by Wahlfeld and accepted their cost estimates. Once a loan had been granted, it paid the dealer directly for materials as they were delivered.[51] Together, a lender and a dealer could offer an attractive and potentially flexible package of assistance (Fig. 11.10).

Of course, the complete package included land. To make this possible, a lender or dealer would have to join forces with a landowner or go into the business of land development themselves. Each was tried in the Peoria area. Before the Second World War ended, People's Federal was offering to help borrowers obtain sites and plans, materials, and financing ("New homes for Peoria" 1945). It appears that their staff members were securing options on likely building lots in scattered subdivisions. Within two years, the company had acquired land and created their own subdivision, Forrest Gardens, which they reserved for W. G. Best. Soon, in Pekin, they joined forces with Reinhard to create a subdivision exclusively for owner-builders. In each case, an informal partnership offered owner-builders a complete do-it-yourself package.

In retrospect, A. D. Theobold, who negotiated these arrangements, concluded that they "worked well" (Theobold 1974: 221). Lots sold quickly, customers were satisfied, and homes have lasted well, but a package that included land took time to put in place and carry through. It could work only where demand was substantial and sustained. Even in Peoria, a more modest package of materials and credit was the most common. Elsewhere, the demand from amateurs gathered momentum later, and assisted self-help was more limited. In general, then, the imprint of the owner-builder in North America took the form of anarchic individualism or of modest forms of private assistance.

FIGURE 11.10 Privately-assisted self-help housing: the King's house, El Vista, Illinois, 1940. Modest houses such as this were built with the material and financial assistance of a lumber dealer and lender. Others are in the right background.

Conclusion

The experience of Peoria suggests that, between the 1920s and the 1950s, the characteristic imprint of the suburban owner-builder changed. Anarchic individualism was steadily replaced by commercialized assistance. Although the driving force was the use and deployment of credit, lumber dealers played a central role. They were one of the two main providers of credit and the most important source of materials, plans, advice, and on-site supervision. They were indispensable partners in a program of assisted self-help, as People's Federal recognized (Zweifel 1955: 7). It was through their agency that owner-builders were incorporated into the commercial mainstream. No longer at the margins of the urban economy, as consumers of plans, materials, and a widening array of services, they had been propelled to its leading edge.

As a result, although owner-builders continued to cluster in specific districts, their dwellings and neighborhoods became less distinctive. Except during the building process, which still often extended over a year or more, by the mid-1950s most owner-built dwellings looked much the same as those built by professionals. They were being erected in areas that were coming under new subdivision controls that regulated street setbacks and under zoning regulations that excluded small businesses. As a result, entire neighborhoods of owner-built homes became indistinguishable from those developed by professionals.

By the mid-1950s, in Peoria as across the country, the tide of owner-building was ebbing. Dealers who had learned to cater to owner-builders turned their attention to servicing more modest forms of Do-It-Yourself, a term popularized by *Time* magazine in their cover article of August 2, 1954 (Harris 2012). Since then, home handymen and women have turned their attentions to renovations and repairs. They have left their mark in the details of almost every dwelling in the country, but today the larger impress of the owner-builder has been largely relegated to the outer and less traveled margins of the metropolitan fringe.

Acknowledgments

I thank those who shared their memories of owner-building (identified in the Notes), Sarah Hardy for help with the interviews, George Zweifel for a copy of his MA thesis, Dennis Powers for a copy of A. D. Theobold's manuscript, John Wahlfeld for access to his company's records, and Nancy Trueblood for running a timely article in the *Peoria Journal.* The Social Sciences and Humanities Research Council of Canada provided financial support.

Notes

(Including reference to all unpublished interviews.)

1 The local newspaper was an invaluable source of information. It was sampled at monthly intervals for the period 1935–55, and intensively for 1939–40 and 1945–50. Additional articles were located in clippings files maintained by local public libraries.
2 This institution was known as People's Savings and Loan until 1935 and as First Federal from 1953.
3 These interviews were undertaken by myself in 1995 and by Sarah Hardy in 1996. In each case, responses were solicited to articles published in the local daily newspaper (Kenyon 1995; Harris 1996b). Initial phone contacts were usually followed by in-person interviews in the respondents' homes. In most cases, these were the original owner-built structures. Many interviewees offered house tours and provided photographs and/or plans. Most interviews lasted between thirty minutes and one-and-a-half hours. Some of those interviewed in 1995 were contacted again in 1996. Summaries of each interview were later transcribed and sent by mail for correction and clarification. Many respondents chose to send additional information, which was incorporated into the relevant file. Where such material is used, it is referenced by the date of the original interview. No names or details have been altered. All information, including illustrative material, is used with permission. Seven other interviews were undertaken with people who had been active in the building industry in the study period, either as builders (1), real estate agents (1), employees of lending institutions (2), or lumber dealers and their employees (3).
4 Interview with Ed Schlaffer, Peoria, Illinois, March 21, 1995.
5 Interview with Lloyd Johnson, East Peoria, Illinois, June 23, 1996.
6 Interview with Mel Schmidt, Peoria, Illinois, March 20, 1995.
7 Interview with Horace C. Mead, Morton, Illinois, June 19, 1996.
8 Interview with J. Spiers, Peoria, Illinois, June 19, 1996.
9 Interview with V. Oedewalt, Morton, Illinois, June 19, 1996.
10 Interview with Dan Letizia, Peoria, Illinois, March 20, 1996.
11 Interview with Ed Schaffler.
12 Interview with Horace Mead.
13 Interview with Horace Mead.
14 Interview with Lloyd Johnson. I have not been able to ascertain whether the members of this group traded labor.
15 Interview with O. Kathus, Peoria, Illinois, March 21, 1995.
16 Interview with O. Kathus.
17 Interview with Floreine Harris, East Peoria, Illinois, June 20, 1996.
18 Interview with Horace Mead.
19 Interview with Joyce McLeod, Pekin, Illinois, June 21, 1996.
20 Interview with Floreine Harris.
21 Interview with Ed Schaffler.
22 Interview with Lloyd Johnson.
23 Interview with Jason Hopkins, Pekin, Illinois, June 20, 1996.
24 Interview with J. Boatman, Peoria, Illinois, June 23, 1996, mentioning dealers; with Mel Schmidt mentioning magazines; and with Rick Post, Peoria, Illinois, March 22, 1995, mentioning national catalogs.
25 Interview with Walter E. Barnevolt, Peoria, Illinois, June 24, 1996.
26 Interview with J. Speirs.
27 Interview with M. Wegner, West Peoria, Illinois, July 1, 1996.
28 Interview with V. Oedewalt.

29 Interview with M. Andrews, Peoria Heights, Illinois, June 24, 1996.
30 Interview with P. Kenyon, Peoria, Illinois, March 19, 1995.
31 These numerous advertisements include, for example, "Attention homebuilders ..." 1946; "1 and 2 bedroom homes..." 1946; "Yes you can move in..." 1947; "Pre cut homes $2,450" 1947; "Now available..." 1947; "Own your home..." 1949; "Build an ideal home..." 1949; "Build a Midwest home..." 1952.
32 Interview with Dennis Powers, Peoria, Illinois, March 19, 1995.
33 Interview with M. Andrews.
34 Interviews with Lloid Brugger, Washington, Illinois, June 22, 1996; Frank Elam, Morton, Illinois, June 19, 1996; M. Wegner, West Peoria, Illinois, July 1, 1996; Rick Post; and Floreine Harris.
35 Interview with Joyce McLeod.
36 Interview with Horace Mead.
37 Interview with Mel Schmidt.
38 Interview with R. Bolam, Pekin, Illinois, March 10, 1995.
39 Interview with Jason Hopkins.
40 Interview with M. Andrews.
41 Interview with Lloid Brugger.
42 Interview with M. Wegner.
43 Interview with J. Speirs.
44 Interview with Horace Mead.
45 Interview with J. Boatman.
46 Interviews with J. Boatman and M. Griffin.
47 Interviews with Ed Schlaffer, P. Kenyon, and Frank Elam.
48 Interviews with Mel Schmidt, Jason Hopkins, and Rick Post.
49 Interview with M. Wegner.
50 Interview with M. Griffin.
51 Interview with George J. Zweifel, Peoria, Illinois, June 23, 1996.

References

Alexander, Z. (1939) Bellevue Acres. *Peoria Journal-Transcript*, 29 October: 15.

Allen Lumber Co., The (1938) U. S. Works Progress Administration (unpublished typescript). Peoria, Ill.: Peoria Public Library.

American Lumberman (1941) Let the pictures speak. *American Lumberman*, 13 December: 46.

American Lumberman (1946) Dealers co-operate with owner-builders to establish profitable new markets. *American Lumberman*, 8 June: 50–1.

Announce suburban homes for veterans in new subdivision (1946) *Peoria Journal-Transcript*, 15 September: A-14.

Architectural Forum (1934) U. S. real property inventory II: Peoria. *Architectural Forum*, 61 (5): 331.

Assets of the Peoria Savings and Loans as of 1 January 1949 (1949) Unpublished typescript. Peoria, IL: Peoria Public Library.

Attention homebuilders and contractors (1946) *Peoria Journal-Transcript*, 28 July: D-3 [advertisement].

Basement homeowners! (1952) *Peoria Journal-Transcript*, 8 June: B-13 [advertisement].

Bellevue Acres (1939) *Peoria Journal-Transcript*, 18 June: Section 4-9 [advertisement].

Big subdivision planned near golf course (1951) *Peoria Journal-Transcript*, 24 June: B-1.

Bodfish, M., and Theobold, A. D. (1938) *Savings and Loan Principles.* New York: Prentice Hall.

Boom town with a future mushrooms from meadow atop bluff at Peoria's front door (1937) *Sunday Morning Star*, 28 March: Section 4-1.

Build a home for yourself and save up to 70% (1951) *Peoria Journal-Transcript*, 18 March: D-3 [advertisement].

Build a Midwest home—compare our price with others (1952) *Peoria Journal-Transcript*, 4 May: D-4 [advertisement].

Build an ideal home like this for $6,900 (1949) *Peoria Journal-Transcript*, 16 October: D-5 [advertisement].

Build in Hilltop extension (1939) *Peoria Journal-Transcript*, 26 November: Section 4-2 [advertisement].

Build new house? Do it yourself says new book (1949) *Peoria Journal-Transcript*, 19 June: A-14.

Building activity in first quarter far ahead of '38 (1939) *Peoria Journal-Transcript*, 7 May: Section 3-10.

Building Supply News (1939) Building costs too much in Peoria. So 3,000 owners build own homes. *Building Supply News*, 57 (6): 20–1.

Building Supply News (1945) 26 product displays in medium-sized store are key to Proctor's postwar plan. *Building Supply News*, 69 (3): 72–5.

Build your own Best built house (1947) *Peoria Journal-Transcript*, 27 April: D-4 [advertisement].

Cemesto house is on display here; pre-engineered (1949) *Peoria Journal-Transcript*, 26 January: C-11.

Cobb, H. (1950) *Your Dream Home: How to Build It for Less than $3,500*, New York: W. H. Wise.

Complete line of building materials (1950) *Peoria Journal-Transcript*, 9 July: D-4 [advertisement].

Corey, P. (1946) *Build a Home*. New York: Dial.

Correct construction (1939) *Peoria Journal-Transcript*, 19 March: Section 3-9.

Drive out to see Knoll Crest: the choice area for Peoria homes (1946) *Peoria Journal-Transcript*, 25 August: C-15 [advertisement].

Dyos, H. J. (1961) *Victorian Suburb: A Study of the Growth of Camberwell, Leicester*. Leicester, U.K.: University Press.

Every convenience in Norwood Park (1940) *Peoria Journal-Transcript*, 26 May: 2 [advertisement].

Fastest growing town in the country (1936) *Peoria Journal-Transcript*, 13 December: Section 4-1.

Going to build? (1940) *Peoria Journal-Transcript*, 18 February: Section 4-5 [advertisement].

Groth, P. (2004) Workers'-cottage and minimal bungalow districts in Oakland and Berkeley, California, 1870–1945. *Urban Morphology*, 8 (1): 13–25.

Harris, R. (1996a) *Unplanned Suburbs: Toronto's American Tragedy, 1900–1950*. Baltimore: Johns Hopkins University Press.

Harris, R. (1996b) Editor finds Peoria rich in facts on owner-builders. *Peoria Journal-Star*, 23 June.

Harris, R. (1997) Reading Sanborns for the spoor of the owner-builder, 1890s–1950s, in A. Adams and S. McMurry (eds.), *Perspectives in Vernacular Architecture*, vol. 7, 251–267 Knoxville: University of Tennessee Press.

Harris, R. (1999) Slipping through the cracks: the origins of aided self-help housing 1918–1953. *Housing Studies*, 14 (3): 281–309.

Harris, R. (2000) 'To market! To market! The changing role of the Australian timber merchant 1945–1965. *The Australian Economic History Review*, 40 (1): 22–50.

Harris, R. (2001) Flattered but not imitated. The Nova Scotia Housing Commission, 1936–1973. *Acadiensis*, 31 (1): 103–28.

Harris, R. (2012) *Building a Market: The Rise of the Home Improvement Industry, 1918–1960*. Chicago: University of Chicago Press.

Hawley, A. (1956) *The Changing Shape of Metropolitan America: Deconcentration since 1920*. Glencoe: Free Press.

Home Planners Institute opens tomorrow night (1945) *Peoria Journal-Transcript*, 8 April: C-8.

Home plans (1950) *Peoria Journal-Transcript*, 19 March: D-5.

Home show to feature builders at work (1949) *Peoria Journal-Transcript*, 27 March: D-1.

Home wiring exhibit in Peoria Loop (1948) *Peoria Journal-Transcript*, 8 August: D-6.

House Beautiful (1946) How 4,000 Peoria families built their own homes. *House Beautiful*, 88 (3): 112–3, 179.

Inexpensive convenience (1939) *Peoria Journal-Transcript*, 29 January: Section 3-12.

Journal of Housing (1952) Bartonville, Illinois has state aided owner builder program. *Journal of Housing*, 9 (12): 434.

Kenyon, T. J. (1995) Owner-builders part of Peoria's past. *Peoria Journal-Star*, 20 March.

Leckey, W. C. (1947) *Your Home and How to Build It Yourself*. Chicago: Popular Mechanics Press.

Livingstone, M. (1946) Come inside the first *Parents' Magazine* expandable home. *Parents' Magazine*, 21 (3) (March): 46–7, 102–6.

Livingstone, M. (1949) The George Mongolds build *Parents' Magazine*'s 2nd expandable house. *Parents' Magazine*, 24 (2) (February): 39, 102–8.

New homes for Peoria (1945) *Peoria Journal-Transcript*, 24 June: C-6 [advertisement].

Nicolaides, B. (2002) *My Blue Heaven: Life and Politics in the Working-Class Suburbs of Los Angeles, 1920–1965*. Chicago: University of Chicago Press.

No matter what you earn you can own a Wahlfeld home (1940) *Peoria Journal-Transcript*, 28 April: 5 [advertisement].

Now available in the $5,000 range (1947) *Peoria Journal-Transcript*, 30 November: 3 [advertisement].

Now you can build this ideal home for $5,900 (1945) *Peoria Journal-Transcript*, 21 October: D-3 [advertisement].

1 and 2 bedroom homes for veterans—"factory bilt" by Strathmoor of Detroit (1946) *Peoria Journal-Transcript*, 3 November: D-2 [advertisement].

Own your home—just $500 down (1949) *Peoria Journal-Transcript*, 24 April: A-12 [advertisement].

People's Federal offers new home building service plan (1939) *Peoria Journal-Transcript*, 16 April: Section 3-7.

Peorian still sold on factory built housing idea (1950) *Peoria Journal-Transcript*, 18 February: 2.

Popular free home builders library (1939) *Peoria Journal-Transcript*, 26 February: Section 1-7.

Pratt, R. (1950) You can build your own home for half the price. *Ladies Home Journal*, 67 (4) (April): 46–9.

Pre cut homes $2,450 (1947) *Peoria Journal-Transcript*, 12 October: D-11 [advertisement].

Prize winning home for city (1940) *Peoria Journal-Transcript*, 2 March: Section 1-10.

Refridgerator car homes—they are well-insulated (1946) *Peoria Journal-Transcript*, 14 April: A-17.

Sanborn (1956) *Sanborn Fire Atlas, Peoria, Illinois*. New York: Sanborn Map Company.

Schneider, S. (*c*.1991) Undated, untitled typescript [a history of the Wahlfeld Mfg. Co.], Wahlfeld Manufacturing Co.

Schweitzer, R., and Davis, M. W. R. (1990) *America's Favorite Homes: Mail Order Catalogues as a Guide to Popular Early 20th-century Homes*. Detroit: Wayne State University.

Sears—immediate delivery to your lot (1947) *Peoria Journal-Transcript*, 25 May: C-17 [advertisement].

Shenkel, W. M. (1967) Self-help housing in the United States. *Land Economics*, 43: 190–201.

Shulist, T., and Harris, R. (2002) Build your own home: state-assisted self-help housing in Canada, 1942–75. *Planning Perspectives*, 17: 345–72.

Small Homes Guide (1951) Families are helping to build their own—and SAVING money. *Small Homes Guide*, 26 (Summer–Fall): 99–100.

Southern Pine Association (1935) *Livable Homes of Southern Pine*. New Orleans: Southern Pine Association.

Standard Homes Company (1950) *Standard Construction Details for Home Builders*. Washington, D. C.: Standard Homes Company.

Teaford, J. (1993) *Cities of the Heartland: The Rise and Fall of the Industrial Midwest*. Bloomington: Indiana University Press.

The Mackemer Lumber Company (1938) U.S. Works Progress Administration (unpublished typescript). Peoria, IL: Peoria Public Library.

Theobold, A. D. (1974) A historical review of First Federal Savings and Loan Association of Peoria 1874–1974. Bound typescript in possession of the author.

Tuomey, D. (1949) *How to Build Your Own House.* New York: Grosset and Dunlop.

U. S. Department of Labor (1954) Structure of the residential building industry in 1949, Bulletin 1170. Washington, D. C.: U. S. Department of Labor.

U. S. FHA [Federal Housing Administration] (1935) *Analysis of the Real Property Inventory and Financial Survey of Housing for Peoria, Illinois*. Washington, D. C.: U. S. FHA.

U. S. FHA (1949) Report on the current housing situation in Peoria, Illinois (unpublished typescript). Office of Housing Market Analysis, FHA, January, National Archives, RG 31, Box 6.

U. S. HHFA [Housing and Home Finance Agency] (1951) *Housing Cooperatives in the United States, 1949–1950*, Housing Research Paper 24. Washington, D. C : Housing Research Division, U. S. HHFA.

Used building material for sale (1940) *Peoria Journal-Transcript*, 10 March: Section 2-10.

Veterans learn secrets of painting and decorating (1946) *Peoria Journal-Transcript*, 3 November: D-4.

Warner, S. B. (1962) *Streetcar Suburbs: The Process of Growth in Boston, 1870–1930.* Cambridge: Harvard University Press.

We built our own (1947) *Peoria Journal-Transcript*, 29 June: A-10 [advertisement].

What we have done for many people we will gladly do for you (1940) *Peoria Journal-Transcript*, 7 April: 5 [advertisement].

Whitehand, J. W. R., and Carr, C. M. H. (2001) *Twentieth-Century Suburbs: A Morphological Approach.* London: Routledge.

Whitman, R. C. (1945) First aid to ailing house. *Peoria Journal-Transcript*, 6 May: B-5.

Wickens, D. (1937) *Financial Survey of Urban Housing.* Washington, D. C.: United States Government Printing Office.

Wil-Mar Knoll subdivision is completed (1949) *Peoria Journal-Transcript*, 20 November: D-16.
Wittick, W. A. (1939) The City Plan. *Peoria Journal-Transcript*, 2 July: Section 3-8.
Yes you can move in—in 30–45 days (1947) *Peoria Journal-Transcript*, 20 July: D-3.
You select the design, we handle all financing details (1939) *Peoria Journal-Transcript*, 22 January: Section 3-9.
Zoning idea moves out into the county (1948) *Peoria Journal-Transcript*, 18 April: D-1.
Zweifel, G. J. (1955) "Sweat Equity" lending—a profitable service (unpublished MA thesis). Bloomington: Indiana University, Graduate School of Savings and Loan.

PART V

Agency in Late Modern and Postmodern Settings

12

MODERNISM AGAINST HISTORY

Understanding Building Typology and Urban Morphology among Italian Architects in the Twentieth Century

Nicola Marzot

In the contentious debate on good urban form and appropriate building types that gripped the Italian architectural profession during the second half of the twentieth century, a crucial issue was the identification of the driving forces behind urban transformation and their interactions. In this debate, the so-called Early Modern period was considered to be an intellectual watershed in relation to which different theories and implicit manifestos arose. They produced a wide range of perspectives through which the reality of the built environment started being systematically investigated and framed via the construction of internally coherent representations, called "types."

With this in mind, it is important to trace back individual research positions to their seminal inception, where ideological premises lie, to follow further developments, methodological maturation, knowledge outputs, and critical decline and resurgence of interest through different forms of metabolism. It is perhaps useful to develop a historiography of morpho-typological studies, to recreate the production of "intellectual worlds" as the result of a conscious interpretation of reality, whose objectivity is not achievable if not in ideal terms. To do that, it is worthwhile to compare a selected range of positions according to an analytical methodology that pays special attention to the "agents of transformation" as a challenging issue. Out of this, we can isolate and define a common attitude, which, however, does not obscure the distinctions among unique, individual perspectives.

The Continuity of Processes in the Transformation of Urban Form

There is a long tradition of urban analysis founded on the idea that everything stems from precedents. This derives from systematically mapping transformations of urban form by direct surveys and the study of cadastral maps over time, combining formal studies with a wide range of extra-disciplinary sources. For a long time, the main focus of this tradition was on the period stretching from initial settlement to the emergence of the bourgeoisie.

This approach formed the basis of the Rome Royal Architectural School during the fourth decade of the twentieth century. Giuseppe Giovannoni, urban designer and holder of the Chair in Survey and Monumental Restoration, traced the origins of the medieval city in Italy to earlier Roman settlements. For him, this offered a way to demonstrate that even Modernity could be seen to stem from urban precedents, physically and metaphorically "grafting" its highly technological infrastructure of mobility to solid historical roots, prompting the well-known *teoria dell'innesto* (Giovannoni 1931). On a similar basis, but at a different scale, Vincenzo Fasolo and Giovanni Battista Milani, respectively, holders of the Chairs of History and of Architectural Styles and Building Construction Techniques, described classical and medieval tectonics as the transformation of preexisting architectural bodies of knowledge made possible through an endless process of learning by doing site-specific experiments, where practice could not be assumed to be separate from theory (Fasolo and Milani 1931–40).

Soon, similar cultural developments occurred in Milan. Giuseppe Pagano, an outstanding exponent of Italian architectural rationalism, studied the enduring Italian agricultural building tradition and showed how even the most humble and recent buildings represent a transformation of existing structures, based on an enduring structural memory passed down through the generations, embodying an ingrained attitude of craftsmanship (Pagano and Daniel 1936).

The intuitions of the earlier scholars in Rome were subsequently developed in full by Saverio Muratori. As the founding holder of the Chair of "*Caratteri Distributivi degli Edifici*" at the Istituto Universitario di Architettura di Venezia (IUAV) from 1950 to 1954, he used his classes to conduct a systematic building survey of Venice to identify characteristics of historical continuity from the settlement's beginnings onward. He gave equal attention to public monuments and to ordinary, vernacular buildings. He reconstructed the history of building types, however, rather than that of architectural styles. With such guidelines, he ultimately succeeded in discovering an almost endless stream of clues to the internal processes by which urban building types were transformed. These he differentiated according to varying levels of complexity in their internal arrangement, which he referred to as "scales" evolving through space and time to host new individual needs and expectations (Muratori 1959–60). Crisis occurred when transformation was prompted by forces external to site-specific conditions and the internal capacity of the city to evolve and develop. Such crises appeared rather suddenly from the Enlightenment period onward, with limited but effective antecedents during the period of the Renaissance, which introduced forms deliberately without, and in opposition to, precedent.

According to Muratori, Early Modern culture deliberately refused to recognize that urban fabric, or urban tissues, had always performed as a "living organism" whose main quality is viability or to recognize the city's capacity to preserve and nurture its own potential for development through transformation, from the territorial scale right down to the level of individual architecture. This argument offers an unintended and surprising parallel to Chomsky's concept of a transformational-generative grammar and implicitly anticipates the issue of environmental sustainability. Once Muratori had come to this realization, the main purpose of his work and that of the school he created was to discover principles and behaviors that transformed urban form, developing an analytical approach he dubbed "operational history" ("*storia operante*"), one of the most controversial and misinterpreted ideas in the field of Italian urban morphology—often confused with an idealistic vision of history (Muratori 1963).

The concept of crisis played a crucial role in the work of his students. To understand major changes occurring in the morphology and building typology of cities in the Early Modern period, Paolo Maretto and Gianfranco Caniggia focused mostly on the rise of the new bourgeoisie from the late eighteenth century. Political imperatives forced the rejection of transformation processes deeply embedded in history and replaced them with a new reality based on stark rationalism, empowered by intellectuals fighting against aristocratic privileges inherited from the past. New economic conditions weakened the traditional role of guilds, which at that time still had the responsibility of managing urban development according to rules deeply rooted in local conventions and strongly shared by the urban community at large. Social claims from the newly prominent bourgeoisie shifted power away from the hierarchical society of the Ancient Regime, strongly anchored in the primacy of time over space. A cultural revolution forced the "project" to assume a leading role in the transformation of urban form, which inevitably led to the supremacy of projects that prefigured the future rather than adapted the existing.

For all these reasons, Paolo Maretto (1960, 1980, 1986) and Gianfranco Caniggia (1963, 1981; Caniggia and Maffei 1978, 1984) suddenly broke away from the prevailing twentieth-century architectural paradigm of Modernity as practiced in Italy. They sought to systematically interweave the role played by Early Modern "agents of transformation" with the autonomous ability of traditional urban tissues to adapt to the appearance in society of new attitudes. Their writings articulated by implication the ideology underlying the experiences of others who similarly questioned the dominant ahistorical assumptions of Modernity and embraced the historic past, albeit later on as an idealized interpretation of it even as it represented a dialectic opposition between New and Old. While fully recognizing that this revolutionary stance would lead to a rupture in contemporary architectural practice that the wider society could easily see, they argued strenuously for a reconciliation between history and Modernity. Such a rapprochement could be achieved if intellectuals, exercising "critical consciousness"—itself a living heritage of the Enlightenment—would begin to pay renewed respect for the existing without rejecting innovation. If they would explicitly accept that continuity could once again be a shared value that played its part in the broadly evolving character of the contemporary city, it would once more demonstrate its capacity to convey the past into the present, refreshing the fundamental processuality of reality.

The notion of type would be the conceptual means of reconciliation. The Muratorian School developed this legacy further through different levels of complexity: Alessandro Giannini (1964, 1976, 1980), Sergio Bollati (1976, 1980), Renato Bollati (1976, 1980), Giancarlo Cataldi (1975, 1977), Attilio Petruccioli (1994), and Marco Maretto (2008) all focused on the territorial, or regional scale; Paolo Vaccaro (1968, 1980; Vaccaro et al. 1987), Gian Luigi Maffei (1981, 1990; Caniggia and Maffei 1978, 1984; Bascià et al. 2000; Maffei and Maffei 2011) and Nicola Marzot (Zaffagnini et al. 1995; Balzani and Marzot 2010) have given special attention to urban and building tissues; while Giuseppe Strappa (1995; Strappa et al. 2003) has worked on the unity of the architectural organism.

A similar attitude, even though it came from a slightly different cultural background closer to the rational milieu of the Milanese bourgeoisie, was displayed by Antonio Monestiroli and Guido Canella. Monestiroli sought to combine the different cultural perspectives that historically claimed and played a role in the transformation of urban form. He suggested viewing the process as a three-step sequence: (1) a neutral acceptance of existing building structures as they effectively occurred in the specific conditions of space and time; (2) a subsequent critical assessment of their socioeconomic and cultural constraints in the light of new community expectations; and (3) an ultimate, morphogenetic phase during which new building types are born from existing ones as substitutions of both material and ideal original conditions. In the light of such evaluation, whether it be implicit or explicit, Monestiroli (1979, 1997) used case studies to demonstrate the process by which the Late Renaissance urban block, for example, was derived from medieval building tissues and how the prior experiences of housing communities were continued through a general rethinking of precedents connected with the formally unitarian public square. To Monestiroli, tracing back the transformative process would create the possibility of understanding the society that facilitated and followed it. Guido Canella projected a similar approach to contemporary issues by describing the emerging urban network as a metropolitan transformation brought about by the modern commercial distribution system, imported to Europe from the United States (Canella 1965).

The Project of Architecture without Precedents

Starting in 1963, Carlo Aymonino taught "*Caratteri Distributivi degli Edifici*" as a lecturer (*professore incaricato*) at the IUAV. Together with his assistants, he stressed the necessity of changing the conventional interpretation of Modern architecture. Echoing the theme of the pioneering master exponents, he emphasized the role played by society itself as an all-embracing agent of transformation (Aymonino 1966). From this point of view, the existing architecture of the city, because of the relationship between urban morphology and building typology, was made an essential prerequisite for investigation. Consequently, the history of architecture was no longer conceived as a sequence of isolated, individual milestones but rather as the result of widely shared urban experiences.

Aymonino's main focus was on the origin of bourgeois society, specifically stressing the importance of the relation between material condition—the limits of property, the logic of production and political ideology—and architecture as a representation of this content (Aymonino 1967, 1971; Aymonino et al. 1967, 1970). To do that, architecture has to divest itself of individual idiosyncrasies to better reflect shared values, made self-evident and recognizable in a wide spectrum of proposals. The "building type," investigated across the face of the city, therefore becomes the template for expressing the common heritage physically, embodying the very soul of the community.

As building type symbolizes the systematic quality of architecture, Aymonino attempted to establish its characteristic range in the eighteenth-century city, at the beginning of the Industrial Revolution, as an expression of an emerging capitalist society. He was especially interested in the definition and development of new prototypes, or "buildings without precedents." To him, when certain activities arise spontaneously and reach a clear degree of inner articulation and subsequent stability in specific historical conditions, it becomes necessary to recognize a new building artifact, peculiarly fitted to serve those activities within its corporeal form. This phenomenon appears in civil architecture with respect to community facilities (*attrezzature collettive*), which are entirely distinct from residential building thanks largely to such efforts of Enlightenment architects as those in France, exemplified by Étienne-Louis Boullée, Jean-Jacques Lequeu, and Claude-Nicolas Ledoux and in Italy by, for example, Francesco Milizia. They all stressed the originality of design parameters used to define the new architecture both in terms of internal arrangement and, indeed, urban location. When those innovative aspects began to diffuse among different places, spreading bourgeois values, they developed into specific types, according to the definition offered by Quatremère de Quincy. They established an independence within the existing urban fabric that prevented any interference with their novel and essential function.

Aymonino's strong interest in civil architecture stemmed from the important role it played from the outset in the capitalist transformation of urban form (Aymonino 1974, 1975). Whereas residential buildings speak to the initiative of private agency, community facilities, on the other hand, belong to the public domain and bear physical witness to collective values. As a result, it is possible to rediscover typological rules that the public administration, as the new client of bourgeois society—replacing the king and his aristocratic court—pursued. The goal was to find the proper urban setting in which to emphasize the inner quality and principled design of public buildings, without any potential limitation, through distinguished architecture. With regard to the private domain, building types soon became constrained by building regulations owing to the necessity of subordinating residential developments to the interests of real estate speculation and its material limitations.

According to Aymonino's writings, his interpretation of building type derives clearly from the ideological assumption that the type itself, being the concept of an "absolute architecture"—that is, an architecture designed to exploit its capacity to represent social expectations without compromise—applies only to public building and cannot be embodied by private enterprises. However, to reestablish a key role for housing in representing contemporary society, because of its obvious contribution to urban form, it is fundamental to bring the public sphere into this field of application as well, precipitating a search for a new equilibrium among critical driving forces. In so doing, Aymonino established a critical distance between himself and Saverio Muratori, who had held the same teaching chair before him.

Notwithstanding this separation, Aldo Rossi had already shown interest in typological analysis during his student apprenticeship, but it was not until he became Aymonimo's assistant in Venice at IUAV that he fully engaged with it. Attending the courses of "*Caratteri Distributivi degli Edifici,*" Rossi clarified his own position. He declared his aim was to investigate the relationship between building typology, defined as the study of building types, and urban morphology, or the study of urban form, with the conviction that from the relation itself there could arise a specific knowledge. The field of investigation is the urban landscape, according to the French geographer Georges Chabot, interpreted as an empirical field of research. To Rossi, there were two different approaches to the issue: the analysis of functional systems, as generators of urban space, and the description of their spatial structure. In the first case, the main focus is on economic, political, and social aspects; in the second, it is on the spatial relation. If the former aspect has already produced a consistent literature, mainly of Marxist derivation, the latter is still open to contribution.

The description of urban form is, therefore, the methodology used by urban morphology. In this respect, we have to face three different scales, or levels of complexity: the street, the district, and the city. All of them have been affected by rational data (a set of building rules and design norms), the impact of economics and real estate structure, and the influence of socio-historical factors. Notwithstanding Rossi's awareness of the city's capacity for self-regeneration, he was more interested in the "city as a project." In the project, he identified the possibility of critically subverting the existing condition, reflecting Aymonino's political and cultural imprint upon him. According to this aim, the "agents of transformation" will no longer be anonymous forces but leading figures in society who claim their role to be evident in the built form itself. In this way, his long-standing interest in the Early Modern period was justified. Here, for the first time, a social revolution manifested itself on a broad scale, assuming the city as a stage (Rossi 1964a, 1964b, 1964c, 1966a, 1969).

Rossi's own position became even more detailed in his highly influential book, *L'Architettura della Città* (Rossi 1966b, 1975). All agents that could transform city form, merely noted in his previous papers, were now systematically described through the critical assessment of already published research in the form of a consistent original essay. Setting himself somewhat apart from Aymonino, Rossi stated that new cities always act toward the existing order by opposing to it some specific and limited features, never sufficient to overwhelm it entirely. This led to the idea of the "city as a patchwork" (*città per parti*), which represents a field of persisting conflicts among groups and individuals. They are affected by specifically occurring facts and events and not by history assumed as an idealistic structure—thereby eliding a misinterpreted position of Saverio Muratori—that sometimes produce important urban elements simultaneously acting as both constraints and agents of progress. These facts emerge through the persistence of building forms, continuity of street pattern, and fundamental ideas shared by old cities and new quarters alike, called primary elements (*elementi primari*).

This definition is crucial in understanding Rossi's idea of the "city as a project," which counteracts the Muratorian one of the "city as organism." Primary elements identify with those public arrangements that preserve their formal integrity through time and behave differently from housing tissues (*aree residenza*), which are completely transformed by individual use and meaning. The distinction between the public and the private domain assumes a clear political significance in Rossi's approach to urban form and building types. The public domain, heavily resisting transformation, implicitly neglects the contributions of the individual, weakening his role in the modification process of what exists, while the private domain's evolution implicitly empowers singular performances whose success is validated by emulation and not by top-down imposition. By not being specific historical products but rational outcomes of humankind, the primary elements stand out as potential components of a design discipline deliberately based on the strategy of opposition—theoretically comparable with Ferdinand De Saussure's notion of the *langue* (general rules) and clearly distinguished from the *parole* (individual executions).

A major consequence of this methodological proposition, spread among the Venice Faculty of Architecture, was the prompt beginning of analytical work by the so-called *Gruppo Architettura* on

FIGURE 12.1 EMPAS headquarters, Via dei Mille 9, Bologna, Italy (designed by Saverio Muratori, 1952–57).

During the Middle Ages Bologna experienced tremendous growth, becoming one of Europe's largest markets. Buildings increased their mass by adding floors, consuming rear garden space and encroaching on the street space with cantilevered frontal extensions. Beyond a certain threshold, overhanging projections need pillars for support, creating the 'portico' or arcade. This evolution can be defined as the portico's typological process, which, through extensive replication over the centuries, came to epitomize Bologna's architectural identity. Saverio Muratori reinterpreted the street-level portico as the basis for a new office building in Bologna, expressed explicitly through a neo-medieval architectural language. Combining projected upper floors with a stable portico, he succeeded in preserving the bond between the building's modern idiom and its typological antecedents. It is a bold example of the New Historicism in architecture, relating particularly well with the nineteenth-century linear buildings next to it.

the conventional quality of the architectural language. Following Rossi's systematic reference to linguistics, the young research group moved beyond the Enlightenment period—with its shared heritage of insights from Aymonino and Rossi gained through urban morphology—and took on the challenge of interpreting Modernity. This called for testing empirically the notion of architecture as an impersonal set of rules and implied a major concern for the rational aspects of the architectural discourse following De Saussure's definition of *langue* based on structure rather than history. From that moment on, the "synchronic" level, or the interpretation of architecture as a system of relations among assigned components, became the paradigm according to which the relation between urban morphology and building typology was addressed (Aymonino et al. 1984).

Special attention should be given to the figure of Giorgio Grassi in Milan. He emphasized the importance of the rational and the methodological in urban and architectural design and embraced the obligation of urban morphology and building typology to construct an analytics of both architecture and the city, reduced simply to their logical internal arrangements. Equipped in this way, Grassi inevitably discovered the *Grand Siècle,* the seminal premise of Modernity, and it led him to establish several positions. He compared the systematic categorization of architectural styles to the rationality of contemporary methodology. He sought, for example, to use the liaisons between the original appearance of the repetitious homogeneity of uniform building façades and the individuality of buildings in the French tradition of the Place Royale to empower the emergence of a State tradition. This included the role that sets of building rules played in the formation of the Modern city, which helped consolidate the former bourgeois sovereignty with the latter-day welfare role in society. And he sought to relate the diffusion of classical treatises on architecture and urban design to a similar resurgence of interest in the contemporary era of Modernity (Grassi 1967, 1979).

Conclusions

The aim of this chapter has been twofold: to reconsider the role played by new leading agents in the transformation of urban form during the Early Modern Period and to clarify the extent to which their different interpretations affected the morphological and typological debate that occurred, especially among architects and planners in Italy during the twentieth century. By comparing the various groups' interpretations—ranging from traditional continuity to modern discontinuity with respect to history—one can observe how the differences let submerged ideologies with strong political dimensions come to the surface. In particular, the emergence of bourgeois society, representing an ideological break with the long-established imprint of the Ancient Regime, sought to substitute the widely dispersed nature of city transformation with the notion of the city as project. Within this framework, a crucial role is subtly revealed by the use of terms employed in the different perspectives just mentioned.

On the one hand, the lemma "organism" as applied to urban and architectural design, and peculiar to the Muratorian School, indicates a major concern for the processual nature of change. In this, building types are the unstable and unpredictable outcomes of an endless transformation of the built environment. They reveal the city's autonomous capacity to evolve and regenerate itself, respecting both individual and communal needs and expectations. The use of this term, therefore, implies a strong association with civil continuity and stability as existed before the emergence of the Enlightenment (Fig. 12.1). On the other hand, the "city as a patchwork," recurrent in the thought and legacy of Aymonino and Rossi, refers to the ability of the new Bourgeoisie to play with "composition" intended as a new rational ability—and as such universal and not conventional, obtained through application and practice—to establish a new kind of authorship in guiding progress from the Early Modern Period onward.

FIGURE 12.2 Monte Amiata housing complex, Gallaratese district, Milan, Italy (designed by Aldo Rossi, 1967–72)

According to Italian tradition, porticos developed from the expansion of existing buildings into the street space, increasing their own density. As a result, they were viewed simultaneously as 'thick' urban frontage, made habitable both to please owners' expectations and to offer comfortable shelter for pedestrians during the rainy and hot seasons. Aldo Rossi saw the portico as an elemento primario, *a permanent and absolute architectural type, capable of giving order to city growth and resisting its chaotic transformation, independent of its historical inception and its relation to existing or prospective private buildings that might be linked by it. For these reasons Rossi designed a low-income suburban housing project reduced to an abstract monumental portico, unified by repeating a single window and structural rhythm. It affirmed the primacy of the collective over the individual, offering a paradigmatic example of architectural Neo-Rationalism.*

Similarly, there is a distinction between "spontaneous consciousness" favored by Muratori and his pupils to refer to ordinary building production in use up to the Enlightenment and fostered by local guilds on the one hand and "critical consciousness" favored by Aymonino, Rossi, and Grassi on the other hand, which promotes self-consciously designed architectural outcomes from the rise of bourgeois entrepreneurs onward. Therefore, the innate body of knowledge concerning how things develop, implicit in the material culture of everyday life and often referred to as vernacular architecture, stands in stark contrast to the rational awareness of it as a value to apply in strategies of architectural and urban design, the chief meme underlying the "city as a project" taken up by Enlightenment architects. Using the rhetorical device of analogy, this approach aims at substituting the reality of the historical process with a fictional world in which rationality artificially reproduces and represents the quality and character of the former. In this respect, Rossi's *città analoga* was intended as a political project in opposition to the Muratorian manifesto *città come organismo*.

In summary, the Muratorian School's typological approach identifies an interest in unplanned transformative processes opposed to the so-called "primary elements" (*elementi primari*) used by Aldo Rossi, whose main significance is to privilege the rational, designed, and stable character of architecture

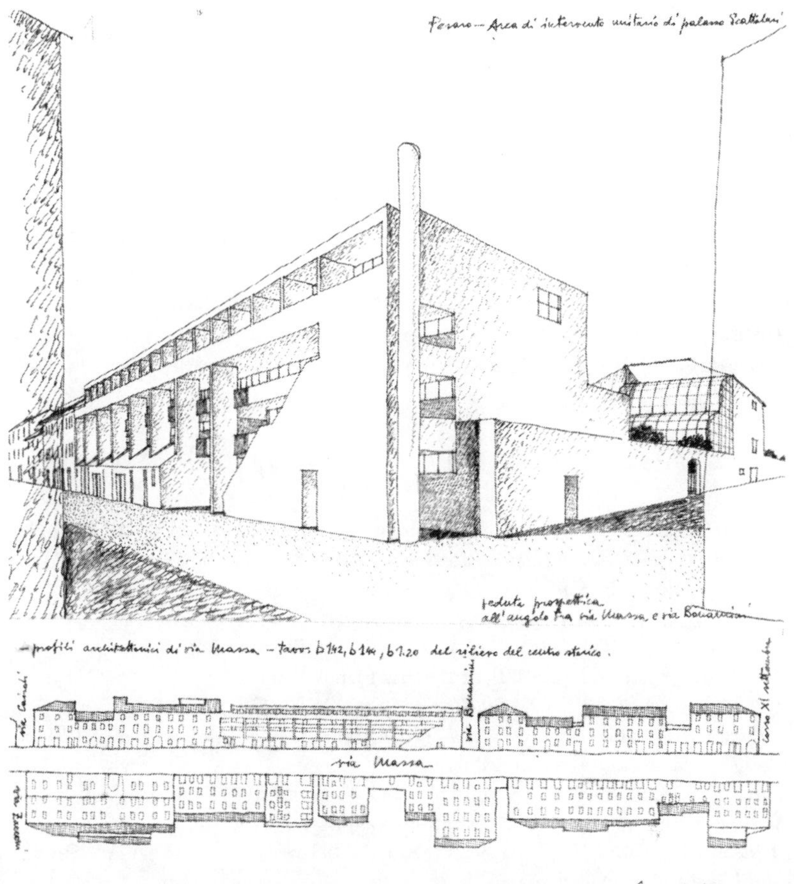

FIGURE 12.3 Casa-Parcheggio (temporary accommodation for residents displaced by historic renovation), via Domenico Mazza 30–48, Pesaro, Italy (designed by Carlo Aymonino, 1978–81)

The quality of historic urban centers is a function of architectural diversity set within the context of a broadly coherent building fabric. While the former results from unpredictable shifts in cultural habits, the latter reflects more stable community values. Within the same morphological period one can observe how individual buildings preserve their own uniqueness, while at the same time sharing the characteristics of a common building type. When asked to replace buildings cleared from a corner portion of a city block, Aymonino studied the historic plot pattern and its relation to street alignment. In this relationship he saw the key to guaranteeing a new combination of unity and diversity. Consequently, he rejected the notion of introducing an alien architectural object, preferring instead a structure with traditional features that could nevertheless invite the unexpected. He adopted the portico to establish a modular rhythm of bearing walls, with shops on the ground floor and a roofline respecting the consensus of the street. This rhythm served to memorialize the age-old relationship between stable plots and changeable built infill. The result is a fine example of modern Architectural Structuralism applied to the historical city.

and which seems so independent of individual, historical uses (Fig. 12.2). To put it another way, craftsmanship describes an artisanal mastery implicit in the way work develops, as a strict behavior shared by individual members of the guild, on behalf of a local community, performing a comparable experience. It is a way of doing that defines itself through its progressions, and this is fundamental to understanding the Muratorian School's concern with the pre-Modern period. In the contrary architectural worldview, discipline frames a set of transmissible rules whose validity is independent of individual work, emphasizing the intellectual and rational competence of the designer compared to the habitual builder, thus substituting real conditions with their intentional representation crucial in the Aymonino and Rossi legacy (Fig. 12.3).

In conclusion, one can assume that, from a phenomenological point of view, agents of change are fleetingly and implicitly recorded in the urban and architectural morphogenetic process, which itself becomes in a generalized way the living witness of their individual, active presence in claiming a role in society. Of course, from a materialist point of view, agents of transformation come into existence by inscribing their general values on a permanent basis in the public scene. How these significations in the urban landscape should be interpreted, especially since the dawn of the Early Modern period, has strongly affected the theoretical debates on urban morphology and building typology—in Italy and beyond—ever since.

References

Aymonino, C. (1966) La formazione di un moderno concetto di tipologia edilizia, in G. Fabbri (ed.), *Rapporti tra la Morfologia Urbana e la Tipologia Edilizia: documenti del corso di caratteri distributivi degli edificei, anno accademico 1965–1966*, 12–51. Venice: Libreria Cluva.

Aymonino, C. (1967) *Lo Studio dei Fenomeni Urbani*. Bari: Libreria Fratelli Laterza.

Aymonino, C. (1971) *Origini e Sviluppo della Città Moderna*. Padua: Marsilio Editori.

Aymonino, C. (1974) *Il Significato della Città*. Bari: Libreria Fratelli Laterza.

Aymonino, C. (1975) *Le Capitali del XIX Secolo: Parigi e Vienna*. Rome: Officina.

Aymonino, C., Aldegheri, C., and Sabini, M. (eds.) (1984) *Per un'Idea di Città: La Ricerca del Gruppo Architettura a Venezia (1968–1974)*. Venice: Libreria Cluva.

Aymonino, C., Giordani, P., and Campos Venuti, G. (1967) *I Centri Direzionali: La Teoria e la Pratica, gli Esempi Italiani e Stranieri, il Sistema Direzionale della Città di Bologna*. Bari: De Donato Editore.

Aymonino, C., Brusatin, M., Fabbri, G., Lena, M., Lovero, P., Lucianetti, S., and Rossi, A. (1970) *La Città di Padova: Saggio di Analisi Urbana*. Rome: Officina.

Balzani, M., and Marzot, N. (2010) *Architetture per un Territorio Sostenibile: Città e Paesaggio tra Innovazione Tecnologica e Tradizione*. Milan: Skira Editore.

Bascià, L., Carlotti, P., Maffei, G. L., and Capolino, P. (2000) *La Casa Romana nella Storia della Città dalle Origini all'Ottocento*. Florence: Alinea Editrice.

Bollati, R. (1976) *Metodo di Lettura delle Strutture Urbane, Attraverso le Fasi Evolutive, Applicato ai Centri Calabresi di Gerace, Cosenza, Reggio Calabria: Ipotesi di Lavoro*. Reggio Calabria: Istituto Universitario Statale di Architettura.

Bollati, R. (1980) *Metodo di Lettura delle Strutture Urbane, Attraverso le Fasi Evolutive*. Reggio Calabria: Istituto Universitario Statale di Architettura.

Bollati, S. (1976) *Tesi Storiche Relative alla Formazione ed allo Sviluppo di un Aggregato Antico Attraverso la Lettura delle sue Strutture allo Stato Attuale*. Reggio Calabria: Istituto Universitario Statale di Architettura.

Bollati, S. (1980) *Formazione e Sviluppo di un Aggregato Antico*. Reggio Calabria: Istituto Universitario Statale di Architettura.

Canella, G. (1965) Relazioni tra morfologia, tipologia dell'organismo architettonico e ambiente fisico, in E. N. Rogers et al., *L'Utopia della Realtà: un Esperimento Didattico sulla Tipologia della Scuola Primaria*, 66–81. Bari: Leonardo da Vinci Editrice.

Caniggia, G. (1963) *Lettura di una Città: Como*. Rome: Centro Studi di Storia Urbanistica.

Caniggia, G. (1981) *Strutture dello Spazio Antropico: Studi e Note*. Florence: Alinea Editrice.

Caniggia, G., and Maffei, G. L. (1978) *Lettura dell'Edilizia di Base*. Padua: Marsilio Editori.

Caniggia, G., and Maffei, G. L. (1984) *Il Progetto dell'Edilizia di Base*. Padua: Marsilio Editori.

Cataldi, G. (1975) *Il Territorio della Piana di Gioia Tauro*. Florence: Teorema, Studi e Documenti di Architettura 4.

Cataldi, G. (1977) *Per una Scienza del Territorio: Studi e Note*. Florence: Uniedit.

Fasolo, V., and Milani, G. B. (1931–40) *Le Forme Architettoniche*. Milan: F. Vallardi Editore.

Giannini, A. (1964) *Corso di lezioni sul territorio*. Rome: Istituto di Metodologia Architettonica.

Giannini, A. (1976) *L'Organismo Territoriale: Corso di Pianificazione Territoriale Urbanistica*. Genoa: Istituto di Progettazione Architettonica.

Giannini, A. (1980) *L'Individuo Territoriale: Corso di Pianificazione Territoriale Urbanistica*. Genoa: Istituto di Progettazione Architettonica.

Giovannoni, G. (1931) *Vecchie Città ed Edilizia Nuova*. Torino: *Unione Tipografico-Editrice Torinese (UTET)*.

Grassi, G. (1967) *La Costruzione Logica dell'Architettura*. Padua: Marsilio Editori.

Grassi, G. (1979) *L'Architettura come Mestiere e Altri Scritti*. Milan: Franco Angeli.

Maffei, G. L. (1981) *La Progettazione Edilizia a Firenze*. Venice: Marsilio Editori.

Maffei, G. L. (1990) *La Casa Fiorentina nella Storia della Città*. Venice: Marsilio Editori.

Maffei, G. L., and Maffei, M. (2011) *Lettura dell'Edilizia Speciale*. Florence: Alinea Editrice.

Maretto, M. (2008) *Il Paesaggio delle Differenze: Architettura, Città e Territorio nella Nuova Era Globale*. Pisa: Edizioni ETS.

Maretto, P. (1960) L'edilizia gotica veneziana. *Palladio*, 3–4: 123–201.

Maretto, P. (1980) *Realtà Naturale e Realtà Costruita*. Florence: Uniedit.

Maretto, P. (1986) *La Casa Veneziana nella Storia della Città: dalle Origini all'Ottocento*. Venice: Marsilio Editori.

Monestiroli, A. (1979) *L'Architettura della Realtà*. Milan: Libreria Clup.

Monestiroli, A. (1997) *Temi Urbani: Cinque Progetti per la Città*. Milan: Editizioni Unicopli.

Muratori, S. (1959–60) *Studi per una Operante Storia Urbana di Venezia*. Rome: Istituto Poligrafico dello Stato.

Muratori, S. (1963) *Studi per una Operante Storia Urbana di Roma*. Rome: Consiglio Nazionale delle Ricerche.

Pagano, G., and Daniel, G. (1936) *Architettura Rurale Italiana*. Milan: Ulrico Hoepli Editore.

Petruccioli, A. (1994) *Il Giardino Islamico: Architettura, Natura, Paesaggio*. Milan: Mondadori Electa.

Rossi, A. (1964a) Aspetti della tipologia residenziale a Berlino. *Casabella–Continuità*, 288: 11–20.

Rossi, A. (1964b) Considerazioni sulla morfologia urbana e la tipologia edilizia, in C. Aymonino et al., *Aspetti e Problemi della Tipologia Edilizia*, 15–31. Venice: Libreria Cluva.

Rossi, A. (1964c) I problemi tipologici e la residenza, in C. Aymonino et al., *Aspetti e Problemi della Tipologia Edilizia*, 15–31.Venice: Libreria Cluva.

Rossi, A. (1966a) Tipologia, manualistica e architettura, in G. Fabri (ed.), *Rapporti tra Morfologia Urbana e Tipologia Edilizia: Documenti del Corso di Caratteri Distributivi degli Edificei, anno accademico 1965–1966*, 13–52. Venice: Libreria Cluva.

Rossi, A. (1966b) *L'Architettura della Città*. Padua: Marsilio Editori.

Rossi, A. (1969) L'architettura della ragione come architettura di tendenza, in R. Bonicalzi (ed.), *Aldo Rossi: Scritti Scelti sull'Architettura e la Città, 1956–1972*, 370–9. Milan: Città Studi Edizioni.

Rossi, A. (1975) Introduzione all'edizione portoghese de "L'architettura della città," in R. Bonicalzi (ed.), *Aldo Rossi: Scritti Scelti sull'Architettura e la Città, 1956–1972*, 443–53. Milan: Città Studi Edizioni.

Strappa, G. (1995) *Unità dell'Organismo Architettonico*. Bari: Edizioni Dedalo.

Strappa, G., Ieva, M., and Dimatteo, M. A. (2003) *La Città come Organismo: Lettura di Trani alle Diverse Scale*. Bari: Mario Adda Editore.

Vaccaro, P. (1968) *Tessuto e Tipo Edilizio a Roma: dalla fine del XIV sec. alla fine del XVIII sec.* Rome: Centro Studi di Storia Urbanistica.

Vaccaro, P. (1980) *Cortona: il Piano del Centro Storico e la Sua Gestione*. Cortona: Comune di Cortona.

Vaccaro, P., Gialluca, B., and Lavagnino, E. (1987) *Cortona Struttura e Storia: Materiali per una Conoscenza Operante della Città e del Territorio*. Cortona: Editrice Grafica l'Etruria.

Zaffagnini, M., Gaiani, A., and Marzot, N. (1995) *Morfologia Urbana e Tipologia Edilizia*. Bologna: Pitagora Editrice.

13

A NEW VISION

The Role of Municipal Authorities and Planners in Replanning Britain after the Second World War

Peter J. Larkham

During and immediately after the Second World War, about 200 "advisory" or "outline" reconstruction plans were formulated for a wide variety of British towns and cities. Some cities had been badly bomb-damaged, others were little damaged or even undamaged. Some plans were written by the most eminent consultants, others by the professional officers or elected councilors of individual local authorities, and a few by local organizations and residents. This chapter uses some of the plans produced, particularly for the Midlands, to review how the future town was being conceived and re-shaped and the processes and actors engaged in this massive urban restructuring; it focuses, however, on the preparation, not on the implementation, of plans.[1]

In terms of British planning, the period 1947–50 was a crucial one in the development of concepts and processes. Reconstruction spurred central government action, even—briefly—through the agency of a dedicated ministry, the Ministry of Town and Country Planning (Cullingworth 1975). The Town and Country Planning Act of 1947 specified the content of development plans, changing the character of published plans considerably by the early 1950s. Many of the plans were "technocentric" (Diefendorf 1989), using major infrastructure investments to overcome problems, particularly of traffic volume and flow, and using the "neighborhood unit" concept to resolve issues of overcrowded and poor-quality housing.

There are several significant issues relating to morphological agency embedded in these plans and their processes of production and consumption. First, who developed the plans? In the case of outside consultants, how much did they know of the character of the places they were replanning? There can be little doubt that the activities of plan making and implementation in this crucial but short period have had long-lasting implications for British towns and cities ever since the war. Similarly, there is no doubt that Jeremy Whitehand's approach to exploring the role of agency in the urban landscape is as applicable here as to the original context he investigated—one of board-room decision-makers remote from, and unfamiliar with, the places affected by their decisions (Whitehand 1984: 4). Although Joe Nasr (2003) has begun to consider such issues, particularly center–local tensions, in the context of French postwar reconstruction, they remain under-explored elsewhere.

Yet researching the personalities behind decision making is problematic. Little biographical work exists on British planners of the time, in contrast to contemporary architects. Gordon

Cherry attempted to raise the profile of individual town planners, editing a volume of biographical contributions (Cherry 1981) and producing a biography of Lord Holford, joint-author of the reconstruction plan for the City of London (Cherry and Penny 1986). Even the most prominent and prolific plan-authors of the period, Thomas Sharp and Professor Sir Patrick Abercrombie, have until recently received little more consideration than chapters in Cherry's book and entries in the *Dictionary of National Biography*.[2] The municipal employees who compiled many plans and coordinated the actual postwar rebuilding have gone largely unrecorded; although Dagenais et al. (2003) have urged further examination of the roles of urban service providers and agents in urban transformation, and of the "municipal experience," and Flinn (2012, 2013) explores more of the political and economic (i.e. largely bureaucratic) realities of the postwar reconstruction in Britain. Initial exploration of center-local tensions, especially via the views of Ministry personnel, have recently been explored by Larkham (2011) and Hasegawa (2013), although their archived words are now bereft of context. This is a fruitful subject for deeper investigation.

The Production of Plans

As "reconstruction plans" were produced for so many towns, including those that were little damaged or even unscathed, it is clear that plan production was seen as a municipal or professional imperative. Early during the war, bomb-damaged towns such as Plymouth were forcefully exhorted by the planning minister, Lord Reith, to "plan boldly and comprehensively" (quoted in the authors' note, Watson and Abercrombie 1943: vii), a message he also seems to have conveyed to officials in Coventry, London, and Manchester.[3] Obviously, the war damage had to be repaired. Even in the worst-hit towns and cities, however, the nature and extent of the replanning far exceeded the damage itself. Opportunities were being seized to address many perceived shortcomings of urban structure and function, including transport and other infrastructure, functional zoning, slum clearance, and urban design. It is also relevant to consider the extent to which these plans were a form of place-promotion, as towns sought to re-position themselves in the changing postwar urban hierarchy (Larkham and Lilley 2003). On the other hand, it should be noted that some places did not formulate "plans" in the same way, with Birmingham being chief among these, given both the amount of bomb damage and the scale of its postwar rebuilding. There, its well-connected city engineer and surveyor, Herbert Manzoni, felt that the prior existence of a range of redevelopment plans, his own involvement in shaping planning legislation, and his conviction that master plans were "often obsolete by the time they were put into effect" positioned the city to begin immediate reconstruction (Sutcliffe and Smith 1974: 448; Larkham 2007a).

Given these very different functions of plans, it is hardly surprising that a wide range of approaches were taken to the production of plans. These include the employment of consultants, the use of in-house municipal staff, the formation of specific committees of elected representatives, the involvement of the local press, and the contribution of third parties, whether local organizations or private individuals (Fig. 13.1).[4] It has been a surprising finding, given the focus of traditional planning histories, that the authorship of known plans is weighted more toward local authority officers than consultants; plans by other types of author—ranging from private individuals to local societies—do exist, but are rare (Table 13.1). In most cases, the final "plan" was a composite, showing influences induced by the nature of the commission, the professional approach or personal idiosyncrasies of the author(s), and even the interpretations of illustrators, photographers, and model makers. Most published commentaries have focused on the individual named author and particularly on the "great plans" of the "great planners."

FIGURE 13.1 Some plan authors—mostly male, mostly established professionals. Clockwise from top left: Max Lock, Donald Gibson, Herbert Manzoni, Patrick Abercrombie

TABLE 13.1 Plan numbers and types of author

Type of author	*Number of plans*	*Percentage*
Consultant	98	37
Local authority	120	45
Unofficial	48	18
Total:	266	100

This chapter seeks to explore the processes of plan making in greater detail. It builds on the plans and experiences of many towns. However, in a significant number of cases, the records of local authorities and their departments have not been preserved. The formal "minutes of councils" and their constituent committees are almost invariably available, but legally these need only be a record of decisions (Arnold-Baker 2002): some are very terse, whereas others contain considerable details of discussions leading to decisions. Therefore, although the clear facts of dates and commissions can usually be found, the minutiae of the plan-making process often remain opaque. It is extremely rare that personal papers of the plan authors survive.[5] This examination is based on documentary evidence from numerous local record offices and a broad range of contemporary publications.

The Selection of Consultant Authors

At the time, it should be remembered that the profession of town planning was young. There were relatively few professionally qualified town planners; much planning was undertaken by architects or architect-planners.

> This raises the important question of the number of experienced town planners available for the work which will be so vital to our well-being after the war. There are not many of them, for although the professor himself [Abercrombie] must have had quite a number of able students under his tuition and guidance, few of them can have had much practical experience. Our best men are likely to be overworked.
>
> (*Architect and Building News* 1941: 140)

This is borne out by the credited authorship of plans. A very small number of consultants were very active. Although most, such as Abercrombie and Davidge, were well-established professionals, several having served as president of various professional organizations, others were relatively junior and made their name through their plans, such as Sharp and Lock. A recent consideration of the Plymouth plan (Essex and Brayshay 2007) uses "actor network theory" to identify the consultant author, Abercrombie, as a "nodal figure" in the networks; this is hardly surprising, although Abercrombie is perhaps an atypical figure, but this analysis is also useful in articulating the separate roles of others: Lord Astor had a local role as Lord Mayor, as the "nodal actor" in persuading Abercrombie to take on the commission, but again is atypical in his national role and connections. The minister, Reith, had a role in "problematization" with his "plan boldly" advice. The Ministry officials and their responses to the plan also played a specific role.

This concentration of planning activity is demonstrated in Table 13.2, although it disregards consultants who worked on only one plan. It reveals some surprising names, including the great Edwardian architect, Sir Edwin Lutyens who, with Abercrombie, took the commission for Hull in the final years of his life, when he was dying of lung cancer; Geoffrey Jellicoe, more famous as a landscape architect; and Clough Williams-Ellis, historian of the Royal Tank Regiment and owner-architect of Portmeirion. It also demonstrates some enduring professional partnerships, including Minoprio and Spencely, who were together at Harrow, Oxford, and Liverpool and went into partnership in 1928 (Reilly 1938: 235); Richard Nickson, in architectural practice in the Wirral, who went into partnership with Abercrombie in mid-1945 with offices in London; and Robert Hening and Anthony Chitty. Hening was educated as an architect but, as noted in an obituary, "did not bother with exams," going instead into partnership with Chitty, formerly with Tecton, in 1937; "their qualities were complementary, Chitty urbane and Hening brusque, neither being designers of star quality" (Powers 1997).

Nevertheless, despite the shortage of planners, this was the "golden age" of British planning (Mandler 1999): a period when, despite the immaturity of planning as a profession, there was a "belief in planning as an overall principle for ordering human affairs" (Ward 1994: 114). As with other professionals, planners were seen as the informed experts and were largely left to get on with the job (Hall 2002: 357). Moreover, there was apparently a view of "the planner as omniscient ruler, who should create new settlement forms, and perhaps also destroy the old, without interference or question" (Hall and Tewdwr-Jones 2010: 53). Though the new profession and new mechanisms, including a new ministry, were fast developing, there was also a broad general consensus in favor of the activity of planning. Turning to an "expert" seemed natural for towns as diverse as London, Macclesfield, Brierley Hill, and Accrington.

TABLE 13.2 Numbers of known plans by named consultant authors[a]

Consultant (with qualifications etc[b])	*Number of plans*
Sharp, Thomas CBE MA DLitt MTPI FRIBA PPILA; TPI President 1945–6	12
Abercrombie, Sir Patrick MA DLitt FRIBA FILA; TPI President 1925–6	10[c] (3 with Nickson)
Davidge, William R. MTPI AMInstCE FRIBA FSI; TPI President 1926–7	7
Chapman, W. Dobson MA MTPI LRIBA FILA; TPI President 1943–4	6
Lloyd, T. Alwyn OBE Hon LLD FRIBA FILA FSA; TPI President 1933–4	6 (3 with Jackson)
Chitty, Anthony M. MA FRIBA AMTPI	5 (3 with Hening)
Holden, Charles LittD FRIBA MTPI	5 (2 with Enderby, 2 with Holford)
Lock, Max ARIBA MTPI	4
Adshead, Stanley D. MA MArch FRIBA; TPI President 1918–19	4 (2 with Needham)
Jellicoe, [later Sir] Geoffrey CBE RA PPILA FRIBA MTPI	4
Edwards, A. Trystan FRIBA	3
Jackson, Herbert	3 (all with Lloyd)
Needham, Charles William Cashmore FRIBA	3 (2 with Adshead)
Nickson, Richard MA FRIBA (Abercrombie's business partner from 1945)	3 (with Abercrombie)
Thompson, F. Longstreth BSc FSI AssocMInstCE PPTPI	3 (but seems not to have written reports)
Williams-Ellis, [later Sir] Clough MC CBE FRIBA MTPI PPILA Hon LLD	3
Gibberd, Frederick ARIBA AMTPI	2
Hening, Robert MBE	2 (with Chitty)
Holford, [later Lord] William BArch MA DCL Hon LLD ARA PPRIBA PPILA; TPI President 1953–4	2 (with Holden)
James, Charles Holloway RA FRIBA	2 (with Pierce)
Lutyens, Sir Edwin OM KCIE PRA FRIBA Hon LLD etc	2 (includes initiating Royal Academy 1942 report)
Minoprio, Anthony BArch MA FRIBA AMTPI	2 (with Spencely)
Pierce, S. Rowland FRIBA	2 (with James) + LRRC membership
Spencely, H.G.C. BArch FRIBA AMTPI	2 (with Minoprio)

Notes:

a. This list omits named authors known to have been officers of local authorities (therefore generally involved only in plans for their area), and named authors of unknown status. It also covers only urban, not regional, plans.

b. The qualifications etc listed may have been gained after this period of reconstruction.

c. Abercrombie's total includes the *County of London* and *Greater London* plans but omits an unconfirmed reference to a Ministry commission for Birmingham, which may refer to his *West Midlands Plan*.

Given the shortage of trained planners, there was a fierce professional demarcation dispute about reconstruction. Which profession was most appropriate to undertake or oversee the job? The architect, campaigner, and polemic-writer Clough Williams-Ellis was so forthright in his assertion that architects could, should, and must plan that the anonymous editor of his contribution to the "Rebuilding Britain" series felt it necessary to add a disclaimer in the Foreword (Williams-Ellis 1941). Despite such declarations, however, he failed to complete his commission to replan Bewdley in 1944–5 (Larkham and Pendlebury 2008: 298–301). The architect S. Rowland Pierce, later to co-author reconstruction plans for Norwich and Leamington Spa, wrote that "For planning in general and for 'Town Planning' and building-planning in particular the fully competent architect is undoubtedly the person for the job, uniting as he does (or should) the qualities of Artist, Scientist and Administrator." And yet Pierce produced a scathing attack on town planning and town planners. Town planning was a "now doubtful term," though there are "many good and qualified Planners outside the ranks of so-called Town Planners." Of the new town planners, "their usefulness is rather as specialists, to be consulted by executant Planners" (Pierce 1941: 79). In contrast, only a fortnight later, the same journal proclaimed that "The town planner requires the supreme gift of creative imagination, which is rarely an attribute of those preoccupied with the architectural side of layouts and buildings" (*Architect and Building News* 1941: 43). Moreover, in 1942 the Institute of Municipal and County Engineers was writing to local authorities, seeking support for its position that it was

> not in agreement with the policy of the Ministry of Works and Planning to control planning through the Ministry"s regional representatives and are [*sic*] of the opinion that qualified Engineers and Surveyors of Local Authorities are fully competent to continue and complete the preparation of planning schemes.
>
> (quoted in the Minutes of Dover's Post War Development Sub-Committee, 23 November 1942: East Kent Archives Center)

Although a number of individual authorities agreed with the Institute and some wrote to the Ministry or even direct to the prime minister,[6] prompting the Ministry's staff to comment acerbically on the abilities of surveyors and engineers to plan properly (Hill to Vincent, 14/6/41: National Archives, hereafter NA, HLG 71/760), three such authorities whose relevant records have been examined (Bromsgrove, Canterbury, and Dover) later employed consultants.

Irrespective of which profession supplied the consultants, it is certain that their employment was not cheap, particularly given the financial stringency of wartime and the immediate postwar period. Table 13.3 compares the advertised fees for a range of consultants and towns (or, in the case of the Clyde Valley, a government-sponsored regional plan). These, taken from news items in professional journals, are only the consultant's fee and usually take no account of expenses or the usual requirement to publish the final report. In the case of Abercrombie's plan for Warwick, the original fee of £530 (in mid-1945) rose to a final invoice of £3,200 (by early 1947), although this included approved additional work and the employment of a professional photographer and perspectivist. In the case of the most prolific plan author, Thomas Sharp, we are able to compare the fees he charged for most of his reconstruction plan commissions to a broad range of sizes and types of town, throughout the main period of plan production (Table 13.4). Warwick was also faced with a further £3,000 to publish the final report (Abercrombie and Nickson 1949), amid some adverse press coverage over escalating costs. One councilor even felt that it was all an awful waste of money ... Ever since they went in for the scheme the costs had increased and he protested against further expenditure ... What do we want 4,000 copies for? Heaven only knows—except for Sir Patrick to send out to his friends to advertise himself at our expense ... I am not decrying the work done. It has been wonderfully done and carefully done, but it will not be very important in 60 years' time ... I think we have had enough of Sir Patrick.

(*Warwick and Warwickshire Advertiser* 1947; see Larkham 2004)

TABLE 13.3 Comparison of fees charged by a range of consultants

Location	*Consultant*	*Date of contract*	*Fee (£)*
Plymouth	Abercrombie	1941	840
City of Westminster	Davidge	1943	1,575
Clyde Valley	Abercrombie	1943 (2-year contract)	5,000
Middlesbrough	Lock	1943	940
Norwich	James/Pierce	1943 (2-year contract)	2,000
Birkenhead	Reilly/Aslan	1944	1,050
Worcester	Minoprio/Spencely	1944	670
Warwick	Abercrombie/Nickson	1945	520; final bill: 3,200
Worthing	Cowles-Voysey	1946	2,625
South Bank area, London	Holden	1947	6,000
Bedford	Lock	1950	1,000*

Notes: Fees exclude travel and other expenses, and publication costs.

* The total fee agreed by Bedford Council was £5,000; of this, Lock's own fee was £1,000.

Source: news items in contemporary professional journals, principally *Architect and Building News* and *The Builder.*

TABLE 13.4 Fees charged by Thomas Sharp for reconstruction plans

Location	*Date (of final report or, where asterisked, of contract)*	*Fee (£)*
Exeter	1944*	1050
Todmorden	1945	525
Oxford	1948	2625
Taunton	1948	787
King's Lynn	1948	1102
Minehead	1948*	1050
Salisbury	1949	1050
Chichester	1949	1312
Stockport	1949*	2625

Source: file of contracts, in Sharp archives, University of Newcastle upon Tyne; news items in contemporary professional journals, principally *Architect and Building News* and *The Builder.*

Costs were such that not all plans reached print (or wide circulation at least). Faced with a potential bill of several thousand pounds for printing Max Lock's Hull Civic Survey and having had personal disagreements with Lock over his headship of the Hull School of Architecture, the City Council chose not to publish the report (correspondence and newspaper cutting file, Hull City Archives).[7] The Dover report, to which Abercrombie and Nickson contributed, was finally made available as seventeen foolscap pages with two-color maps, at the high price of four guineas (Minutes, Dover Planning Committee, 17 April 1947, East Kent Archives Centre). The cost of printing 2,000 copies of the Birkenhead report would be about £2,300; an equivalent of a 1d or 2d rate (local property tax) (*Liverpool Daily Post* 1945).

Some of the established local authority officers, especially engineers and surveyors, made strenuous efforts to resist "outsiders." A 1944 Ministry memo on the replanning of the Tyneside area noted that "it is evident that Parr [of Newcastle] and Lewis of Sunderland, and probably Minders of Darlington as well, are determined to prevent an outside planner from trespassing on what they consider is their own domain" (NA HLG 71/1205).

In a few cases it is clear that consultants—planners or architects—were selected because of their prior connection with a place and thus, inevitably, their development of good working relationships with either the local politicians or senior municipal officers (perhaps both). Abercrombie was approached by the Bath and District Joint Planning Committee to prepare a plan for Bath, damaged in one of the 1942 "Baedeker raids." He had been employed as a consultant by the Bristol and Bath Regional Planning Committee since about 1928 and as consultant town planning officer by the Bath and District Joint Planning Committee since March 1935 and so was well known to at least one of his co-authors, H. A. Mealand (Lambert 2000). The three became "something like a secret society who had been working since July 1943 on a plan for the future of Bath" (Mealand, quoted by Lambert 2000: 182). Likewise the architects C. H. James and S. Rowland Pierce were engaged to produce a plan for Norwich, which had also suffered a Baedeker raid. They had designed its City Hall (in 1930; built 1938) and were commissioned to extend it in January 1945. Some were simply "on the spot": W. Dobson Chapman's practice was based in Macclesfield and, in the inevitable downturn of work in wartime but at a point when he was elected as the youngest president of the Town Planning Institute, he acted as Honorary Consultant to produce the short but graphically striking Macclesfield plan, which was "the result of two years' work at odd hours" (Chapman 1944).

In some cases where no direct personal relationship existed, local authorities seem to have worked on a word-of-mouth basis. There is one very striking example of this in the West Midlands (although, sadly, detailed records are virtually nonexistent). The Cardiff-based architect-planner T. Alwyn Lloyd, a senior professional who had been president of the Town Planning Institute in 1933–4, produced several reconstruction plans in a very sharply defined geographical cluster during a very short period. These included Brierley Hill (1943), Bromsgrove (1943), Bilston (1944), Dudley (1944), and Stourbridge (1945), some in conjunction with the Birmingham-based Herbert Jackson. This cluster seems to originate in his being invited to report "as to the practicability of engaging upon a comprehensive planning scheme" for an area of Bilston in early 1943, two-and-a-half months before the press report of his Bromsgrove commission. By October 1943, he had been invited to design two major housing estates in Bilston and, by June 1944, to prepare a Borough-wide plan in which his estates were integrated (Minutes, Bilston Development and Reconstruction Committee: in Wolverhampton Archives & Local Studies collection). However, his Bilston plans were not implemented. The then town clerk noted,

> I wrote to Lloyd yesterday and did my best to make our change of heart appear not too unkindly. I like Lloyd. This business of planning however is quite ruthless and I never felt that his vision of Stowlawn was my idea of an organic community.
>
> (A. V. Williams to C. Reilly, in Reilly's archive at the University of Liverpool; Larkham 2006)

In yet other cases, local authorities sought advice directly from the professional bodies: the Town Planning Institute or Royal Institute of British Architects. Although their letters were almost invariably addressed to the presidents of these institutions, the responses came from various officers. A pre-war comment by Charles Reilly about Edward Carter, then RIBA librarian and editor of the *RIBA Journal*, sheds an interesting light on the influence of these officers:

> I feel Carter is already a power behind the scenes who will do much to steer the Institute, largely without its realizing it, into the key position it must now take up. He knows all the young men and sympathizes with their work, and better still, helps them to get positions and influence.
>
> (Reilly 1938: 310)

In un-bombed Warwick, the Borough Surveyor was "instructed to approach the Town Planning Institute to enquire whether it is possible to engage a Town Planning Expert for the Borough" (Minutes, Housing Inspection Sub-Committee, Warwick County Record Office, 12 January 1945). A list of names was reported on March 9 (unfortunately this has not survived). Abercrombie appears to have been the first choice, for he had visited the borough with an assistant before early June, when he wrote stating that he would be "willing to accept the position of Town Planning Consultant at the usual fees, namely about £500" (Minutes, Public Health and Housing Committee, 8 June 1945).

Worcester—also un-bombed—took a more roundabout route. The city council formed a Reconstruction and Development Committee on February 2, 1943 (Minutes, Warwick County Record Office). On June 11, under pressure from the Dean of Worcester, the Committee agreed that "it might be advisable to call in someone ... to advise at what stage it would be most profitable to call in a planning expert," and the borough surveyor approached H. C. Bradshaw, secretary of the Royal Fine Art Commission. Bradshaw reported at some length on August 27, concluding that

> The Royal Fine Arts Commission would not recommend any names for appointment as consultant; application should be made to the Presidents of the Town Planning Institute and the Royal Institute of British Architects, who would be willing to submit the names of qualified members of those bodies.

At the same time, the Committee was also discussing commissioning city-wide economic, social, and industrial surveys. Yet it was not until June 27, 1944, that "tentative consideration was given to the question of the appointment of a town planning consultant, and the chairman was requested to make enquiries in that direction." By September 22, "The Chairman reported that through the kindness of Lady Atkins he had been put in touch with Sir Montague Barlow who had acquaintance with many Town Planners." Barlow had consulted Abercrombie, who had recommended five names; the Worcestershire branch of the Campaign for the Preservation of Rural England had suggested a further two. Of the seven, two were ill and unable to undertake the work; a further two had been interviewed. C. H. James, then working on the Norwich plan, was not appointed. Anthony Minoprio and High Spencely, who had quoted a lower fee and were recommended by Abercrombie (both former students of his), were appointed. Minoprio was then working on the plan for Chelmsford, an independent plan commissioned by the Chelmsford Area Planning Group: Abercrombie wrote its Foreword and opened the public exhibition.

There remain some traces of unsolicited approaches, usually by younger or less-successful consultants. For example, I. Massey, LRIBA, describing himself as a chartered architect and quantity surveyor, wrote to Coventry shortly after its major raid: "It may be that I could render you some assistance at some date in re-designing your City and Buildings" (Coventry Record Office CCD/CE/7/1). No such approach is known to have been successful.

However appointed, the working relationships between consultants, local officers, and politicians were not always easy. Evidently there were problems between Sharp and officials in Exeter for, discussing forthcoming work at Oxford, H. C. de Cronin of the Architectural Press wrote to Sharp, "Ought we not to start taking photographs this summer, to avoid the Exeter trouble? ... what sons of bitches that Exeter council is composed of—don't let them get you down" (25 May 1945, letter in Sharp archive, University of Newcastle upon Tyne). Sharp was an idiosyncratic character: a loner who never hesitated to speak (or write) his mind (Stansfield 1981; Cherry 1983). Some consultants had low opinions of local officers, typified by Charles Reilly's conflict with Bertie Robinson, borough engineer and surveyor of Birkenhead. Reilly did not mince words on the ineptness of his "typical" housing designs (cf. Potter 2003) although he seems to have made an exception for Manzoni (Reilly 1944: 182). Max Lock had similar problems with the borough engineer at Middlesbrough, despite the Housing Subcommittee's instructions that they should collaborate; he wrote to the borough engineer that "I was very disappointed to hear from you ... that you could not consider discussing any amendments to either of the schemes in such a way that we can present a combined scheme to the Housing Committee" (Max Lock Archive 17.4, University of Westminster).

On the other hand, a successful and unusual arrangement was developed at the end of the reconstruction planning period for W. G. Holford and H. Myles Wright (later Professor Lord, and Professor, respectively) acting for Cambridge.

> A consultant of the first order [Holford] was appointed for Cambridge Borough under what I believe is a unique arrangement, namely, that he used the staff of the county planning department, and was represented locally by a partner [Myles Wright] who during the preparation of the report gave his whole time to the work and worked inside the department, not in an office fifty miles away. It is believed that in this way continuity will be preserved and the consultants' proposals will not become just another seven days' local planning wonder.
>
> (Orbell 1950: 323)

The contrast with other working practices, to be discussed below, is noteworthy. Another advantage of engaging a consultant is also explained: the relevant planning officer (the county planning officer, at this point) was not the plan author and could, therefore, act independently, especially if amendments were deemed necessary; however, the experience of those who worked on the plan preparation was retained within the department.

In the cases of the consultants, their authorship is plainly and prominently credited on covers and title pages. Indeed, as the town clerk of Hartlepool wrote to Max Lock, "I think I am right in saying that the plan became known to the public as 'The Max Lock Plan'" (18 March 1952; Max

Lock Archive, University of Westminster). Yet they rarely carried out all of the work alone. In the case of the Bath plan, "while Abercrombie laid down the framework ... it is likely that most of the detailed work was done by Mealand and Owens, with a team of about forty employees at the City Council and other consultants" (Lambert 2000: 182). Speaking of the *County of London Plan*, Arthur Ling referred to Abercrombie—by whose name the report is commonly known—as coming in periodically (Gold 1997: 180). Perhaps Thomas Sharp comes closest in this respect, as his was virtually a one-man practice: he even drew many of his own maps and illustrations. Nevertheless, he also used other model makers, photographers, and perspectivists, including A. C. Webb, who was in great demand by architects as prominent as Sir Giles Gilbert Scott. Much of the impact of, and positive critical and professional response to, Sharp's plans (including Durham, 1944; Exeter, 1946, and Oxford, 1948) came from their publication by the Architectural Press and the strong relationship he developed with Raymond Philp, who minutely scrutinized the publication process. Even Abercrombie never ran a large office. He would apparently employ a relatively small number of familiar people, usually past students from Liverpool or London, on individual contracts. They sometimes, but not necessarily, moved with him from contract to contract. Naim Aslan, for example, seems to have worked with Abercrombie on the Plymouth and London plans, before moving to collaborate with Reilly on the Birkenhead plan (Wildman 1989: 113).

The Use of in-House Professionals

The work of the consultants, where these were engaged, would have been much more difficult without the cooperation of existing in-house staff. Bradshaw had advised Worcester officials that, although the Town Planning Institute operated a fixed scale of costs, "much would depend ... on the amount of assistance which could be given by the authority's own department" (Minutes, Planning and Siting Sub-Committee, 27 August 1943). Yet there were also significant cost implications of using in-house staff. In 1943, Manchester Corporation appointed twenty-nine temporary planning assistants at a cost of at least £7,000 per year, most of whom were employed on the city or the regional plans (*Architect and Building News* 1943: 139). Suitably qualified professionals were often as expensive per year as consultants: when F. H. C. Maunder, ARIBA, was appointed city planning officer and reconstruction architect for Portsmouth City Council in 1944, his annual salary was £1,250 (*The Builder* 1944: 42).

Indeed, many consultants' reports were produced in such close cooperation that the relevant chief officer is cited as a co-author. Abercrombie's reports for Plymouth, Bath, and Edinburgh are examples. In the case of the Edinburgh plan, the Town Planning Officer, Derek Plumstead, is credited as co-author (Abercrombie and Plumstead 1949). Plumstead had been appointed as a temporary town planning assistant at Plymouth, then became involved in the Hull plan after the death of Abercrombie's co-author, Sir Edwin Lutyens—being described by Abercrombie (in the Edinburgh plan) as "resident planner" for the Hull plan—but it is unclear whether he was ever directly employed by Abercrombie.

Some reports bear only the names of the chief officer. Many of these are now virtually unknown, although a few were prominent in their professions, and their experience was such that no thought was given to bringing in expensive consultants. Among these would be counted Herbert Manzoni, CBE, MICE, MIM&CE, later knighted, the city surveyor and engineer of Birmingham from 1935 to 1969. He was a very powerful figure within the municipal structure: "It was through him that the rebuilding programme was accomplished, and through him that it had the character and qualities that it did." Even after the appointment of a city architect in 1952, "major decisions and the real power remained with Manzoni" (Higgott 2000: 152). Likewise, J. Nelson Meredith, FRIBA, Bristol's city architect, was well connected and served as editor of the journal *Official Architect*. He was deeply involved with Bristol's replanning, writing several conference and journal papers about it (e.g. Meredith 1941). Even officials of much smaller towns could be well-connected in professional organizations: M-E. Habershon, OBE, MEng, MIM&CE, borough engineer and surveyor of Walsall, spoke on the replanning of central areas (his diagrams were a very thinly-disguised Walsall) to the Institute of Municipal and County Engineers (Habershon 1942). Neither Birmingham, Bristol, nor Walsall employed consultants for their reconstruction planning (Sutcliffe and Smith 1974; Punter 1990; Larkham 2003, 2007a).

However, in these cases, even more than with the consultants, it is plain that the actual plans were the result of many hands. Percy Parr, OBE, BSc, MTPI, city engineer and planning officer of Newcastle upon Tyne, is named as the principal author of the city's plan (Parr 1945), although the acknowledgements thank several staff, and a title page suggests that it is actually a report of the Town Planning Sub-Committee. The substantial number of new staff recruited by Manchester Corporation has already been mentioned. The prevailing bureaucratic tradition of all departmental work being credited to the senior officer was roundly criticized by Reilly, writing about pre-war architectural practices:

> When ... the real author of some municipal building, as so often happens, is an anonymous, unknown young architect in the Borough Surveyor's or Borough Engineer's office, with one of those officials signing his drawings and taking to himself the credit for his work, it is not to be wondered at if, after a while, he loses his enthusiasm and initiative ... This fraud as regards architecture ... on the part of the Borough Engineers and Borough Surveyors of the country, is a thing which needs hammering at and exposing.
>
> (Reilly 1938: 304)

Again, little information survives on how junior staff members were recruited. The experience of Percy Johnson-Marshall at Coventry is instructive (from correspondence and autobiographical notes in the Johnson-Marshall collection, University of Edinburgh Archives). He refers to Donald Gibson's appointment as the first city architect in 1938 and the impact on young radical professionals. Johnson-Marshall himself was left-wing, indeed a card-carrying member of the Communist Party certainly in the 1940s (when working at the Ministry and the London County Council: his membership cards survive).

> Donald had to accept some handovers from the City Engineer's empire, but also advertised for his new men. It was the moment for which we had been waiting, and I applied immediately I saw the advertisement. I was fortunate to be appointed out of a shortlist of over 500. It was a big moment, and I shook the dust of London off my feet without any qualms (archive box FR38) ... a group of us went from London to Coventry ... We thought a small city might present an opportunity as a test case (archive box FR30)

The young radical staff almost immediately set about replanning the city center and exhibited their proposals even before the major air raid of 1940. Thereafter, Johnson-Marshall became the senior architect responsible for the city-center reconstruction.

The Unusual Role of the Town Clerk

In the small Midlands town of Bilston, the problem was not bomb damage but the combination of industrial dereliction and slum housing. The prime mover in attempts to resolve these problems during the reconstruction planning era was A. M. Williams, the town clerk (Larkham 2006). As did most town clerks, Williams had a legal training. His role is significant because, in most other cases, it was the borough surveyor, architect, or engineer (i.e. with qualifications in and experience of the built environment) who promoted action. Reilly later wrote of Williams that

> I think he is unique. I have never before met a man with such fine sociological ideals, such administrative capacity and such quick decision. The idea of the carrying out of Bilston, as it will be one day, is more his than mine. He saw in the *Architects' Journal* that my Woodchurch suburb for Birkenhead gave form to his ideas and the thing was done.
>
> (Reilly to Williams-Ellis, 23 August 1946: all Reilly correspondence is from his archive at the University of Liverpool)

Williams wrote inviting Reilly to Bilston, stating that he had read Wolfe's polemic advocating Reilly's radical housing layout and way of life; he later also wrote that he had read Lewis Mumford's books many times, and this was one of the major influences on his thinking about urban redevelopment (Williams to Reilly, 5 February 1946; 3 July 1946). Interestingly, the local newspaper told a slightly different story, crediting a politician rather than the civil servant:

> Some months ago Mr A.V. Williams, town clerk of Bilston, and Alderman Ben Bilboe were glancing through some old copies of an architectural trade paper when simultaneously they spotted an unusual lay-out of houses set round and facing on to a village green. "That's exactly what we want on Bilston's new housing estates," said Alderman Bilboe, and Mr Williams agreed.
>
> (*Express and Star* 1946)

Reilly was appointed as consultant to design several new communities and managed to obtain commissions for several friends and former students to design the buildings and detail layouts. He worked closely with Williams. He also exerted personal influence with the Minister of Housing, Aneurin Bevan; when, in 1947, expenditures were cut, Bilston's house building program was also slashed. Indeed, he even wrote to Bevan that his community design "with its abolition of the ordinary isolationist house, breeding Conservatives whose aim in life is to keep themselves to themselves, goes right to the heart of Socialism" (23 February 1947).

However, in mid-1946 and just as the Reilly designs were about to be implemented, Williams, who appears to have become something of a family friend to Reilly—who stayed at Williams's home on several occasions—resigned as town clerk of Bilston, having been appointed to the same position in neighboring Dudley. In his first letter to Reilly after announcing his resignation, Williams noted, "PS I have already indicated to the Dudley people that they have got to do something about the Reilly plan in Dudley. When you are over, perhaps we might pop in and have a word with the Mayor" (3 July 1946). Reilly was duly appointed.

In both Bilston and Dudley, however, the impetus for Reilly's radical vision was short-lived, and what was built was a very debased version of the original. For Williams also left Dudley, being appointed first general manager of Peterlee New Town in mid-1948, and Reilly had died earlier that year. In this instance, it was, clearly, the vision of the legally trained town clerk, evidently well read in contemporary urbanism, architecture, and sociology, who promoted this radical replanning. The borough engineers were less interested.

Some Problematic Personalities

The Local Level

There are some examples of tension between consultants and local officers, and, indeed between officers themselves. In Dover, where Abercrombie was appointed as consultant by May 18, 1945 (Minutes, Dover Planning Committee, East Kent Archives Centre), it is probable that most work was carried out by his new partner, Richard Nickson. Yet the final report, accepted by the full Council on January 29, 1946, carried the sole name of P. V. Marchant, the borough engineer and surveyor. It was noted simply in the press that "Frequent consultations have taken place between Professor Abercrombie and Mr Marchant" (*Estates Gazette* 1947: 445). The Norwich plan more directly betrays uneasy relationships between the consultants and the locals. This is even seen in the Foreword, where the chairman of the Town Planning Committee begins "Town Planning in England is a new science," while the second paragraph of the main text begins "Planning is no new activity" (James et al. 1945). The tone of the main text seems to be that of the consultants and, although H. C. Rowley, the city engineer, is credited on the title page, his only clear contribution is in the form of a forthright Appendix, "Reservations on report by City Engineer" (James et al. 1945: 126–30 and fold-out plan). This has recently been described as a "crude plan" which "was, of course, much more destructive" than the consultants' "sane and conservative approach" (Stamp 2007: 153).

At Southampton, there was a complex relationship between consultant, officials, and politicians (Hasegawa 1992: chapters 5 and 7). The city had a town planning assistant, H. T. Cook. He was regarded by the deputy leader of the local Labor group, experienced in planning issues, as "a first class man" but

> handicapped by his subordination to the Borough Engineer and by the prevailing attitude of Council members to any drastic planning proposals. That is why the appointment of an eminent Town Planning consultant is essential. But in addition to this the Town Planning work of the Council should be constituted either as a separate Department, or Mr Cook, as Town Planning Officer, be given special status.
>
> (Councillor Matthews, private note, Southampton Record Office D/Mat/10/4)

An eminent consultant was called in, apparently on the recommendation of the then minister, Lord Reith (*Southern Daily Echo* 1941). This was Professor Stanley Adshead, who, although then at the end of his career, had been the country's first professor of town planning at the University of Liverpool and then the University of London. Cook was promoted to head a new Town Planning and Development Department. A city-wide plan was speedily produced (Adshead and Cook 1942). Following its consideration by councilors, Cook was then asked to prepare a revised plan with H. Bennett, appointed as borough architect in 1943 (Adshead's contract was not renewed), and a new Reconstruction Committee was set up, but Cook found difficulties in working with Bennett, writing that "you prefer to work out your own scheme independently" (letter, 7 April 1944, Southampton Record Office SC/EN/13/5/4/2; see Hasegawa 1992: 148, note 68). A newly appointed borough engineer, F. L. Wooldridge, sided with Bennett; although his own proposals were criticized by the Ministry of Town and Country Planning. Nevertheless, the Council accepted Wooldridge's proposals as the way forward in January 1946, and Councilor Matthews noted that "Where experts differ the layman has to make a decision ... and having made it the officers must loyally accept it and get to work on the details so that the reconstruction of the central area can proceed rapidly" (quoted in *Southern Daily Echo* 1945). Cook did not "loyally accept" the decision and resigned, instead joining a local business association that fought the Council's plans as far as the Public Local Inquiry in September 1946. Shortly after, he left and, probably caused to a large extent by the breakdown of personal and professional relations, the city's Town Planning and Development Department was disbanded.

National-Local Relationships

Not only were relationships within individual authorities sometimes problematic, but those between authorities and central government were often poor. The Ministry in its various guises, and indeed the various ministers themselves, could be autocratic. The first minister with responsibility for reconstruction was Lord Reith and, as has been mentioned (see Note 3), he forcefully encouraged towns to "plan boldly," causing some confusion. W. S. Morrison, the first minister of the new Ministry of Town and Country Planning formed in 1943, was equally forceful in pushing the City of London Corporation to abandon the plan produced by its own staff and engage consultants. His senior staff felt that "an entirely new plan prepared by a competent planner was required" (quoted in Hasegawa 1999: 129). In the early years of reconstruction, of course, building material was rationed and controlled by the Ministry, so the aspirations of individual authorities were frequently dashed. All reconstruction plans had to be approved by the Ministry, and the processes of consultation and approval were often extremely lengthy, as Coventry in particular found, having drafted its master plan in February 1941 but receiving no formal comment until 1947: the regional planning officer noted that "the officials were disturbed to receive our comments on their scheme so long after its preparation and submission" (Ministry of Town and Country Planning 1947a). Furthermore, all plans concerning housing design or layout had to be approved by the Ministry of Health. Such approvals were largely to release grants or loans. The impact of such refusal on purely financial terms is shown by Bilston's problems with house building and its consultant Reilly's dramatic personal intervention with the minister (Larkham 2006).

Communications from the Ministry could also be terse and dismissive. Max Lock, Middlesbrough's planning consultant, wrote in April 1944 seeking the Ministry's advice over the borough surveyor's continued submission of plans despite Lock's appointment. He received from George Pepler a two-line response: "To a Ministry a local authority is supposed to speak with one voice" (letters, Lock files, University of Westminster Archives). In belatedly commenting on Coventry's plan, the Ministry's report noted that "the plan of the proposed redevelopment is badly presented and indefinite ... the statement in support of the application is little more than a description of the redevelopment plan," bemoaning the fact that the proposal would have been far better if Coventry had complied with the forthcoming guidance notes (as this was essentially a 1941 plan, this criticism seems unreasonable, especially as the guidance was not finally made available until 1947!) (Ministry of Town and Country Planning, undated).

Ministry officials were also not averse to writing equally dismissive internal reports and memoranda (Larkham 2011), such as the note by H. Gatliff, assistant secretary at the Ministry, that

> Generally, it seems to me a tragedy both for Hull, Sir Patrick Abercrombie and planning generally that he ever went near the place, and the sooner Hull gets away from his wilder ideas and faces up to the practical job of replanning ... in a sound, decent, ordinary way the better .
> (14 February 1946; National Archives HLG 79/226)

Sometimes these comments were very personal, such as Wells's comment of 14/3/44 that "the City Surveyor [of Exeter], Mr Dymond, is not very imaginative but confesses to his own limitations" (HLG 71/1284), and Hughes's comment of 16/8/49 that H. T. Hough, City Engineer of Liverpool, "is rather a weak character" (NA HLG 79/307). Indeed, the Ministry seems to have held low opinions of most local borough engineers and surveyors: the surveyor of Welshpool, for example, presented "the usual rather amateur attempt at a planning scheme [which] serves no useful purpose" (NA HLG 79/810). The comments from THS (the permanent secretary) to the minister about Great Yarmouth are not only personal but also patronizing: "They are not a good Council and their professional officers are weak. The Town Clerk is quite a good young man in his way but is not, I suspect, really interested in town planning" (26/11/46; NA HLG 79/202). There are equally dismissive comments about Yarmouth's planning officer, K. K. Parker; ironically, he joined the staff of the Ministry in August 1945. Gatliff also wrote acerbically of the West Sussex county clerk in the case of Sharp's plan for Chichester: "One cannot write chatty human letters to a mummy which is about what the County Clerk seems to be, though he is an exceedingly courteous one"; and this memo has a manuscript PS, "or should we say an embodied rubber stamp" (Gatliff to Walsh, 6/10/50, NA HLG 79/875). Ironically, the architect S. E. Dykes Bower, then working for the Ministry, wrote in a report on Carlisle that "it is important, in reports of this kind, to avoid any appearance of being critical and still more of trying to dictate how a local authority should plan" (report to Hughes, Regional Planning Officer, 28/7/44; NA HLG 79/95).

Although Cullingworth's official history (1975) exhaustively reviews the development of policy prior to the 1947 Act, and Cherry and Penny (1986) discuss Holford's contribution within the Ministry, there is no clear rationale for this extremely critical perspective from the center—"Headquarters," as the Ministry's London office referred to itself—of the individual local authorities, their officers, and consultants. No one, however experienced, seemed exempt. Perhaps the senior members of Ministry staff were more imbued with a civil service mentality? Although the regional planning officers were all members of the Town Planning Institute or Royal Institute of British Architects by 1947, the regional controllers certainly were not (Table 13.5).

Conclusions

This exploration of agents and agency sheds new light on a period of unparalleled activity in British planning, architecture, and urban design. More towns and cities were replanned in a shorter period than ever before, and this involved the widespread introduction of radical new concepts of architectural and urban form and a technocentric, scientific approach to planning. The view of the planner as independent scientific expert was nurtured in this process.

Using a wide range of plans produced through the 1940s and into the early 1950s, which in many cases have had long-term impacts, the evidence discussed here suggests that the actual process of reshaping urban form was very different from the processes introduced by the 1947 Town and Country Planning Act, with its prescriptive vision of the format and content of the "Development Plans" required; the contribution of external consultant plan authors declined very quickly thereafter.

TABLE 13.5 Regional Controllers of the Ministry of Town and Country Planning, 1947

Regional Controller (with qualifications etc)	*MTCP Region*
M. B. Tetlow BA ARIBA AM TPI	North-East
H. E. C. Gatliff	Leeds
Sir H. Prior NCSI C&E	Nottingham
P. T. Mansfield CSI CIE	Cambridge
Major-General M.A. Coxwell-Rodgers CB CBE DSO	Reading
Brigadier R. Peters CBE	Bristol
D. T. Williams MA	Cardiff
L. P. Ellicott ARIBA MTPI	Birmingham
P. L. Hughes ARIBA AMTPI	Manchester
A. P. Hughes-Gibb OBE	Kent

Source: Ministry of Town and Country Planning (1947b)

Who did the planning—consultant or local official—depended more on local politics and spheres of influence than objective assessment of plan-making abilities or experience. Advertising for consultants, competitive tendering, or searching interviews—in short, an open and transparent selection process—played only minor roles and in only a few cases. People were selected because of whom they knew (or who knew them) or because of press coverage of their work. Owing to the small pool of suitably qualified people, "who knew them" was often determined by their place of education. The University of London and, most particularly, the School of Architecture and Department of Civic Design at the University of Liverpool, generated high numbers of reconstruction planners, with Professors Abercrombie and Reilly active in promoting their former students or, indeed, employing them directly.

The recent use of actor network theory in the context of Plymouth's plan (Essex and Brayshay 2007) does articulate the functionally separate roles of actors and agents, but networks are not static, and outside influences change. The roles of Astor and Abercrombie diminished, and the new 1947 Act and other national political and economic considerations shaped the plan's implementation. The simpler consideration of types of actor used in earlier morphological studies ("direct" and "indirect"; see Chapter 1 and Larkham 1988) remains a helpful concept in exploring these plans, although it would be helpful to separate the process of plan formation, in which the author is a powerful direct actor, with the plan implementation, when many other factors are involved and where, as with Plymouth, the original author's concepts may be overtaken by events, become dated, and usually implemented in very dilute form.

The plan production process was often shaped by personal, political, or professional tensions. These operated at a local scale, with Reilly's experiences at Birkenhead being perhaps the most overt political clash, and the problems in Southampton between Cook, Bennett and Wooldridge, and also in Coventry between Ford and Gibson, being both professional and, the written evidence suggests, personal conflicts. Cook's resignation, and his subsequent work in opposition to his former employer, is an extreme reaction. Yet both Donald Gibson and A. G. Sheppard Fidler (Birmingham's city architect) resigned in 1955 and 1964, respectively, in what might be termed demarcation disputes over the implementation of reconstruction schemes. Similar tensions also existed between local authorities and the Ministry's civil servants at both regional and "headquarters" level, with the Ministry files and correspondence in the National Archives being littered with disparaging comments such as that about Abercrombie's involvement in Hull. Even the most experienced consultant, commissioned repeatedly by the same Ministry for some of the largest-scale regional reconstruction plans, was not immune from vitriolic criticism, of which he was presumably unaware.

Professional publicity and self-promotion, planning histories, and bibliographic conventions have tended to represent many plans as being the sole product of just one or two people—especially consultants and, with perhaps only one or two exceptions, males. This is a far from accurate view of the range of activity and contributors to these plans. For example, the pioneering sociological contributions of Ruth Glass to the plans of the Max Lock Group, fully acknowledged in the printed versions, seem too often forgotten. The plans were truly the products of many minds. Planning solutions emerged from a labor-intensive Geddesian process of survey and analysis. They were filtered through consultation with the local politicians, local officers and, often, the wider public. They were often further interpreted for communication purposes by artists and model makers (cf. Larkham 2007b).

In terms of the consumption of reconstruction plans, the period was marked by an unparalleled rise in public consultation (Lilley and Larkham 2007). Large-scale exhibitions were mounted, some of which were attended by tens of thousands of visitors, including organized school visits. Many, but by no means all, plans were published, some even in specially written précis form for a general readership. Yet, when the terms of reference of both exhibitions and publications are examined, in many cases, the aim is not simply to inform the public of what is to happen but actively to solicit views and (constructive) criticism about what were generally seen by their authors as draft proposals. These represent early large-scale planning consultation exercises and were higher up Sherry Arnstein's "ladder of public participation" (1969) than is often credited.

In short, the numerous British reconstruction plans of the immediate postwar period have proved a fertile source for the consideration of morphological agency at the city-wide scale, reassessing the processes of plan production and consumption and challenging the myth of the postwar planner as wholly objective scientist. This period of radical urban reshaping owes far more to the influence of human behavior, including politics and personality, than is commonly credited. Those who replanned our cities were all too human and suffered all of the foibles of humanity. This reappraisal sets the scene for the detailed explorations of morphological agency at the micro-scale by Whitehand and others, which have covered the actual implementation of changing urban forms throughout the postwar period.

Notes

1 Citations to archival material appear complete within the text and are not separately listed in the References.
2 On Abercrombie and his plans, see Dix (1981); Hall (1995); Jones (1998); Lambert (2000); Larkham (2004); Essex and Brayshay (2005, 2007). John Pendlebury has been re-appraising Sharp's plans (Pendlebury 2009), but Stansfield (1981) remains the main biographical source.
3 It is interesting that Reith later wrote that:

> I told them that if I were in their position I would plan boldly and comprehensively, and that I would not at that stage worry about finance or local boundaries. They had not expected such advice … but it was what they wanted and it put new heart into them (Reith 1949: 424).

And that his successor in 1947, Silkin, was trying to encourage progress in rebuilding the bombed cities and said at a conference, "Whether you plan boldly or timidly, and I sincerely hope you will plan boldly ..." (typescript speech, 18/9/47: NA HLG 71/34).

4 The role of local voluntary planning groups is un-researched, although two of them commissioned professional planners to produce their plans: Chelmsford, formed 1935, employed Minoprio (1946), and Sudbury, formed 1944, employed Jeremiah. By 1950, Whittick was extolling the virtues of such local groups and plans using the example of Beckenham (Whittick 1950).
5 Though personal papers of the plan authors are extremely rare, there are archive holdings of the papers of Percy Johnson-Marshall, Max Lock, and Thomas Sharp. The collection of Professor Percy Johnson-Marshall is in the Archives of the University of Edinburgh. Johnson-Marshall was a senior architect at Coventry to *c.* 1942 and worked after the war at the Ministry of Town and Country Planning and at the London County Council on reconstruction matters. The Max Lock Centre at the University of Westminster has many of his papers, stored at the University's Archives. Lock and his practice produced plans for Middlesbrough, Hartlepool, Portsmouth, and Bedford, and a civic survey for Hull. A selection of Thomas Sharp's papers is held by the Library of the University of Newcastle: Sharp was the most prolific of the reconstruction plan authors. Personal papers of Professor Sir Patrick Abercrombie, probably the most famous planner of the period, also exist, currently held by Professor Gerald Dix.
6 The authorities writing in support of the Institute of Municipal and County Engineers included Fleetwood, Ramsgate, Nelson (Lancs), East Dereham, Ryde, Derby, Windermere, Newton Abbott, Exmouth, Maltby, Stanley (Co. Durham), and Tynemouth. These were, with the exception of Derby, not seen as "important" towns and the correspondence was virtually ignored (NA HLG 71/760).
7 Likewise Hull City Council did not receive the Lutyens/Abercrombie report with any great enthusiasm and chose to retain very little evidence of it for preservation in the City Archives.

References

Abercrombie, P., and Nickson, R. (1949) *Warwick: Its Preservation and Redevelopment*. London: Architectural Press.

Abercrombie, P., and Plumstead, D. (1949) *A Civic Survey and Plan for the City and Royal Burgh of Edinburgh*. Edinburgh: Oliver and Boyd.

Adshead, S. D., and Cook, H. T. (1942) *The Replanning of Southampton*. Southampton, U.K.: Council of the County Borough.

Architect and Building News (1941) It needs to be said (editorial). *Architect and Building News*, 24 October: 43.

Architect and Building News (1942) Comment. *Architect and Building News*, 20 February: 140.

Architect and Building News (1943) News item on additional Manchester Corporation employees. *Architect and Building News*, 3 September: 139.

Arnold-Baker, C. (2002) *Local Council Administration*, 6th ed. Oxford: Butterworth.

Arnstein, S. (1969) A ladder of citizen participation. *Journal of the American Planning Association*, 35: 216–24.

The Builder (1944) News item on Maunder's appointment to Portsmouth. *The Builder*, CLXVII (5294), 21 July: 42.

Chapman, W. D. (1944) *Towards a New Macclesfield: A Suggestion for a New Town Centre.* Macclesfield: Cloister Press, for Macclesfield Borough Council Planning Committee.

Cherry, G. E. (ed.) (1981) *Pioneers in British Town Planning.* London: Architectural Press.

Cherry, G. E. (1983) *Thomas Sharp: The Man Who Dared to Be Different* (text of Sharp Memorial Lecture). Newcastle upon Tyne, U.K.: University of Newcastle upon Tyne, Department of Town and Country Planning.

Cherry, G. E., and Penny, L. (1986) *Holford: A Study in Architecture, Planning and Civic Design*. London: Mansell.

Cullingworth, J. B. (1975) *Reconstruction and Land Use Planning 1939–1947*. London: HMSO.

Dagenais, M., Maver, I., and Saunier, P.-Y. (eds.) (2003) *Municipal Services and Employees in the Modern City: New Historic Approaches*. Aldershot, U.K.: Ashgate.

Diefendorf, J. M. (1989) Artery: urban reconstruction and traffic planning. *Journal of Urban History*, 15: 131–58.

Dix, G. (1981) Patrick Abercrombie, in G. E. Cherry (ed.), *Pioneers in British Town Planning*, 103–30. London: Architectural Press.

Essex, S., and Brayshay, M. (2005) Town versus country in the 1940s. *Town Planning Review*, 76: 239–63.

Essex, S., and Brayshay, M. (2007) Vision, vested interest and pragmatism: who re-made Britain's blitzed cities? *Planning Perspectives*, 22: 417–41.

Estates Gazette (1947) News item on Dover plan. *Estates Gazette*, 21 June: 445.

Express and Star (1946) News item on appointment of Reilly to Bilston. *Express and Star*, 15 May.
Flinn, C. (2012) "The city of our dreams?" The political and economic realities of rebuilding Britain's blitzed cities, 1945–54. *Twentieth Century British History*, 23(2): 221–45.
Flinn, C. (2013) Reconstruction constraints: political and economic realities, in M. Clapson and P. J. Larkham (eds.), *The Blitz and Its legacy*, 87–97. Farnham, U.K.: Ashgate.
Gold, J. R. (1997) *The Experience of Modernism*. London: Spon.
Habershon, M. E. (1942) Replanning of central town areas. *Proceedings of the Institute of Municipal and County Engineers*, 69: 312–20.
Hall, P. (1995) Bringing Abercrombie back from the shades: a look forward and back. *Town Planning Review*, 66: 227–43.
Hall, P. (2002) *Cities of Tomorrow*, 3rd ed. Oxford: Blackwell.
Hall, P., and Tewdwyr-Jones, M. (2010) *Urban and Regional Planning*, 5th ed. London: Routledge.
Hasegawa, J. (1992) *Replanning the Blitzed City Centre*. Buckingham, U.K.: Open University Press.
Hasegawa, J. (1999) Governments, consultants and expert bodies in the physical reconstruction of the City of London in the 1940s. *Planning Perspectives*, 14: 121–44.
Hasegawa, J. (2013) The attitudes of the Ministry of Town and Country Planning towards blitzed cities in 1940s Britain. *Planning Perspectives*, 28: 271–89.
Higgott, A. (2000) Birmingham: building the modern city, in T. Dekker (ed.), *The Modern City Revisited*, 150–66. London: Spon.
James, C. H., Pierce, S. R., and Rowley, H. C. (1945) *City of Norwich Plan*. Norwich, U.K.: City of Norwich Corporation.
Jones, P. N. (1998) "... a fairer and nobler City"—Lutyens and Abercrombie's plan for the City of Hull 1945. *Planning Perspectives*, 13: 301–16.
Lambert, R. (2000) Patrick Abercrombie and planning in Bath', *Bath History*, 8: 172–96.
Larkham, P. J. (1988) Agents and types of change in the conserved townscape. *Transactions of the Institute of British Geographers*, 13: 148–64.
Larkham, P. J. (2003) Walsall: the origin, promotion and disappearance of a wartime "reconstruction" plan. *Planning History*, 25: 5–11.
Larkham, P. J. (2004) Professor Sir Patrick Abercrombie and the replanning of Warwick, 1945–1949. *Midland History*, 29: 124–38.
Larkham, P. J. (2006) People, planning and place: the roles of client and consultants in reconstructing postwar Bilston and Dudley. *Town Planning Review*, 77: 557–82.
Larkham, P. J. (2007a) *Replanning Birmingham: Process and Product in Postwar Reconstruction*, Working Paper 2. Birmingham, U.K.: Birmingham City University, Faculty of Law, Humanities, Development and Society.
Larkham, P. J. (2007b) Selling the future city: images in UK postwar reconstruction plans, in I. B. Whyte (ed.), *Man-Made Future: Planning, Education and Design in Mid-Twentieth-Century Britain*, 99–120. London: Routledge.
Larkham, P. J. (2011) Hostages to history: the surprising survival of critical comments about British planning and planners c.1942–1955. *Planning Perspectives*, 26: 487–91.
Larkham, P. J., and Lilley, K. D. (2003) Plans, planners and city images: place promotion and civic boosterism in British reconstruction planning. *Urban History*, 30: 183–205.
Larkham, P. J., and Pendlebury, J. (2008) Reconstruction planning and the small town in early postwar Britain. *Planning Perspectives*, 23: 291–321.
Lilley, K. D., and Larkham, P. J. (2007) *Exhibiting Planning: Communication and Public Involvement in British Postwar Reconstruction*, Working Paper 4. Birmingham, U.K.: Birmingham City University, Faculty of Law, Humanities, Development and Society.
Liverpool Daily Post (1945) News item on costs of Birkenhead plan. *Liverpool Daily Post*, 12 October.
Mandler, P. (1999) New towns for old: the fate of the town centre, in B. Conekin, F. Mort, and C. Waters (eds.), *Moments of Modernity: Reconstructing Britain 1945–1964*, 208–27. London: Rivers Oram Press.
Meredith, J. N. (1941) The reconstruction of Bristol. Presentation at the Housing Centre, 30 September, briefly excerpted in *Architect and Building News*, 10 October: 19.

Ministry of Town and Country Planning (undated, probably 1946) *Reconstruction Areas Technical Examination Committee: Report on Coventry's proposals*. Copy in Johnson-Marshall archive, University of Edinburgh, GB 0237/PJM/CCC/A/1/1.

Ministry of Town and Country Planning (1947a) Minutes of the 57th Technical Meeting of Regional Planning Officers, 23 October. Copy in Johnson-Marshall archive, University of Edinburgh, box SR4.

Ministry of Town and Country Planning (1947b) *Circular 30*, 7 February. London: Ministry of Town and Country Planning.

Minoprio, A., and Spencely, H. (1946) *Worcester Plan: An Outline Development Plan for Worcester*. Worcester, U.K.: Worcester City Council.

Nasr, J. (2003) Local wishes and national commands: planning continuity in French provincial towns in the 1940s, in J. Nasr and M. Volait (eds.), *Urbanism Imported or Exported? Native Aspirations and Foreign Plans*, 230–64. Chichester: Wiley-Academy.

Orbell, W. (1950) The new planning system in Cambridgeshire. *Town and Country Planning*, 18: 323–6.

Parr, P. (1945) *Plan—Newcastle upon Tyne 1945*, report of the Town Planning Sub-Committee. Newcastle upon Tyne, U.K.: Newcastle City Council.

Pendlebury, J. (2009) The urbanism of Thomas Sharp. *Planning Perspectives*, 24: 3–27.

Pierce, S. R. (1941) Organization of town planning (letter to the editor). *Architect and Building News*, 8 August: 79.

Potter, L. (2003) The Woodchurch controversy, 1944. *Transactions of the Historical Society of Lancashire and Cheshire*, 150: 145–69.

Powers, A. (1997) Obituary of Robert Hening. *The Independent*, 26 August.

Punter, J. V. (1990) *Design Control in Bristol 1940–1990*. Bristol, U.K.: Redcliffe Press.

Reilly, C. H. (1938) *Scaffolding in the Sky: A Semi-Architectural Autobiography*. London: Routledge.

Reilly, C. H. (1944) review of Watson and Abercrombie (1943) in *Building*, July: 182–3.

Reith, J. C. W. (1949) *Into the Wind*. London: Hodder & Stoughton.

Southern Daily Echo (1941) News report of appointment of Adshead to Southampton. *Southern Daily Echo*, 12 August.

Southern Daily Echo (1945) News report of Councillor Matthews's views, Southampton. *Southern Daily Echo*, 28 September.

Stamp, G. (2007) *Britain's Lost Cities*. London: Aurum.

Stansfield, K. (1981) Thomas Sharp 1901–1978, in G. E. Cherry (ed.), *Pioneers in British Town Planning*, 150–76. London: Architectural Press.

Sutcliffe, A. R., and Smith, R. (1974) *Birmingham 1939–1970*. London: Oxford University Press.

Ward, S. V. (1994) *Planning and Urban Change*. London: Paul Chapman.

Warwick and Warwickshire Advertiser (1947) News items about costs of publication of Abercrombie plan. *Warwick and Warwickshire Advertiser*, 1 August: 1.

Watson, J. Paton, and Abercrombie, P. (1943) *A Plan for Plymouth*. Plymouth, U.K.: Underhill, for the City Council.

Whitehand, J. W. R. (1984) *Rebuilding Town Centres: Developers, Architects and Styles*. Birmingham, U.K.: University of Birmingham, Department of Geography, Occasional Publication 19.

Whittick, A. (1950) Planning and the voluntary organization. *Town and Country Planning*, 18: 504–8.

Wildman, D. (1989) Obituary of Naim Aslan. *Journal of the Royal Institute of British Architects*, 96: 113.

Williams-Ellis, C. (1941) *Plan for Living: The Architect's Part*. London: Faber.

14

IN SEARCH OF NEW SYNTHESES

Urban Form, Late Flowering Modernism, and the Making of Megastructural Cumbernauld

John R. Gold

> All the while—like a jeweller fashioning precious metal—I hammered the cross-sections and shaped landscape to forge an urban morphology
>
> (Copcutt 1997).

These words, taken from reminiscences recorded by Geoffrey Copcutt, remind us of a short-lived but fascinating episode in both the development of the British New Towns and the history of modern architecture. Copcutt was the Group Architect of the town center or "Central Area" at the Scottish New Town of Cumbernauld. Although Cumbernauld broke with many of the established practices of the existing generation of fourteen Mark I British New Towns (founded between 1947 and 1950), its most revolutionary feature was the design of its Central Area (Fig. 14.1). With its car parks and service areas at ground level linked by stairs and lifts to shops, offices, leisure facilities, and dwellings located above, the Cumbernauld Central Area represented perhaps the most comprehensive example of vertical separation of pedestrians and vehicles seen anywhere in Britain in the postwar period (Houghton-Evans 1975: 106). Its aesthetics, especially the use of raw concrete and unadorned geometric shapes in its external surfaces, resonated with the then-prevailing preoccupations of modern architecture. Its monumentality also attracted attention, spectacularly dominating the skyline in a manner that many compared with the citadel of a medieval hilltop town (Ravetz 1980: 125).

Yet, the feature that excited greatest interest was that this scheme met the criteria necessary for it to be described as a "megastructure," a term that, while only coined in the early 1960s (Maki 1964), effectively codified features that had emerged far earlier.[1] Megastructures briefly captured the imagination, due both to their supposed advantages for addressing problems of new urban development and to their possible role in reinvigorating modernist approaches to urban form. For something to be defined as a "megastructure" is not dependant on its size or corresponding to a specific urban form, because the term maps out a category that can include anything from open-ended linear grids to huge and integrated multi-story urban complexes. Rather, it constitutes a category in which buildings and other structures rely on a shared and extensible framework that enables them effectively to function as a single entity. Its extensibility is particularly important. Designing structures around such a framework supplies an innovative way of responding to the uncertainties of future urban development by allowing units to be added or removed to accommodate changing

FIGURE 14.1 Photograph of Cumbernauld Central Area, Stage 1, *c.*1980

needs. From the standpoint of the 1960s, these advantages exerted a powerful intuitive appeal, but it did not take long before practice revealed the contradictions present in much megastructural thinking. Indeed, by the early 1970s, when modernism in general was under attack, megastructures encountered particularly fierce criticism as being grandiose, impractical, and inhuman. The few schemes that had been attempted were mostly abandoned or trimmed back. Henceforth, it was only when engagement was made with commercial realities, such as with the design of combined leisure, sporting, and shopping complexes, that any aspect of megastructural thinking was retained.

At first glance, the story of Cumbernauld's town center would seem to illustrate these themes perfectly. Chosen as the preferred form for the New Town's Central Area around 1960, its designers envisaged an integrated structure that would house the town's social, retail, and commercial facilities. Construction began in 1963, but only the first two of the five phases of construction proceeded according to initial intentions. The piecemeal development that characterized the three final phases effectively stripped the logic from the earlier megastructural developments, leaving the latter to be increasingly depicted as, at best, white elephants and, at worst, expensive aberrations. These underlying judgments also helped to justify recent decisions to demolish sections of the original structure, despite active campaigns by national and international bodies for its conservation (McBeth 2002). Yet, as is often the case with architectural modernism, a more complex narrative underpins the history of the engagement between modern architecture and the design of the urban environment. Though in no way disputing the current dysfunctional state of the megastructural portions of the town center, at least part of the responsibility for its problems lay not in the architectural field but in poorly judged political decisions over initial land allocations, resources, and location.

This chapter, which draws on and extends earlier work (Gold 1997, 2006, 2007), revisits the early development of Cumbernauld's Central Area to explore these issues further. Using oral history, primary documentation, and contemporary reportage, it examines the conscious efforts made by the design team at Cumbernauld to reconceptualize the traditional morphology of the city center and their attempts to craft a technologically advanced, but socially responsive, environment that might meet the needs of the new age. The first section of this chapter creates context by sketching the origins and development of megastructural concepts within contemporary architecture. The next sections discuss the circumstances that led to the adoption of a megastructure for Cumbernauld's town center and examine its implementation through to the abandonment of the megastructural concept. The conclusion reflects on the lessons to be learned, especially in terms of constructing narrative, from the experience of one of the few megastructural schemes that ever made the transition from paper vision to built form.

Megastructural Thinking

At the outset, it is important to stress that megastructuralism is not inherently utopian. Not all megastructural visions for new urban environments are overlain with the socially transformatory urge that is an essential part of utopian endeavor (Gold 2008; Pinder 2010); paper is cheap, and there is no obligation to ask soul-searching questions about supplying the basis for the Good Life before designing schemes primarily intended for discussion or exhibition purposes. Moreover, the history of architecture reveals that many developments that have incorporated the size and infrastructural elements typical of megastructures have proved to be successful and adaptable features of the cities where they were built. The huge sports complexes at the Coliseum and Circus Maximus in ancient Rome, the inhabited bridges of medieval European cities, and the vast iron-and-glass pavilions built at nineteenth-century international expositions all have claims to be antecedents of more recent practice.[2] For example, Old London Bridge, which existed for more than six centuries (1176–1831), incorporated an ever-changing assortment of houses, shops, workshops, a two-story chapel, watermills, warehouses, gates and fortifications, and even a colonnaded town square. As a "multi-functional and multi-layered" framework, this twenty-arch bridge was "an organic thing," with "the structures on it evolving in response to the people, the times, [and] the disasters" (Pierce 2001: 4).

More recently, analogous thinking can be said to have underpinned the rise of the modern shopping mall as an "entity characterized by comprehensiveness and completeness...[that] is designed, built and operated as a single unit" (Longstreth 2010: 170). As Rodney Gordon observed, commercial developers in the late 1950s and 1960s approached their potential projects primarily from the viewpoint of floor space, allowing architects remarkable degrees of freedom in design provided they maximized the amount of space to let. They were particularly fond of mixed developments that could attract a broader cross-section of users. Major users took the prime sites within the complex at the highest rents, with lower rent-yielding activities, like leisure amenities or dwellings, filling the remaining spaces that the prime commercial users did not want.[3] The original redevelopment of the Bull Ring Centre in central Birmingham (by Sydney Greenwood and T. J. Hirst, 1961–4), for instance, saw the developers' architects fit an integrated structure to an awkward four-acre sloping site that spanned the inner Ring Road. Once the cross-section was decided, it was possible to make use of the sixty-five-foot slope by constructing a shopping center on six levels; three of which were devoted to retailing and leisure services, one to car parking and access, one to delivery, and one that comprised a ballroom. Delivery systems, including lifts and access corridors, were incorporated at the rear. The parallels with Cumbernauld, as we shall see, are sufficiently striking to indicate that its megastructural Central Area was not wholly the product of blue-sky avant-gardism.

Yet, as Reyner Banham (1976) indicated in his highly perceptive survey of an idea that fell from grace, it cannot be denied that expressions of megastructuralism have tended to be overlain with aspirational anticipations of the future. This was already evident in the period immediately before the First World War. In 1914, for instance, the Futurist architects Antonio Sant'Elia and Mario Chiattone offered visions of megastructural forms in sketches that they showed at Milan's "Nuove Tendenze" exhibition. Their depictions of a *Città Nuova* (New City) featuring multi-story buildings with stepped-back profiles, cathedral-like power stations, and cavernous roadways (see da Costa Meyer 1995: 89–168) contain extraordinary glimpses of how new building techniques and materials might reshape the urban future but remained fragments with no interconnecting schema. Around the same time, the American writer Edgar Chambless (1910) devised a scheme for guiding urban growth in the form of a hypothetical linear settlement known as "Roadtown." This envisaged laying the modern skyscraper on its side and running "the elevators and the pipes and the wires horizontally instead of vertically. Such a house would not be limited by the stresses and strains of steel; it could be built not only a hundred stories, but a thousand stories or a thousand miles" (Chambless 1910: 19; see also Reiner 1963; Segal 1985).

Interest in megastructuralism grew steadily in the next half-century,[4] with the underlying principles steadily becoming an essential ingredient in the imaginings of avant-garde architects when contemplating what might be achieved through the creative alliance of new technology with imaginative design and planning. In the 1920s, Bruno Taut's Expressionist crystalline structures (Taut 1919, 1929) hinted at what might be achieved with "space-frame" buildings—three-dimensional frameworks for enclosing spaces "in which all members are interconnected and act as a single entity, resisting loads applied in any direction" (Makowski 1965; cited by Curl 1999: 626–7). Ludwig Hilberseimer's *Hochhausstadt* (Skyscraper City) combined work, residence, and basic services in huge slab blocks of flats placed on a grid, with five-story podia beneath them (Larsson 1984: 203; Hays 1992). Yet, perhaps the most iconic and influential of pre-1960 applications of mega-forms came from Le Corbusier. His Montevideo and Rio de Janeiro Plans (both 1929) and Algiers Plan (1930–1) contained powerful visions of buildings designed integrally with communication systems. The Algiers Plan, for instance, featured a sinuous building known as the Fort l'Empereur, fifteen kilometers long, twenty-six meters wide, and fourteen stories high, with a motorway on its roof (Le Corbusier 1935: 233–61). Just after the Second World War, his design for a fifteen-story slab, which was built in Marseilles between 1947 and 1953 and known as a *unité d'habitation*, saw an entire neighborhood brought together within one building, replete with shops, restaurant, kindergarten, and hotel accommodation (Curtis 1996: 437–40).

The 1950s and early 1960s produced a new clutch of schemes. Sergei Kadleigh and Patrick Horsbrugh (1952), for example, produced an unrealized but highly influential scheme for "High Paddington," a glass-towered vertical city for 8,000 people to be built above railway tracks in west London. The CIAM Congress at Otterlo in 1959 saw Ralph Erskine exhibit his megastructural ideas for ideal Arctic settlements, proposing "continuous faceted buildings" to maximize energy efficiency (Collymore 1995: 22–4). At a similar time, the Japanese Metabolist movement, led by Kenzo Tange, envisaged urban development in a series of gigantic cylinders on reclaimed land in Tokyo Bay (Riani 1969: 26–34). On an even larger scale, the composer and architect Iannis Xenakis (1965) proposed a "Cosmic City" in which 5 million inhabitants would be housed in "slender hyperbolic shells of more than 3,000 metres high and 50 metres wide" (Sterken 2003: 1).

Yet perhaps the foremost expression of this breezy, anything-is-possible approach came with the work of the six-man British group known as Archigram (Sadler 2005). Their completed schemes, for example, included "Plug-in City." Designed between 1962 and 1966, "Plug-In City" was designed around an infrastructural framework of tubes that would contain the city's electricity, water, and sewage services and passenger lifts and goods distribution systems. Buildings would be factory-produced modular units that would be brought to the site and simply clipped onto the framework in whatever manner was required. The city, therefore, could be almost any shape, density, or size required. Given that the megastructural framework itself had built-in obsolescence through having a projected life-span of only forty years, it was argued that "Plug-In City" would allow people maximum freedom to indulge their new-found affluence and supposed desires for novelty, change, and leisure.

This casual attitude toward questions involving urban society fitted the mood of a time predisposed to treat the canon of feasibility as tantamount to an irrelevance. Enthusiastic supporters of megastructures saw them as a potent design solution capable of bringing the alchemy of technology to bear on pervasive urban problems. For example, they could be drawn into proto-environmentalist debate by facilitating housing the population in higher-density settlements, thereby allowing society to enjoy the extra land left free from building (e.g. Blake 1961; Soleri 1969). Megastructures might address problems of urban anonymity by providing imposing symbols that expressed the identity of the town and its citizens (e.g. Banham 1976: 16–69). Pushing the envelope of credibility yet further, it was opined that megastructures might even help to invigorate social and communal life in that they had:

> the potential of making greater change and variety possible in life, the liberation and ecological recreation of more open land, and even the more immediate response of the community to citizen and vice versa on a newly revealed interface of the individual with his social, political, and cultural, as well as his physical, environment.
>
> (Burns 1972: 135)

Origins

The vibrant and multi-faceted debate that surrounded adoption of megastructures was paralleled by more specific but fiercely contested debates arising from the designation and planning of Cumbernauld. As one close observer laconically noted, the designation process for Cumbernauld New Town was surrounded by a "certain amount of turmoil"[5] that, in turn, had a long-term impact on decisions made about the town center. The original idea for the New Town stemmed from the Clyde Valley Regional Plan, which recommended the creation of four self-contained New Towns within Glasgow's Green Belt. These would have been at East Kilbride, Cumbernauld, Houston, and Bishopton (Abercrombie and Matthew 1949). The Conservative governments of the 1950s, however, had little time for New Towns, preferring the more limited alternative of Town Development ("Expanded Town") schemes. Nevertheless, they were prepared to make an exception to cope with Glasgow's severe housing shortage. The possibility was canvassed of a New Town to the west of the city at Houston (Renfrewshire), but local political interests—backed by Sir Hugh McNeill, the Secretary of State for Scotland and Member of Parliament for the area—successfully opposed the scheme. Alternative sites with reasonable proximity to Glasgow were hard to find. A Draft Order by the Department of Health for Scotland in 1955 allowed for a parcel of 8,000 acres—much the same size as previous New Towns—to be centered on Cumbernauld, fifteen miles northeast of the city. This would then act as a reception point for 50,000 people, 40,000 of whom would come from Glasgow's housing lists.

Crucially, however, the proposed designated area overlapped the county jurisdictions of Lanarkshire and Dunbartonshire, with Lanarkshire objecting to the New Town designation. Although prepared to accept industry, its County Council had no wish to give up land for other purposes. Choosing not to put the issue to a Public Inquiry,[6] the Scottish Office decided to press ahead with the New Town in February 1956 on the segment of just 4,150 acres that lay in East Dunbartonshire (this was a detached portion of a county that principally lay to the north of Glasgow, about which the County Council had little apparent interest). This would have immediate implications for density, given that the population target was retained (and would be increased to 70,000 in 1959), but problems were compounded by the poor quality of the Dunbartonshire land. Much of it comprised ridges, steep slopes, deep glens, peat bog, and the remains of coal and fireclay workings. After review, it was decided that development would primarily take place in an oval-shaped area of around 930 acres (376 hectares). This was dominated by the hogback Cumbernauld Hill, about one mile wide and two-and-a-half miles long (1.6 × 4 kilometers), which rose approximately 260 feet (79 meters) above the surrounding area.

The reduced land allocation set parameters for the New Town. At 8,000 acres (3,238 hectares) it might have been possible to construct a New Town like Vällingby in Sweden, a satellite town for Stockholm and a prototype that aroused considerable interest given the favorable press coverage then enjoyed by Swedish design. With only 4,150 acres (1,680 hectares) of poor-quality land, the designers of Cumbernauld made a virtue of necessity by embracing cohesion and compactness for their New Town, with commensurately higher densities than in the first generation New Towns and limited use of high-rise buildings. This would contribute to the town's abandoning the neighborhood planning of its predecessors—decried as emphasizing "pseudo-village-greens" that encouraged residents to look inward to a local center rather than "visualising the town as a whole" (Houghton-Evans 1975: 103). There were also changes stemming from the planning team's acceptance that future society would expect to take advantage of its greater mobility made possible through the spread of the private car. Planning for Cumbernauld, therefore, absorbed new levels of traffic forecasts and ideas of traffic planning, particularly from the United States, to create a town *engineered*—a verb commonly applied at the time—to meet the needs of the motor age. Indeed, when implemented, Cumbernauld's high-capacity roadways resembled American "urban freeways," one of which would pass under the town center.

From the beginning, then, Cumbernauld was not designed on the basis of the cellular neighborhood pattern adopted in the previous New Towns but as a single unit, with housing areas clustered around the Central Area and connectivity provided throughout by its advanced road system. The location chosen for the town center, therefore, was of the greatest importance. The first Preliminary Planning Proposals, published in late May 1958, envisaged a T-shaped Central Area in the hollow immediately north of the railway station and rising to a point below the crest of the hill (*Architects' Journal* 1958: 858). Although the text promised a multi-function town center with adjacent "high blocks of flats" (*Architects' Journal* 1958: 859), there was no suggestion of megastructural principles. Several of the planning team continued to press for the valley site—an option that was also favored by the planners working on the later abandoned private New Town project for the London County Council at Hook (Hampshire).[7] However, Hugh Wilson, Cumbernauld's Chief Planner, favored a site that would be geographically central to the residential area, and this was formally selected (Wilson 1959a). Placing the town center in this position would permit Cumbernauld to be a pedestrian town in which no dwellings would be more than three-quarters of a mile from the shops, with full separation of pedestrians and traffic. At the same time, it meant basing the New Town around Cumbernauld Hill.

The town center was now earmarked for a 150-acre (60 hectares) strip running along the top of the ridge that would create a readily visible feature in the surrounding landscape.

It was immediately recognized that this location was problematic. The site was narrow and elongated, which placed immediate limitations on the chosen design in terms of the disposition of roads and buildings. Any pedestrians visiting the city center in its hilltop site would need to cope with the stiff gradients on the way there regardless of the direction from which they approached. There were also microclimatological problems. The southwest to northeast alignment of the central ridge coincided with the direction of the strong and frequently rain-bearing prevailing winds. Development there would need to take into account probable wind channeling and might require the construction of substantial windbreaks; something that would have been unnecessary if the alternative valley site had been chosen.[8]

Design

At one level, what followed would seem wholly in line with the Modern Movement's favorite mantra, namely, that form follows function. Those who had worked on the scheme in the early days insisted that the design of the megastructure evolved only after developing the cross-section of levels for the town center on the hill and having conducted research to forecast traffic levels and the likely demand for retail space. According to Alex Kerr,[9] for example, the exercise began by asking basic questions about the nature of shops, the form of access required, the respective uses of private and public transport, and the likelihood of changes in the foreseeable future. It was noted, for instance, that the earlier New Towns had traditional single- or double-fronted shops, with street access for customers at the front and delivery at the back, but that the very narrow configuration of the center on the ridge made this pattern more difficult. Teams were established within the design team to create the basic pattern for the town's road system and to study how this could best give access to the center. Outside consultants were employed where necessary, and Copcutt and other senior staff paid visits to the United States and Canada to study North American experience. Once the basis of the cross-section was also decided, the ingredients were apparently then in place to design the Central Area.

Yet it is difficult to accept that the megastructural form followed entirely from this analysis of function. There would have been other ways to build a center, even given the constraints of the site and the functional requirements placed on it. Nevertheless, the decision had been taken by the start of 1959 that the Central Area would probably be "multi-level in character" (Wilson 1959b: 14), a preference that would have helped to create the center's citadel-like appearance. Moreover, the Preliminary Report on the Town Centre, prepared before the statistical surveys and other studies were carried out, makes it clear that the decision to build the town center as a megastructure had already been taken. Arguing that the town center needed to be the focus for town life, the report's writer stated that it was necessary "for the design and structure of the town centre, the buildings and facilities they will contain, to portray and amplify this concept" (CNTDC undated: 3). The account went on to note the importance of estimating "at this stage what the accommodation of the Town Centre should be because the Town Centre envisaged for Cumbernauld is *one huge multi-storey building*, to be built in phases" (CNTDC undated: 4, author's emphasis).

The design work was the responsibility of the small Town Centre team led by Geoffrey Copcutt, an Edinburgh-trained architect who arrived in 1959. Copcutt had been identified in 1958 as one of Britain's most promising young architects by a reviewer in the avant-garde *Zodiac* magazine: an accolade thought to have helped him gain the job at Cumbernauld.[10] Although a former colleague argues that Copcutt's designs were "seminal,"[11] others recognize that ideas about megastructures were certainly "in the wind"[12] and both the scale and unique properties of the hilltop location appealed to his known sensitivities as a designer. Copcutt was a compulsive visualizer, "always accompanied by a 10 inch roll of tracing paper, 20 yards long. On this, he produced loads of ideas and basic sketches which could be taken forward by others."[13] Unusually, he did not execute line drawings himself, with the type of attention to detail that this demands, but rendered sketched ideas into three-dimensional form through scale modeling in paper (*pocher*), cardboard, or plywood; the finished line drawings were normally completed by Copcutt's associates. The early versions produced by these methods exuded a tangible excitement for the sculptural possibilities of building on this site: one example showing shopping and other central uses under a vast ramped canopy of housing, using the profile of the hillside to bring the closest possible connection between residents and the facilities of the town center (an example is shown in Copcutt 1963: 210). By stages, however, this gradually transmuted into a multi-story structure arranged in a series of "decks".

By January 1962, a prototype scheme envisioned shopping located on three levels, with other communal uses above and surmounted by three ranges of penthouses.[14] The entire edifice would be placed over a one-way system of roads, with separate lanes for different types of vehicles and car parks. The layout in the center included two squares, civic buildings, a hotel, and spaces for entertainment buildings. By this stage, any significant use of the railway had faded from the picture, but enthusiasm for innovation continued by conducting feasibility studies of various innovative methods for handling traffic and circulation. These included tracked magnetic-levitation systems, parcel pick-up, and gravity parking.[15] Studies of regional shopping centers in North America helped to refine the pattern for retail provision but brought home the uncomfortable fact that U.S. shopping centers were enclosed, whereas that at Cumbernauld was largely open to the elements. Windbreaks were clearly necessary. After a consultant's report by Professor A. Hendry of Liverpool University, proposals for artificial earthen mounds at each end of the structure were abandoned, and the design changed to long, high buildings with air gaps beneath.

Plans and models for Phase 1 (Fig. 14.2), along with artists' impressions (Fig. 14.3) and diagrams of the cross-section, were unveiled in late November 1962. The scheme had been considerably simplified from the earlier version with, for example, the principal shopping elements placed on one deck, at the level of the ground on the north side, with an additional deck at one floor below on the south side. Yet, despite the manifest complexity involved in fitting the decks to the hilltop site, Phase 1 comprised just two main architectural elements. As described by Miles Glendinning (1992), the larger segment comprised the main commercial, administrative, and housing block located to the south of the dual carriageway—in profile representing "a gigantic, squat, tiered structure progressively stepping up from south to north, and crowned by a range of penthouses." By contrast, the second element was a spur to the north that directly continued the main shopping concourse for a short distance across the dual carriageway. There were also sites adjacent to the northwest, where other agencies would be able to build a hotel and the parish church (St. Mungo's).

As befitted a center destined to be built in distinct stages, the keynote was flexibility. Copcutt (1963: 210) described the scheme as comprising "demountable enclosures." Its future managers might rearrange its interiors or expand in planned fashion, either within the structural grid or in spaces beyond. In a remote future, if certain central area functions declined, the center could become "a giant vending machine through which the motorized user drives to return revictualled." In language that parallels the celebrations of mobility and consumerism associated with Archigram, this was "a drive-in center," "a vast terminal facility" where levels interpenetrate, forms "erupt,"

FIGURE 14.2 Model of Cumbernauld's first phase

FIGURE 14.3 Artist's impression of the different deck levels. Drawing by Michael Evans

sections are revealed to the "mechanically propelled" visitor, and advertising presents a "kaleidoscope" (Copcutt 1963; see also Glendinning 1996: 125). Playfully, too, Copcutt also added an illustration of a landscape view of the future town center with a large American car in the foreground. Its registration plate was "GC 1963."

The chosen aesthetic for the center merits consideration. The plastic, almost sculptural quality suggested by the early models came to be replaced by a harsher aesthetic of angular geometries and unfaced concrete finishes. Some of the geometric features would make greater sense once the later stages were built—this was, above all, a scheme that was intended to realize the megastructure's vaunted characteristics of flexibility and extensibility. The abrupt ends of the building were intended as no more than a temporary stage before the next sections were constructed. The use of concrete, however, was an expression of the austere style and aesthetics known as "New Brutalism." Although it is not possible to discuss the New Brutalist movement in detail here,[16] it was characteristically a blend of design preferences and sociological presumptions. Its proponents asserted the primacy of space, structure, and materials displayed in their untrammeled form, with concrete bearing the marks of its timber shuttering, brickwork left unplastered, and steel frames exposed. This version of the Modern Movement's hallowed maxim "truth to materials" gave architecture an alluring moral content. New Brutalism stood for an attempt to face up to what were regarded as the new realities of "mass-production society," to "drag a rough poetry out of the confused and powerful forces which are at work" and provide an aesthetic that is that society's "visual equivalent" (Banham, quoted in Jencks 1973: 257). The looseness of this conception proved entirely suitable for most designers' needs. Though its use of concrete may have been seen as a cheap way of providing texture,[17] there was an image inseparably linked to New Brutalist buildings in architectural discourse: uncompromising, pioneering, forward-looking, and expressive of modernity. Those values seemed eminently suitable for the megastructure that was due to appear.

Implementation

Moves to implement Phase 1 followed relatively smoothly, notwithstanding the bankruptcy of the contractors Duncan Logan and the early departure of the key staff—Hugh Wilson having left in October 1962 and Geoffrey Copcutt in February 1963. The national Conservative government had modified its position on the New Towns, and the Scottish Office gave financial and moral support to what was now regarded as a showpiece to kick off a second generation of British New Towns. Phase 1 was built between 1963 and 1967. The scheme proceeded according to Copcutt's plan and chosen aesthetic but was implemented by his successors Philip Aitken and Neil Dadge. Although the Cumbernauld staff contributed working diagrams, the detailing was handled by the contractors, who had been hired on a "design and build" basis.

The early response seemed encouraging. The Institute of American Architects' decision to make Cumbernauld the first recipient of its R. H. Reynolds Memorial Award for Community Architecture testified to its reputation in international architectural circles. Indeed, at the prize-giving ceremony held on May 19, 1967, the day after the official opening of the town center, the jury's citation stressed the significance of the new "concept of community living" employed at Cumbernauld for the future development of community architecture in the Western world generally and praised the town center as being "designed for the millennium" (*Architects' Journal* 1968a). The architectural press, too, broadly approved. Michael Webb's influential review of *Architecture in Britain Today* referred to the center as a "much vaunted showpiece." While declaring that it was too early to judge the success of the plan, it was judged "certainly an improvement on the early New Towns" (Webb

1969: 150). The reviewer for the *Architects' Journal* concluded that "its final worth and justification exists in the powerful identity it gives to those who live in Cumbernauld. They do not believe, not even the critical, that they have been given something which is second rate" (*Architects' Journal* 1968b: 304). Furthermore, "it has, already, a bookshop"—clearly a sign of success. Despite the problems of microclimate, detailing, and construction workmanship, "all this is nothing against the positive contribution it will make to those who live in Cumbernauld new town and to those of us whose concern is making new environment fit for this century" (*Architects' Journal* 1968b: 307). The architectural historian Patrick Nuttgens, writing in the *Architectural Review*, gave a guarded approval that careful reading suggests was more an expected response than a rapturous endorsement. Full of faint praise, the catalog of reservations catches the eye, for example:

> it is sometimes coarse and verging on the megalomaniac; here and there it ignores simple needs in favour of some private aesthetic. And yet with ironic justice it is the occasional pieces of pure architecture that in the end are the most irritating aesthetically, communicating a lively sense of the unnecessary. ... The next phase ... must inevitably correct what appear at a superficial glance to be major faults.
>
> (Nuttgens 1967: 444)

It was a symptom of changing times. The building of Phase 2 of the Central Area began in 1968—a time when the political and economic context had already changed dramatically. As Dudley Leaker, Hugh Wilson's replacement, recognized:

> the Town Centre is a case in point where the climate of high hope and financial backing changed before the second stage had a chance to get started and before the right quality of materials and finishes could be applied.[18]

This was not helped by the more strident criticism of modernism that was starting to surface. The *Architectural Review*, for example, published its "Housing" issue in November 1967, which revealed profound disquiet about aspects of social housing influenced by modernism. The climate of opinion about megastructures was also changing. Peter Hall, who in his book *London 2000* had envisaged the future settlement of Hamstreet as having a megastructural town center (Hall 1963: 268–73), had completely changed his mind by 1968. Condemning them as "monumental follies," he noted how these and similar utopian expressions of urban futures omitted characteristic urban problems of the 1960s such as poverty, pollution, and social inequality—apparently abolished by the beneficent powers of technology (Hall 1968). Broader criticisms came from those who recognized the banal and potentially dangerous assumptions being made. Certainly by the time that Phase 2 was completed, megastructural concepts were widely condemned as representing some of the worst follies of grandeur committed by the Modern Movement.

Phase 2 would indeed be the last to proceed in broad conformity to Copcutt's original design, albeit with what Glendinning (1992) calls a "marked dilution of the visual ferocity of the previous phase." Phase 2 almost completely swallowed up the previous phase's northern spur across the dual carriageway. It consisted of a single block, aligned north-south, and between three and four stories high. Its lowest levels were occupied by the north car park and its upper stories by offices, shops, and a small market hall (Glendinning 1992). By the time of its completion, it was clear that the town needed a larger store, but "the unorthodox layout of the Centre, with both ends unfinished and awaiting further development, did not encourage developers."[19] Woolworths eventually agreed to build a Woolco superstore, with two levels of car parking underneath, but they did so as a discrete project. Although the resulting box-like building was called Phase 3, neither it nor the two phases that followed—which lie beyond the scope of this chapter—were developed as an integral part of the megastructure. That experiment had ended with Phase 2; the megastructural concept was effectively dead.

Conclusion

Any visitor to Cumbernauld wishing to look at the megastructural portions of the Town Centre faces two problems. In the first place, the addition of such structures as the Antonine Shopping Centre (opened in 2007) and the new Tesco Extra and Asda superstores make it increasingly difficult to discern where the original sections are actually located—especially as the superstores occupy what should have been open spaces left around the Central Area. Second, substantial parts of the early phases of development are no longer there (Fig. 14.4). The Golden Eagle Hotel, which had proven unprofitable and had stood empty for some years, was quickly demolished when constructional faults with the panelling appeared. The North Car Park and adjacent sections of Phase 1 were pulled down in 2002–3. The penthouse deck narrowly avoided the same fate after major flaws developed in one of the massive supporting concrete beams. Here, demolition was rejected primarily because of the virtual impossibility of its being done on top of an active town center.

These, however, were just part of a raft of constructional and functional problems that have turned the scheme that Banham (1976: 170) once referred to as the "most comprehensive paradigm of what an urban megastructure should be" into a paradigm of the more general failings of 1960s town center renewal (Gold 2013). The Centre still suffers from the legacy of cost cutting, especially manifested in poor-quality work and finishes. The contractor, Logan, had left no records of major

FIGURE 14.4 Demolitions on north side, Cumbernauld

elements of design, such as with regard to the steel reinforcement in the main concrete structures.[20] The concrete finishes were unable to cope with water percolation. The microclimate proved every bit as inclement for users as had been forecast, requiring enclosure to make conditions more hospitable. Considerable sums, therefore, had to be spent on glazed roofing and side enclosure to rectify the wind tunnel effects along the semi-open malls (Cowling 1997: 59). Lifts and escalators broke down. Vandalism created problems until surfaces were refinished with graffiti-proof materials and the main areas were enclosed and fully patrolled. Potential developers found the center unattractive internally and externally. Even the much-vaunted extensibility turned out to be a myth, with any significant change to the center's concrete carapace proving uneconomic and disruptive.[21]

Yet care is needed before Olympian judgments are made that relate the fate of Cumbernauld's megastructure to the architectural prototypes that underpinned its construction. Any such narrative has to recognize that development was hamstrung from the outset by a series of decisions that lay outside the architectural field. These included the initial location (Cumbernauld, not Houston); the amount and quality of land left after the loss of the Lanarkshire portion; choosing the hilltop site and failing to tackle its inherent problems adequately; and the decision to permit building in the open spaces.[22] To these should be added the problems of undertaking a project with a twenty-year or greater time horizon in the light of changing economic and cultural circumstances. Official willingness to back the town center scheme soon evaporated, with a commensurate diminution of resources. This was particularly so after the financial crises of the late 1960s placed general pressures on major capital projects in the public sector. The resulting economizing adversely affected constructional work across the sector but was particularly serious for unconventional buildings using materials like concrete—which needed exacting standards of workmanship if it was to function effectively. By the early 1970s, changes in personnel, functional needs, and aesthetic tastes also contributed to an unwillingness to complete Cumbernauld's Central Area as originally envisaged. The net result was that, iconic though Phase 1 and the reduced Phase 2 might have been, they were not the full megastructure but just "a tiny wee bit of it."[23]

The countervailing comments, of course, are not made to absolve the architect from responsibility for the list of problems that had arisen from this particular application of modernist principles to urban development. Naturally Copcutt and his team, like many of their professional colleagues, relished the opportunity "to forge an urban morphology" (Copcutt 1997) for the emerging society and drew on their skills to craft an appropriate modernity. They also sought the freedom to implement their creativity. Yet, here as elsewhere, their ability to execute their chosen designs was severely and, in many respects, properly constrained. What the saga of Cumbernauld's town center shows is not the heroic exercise of untrammeled vision but the relationship between architectural creativity and the contexts—economic, political, professional, social, and cultural—in which the architects worked. Above all, it also shows the need to situate an understanding of the practice of modernism in terms of those wider contexts and to recognize, in a sophisticated manner, the thoroughgoing importance of the complexities inherent within them.

Acknowledgments

This chapter builds on research originally funded by the Arts and Humanities Research Board. I acknowledge this support as well as the assistance of David Whitham and Miles Glendinning, who generously loaned me unpublished materials.

Notes

1 In passing, it is worth noting that even then it only gradually ousted such rival terms as "omnibuilding" (e.g. *Progressive Architecture* 1968).
2 Indeed, it may be argued that the Crystal Palace, built for the 1851 Great Exhibition in London's Hyde Park, was one of the century's most influential structures for the nature of its encompassing structure and its innovatory use of large interior spaces, (see Gold and Gold 2005).
3 Interview with Rodney Gordon, November 11, 2004. See also Oxman et al. 2002.
4 A sample of the extraordinary range of schemes suggested can be found in Habraken 1972; Lampugnani 1982; Pawley 1990: 102–11; Thomsen 1994; Sadler 1998; Wigley 1998; Burden 2000; Eaton 2001; Pinder 2005; Friedman 2006; Alison et al. 2007; Gold 2007: 246–64.
5 Interview with Alex Kerr, December 2, 2004. For further information on Cumbernauld, see *Architects' Journal* 1958, 1962, 1963, 1966, 1968a, 1968b; *Architectural Review* 1964, 1967, 1968; Nuttgens 1967; Johnson 1973; Johnson and Johnson 1977; Wilson and Gibbs 1962.
6 Interview with Dr. Derek Lyddon, December 3, 2004.
7 A contrast drawn by Oliver Cox, interviewed November 2, 2004. For details of the Hook project, see London County Council (1961): an extraordinary text that explains better than any other available source the philosophy behind not only Hook but also Cumbernauld, from which its designers had drawn considerable influence.
8 Interview with Alex Kerr, December 2, 2004.
9 *Ibid.*
10 Copcutt (1997) seems to dispute this and stated that tasks were assigned by tossing a coin. Derek Lyddon has no recollection of this and suggests that it was highly unlikely: interview with Dr. Derek Lyddon, December 3, 2004.
11 Interview with Alex Kerr, December 2, 2004.
12 Interview with Dr. Derek Lyddon, December 3, 2004.
13 Unpublished handwritten note to the author from Alex Kerr, December 2004.
14 Much of this and the following paragraph come from the manuscript draft of chapter 6 of *Building a New Town*, an unpublished edited collection of essays compiled in 1963–4 by Rod Hardy (I am grateful to David Whitham for giving me access to this material). The chapter in question carries Hugh Wilson's initials. This point also draws on CNTDC (1962).
15 Interview with Alex Kerr, December 2, 2004. Each was ruled out on grounds of cost.
16 Originally coined in 1950 as a joke by the Swedish architect Hans Asplund, the word "Brutalism" had been appropriated with enthusiasm by younger British architects, such as Peter and Alison Smithson, to describe their work (see Gold 1997).
17 Interview with Alex Kerr, December 2, 2004.
18 Quoted in an unpublished memorandum written in April 1995 by Brigadier Colin H. Cowan entitled "Individual thoughts on Cumbernauld Town Centre." Cowan was the General Manager/Chief Executive of Cumbernauld Development Corporation, 1970–85. I am grateful to Miles Glendinning for permitting me access to this document.
19 *Ibid.*
20 *Ibid.*
21 *Ibid.*
22 Interview with Alex Kerr, December 2, 2004.
23 This comes from an anecdote told by Alex Kerr (interviewed December 2, 2004). He recalled visiting Cumbernauld with Copcutt in the mid-1960s after he had moved to the Scottish Office and Copcutt had moved to Dublin. Inspecting the scene when Phase 1 was being constructed, Copcutt noted wistfully that "at least we got a tiny wee bit of it,"

References

Abercrombie, P., and Matthew, R. H. (1949) *The Clyde Valley Regional Plan 1946*. Edinburgh: HMSO.

Alison, J., Brayer, M. A., Migayrou, F., and Spiller, N. (eds.) (2007) *Future City: Experiment and Utopia in Architecture*. London: Thames and Hudson.

Architects' Journal (1958) Cumbernauld New Town: preliminary planning proposals. *Architects' Journal*, 127: 858–9.

Architects' Journal (1962) Cumbernauld: new town centre. *Architects' Journal*, 136: 1279–88.
Architects' Journal (1963) Cumbernauld—worth a blow. *Architects' Journal*, 139: 1116.
Architects' Journal (1966) Dream and reality. *Architects' Journal*, 144: 718.
Architects' Journal (1968a) Cumbernauld wins for "community architecture." *Architects' Journal*, 145: 1149.
Architects' Journal (1968b) Town centre: Phase 1. *Architects' Journal*, 147: 293–310.
Architectural Review (1964) Hill-top living: housing at Cumbernauld New Town. *Architectural Review*, 135: 93–9.
Architectural Review (1967) Town centre: Cumbernauld. *Architectural Review*, 142: 445–51.
Architectural Review (1968) Central area: Cumbernauld, Scotland. *Architectural Review*, 43: 20–1.
Banham, P. R. (1976) *Megastructure: Urban Futures of the Recent Past*. London: Thames and Hudson.
Blake, P. (1961) The fantastic world of Paolo Soleri. *Architectural Forum*, 114: 104–9.
Burden, E. (2000) *Visionary Architecture: Unbuilt Works of the Imagination*. New York: McGraw-Hill.
Burns, J. T., Jr. (1972) Social and psychological implications of megastructures, in G. Kepes (ed.), *Arts of the Environment*. London: Aidan Ellis.
Chambless, E. (1910) *Roadtown*. New York: Roadtown Press.
CNTDC (Cumbernauld New Town Development Corporation) (undated) *Cumbernauld Town Centre: preliminary report*. Cumbernauld, U.K.: CNTDC.
CNTDC (1962) *Planning Proposals—Second Revision: Second Addendum Report to the Preliminary Planning Proposals*. Cumbernauld, U.K.: CNTDC.
Collymore, P. (1995) *The Architecture of Ralph Erskine*. London: Academy Editions.
Copcutt, G. (1963) Cumbernauld New Town central area. *Architectural Design*, May: 210–1.
Copcutt, G. (1997) Reflections on Cumbernauld town centre, in A. Burton and J. Hartley (eds.), *New Towns Record*, CD-ROM 1. Glasgow: Planning Exchange.
Le Corbusier (1935) *La Ville Radieuse*, trans. (1966) as *The Radiant City*. London: Faber and Faber.
da Costa Meyer, E. (1995) *The Work of Antonio Sant'Elia: Retreat into the Future*. New Haven: Yale University Press.
Cowling, D. (1997) *An Essay for Today: The Scottish New Towns, 1947 to 1997*. Edinburgh: Rutland Press.
Curl, J. S. (1999) *A Dictionary of Architecture*. Oxford: Clarendon Press.
Curtis, W. J. R. (1996) *Modern Architecture since 1900*. Oxford: Phaidon.
Eaton, R. (2001) *Ideal Cities: Utopianism and the (Un)Built Environment*. London: Thames and Hudson.
Friedmann, Y. (2006) *Pro Domo*. Barcelona: Actar.
Glendinning, M. (1992) Cluster city (unpublished manuscript).
Glendinning, M. (1996) Megastructure and genius loci: the architecture of Cumbernauld New Town, in *Proceedings Fourth DOCOMOMO International Conference*. Bratislava: DOCOMOMO.
Gold, J. R. (1997) *The Experience of Modernism: Modern Architects and the Future City, 1928–53*. London: Spon.
Gold, J. R. (2006) The making of a megastructure: architectural modernism, town planning and Cumbernauld's central area, 1955–75. *Planning Perspectives*, 21: 109–31.
Gold, J. R. (2007) *The Practice of Modernism: Modern Architects and Urban Transformation, 1954–72*. London: Routledge.
Gold, J. R. (2008) Modernity and utopia, in P. Hubbard, T. Hall, and J. R. Short (eds.), *The Sage Companion to the City*, 67–86. London: Sage.
Gold, J. R. (2013) Modernist narratives of renewal and the historiography of cross-national urban regeneration, in M. E. Leary and J. McCarthy (eds.), *Handbook of Urban Regeneration*. London: Routledge.
Gold, J. R., and Gold, M. M. (2005) *Cities of Culture: Staging International Festivals and the Urban Agenda, 1851–2000*. Aldershot, U.K.: Ashgate.
Habraken, N. J. (1972) *Supports: An Alternative to Mass Housing*. New York: Praeger.
Hall, P. (1963) *London 2000*. London: Faber and Faber.
Hall, P. (1968) Monumental follies. *New Society*, 12 (24 October): 602–3.
Hays, K. M. (1992) *Modernism and the Posthumanist Subject: The Architecture of Hannes Mayer and Ludwig Hilberseimer*. Cambridge: MIT Press.
Houghton-Evans, W. (1975) *Planning Cities: Legacy and Portent*. London: Lawrence and Wishart.
Jencks, C. (1973) *Modern Movements in Architecture*. Harmondsworth: Penguin.

Johnson, J. H. (1973) Cumbernauld extended. *Architects' Journal*, 157: 1095–7.
Johnson, J. H., and Johnson, K. (1977) Cumbernauld revisited. *Architects' Journal*, 166: 637–49.
Kadleigh, S., and Horsbrugh, P. (1952) *High Paddington: A Town for 8,000 People*. London: Architect and Building News.
Lampugnani, V. M. (1982) *Visionary Architecture of the 20th Century: Master Drawings from Frank Lloyd Wright to Aldo Rossi*. London: Thames and Hudson.
Larsson, L. O. (1984) Metropolitan architecture, in A. Sutcliffe (ed.), *Metropolis, 1890–1940*, 191–220. London: Mansell.
London County Council (1961) *The Planning of a New Town: Design Based on a Study for a New Town of 100,000 at Hook, Hampshire*. London: LCC.
Longstreth, R. (2010) *The American Department Store Transformed, 1920–1960*. New Haven: Yale University Press.
Maki, F. (1964) *Investigations in Collective Form*. St. Louis: Washington University, School of Architecture.
Makowski, Z. S. (1965) *Steel Space Structures*. London: Michael Joseph.
McBeth, J. (2002) Cumbernauld goes from joke to World Heritage Site. *The Scotsman*, 21 June.
Nuttgens, P. (1967) Criticism: Cumbernauld town centre. *Architectural Review*, 142: 441–4.
Oxman, R., Shadar, H., and Belferman, E. (2002) Casbah: a brief history of a design concept. *Architectural Research Quarterly*, 6: 321–36.
Pawley, M. (1990) *Theory and Design in the Second Machine Age*. Oxford: Blackwell.
Pierce, P. (2001) *Old London Bridge: The Story of the Longest Inhabited Bridge in Europe*. London: Headline.
Pinder, D. (2005) *Visions of the City: Utopianism, Power and Politics in Twentieth-Century Urbanism*. Edinburgh: Edinburgh University Press.
Pinder, D. (2010) Necessary dreaming: uses of utopia in urban planning, in J. Hillier and P. Healey (eds.), *Ashgate Research Companion to Planning Theory: Conceptual Challenges for Spatial Theory*, 343–64. Farnham, U.K.: Ashgate.
Progressive Architecture (1968) Omnibuilding: special section. *Progressive Architecture*, 44: 89–158.
Ravetz, A. (1980) *Remaking Cities*. London: Croom Helm.
Reiner, T.A. (1963) *The Place of the Ideal Community in Urban Planning*. Pittsburgh: University of Pittsburgh Press.
Riani, P. (ed.) (1969) *Kenzo Tange*. London: Hamlyn.
Sadler, S. (1998) *The Situationist City*. Cambridge: MIT Press.
Sadler, S. (2005) *Archigram: Architecture without Architecture*. Cambridge: MIT Press.
Segal, H. P. (1985) *Technological Utopianism in American Culture*. Chicago: University of Chicago Press.
Soleri, P. (1969) *Arcology: The City in the Image of Man*. Cambridge: MIT Press.
Sterken, S. (2003) Between the Visionary and the Archaic: Iannis Xenakis's Cosmic City. *Proceedings of the ISUF International Conference*. Online. Available HTTP: <https://biblio.ugent.be/input?func=downloadFile&fileOId=552954> (accessed 29 December 2011).
Taut, B. (1919) *Alpine Architektur*. Hagen: Folkwang-Verlag.
Taut, B. (1929) *Modern Architecture*. London: The Studio.
Thomsen, C. W. (1994) *Visionary Architecture: From Babylon to Virtual Reality*. Munich: Prestel.
Webb, M. (1969) *Architecture in Britain Today*. Feltham, U.K.: Country Life Books.
Wigley, M. (1998) *Constant's New Babylon: The Hyper-Architecture of Desire*. Witte-de-With: 010 Publishers.
Wilson, L. H. (1959a) *Cumbernauld New Town: Preliminary Planning Proposals*. Cumbernauld: Cumbernauld New Town Development Corporation.
Wilson, L. H. (1959b) Cumbernauld. *Prospect*, 13 (Spring): 13–4.
Wilson, L. H., and Gibbs, A. K. (1962) Cumbernauld New Town, mark II: a plan to master the motor car. *Architects' Journal*, 136: 276–84.
Xenakis, I. (1965) La ville cosmique, in F. Choay (ed.), *L'Urbanisme: Utopies et Réalités*, 335–42. Paris: Seuil.

15

MORPHOLOGICAL PROCESSES, PLANNING, AND MARKET REALITIES

Reshaping the Urban Waterfront in Auckland and Wellington

Kai Gu

Port cities all around the world face great challenges as they seek to redevelop their urban waterfronts in the interest of economic competitiveness and place promotion. Research on urban waterfront transformation, since at least the 1960s and 1970s, has been concerned with changing political-economic frameworks and waterfront revival; urban waterfront planning and design; spatial and land-use changes in waterfront districts; the role of history and heritage in waterfront revitalization; and ecological and environmental issues concerning waterfronts (Forward 1969; Gordon 1999; Hoyle 1994). Much of this research, by both researchers and practitioners, has been multidisciplinary and regionally comparative. Although waterfront redevelopment has many dimensions (Hoyle et al. 1988; Marshall 2001), it is concerned essentially with the spatial impact on the physical environment of proposals for new development and the spatial coordination of the various functions and activities that they would require in relation to the urban fabric at the all-important junction of land and water. In this connection, a morphologically-based inquiry into the modes of decision making that underlie the spatial character and dynamics of the waterfront landscape offers the possibility of providing a sound footing for accountable waterfront planning and design.

The urban morphological approach, notably that part of it relating to the evolutionary method of plan analysis, was especially developed in the mid-twentieth century by M. R. G. Conzen. According to Conzen (1960: 4–5), the urban landscape comprises three morphological elements: the ground plan (comprising streets, plots, and the block plans of buildings); the building fabric; and land and building utilization. It is possible to divide an urban area, based on one or all of these morphological elements, into landscape divisions that each have a unity distinguishing them from adjoining areas (Whitehand 1967: 223). Distinguishing and characterizing such urban landscape divisions and the relations between them, based on their historico-geographical development, not only helps to understand the spatial structure of towns and cities but serves as a basis for creating and managing urban landscapes. In particular, its practical significance has been discussed and demonstrated in the fields of urban conservation, urban design, and land-use planning (Baker 2010; Samuels 2008; Whitehand and Morton 2004).

Commercial waterfronts in cities frequently comprise important segments of an even broader subtype of cityscape known as *urban fringe belts*. Fringe belts derive their unity from certain common factors that influenced their original location near the margin of the built-up area (Whitehand 1967:

223). Such belts are zones of heterogeneous land use initially seeking peripheral locations during periods of minimal outward residential growth. They eventually become embedded within the urban area when residential growth resumes (M. P. Conzen 2009). Fringe belts are distinguished from other parts of the city by their generally larger ownership parcels, lower residential presence, higher proportion of open ground and lower building coverage, lower street density, and greater vegetative cover (Whitehand and Morton 2004). A fringe belt frequently includes important ecological and heritage features and open spaces, which are normally important public amenities. Applying the fringe-belt concept in urban planning and design began to be explored after the late 1990s. In particular, urban morphologists have explored the fringe-belt idea as an integrated planning approach, as significant for urban design policy, and as having strong implications for urban ecology and sustainable development (Hopkins 2004; Kropf 2001; Whitehand and Morton 2004). Though the logical and empirical bases for such investigations may be clear, more explicit operational methods and examples from more diverse geographical settings are needed to reveal the value of the fringe-belt concept to policy makers and urban designers.

Well-established urban fringe belts exist surrounding the central business districts (CBDs) of most cities and coincide with what has been called the CBD frame (Horwood and Boyce 1959: 9–26). In an early classic fringe-belt study in Newcastle upon Tyne, M. R. G. Conzen (1962) noted that the city's expanding CBD was a major influence on the development of the city's adjacent "inner fringe belt." The CBD reflects the centralizing forces that concentrate economic activities at the urban core, whereas fringe belts record those portions of the urban area conditioned by accumulations of larger space-using sites and structures, such as institutions, transport facilities, market gardens, nurseries, allotment gardens, cemeteries, parks, and playing fields (M. P. Conzen 2009: 30). The original land uses of commercial waterfront areas adjacent to the CBDs of many port cities include cargo and passenger transfer facilities and marine industries and services, all essential for urban growth. It is not surprising, therefore, that such waterfront areas are frequently full of such typical fringe-belt elements. This is particularly well illustrated in New Zealand, where the commercial waterfronts of Auckland and Wellington were created mainly from land reclamation schemes after the mid-nineteenth century and largely retained their original land uses until the late 1980s. Though fringe belts have been identified as structural components of many cities around the world (M. P. Conzen 2009), there has been very little examination of this concept in Australasia. This chapter seeks to fill this lacuna, particularly in light of the challenges and opportunities for planning that are facing the central areas of these two New Zealand cities (Morrison and McMurray 1999; Murphy 2008).

Auckland and Wellington's economic prosperity has always been intimately linked with the trade through their ports. The commercial waterfront areas of the two cities are also rich in Maori and European colonial heritage (Auckland Regional Council and Auckland City Council 2005; Waterfront Leadership Group 2001: 11–12). The dynamic relationship between city and sea resembles that in other cities, such as Sydney, Cape Town, Vancouver, and San Francisco. The commercial waterfront areas in Auckland and Wellington are similar in their size, history, and political-economic contexts. However, the contrasting dynamics of waterfront redevelopment in the two cities, especially in the past two or three decades, has resulted in quite different patterns in their built environment and different socioeconomic consequences. To what extent can the fringe-belt idea contribute to the understanding of the character of the urban waterfront landscape and its changing dynamics? Can this strengthen waterfront planning and design practice? These and related questions will be explored in an examination of the changing forms of, and varying pressures for change within, Auckland and Wellington's commercial waterfront areas.

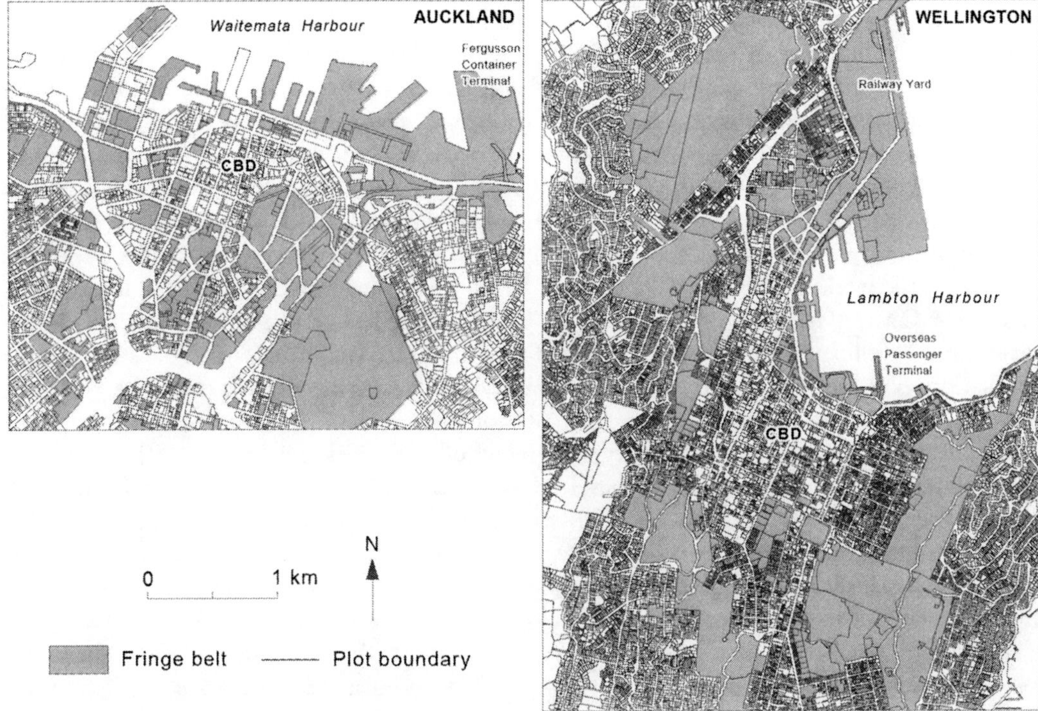

FIGURE 15.1 The inner fringe belts of Auckland and Wellington, New Zealand. Based on Auckland and Wellington GIS data (Auckland City Council 2010; Wellington City Council 2010) and author's field survey, 2008–10

Inner Fringe Belts and Commercial Waterfront Areas in Auckland and Wellington

Auckland, with a population of 1.46 million in 2010, is the largest conurbation in New Zealand. The geographical boundary of its CBD is traditionally defined by the southern edge of Waitemata Harbour on the north and the region's motorway system on the other three sides (Fig. 15.1). Wellington, New Zealand's national capital, has about one-third of Auckland's population. Its CBD is generally defined by a motorway to the west and south, a railway yard to the north, and Lambton Harbour to the east (Page 1996a; see Fig. 15.1). Both Auckland and Wellington have about a 170-year European urban history, and the different periods of development have left their marks on the ground. The succession of forms from 1840 onward, particularly in terms of ground plans and building types, reflects the evolution of the society from its early colonial days.

The methods of delimiting fringe belts in this study are derived mainly from town-plan analysis (Conzen 1960), notably the reconstruction of the urban development process through analyses of historical series of ground plans and documentary records. A plot-by-plot field survey established the current characteristics of fringe-belt land uses, focusing here on the high-density city core and residential areas developed up to the early twentieth century. In the case of Auckland, a recent study has traced the formation of a set of three concentric urban fringe belts on the metropolitan isthmus (Gu 2010). Here the focus is on the inner fringe belts of both Auckland and Wellington that circumscribe their CBDs—the most extensive historical areas of the two cities—and on the agents of change that have recently been transforming them.

The way in which the inner fringe belts surrounding the CBDs of Auckland and Wellington developed resembles that of numerous other cities. In addition to fluctuations in socioeconomic development and the adoption of new transport modes, it is topography and land reclamation that have been the major factors influencing inner fringe-belt formation in the two cities. In Wellington, the inner fringe belt largely overlaps with its historic "town belt"—a belt of reservation land designated during the design of the town in the 1840s—and provides a green, open space for the pleasure and health of its citizens. The town belts established around the settlements planned on the Wakefield model in Australia and New Zealand (Bunker 1988; Reed 1952: 182) were unique for their time anywhere in the world (Wellington City Council 2010). Like fringe belts generally (see, for example, Barke 1974; Carter 1983; Carter and Wheatley 1979), the fringe-belt zones surrounding the CBDs of Auckland and Wellington have inherited much of their character, particularly their low street density and spacious plots, from the time when these zones stood at the fringes of the cities (see Fig. 15.1). The commercial waterfronts adjacent to the CBDs of Auckland and Wellington, which have been undergoing major transformation, are integral segments of these cities' inner fringe belts (Fig. 15.2).

Both waterfronts were created by a series of land reclamation schemes starting in the mid-nineteenth century. Their development before the 1980s can be divided generally into three phases. The first extended from the mid- to the late-nineteenth century, dominated by an augmentative process of land reclamation to satisfy increasing demands for marine transport, industries, and services. Beginning already in the 1880s, the reclaimed land began to be used to accommodate the early railway development of both cities. The second phase extended from the early twentieth century to the 1950s, when rapid economic growth, especially during the inter-war period, stimulated further waterfront expansion. The third phase lasted from the 1960s to the late 1970s, when containerization led to the expansion of existing loading areas and the creation of larger wharves (Anderson 1984; Auckland Harbour Board 1973: 4–6; Wellington City Council 2005; McClean 1997; Fig. 15.3). By the late 1970s, the major land reclamations were complete in both cities. By the early twenty-first century, the extent of land reclaimed amounted to about 328 hectares and 360 hectares respectively in Auckland and Wellington. Though Wellington has just one-third of Auckland's population, its land reclamation area is slightly larger than that of Auckland's harbor region. The scarcity of flat land in Wellington's central area largely explains its pressing need to reclaim land. These zones of made land neatly define the waterfront portions of both cities' inner fringe belt.

A striking outcome of the dynamics of these waterfront expansions is the formation of contrasting "plan units," to use Conzenian terminology, within them. Nine plan units (1–9) and seven plan units (A–G) can be identified in the waterfronts of Auckland and Wellington, which largely define their landscape character (Fig. 15.4). Each unit represents an individualized combination of streets, plots, and buildings distinct from its neighbors, unique in its site circumstances, and endowed with a measure of morphological unity or homogeneity. Following Conzenian methods (Conzen 1960), Tables 15.1 and 15.2 summarize the characteristics of streets, plots, and buildings of the plan units in the two cities' waterfront areas. In both Auckland and Wellington, an extensive railway yard unit lies adjacent to a large port unit; the combined land area of the two units dedicated to transport accounts for about 50 percent of the total waterfront area. The plan units directly bordering the CBDs in both cities have smaller plots and higher building density. The built environment of these units, especially the Fort Street unit in Auckland and the Central Area unit and the Wakefield Street unit in Wellington, appear to be natural extensions of their CBDs.

Further analysis of the strengths and weaknesses of the plan units in terms of their physical characteristics is important for site-specific planning and design. In contrast to the two plan units

FIGURE 15.2 The waterfront areas adjacent to the CBDs in Auckland and Wellington. A) Auckland, the Fergusson Container Terminal is in the foreground to the right (Port of Auckland 2010); B) Wellington, the Overseas Passenger Terminal and Waitangi Park are in the mid-ground to the right and left respectively

along Wellington's harbor edge, fully four plan units can be identified along Auckland's harbor edge. This difference presents a variable challenge to waterfront planning and design, if the aim is to develop more continuous and cohesive space along the harbor edge. In addition to enhancing the connectivity between the CBD and the waterfront, planning strategy that focuses on the links between the plan units will help to maintain and improve the integrity of the waterfront landscapes.

Fringe-belt zones, like other parts of a city, are subject to cycles of adaptation and redevelopment, which usually involve a change of land use. In Auckland and Wellington, while significant

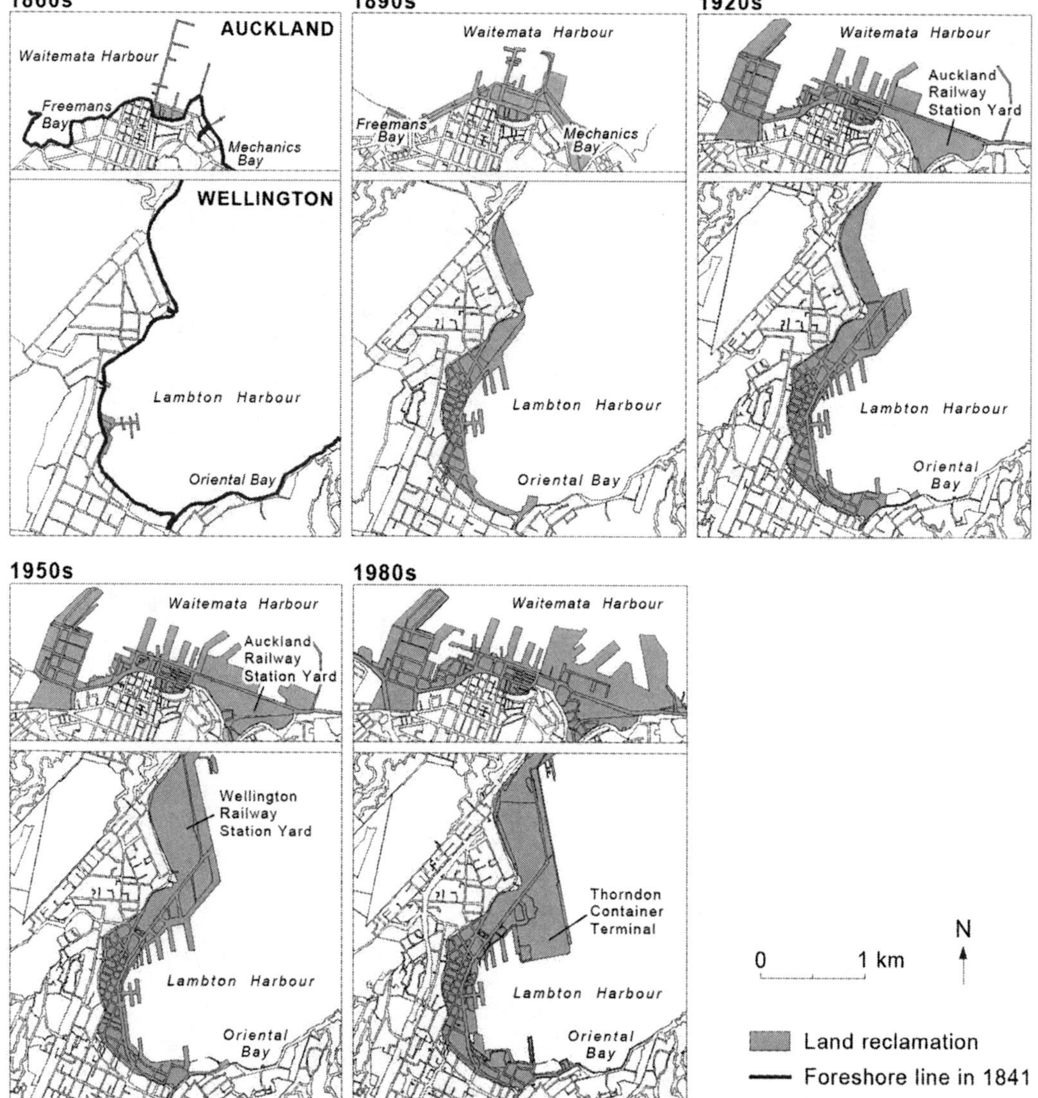

FIGURE 15.3 The formative processes of the waterfront areas in Auckland and Wellington. Based on Gu (2010: 54) and Anderson (1984: 124–6)

waterfront territory, especially the docks and railway yards, remains in original use, many traditional land uses along the waterfront have begun to be replaced by alternative uses since the early 1990s. The remainder of this chapter examines what has become a major phenomenon in Auckland and Wellington—waterfront redevelopment. It describes the changing waterfront landscapes and seeks to explain the physical changes in terms of the key morphological agencies at work and their evolving roles in the development and implementation of waterfront planning and design.

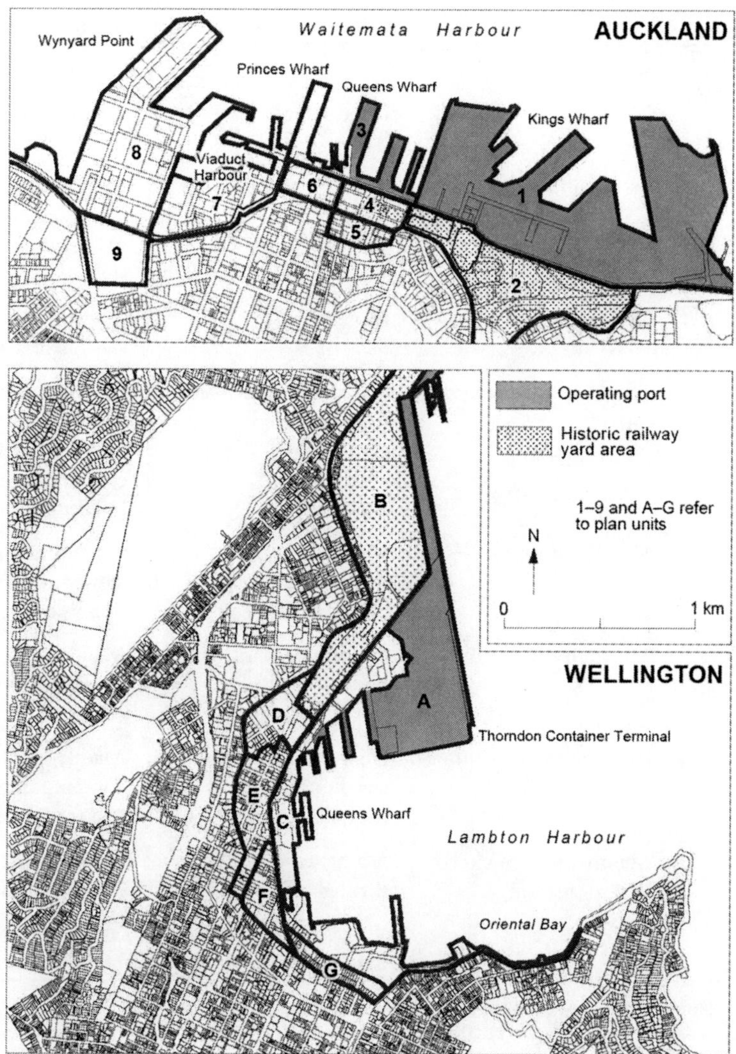

FIGURE 15.4 Principal plan units in Auckland and Wellington's waterfront areas. 1) Port unit; 2) Quay Park unit; 3) Central wharfs unit; 4) Britomart unit; 5) Fort Street unit; 6) Central area unit; 7) Viaduct Harbour unit; 8) Wynyard Point unit; 9) Victoria Park unit. A) Port unit; B) Railway yard unit; C) Harbour edge unit; D) Whitmore Street unit; E) Central area unit; F) Civic center unit; G) Wakefield Street unit. Based on author's field survey, 2008–10

Auckland's Waterfront Redevelopment: A Process of Urban Intensification

With changes in port operations, transport modes, and the progressive expirations in the industrial leases in the reclamation land in the 1980s, many waterfront areas in Auckland deteriorated, and authorities began to search for alternative uses. Waterfront redevelopment attracted wider public attention in 1989 when the City Council's Harbour Edge Project was announced. Substantial changes did not begin until 1993 when the "Whitbread around the World Race" led to the

TABLE 15.1 Characteristics of streets, plots, and buildings of the plan units in Auckland's waterfront area

	Streets	*Plots*	*Buildings*
Port unit	Occupation streets	Large singular plot	Mainly low-rise buildings serving cargo transport
Quay Park unit	Irregular curving streets	Medium-sized irregular plots	Mixture of commercial and residential buildings, mainly in contemporary style
Central wharf unit	Occupation streets	Large plots	Mixture of contemporary and historical buildings
Britomart unit	Through streets in grid pattern	Mixture of small- and medium-sized plots	Mixture of historical warehouses, public buildings and modern and contemporary commercial buildings
Fort Street unit	Mainly through streets	Mixture of small through plots and irregularly shaped plots	Mixture of historical and contemporary commercial buildings
Central area unit	Through streets	Mainly medium-sized plots	Mainly modern and contemporary high-rise commercial buildings
Viaduct Harbour unit	Irregular through streets	Mixture of medium-sized through plots and irregularly shaped plots	Mainly mid-rise contemporary commercial and residential buildings
Wynyard Point unit	Mainly through streets in grid pattern	Mainly medium-sized through plots	Mainly low-rise marine service and industrial buildings
Victoria Park unit	N/A	Large singular plot	N/A

Sources: Based on author's field survey, 2008–10

redevelopment of the inner wharf area by the Port of Auckland Limited. The redevelopment projects along the waterfront that followed were related to increasing demand for business growth and urban living. Urban intensification and mixed-use redevelopment have been key processes. Fringe-belt alienation—the acquisition of fringe-belt sites by land uses of quite different character (in this case, mainly multi-story commercial and apartment buildings and office blocks)—has eroded the integrity of the waterfront urban landscape and has had adverse effects on the public access to the city's harbor edge.

Land uses in the Viaduct Basin before the late 1990s included timber milling, boat building, cargo handling at the port, and fish processing (Fig. 15.5). Major redevelopment took place after the first running of the America's Cup yacht races in 1998. A large proportion of land was then transformed into apartments and commercial areas. Princes Wharf was built in 1923 to accommodate wool bale stores. The resulting concrete structure was adapted in 1960 as a passenger ship terminal and parking garage. The redevelopment project created between 1999 and 2001 a high-density, multi-

TABLE 15.2 Characteristics of streets, plots and buildings of the plan units in Wellington's waterfront area

	Streets	Plots	Buildings
Port unit	Occupation streets	Large plots	Mainly low-rise buildings serving cargo transport
Railway yard unit	Occupation streets	Medium- and small-sized plots along the edge of a large irregular plot	Mainly large public buildings
Harbour edge unit	Irregular through and occupation streets	Irregular medium- and small-sized plots	Mixture of public and commercial buildings
Whitmore Street unit	Irregular through streets	Medium-sized irregular plots, but small plots at south and west ends	Mainly historical, modern and contemporary public buildings
Central area unit	Through streets in grid pattern	Mixture of medium-sized through and small plots	Mixture of contemporary high-rise and historical commercial buildings
Civic center unit	Irregular through streets	Mixture of medium- and small-sized plots	Mixture of contemporary and historical public buildings
Wakefield Street unit	Through streets	Mainly back-to-back plots	Mixture of contemporary and historical commercial buildings

Sources: Based on author's field survey, 2010

use complex that included restaurants, retail shops, apartments, a car park, and a hotel. On the southern side of the port unit is the Quay Park. Much of the land was formerly owned by the New Zealand Railway Corporation and subsequently administered by the Department of Survey and Land Information. It is entirely reclaimed land and was the site of Auckland's former Central Rail Station, rail yards, and associated warehouse and industrial uses. In the past decade, contemporary apartments, an office park, Vector Arena, and intensive housing communities have been built, mainly along the edge of the Quay Park. Land-use changes to the Viaduct Basin, Princes Wharf and the Quay Park are characteristic of the fringe-belt alienations that have occurred. Privatization of the waterfront areas has been obviously dominant in Auckland. These developments have failed to improve public access to the city's harbor edge. In the total land area involved in the redevelopment by 2010, fringe-belt alienation accounts for about 27 hectares, which is more than ten times the land area that has maintained its fringe-belt character (see Fig. 15.5).

The vision for the waterfront set out by the City Council was that of "a world class destination that excites the senses and celebrates our sea-loving Pacific culture and our maritime history, commercially successful and innovative, a place for all people, rich in character and activity that truly links people, city and the sea" (Auckland City Council 2006: 12). However, the redevelopment projects implemented have not adequately protected historical landscapes and public amenities. Recent opportunities for redeveloping Auckland's waterfront area, which was still a largely public asset by the 1990s, could have created more generous and inviting places adjacent to the city's CBD, but redevelopment projects are frequently enclosed and segregated from neighboring urban

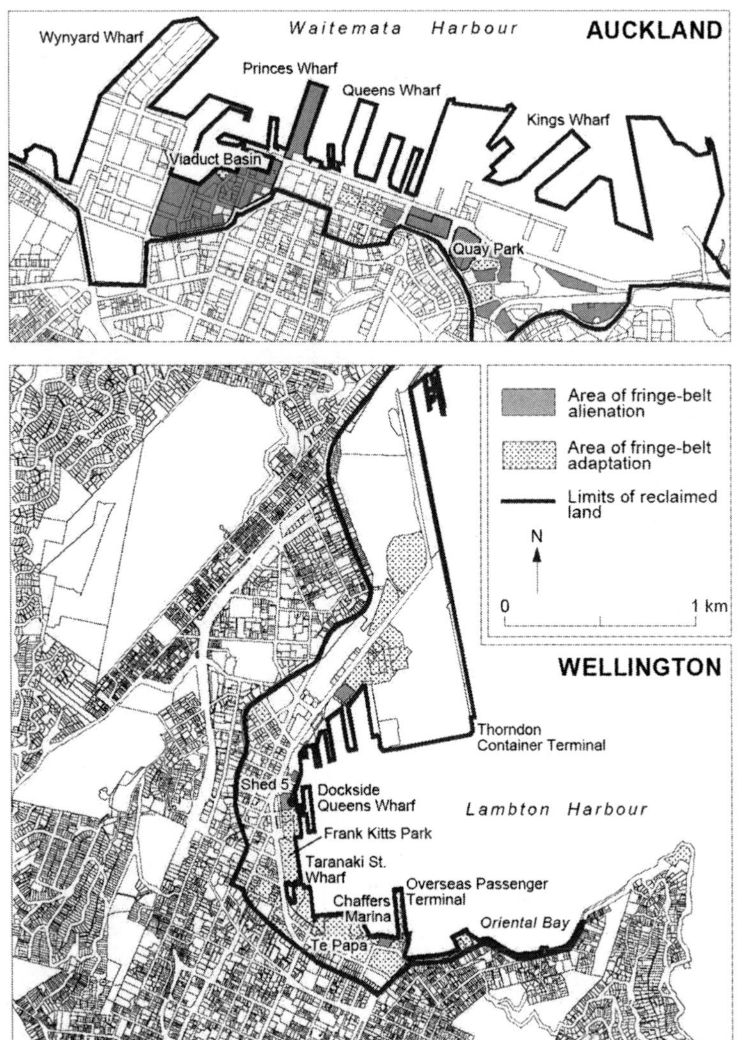

FIGURE 15.5 Areas of fringe-belt alienation and adaptation in Auckland and Wellington. Based on author's field survey, 2008–10

fabric, and the new plans give little consideration to maintaining the valuable historical, frequently highly permeable, urban landscape. According to a recent publication by the Royal Commission on Auckland Governance (2009), a government body responsible for making suggestions regarding future urban development, the poor quality of much of the built environment in the waterfront area has significantly reduced the amenity value of what could be the region's, and one of New Zealand's, most important areas (Royal Commission on Auckland Governance 2009: 196). This situation is in stark contrast to the new patterns of the built environment in Wellington's waterfront, which has contributed remarkably to public life and the socio-cultural development of the city.

Wellington's Waterfront Redevelopment: Creating a Landscape Servicing the Public and Tourism

In 1982, the Wellington Harbour Board and the City Council sponsored the Wellington Civic Trust to organize a competition and conference to plan the future of redundant port land resulting from the technological change that occurred in the shipping industry (Doorne 1998: 137). Redevelopment of Wellington's commercial waterfront commenced in 1987, when the Lambton Harbour Development Project was established as a partnership between the Wellington City Council and the Wellington Harbour Board. As a result, major redevelopment projects took place during the 1990s. Adaptive reuse of historical buildings and creation of a landscape of services and tourism were the key transformations.

Unlike the predominant process of fringe-belt alienation in Auckland's waterfront transformation, Wellington's waterfront has largely maintained its fringe-belt character. In particular, Frank Kitts Park was remodeled in 1990, along with the development of a lagoon. The Dockside and Shed 5 restaurants and bars opened in the early 1990s. The Overseas Passenger Terminal was transformed into an event facility in 1992. Chaffers Marina was completed in 1993. The creation of Queens Wharf events center, with underground parking and the development of Queens Wharf Square, were finished in 1995. A new National Museum, Te Papa, was opened in 1998 (Waterfront Leadership Group 2001: 8). The major waterfront redevelopment projects implemented in Wellington are characteristic of fringe-belt adaptation—the acquisition of fringe-belt sites by land uses of similar type and character. These developments have improved public access to open spaces. In contrast to the 2.4 hectares that can be characterized as fringe-belt alienation by 2010, the total land area of fringe-belt adaptation is about 24 hectares (see Fig. 15.5).

In Wellington, the City Council deliberately chose a path toward redevelopment that emphasized the attraction of the waterfront (Page 1996b). The waterfront development is designed to enhance the city's role in tourism and complement the promotion of itself as the events capital of New Zealand (Page 1993, 1996b: 341). Many old warehouses, sheds, and maritime industrial facilities have been redeveloped as art galleries, event arenas, museums, theaters, and sports clubs. Some vacant land and former public institutions have been transferred to individual commercial and residential developments on a much smaller scale compared with Auckland's urban intensification projects (see Fig. 15.5). Waterfront redevelopment in Wellington has demonstrated that a successful waterfront does not need to be expensive and luxurious but rather a vital focal point for community identity and an important catalyst for inner city improvement.

The redevelopment processes in the past two to three decades have set the built environments of the two New Zealand cities' waterfronts on divergent paths, with predictably different socioeconomic consequences (Gibson 2010). In Auckland—the largest commercial center in the country—the process of CBD colonization has come to dominate waterfront redevelopment. The waterfront fringe-belt zones are more susceptible than ever to the pressures for change, and in most cases they have succumbed to high-density commercial and residential developments—and not always with adequate coordination. The waterfront landscape in Auckland is, therefore, fragmented and lacks integration. In Wellington—New Zealand's governmental and cultural capital—the waterfront fringe-belt zones are more resistant to urban intensification and, consequently, the waterfront landscape is continuous and coherent. Wellington's waterfront has been reinvented by its custodians, who have thereby attracted new flows of global capital, achieved a balance of economic growth and public benefits, and visibly strengthened the relationship between the city and its waterfront. The differences in political economy and planning culture between Auckland and Wellington go some way to explaining the contrasts between their new waterfront landscapes. In common with many port cities around the world, the morphological agents of change in transforming the waterfronts of Auckland and Wellington include a mixture of government agencies, port authorities, the development industry, professional groups, and the general public. It is appropriate now to take a closer look at the interplay of these "actors" in the drama of waterfront redevelopment.

Managing Changes to the Waterfront Landscapes in Auckland and Wellington

In contrast to Wellington's clearly established institutional framework for waterfront management and a corresponding planning and design strategy from the beginning of the redevelopment cycle, in Auckland there has been a lack of sound leadership and effective management. In Wellington, a joint venture agreement was signed by the Wellington Harbour Board and the City Council in 1986. The agreement established a Special Development Zone, a Concept Plan, and the formation of two companies to provide the management and administration of the project—Lambton Harbour Overview Limited and Lambton Harbour Management Limited. The Lambton Harbour Development Concept Plan allowed for the creation of generous open spaces and retention and enhancement of existing buildings, together with provisions for new buildings (Lambton Harbour Group and Gabites Porter and Partners 1989). The developments undertaken were reviewed from 1996 to 1998 and a revised concept plan concluded, along with new funding arrangements. A three-stage process for developing and implementing a new plan for the waterfront was proposed and approved by the Council in 2000. Stage One was to develop a framework for the waterfront; Stage Two was to decide more detailed plans for each area; and Stage Three was to implement and monitor the plans. The Waterfront Leadership Group, established in 2000, produced the Wellington Waterfront Framework the following year (Waterfront Leadership Group 2001). In addition to the creation of a new waterfront vision with a greater emphasis on quality urban design, extensive public access, and greater connectivity with the CBD, a special priority for the future was placed on public engagement and transparency and the specific separation of planning and implementation with respect to waterfront management. The document was adopted in April 2001 and was followed by the creation of detailed development plans. The key planning and design documents guiding Wellington's waterfront redevelopment are shown in Table 15.3.

Although the redevelopment of Wellington's waterfront has been successful in developing public spaces and place identity, the processes have not always run smoothly. The 1989 Lambton Harbour Combined Scheme contained proposals for construction of a thirty-one-story building north of Queens Wharf known as Landmark Tower, a hotel and conference center on Taranaki Street Wharf, and an intensive housing development at Chaffers (Waterfront Leadership Group 2001: 8). These proposed projects can be characterized as fringe-belt alienations. The Landmark Tower project fell by the wayside after the stock market crash in 1987 (Waterfront Leadership Group 2001: 8). After a significant community outcry following the construction of the Retail and Event Centers, especially its Retail Center (subsequently used largely as an office precinct), there was a further review of development plans, which resulted in the withdrawal of the proposal for commercial developments at Taranaki Street Wharf and Chaffers Park. Open space development currently underway is focusing around the new Waitangi Park (previous Chaffers Park), a 6.5-hectare area adjacent to Chaffers Marina and close to Te Papa (Mistry 2005).

The key documents and proposals relating to overall waterfront planning and design prepared by various Auckland agencies involved in waterfront issues are presented in Table 15.4. It is evident

TABLE 15.3 Key urban planning and design documents prepared for Wellington's waterfront redevelopment

Year	*Title*	*Prepared by*	*Summary*
1986	Lambton Harbour Development Concept	Lambton Harbour Group and Gabites Porter and Partners	Urban planning and design concepts and proposals for Wellington's waterfront and its character areas
1989	Lambton Harbour Combined Scheme	Lambton Harbour Group and Gabites Porter and Partners	Urban planning and design principles and management strategy for waterfront transformation
1998	Wellington Waterfront Public Spaces Concept Plan	Wellington City Council	Provision and design of public open spaces and retention and enhancement of existing buildings
2001	The Wellington Waterfront Framework	Waterfront Leadership Group	Visions, principles and values that should govern future development and urban design of the waterfront and its character areas
2003–2010	Annual Waterfront Development Plan	Wellington Waterfront Limited	A work program to implement the objectives of the Framework, including how developments will be implemented, a phasing schedule and a financial model for the proposed work

TABLE 15.4 Key urban planning and design documents prepared for Auckland's waterfront redevelopment

Year	Title	Prepared by	Summary
1989	Auckland Harbour Edge Investigation Committee Report	Auckland Harbour Edge Investigation Committee	Detailed survey of Auckland's waterfront area and recommendations for future development opportunities
1991	Joint Harbour Edge Study Interim Report	Auckland Regional Council and Auckland City Council	Planning and design framework for waterfront redevelopment
2005	Auckland Waterfront 2040	Auckland Regional Council and Auckland City Council	Principles and implementation strategy to guide the future development of the waterfront
2009	Auckland City Centre Waterfront Masterplan	Auckland City Council	A strategic framework to guide future proposals for buildings, spaces, movements and water and land-based activates

that systematic studies of Auckland's harbor edge and future development opportunities had been undertaken before the large-scale redevelopment projects began (Auckland Harbour Edge Investigation Committee 1989; Auckland Regional Council and Auckland City Council 1991). However, the research findings and recommendations were not incorporated into planning and design proposals and policies. The early waterfront redevelopment projects were propelled by individual development proposals and managed by separate project corporations (Auckland City Council 1996, 2006). Auckland did not have a comprehensive planning and design guide for the entire waterfront until 2005 (Auckland Regional Council and Auckland City Council 2005) by which time the major redevelopment projects had been completed. In the absence of an agreed long-term plan and a clear investment direction, because politicians and owners change (Cormack 2009), it is not surprising that the new waterfront landscapes are fragmented and lack consistency. Although an integrated approach to waterfront development has been indicated in Waterfront Vision 2040 (Auckland Regional Council and Auckland City Council 2005), an effective management and policy framework has still been lacking. The City Council prepared the Auckland City Centre Waterfront Masterplan in 2009, but very limited research and plan implementation details have been included in this document (Auckland City Council 2009). Wellington's effective system of waterfront planning and design, including a waterfront framework, development plans, performance briefs, and detailed design, is unfortunately absent in Auckland.

In Auckland, the main public agencies involved in waterfront issues have been the Auckland Regional Council and the Auckland City Council. The former had a regulatory role with regard to the coastal marine area below the mean high water mark through its Regional Coastal Plan, while the latter agency was responsible for managing natural and physical resources above this mark through its District Plan. Those areas connecting water and land were the joint responsibility of both jurisdictions. The Auckland Regional Council included representation from the Auckland Regional Transport Authority and Auckland Regional Holdings (ARH), which were established in 2004. The ARH successfully completed its bid for 100 percent ownership of the Ports of Auckland Ltd in 2005. Most land and properties in the port area were handed over to be owned and managed by the ARH. However, one of the ARH's main functions was to generate returns from its investments to fund regional transport and stormwater programs. The financial targets and objectives of the ARH contributed very little to the realization of the City Council's socio-cultural objectives of waterfront redevelopment. The poor coordination between the management authorities and the absence of an effective urban landscape management and policy framework have been key problems. Those problems are particularly exemplified by the Wynyard Point project.

Wynyard Point, also known as the tank farm, is located on the western end of Auckland's waterfront area. It was zoned predominantly for port- and marine-related industrial activities. Wynyard Point is a beacon of Auckland's industrial past and is a prominent harbor landmark. Redevelopment of the area of thirty-five hectares that was originally reclaimed between 1905 and 1930 (Auckland Harbour Board 1973) has been proposed by the local authorities (Auckland Regional Council and Auckland City Council 2005). The aim of the project is to "optimize revenues" while delivering a "world class waterfront development" (Cayford 2008). The urban design proposals and planning documents for the future development of Wynyard Point reveal that some relatively unconstrained open spaces are to be provided. This is much needed in Auckland's waterfront, though its size could be more generous. Future development will, to a large extent, continue the previous patterns of urban intensification (Auckland City Council 2006).

Waterfront redevelopment in Auckland and Wellington has been directly influenced by statutory planning, including the Regional Coastal Plan and the District Plan. The statutory planning provisions are largely defined by the Resource Management Act (RMA), which was invented as part of a radical liberalization agenda of New Zealand in the early 1990s (Kelsey 1995). In contrast to the conventional "conforming land use" regulation, the current statutory planning adopts a "performance-based" approach, expressed as the management of the environmental effects of land uses. The RMA establishes a planning regime that has in practice been more reactive than strategic, and this has limited the ability of local authorities to pursue socioeconomic or cultural goals (Oram

2007). The consequences of this neo-liberal shift have become especially evident in the early waterfront redevelopment in Auckland, for example, the Princes Wharf (Cayford 2009) and Viaduct Basin projects (Eisenhut 2008), in which developer-driven market processes have been dominant.

At a more operational level, however, if waterfront development is to succeed, it is essential that an urban landscape management plan be based on an understanding of the spatial coherence and context of the built environment. The lack of a sound theoretical basis for interpreting and representing the urban landscape and its morphological processes contributes to the disjunction between plan and reality, which is a main source of frustration for urban planners and designers. It is unlikely that urban managers, planners, and designers in both Auckland and Wellington are aware of the fringe-belt concept. However, the practical significance of the fringe-belt idea lies in its potential to clarify and reinforce the rational and cultural basis for understanding the urban landscape as the meaningful outcome of general and place-specific historico-geographical development (M. R. G. Conzen 2004). Such a viewpoint is fundamental in formulating planning and design recommendations for the sensitive management of urban landscapes. Both Auckland and Wellington are striving to promote themselves as regional and international centers of culture, business, and tourism. Establishing a systematic understanding of the physical form of, and change to, their fringe belts and creating sound bases for urban waterfront landscape management are both much-needed objectives.

Conclusion

Fringe belts have been recognized as a powerful means of understanding the physical structure of urban areas in relation to the process of outward growth and internal change (Whitehand 1988). Fringe-belt zones are always subject to cycles of adaptation and redevelopment, which usually involve a change of land use. Different types of fringe-belt modification have direct planning implications. This chapter contributes to the exploration of fringe-belt evolution, especially its relevance to and value for contemporary urban planning and design.

The early growth of many towns and cities in New Zealand was fundamentally influenced by maritime history. Waterfront areas, therefore, have always been essential in the economic and socio-cultural development of the country. As in many port cities, a striking fringe belt that borders the CBD can clearly be recognized in Auckland and Wellington. The waterfronts of the two cities are integral segments of their inner fringe belts. Fringe belts frequently contain important urban heritage features, urban ecological corridors, and places for less restricted movement by urban populations. Recognition of these characteristics in the form of planning and design policy would benefit not just the tourist potential of the two cities but their residents' sense of tradition and continuity. In the processes of rapid waterfront transformation over the past two to three decades, reconciling the historical and cultural legacies embodied in that urban form with the accelerating stream of functional and economic impulses has been a challenging task.

As the waterfronts in Auckland and Wellington were still largely public assets before the beginning of the large-scale redevelopment, the government agencies and port authorities have been the key morphological agents of change in influencing the waterfront redevelopment. Though Auckland and Wellington are similar to each other in their planning and institutional contexts, the two cities have created contrasting new waterfront landscapes. In Auckland, waterfront privatization and the subsequent developer-driven development took place more widely than that in Wellington. It is evident that in the decision-making process, the influences of the "hidden" agendas and the individual leadership within organizational structures are considerable. To achieve an objective and accountable policy process, transparency, dialog, and debate are fundamental, and the media and public involvement should play a more critical role.

At an operational level, the lack of a theoretical basis for waterfront planning and design and an effective implementation strategy has directly contributed to the discrepancy between vision and reality. This is particularly evident in Auckland's waterfront redevelopment, in which a process of fringe-belt alienation has dominated the waterfront landscape change. It is argued that an appreciation of the importance of maintaining the integrity of the inner fringe belt as a whole and treating waterfront character on a scale beyond that of isolated parcels are essential for sound redevelopment management. A more comprehensive waterfront redevelopment and management framework that is based on a systematic investigation of the waterfront landscape characteristics and on an objective assessment of recent developments is fundamental to the future success of the waterfront.

Auckland's waterfront has been bedeviled by the complex governance and uncoordinated redevelopment objectives of the morphological agencies involved in the preparation and implementation of waterfront planning and design. The Royal Commission on Auckland Governance has recommended that any future development of the waterfront should be carried out by a waterfront agency with the capacity to design and implement a "master plan" for the area, as opposed to the piecemeal approach taken to date (Royal Commission on Auckland Governance 2009: 11–12). In response to the report, the Auckland Waterfront Development Agency was established in 2010 after the creation of the new Auckland Council, which combines the operations of the previous Auckland Regional Council and the city and district councils. It is expected that the Auckland Waterfront Development Agency will adopt a strategic approach to the development of Auckland's entire waterfront (Auckland Waterfront Development Agency 2010). However, it is likely that using waterfront redevelopment opportunities to promote immediate economic growth, as it has been pursued in the past two to three decades, remains one of the dominating development ideologies (Goodall 2010).

Comparative urban research has been used in studies of urban waterfront transformation. It has helped to overcome the problem of idiographic studies in which particular findings fail to yield useful generalizations. Comparative urban morphology makes it possible to identify urban landscapes common to different geographical regions; it also helps to distinguish unique historical characteristics and developments that are important for cities in seeking place identity. The fringe-belt concept provides a frame of reference for depicting, explaining, and comparing the physical structure and change of urban landscapes and the dynamics of morphological agencies. To prove the wider validity and significance of fringe belts for waterfront redevelopment as revealed in Auckland and Wellington, more empirical investigation from other geographical regions will be needed, but it should prove highly beneficial in the longer term.

Acknowledgments

The research on which this chapter is based was supported by the Performance Based Research Fund of the School of Architecture and Planning, University of Auckland. The author is grateful for research assistance from Jimmy Zhuang.

References

Anderson, G. (1984) *Fresh About Cook Strait: An Appreciation of Wellington Harbour*. Auckland: Methuen Publications NZ Ltd.

Auckland City Council (1996) *Viaduct Basin Update*. Auckland: Auckland City Council.

Auckland City Council (2006) *Draft Wynyard Point Concept Vision*. Auckland: Auckland City Council.

Auckland City Council (2009) *Auckland City Centre Waterfront Masterplan*. Auckland: Auckland City Council.

Auckland City Council (2010) *Auckland Council GIS Viewer*. Auckland: Auckland City Council. Online. Available HTTP: <http://maps.aucklandcouncil.govt.nz/ AucklandCouncilViewer/> (accessed 29 November 2010).

Auckland Harbour Board (1973) *Waitemata Harbour Study: Preliminary Report on Fill*. Auckland: Auckland Harbour Board.

Auckland Harbour Edge Investigation Committee (1989) *Auckland Harbour Edge Investigation Committee Report*. Auckland: Auckland Harbour Edge Investigation Committee.

Auckland Regional Council and Auckland City Council (1991) *Joint Harbour Edge Study Interim Report*. Auckland: Auckland Regional Council and Auckland City Council.

Auckland Regional Council and Auckland City Council (2005) *Auckland Waterfront 2040*. Auckland: Auckland Regional Council and Auckland City Council.

Auckland Waterfront Development Agency (2010) Our role in Auckland's waterfront. Auckland: Auckland Waterfront Development Agency. Online. HTTP: <http://www.waterfrontauckland.co.nz/About-AWDA/Our-Role.aspx> (accessed 30 November 2010).

Baker, N. (2010) *A Characterisation of the Historic Townscape of Central Hereford*. Hereford, U.K.: Herefordshire Council, Herefordshire Archaeology Report 266.

Barke, M. (1974) The changing urban fringe of Falkirk: some morphological implications of urban growth. *Scottish Geographical Magazine*, 90: 85–97.

Bunker, R. (1988) Systematic colonization and town planning in Australia and New Zealand. *Planning Perspectives*, 3: 59–80.

Carter, H. (1983) Suburbs, estates and fringe belts: the structure of urban extension, in H. Carter (ed.), *An Introduction to Urban Historical Geography*, 130–49. London: Edward Arnold.

Carter, H., and Wheatley, S. (1979) Fixation lines and fringe belts, land uses and social areas: nineteenth-century changes in the small town. *Transactions of the Institute of British Geographers*, NS 4: 214–38.

Cayford, J. (2008) Wynyard Point waterfront plan. Online. HTTP: <http://www.places4people.org.nz/Wynyard.htm> (accessed 26 April 2008).

Cayford, J. (2009) 'How sad is Princes Wharf (Part 1 and 2)?' Online. Available HTTP: <http://joelcayford.blogspot.com/2009/02/how-sad-is-princes-wharf.html> (accessed 3 October 2011).

Conzen, M. P. (2009) How cities internalize their former urban fringes. *Urban Morphology*, 13: 29–54.

Conzen, M. R. G. (1960) *Alnwick, Northumberland: A Study in Town-Plan Analysis*. London: George Phillip, Institute of British Geographers Publication 27.

Conzen, M. R. G. (1962) The plan analysis of an English city centre, in K. Norborg (ed.), *Proceedings of the IGU Symposium in Urban Geography, Lund 1960*, 383–414. Lund: Gleerup.

Conzen, M. R. G. (2004) *Thinking about Urban Form: Papers on Urban Morphology, 1932–1998*, M. P. Conzen (ed.). Oxford: Peter Lang.

Cormack, G. (2009) *The Auckland Waterfront Case Study*. Auckland: Committee for Auckland.

Doorne, S. (1998) Power, participation and perception: an insider's perspective on the politics of the Wellington waterfront redevelopment. *Current Issues in Tourism*, 1(2): 129–66.

Eisenhut, K. G. (2008) A critical evaluation of local government influence on waterfront development: a case study of Auckland and Melbourne (unpublished Master's thesis). Auckland: University of Auckland.

Forward, C. N. (1969) A comparison of waterfront land use in four Canadian ports: St. John's, Saint John, Halifax and Victoria. *Economic Geography*, 45: 155–69.

Gibson, A. (2010) Absolutely positively a harbor to envy. *The New Zealand Herald*, Saturday 13 March. Online. Available HTTP: <http://www.nzherald.co.nz/property/news/article.cfm?c_id=8&objectid=10631778&ref=rss> (accessed 13 December 2010).

Goodall, K. (2010) Project Auckland: Wynyard Quarter is not just a pretty face. *The New Zealand Herald*, Tuesday 21 September. Online. Available HTTP: <http://www.nzherald.co.nz/business/news/article.cfm?c_id=3&objectid=10674806> (accessed 13 December 2010).

Gordon, D. L. A. (1999) Implementing urban waterfront redevelopment in an historic context: a case study of the Boston Naval Shipyard. *Ocean and Coastal Management*, 42: 909–31.

Gu, K. (2010) Exploring the fringe-belt concept in Auckland: an urban morphological idea and planning practice. *New Zealand Geographer*, 66: 44–60.

Hopkins, M. I. W. (2004) Using fringe belts to examine the relationships between urban morphology and urban ecology (unpublished PhD thesis). Birmingham, U.K.: University of Birmingham.

Horwood, E. M., and Boyce, R. R. (1959) *Studies of the Central Business District and Urban Freeway Development*. Seattle: University of Washington Press.

Hoyle, B. S. (1994) A rediscovered resource: comparative Canadian perceptions of waterfront development. *Journal of Transport Geography*, 2: 19–29.

Hoyle, B. S., Pinder, D. A., and Husain, M. S. (1988) *Revitalizing the Waterfront: International Dimensions of Dockland Redevelopment*. London: Belhaven Press.

Kelsey, J. (1995) *The New Zealand Experiment: A World Model for Structural Adjustment?* Auckland: Auckland University Press.

Kropf, K. (2001) Testing the fringe belt concept in the planning process. Unpublished paper presented to the Eighth International Seminar on Urban Form, Cincinnati, Ohio, September 2001.

Lambton Harbour Group and Gabites Porter and Partners (1989) *Lambton Harbour Combined Scheme*. Wellington: Lambton Harbour Group.

Marshall, R. (ed.) (2001) *Waterfronts in Post-industrial Cities*. London: Spon.

McClean, R. A. (1997) *Te Whanganui-A-Tara Forshores Reclamations Report*. Wellington: Waitangi Tribunal.

Mistry, R. (2005) Chaffers Park redevelopment in Wellington—an analysis. *New Zealand Geographer*, 61: 54–60.

Morrison, P. S., and McMurray, S. (1999) The inner-city apartment versus the suburb: housing sub-markets in a New Zealand city. *Urban Studies*, 36: 377–97.

Murphy, L. (2008) Third-wave gentrification in New Zealand: the case of Auckland. *Urban Studies*, 45: 2521–40.

Oram, R. (2007) The Resource Management Act: now and in the future, in *Beyond the RMA: An In-Depth Exploration of the Resource Management Act 1991, Conference Proceedings 30–31 May 2007*, 5–37. Auckland: Environmental Defence Society.

Page, S. J. (1993) Perspectives on urban heritage tourism in New Zealand: Wellington in the 1990s, in C. M. Hall and S. McArthur (eds.), *Heritage Management in New Zealand and Australia: Visitor Management, Interpretation and Marketing*, 17–20. Auckland: Auckland University Press.

Page, S. J. (1996a) Wellington. *Cities*, 13: 125–34.

Page, S. J. (1996b) Wellington waterfront, in R. Le Heron and E. Pawson (eds.), *Changing Places: New Zealand in the Nineties*, 341–3. Auckland: Longman Paul Limited.

Port of Auckland (2010) Image gallery. Online. Available HTTP: <http://www.poal.co.nz/news_media/gallery.htm> (accessed 26 November 2010).

Reed, A. H. (1952) *The Story of New Zealand*. Wellington: A. H. and A. W. Reed.

Royal Commission on Auckland Governance (2009) *Report of the Royal Commission*. Auckland: Royal Commission on Auckland Governance. Online. Available HTTP: <http://www.royalcommission.govt.nz> (accessed 22 April 2009).

Samuels, I. (2008) Typomorphology and urban design practice. *Urban Morphology*, 12: 58–62.

Waterfront Leadership Group (2001) *The Wellington Waterfront Framework*. Wellington: Wellington City Council.

Wellington City Council (2005) *Old Shoreline Heritage Trail*, 2nd ed. Online. Available HTTP: <http://www.wellington.govt.nz/services/heritage/pdfs/ oldshorelinetrail.pdf> (accessed 8 July 2009).

Wellington City Council (2010) *WebMap*. Online. Available HTTP: <http://www.wellington.govt.nz/maps/webmaps/webmap/wccmap.html> (accessed 8 July 2009).

Whitehand, J. W. R. (1967) Fringe belts: a neglected aspect of urban geography. *Transactions of the Institute of British Geographers*, 41: 223–33.

Whitehand, J. W. R. (1988) Urban fringe belts: development of an idea. *Planning Perspectives*, 3: 47–58.

Whitehand, J. W. R., and Morton, N. J. (2004) Urban morphology and planning: the case of fringe belts. *Cities*, 21: 275–89.

16

"BIRMINGHAM NEEDS YOU. YOU NEED BIRMINGHAM"[1]

Cities As Actors and Actors in Cities

Tim Hall and Phil Hubbard

Something significant happened to the form of Western cities in the last quarter of the twentieth century, with landscapes of production giving way to landscapes of consumption. The phenomenon of industrial sites transformed by commodification and aestheticization was noted throughout the urban West as former manufacturing spaces gave way for nouvelle cuisine restaurants, heritage centers, coffee shops, art galleries, science parks, shopping malls, and high-tech landscapes (Zukin 1998). One spatial corollary of this was that the city appeared to be turning "inside out," as previously centralized functions of urban retailing, business, and leisure became de-centered, unraveling in their path memories of more familiar industrial districts (Soja 1996). Describing the emergence of *exopolitan* edge cities, Edward Soja accordingly suggested that the city center was no longer the primary focus of urban life but was joined by a multiplicity of new "centers" that were, conversely, distanced from the traditional city center. As the city turned inside out, rituals of urban recreation also become de-centered; urban dwellers increasingly sought distraction in spectacular, peripheral landscapes located away from the "inner city" (Hannigan 1998). Yet, for all that, it was evident there were significant countervailing tendencies, with the emergence of "twenty-four-hour city" policies aimed at reversing the decline of city centers, chiefly by attracting affluent, youthful consumers. In the twenty-first century, such "neoliberal policies" of gentrification became ever more entrenched, bequeathing a variegated urban landscape of investment and decline.

Often described by geographers as "post-modern," contemporary urban landscapes, therefore, both look and feel very different from their modern predecessors. Los Angeles is, of course, the "ur-city" of post-modernity: once the exception, its amorphous landscape (and barely concealed social tensions) now seems the rule (Dear and Flusty 1998). Critics of the "Los Angeles School" have pointed out that cities like New York, Miami, and Las Vegas—and, for that matter, London, Paris, or Toyko—are not Los Angeles, and that locally sensitive models and theories are needed to make sense of post-modern urbanism in "ordinary cities" (Amin and Graham 1997). Yet, as a heuristic device, Los Angeles-style post-modernism still holds great appeal for researchers.

In an effort to provide a locally sensitive investigation of post-modernity in a more representative urban context, this chapter explores the contemporary cityscapes of Birmingham, in the heart of the English Midlands, and assesses the city's putative claim to be a post-modern city. Shaking off the last traces of its nineteenth-century ethos, by the 1990s Birmingham appeared to have transformed into something completely new, characterized by gentrified retailing, heritage parks, conference centers, showpiece sporting arenas, museums and galleries, up-market shopping malls, "superclubs," and a plethora of cosmopolitan cafés and bars. At the same time, its industrial eyesores were demolished, obsolete waterfronts scrubbed clean, and its public spaces enhanced with suitably boosterist public art (Hall 1997; Kennedy 2004). The result was, on the surface, the creation of a playful, post-modern, and assuredly affluent city dedicated to the pleasures of conspicuous consumption on a twenty-four-hour basis (mirroring similar trends occurring in Glasgow, Manchester, Leeds, and the other former powerhouses of British manufacturing). This post-modernism, however, appeared to be masking serious problems in the city (problems that remain sharply evident in the new millennium as under-employment, dependency, and marginalization fuel criminality and gun crime). As such, the transformation of Birmingham's urban landscape has been subject to critique, with numerous commentators suggesting that its "entrepreneurial make-over" was designed to gloss over serious urban problems (Hall 1997; Hubbard 1996; Ward 2003; Loftman and Nevin 2003), with the re-vivification of the city center tied into particular agendas of corporate investment and middle-class revanchism (Smith 1996).

Starting in the early 1990s, we set out to investigate the emergence of this "post-modern" urban landscape. When this chapter was conceived, the concern with identifying those "agents of change" and shapers of urban form who were pivotal in the development of the "new" Birmingham was minimal. In part, this was because the focus was more on the consumption of the cityscape rather than its production; it was also because untangling the webs of agency in a city of Birmingham's size seemed formidable in the extreme. While the city council was certainly a key player (with the council leader Dick Knowles, later Sir Richard, a brash advocate of boosterist politics), fiscal retrenchment meant that it was largely reliant on private-sector and corporate interests to enact what were characterized as "entrepreneurial" policies (Harvey 1989). Hence, local property companies, new investors, the universities, the local media, architectural practices, consultancies, and retailers were also involved in specific projects of urban promotion. So, too, were local artists, retailers, businesses, and community groups. Given this complexity and the absence of a clear driving force behind the remaking of the city—compared with Michael Bloomberg's New York, or even Ken Livingstone's London—many media commentators, therefore, simplified the process to the extreme, suggesting that Birmingham had "reinvented itself." Though this reification of the city may seem absurd to many urban geographers, it can be suggested that, in some ways, it is true that cities are actors. The remainder of this chapter, therefore, returns to the 1990s to offer some thoughts on who was responsible for Birmingham's redevelopment by exploring the network of agents who came to act and speak for the city.

Theorizing Urban Governance

It has been widely argued that the increasing emphasis placed by geographers and others on questions of urban governance has been provoked by recent transitions in the nature of Western politics and the contested process by which we have arrived in a post-welfare era (Hall and Hubbard 1998). Particularly important in effecting this transition have been trends toward privatization and political conservatism that have encouraged "neo-liberal" thinking. Although this term covers a range of disparate ideas, the key thread running through neo-liberalism is that free markets are the most efficient mechanisms for regulating the production and distribution of goods and services in society.

Proponents argue, accordingly, that state intervention in the market should be minimized on the grounds that it undermines the efficiency of markets and that only minimal state intervention is necessary to ensure the fairness of business practice. The consequences of such shifts are sharply etched in the urban arena, where privatization and the "hollowing out" of the state are dominant leitmotifs. Under such fiscal and political pressures, city governors have been increasingly forced to adopt the language and attitudes of the private sector, working alongside the private sector in an attempt to stimulate local growth and prosperity. This has often involved the introduction of new political-administrative arrangements, such as public-private partnerships, and the creation of quasi-autonomous organizations ("quangos") including Urban Development Corporations or Training Enterprise Councils. Such partnerships exhibit varied geographies, being spatially diffuse in some cases, locally embedded and focused in others. They can also cross sectoral divides to unite groups or agencies with different functional remits or interests. Most notably, from the point of view of urban governance, they draw together public and private sector actors around a shared strategic focus and sense of civic vision.

Described in the 1990s in terms of a transition from managerial and strongly interventionist government to more flexible forms of "entrepreneurial" governance, public-private efforts to enhance the asset base of cities came to rely upon pro-growth strategies of urban promotion and place-marketing that embraced the logic of neo-liberalism:

> The new entrepreneurialism has as its centerpiece the notion of public-private partnership in which a traditional local boosterism is integrated with the use of local governmental powers to try and attract external sources of funding, new direct investments or new employment sources.
> (Harvey 1989: 7)

As Gordon MacLeod and Kevin Ward (2002) have shown, such strategies typically attempted to reinvent cities as profitable spaces of leisure and commerce, with the re-aestheticization of the city through showpiece redevelopment and prestige projects and explicit means by which corporate capital is enticed to "come to town" (see also Hall and Hubbard 1996; Loftman and Nevin 1996). Much cited examples include the redevelopment of London's Docklands, New York's Battery Park, Barcelona's Olympic Marina, Birmingham's Brindleyplace, Berlin's remodeled Potsdamer Platz, Lisbon's Expo Centre, and so on. Spectacular in form, these developments were—and are—intensely promoted and heavily mediated. Though there was no guarantee that such schemes, or the publicity they generate, would create additional revenue for the city, the assumption was that such urban flagships wave the flag for new investment.

Academic commentators were, however, quick to note the limitations of entrepreneurial policy, making important interventions in policy debates surrounding place marketing (Loftman and Nevin 2003). Yet, they also sought to dissect the partnerships that drive entrepreneurialism, theorizing their formation in relation to the changing interests of both the state and private business (Newman and Thornley 1997). Key questions here included how cities and regions were able to create sufficient "institutional capacity" to promote and govern themselves, given that many previously centralized urban functions are being devolved and privatized. "Growth coalition theory" was, therefore, used extensively in the fields of political science, sociology, and urban geography to explore this process of political devolution (Stoker 1998). Closely allied to "élite" theories in political science (which can be traced back to Marx), coalition theory draws mainly upon the experiences of North American cities to suggest that it is urban élites—that is, coalitions of dynamic businessmen, real estate developers, banks, newspaper proprietors, and pro-active city hall politicians, led usually by a charismatic mayor or politician—who transform "their" city. From the perspective of Marxist political science, growth coalitions are read as place-bound phenomena, having a vested interest in embedding capital in "their" locale (Cox and Mair 1998).

Perhaps the most important statement on growth coalitions is found in the work of John Logan and Harvey Molotch (1987). They defined élite "growth coalitions" as groupings of influential actors who seek growth at almost any cost. They argued that such actors usually stand to benefit from the population expansion and increased land values associated with "growth strategy." However, growth coalitions usually extend their influence by actively working to persuade others that growth will benefit everyone. Typically, a consensus is sought through persuading the wider public of the benefits of the idea of the city as a "growth machine," the potential of which is captured in a combination of visionary development projects and boosterist imagery. The importance of the local media in such growth coalitions is, therefore, obvious, playing an important supportive role in highlighting the wider merits of the projects and creating a positive environment for investment (and persuasively preempting local criticism by selling the growth vision to the local population). In effect, the "story" narrated by the élite becomes the dominant narrative of city development and receives widespread approval from the general populace. In this view, a "unified" city interest is achieved that purports to benefit all residents of the city including the members of the élite coalition. Where opposition to the growth coalition is expressed, the media typically represents its multiple voices as a unified group with the single interest of opposing the growth machine. Thus, the overall picture is one of either universal support for the growth machine or a very polarized situation comprising two camps that are either pro- or anti-economic development. There are, then, important links between the perspectives of coalition theory and the ideas of hegemony proposed by Gramsci: the symbolic framing of the city becomes all-important in the legitimation of urban policy (Boyle 1997).

Critics of growth coalition theory have, nonetheless, argued that its narrow conceptualization of power obscures the multitude of conflicts, compromises, and other political maneuverings that constitute the policy-making and implementation agenda of cities (Stone and Sanders 1987). They argue that the naive view of power in growth coalition theories, which assumes the ability of a growth coalition to exercise control over resources and people, fails to account for the processes that create and shape this power. In many ways, it draws on Marxist ideas of social relations that have been accused of eviscerating urban politics by ignoring the cultural creativity and bargaining explicit in city politics (Collinge and Hall 1997). Arguably, the variety of forms of coalition and the motivations of their members are far more diverse than are allowed for in growth coalition theory (Stone 1989; Stoker 1995). Consequently, growth coalition theory often fails to account for the diversity of coalitions found in different cities. In Britain, for example, there are many examples of local authorities and partnerships committed to no-growth, low-growth or anti-growth development strategies (Hall and Hubbard 1996). As such, Logan et al. have admitted that "after two decades of research, we are still unsure whether growth machines make a difference to urban development" (Logan et al. 1997: 624).

Since its inception in the United States in the late 1980s, through the pioneering works of Richard Elkin and Clarence Stone, "regime theory" has flourished as an alternative approach to analyzing city politics in North America and beyond. In contrast to élite theories that see power as consolidated, regime theory views power as a diffuse resource and draws upon Weberian pluralist traditions in political science that conceive of political power as negotiated and dispersed (being derived from the work of the sociologist Max Weber). Here, different "power clusters" control different spheres of urban life and are granted the power to act through popular consent (as expressed at the ballot box). Grounded empirically in a host of detailed single-city case studies, "regime theory" claims to offer a more sophisticated account of urban politics than growth coalition theory. Regime theory acknowledges that urban decision making is diffuse, fragmented, and non-hierarchical and recognizes the "meshing of interests" that brings both governmental and non-governmental actors within the ambit of governance. It also acknowledges the importance of local business interests in local governance but without succumbing to the economic determinism or structuralism of coalition theory:

> Specifically [regime analysis] recognises the enormous political importance of privately controlled investment, but does so without going so far as to embrace economic determinism. In assuming that political economy is about the relationship between politics and economics, regime analysts explore the middle ground between, on the one side pluralists ... and on the other side structuralists.
>
> (Stone 1993: 2)

Regime theory differs importantly from élite conceptions by focusing on the ways that diverse groups compensate for their individual lack of power by combining to form a more powerful collective regime. These regimes are rarely formed from scratch but are ongoing and constantly shifting phenomena, taking different forms as structures of capitalism mutate. Here, a decisive shift has been that from Fordist production to post-Fordism: from a political economy based on economies of scale to one based on economies of scope.

The argument of regime theory is that political power is not inherently available to any specific individual or agency but has to be created by the members of a regime coming together to blend their resources, skills, and purposes over a long period to produce the capacity required to achieve agreed aims. As Clarence Stone (1989: 229) suggests, "what is at issue is not so much domination and subordination as a capacity to act and accomplish goals—power *to*, not power *over*." In regime theory, politics is not restricted to acts of domination by an élite and consent or resistance from the ruled. It recognizes that, in a complex and fragmented society, no single group can exercise complete control over its environment, and all groups, including governmental institutions, are driven to cooperate with others who may have resources essential to the achievement of policy aims. As the task of government becomes more complex, effective government institutions must cooperate, and blend their capacities, with more non-governmental actors. Thus the establishment of a viable regime is the ultimate act of power in the context of an emerging system of governance (Stoker 1998). There are, then, clear parallels between the issue-focused "capacity-building" dimension of regime theory and the current trend of "enabling" partnership formation in cities.

Though coalition and regime theory have many adherents in the search for theories that might explain emerging forms of urban governance, the limitations of both have been noted:

> There is ... an underlying difference between neo-Marxist theories of hegemony [*coalition theory*], with their formal analysis of the state and its relationships to the structures of capital and class in which empirical investigation is neglected, and regime theory with its more open-ended investigation of political process in which there is greater empirical emphasis, but in which the form of the state apparatus and its structural relationship to economic interests are neglected.
>
> (Collinge and Hall 1997: 135)

The suggestion here is that regime theory provides useful ideas about the making of social relations at the local level, whereas coalition theory furnishes the researcher with key concepts that help us understand the more abstract relationship between state and city space. Gerry Stoker (1995), in contrast, has little positive to say about coalition theory but does argue that the framework for analysis provided by regime theory lends itself to sophisticated classifications of a variety of different types of regime that can be employed heuristically for purposes of research and analysis (Stone 1993, has himself provided a working classification matrix). Nevertheless, even Stone (1993) concedes that it is a theory in need of development. In particular, he suggests that regime theory needs to avoid the "localist" trap and place its micro-political analysis in the context of the broader political environment.

Exploring City Networks

Though there appears to have been some continuity in the coherence of governance itself as a practice over the last thirty years, the debates between regime theorists and coalition theorists have hindered the understanding of how urban governance is enacted, and by whom. Indeed, the literature theorizing governance is the source of more than a little methodological anarchy and definitional chaos. Certainly, coalition and regime theories, though underpinned by certain key ideas about the state, differ widely in their conception of power and their scale of analysis. Another common problem is that the tripartite distinction between the state, market, and civil society is assumed in all approaches, even though the distinctions between them are increasingly blurred as all sectors are fused in the melting pot of mutated governance. As our introductory remarks on Birmingham suggested, the three categories are, in fact, enmeshed and overlapping. Further, the search for coalitions or regimes seems fraught with difficulty, given that partnerships between different actors may be unstable and short-lived. Certainly, unpacking the production of a multitude of partnerships that may coexist at various scales in overlapping and nested webs of networks presents analysts with an increasingly mutable and difficult-to-pin-down research target.

One important theoretical impetus for understanding how policy and decision making are produced on a variety of inter-related scales is "actor network theory." Bingham and Thrift (2000) argue that actor network theory originates within studies of science, French intellectual culture and, above all, the writing of Michel Serres and Bruno Latour. Latour developed an account of networks on the basis that these intermediary arrangements are much more interesting than the two "extremes" of micro- and macro-level analysis. He also argued that it was essential to develop an account of networks that incorporates non-human elements as active entities or "actants" on the grounds that they can be just as important as human actors in any particular study. In Latour's work, power is viewed as the immanent and "performative" ability to get others to perform action rather than as a stock of influence residing in any particular person or institution. It is not the inevitable outcome of irresistible forces but the fluid effect of a mobilizing capacity to achieve aims through enacted interactions between the agents of a network. Power is creatively composed and reproduced not through unchangeable structures or institutions but through the recurring performance of networks of interaction. Though these enacted patterns are inherently unstable and mutable, they can, nevertheless, congeal into discernible channels through which the continually reproduced power configurations flow. The durability of certain arrangements is sustained by the enrollment of actants who subscribe to, and produce, apparently stable and orderly patterns of action (see also Bingham 1996).

In essence, actor network theory offers an analytical framework for making sense of social relations and struggles of all kinds, avoiding over-generalization or the search for "deep" structures in favor of descriptions of the associations that bring society into being. From the perspective of this theory, the key to the stability and transformation of "coherent" social configurations is to understand how actors are enrolled to perform within them. The theory suggests that power does not belong to particular groups, politicians, or individuals but is a composition produced by a network composed of a combination of heterogeneous entities (even though it might be attributed to one of them).

Actor network theory recommends itself for the analysis of urban governance. Its emphasis on networked interaction coincides conveniently with the increasingly explicit promotion of the partnership approach to governance with its associated emphasis on the incorporation of non-governmental actors into the formulation of policy making through networking, negotiation, and bargaining. As Jonathan Murdoch and Terry Marsden (1995) argue, the powerful are not those who hold political power but those who are able to enroll, enlist, and coerce people and things into networks and associations that allow them to enact their policies. These networks are not spatially constrained, so that a network that allows particular policies to be pursued in a specific city may extend globally, involving representatives of local community groups, global corporations, national media companies, visitors, and so on (Doel and Hubbard 2002). This means that non-local actors can often exercise power at a distance and that those located in the center of a network may be physically distant from those with whom they are associated. Hence networks can be "fat" or "thin," "deep" or "shallow," but their effectiveness does not depend on their size or shape but the extent to which they create ability to act.

This emphasis on the capacity to act being created through associations between different actors in the network points to the importance of the discourses and representations that give those in the network a sense of identity. Crucial here are the "policy" documents, brochures, press releases, promotional paraphernalia, and videos that act as a marshalling point in the formation of meaningful city networks. This emphasizes that materials, technologies, and texts are a crucial part of networks and that "actants" in networks may be non-human and human (for example, "town plans" are just as enmeshed in city networks as are urban planners). Actor network theory recognizes that the capacity to catalyze change or maintain stability is not limited to human beings and that a wide variety of things can bring a situation or condition into existence and sustain it. Accordingly, examining the circulation of things and people through networks is an essential feature of the theory. When enrolled in networks, these actants hold one another in positions that define the identities of subject/objects and their ability to do things (Murdoch 1997). In the context of political life, this means considering the management of networks and flows of information, discourse, documents, ideas, and representations as much as it involves thinking about the social relations between people.

Actor network theory has thus ushered in a new language of "actants" enrolled in the networks of "immutable mobiles" that bring circumstances into being. Open to notions of complexity, and mindful of the fact that the world is always in flux or in the process of becoming, this theory avoids making totalizing claims—meaning that it is very much in keeping with post-modern, and, arguably, post-structural thought. As Sarah Whatmore (1999: 27) argues, for those working with actor network theory, "agency, and by implication, power, is decentered, spun out between social actors rather than seen as a manifestation of unitary intent". Moreover, given that Serres and Latour have used geographical metaphors frequently in their work, the theory seems to offer a distinctly spatial way of describing or mapping—rather than specifically understanding—the world. In relation to urban politics, such insights have been taken up primarily in policy network studies, which combine detailed and sometimes quantitative analysis of relations between agents, politicians, and institutions with an attempt to specify what is actually important in shaping urban policy (Rhodes

1997). As well as thinking about the associations between local and non-local actors, this has involved examination of the power of marketing brochures, planning documents, videos, websites, and e-mail communications to bring networks into being. Thinking about how actors such as city councils enroll key organizations (chambers of commerce, tourist boards, training and enterprise councils, regional development agencies), individuals (local celebrities, dignitaries, visitors, residents), and collectivities (community groups, residents' associations, traders' associations) into a network that speaks and acts for the city, therefore, represents an important avenue for research in urban governance. At the same time, recognizing that such networks need constant attention and maintenance, actor network theory alerts us to the way in which apparent transitions from one capitalist mode of regulation to another are brought into being—not from "above" or "below" but through networked acts of weaving and pleating (Bingham and Thrift 2000).

As well as posing important questions about who are the key "agents of change" in urban politics, actor network theory problematizes questions of scale and boundedness in spatial analysis that are often taken for granted. Ash Amin and Stephen Graham (1997) underline this when they refer to the "within-ness" and "without-ness" of cities, suggesting that cities are manifold formations created in the midst of tangled networks that exist at different scales simultaneously. In part, the realization that cities exist at different scales simultaneously has emerged in response to ideas of globalization that show that cities are not local spaces in the thrall of global trends but are implicated in the making of global space economy in a multitude of ways. In this context, it is the explanatory theory of the "network society" developed by Manuel Castells (2000) that offers perhaps the most convincing analytical framework for exploring the "worlding" of cities. Based on his tentative identification of the network as the key social form (or social morphology) organizing people in relationships of production, consumption, experience, and power, Castells holds to the idea that people live in a network society, reproduced unevenly by "flows of capital, flows of information, flows of technology, flows of organizational interaction, flows of images, sounds and symbols" (Castells 2000: 418). This network requires constant attention and mediation, hence the existence of a key layer in the "space of flows" – the city networks that provide the infrastructure through which these flows are mediated. This perspective on cities suggests the need for a revised ontology of space: one that escapes taken-for-granted notions of "local" and "global," "concrete" and "abstract," "fixed" and "mobile," and "embedded" and "ethereal" to explore space in relational and networked terms (see Hubbard 2006).

Re-scaling City Politics: When Birmingham "Went Global"

The dramatic redevelopment of Birmingham in the late 1980s and 1990s thus provides a vivid example of how the leadership of a provincial English city sought to internationalize it by "extending" its city network over time and space. In the case of Birmingham, the attempt to take Birmingham to the world (i.e. promote globalization from below) and, in turn, bring the world to Birmingham (i.e. globalization from above) was played out against a backdrop of de-industrialization and dereliction (Mawson and Taylor 1983; Spencer et al. 1986; Henry et al. 2002). This transformation involved both a physical reconstruction and a symbolic one: the replacement of parochial spaces of industry with outwardly oriented spaces as well as a vigorous advertising campaign designed to promote Birmingham as a post-industrial and assuredly "international" city. To this end, the city's marketing slogan "Birmingham—the big heart of England" was rapidly replaced by "Birmingham—Europe's meeting place." Additionally, a number of hallmark, place-marketing events were held designed to raise the profile of the city. These included the annual jazz festival, the Birmingham Science Festival, the short-lived Birmingham Super Prix, and the unsuccessful bid for the Olympic Games. All were clearly targeted at creating an aura of cultural dynamism and sophistication about the city and, more specifically, at attracting particular forms of international corporate investment.

An integral part of Birmingham's entrepreneurial strategies was, therefore, a comprehensive package of aesthetic improvements designed to create an environment that appeared safe, attractive and, above all, profitable. This re-aestheticization of the city was seen as an urgent priority, given that the city was generally perceived to have a poor city image and was subject to criticism from residents and visitors alike. Most of this criticism was aimed at the legacy of the physical transformation that occurred between 1947 and 1973, typified by overpowering highway engineering projects that came to be cited as the archetypal "concrete jungle" (Hubbard 1996; Kennedy 2004). Although it could be argued that this redevelopment resulted in commercial vitality, it certainly resulted in a physical landscape that fell short of public aspirations and, according to one vociferous critic—the Prince of Wales (1989)—had become a vast concrete maze where only cars felt at home. Furthermore, "reactions, especially from abroad were harsh. Birmingham's environment was seen as uncomfortable for pedestrians, impossible to "read," dirty, ugly, down-market and dangerous" (Simms, in Highbury Initiative 1988, unpaginated).

Consequently, the pro-growth city center strategy involved substantial redevelopment of a number of key areas with an eye to creating a more appealing city for affluent consumers and investors. These areas included—in the late 1980s in particular—the Broad Street redevelopment axis (home to the International Convention Centre and National Indoor Arena) and Heartlands—an 890-hectare site of mainly derelict and contaminated industrial land in Aston and Duddeston that was given over to new light-industrial, residential, and leisure development. Into the late 1990s, the focus of redevelopment shifted to the east of the city center, particularly the Millennium Point site in Digbeth and the redevelopment of one of Birmingham's archetypal modern landscapes, the Bull Ring shopping center (completed in September 2003; Fig. 16.1). Throughout, the local press in Birmingham (primarily the daily newspapers the *Birmingham Post* and *Evening Mail*) were active in constructing a rhetoric of rebirth, growth, and renaissance around these projects. This reached a crescendo in 1991 when the International Convention Centre was opened (Fig. 16.2).

Given that the spatial and symbolic imprints of these new developments have been well documented (Tinworth 1998), the question to be explored here is: who was responsible for this new Birmingham? Significantly, Patrick Loftman and Brendan Nevin (2003) place great emphasis on the influence of successive leaders of the city council in shaping pro-growth strategies. Noting important shifts in the form and content of pro-growth strategy under Dick Knowles (1984–93), Theresa Stewart (1993–9), and Albert Bore (1999–2004), their account suggests that these figures were crucial in reconciling factions within the city council's Labour Party group, gaining bipartisan support for pro-growth strategies that were expensive and, to some extent, risky. Recognizing the local tradition of great municipal leaders such as Joseph Chamberlain, the Birmingham media latched on to each of these figures in turn, reporting their pro-growth rhetoric.

Notwithstanding the role that these figures played in shaping policy networks, it is too simplistic to suggest that one figure controls the destiny of the city: actor network theory suggests that the reality is inevitably more complex. This is illustrated, for example, through the "Championing Birmingham" initiative, launched in February 2003 (Marketing Birmingham 2003). Championing Birmingham is an initiative developed by the city's strategic marketing partnership, Marketing Birmingham, to encourage companies and organizations within the city to act as ambassadors for Birmingham. Bob Gilbert, the Chairman of Marketing Birmingham, outlined the vision for the campaign:

FIGURE 16.1 The Bull Ring Shopping Centre in Birmingham, England (completed in 2003), including the silver Selfridge's department store and St. Martin's parish church (rebuilt 1873), complete with church shop and tea lounge

'TAKING BRUM INTO THE 21st CENTURY'
Uncredited (1986) *Sunday Mercury*, 16 February

'THIS IS OUR NEW HEART'
Uncredited (1990) *Evening Mail*, 29 March

'JEWEL IN OUR CROWN'
Uncredited (1991) *Evening Mail*, 28 March

'A WORLD BEATER... The ICC itself stands sentinel in Broad Street. William Wordsworth wrote, viewing London from Westminster Bridge: "Dull would be he of soul, who could pass by a sight so touching in its majesty". Perhaps somebody will pen equally memorable words about the International Convention Centre ... WELL DONE BRUM.'
Uncredited (1991) *Evening Mail*, 28 March

'PROUD DAY FOR NATION'S MOST PROGRESSIVE CITY... To walk along Colmore Row to the ICC is to see before one's eyes the renaissance of a city'
N. Hastilow (1991) *Birmingham Post*, 12 June

'ROYAL VISITORS SET SEAL ON CITY'S REBIRTH'
Uncredited (1991) *Birmingham Post*, 12 June

'A SYMPHONY OF NEW LIFE FOR THE CITY... It [the symphony *Momentum*, by Mark-Anthony Turnage, written for the opening of Symphony Hall] could almost be a picture of the positive spirit which the advent of the ICC is breathing into Birmingham'
C. Morley (1991) *Birmingham Post*, 13 June

FIGURE 16.2 Press hyperbole? Mediating the new Birmingham

> Having pledged their support, a named individual within each company or organisation will be required to roll up his or her sleeves, fronting Marketing Birmingham"s ambassadorial initiatives and, at the very highest level, championing the Birmingham advantage. The financial stake of each and every Championing Birmingham supporter will be matched pound for pound by Advantage West Midlands [the Regional Development Agency]. This will significantly boost the operating budgets available to Marketing Birmingham as it undertakes promotions of the city that will capitalise on its regeneration, positioning it as one of Europe's great cities. As an acknowledged stakeholder in the city, this will in turn help your business attract clients, customers and employees.
>
> (Gilbert 2003: 1)

Championing Birmingham sought a three-year commitment from companies and institutions in the region and a contribution of up to £15,000 per annum. It is argued that in more effectively promoting the city, the companies involved would directly benefit from the growth of the city. In addition, Championing Birmingham supporters would have access to "exclusive networking opportunities which will fully engage them with the leadership of the city and its ongoing regeneration and renaissance" (Marketing Birmingham 2003: 8). These opportunities comprise six high-profile events including lunches and workshops. By 2004, there were around seventy companies and organizations committed to Championing Birmingham. Examples include Aston Villa Football Club, BRMB/Capital Gold Radio Stations, Central Trains, Pallasades Shopping Centre, Stanley Casinos Ltd, Cadbury Trebor Bassett, University Hospital Birmingham, Birmingham International Airport Ltd, British Waterways, City Centre Partnership, Anthony Collins Solicitors, Birmingham Post and Mail newspapers, Tempus Computers, Aston University, PricewaterhouseCoopers LLP, and Birmingham City University. Championing Birmingham has been a key marketing and development initiative within the city and well demonstrates the complexities of mapping the processes of city governance. The approach to marketing the city demonstrated by the Championing Birmingham initiative is not an isolated case but can be seen as reflective of a wider trend toward the "downloading" of city marketing along with its associated costs and risks. Norma Rantisi and Deborah Leslie (2006), for example, discuss Montréal's annual competition for architecture and design (Commerce Design Montréal) launched in 1995, which has become a major initiative through which the city is branded. Initiatives such as these tend to require relatively little public funding but generate extensive media coverage while enrolling a variety of actors, particularly from the commercial sector, into the marketing/branding process.

It is possible to read this initiative easily in growth coalition terms as a coherent, urban élite consisting of prominent public and private sector interests united around a set of common goals and aspirations for the city, the most important of which have been to be promote Birmingham globally. This reading appears to be confirmed by the representation of this "coalition" in documents such as the Championing Birmingham prospectus and numerous press releases. For example, Sue Battle, the Chief Executive of Birmingham Chamber of Commerce and Industry, says in the Championing Birmingham prospectus:

> Marketing Birmingham is working hand in glove with the city's business community, and this is reflected in its Championing Birmingham project. Birmingham Chamber puts a high value on the ambitious plan to develop a network of city companies and institutions to promote the Birmingham advantage in the UK and further afield.
>
> (Marketing Birmingham 2003: 1)

The coherence of this coalition is further solidified in a text located prominently within the city. VUBE is a giant (twenty-three meters) plasma cube that displays the Championing Birmingham supporters as they are recruited to the project. Placed at strategic points in the city, these displays emphasize the local embeddedness of the companies and institutions involved in Championing Birmingham, all of which appear to have a vested interest in bringing new investment to the city.

Despite the intuitive appeal of a perspective that emphasizes the local embeddedness of coalition members, it oversimplifies and masks the diversity of relationships within this apparently coherent grouping. For example, the supporters of Championing Birmingham contain companies and organizations that operate at all scales, from the global to the local, from the public and private sectors, and are of vastly different sizes and natures. Indeed, the relationships between certain members of the initiative might as likely be ones of ambivalence or competition as of cooperation. The very diversity of interests within the network makes it unlikely that the images of Birmingham—the versions of the Birmingham advantage, promoted through the network's activities—would be uniform. It is difficult, for example, to imagine how Aston Villa Football Club, British Waterways, and University Hospital Birmingham could speak of the city with one voice. The grounded realities of their positions in and relationships to the city would seem to preclude this possibility. Thus the performed realities of networks such as Championing Birmingham cannot be captured through the simplified imagery of a growth coalition or urban élite.

Many of the characteristics explored through regime theory also appear to be present in the Championing Birmingham network. It can be read as a "power-cluster" with control over the marketing of the city. It appears to demonstrate the diffuse, fragmented, and non-hierarchical nature of power in the post-industrial city; it demonstrates how non-governmental actors have been brought into the sphere of governance and how local government cooperates with these non-governmental actors to achieve its aims, in this case partly to explicitly boost its operating budgets in certain areas. Further, the regime talks explicitly of the blending of skills and capacities to achieve common goals. While this offers a more sophisticated picture of the increasingly complex nature of urban governance, it still fails to capture the complexities within the relationships of the network discussed above.

The fact that many of the business interests influential in the redevelopment of Birmingham are actually transnational companies alerts us to the fact that the power in Birmingham's city network is actually dispersed in networks that may be of great spatial extent. This should lead us to be skeptical of a rhetoric lauding local heroes who seek to take on the "outside world." Indeed, many of the actors who shaped Birmingham in this period were not "Brummies" in any sense at all, either having come to the city from elsewhere or living even at a distance from the city but having a vested interest in promoting the city as a good place in which to live and work. This is clearly apparent from the list of supporters who have been recruited to the Championing Birmingham initiative. Unfortunately, given the tendency for urban geographers to focus on what exists within places, rather than on what individuates them within a wider system (see Hubbard 2006), there is a serious deficit of data about the actors who might have been enrolled in Birmingham's city network yet who did not circulate in local "corridors of power." Yet here one can at least speculate that many "non-Birmingham" firms (including major foreign banks, accountants, lawyers, and advertising agencies) might have a vested interest in ensuring that Birmingham remained Britain's successful second city. After all, it is to the advantage of a London-based lawyers' office that its Birmingham office has plenty of clients or to a Hong Kong-based bank that its Birmingham branch is doing good business. This is why it is important to emphasize that a firm, like any other actor, only exists as a networked formation primarily organized through city networks. The interpretive mistake comes when one separates an economic sector (such as investment banking) from its network of offices. This is to say that sectors and cities are both intertwined in the making of the global space economy (Beaverstock et al. 2002).

Nick Henry and his co-authors (2002) make a similar point about the globalization of Birmingham when they detail the diasporic ethnic networks that contribute to the city's life and prosperity. They note, for example, that the entrepreneurial policies of the 1980s and 1990s made great play of cultural diversity, promoting certain spaces and events associated with ethnic groups. For example, foodscapes associated with the Bengali populations of Ladypool Road and Chinese populations around Highgate were promoted vigorously in the promotional literature for the city, while religious festivals and holy events were seized upon by the city council in their attempt to promote multiculturalism (Christmas being, briefly, reinvented as "Winterval" in an attempt to play up to Birmingham's culturally inclusive reputation). Yet here, Henry and his co-authors point out that ethnic populations were not simply "used' by the city council as they sought to internationalize Birmingham: there were many ethnic entrepreneurs who were themselves internationalizing Birmingham through their own initiatives and efforts. Here one might cite the success of the Birmingham-based company Wing Yip in establishing Chinese supermarkets around the country, drawing on import/export linkages with China and its surrounding regions (Chan 2005). In addition, there are many other Birmingham-based examples of ethnic food industries that have proliferated during the 1990s. These include East End Foods of Smethwick, set up in 1969 and now one of the largest importers/exporters of Indian foods in the United Kingdom. Another example was Wine and Dine, which grew from its origins as a Greek restaurant that began making dishes and dips in response to customer demand and by the early 2000s supplied 40 percent of the U.K. retail chilled salad dressings market. At its height, it concentrated on manufacturing and employed a workforce of nearly 100 people (with a turnover of £6 million).

Taken together, these perspectives on the redevelopment and globalization of Birmingham in the 1980s and 1990s stress that the actor network responsible for shaping the city's destiny is potentially vast. It is not simply firms that are locally based or have local origins that have a stake in seeing Birmingham perform well; it is also those who serve the city, trade with it, or who have economic linkages through and beyond the city. This includes those politicians who actively promote Birmingham globally, yet do so at a distance. For instance, through its participation in the English Core Cities group and the Eurocities program, Birmingham City Council has also been caught up in a multiplicity of inter-city connections, twinning programs (through the TACIS program, for instance) and exchanges of staff and resources. Because of the nature of such programs, it can be suggested that one of Birmingham's key rivals in the global battle for jobs and capital—Lyon (France)—is now a collaborator, with the fortunes of Lyon and Birmingham tied together through a series of business and civic exchanges: They are formally "partner cities." As stakeholders in the city's future, it is possible to argue that Lyon's politicians and business leaders are now significant actors in shaping Birmingham, playing a role in the articulation of a strategic vision that is constructed through and by a city network of international dimensions (and rarely the voice of one key actor).

Conclusion

This chapter began by presenting the oxymoronic statement that cities act. However, rather than seeking to reify the city as an agent in and of itself, it has been argued that the city gains its evidential agency by virtue of a complex city network that comes to speak and act, collectively, as if it were the city. This network does not simply consist of those businesses and institutions recruited by leading politicians to endorse a rhetoric of civic pride and progress. Rather, it consists of a more-or-less diffuse network of actors who come together around a shared agenda of promoting and enhancing the flow of capital through the locality. Exactly how this is achieved is something about which different actors in the network will not necessarily agree. Such disagreement can, of course, be accommodated within the network, so long as the latter does not "break down" entirely and lose its capacity to act. Emphasizing the ongoing and contested nature of city politics, an actor network theory perspective stresses the polycentric and dispersed nature of power within networks and thus allows for resistance within networks. The power of the electorate at large, however, remains limited: frozen out from these city networks, it appears that citizens succeed in shaping the city only when they come together in the trade, retail, business, or community groups that are drawn into networks of city government.

The case study of Birmingham has, therefore, highlighted some of the inherent problems in identifying the dominant shapers of Western urban landscapes. Though one cannot discount local politicians, it is apparent that they can develop the power to act only when they network with local businesses. Yet to fixate on the local is to ignore the "worlding" of city governance. Birmingham's city network is of global dimensions and involves actors who may reside on the other side of the world from the city. What brings together this diversity of actors and institutions is a vested and seemingly common interest in maintaining and improving Birmingham's position in a global space of flows. The morphology of this city network is, thus, as complex and contradictory as the urban landscapes it creates. Exploring the variable constitution of city networks thus presents a considerable challenge but a necessary one in identifying the shapers of the post-industrial city.

Note

1 This is a slogan taken from the marketing initiative "Championing Birmingham," discussed in detail later in the chapter.

References

Amin, A., and Graham, S. (1997) The ordinary city. *Transactions of the Institute of British Geographers*, 22: 411–29.

Beaverstock, J., Doel, M., Taylor, P., and Hubbard, P. (2002) Attending to the world: co-efficiency and collaboration in the world city network. *Global Networks*, 2 (2): 96–116.

Bingham, N. (1996) Object-ions from technological determinism towards geographies of relations. *Environment and Planning D: Society and Space*, 14: 635–58.

Bingham, N., and Thrift, N. (2000) Some new instructions for travellers: Michel Serres and Bruno Latour, in M. Crang and N. Thrift (eds.), *Thinking Space*, 281–301. London: Routledge.

Boyle, M. (1997) Civic boosterism in the politics of local economic development: institutional positions and strategic orientations in the consumption of hallmark events. *Environment and Planning A*, 29: 1975–97.

Castells, M. (2000) *The Information Age*. Oxford: Blackwell.

Chan, W. F. (2005) A gift of a pagoda: the presence of a citizen and the possibilities of hospitality. *Environment and Planning D: Society and Space*, 23: 11–28.

Collinge, C., and Hall, S. (1997) Hegemony and regime theory in urban governance: towards a theory of the locally networked state, in N. Jewson and S. MacGregor (eds.), *Transforming Cities: Contested Governance and New Spatial Divisions*, 129–40. London: Routledge.

Cox, K., and Mair, A. (1998) Levels of abstraction in locality studies. *Antipode*, 21: 121–32.

Dear, M., and Flusty, S. (1998) Postmodern urbanism. *Annals, Association of American Geographers*, 80: 50–72.

Doel, M., and Hubbard, P. (2002) Taking world cities literally: urban competition and the spatialities of a global space of flows. *City: A Journal of Urban Analysis*, 6 (3): 351–68.

Gilbert, B. (2003) Foreword, in Marketing Birmingham, *Championing Birmingham Prospectus 03/04*. Birmingham: Marketing Birmingham.

Hall, T. (1997) Images of industry in the post-industrial city: Raymond Mason and Birmingham. *Ecumene*, 4: 46–68.

Hall, T., and Hubbard, P. (1996) The entrepreneurial city: new urban politics, new urban geographies? *Progress in Human Geography*, 20: 153–74.

Hall, T., and Hubbard, P. (1998) The entrepreneurial city: geographies of politics, regime and representation, in T. Hall and P. Hubbard (eds.), *The Entrepreneurial City*, 1–23. Chichester, U.K.: Wiley.

Hannigan, J. (1998) *Fantasy City: Pleasure and Profit in the Post-Modern Metropolis.* London: Routledge.

Harvey, D. (1989) From managerialism to entrepreneurialism: the transformation of governance in late capitalism. *Geografiska Annaler*, 71B: 3–17.

Henry, N., McEwan, C., and Pollard, J. S. (2002) Globalization from below: Birmingham – postcolonial workshop of the world? *Area*, 34: 118–27.

Highbury Initiative (1988) Proceedings of the Birmingham City Centre Challenge Symposium (25–27 March). Birmingham: unpublished report for the City Council.

Hubbard, P. (1996) Urban design and city regeneration: social representations of entrepreneurial landscapes. *Urban Studies*, 33: 1441–61.

Hubbard, P. (2006) *Key Ideas in Geography – the City*. London: Routledge.

Kennedy, L. (2004) *Remaking Birmingham: The Visual Culture of Urban Regeneration*. London: Routledge.

Loftman, P., and Nevin, B. (1996) Going for growth prestige projects in three British cities. *Urban Studies,* 33: 991–1019.

Loftman, P., and Nevin, B. (2003) Prestige projects, city centre restructuring and social exclusion—taking the long-term view, in T. Hall and M. Miles (eds.), *Urban Futures*, 76–91. London: Routledge.

Logan, J., and Molotch, H. (1987) *Urban Fortunes*. Berkeley: University of California Press.

Logan, J., Whaley, R. B., and Crowder, K. (1997) The character and consequences of growth regimes: an assessment of 20 years of research. *Urban Affairs Review*, 32: 603–30.

MacLeod, G., and Ward, K. (2002) Spaces of utopia and dystopia: landscaping the contemporary city. *Geografiska Annaler*, 84B: 153–70.

Marketing Birmingham (2003) *Championing Birmingham Prospectus 03/04*. Birmingham: Marketing Birmingham.

Mawson, J., and Taylor, A. (1983) *The West Midlands in Crisis: A Profile of Decline*. Birmingham, U.K.: University of Birmingham, Centre for Urban and Regional Studies/Institute of Local Government Studies.

Murdoch, J. (1997) Inhuman/nonhuman/human actor-network theory and the prospects for a nondualistic and symmetrical perspective on nature and society. *Environment and Planning D: Society and Space*, 15: 731–56.

Murdoch, J., and Marsden, T. (1995) The spatialization of politics: local and national actor spaces in environmental conflict. *Transactions of the Institute of British Geographers*, 20: 368–80.

Newman, P., and Thornley, A. (1997) Fragmentation and centralization in the governance of London. *Urban Studies*, 34: 967–88.

Prince of Wales (1989) *A Vision of Britain*. London: Doubleday.

Rantisi, N. M., and Leslie, D. (2006) Branding the design metropole: the case of Montréal, Canada. *Area*, 38: 364–76.

Rhodes, R. A. W. (1997) *Understanding Governance: Policy Networks, Governance, Reflexivity and Accountability*. Buckingham, U.K.: Open University Press.

Smith, N. (1996) *The New Urban Frontier.* London: Routledge.

Soja, E. (1996) *Thirdspace*. Oxford: Blackwell.

Spencer, K., Taylor, A., Smith, B., Mawson, J., Flynn, N., and Batley, R. (1986) *Crisis in the Industrial Heartland: A Study of the West Midlands*. Oxford: Clarendon Press.

Stone, C. (1989) *Regime Politics Governing Atlanta*. Lawrence: University of Kansas Press.

Stone, C. (1993) Urban regimes and the capacity to govern: a political economy approach. *Journal of Urban Affairs*, 15: 1–28.

Stone, C., and Sanders, H. (1987) *The Politics of Urban Development*. Lawrence: University of Kansas Press.

Stoker, G. (1995) Regime theory and urban politics, in D. Judge, G. Stoker, and H. Wolman (eds.), *Theories of Urban Politics*, 54–71. Beverley Hills: Sage.

Stoker, G. (1998) Governance as theory: five propositions. *International Social Science Journal*, 155: 17–28.

Tinworth, A. (1998) Metamorphosis—Birmingham. *Estates Gazette*, 9839, 26 September.

Ward, K. (2003) The limits to contemporary urban development: doing 'entrepreneurial urbanism' in Birmingham, Leeds and Manchester. *City*, 7: 199–211.

Whatmore, S. (1999) Hybrid geographies: rethinking the human in human geography, in D. Massey, J. Allen, and P. Sarre (eds.), *Human Geography Today*, 22–39. Cambridge: Polity.

Zukin, S. (1998) Urban lifestyles: diversity and standardisation in space of consumption. *Urban Studies*, 35: 825–39.

PART VI

Envoi

17

AGENTS AND AGENCY, LEARNING, AND EMERGENCE IN THE BUILT ENVIRONMENT

A Theoretical Excursion

Karl Kropf

The city is often cited as the supreme human creation, the most complex product of a deliberate, intentional act of planning. Yet, the language used to describe cities often suggests that they grow and change autonomously, without clearly identifiable human intentions. For example, on the Web site "thisbigcity," an article begins as follows: "How Amsterdam's Urban Form *Created* the Ideal Cycling City. Before the bicycle arrived in Amsterdam in the 19th century, the city had undergone six centuries of development, *inadvertently creating* a compact urban environment ideal for bicycle use" (Peach 2011; *my emphasis*). Who is doing the creating? The city in all its complexity seems to be neither entirely intentional nor entirely emergent but both at the same time. Such a view is at once intuitively satisfying and awkwardly contradictory.

Because we are intentional creatures, it is easy to impart intention to the objects we see around us. We are inveterate storytellers (and listeners), and we keep on listening because we want to find out what happens. We want to find out why the characters behave the way they do. So it is a general habit to think that when something changes, there is some intention involved. Our normal model of intentionality is based on the individual organism—by default, other human beings. This is why it is so easy, and often necessary, to speak *as if* a city is an individual (see Dennett 1995: 205, 398–9 on "as if" intentionality), but a city is self-evidently not the product of an individual. It is the product of a community or group of people.

One of the ways in which people have attempted to understand the city as the product of a group is through the idea of emergence (see Johnson 2001 for a broad survey of the idea and Hacking 1990 for some of its origins). At least since Jane Jacobs identified the city as a problem of *organized complexity* (1961: 433–40), the concept of emergence has developed and been applied in a number of different ways to come to terms with the phenomena of how cities work and change (see, for example, Hillier 1996; Kropf 2001, 2003; Hensel et al. 2004; Salingaros 2004; Batty 2005; Marshall 2009; Coates 2010, Weinstock 2010).

Some of this work, particularly that of Hillier, Batty, Coates, and Hensel, has been pursued through the medium of computer modeling. This is due in part to the fact that the concepts and tools for elaborating emergence have been borrowed from other fields that routinely use quantitative methods and in particular non-linear mathematics, which is only tractable with the use of computers.

Though some of the computational methods actively incorporate the idea of agency, the full scope of how agency operates within the built environment remains obscure. There are numerous "agent-based" models that seek to either simulate aspects of formation, transformation, and use of the built environment or, alternatively, to generate new forms (see Batty 2005 for a very good survey). To be computationally workable, however, models of agency necessarily make assumptions about the nature and character of the agents as entities. The basic assumption is that the agent is an individual, that is, equivalent to an individual human being. It is also generally assumed that the individual agent operates independently within the bounds of a fixed set of behavioral rules, and the agents are limited to a narrow range of behavioral options.

Perhaps more fundamentally, there is a limit on what the agent is able to "see" or perceive in the environment, and so the feedback loops that are central to emergent behavior are equally limited. This issue is of particular importance given the multi-scalar structure of the built environment. An underlying assumption in many models of emergence in the built environment is that global structure arises from the actions of agents following local rules, but is it correct to assume that an agent is able to see and respond to only a single level (for example, adjacent cells in a cellular automaton)? Do we get an adequate picture of agency in the built environment if these limits are imposed? Could we improve our understanding of the built environment and agent-based systems more generally if we extended the range of what an agent sees and what an agent is?

The purpose of this closing chapter is to explore the nature and character of agency in the built environment in an effort to improve our understanding of the balance between intention and emergence in the way towns grow and change. A principal tool in this effort is the concept of the *typological process* as put forward by Muratori (1959), Caniggia and Maffei (2001), Cataldi (1981), Petruccoli (2007), and others. Scrutiny of the typological process shows that the principles of emergence have been integral to it from the start (see also Kropf 2001). The analysis will be illustrated by a case study of an urban extension proposed for the market town of Leighton Buzzard in Bedfordshire, England (Fig. 17.1). The context for the case is, thus, the British planning system.

Agency

Agency at its most basic involves some entity able to construct a picture of the world (through "perception" of external stimulus) and who has an aim, need, desire, or a range of desires or needs (see Dennett 1997). Construction of towns and cities necessarily assumes the idea of agency. Cities are built by people to meet their needs. It is on this basis that it can be said that "space is social" or "space is the embodiment of social constructs," but these formulations leave out the agent. Rather, seen through the lens of agency, they become "structure is the product of a social process enacted by social agents." The idea of agency implies looking not merely at the product—the structure and configuration—but also at the process.

In looking at the example of the urban extension at Leighton Buzzard, it becomes evident fairly quickly that there are a number of different individual agents involved, each with a different set of aims, desires, and needs. Broadly, there are four main "parties' involved: the landowners/developers, the designers/technical professionals, the local authority, and the local community (the current residents of Leighton Buzzard and those who work there). So, already, there are not just individuals but also organizations involved. The issue of different types of agent—individual or corporate—is dealt with in more detail below. Irrespective of whether an individual represents an organization or not, he or she participates on the basis of seeking to achieve some aim and has to work toward that aim on the basis of how he or she perceives and understands the situation.

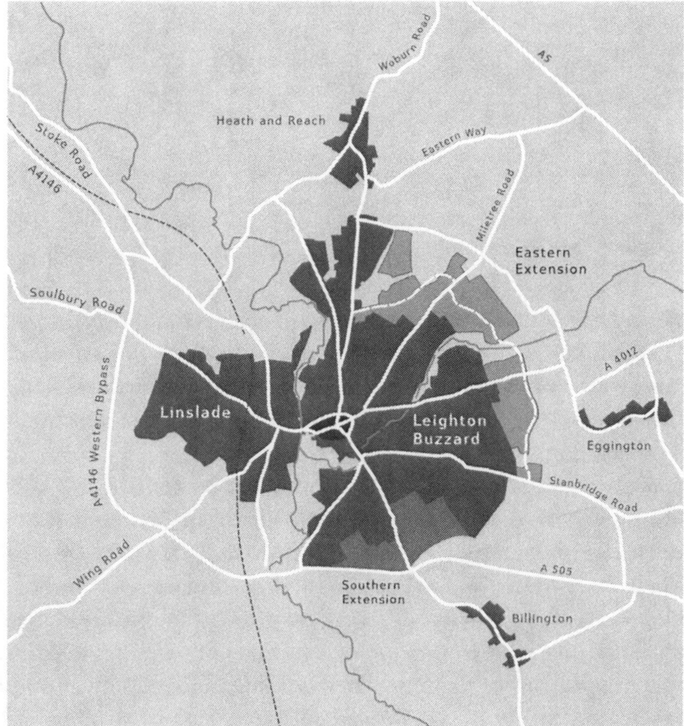

FIGURE 17.1 Leighton Buzzard is a market town in Bedfordshire, England, located between Milton Keynes and Luton/Dunstable

The population of the main built-up area is about 32,000. The town is 45 minutes from London by train and lies in the Milton Keynes South Midlands sub-region, which was identified as a growth area in the regional plan from the 1990s–2000s. Initial development in response to the plan took the form of a southern extension, nearing completion in 2012. Further growth to the east is agreed in policy to meet identified housing need. Planning applications for the eastern extension were being considered in 2012, nearly ten years since the first diagrammatic ideas were put forward.

Learning

The behavior of agents broadly falls into the category of "learning" and/or adaptive behavior. Learning at its most basic involves an agent with its world picture and desires and (1) the perception of a particular stimulus, (2) a response to that stimulus, and (3) a further stimulus that reinforces the response either negatively or positively (Fig. 17.2). It goes without saying that the agents involved in the Leighton Buzzard extension are all the *product* of learning. To get to their respective positions, they will have gone through formal and informal education and training and continue to learn and use their experience to achieve their aims. One example of the continued operation of learning and adaptive behavior in this case is the negotiating that goes on between land owner and local authority. In the early stages of the process, the area for the urban extension had not been finalized, and discussions were held between the two main land owners and the local authority to agree upon the extent of the area to be included. At individual meetings, the discussions amounted to a negotiation between the parties, with the land owners seeking to get as much of their land

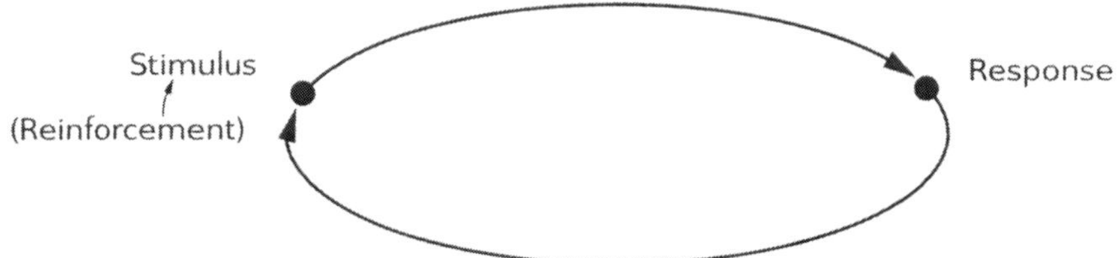

FIGURE 17.2 The simple circuit of learning

included as possible and the local authority working to achieve its policy aim of limiting the size of the extension. The actions of each of the parties can be seen as part of an adaptive circuit: watching and listening to the others (stimulus), making verbal and gestural statements (response), and watching and listening to the responses of others (reinforcement), responding in turn, and so on for any number of iterations.

The complexity of even this simple example is hinted at by comparison with the "three-body problem" in classical physics (analyzing the motion of three interacting bodies is mathematically unsolvable with general formulas; see, for example, Wolfram 2002). The land owners, who are in competition, necessarily have to respond to both one another and the local authority to achieve their aims. The local authority has to take in the differing positions of the two landowners and formulate responses that satisfy both. Not surprisingly, it took a number of meetings to come to an agreement.

Behind the simple pragmatism of that last statement lies an extremely important and profound distinction. Learning is not by any means limited to the single circuit illustrated in Figure 17.2. Rather, a more common interpretation would say that the single circuit is simple *feedback*, and you only get "learning" with the repetition of the circuit to achieve some lasting form of behavior. We all learn a language by listening, trying it out, making mistakes, getting corrected, and trying again, repeatedly. The essence of learning is in the *repetition*.

The better negotiator in the discussions between the land owners and local authority will have had significant experience to draw on, reflecting back on previous negotiations and the success of different strategies and tactics. The profound shift here is between an *individual instance* of feedback and an *aggregate or class* of events. Learning to negotiate means making use of accumulated experience of many single sessions of negotiation. The negotiator is, consciously or not, taking in the immediate stimulus of the meeting (within the single circuit) and also his or her memory of previous meetings (multiple repetitions of the circuit). He or she is looking at the process of feedback as a whole. The negotiator uses feedback in an individual session to get a result in a specific case and uses what Gregory Bateson calls "calibration" to become a better negotiator (1980: 209–224; see also Bateson 2000). Repeated rounds of feedback allow the negotiator to adjust or calibrate his or her responses in a given case in an effort to improve. This is illustrated in Figure 17.3, which shows a higher-level loop that is built on, and feeds into, the lower-level circuit.

The distinction between individual and aggregate is central to the entire discussion of agency in the built environment. It is particularly relevant in seeking to understand the relationship between intention and emergence. There are a number of different ways in which the distinction applies, but its importance lies in a simple point. What is true of an individual is not necessarily true of the aggregate and vice versa.

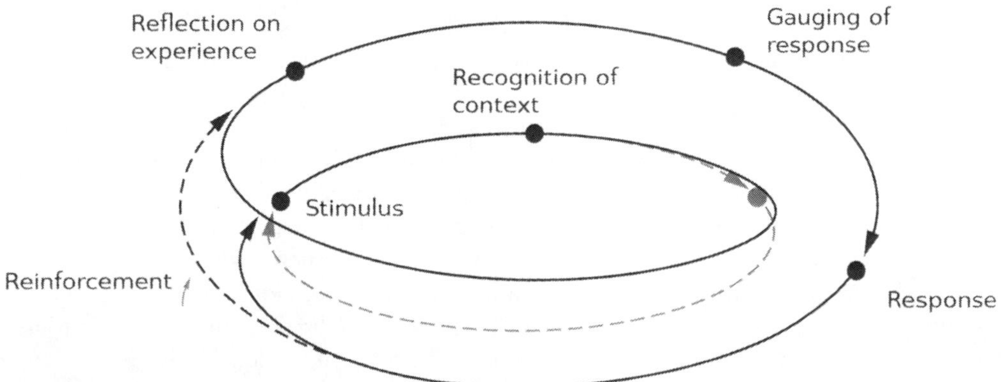

FIGURE 17.3 The loop of calibration, which is built on and feeds into the simple circuit of learning shown in Figure 17.2

Group Agents

Probably the most obvious form of the distinction between individual and aggregate is with respect to the agent. The simple interpretation of "agent" is "a single person," but the example of the Leighton Buzzard extension shows that the agents involved in transforming the built environment are more often than not groups or, strictly, individuals acting as representatives of a group. In some ways, the idea of a representative is probably the more common interpretation of "agent." For analytical clarity, agents can be distinguished by whose interest they serve:

- individual (simple self-interest),
- corporate (self-interest of group members),
- charity (interest of non-members—individuals or groups),[1] and
- government (interest of the public).[2]

A sub-group within most groups is the *leadership*. Strictly speaking, "the public" or "community" as *un-organized* statistical aggregates are not agents. In the Leighton Buzzard case, the land owners are constituted as limited companies, and the designers and technical professionals work for either the land owner or the local authority. In turn, the technical professionals work either in the capacity of a private practice consultancy (a separate group) or as "in-house" specialists. The professionals are also members of professional bodies that represent, monitor, and control the interests and activities of the individual members of the profession.

The local authority is one of at least three levels of government in Britain. The hierarchy of government includes Parliament, county councils, district councils, and town or parish councils (with limited powers). In some cases, the county and district are merged into one unitary authority. All the councils are made up of elected representatives who, in principle, represent their constituencies and are supported by appointed officers. Between 1998 and 2010, there were also Regional Assemblies made up of appointees from the constituent councils. In the case of Leighton Buzzard, at the start of the process, the relevant authorities were the East of England Regional Assembly, Bedfordshire County Council, and South Bedfordshire District Council. With a subsequent reorganization, the County and District were merged, along with another District to form Central Bedfordshire

Council, a unitary authority. In effect, the hierarchy of government acts as a hierarchy of control, with the bodies higher up giving direction to and setting limits on the actions of those lower down.

As an illustration, over the period in which the plans for the Leighton Buzzard extension were developed, a general election was held. National leadership changed from one party (Labour) to a coalition (Conservative/Liberal Democrat). The change in government resulted in substantial changes to legislation and planning policy, in particular, a move to shift control from higher to lower levels in the hierarchy. One part of that move was to scrap regional assemblies and regionally based targets for house building imposed from above. At the same time, the new government had to respond to the severe economic downturn and has sought to stimulate the economy, in part by encouraging house building to meet identified housing needs. The unitary and district authorities responsible for planning have had to adjust their policies to conform with emerging national legislation and policy. It is worth considering that the intention behind some shifts of policy at higher levels is driven by a range of intentions or motives some specific to the issue, some more political and ideological.

Specialization

In addition to the vertical differentiation of groups in the hierarchy of control, there is also a horizontal differentiation by specialization within groups and between groups. Within the local authority, in addition to the split between elected members and officers, the different departments of the local authority are staffed by sub-groups of different professionals. The most relevant to the case of the Leighton Buzzard extension are the planners, urban designers, landscape architects, highway/civil engineers, ecologists, historic conservation officers, archaeologists, environmental health officers, police, education officers, recreation officers, and housing officers. For each profession or "topic area," there are often also specialist organizations functioning as "statutory consultees" at a higher level either as a government agency, quango, civic society, or charity. These include the Highways Agency, Environment Agency (flooding and pollution), Natural England (ecology, biodiversity, and landscape), English Heritage (the historic environment), and Sport England (recreation), among many others. In addition, as noted above, there are the professional associations whose role is variously to promote the interests of the profession, regulate it in accordance with defined standards, develop and promote best practice, and advise other bodies including government on legislation, policy, and guidance.

Also participating in the overall process of taking a project such as an urban extension from initial idea to implementation are many other sub-groups outside of the local authority. These are, in general, self-selected community action or special interest groups who campaign on either a specific project or a specific topic. Examples in the case of Leighton Buzzard include Leighton Linslade Opposes Unsustainable Development (LOUD) and Friends of the Earth. As its name suggests, LOUD opposed the urban extension while Friends of the Earth sought to ensure any development achieves identified principles of sustainable development such as better public transport, lower carbon emissions, better community facilities, and better access to facilities and open space, among other things.

An important point to raise with respect to some of the specialist agents is the scope of their interests. One example is the public highway. In Britain, the public highway is the responsibility of the highway authority (though strategic roads are the responsibility of the Highways Agency). The scope of the authority's interest is not limited to the boundary of a development site. It is responsible for managing the highway network as a whole within the authority's boundary. This wider remit will be fundamental to the aims of the authority in contributing to the project. The principles that they will be trying to achieve will take the entire network into account and so will be following "global" rules and "local rules." To a certain extent, the public highway functions as a quasi-autonomous element managed by a defined group of agents. Other groups such as service providers (the education authority, water, sewerage, etc.) and food retailers may similarly have a more global scope and so act according to both global and local principles.

A further agent indirectly involved in the process is the end user. It is the habits and behavior of the users that the designers must take into account in their designs and to whom the developer must, in the end, appeal if the development is to go forward, most particularly within a market economy. Users include both individual residents and groups, including commercial corporate bodies that will purchase and/or occupy the development. In general, the interests of the users will be championed by different agents directly involved in the process. Some of those interests may be fairly limited, in particular the commercial corporate interests, for example, food retailers. The focus of their interest is the health of their business and can work to adapt the design to suit those interests rather than any wider aim for the development as a whole. In some cases, the users' interests are represented by a proxy reference to "the market."

Hierarchy of Learning

The proliferation of interested agents in the process begins to obscure the roles each might play, how they fit together, and where the "intention" in the process might lie. The looped circuit of learning discussed above and illustrated in Figures 17.2 and 17.3 provides a useful framework for giving the process some coherence.

That is to say, one way to make sense of the complexity and diversity is to see the social process involved in producing the built environment as a form of learning. The collective, social response to environmental, political, and economic issues can be seen as an example of the circuit of stimulus, response, and reinforcement. Climate change is a stimulus, proposals for sustainable development—however defined—are a response, and the policy and practical decisions to deliver those proposals on the ground (or not to) is reinforcement. And it is here that care needs to be taken in identifying the "learning agent." In a manner of speaking, it is not just an individual or single group that learns but the aggregate of groups involved in transforming the built environment. In strict terms, however, the aggregate learns only when the relevant individuals and groups *all learn the same thing*—individuals learning to work together in different ways—as a team learns to improve its game by practicing *together as a whole*. For the less homogeneous and formally organized groups such as all the agents involved in urban development, it will only ever be some statistical portion of the entire aggregate that "learns together." Not everyone agrees on what sustainable development should be or that it is even necessary in the first place. Though there is a hierarchy of learning, it increases in abstraction with each rise up the hierarchy.

Habit, Crisis, and the Roots of Learning

Again, we can only begin to see the higher levels because of the actions of individual people and groups working on individual projects. The stimulus for starting the project is some *need* (in the case of Leighton Buzzard, a housing shortage), and the stimulus for looking at new ways in which it might be done is a consciousness that something is not working as it should or is in danger of not working—the need to *adapt* to changing circumstances. Another part of the "need" stimulating the project in the case of Leighton Buzzard is the necessity for the landowners/developers to sustain their businesses by selling land at a profit to generate income. The need or *crisis* in the circuit stimulates the response, which is a new project to relieve the crisis: an urban extension.

At the same time, the starting point for any individual project is always "the way we did it the last time." No project starts entirely from scratch but necessarily makes use of the accumulated knowledge and practical experience (usefully referred to as *habits*[3]) gained until the time a new project begins.

Muratori (1959) and Caniggia and Maffei (2001) refer to that product of learning and habit as the *type*. For them, the type is the *idea of the building* (or *urban tissue*) in all its detail in the mind of the builder, compiled from all his or her experience. It is important to note that one way or another, the idea is *social*. It is not limited to the mind of one person. It will always involve the work of precursors (however primitive) and, in most cases, will involve contemporaries. Humans are social, and the built environment is a social endeavor, an endeavor that has developed over time.

The Distributed Idea

Looking at the range of competencies involved in urbanization as set out above, it is highly unlikely that the full, detailed idea of an urban extension can be held in the head of one person. The idea, in all its detail, is better considered to be *distributed* among the various individuals and groups, operating in the various specialisms and at various levels in the hierarchy of control. Given the different training, interests, and aims of the agents, the idea will be composite and as such not entirely internally consistent.

The lack of internal consistency is illustrated by (but not limited to) the diversity of views held by the different specialisms within the local authority. For example, the urban designers advocate as a basic principle of "good design" a street layout of interconnecting, "permeable" streets (thoroughfares; see, for example, Bentley et al. 1985). The rationale for permeable layouts is that connected streets allow for more choice of route and make it easier for pedestrians and cyclists to get to various destinations more easily. This is deemed more sustainable because it reduces reliance on the motor car for short journeys and is better for social cohesion. A permeable layout is counter-posed with cul-de-sac layouts, in particular multi-headed cul-de-sacs. The police, in contrast, *advocate* the use of cul-de-sacs on the basis that they are less "criminogenic" (a controversial term in itself). That is, some statistical analyses suggest that there is a higher incidence of crime in permeable layouts (see Knowles 2003).

The principal point here is that two sub-groups within the local authority do not agree on the "best" form of street layout and when "the local authority," as a single entity, responds to plans submitted to the authority, "it" gives contradictory advice. Similarly, there are often disagreements between urban designers and highway engineers as to the "best" forms of development. The engineers advocate designs for streets that minimize congestion and accidents by providing more highway space and junctions that allow for full visibility and "uninterrupted flow" of vehicles. The urban designers, in contrast, put forward designs that allow for "continuous pedestrian access" along barrier free routes for pedestrians, ensuring easy movement for the less mobile and disabled members of the community (concerted effort in recent years has reduced the gap between the two groups).

There are many other instances of conflicts between different professions such as the most suitable location for schools, shops, and parking. The conflicts noted can lie *within* the local authority and within consultant teams working for landowners/developers. Needless to say, the same conflicts can arise between the developer team and the local authority and points such as the total amount of land included for housing and commercial premises (income generating) and for community facilities (income consuming).

These conflicts are usually resolved through an iterative process of trial and error in which the developer team submits proposals, the local authority comments, and the proposals are revised (another instance of the learning circuit). In some cases, the process also involves community groups participating through workshops and other events to identify issues, suggest solutions, and comment on proposals.

An important point to note here is that like the early negotiation between landowners and local authority, the various agents involved in settling the final form of the development are all employing their own circuits of learning that interact with one another. That is, what is taken as the stimulus by one agent is, from the standpoint of another, a response to a previous stimulus, which was, in turn, the first agent's (or another's) response to a previous stimulus. The interaction is *mutually modifying adaptive behavior*.

Design by Committee: One Kind of Emergence

The end result of this process can be characterized as a particular kind of emergence, in this case "design by committee" (Fig. 17.4). In essence, there is no single source for the generating idea, and the final design that emerges is a compromise between the various ideal principles held by the different agents involved. The design is the result of the interactions between the agents. There is no way to predict the specific outcome because it is the product of a particular run through the process of negotiation and the contingent performance of all the agents, each responding to some or all of the others.

Though "design by committee" has pejorative connotations, it would seem that it is an instance of mutually modifying adaptive behavior that is essential in getting something like an urban

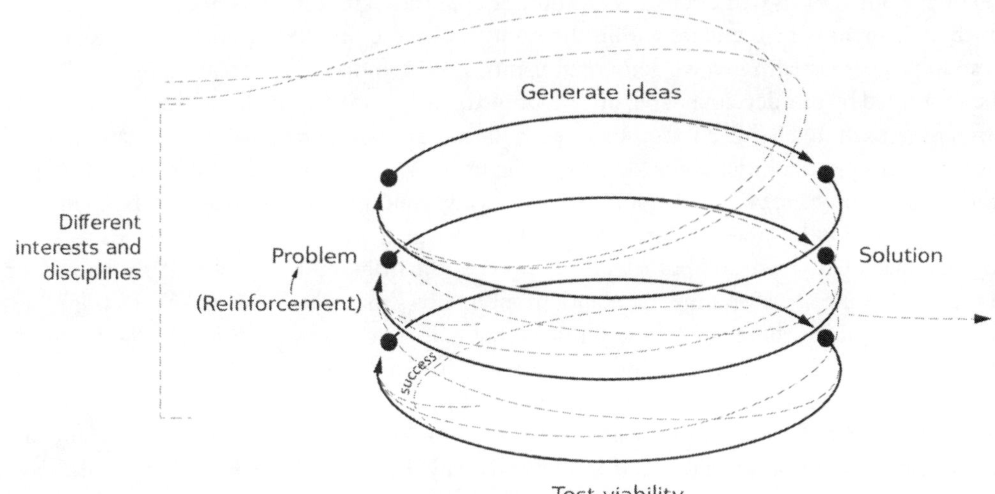

FIGURE 17.4 'Design by committee': mutually modifying circuits of learning

extension to work. In this respect, it is also important to note that the mutually adaptive behavior necessarily involves the specifics of the site. This is particularly true for the agents looking after quasi-autonomous elements that function at a scale larger than the urban extension itself (for example, the street network, utilities, educational facilities, retailing). The highway engineer starts with fairly rigid principles and objectives based on the performance of the highway network as a whole. In practice, the principles have to be interpreted to fit local circumstances and to a greater or lesser degree, the aims and objectives of other agents. Integrating the local part of the system necessitates accommodating and adapting to the global or larger-scale systems to keep the larger-scale system working. At the same time, getting the local part to work means interpreting and sometimes bending the rules to accommodate local conditions and circumstances. There is a necessary interaction between the local and the global. Longer distance routes need to meet the needs of longer distance travelers, but those routes need to be adapted to fit into settlements to get travelers onto them in the first place.

Distribution in Time

In addition to being distributed over many agents, the generating idea for something like an urban extension can also be distributed in time. Initial ideas for urbanization are likely to be generalized and only developed in site-specific detail over time. In the case of Leighton Buzzard, the process started, from the perspective of the landowner, with a general study of the town as a whole and the identification of key characteristics and constraints. This led to a broad strategy represented only by a plan with arrows pointing in the direction of growth. The initial diagram was progressively refined and submitted to the local authority as part of its own effort to identify a growth strategy for the wider region. Further, more detailed assessments were then carried out, and additional detail was added, including areas and locations of different land uses and principal routes. These were tested by the landowner team for financial viability and conformity with general policy and best practice. The progress from initial diagram to a planning application took about five years.

In the British planning system, the spread in time of the "idea" for larger-scale development is formalized by the distinction between two types of planning application: *outline* on the one hand and *detailed* on the other. As its name suggests, the outline application requires less fixed detail and allows for further elaboration of the ideas within the limits set by the outline application. The two-stage application process can also involve additional agents. It is often the case that an outline application will be submitted by one developer and, once approved, the site will be divided and sold to a number of different house builders. Each additional agent then submits a *reserved matters* application, which requires providing the additional detail. One of the implications of the spread in time is that, over the course of the process, policies or priorities can change, and the design is likely to be changed as a result. The initial idea is modified in part to suit a new situation.

To generalize the process and put it in the context of the diagram in Figure 17.2, the movement from the "generating ideas" to implementation itself involves many iterations of (interacting) "sub-circuits" within which there are two key roles. One role is to propose an idea (however partial relative to the whole project) and the other is to test that idea against various criteria of "viability": physical, technical, economic, and cultural (see Fig. 17.5). The forum of the proposal and testing can vary from the brain of an individual (turning ideas over in his or her head), a small design team, or to the submission of a planning application and its review by the specialists as part of the consultation process. In terms of roles, all agents test in some capacity (if only in their heads), some agents mainly propose, and some, officially, only test (for more on "generate and test" see Dennett 1995).

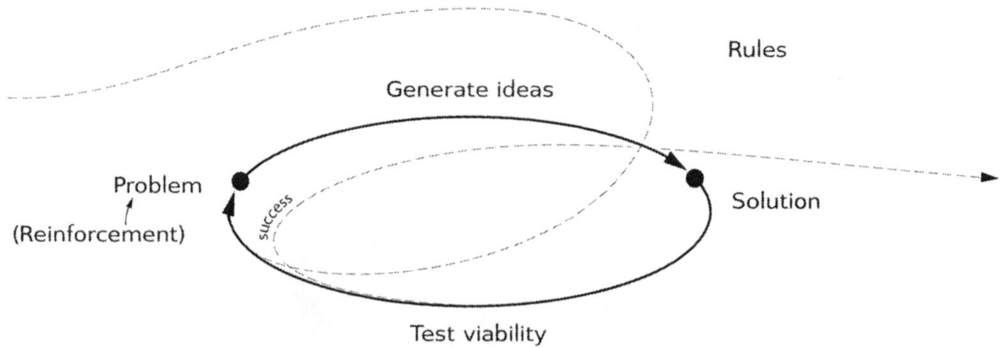

FIGURE 17.5 The sub-circuit of 'generate and test' as part of a larger circuit of learning

As noted above, for a project such as an urban extension, many ideas are involved, and they come from many sources. Though the ideas may come from anywhere, and a wide range of agents might come up with ideas, the role of official testing in the case of Leighton Buzzard corresponds to the regulatory system. The sources of many of the rules against which ideas are tested are regulatory bodies higher up the hierarchy of control: national legislation, policy and guidance covering planning, highways, flooding, habitat and protected species, the historic environment, carbon emissions, building regulations, and health and safety, among others. The "rules" embodied in the regulatory system are to a large extent based on an aggregate of accumulated experience and research (circuits of learning) and so constitute a form of calibration. In terms of the diagram in Figure 17.5, the rules lie a level up from the circuit representing the act of applying the rules in the production of a particular example such as the Leighton Buzzard extension. This could be represented as a higher loop of calibration, as in Figure 17.3, for the entire process or for each of any number of sub-circuits representing the proposal and testing of different elements of the design.

The actual process of construction is a further form of testing in which inevitable adjustments (on-the-job decisions) are made to accommodate unforeseen or overly idealized details and circumstances. It is at this stage that any innovative, untested elements can prove unworkable and so be changed, adapted, or replaced.

Forms in Use

The ultimate test of viability is putting the finished product to use. For an urban extension, that means occupying the houses and using the facilities. A design can pass the initial tests of adhering to policies and regulations and getting built but may still not fit with the habits and expectations of the individuals who move into the houses. If the fit is poor, there are two main responses new residents might make. One is to adjust their habits; the other is to modify the physical form of the buildings within their control.

An aspect of agency that is easy to overlook in this respect is the sensory. An essential part of the learning circuit is the ability to sense and process the stimulus. This means that all users of the built environment are agents in this capacity. It is the behavior of individuals and their judgments and expressions of contentment or discontent that provides the signal to do something about it one way or another.

An example from Leighton Buzzard is the issue of parking. In recent schemes, one of the design principles insisted on by the local authority was that streets should not be visually dominated by

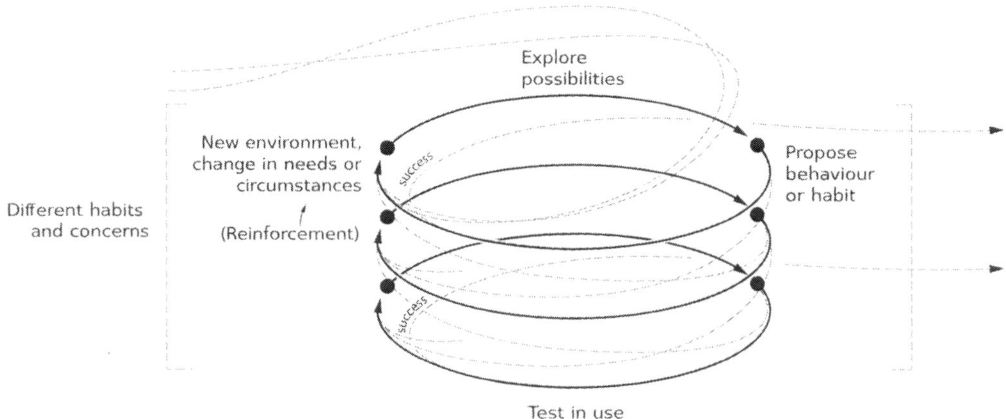

FIGURE 17.6 Form in use by a group: mutually modifying circuits can lead to common forms of behavior

parked cars. Parking spaces were, therefore, located to the side or behind the houses and on-street parking essentially "forbidden." In an effort to keep vehicle speeds down, the highway officers for their part insisted on minimum width carriageways so there was no space to park without blocking one or another lane of the carriageway.

Another policy aim was to achieve higher densities using terraced forms of housing, which allow only limited parking spaces to the side of the houses. As a result, the bulk of the parking was located behind the houses in "parking courts." A further policy aim was to require that all streets have "active fronts," which means in practice that the "front" door of the house should face the street.

This combination of features then poses a potential dilemma for the residents. A strong habit in most residents is to park as close as possible to the front door of their house. To maintain that habit, people ended up either using their back door as the main entrance to their house, or they parked their car in the street, half on the footway, half on the carriageway (known in the United Kingdom as "footway parking"). One way or another, it should be clear that the situation described is another instance of a circuit of learning, illustrated diagrammatically in Figure 17.6.

Exploratory Emergence

The encounter between new resident and house (in its physical context) is the stimulus and takes the form of an exploration of possibilities: what will work? The response is to decide on a particular way of doing things and test it out in practice. The reinforcement is the judgment that it works or not. If the option chosen has not been tried before it can be said to arise by *exploratory emergence* when an agent and environment are put together. The new form of behavior cannot be predicted from either element on its own. There are three central qualifying points here: first, each of a number of households necessarily makes a choice of how to "behave"; second, options will be constrained by habit and perceptions of social pressures; and third, choices can be affected by seeing what other people do (another form of stimulus). People often copy their neighbors, an instance of what Whitehand and Carr (2001) call the "neighbor effect." The result is that despite the exploration, common or predominant forms of behavior can arise from the interaction of individuals with their environment and with one another. Like design by committee, it is a case of mutually modifying behavior, and the result depends on the nature and character of the particular agents involved. The exploratory divergence is countered by social convergence but not entirely. New forms of behavior can catch on to become the norm.

In Leighton Buzzard, residents explored the options for parking, and many chose footway parking. This in turn gave rise to a significant issue for the neighborhood as a whole. In particular, there was an incident when a fire engine needed to get down a street and could not because the parked cars created a barrier. This result provided further stimulus to keep the sub-circuit going. New forms of behavior can lead to the need for new physical forms.

The various examples of "sub-circuits" described so far, including design by committee, and generate and test can be generally characterized as forms of *developmental emergence*. They are examples of emergent behavior because the distinct effect or pattern—an agreed design or car-lined streets—cannot be attributed to any one individual (or single group acting as a unit) but only to the aggregate of agents acting semi-autonomously. The examples can be distinguished as "developmental" forms of emergence because they arise out of the development and ongoing life of a single, individual place.

Emergence and the Hierarchy of Elements

Another form of developmental emergence is related to the physical implications of distinguishing individual and aggregate. The distinction is fundamental to the urban morphological concept of the hierarchy of elements (levels of scale). Both Conzen's identification of buildings, plots, and streets as the main plan elements (1960) and Caniggia and Maffei's double, four-level hierarchy encompassing materials, structures, rooms and buildings, tissues, districts and settlements (2001) are based on seeing the constituent elements as both individual objects and aggregates of parts. The *objects* of one level are the *parts* that are aggregated to form the objects of the next level up the hierarchy. Rooms are aggregated to form buildings, and plots are aggregated together to form plot series.

Viewed in the abstract, this principle can be seen as central to the underlying generative process that results in the hierarchy of elements itself, as suggested in Figure 17.7. The act of aggregating single rooms results in a range of viable or "stable," workable buildings, the combination of one or more buildings, and a bounded area of ground results in a range of viable plots, and the aggregation of plots results in a range of plot series, which, together with a route, results in a street.

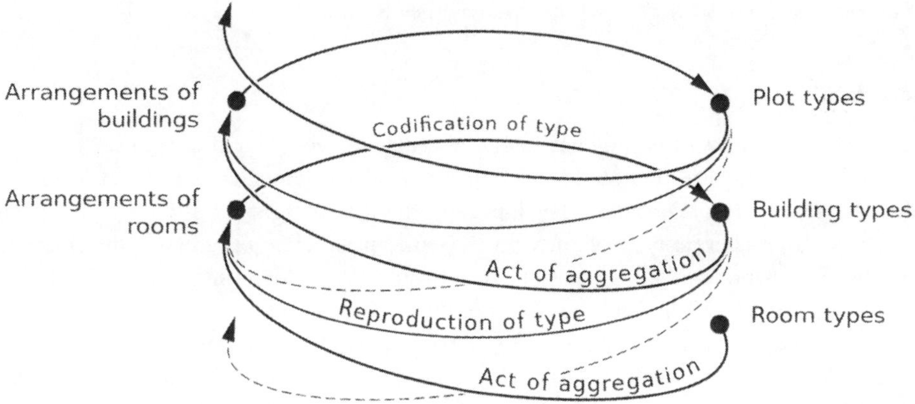

FIGURE 17.7 The hierarchy of scale emerges from alternating acts of aggregation and codification of types fed by reproduction

Whether there is any case to argue that this generative process corresponds to an identifiable historical process is an open question. Did the higher-level elements in the hierarchy such as the street develop from *ad hoc* aggregations of more primitive elements? Before there was any codified idea of the "street," were there plots or buildings ranged either side of a preexisting route due to the common locational choices of a number of individuals?

Caniggia and Maffei do in fact posit this basic principle for the development of urban form and in particular the idea of the grid settlement (2001). In their view, the grid is a form that emerged from the progressive construction of individual but interconnected streets. First there is a main "matrix" route with plots either side. An example would be a single "high street" settlement such as in some medieval planted towns. With the later need for more houses, side streets are then built as extensions more or less at right angles to the main street. Finally, with further growth of the town, streets are built to connect up the side streets, set back from and parallel to the high street. The grid emerges from the progressive construction of "single" streets.

What is important with respect to agency is that the emergent form, once established, can be seen as the basis of a new design. The experience of a grid formed by steps can be used to deliberately design a grid-form settlement *from the outset*. The emergent form "proposes" the design, which can be "selected" by the designer for the next settlement. This is fundamentally the same sequence as set out by Muratori (1959), Caniggia and Maffei (2001) in the typological process. In the standard typological process, the modifications of buildings over time are used as a basis for the design of a new version of the same generic type. If, for example, the predominant house type at a given moment is two story but enough are modified over time by the addition of a third story to fit the habits and expectations of builders and residents, the three-story version becomes the common or leading type and is used as the basis for any new house.[4]

An example of the process can be found in Leighton Buzzard in a housing area from the 1970s. Each plot in the development had a "car port" to the side of the house but no garage. In time, a resident applied to convert the car port to a garage. Many other residents followed suit, with the result that most of the area was transformed by the neighborhood effect. Each modification was done individually but following the same basic principle, copied from the first instance. Once enough people make the change, it becomes obvious that an integral garage is a desirable feature, and new houses in other areas are designed from the outset with an integral garage. Over the long term, the street changes, and a new local building type emerges.

Scalar and Evolutionary Emergence

There are at least two forms of emergence being described above—in addition to the examples of developmental emergence already noted. In the first case, a form emerges at a higher level of scale when *physical aggregates* are created and developed by the acts of agents building and combining a number of the same generic type of form in the same place. The progressive development of a gridded settlement from individual streets, for example, or a plot series from individual plots involves a step up in the physical level of scale: street to settlement, plot to plot series.

In the second case, an entity emerges at the same physical level of scale by the acts of agents reproducing a common type to form a *population* or *class* of individual buildings. Strictly, that emergent entity is an idea. There is a step "up" not in physical scale but from individual examples to the type, from member to class (see Bateson 1980 and Hofstadter 1999 for expositions on this concept of "logical type").

While these are both generically cases of emergence, they are different in an important respect that deserves emphasis. In the first case, the emergence can occur in a single instance where a new form emerges at a higher level of scale from the aggregation of parts at the next lower level. Because it occurs in the development of a single instance, it is a form of developmental emergence. Because it involves a step up in scale, it can be more specifically distinguished as *scalar emergence*.

In the second case, the emergence occurs when modifications are made to a *population* of forms, or a new population is created. The move is from individual to population (example to type). For this reason, it can be termed *evolutionary emergence*. It operates at the level of the population.

It is important to make the distinction because it allows us to put together a clearer picture of how the diversification of form occurs. It allows us to trace out the actions and interactions of individuals that give the impression of intentionality on the part of an entity such as an entire city. The distinction is also key to qualifying the notions of "local" and "global" rules to sketch out a richer and more powerful picture of morphogenesis that better explains the different kinds of order we find in urban form.

Emergence and the Diversification of Form

Once identified, it becomes clear that developmental and evolutionary emergence are necessarily intertwined. They work together and feed off each other. The interaction is exemplified by the progressive creation of the gridded settlement as proposed by Caniggia and Maffei. The results of scalar emergence through the physical aggregation of streets is consciously identified as a "new idea" and deliberately used as the basis for the design of an entire settlement. The emergent form at the higher level of scale becomes codified as an idea. The evolutionary emergence occurs when the idea is taken up in enough cases and emerges as a type or population. That new form may then evolve by modification of existing examples and the creation of new, modified versions of the type. This double emergence can occur at other levels in the hierarchy. Rather, it could be said that the double process created the hierarchy. The reproduction of many examples of the same kind of object according to the shared idea of the type at one level provides the substance for making up physical aggregates at the next level up.

This double process of emergence follows the two interrelated circuits of learning illustrated in Figures 17.2 and 17.3. As shown in Figure 17.8, the developmental stage corresponds to the simple circuit of learning, and the evolutionary stage corresponds to calibration. The initial stimulus is the need for a building and the response a finished house or street. This is put to use, and the reinforcement is the judgment that the form fits with the habits of the user and the subsequent choice to continue as is or change. If circumstances change, forcing a change in habit (a new stimulus), the response might be to adjust behavior to suit the form. If the habits change enough, a decision is made at some point to modify or add to the form, which sends the process around the circuit again. A new story is added to the house or new streets are added to the settlement. If the same change is followed by enough agents, a population is created or changes. *Reproduction* is the essential trigger for evolutionary emergence.

The intertwining of developmental and evolutionary processes occurs when the "calibration loop" feeds back into the lower circuit. The emergent building type is used as the basis for the design of new individual buildings, and the consciousness of the aggregate informs the design of the constituent elements further up the scale.

The fruits of emergence cannot feed diversification unless the agents shift their view up a level from the individual, to the population or to the physical aggregate. Someone, somewhere had to move his or her attention from the building to the street and from the street to the settlement as a

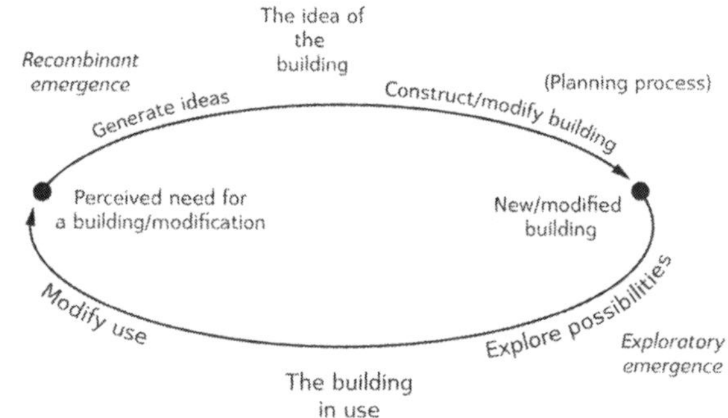

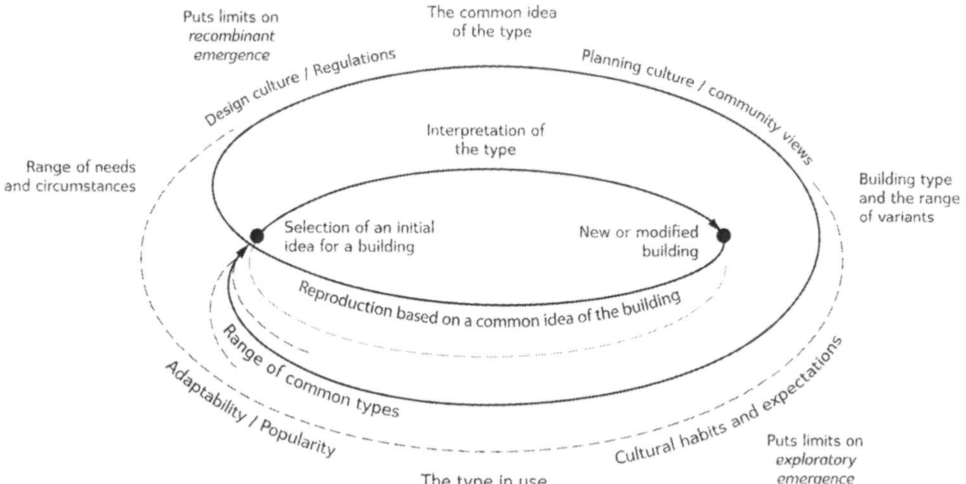

FIGURE 17.8 The typological process. The development circuit, top, and the evolutionary loop, below, are essential elements of the same process

whole. This shift may or may not be conscious, but the ability to do so is an essential capacity of an agent in the creation of the built environment.

And though the idea of an historical "first recognition" is necessarily speculative, the principle of *recognition* of forms as opposed to any kind of pure *de novo* creation becomes more compelling if we return to the maligned notion of design by committee.

As suggested earlier in the account of the Leighton Buzzard urban extension, design by committee is a kind of emergence. When compared with either recognition or *de novo* creation as sources of diversity, design by committee, in principle, appears not as a degenerate, poor substitute for some pure form of creation but rather an essential element in the development and diversification of the built environment. Recognition on its own would be too limited and conservative, reproducing only things that have been done before. Pure de *novo* creation on its own would be too profligate, producing too many untested and ultimately unsuccessful products.

The notion of design by committee is pejorative not because it involves mixing together different ideas but because of the way in which they are mixed together—the institutional structures and personalities of the people who do the mixing. For the diversification of form, the mixing of ideas is of the essence. Whether in a committee, a team, or an individual brain, mixing results in the emergence of the new and unpredictable but, at the same time, preserves some of the proven successes of the individual ideas. The process involves the combination or recombination of a number of ideas to form a more-or-less coherent single idea. What can be termed *recombinant emergence* is distinct because it involves a step up from a plurality of ideas to a single idea: for example, from a range of possible houses or elements of houses to a specific design. There is no step up in physical level from individual to aggregate (such as plot to plot series), nor is there a step up from member to class (for example, individual house to house type).

Hierarchy of Agency and Control

The three kinds of developmental emergence (recombinant, exploratory, and scalar) and evolutionary emergence all work together in the overall process that leads to the diversification of urban form. And with the emergence of deliberate design and planning at higher levels of scale comes the parallel emergence of agents with the power and authority to undertake a project at the higher level. Building a new town requires someone or some group to bring together and control sufficient resources to complete the project. Such an undertaking does not happen by itself.

One way or another, a hierarchy of control sets up the possibility and likelihood of competition between those in control and those subject to control. Petruccioli puts it very elegantly when he says, "the crystalline form of an original city is to be found only in illustrated treatises. In the reality of the historical process, the inhabitants of a city quickly see to the deformation of the plan with individual acts of appropriation" (2007: 223. On this general issue, see also McClain et al. 1994). The development of planning laws and regulations has to a large extent been a response to the activities and emergent forms generated by the many individuals (and groups) operating at various levels of scale. The rules are enacted to deliberately direct, control, and limit the "creativity" driving such things as overbuilding, back-to-back housing, the appropriation of public space by individuals, or the creation of squatter settlements.

The Basic Unit of Control

The emergence of form occurs at all levels, but there is, however, a distinct difference in kind at the level of the plot or lot. This element of form corresponds (generally but by no means as a hard and fast rule) to a unit of control, most basically occupation and ownership. Changes that occur within that unit are, in general, under the control of a single agent, the owner or occupier.

Once one steps up to a level that involves an aggregate of plots, a street, for example, the element as a whole is not in the control of a single agent but an aggregate of agents, in principle, one agent per plot, and one or more regulatory agents further up the hierarchy of control. Changes to a street can follow from the aims and intentions of a number of agents each acting independently of one another or at least semi-independently, only seeking to act on and change his or her own plot within the street. The changes to the street might be *convergent* or *divergent* depending on whether individual changes are based on the same or different ideas.

Design, Control, and Different Kinds of Agent

From this perspective, planning control is not a deliberate act of design or creation but a channeling of effort and energy running "of its own accord," which is to say, running on the energy of individual agents operating at lower levels taken together. The controls limit but do not determine the forms, but neither is it the case that there is no top-down design. The simple model of many agents, all of the same kind, acting at the lowest level, following "local rules," is neither satisfying nor adequate. The example of the Leighton Buzzard urban extension illustrates, however, that the design of higher-level forms is not a straightforward "top-down" exercise, either. This is true in terms of the different kinds of emergence set out above and also in terms of the different kinds of agents involved in their different roles.

Conclusion

In a quick summary of the foregoing, it is possible to distinguish different general roles for the different agents in the process. The range includes those who drive it by making and pressing forward proposals for change (*motive agents*), those who generate the specifics of the proposal (*generative agents*), those who control or limit proposals (*regulatory agents*), those who oppose them (*resistive agents*), and those who use them (*sensory agents*). Any one agent may play several or all of the roles. All of these types are also potentially *testing agents,* those who make judgments by comparison with previous experience, principles, or standards.

The aim of this "theoretical excursion" has been to show that agency can be seen not as a seemingly random collection of acts but part of a coherent process. The coherence is not, however, the process or product of deliberate design. Rather, the coherence arises out of basic habitual behavior on our part as human beings: the habit of learning. The chapter has "mapped" a description of the development process onto the basic circuit of learning. This has shown that there are loops and sub-circuits within the overall process corresponding to the different kinds of emergence.

Understanding the full diversity of the process also requires acknowledging that there is not just one type of agent and not just one type of agency. Rather, agency involves different roles potentially operating at different levels, within both the hierarchy of control and levels of scale. Diversity also arises with specialization of agents acting on the basis of complementary but potentially competing principles and aims.

The example of Leighton Buzzard shows that the generating idea of the project may be distributed between the different agents. This situation can result in the *recombinant emergence* of designs by the application of independent standards and principles pursued by the different agents participating in the process. The end design may not be the deliberate choice of any one agent or group but the mutually acceptable compromise arrived at by mutually modifying adaptive behavior of the agents. Distribution of the idea in time can also result in less "control" over the generating idea. What is produced in the end may differ significantly from what was envisaged in the early stages because of changes in circumstances or policy.

The generation of designs, and their implementation through a regulatory process leading to construction is only one half of the overall circuit. As the chapter has attempted to show, the second half involves the active occupation and use of the completed project. Agency does not end with completion. It is only possible to determine whether the *proposal* of a particular design actually works by putting it to the *test* of use. And it is the users, as sensory and testing agents, who provide the signal that is either an implicit or explicit judgment that the design is and remains a success or not. Active use provides the stimulus for modification and growth through *exploratory emergence*: new forms of behavior requiring new physical forms. It is then the choice of motive agents to initiate change. As the chapter has sought to demonstrate, when the circuit operates at a level above the individual plot, there will necessarily be more than one agent involved, and roles will begin to be separated.

The result of mapping the longer-term development process onto the circuit of learning shows clearly where emergence occurs. With the repetition of the circuit over many iterations, there are in fact two interrelated forms of emergence involved. One type, *developmental emergence*, occurs in the life of an individual element (encompassing recombinant, exploratory, and scalar emergence). The other kind, *evolutionary emergence*, arises out of the repetition and reproduction of the developmental circuit and occurs at the level of the population or type. The interaction lies in the fact that any given circuit of development is informed by the experience of previous versions of the type, either by unconscious or conscious recognition. The connection is directly analogous to the chicken and egg. It is not, however, a paradox, because the process occurs over time. Each step has its precursor in a previous, likely simpler version, down to the primitive exploratory accidents that allowed for some initial recognition of "shelter."

It would, thus, appear that an essential aspect of agency in the built environment is the capacity to shift attention from an object to its relationship with others (context) and from object to a class. There would seem to be a native though often unconscious ability to look up and down the hierarchy of elements, between individual and aggregate, between general rules and their application in a particular instance, and so between individual and type. Equally, it is essential to understand the threshold of the plot as the transition point where agency proliferates and begins to generate more obvious forms of emergent behavior.

One way or another, these various acts are fundamentally *social*. The built environment is social in the same way that language is social, in a radical yet paradoxical way. Both rely on an interaction between individuals (our conversations) but also on a relationship between the individual and the group (learning and being taught the results of accumulated knowledge). On the one hand, language and the built environment are built by the acts of individuals but, on the other hand, the individual act is built out of elements that are provided and given currency by the group. Though it is only individuals who ever actually speak, a language is necessarily spoken by a community. The ideas on which language and the built environment are based must be shared to be effective and to have meaning. They would not be generated at all if it were not for our need to cooperate to survive. We speak and build for mutual benefit.

Notes

1 The size of the non-member group served by a charity varies considerably, as does the extent to which the activities of the charity serve members and non-members. There would seem to be a spectrum between a quasi-corporate group and a pure charity, whose activities provide no benefit to the members other than the act of helping others.
2 This naïve formulation clearly begs many questions that are at the root of much political debate.
3 Habits can be good and bad and certainly encompass accumulated knowledge and experience. A concert pianist or fluent speaker of a foreign language has established good habits or a "second nature."
4 This is the idealized process. As suggested by the concept of recombinant emergence, ideas for new types may come from many sources. One way or another, the emergent type is an idea and is always subject to *interpretation* in the move from idea to a built form.

References

Bateson, G. (1980) *Mind and Nature: A Necessary Unity.* New York: Bantam.

Bateson, G. (2000) *Steps to an Ecology of Mind.* Chicago: University of Chicago Press.

Batty, M. (2005) *Cities and Complexity: Understanding Cities with Cellular Automata, Agent-Based Models, and Fractals.* Cambridge, MA: MIT Press.

Bentley, I., Alcock, A., Murrain, P., McGlynn, S., and Smith, G. (1985) *Responsive Environments: A Manual for Designers.* London: Architectural Press.

Caniggia, G., and Maffei, G. L. (2001) *Architectural Composition and Building Typology: Interpreting Basic Buildings,* trans. S. J. Frazer. Florence: Alinea Editrice.

Cataldi, G. (1981) *Lezioni di Architettura,* Biblioteca di Architettura / Saggi e Documenti 26. Florence: Alinea Editrice.

Coates, P. (2010) *Programming Architecture.* London: Routledge.

Conzen, M. R. G. (1960) *Alnwick, Northumberland: A Study in Town-Plan Analysis.* London: George Philip, Institute of British Geographers Publication No. 27.

Dennett, D. (1995) *Darwin's Dangerous Idea: Evolution and the Meanings of Life.* New York: Simon and Schuster.

Dennett, D. (1997) *Kinds of Minds: The Origins of Consciousness.* London: Phoenix.

Hacking, I. (1990) *The Taming of Chance.* Cambridge: Cambridge University Press.

Hensel, M., Menges, A., and Weinstock, M. (eds.) (2004) *Emergence: Morphogenetic Design Strategies.* London: Wiley.

Hillier, B. (1996) *Space Is the Machine: A Configurational Theory of Architecture.* Cambridge: Cambridge University Press.

Hofstadter, D. (1999) *Gödel, Escher, Bach: An Eternal Golden Braid.* London: Penguin.

Jacobs, J. (1961) *The Death and Life of Great American Cities.* New York: Random House.

Johnson, S. (2001) *Emergence: The Connected Lives of Ants, Brains, Cities and Software.* London: Penguin.

Knowles, P. (2003) The cost of policing new urbanism. *Safer Communities,* 2 (4): 33–7.

Kropf, K. (2001) Conceptions of change in the built environment. *Urban Morphology,* 5 (1): 29–42.

Kropf, K. (2003) Between the intentional and the emergent, in A. Petruccioli, M. Stella, and G. Strappa (eds.), *The Planned City?* 291–5. Bari: Uniongrafica Corcelli Editrice.

Marshall, S. (2009) *Cities, Design and Evolution.* London: Routledge.

McClain, J. L., Merriman, J. M., and Ugawa, K. (eds.) (1994) *Edo and Paris: Urban Life and the State in the Early Modern Era.* Ithaca: Cornell University Press.

Muratori, S. (1959) Studi per una operante storia urbana di Venezia, in *Palladio: Rivista di Storia dell'Architettura* Nuova Serie, anno IX–1959, Fasicolo III–IV. Rome: Istituto Poligrafico dello Stato.

Peach, J. (2011) How Amsterdam's Urban Form Created the Ideal Cycling City, on *thisbigcity*. Online. Available HTTP: <http://thisbigcity.net/amsterdam-urban-form-created-ideal-cycling-city/> (posted 18 November 2011, accessed 7 March 2012).

Petruccoli, A. (2007) *After Amnesia: Learning from the Islamic Mediterranean Urban Fabric.* Bari: Politecnico di Bari, Dipartimento di Ingegneria Civile e Architettura (ICAR).

Salingaros, N. (2004) Design methods, emergence and collective intelligence. *Katarxis,* 3. Online. Available HTTP: <http://www.katarxis3.com/Salingaros-Collective_Intelligence.htm> (accessed 7 March 2012).

Weinstock, M. (2010) *The Architecture of Emergence: The Evolution of Form in Nature and Civilisation.* London: Wiley.

Whitehand, J. W. R., and Carr, C. M. H. (2001) *Twentieth-Century Suburbs: A Morphological Approach.* London: Routledge.

Wolfram, S. (2002) *A New Kind of Science.* Champaign, Ill.: Wolfram Media. Online. Available HTTP: <http://www.wolframscience.com/nksonline/toc.html> (accessed 7 March 2012).

INDEX

abbey precincts 51–5; *see also* ecclesiastical precincts, monastic precincts
abbeys *see* religious houses
Abercrombie, Sir Patrick (1879–1957), British urban planner 231, 235
Aberystwyth, Dyfed, Wales 32, 36
absolutist rulers, urban visions of 83
absolutist states 13
actor-network theory 10, 233, 290–2
administrative skills 101
administrators: as cultural heroes 102; necessary qualifications 100
admiralty (navy yard) 116, 129
agency *see* morphological agency
agent-based modeling 11, 304
agents of change (transformation) 10, 11, 219
agents *see* morphological agents
Aigues Mortes, Gard, France 39
Alaska 115–32; transfer from Russia to the U.S. (1867) 119
Alnwick, Northumberland, England 7
American Civil War (1861–1865) 119
Amsterdam, The Netherlands, bicycle in 303
archaeological evidence 6, 47, 50; on strip plots 53; plot subdivision 76; in Lübeck 79n5; on street patterns 6
archaeologists 9, 308; dating of monastic housing 48
archaeology 5, 7
architects: cultural perceptions among 221; in court towns 14; foreign architects employed in court towns 88; interaction with industrialists 170; interaction with urban planners 17; interest in historical urban form 6; limited independence of court-town architects 89; as morphological agents 16; as a profession 16; *see also* Italian architects
architctural style *see* building style
architectural theory and ideology 16
architectural type 17; *see also* building type, Muratorian terminology
architecture, as a local profession 9
Ardres, Pas-de-Calais, France 39
aristocracy, relations with burgesses in medieval towns 70
aristocratic families: founders of universities and religious houses 78; impact on urban form 9; palaces 67, 83
Armagh, County Armagh, Ireland 48
artisan production 15
assembly rooms 13
Assisi, Umbria, Italy 47
Auckland, New Zealand 18, 267–82; lack of comprehensive planning and design guide 279; waterfront élite privatization issues 275; waterfront redevelopment 273–6
Augsburg, Bayern, Germany 66
Australia, British town-making in 14
Austria, Duchy of, in the thirteenth century 11
authoritarian landscapes, dominant role of the potentate in 94
authorship, of buildings and environments 3–4
automobiles, acquired 197; parked 314–5
Aymonino, Carlo (1926–2010), Italian architect and historian 222–3; as proponent of architectural structuralism in the historical city 227

Baa, near Bordeaux, Aquitaine, France (bastide town) 34, 35, 39
balloon-frame construction 121

Baltimore and Ohio Railroad (B&O) 137, 143, 145, 149
Baltimore, MD, U.S.A. 15, 137, 143–5; precedent for railroads in city streets in America 144
Banham, Reyner (1922–1988), British architectural critic 253
bankers 100, 162
Barcelona, Catalonia, Spain 99
bastide towns 36, 79
Bath, Somerset, England 4, 38
Battle, Sussex, England 51
Beaumaris, Angelsey, Wales 37, 40–2
behavioral environment: attitudes towards 8; theory of 8
beltline railroads 145, 147
Bere, Merionethshire, Wales 35, 37
Beresford, Maurice (1920–2005), British historian 9, 28, 30, 35
Berkeley school of cultural geography 6
Berlin, Germany 13, 14
Bern, Switzerland 64, 67
Berwick upon Tweed, Northumberland, England 32
Birka (Ekerö), Björkö, Sweden, Viking town 63
Birmingham, England 285–98: Bull Ring Shopping Centre 253, 293–4; "Championing Birmingham" iniative (2003) 293; postindustrial 18; urban landscape 7, 293
bishops, as morphological agents 46–61; relations with kings regarding town development 52
bishops' palaces 48, 50, 67, 116
boardroom decisions 10
Bobek, Hans (1903–1990), Austrian geographer 6
Bohemia, Kingdom of 11
Bois de Boulogne (pleasure park), Paris 103
Bonel, Nicholas (active 1270s), English surveyor 39
borough privileges 35
Boston, MA, U.S.A.: élites in 10; estuarine solutions for railroads 15; retail districts in 10
boulevards haussmanniens 97
bowling alleys 123
breakthrough streets (*grandes percées*), distinctiveness of Haussmann's in Paris 104
bridges, 67; footbridge 177; inhabited 253; for railroads 140, 142; over railroads 184; *see also* viaducts
Britannia, Roman province 46
brown-fields 18
builders: master-builders 14; in U.S. 16; *see also* house builders
building fabric: brick factories 156; brick workers' housing 158, 164; German *rohbau* 156; log 121; transition from log to frame 122; *see also* building materials
building inspectors 194
building materials: brick 71, 78, 88, 158, 164, 168; concrete 187, 251; log (wooden) 114, 119, 125; stone 56, 63, 70, 77–8, 86, 108, 185; "truth to materials" maxim 260; wood 88
building permits 194
building plans: in Britain 9; owner-built housing (U.S.) 200–2
building regulations, 94, 193, 222, 313, 319; absence of 115, 132, 194–5, 198; against fire 70, 92; in court towns 13, 84, 86; in Haussmannian Paris 108; in medieval towns 67, 70; privately enforced 199; suburban 193, 196; *see also* planning regulations, street lines
building styles: Anglo-Saxon 54; Classical 181; Dutch 88; Eclectic 166; English Gothic 159; Glasgow 181; Gothic 71, 78; Italian Renaissance 159; Italianate 181; Modernist 168; Neoclassical 119; neo-Gothic 156; New Brutalist 260; Norman 50, 54; Old English 181; Postmodern 285; Romanesque 54, 78; Scots Baronial 181; Second Empire 108; Swiss 159, 166
building type, fundamental nature of 220
building types (other than residential): balloon-frame construction 121; city halls 237; log buildings 114, 119, 125; megastructures, 251–63; town halls 66, 70–2; *see also* church buildings, house types (residential), factory buildings
building typology 219
built environment: conflict over form of 8; emergence of 303–21; *laissez-faire* development 154; social production of 9; *see also* urban form, urban morphology
burgages 7; burgage cycle 7; burgage plots, 16, 39, 64, 68–9; repletion 7
Burgess, Ernest (1886–1966), American urban sociologist 7
burgesses: as planners 67; relations with aristocracy in medieval towns 70; as urban patricians 66
Burton-on-Trent, Staffordshire, England 51, 54
Bury St. Edmunds, Suffolk, England 55, 57
businessmen, as morphological agents 14, 126; *see also* merchants

cadastral map 120, 219
Cadbury Brothers, owners of Bournville, Birmingham, England 159
Caernarfon, Gwynedd, Wales 32, 37
Caerwys, Flintshire, Wales 37
canal engineers 143
canals: impact on urban morphology 143; and railroads 139–40, 143
Caniggia, Gianfranco (1933–1987), Italian architect, architectural theorist and urban morphologist 17; championed Muratori's ideas, 220–1
Canterbury, Kent, England 49

capital flows, through cities 18
cars *see* automobiles
Carter, Harold (b.1925), British geographer and urban morphologist 8
castle towns 27–44, 48, 79
castles 12, 32, 34, 39, 48, 58; prohibitions on building 63
cathedrals 49–60, 67, 70, 118; built of logs 125; stone-built 48
CBD (central business district) frame 268; encroachment on waterfront 277; *see also* downtown
cellars: apartments 67, 73–5; housing with and without 166; wine 57; prison in 73
cemetery 119
central government officials 115
central place theory 6
Cerdà, Ildefons (1815–1876), Catalan urban planner 99
Chabot, Georges (1890–1975), French urban geographer, 223
Chandigarh, India 99
Chapin, F. Stuart (b.1944), American ecologist and planner 8
charters 68–9; railroad 139, 143, 145, 149; Russian-American Company (from the Russian government) 115–16; town 13, 30–1; 64, 67, 78, 122
Chester, Cheshire, England 47, 55
Chicago school of sociology: land-use models of 9n; little concern for physical form 7
Chichester, Sussex, England 49
China, morphology and conservation in 10
Chinese communism, cultural and economic control of 10
Chinese culture and urban form 10
Chinese frontier regions, urban form in 10
Christaller, Walter (1893–1969), German economic and urban geographer, developer of central place theory 6
Christian-Erlang (Erlangen) *see* Erlangen, Germany 84
Church (institution), role of in urban form 9, 46
church authorities, as morphological agents 12–13
church-building, as chief motive for ecclesiastical town-founding 60
church buildings 34; as "central places" 46; locations in towns 34, 40, 46; as significant buildings in early medieval towns 46
church cemeteries 50
churches: as early urban nuclei 47; official 13
church leaders 115
church-town relations 50
citadel 116; appearance of 251
city-center revival, financing and promotion of 286
city and cosmos 29
city gates 38, 50, 70, 76
city halls 147, 237; *see also* town halls
city politics 292–7
class, role of in urban form 9
clergy *see* bishops, ecclesiastical authorities
coalition theory 289
Cologne (Köln) Nordrhein-Westfalen, Germany 66
colonial economies 11
colonial margins of empire 10, 14
colonial regimes, transfers between 114–5
colonial town founding 11; Portuguese 14; Russian 115; Spanish 14
commercial development 9
communities of interest 18; *see also* urban stakeholders
company charters *see* government charters
company housing 15
company towns: community buildings 159; design authorship 160–1, 168–9; owners' villas 159–60; in Poland 15; Scheibler's district in Łódź 155–161; Sitka 115; workers' housing 158, 163–6
compulsory purchase 187; *see also* expropriation laws
Congress Kingdom of Poland 153
conservation: neighborhood 187; restriction of to major monuments 107
conservation planning 9; conservation area designation 187
contract employees, as morphological agents 14
convention business 18
Conwy, Clywed, Wales 32, 33, 37, 40–2
Conzen, M. R. G. (1907–2000), British geographer and urban morphologist 6; concept of urban fringe belt 189; developer of morphological plan-analysis 7, 267–9, 315; ideas championed by Jeremy Whitehand 7–8; interest in medieval towns 27; laid foundation for British school of urban morphology xxiii; mentor to Jeremy Whitehand 27, 63; seminal contributions to urban morphology xxii, 189
Conzenian terminology (concepts), in urban morphogenesis xxiii, 270
Copcutt, Geoffrey (1928–1997), Scottish architect of Cumbernauld Town Centre, Cumbernauld, Scotland 251, 257–8
cosmos and city 29
courts, judicial 13
court-town building: architect interactions with the potentate 87; often piecemeal 85
court-towns 13, 83; accommodation for standing army 88; founded for personal reasons 84; building regulations 84; façade regulation 92; limits to grandiose plans 95; longterm results reflected both power and negotiation 95;

motives to dazzle 84; potentate's involvement in design 87–9; potentates' wishes often disregarded 92–4; residents' chaotic conversions 92; strategies and incentives to populate and provide a laborforce 91–2; from timber-frame to stone houses 86; uniformity of streetscapes and building lines 84–5; villas and palaces often copied from biggest cities in Europe 89; without defenses 83
covenants, 176
craft guilds *see* guilds
Criccieth, Gwynedd, Wales 37
Cullen, Gordon (1914–1994), British urban planner xxii, 19n
cultural choices 77–8, 138, 227, 280
cultural collision, between Russia and America 115, 130
cultural geography, Berkeley school of 6
cultural landscape 5
cultural perceptions 18, 102; among architects 221
cultural shift 115
Cumbernauld, Lanarkshire, Scotland 17, 251–63; American architectural award 260; design 257–60; early demolitions 262; implementation 260–2; limitations of architectural freedom 263; microclimatic problems 257, 261, 263; New Brutalism aesthetic 260; planning origins 255–7; problematic location of the town center 256–7
customary law, medieval 63

decision-making 8–9; converting court town plans into reality 83; elusive nature of 8; extreme concentration and its implications 170; in founding of medieval Salisbury 59; role of medieval bishops and abbots 60; role of medieval masons and carpenters 60; top-down or bottom-up in medieval town planning 43
defenses 35, 37, 39, 120; Roman 52; timber 52
de la Tour, Master Gérard (active 1280s), French town surveyor 35, 39
demolition 91, 94; in Cumbernauld 262; in Paris 107; in Sitka 125
design authority, in factory towns 170
design plans, for suburban developments 181; *see also* feuing, urban platting
Dickinson, Robert E. (1905–1981), British geographer and urban morphologist 6
dioceses, spread of: in Gaul 46; in Iberia 46: in Italy 46
distance decay 10
dockland redevelopment 18
documentary sources, evidence for morphological agency 27
downtown 119, 127, 129; *see also* CBD
Dresden, Sachsen, Germany 67
Dubai, United Arab Emirates 10
Dublin (Âth Cliath), Ireland 64
Dukes of Zähringen (Switzerland) 64

Earl of Surrey (vassal of King Edward I) 34, 40
ecclesiastical authorities, as morphological agents 46–61
ecclesiastical buildings, fringe-belt locations of 55
ecclesiastical precincts 49–51, 118–9; gates of 50–1, 61; walls of 47, 50–1
ecclesiastical towns, distinctive character of 13
economic constraints 189, 198, 231
economic cycles xxii, 105, 308
economic development 52; in balance with public benefits 277; pace of 115, 270; prospects for 120
economic goals: of public authorities 280; of town founding 13, 60; of town residents 94
economic power 9; of Chinese communism 10
economic stagnation 4, 115, 121, 123
economics, urban 7
economic vitality 15, 18, 78, 196, 268
edicts: military 122; presidential 132; royal 63, 67
Edward I, King of England (1239–1307) 12, 57; and his new towns 27–45
engineers, 35, 39, 149, 308; canal 143; city 231; cooperation with merchants and government officials 149; critical to town design 153; highway 310, 312; housing for 166; municipal 235, 237–44; in Paris 100; in Poland 161; George Stephenson 140; railroad 147; street design by 198; as surveyors 31; team members 101; U.S. navy 120; *see also* surveyors
engineering 3; civil 52; innovations 140, 142; projects 293; reports, American on British railroads 143–4
entrepreneurial activity: as "makeover" of cities 286; governmental inducements for 169
entrepreneurial policy (stategies) 287
entrepreneurs 142, 150; bourgeois 226; commercial 115, 130; ethnic 297; industrial 15, 152, 154; homes close to their factories 159
Erlangen, Bayern, Germany 84
estate agents (realtors in U.S.) 10; as morphological agents 16
estate development (at the urban fringe) 180
estates, gates to 158
European Historic Towns Atlas 66
Exeter, Devon, England 49
expropriation, compensation for in Paris 101, 105

factory buildings 15; cotton 153, 155–8 161–3; linen 153; textile 152
factory owners' mansions 15, 159–60
factory towns 153; community buildings 159; owners' villas 159–60; tripartite spatial organization 170; workers' housing 158, 163–6
fashionable districts, risk of demise 177–8

feudal lords *see* town lords
feuing (Scottish method of land subdivision and development) 178–84
field patterns, as templates for planned urban extensions 54
finance, in Haussmann's theory of productive expenditure 101
fixation lines 7, 189
Flint, Flintshire, Wales 32, 34, 36, 57; burgages at 39; orthogonal plan 40
Florence (Firenze), Toscana, Italy 67
fortifications 67, 71; as megastructures 253; around Paris 107; Sitka 120
fossatores (diggers of defensive works) 37, 43
Freiburg im Breisgau, Baden-Württemberg, Germany 67
French state, governance culture of 102
Friedrich II (1194–1250), Holy Roman Emperor (House of Hohenstaufen) 66
Friedrich II (1712–1786), "Frederick the Great," King of Prussia 83
Friedrich Wilhelm I (1688–1740), King of Prussia 13, 84
fringe belts *see* urban fringe belts
Fritz, Johann (active 1890s), early German urban morphologist 5
fur trade 14

garden city, significance of for social reform 174
garden suburbs 16, 173–90; distinct from garden city 174; origins of 175
garden walls 176
gardens *see* garden suburbs
garrisons 13
Gascony (Gascogne), France 29, 30, 33
gates *see* city gates, ecclesiastical precincts, estates
Gaul, spread of dioceses in 46
Geisler, Walter (1891–1945), German urban morphologist 5–6
gentrification 285
geographical isolation: effects of 115; enhanced industrialist's control in 170; from central government 121
geography, discipline of 5
geology 6
geometrical knowledge: transfer from church building to town layouts 57, 70
geomorphology 6
German academic tradition 5
Giedion, Sigfried (1888–1968), Bohemian-born Swiss architectural critic 97
Giovannoni, Giuseppe (1903–1981), Italian urban designer 219
Girard, Philippe de (1775–1845), French engineer in Poland 161–2
Glasgow, Scotland 173–90
globalization 10, 11
Gloucester, Gloucestershire, England 49–50
Göttingen, Niedersachsen, Germany 76
governmental minimalism 121, 131, 170
governmental transfers *see* regime change
government bureaucrats, as morphological agents 14
government charters *see* charters
government incentives, for industrial investment 15, 152–3
governance 130, 154; ecclesiastical 47; "entrepreneurial" (public-private) 287; local 120; mayoral 50; medieval corporate 46, 63–79; model of modern urban 18; municipal 282; values underlying 130; *see also* urban governance
grade separation (of streets and railroads) 144, 150
Grand Prefét see Haussmann
grandes percées (breakthrough streets) of Paris 97–110
Grands Travaux (of Haussmann) 14, 98; authorship discussed 99; disparities between districts in Paris 104
Grassi, Giorgio (b.1935), Italian architectural theorist, 225
Great Men, relationship to broad societal processes 105
Greco-Russian Orthodox Church 116, 119–20
grid pattern *see* street patterns
grid planning 57
ground plans 5; *see also* town plans
growth coalition theory 287
guilds 13, 78; craft guilds 66, 173; custodians of urban development on evolutionary lines 220; merchant guilds 66, 76; weakening of facilitated court town construction 84

Haithabu (Viking town), Germany *see* Hedeby
Halbwachs, Maurice (1877–1945), French sociologist 104
Hall, Sir Peter (b.1932), British geographer and urban critic 261
Hamburg, Germany 66
Hanseatic League 71
harbors, railroad service in 144; *see also* ports
Harlech, Gwynedd, Wales 37
Haussmann, Georges-Eugène (1809–1891), Prefect of the Seine Department 14; criticism over project costs 101; early criticism of 98; as "executing agent" 102; legacy reconsidered 97–110; opposition to industrialization 107
Haussmannian block (triangular) 109
haussmannisation 97
Headingly, Leeds, Yorkshire, England 9
Hedeby (Haithabu), Schleswig-Holstein, Germany, Viking town 63
hereditates (early property units) 75

historical map series 5
Holford, Lord William Graham (1907–1975), British architect and town planner 231
Holt, Flintshire, Wales 34, 40
Hoskins, William George (1908–1992), British landscape historian 4
hospitals 13, 73, 118
hotels 9
house builders 193; general contractors 193, 198; self-builders 193–211; speculative builders, 178, 181, 189
house forms *see* house types
house kits 202–3
house purchasers: as morphological agents 16
house types (residential) 88, 94; apartment buildings 131; bungalows 208; English 187; gable-ended 73; half-houses (*Buden*) 74; local authority flats 187; log houses 116; ranch-style homes 208; rowhouses (townhouses) 86; semi-detached villa 176; social housing 189; suburban villa 176; tenement flats 181–2; terrace houses 181; wood-frame buildings 116; *see also* building types (other than residential)
house walls, 68, 76–7, 85, 119, 168, 198, 227
housing conversions (internal subdivision) 187
housing (social aspects): middle-class 173; regimented 13; self-built 16; subsidized 84; *see also* social housing, workers' housing
Howard, Ebenezer (1850–1928), British garden city planner 174
Hoyt, Homer (1895–1984), American urban economist 7
human agency, passive view of 8

Indians (U.S.) *see* Native Americans
individuals as agents, relationship of to general social dynamics 109; *see also* Great Men
industrial architecture *see* factory buildings
industrialists, interaction with architects 170; *see also* entrepreneurs
industrialization: non-local sources of capital and labor 152; policy 153; as a transformative process 15
ingeniatores (engineers) 39, 43
inner fringe belts *see* urban fringe belts
innovation diffusion 10
International Seminar on Urban Form (I.S.U.F.) xxi
investors, multiple generations of 169
Islamic world, source of mathematical knowledge in medieval Europe 55
Italian architects: concept of post-Enlightenment architectural crises 219–20; rationalist idiosyncracies versus societal values 222; "spontaneous consciousness" versus "critical consciousness" in architecture 226; theoretical debates 17, 219–28
Italian typomorphological school xxii–xxiii; *see also* Muratori, Saverio

Jacobs, Jane (1916–2006), American-Canadian journalist and urban critic 303
James of St. George (c.1230–1309), Savoyard master castle-builder 32, 39, 40

Kalkar, Nordrhein-Westfalen, Germany, 67–70
Karl III Wilhelm (1679–1738), Margrave of Baden-Durlach, founder of Karlsruhe 90
Karlsruhe, Baden-Württemberg, Germany 14; court-town ideals embodied in town plan 92; orderly façades and disorderly backyards 92
Kaupang (Viking town), Tjølling, Vestfold, Norway, 63
Kells, County Meath, Ireland 48
Keyser, Erich (1893–1968), German historian and urban morphologist 5
Kilkenny, Leinster, Ireland 67–9
kings: divine right of 29; as morphological agents 27–44; relations with bishops regarding town development 52
Księży Młyn, Łódź, Poland 15, 152, 155–161; community buildings 159; design authorship 160–1; workers' housing 158
Kulturgeographie 5
Kulturlandschaft 5

land allocation 10
landowners: impact on urban form 9; medieval 75-6; as morphological agents 16
landownership, in industrial towns 9
land reclamation schemes 270, 272
land reserves: for factory development 153–4; for public use 124
landscape parks *see* parks
land speculation 9
land surveying *see* surveying
land-use models: American 7, of the Chicago school of sociology 9n
land-use patterns, study of in the U.S. 7
land use, redundant 17–18
land-use regulation 280; *see also* zoning regulation (U.S.)
lanes *see* streets
laws *see* customary law, town laws
Le Corbusier (Charles-Édouard Jeanneret-Gris) (1887–1965), Swiss-French architect 99; high opinion of Haussmann 102; megastructures 254
Leeds and Liverpool Canal, England 140
LeFebvre, Henri (1901–1991), French sociologist 9
Leighly, John (1895–1986), American geographer and urban morphologist 6
Leighton Buzzard, Bedfordshire, England 18, 303–21

L'Enfant, Pierre Charles (1754–1825), French-born American architect and civil engineer 99
Lhasa, Tibet 10
Liège, Belgium 56
Liverpool, England 15, 137, 139–43
Liverpool and Manchester Railway (L&M), England 137, 147
Llandudno, Clwyd, Wales 8
local authority planning *see* urban planning
local government officials 115
Łódź, Poland 15–16, 152–3; *see also* Księży Młyn
log buildings 114; lifespan 119; slow disappearance 125
log town 14, 118; log houses covered with clapboard 123–4
London, England 33, 49
Louis XIV (1638–1715), King of France 14; 83–4
Lübeck, Schleswig-Holstein, Germany 66; medieval landowners in 75; town hall 72
Ludwigsburg, Baden-Württemberg, Germany 91
Lynch, Kevin A. (1918–1984), American urban planner xxii
Lyon, Rhône, France 106

Maksoutoff, Prince Dmitrii Petrovich (1832–1889), Russian Governor of Alaska 120
managerial class, as morphological agent 16
Manchester, England 15, 137, 139–43; merchants in 139
Manzoni, Herbert J. B. (1899–1972), British civil engineer 231, 240
Maretto, Paolo (1931–1998), Italian architect, student of Muratori, 220–1
market concretion (concept) 7
market halls 13
market place 60, 67, 68–9, 71–3, 78; in early medieval towns 52–3; *see also* street market
market settlements, planned 6
market square 76
masons, 35, 39, 64; master masons 54, 57, 59
master builders *see* builders
master plans 174, 231, 244, 282
mathematical models 11
Maxwell family of Pollock, developers of Pollockshields, Scotland 180–5
medieval towns 27–79; British 6; documentary evidence about 9, spatial development of 27
megastructures, 251–63, 274–5; Bull Ring Centre (Birmingham) 253; Cumbernauld, Scotland 251–63; fortifications 253; in history 253; and new towns 17; *see also* castles, cathedrals
Mémoires du Baron Haussmann 98
merchant guilds *see* guilds
merchants: as key supporters of railroads 143; as morphological agents 13, 115; Quaker 139, 149
metrological analysis: in towns 9; of plot patterns 54
Middle Ages: architects in 16; importance of institutions in 12; re-emergence of towns in 12
middle class, retreat of to the suburbs 176
migrant communities 11
military administration, edicts of 122
military defenses 120; *see also* castles, town walls
military officers, as morphological agents 14
model factory towns *see* company towns
modèle haussmannien 97
models *see* agent-based modeling, governance, land-use models, mathematical, morphological agency, new towns, urban governance, urbs-suburbium model
Modernist Movement (Modernism), in architecture 16, 251–63; rejection of historicism 219, 221
monarchs, as morphological agents 12; *see also* kings
monasteries *see* religious houses
monastic precincts 50; *see also* abbey precincts, ecclesiastical precincts
monastic towns, in Ireland 48
Morizet, André (1876–1942), French politician 99–100
morphogenetic approach: to garden suburbs, 173–90; spatial development of medieval towns 27
morphogenetic regions (within towns) 7
morphographical classification 8; description of towns 5, 7
morphological agency and agents 303–21; balance between public and private 189; documentary sources as evidence for 27; model of 18; recombinant emergence of multiple agency 320; rise in study of 3–4; town plans, as evidence for 12, 27; types of 18
morphological agency, Kropf's model of a coherent process to produce a built environment (*topics in this entry listed in order of Kropf's discussion*) agents 304–5; learning behavior of agents 305–6; group agents 307–8; specialization 308–9; hierarchy of learning 309; habit, crisis, and roots of learning 309–310; distributed idea 310–11; designs by committee 311–12; distribution in time 312–13; forms in use 313–314; exploratory emergence 314–15; emergence and the hierarchy of elements 315–16; scalar and evolutionary emergence 316–317; emergence and the diversification of form 317–19; hierarchy of agency and control 319; basic unit of control 319; design, control and different kinds of agents 320
morphological agents: anonymity of 12; architects 16; aristocratic families 9; bishops

46–61; builders 16; businessmen, 14; church authorities 9, 46–61; conflicts among 115; contract employees 14; direct and indirect 10; ecclesiastical authorities 46–61; entrepreneurs 170; estate agents 16; government bureaucrats 14; house purchasers 16; importance in periods of changing attitudes 108; industrialists 152–71; kings 27–44; landowners 16; in medieval Kalkar 68–9; in medieval Kilkenny 68–9; in medieval Sopron 68–9; merchants 13; motives of 8; native Indians 14; organizations and individuals as 8; roles of (Kropf's concept of motive, generative, regulatory, resistive, sensory, and testing agents) 320; royal officials 12; Tlingit Indians 14; town corporations 9; town councils 12, 13; trading company officials 14
morphological frame 7; persistence of 131; *see also* field patterns
morphotopes (smallest morphological unities) 7
morpho-typological studies 219; emergence of new building types 222
mortgage lenders 194–6
Moscow, Russia, imperial court moved from 84
multiculturalism and urban form 10, 297
municipal administration, by the military 121
municipal planning *see* urban planning
Münster, Nordrhein-Westfalen, Germany 48–9
Muratorian terminology (concepts) 220
Muratori, Saverio (1910–1973), Italian architect, architectural historian and urban morphologist 17; concept of operational history 220; champion of unplanned transformative processes in architectural history (*contra* Rossi) 226; emphasis on the city as "organism" 220–2, 225; exponent of the New Historicism 224; typological process 304, 309–10
museums 277
Muslim culture and urban form 10

Nantes, Loire-Atlantique, France 106
Napoléon III, Louis (1808–1873), Emperor of France 14, 98; importance in shaping the *Grands Travaux* of Paris 100
Native Americans, as morphological agents 14
neighborhood conservation 187
neighborhoods, perceptions of status of 189
neo-haussmannisme 97
neo-liberal urban policies 286
Neomodernism, as an architectural movement 16
Newborough, Anglesey, Wales 37
Newcastle upon Tyne, Northumberland, England 7, 268
new streets (in Paris) *see Grandes percées*
new towns (medieval) 9; agent-based model of (Edward I's reign) 29–31; decisions about designing and surveying 34–5; ecclesiastical role in founding 46; populating and chartering, 35–6; site selection 12; timing and locating of (Edward I's reign) 31–4; in thirteenth-century Florentine republic 28
Newton, Dorset, England 35
new towns (modern): Cumbernauld, Scotland 251; as population overflow 17, 255; twentieth-century British 251
New Winchelsea, Sussex, England *see* Winchelsea
New York City, U.S.A.: élites in 10; railroads in 145; retail districts in 10
Novoarkhangel'sk (new Archangel) *see* Sitka

orthogonal urban planning, medieval 55; 78–9
Overton, Clwyd, Wales 37
Owen, Robert (1771–1858), Welsh-born social reformer and owner of New Lanark industrial village, Scotland 159
owner-builders 193–211; amateurs displaced by professionals 193; cooperative activity 198; preference for unincorporated areas 194; ubiquity 193; variable embeddedness in development process 196
owner-built settlement patterns: clustered 198; scattered 197; spectrum from individualistic anarchy to constrained uniformity 207–10; variable landscape imprint 211
own-house-building: building plans 200–2; house kits 202; magazines 204; materials 202–4; obtaining land 197–9; recycled building materials 203; role of lumber dealers 200, 202, 204, 206–7, 211; sources of credit 206–7; tools, knowledge and advice 204–6

Pacific Ocean 14, 115
Pagano, Giuseppe (1896–1945), Italian architect 220
palace parks *see* parks
palaces: of aristocratic families 67, 83; of bishops 48, 50, 115; centrality of 13; inspiration for 89; royal 83–4; Potsdam 84, 87, 89; summer 84; Versailles 83; Whitehall 87
Paris, France 4; central 14; transformation of the built environment 97–110
parish churches 13, 50, 52, 67–9, 71, 167–8; dedications reflect urban evolution 77; *see also* churches, church buildings
parking: on-street 314; car-lined streets 315
parks: landscape parks 13, 103; palace parks 83; remodeled 277; Russian tea garden 116; *see also* garden suburbs
pedestrians, separation of from vehicles 251
Penecestre, Stephen de (d.1299), warden of the Cinque Ports, England 34
Penn, William (1644–1718), founder of Philadelphia, U.S.A. 147

Peoria, IL, U.S.A. 16, 194
Peterborough, Cambridgeshire, England 54
Peter the Great (1672–1725), Tsar of Russia 84, 86, 91
Philadelphia, PA, U.S.A. 9, 15, 137, 145–7; terminal stations at city limits of 145
physical fabric of towns *see* built environment, urban form, urban morphology
Piast kingdom (Poland) fortress (*gród*) 47–8
place-promotion (marketing): "Championing Birmingham" iniative (2003) 293; concept 18, 267, 292; postwar replanning as 231
plan analysis (morphological) *see* town-plan analysis
plan types, urban (morphological) 6
plan units (morphological) 5, 52, 116, 128; hierarchically nested 7; significance for planning 270; waterfront 270–1, 274–5
planners: interaction with architects 17; political influence in selecting 246
planning departments, local authority 9
planning regimes: developer-driven 280–1; reactive *vs.* strategic 280
planning regulations 4, 67, 190; *see also* building regulations, urban planning, zoning regulations
Plato's *Timaeus* 29
plot amalgamation 7
plot dimensions 9
plot patterns: deep plots in Łódź 153; in Dublin 64; in ecclesiastical towns 52; medieval Scandinavian origins 64; plot demarcation 122; in Sitka, Alaska 127; *see also* street patterns
plot series 37–42, 316
plot subdivision, competition for prestigious locations 76
Plymouth, Devon, England 10
political atmosphere 105; in 1848 155
political control 17
political decisions 252
political opponents 99
political power 9, 289, 291; distance from centers of 131
political regimes 114
politics: boosterish 286; city 292–7; influence in selecting planners 246; postwar 10
Pollockshields, Glasgow, Scotland, Britain's first garden suburb, 180–5
pope, petition to, to relocate an English cathedral 58–9
portico: modern reinterpretation 224, 226; origins in Bologna 224, 226
port cities 18
ports 267; *see also* harbors and waterfronts
Portuguese town-founding in the New World 14
post-colonial economies 11
Postmodernism (postmodernity) 285; as an architectural movement 16
Potsdam, Berlin, Germany 13–14; 83–95
Prague, Czech Republic 76
precincts *see* abbey precincts, ecclesiastical precincts, monastic precincts
pre-urban nucleus 6, 47
principle of precedents (concept of) 219–20
private property market, emergence of 119
privatization of public structures 126, 131–2
promyshlenniki (contract workers) 116, 118
property plots 67
property speculators, 179
property tenure, systemic changes in 120
public art 287
public consultation, in urban planning 17
Pullman, George Mortimer (1831–1897), American industrialist 16, 159

Quaker merchants: early supporters of railroads 139; networks of in London, Liverpool and Baltimore 149

race, role of in urban form 9
Radburn, NJ, U.S.A., garden suburb 174
railroad charters *see* charters
railroad stations: Saint-Lazare station (Paris) as magnets for development 103; stimuli for urban development 149; stubborn effects on urban morphology 147; union stations 142
railroads: Baltimore precedent for railroads in U.S. streets, 144; beltlines 145, 147; bridges 142; and canals 139–40; and canals in the U.S 143; conflicts between merchants and city councils 144; emergence of railroad corridors 142; entry routes into cities 140; freight terminals in waterfront industrial districts 138, 140; insertion into existing cities 15, 137–50; passenger terminals near city centers 138, 140; restricted routes 142; retrospective grade separation in U.S. cities 144; surveys 139; terminal stations at city limits (Philadelphia) 145–7; tracks in city streets 142, 144; tramroads 138–9, 143; urban tunnels 140–2, 149; viaducts 141–2, 149; waterfront rail yard 270, 272
railroad tracks (in streets), grooved 143–5, 149
Ratzel, Friedrich (1844–1904), German geographer 5
re-aestheticization of cities 292
realtors (estate agents in Britain): 10; as morphological agents 16
reconstruction plans (for war-damaged cities), in Britain 17
recycled building materials 203
regime change (sovereign governments), and urban form 114–32
regime theory 288–9

religious houses 67, 119; abbeys 47, 49–52; endowed by aristocratic families 78; loss of state privileges 130; monasteries 50, 70, 74–5
Renaissance era 13; architects in 16
residential differentiation, in a garden suburb, 173–90
residential neighborhoods: fashionable districts 177–8; in the U.S. 16
residential segregation 187–9; in Glasgow, Scotland 16; reflection of class-consciousness 175
residential utilities, uncoordinated 195
Resource Management Act (New Zealand) 280
retail districts 10
Rhuddlan, Denbighshire, Wales 32, 34; first burgages at 36, 39
Ribe, Esbjerg, Denmark, origin as a Viking town 63
river access, for new towns 39
roads: curving 176, 181; extramural 48; gravel 198; high-capacity 256; livestock damage to 91; nonalignment of 59; palace alignment of 83, ring 253; Roman 53; stone-paved 158; uncoordinated, outside Paris 107; wagonways 139; *see also* streets
road system 257; one-way 258; as morphological frame 59
Robert of Ely (active twelfth century), English cathedral architect 59
Rokesley, Gregory de (d.1291), mayor of London 34
Roman Empire 12
Roman towns, as quarry material for medieval churches 47
Rome, Italy 4
Rome Royal Architectural School 219
Rossi, Aldo (1931–1997), Italian architect, 223; concept of city as project 223; emphasis on the city as "patchwork" or composition 225; champion of rational architecture independent of history (*contra* Muratori) 226; views on public and private domains 223–4
Rostock, Mecklenburg-Vorpommern, Germany 66–7; topographical description in late Middle Ages 71–5
Rouen, Seine-Maritime, France 70, 106
royal authority 83; over medieval towns 63; and urban formation 27–45
royal edicts 63, 67
royal officials: as morphological agents 12; role in town founding 43
royal palace at Versailles 83–4
Russian-American Company 116, 119–20, 123, 132
Russian Empire 115
Russian Orthodox Church *see* Greco-Russian Orthodox Church

St. Albans, Hertfordshire, England 52; abbey as early urban nucleus 47
St. Petersburg, Russia 14, 84, 86, 116
Salisbury, Wiltshire, England, medieval planning of 57–60
savings and loan associations 194–6, 207
Savoy (Savoie), France 39
Saxony (Sachsen), Germany 63
Scheibler, Karl (1820–1881), German industrialist in Poland 15–16,154–61
Schlüter, Otto (1872–1959), German geographer and urban morphologist 5
schools 13
Schorler, Vicke (c.1560–1625), pictorial chronicler of Rostock 71
self-builders *see* owner-builders
self-built housing 16; assistance for 308–10
Sharp, Thomas Wilfred (1901–1978), British urban planner 19n1, 231, 235
shell homes (owner-built) 198
Siena, Toscana, Italy 56; medieval building regulations 67; Office for Beauty 67
Simon, Jules (1814–1896), French prime minister 99
site selection, for new towns 12
Sitka, AK, U.S.A. 14, 114–32
skyscrapers 10, 254
social conductors (facilitators of social movements) 105
social housing *see* house forms
social production 9
social segregation 173
social status, redefined by industrialization 173
socio-morphological patterns 187–8
Sopron (Ödenburg), Hungary, founded by royal edict 67–9
Spanish town-founding in the New World 14
speculative builders *see* house builders
speculative design 9
Spoleto, Umbria, Italy, church of San Salvatore in 47
Stadtlandschaft 5
stakeholders *see* urban stakeholders
Stratford-upon-Avon, Warwickshire, England 54
steam railroads *see* railroads
Stephenson, George (1781–1848), British railroad engineer 139
stockade 118–20; *see also* town walls
Stockholm, Sweden 208
Stockton and Darlington Railway, England 139, 143
straight streets 13, 37; for military purposes 109
street alignments, evidence for town growth stages 5
street commissioners, 122
street density 268, 270
street hierarchy 316
street layouts *see* street pattern
street lines: demarcated 87, 122, 124–5, 127, 211; residents ordered to build along 85
street market 51

street pattern 68–9: concentric (around a church nucleus) 78; continuity of 223; curved 40; curvilinear 181; in ecclesiastical towns 52; grid 36, 52, 55, 59, 181, 183, 316; medieval 28; orthogonal 13, 37, 59–60; regular 6, 64; straight 13, 37; T-shaped 40, 42; *see also* plot patterns
streets: absence of 118; and lanes 34; as landscape evidence of morphological agency 12; paved 70, 86; "permeable" 310; quasi-streets 118; repair 67; retrospective provision 122; straight 13, 37, 109; unplanned 93; views protected 67; *see also* roads
streetscapes, harmonious 86, 88, 92
street setbacks 194, 197–8, 211
street space encroachment (porticos) 224
street width 108; in Łódź, Poland 163; in Sitka, Alaska 122; undefined margins 118; in the U.S. compared with Britain 15
Stuttgart, Baden-Württemberg, Germany, court-town 90
subdivision development (in the U.S.) 16
suburban developers: controls on before land-use planning 189; in the nineteenth century 177
suburban development 9; limited regulation of 194
suburbanization of the middle-class 173
suburbium (*Stadt*, *bourg*), as medieval community of craftsmen and traders 47
surveying 12; delayed 121; establishing a town plat (U.S.) 127–8; medieval manuals of 70
surveyors: employed by church officials 54; in medieval towns 31, 35, 39, 57, 70; municipal 178, 235, 237–8, 241–5; railroad 138, 144; surveyor-general 121; U.S. surveyor 127; *see also* engineers
sweat-equity *see* owner-builders
Swedish towns 6

tenement housing *see* house forms; *see also* workers' housing
textile factories 15
Thirty Years War (1618–48) 84
Thuringia, Germany 5
Tibetan culture and urban form 10
Tlingit Indians: 116; houses 118; as morphological agents 14
topography, in relation to urban form 5; *see also* urban constitutional topography
tourism 18
Tout, Thomas Frederick (1855–1929), British historian 28
Town and Country Planning Act (1947), British, 17, 230
town architect, as nominal position 154
town builders, medieval 12
town center planning 17
town charters *see* charters
town corporations, as morphological agents 9
town councillors 10
town councils 13, 66; concern for infrastructure 70; creative force in medieval period 79; early autonomy in Germany 66; fire prevention 70; as morphological agents 12, 13; morphological influences on medieval towns 63; role in medieval urban extensions 70
town defences 12, 37, 39
town founding 6; ecclesiastical, as economic development 46, 54; Portuguese, in the New World 14; Spanish, in the New World 14; *see also* colonial town founding
town gates *see* city gates
town halls 49, 66–74, 94; *see also* city halls
town laws: medieval 64; Law of Bristol 64; Lübeck Law 64, 71; Magdeburg Law 64
town layouts 5, 11
town lords 64; bishops as 66; ecclesiastical 51; feudal lords 13; kings as 34; morphological influences on medieval towns 63; as owners of towns 63; provided security 78; regained power in early modern period 71; relations with townspeople in the Middel Ages 63–4, 66; role in founding and locating a town 31
town-plan analysis (morphological) 7; Battle 51; Conwy and Beaumaris 40–2; Flint and Rhuddlan 37–40; new towns of King Edward I's reign 37–42; Salisbury 57–60; Winchester 49–50; Worcester 52–3; to characterize waterfront character 267–8
town planning *see* urban planning
town plans (detailed topographical plans): as evidence for morphological agency 12, 27; as evidence of urban design 36–42; study of 5, 269; *see also* urban plans (for planning)
town plans (for planning) *see* urban plans
town records 6
townscapes: basic elements 7; specialized meanings of 19n1; *see also* urban landscapes
townspeople 13, 33, 40; churches founded by 71; as founders of hospitals 78; as founders of religious houses 67; limited self-government in the Middle Ages 67; as morphological agents 30–1, 63–79, 91–4; relations with town lords in the Middle Ages 35, 50–1, 63–4, 66; relations with town overlords in the Absolutist era 88, 91–4
town square 76; *see also* market place
town walls 39, 63, 66–71, 77–8, 87, 94; *see also* stockade
trading company officials: as morphological agents 14; as town-founders 14
tramroads *see* railroads
Trani, Puglia, Italy 47
transfers between empires 115

Trier, Rheinland-Pfalz, Germany, with Porta Nigra town gate 47
Tsar of Russia 84, 86, 91, 116, 119, 170
tunnels 15; for railroads 140–2, 149
Tuscany (Toscana), Itay, medieval planning regulations in 67
twenty-four-hour cities 18, 285
typological process *see* Muratori, Saverio
typomorphology, in urban morphology 17

unfortified towns 84
United States Congress 119
United States federal government 119
universities 13, 73; endowed by aristocratic families 78
urban assets, revalorization of 18
urban constitutional topography 6; *see also* topography
urban cosmopolitanism 285
urban environment, personal involvement in shaping 4
urban form: the Church's role in 46; good urban form 219; regime change and 114–32; relation to topography 5; as a stage with actors upon it 9; study of 3–5; *see also* urban morphology
urban fringe belts xxii, 7; adaptation 277; alienation 274–5; ecclesiastical buildings in 55; industrial 119, 129; inner fringe belt 268–9; knowledge of valuable for planners 281; waterfronts as components of 267
urban governance: models 18; shift from managerial to entrepreneurial 287
urban historians 9
urban history 7; study of 6
urban imagery 18
urbanism (urban way of life): changes in 115; postmodern 285
urban landowners *see* landowners
urban landscape management 10
urban landscapes: authoritarian 13, 83–95; commodification and aestheticization 285; industrialized 152; making of 4; relation to land uses 7; shift from production to consumption 285; transformation from Russian to American, 129
urban modernity, in nineteenth-century Paris 14
urban morphogenesis, agency in 27
urban morphologists: British 7; geographical 6; *see also* Italian typomorphological school
Urban Morphology (journal) xxi
urban morphology (concept): conceptual development xxi, 5–11; definition of 19n; first use of the term 6; intellectual roots 5; principle of precedents 219–20; relation to professional disciplines 3; *see also* urban form
Urban Morphology Research Group xxii
urban occupations, spatial clustering of 76
urban origins, interest in medieval 6; *see also* urban morphogenesis
urban planner, as informed expert 233
urban planning: adjustment to American norms 127; administrative systems of 10; ecclesiastical 51–60; growth of legislation for 189; Haussmannian legacy 109; *haussmannisation* 100; medieval 67–71; municipal planning 17, 230–47; postwar reconstruction 230–47; public consultation in Britain 17; whatever entrepreneurs want 154; *see also* building regulations, planning regulations
urban plans (for planning): distinction between plan formation and implementation 246–7; "neighborhood unit" concept 230, 256; multiple-authorship 247; postwar reconstruction 230–47, public participation 247
urban platting (in U.S.) 127
urban policies: actor network theory 290–2; growth coalition theory 287; opposition to 99; regime theory 288–9
urban reconstruction planning (post-Second World War): consultant fees 236; in-house professionals 240–1; national-local relationships 244–5; outside consultants 230, 233–40; personal connections in consultant selection 237–9; problematic personalities 243–4; replanning outstripped damage 231; town clerk 242–3; turf wars between consultant architects and engineers 234, 237; type of authorship 231
urban re-invention: Birmingham as leisure-based cultural machine 287; Sitka as American 116
urban renewal: of Paris in the nineteenth century 97; relation to beliefs about hygiene 107
urban representation, bird's-eye view of medieval Rostock as 71–5
urban residents *see* townspeople
urban stakeholders, realignments among 18; *see also* communities of interest
urbs (*burg*, *cité*) as center of medieval urban power 47
urbs-suburbium model 47–9
Utrecht, The Netherlands 66

Vaison-la-Romaine, Vaucluse, France 48
Vaïsse, Claude-Marius (1799–1864), renovator of Lyon, France 106
Versailles, Yvelines, France: court-town 14, 83; slow construction 86
viaducts (railroad) 15, 149; in Manchester 141–2; in Philadelphia 147
Vienna (Wien), Austria, origins of medieval town in 70
Viking period 63

Viking towns (Birka, Sweden; Haithabu, Germany; Kaupang, Norway; Ribe, Denmark) 63
villa, as modern suburban ideal 176

wagonways *see* roads
walls *see* house walls, precinct walls, town walls
war damage 230
Warsaw (Warszawa), Poland 152, 162
Washington, DC, U.S.A. 14, 99
waterfront redevelopment: concept plans 278–9; government agencies and port authorities key actors 281; intergovernmental cooperation 278; management and administration 278; mixed-use 274; revenue-driven agencies 280; urban intensification 274
waterfronts 18, 138, 140; as components of urban fringe belts 267; contrasts in redevelopment policies in Auckland and Wellington, New Zealand 277; obsolete 286; planning and design 267; rail yard 270, 272; revival 267; redevelopment 273–8; transformation 267–82
weigh-stations 13, 73
Wellington, New Zealand 18, 267–82; piecemeal waterfront redevelopment 277–80; redevelopment success 275; remodeled park 277
Wells, Somerset, England 38
Wetzlar, Hessen, Germany 78
wharves 273–4 *see also* harbors
Whitehand, Jeremy W.R. (b.1938), British geographer and urban morphologist: analytical approach to landscape development 4; broad research interests in urban morphology xxii; championed Conzen's ideas 7, 27; decision-making as morphological agency 10, 27, 230, 247; developed ideas about agency in urban morphology xxiii, 19, 44, 63, 94, 189; editor of *Urban Morphology* xxi; research program on Chinese cities xxii, 10
William I (1028–1087) "the Conqueror," King of England 51
Wilson, Hugh (1913–1985), architect and initial planner of Cumbernauld New Town, Scotland 256–7
Winchelsea, Sussex, England: Norman cathedral 49–50; relocation of 30–1, 33–5; 57
Worcester, Worcestershire, England 49, 52–3
workers' housing 15; in Księży Młyn (Łódź) 158; at Żyrardów 163–6
Worms, Rheinland-Pfalz, Germany 66
Wrocław (Breslau, Lower Silesia), Dolnośląskie, Poland 76
Wroxeter, Shropshire, England 47

Xanten, Nordrhein-Westfalen, Germany 47

York, Yorkshire, England 47

zoning regulation (land-use in the U.S.) 194, 211; *see also* land use regulation
Żyrardów, Mazowieckie, Poland 15, 152–3; community facilities 167–8; design authorship 168–9; factory buildings 161–3; model factory town 161–9; rescued by German businessmen 163–6; spatial reflection of social structure 166–7; workers' housing 163–6